# Modern British History
# since 1900

# Macmillan Foundations

*A series of introductory texts across a wide range of subject areas to meet the needs of today's lecturers and students*

*Foundations* texts provide complete yet concise coverage of core topics and skills based on detailed research of course requirements suitable for both independent study and class use – *the firm foundations for future study.*

## Published

*Biology*
*Chemistry*
*Contemporary Europe*
*Economics*
*A History of English Literature*
*Modern British History since 1900*
*Physics*
*Politics*

## Forthcoming

*British Politics*
*Economics for Business*
*Mathematics for Science and Engineering*
*Modern European History*
*Nineteenth-Century Britain*
*Sociology*

# Modern British History since 1900

JEREMY BLACK

First published 2000 by
MACMILLAN PRESS LTD
Houndmills, Basingstoke, Hampshire RG21 6XS
and London
Companies and representatives
throughout the world

ISBN 0–333–71954–9

A catalogue record for this book is available
from the British Library.

This book is printed on paper suitable for recycling and
made from fully managed and sustained forest sources.

10  9  8  7  6  5  4  3  2  1
09  08  07  06  05  04  03  02  01  00

Typeset by Footnote Graphics, Warminster, Wilts
Printed in Great Britain by
Antony Rowe Ltd
Chippenham, Wilts

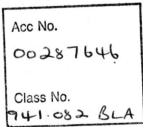

*For Harald Kleinschmidt*
*in appreciation of his friendship*

# Contents

# *Preface*

This book seeks to provide a comprehensive and up-to-date introduction to twentieth-century Britain. It is designed to be of use to students taking courses on the subject and to general readers concerned about the recent past and the way it affects our present. Such a book necessarily involves choices of what to include. The General Strike of 1926 is here, but not the Prayer Book reform that took so much parliamentary time in the 1920s. There is no point pretending some Olympian detachment or Delphic omniscience. These choices are personal. They reflect my views as a historian faced with the difficult tasks of trying to cover such a vast subject and of writing about a world that both writer and readers have experienced in person. I hope my decisions on what to include and how best to cover it prove as stimulating for the readers as they have done for the writer, and that they can be seen as individual (as all history is), but not eccentric. It is important for the reader to be aware that what is here, how it is treated and organised, and what is omitted reflects a process of choice. The past is viewed very differently by commentators and these differences should lead us to more searching questions about what is being discussed and about the process of writing history. This is most apparent and valuable when discussing the recent past. Then reading any work of history necessarily throws light on both subject and process.

All periods of history centre on the interplay of change and continuity, an interplay that is sometimes dramatic but always as insistent as the rhythm of the seasons and the course of generations. The twentieth has been the century that, *so far*, has involved the most striking changes and the greatest pressure of change. It is the modern age. This process of change is the major theme of the book.

The text reflects this emphasis, but the organisation is thematic, not chronological. This is the best way to tackle the range of human experience. One aspect of change after all is that the range that invites attention is now far wider than for a scholar writing in 1799 or 1899 about the recent past. In particular, rather than the focus being confined to politics, economics and 'society', the last is now widely defined, and due attention is also paid to cultural history – culture understood as *EastEnders* as much as the operas of Benjamin Britten. Furthermore, the environment, both natural and human, is now seen as an important topic.

This broadening of range became more apparent in writing about current trends and the recent past during the twentieth century, especially in the second half of the century, and is thus at once part of the history covered in this book, as well as part of its method. For example, it became less convincing to discuss social structure in terms solely of class or occupation-based criteria. Instead, it became increasingly clear that issues of gender and ethnicity played a central role in social structure and, furthermore, that they could not be discussed simply as adjuncts to class-based analysis. More generally, an analysis or narrative that focused on Westminster and Whitehall – the centres of national politics and government – could no longer be seen as *the* defining feature of modern British history.

Such a broad range can only be handled in a thematic fashion, for that prevents a repetitive discussion of, for example, the impact of cars or public health in chapters devoted to periods of time, such as the 1960s and 1970s. Furthermore, the use of thematic chapters, rather than continuous narrative, will enable students to use the book in response to specific subject needs. It is sometimes, however, easy to get lost if a chronological framework is missing. As a result, the text is preceded by a list of dates, with a separate, more detailed, listing of Prime Ministers and of elections. Readers who may prefer to begin with a political narrative should turn to Chapters 9 and 10. These chapters have deliberately not been put first, because, although political developments are central, they are generally over-emphasised in books of this type. Instead, preference is given to issues such as demographic (population) history, or environmental considerations. These were obviously affected by government policy, as in the establishment of the National Health Service (NHS) in 1948 and the National Parks from 1951. Yet, it is important not to focus excessively on such government interventions. Antibiotics and ageing arguably had more of an impact than the NHS.

Furthermore, a stress on government policy can lead to a focus on domestic/internal factors and a notion of 'exceptionalism' that underrates the extent to which the broad thrust of the period's history was not restricted to Britain. For example, secularism, the decline of the landed interest, and the complex and often difficult interrelationship between 'high' and 'low' culture, were all general trends in the Western world. As a consequence, the narrative and exposition of change has to be aware of factors outside the scope and control of Britain's government. In addition, it is necessary to remember that political history should be understood as having a wider focus than merely Prime Ministers and elections. Politics is about the nature, distribution and use of power, and thus involves an understanding of developments in society, the economy and public culture, for example the decline in the influence of the Church of England. These developments are covered throughout the book, but more particularly in Chapters 6–8.

'Modern' is a term that is worth considering. It is necessarily both subjective and transitory and its application is obviously open to debate. In 1976, this writer can recall, the distinguished medievalist Walter Ullmann declared that Britain was still in the Middle Ages because the sovereign was a hereditary monarch. Most commentators would have a less rigid view, but what is modern and where do modern times start? With the creation of a global economy in the sixteenth century, or the cult of progress in the eighteenth-century Enlightenment, or the Industrial Revolution, which may itself be variously dated and defined, or the creation of an overwhelmingly urban and industrial society in the nineteenth century? All these were important changes and, at least in part, valid definitions. They also spread out over centuries. Traditionally, modern history has been treated as that which follows the medieval period. Again there is no clear divide, but, wherever it is found, the resulting modern period is generally a long one. It is frequently divided into early modern and late modern, both, of course, artificial constructs. They are also not terribly helpful in terms of current general suppositions. To refer to the second half of the eighteenth century as part of the late modern period would surprise many who would not think of the conditions and suppositions of the period as modern. The major transformations in theoretical and applied science and technology in most fields, whether transport, the generation and distribution of power, medicine, contraception or agricultural yields, were yet to come. For most, life was a struggle similar to that of their grandparents. For most, there was insufficient food, especially that rich in protein, labour was arduous, and the consequences of injury or disease serious.

Consolation was provided by religious beliefs and the intermediary role of the churches. The wealth had not yet been created that would make it feasible to suggest that humanity's lot on earth could be substantially improved.

Possibly this approach to defining modernity is not a helpful one, as what is modern to one generation generally (although not always) dates rapidly. Furthermore, it can be misleading as such an approach is inherently teleological and present-minded. It tends to assume a process of modernisation, becoming modern, and makes that the central theme and organising principle of study. This does violence to the variety of the past and the complexity of the processes of change.

Instead, the question of how to define the modern can be approached in a different way. Modernity can be understood as a period of experience, that which is contemporaneous with those who are alive, and, in addition, that which immediately precedes this period and actively shaped it. This is the working definition adopted for this book. By focusing on a period of time – the twentieth century – it avoids the problem of adopting a thematic definition of modern, modernity and modernisation that might in fact be partial, not to say partisan. The political, economic, social and cultural history of the country in the twentieth century indeed indicates that very different definitions of modern have been offered.

Having adopted this working, chronological definition of modern, there is still the question of whether the major subjects and themes of the century as laid out in the chapter organisation and coverage of this book are in some way obvious. The answer, as already suggested, is no. It is possible to suggest different subjects, other themes, and contrasting approaches and organisations. It would be worrying if this was not the case. The past is not fixed, a monolith capable of only one interpretation. Indeed readers should consider how *they* would organise the book and approach writing about the twentieth century as an active part of studying the period.

A note of explanation on the use of the term 'Britain' is required. The Act of Union of 1800 with Ireland created from 1801 the state termed the United Kingdom (UK) of Great Britain and Ireland. After southern Ireland became the Irish Free State (from 1937, Eire) following the Anglo-Irish treaty of 1921, the United Kingdom became the United Kingdom of Great Britain and Northern Ireland. Great Britain therefore refers to England, Scotland and Wales. However, neither 'United Kingdom' nor 'Great Britain' lend themselves to use as adjectives, and the term 'Britain' is frequently applied to both. This may be misleading, but it captures the degree to which there has been a central governmental thrust coming from the government in London throughout the century. Throughout this book, the term 'Britain' is used to refer to the then United Kingdom, while, after 1921, the 'British Isles' refers to the former United Kingdom.

The organisation of the chapters also requires some understanding. The book should be read sequentially, moving, after an introductory chapter on the Victorian background, from the 'structural', or fundamental, factors of demographics (population), the environment, and material culture, to a treatment of society, ideology, government, politics, economics, the major parts of the British Isles, Britain and the wider world, and British culture. Such an approach offers a framework for understanding the analysis and seeing the text as a whole. Alternatively, those who would prefer a more chronological background should begin with the chapters on Politics.

Each chapter begins with an outline of its major themes and, also, a number of questions that indicate the key topics that are discussed in the chapter. At the end of each chapter there is a summary, a list of questions for discussion, and suggestions for further reading. Additional material is provided throughout the text in the form of boxed information. At the end of the book there is a Bibliography that provides guidance to some of the wealth of material available for the subject. However, also remember the vast range of information offered by oral history, the legacy of the built environment, and the massive amount of relevant material on radio, television and film.

This book will work if it makes you think – think not only about what is written here, but about what you have experienced, and the world around you. If you disagree, good, but think why. What do you disagree with: observations, analysis, explanation? Look around and consider the significance of the changes you see. Then try to account for them. The historian is not a magician figure able to unlock the past, but a guide who stimulates you to see with your own eyes.

# *Acknowledgements*

I would like to thank Nigel Aston, Anne Borsay, Alistair Davies, Simon Dentith, Stephen Evans, Hamish Fraser, John Gardiner, Bill Gibson, Sheridan Gilley, David Gladstone, Sean Greenwood, Peter Gurney, Anne Hardy, Don MacRaild, Murray Pittock, Nick Smart, David Taylor, as well as George Boyce, Mark Jackson, Tony Kirby, Bill Lancaster, John Martin, Roger Middleton, Graham Mooney, David Powell, Jeffrey Richards, John Sheils, Alan Sykes, Neil Tranter, Graham Walker, Ian Whyte, Ian Wood, and two anonymous reviewers for their comments on earlier drafts of all or part of the book. Houri Alavi and Frances Arnold at Macmillan provided valuable support, and Valery Rose was a very helpful copy-editor. I have benefited from the opportunity to develop some of the arguments advanced in the book offered by invitations to give lectures at Stillman College and the University of Virginia's Alumni Summer School programme in Oxford.

# *Chronology*

| | |
|---|---|
| 1884 | Third Reform Act. |
| 1886 | Gladstone introduces first Home Rule Bill for Ireland. Liberal Party splits. |
| 1888 | County Councils Act leads to elected county authorities. |
| 1889 | London dock strike. |
| 1893 | Second Home Rule Bill rejected by the Lords. Independent Labour Party founded. |
| 1898 | Battle of Omdurman, crucial to conquest of Sudan. |
| 1899–1902 | Second Anglo-Boer War. |
| 1900 | Formation of Labour Representation Committee; Commonwealth of Australia Act. |
| 1901 | Death of Victoria; accession of Edward VII. |
| 1902 | Balfour's Education Act. |
| 1904 | Anglo-French *Entente*. |
| 1905 | Liberals replace Conservatives in power. |
| 1906 | Landslide Liberal win in general election. |
| 1909 | Lloyd George's budget rejected. |
| 1911 | Parliament Act curtails power of the House of Lords; Lloyd George's National Insurance Act. |
| 1911–12 | Railway, mining and coal strikes. |
| 1914 | First World War begins. |
| 1915 | Asquith coalition government brings Labour and Conservatives into government alongside Liberals. |
| 1916 | Conscription introduced. Easter Rising in Dublin. Battles of the Somme and Jutland. Lloyd George becomes Prime Minister. |
| 1917 | Communist revolution in Russia. |
| 1918 | Representation of the People Act gives vote to all men over 21 and most women over 30. New Labour Party constitution. End of First World War. 'Coupon' election. |
| 1919 | Treaty of Versailles |
| 1920 | Communist Party of Great Britain formed. |
| 1921 | Miners' strike. Treaty with Irish nationalists. Foundation of Irish Free State. |
| 1922 | Geddes report calls for large public spending cuts. Lloyd George coalition replaced by Conservative government under Bonar Law. Large Conservative majority in general election. |
| 1923 | Bonar Law replaced by Baldwin. General election without overall majority. |
| 1924 | First (minority) Labour government under MacDonald. Conservatives return under Baldwin. |
| 1925 | Britain goes back on the Gold Standard. |
| 1926 | General Strike. |
| 1927 | Trade Disputes and Trade Unions Act. |

| 1928 | Vote given to all women over 21. |
|---|---|
| 1929 | MacDonald becomes Prime Minister as head of minority Labour government. Wall Street crash. |
| 1931 | Financial crisis. National Government formed. Britain abandons the Gold Standard. National Government wins general election. |
| 1932 | Import Duties Act sets up tariffs. Ottawa Imperial Conference leads to imperial preference in trade. British Union of Fascists formed. |
| 1933 | Hitler comes to power. |
| 1935 | Government of India Act. Baldwin becomes Prime Minister. Abyssinia crisis. National Government wins general election. |
| 1936 | Year of three kings: death of George V, abdication of Edward VIII, accession of George VI. Public Order Act. |
| 1937 | Chamberlain succeeds Baldwin. |
| 1938 | Munich crisis. |
| 1939 | Second World War begins. |
| 1940 | Churchill becomes head of wartime coalition. Battle of Britain. |
| 1941 | Japan attacks Britain and USA. |
| 1942 | Fall of Singapore. Beveridge Report. |
| 1943 | Anglo-American invasion of Italy. |
| 1944 | D-day invasion of France. Butler's Education Act. |
| 1945 | End of Second World War. First Labour majority government formed. |
| 1947 | Coal nationalised. Convertibility crisis. India and Pakistan gain independence. Agriculture Act provides state subsidies. |
| 1949 | NATO founded. Devaluation of the pound. |
| 1950 | Korean War begins. Labour re-elected. |
| 1951 | Festival of Britain. Conservatives return to power under Churchill. |
| 1952 | George VI dies. Accession of Elizabeth II. |
| 1955 | Eden replaces Churchill as Prime Minister. |
| 1956 | Suez crisis. C. P. Snow discerns 'Two Cultures'. |
| 1957 | Macmillan replaces Eden as Prime Minister. |
| 1959 | Macmillan wins third successive Conservative electoral victory. |
| 1963 | Application to join the Common Market vetoed. Home replaces Macmillan as Prime Minister. |
| 1964 | Labour gains power under Wilson. |
| 1966 | Labour re-elected with larger majority. |
| 1967 | Devaluation of the pound. |
| 1970 | Conservatives under Heath gain power. |
| 1972 | Miners' strike. |
| 1973 | Britain enters Common Market. Stormont government abolished in Northern Ireland. |
| 1974 | Miners' strike. Heath replaced by Wilson. |
| 1975 | Referendum confirms membership of the Common Market. |
| 1976 | Economic crisis. Help obtained from International Monetary Fund. |
| 1979 | Devolution referenda in Scotland and Wales. Conservatives under Thatcher come to power. |
| 1982 | War with Argentina over Falkland Islands. |
| 1983 | Thatcher re-elected. |
| 1984–5 | Miners' strike. |
| 1987 | Thatcher re-elected. |

| | |
|---|---|
| 1990 | 21.9 million cars. Thatcher falls from power, replaced by John Major. |
| 1990–1 | Gulf War with Iraq. |
| 1992 | Major re-elected. |
| 1997 | Conservatives replaced by Labour Party under Tony Blair. |
| 1999 | Kosova war with Serbia; Scottish Parliament and Welsh Assembly meet. Northern Ireland Executive meets. |

# List of Prime Ministers

| Date of taking office | Prime Minister | Party |
| --- | --- | --- |
| 25 June 1895 | 3rd Marquess of Salisbury | Conservative |
| 12 July 1902 | Arthur Balfour | Conservative |
| 5 December 1905 | Sir Henry Campbell-Bannerman | Liberal |
| 5 April 1908 | Herbert Asquith | Liberal; Liberal head of Coalition from 25 May 1915 |
| 6 December 1916 | David Lloyd George | Liberal head of coalition |
| 23 October 1922 | Andrew Bonar Law | Conservative |
| 22 May 1923 | Stanley Baldwin | Conservative |
| 22 January 1924 | Ramsay MacDonald | Labour |
| 4 November 1924 | Stanley Baldwin | Conservative |
| 5 June 1929 | Ramsay MacDonald | Labour; from 24 August 1931, head of Conservative-dominated coalition National Government |
| 7 June 1935 | Stanley Baldwin | Conservative head of Conservative-dominated coalition National Government |
| 28 May 1937 | Neville Chamberlain | Conservative head of Conservative-dominated coalition National Government |
| 10 May 1940 | Winston Churchill | Conservative head of wartime coalition |
| 26 July 1945 | Clement Attlee | Labour |
| 26 October 1951 | Winston Churchill | Conservative |
| 6 April 1955 | Sir Anthony Eden | Conservative |
| 10 January 1957 | Harold Macmillan | Conservative |
| 19 October 1963 | Sir Alec Douglas-Home | Conservative |
| 16 October 1964 | Harold Wilson | Labour |
| 19 June 1970 | Edward Heath | Conservative |
| 4 March 1974 | Harold Wilson | Labour |
| 5 April 1976 | James Callaghan | Labour |
| 4 May 1979 | Margaret Thatcher | Conservative |
| 28 November 1990 | John Major | Conservative |
| 2 May 1997 | Tony Blair | Labour |

# Table of General Elections

| Date | Electorate (millions) | Turnout (%) | Winning party | Unionist/ Conservative % of vote | Liberal/Liberal Democratic % of vote | Labour % of vote |
|---|---|---|---|---|---|---|
| 28 September/ 24 October 1900 | 6.7 | 75 | Unionist | 50.3 | 45.0 | 1.3 |
| 12 January/ 7 February 1906 | 7.2 | 83 | Liberal | 43.4 | 49.4 | 4.8 |
| 14 January/ 9 February 1910 | 7.7 | 87 | Liberal | 46.9 | 43.5 | 7.0 |
| 12–19 December 1910 | 7.7 | 81 | Liberal | 43.6 | 44.2 | 6.4 |
| 14 December 1918 | 21.4 | 59 | Coalition | *Coalition:* 53.2 | 13.0 | 20.8 |
| 15 November 1922 | 21.1 | 71 | Conservative | 38.2 | 28.3 | 29.7 |
| 6 December 1923 | 21.3 | 71 | Labour | 38.0 | 29.7 | 30.7 |
| 29 October 1924 | 21.7 | 77 | Conservative | 48.3 | 17.6 | 33.0 |
| 30 May 1929 | 28.9 | 76 | Labour | 38.1 | 23.6 | 37.1 |
| 27 October 1931 | 30.0 | 76 | National | *National:* 60.5 | 7.2 | 30.8 |
| 14 November 1935 | 31.4 | 71 | National | *National:* 53.3 | 6.8 | 38.1 |
| 5 July 1945 | 33.2 | 73 | Labour | 39.6 | 9.0 | 48.0 |
| 23 February 1950 | 33.2 | 84 | Labour | 43.5 | 9.1 | 46.1 |
| 25 October 1951 | 34.6 | 83 | Conservative | 48.0 | 2.6 | 48.8 |
| 26 May 1955 | 34.9 | 77 | Conservative | 49.7 | 2.7 | 46.4 |
| 8 October 1959 | 35.4 | 79 | Conservative | 49.3 | 5.9 | 43.9 |
| 15 October 1964 | 35.9 | 77 | Labour | 43.4 | 11.2 | 44.1 |
| 31 March 1966 | 36.0 | 76 | Labour | 41.9 | 8.5 | 47.9 |
| 18 June 1970 | 39.3 | 72 | Conservative | 46.4 | 7.5 | 43.0 |
| 28 February 1974 | 39.8 | 79 | Labour | 37.9 | 19.3 | 37.1 |
| 10 October 1974 | 40.1 | 73 | Labour | 35.8 | 18.3 | 39.2 |
| 3 May 1979 | 41.1 | 76 | Conservative | 43.9 | 13.8 | 36.9 |
| 9 June 1983 | 42.2 | 73 | Conservative | 42.4 | *Alliance:* 25.4 | 27.6 |
| 11 June 1987 | 43.2 | 75 | Conservative | 42.3 | *Alliance:* 22.5 | 30.8 |
| 9 April 1992 | 43.2 | 78 | Conservative | 41.9 | *Lib. Dem.:* 17.9 | 34.4 |
| 1 May 1997 | 43.8 | 71.5 | Labour | 30.7 | *Lib. Dem.:* 16.8 | 43.3 |

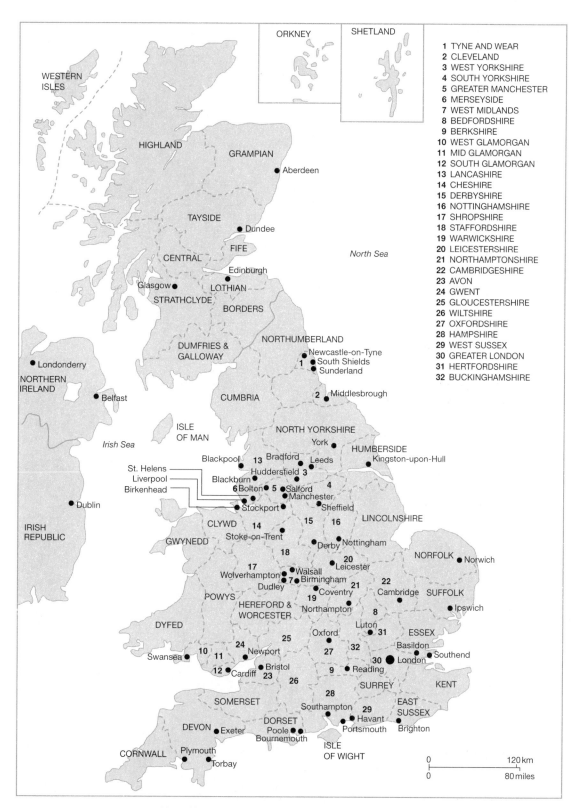

ORKNEY

SHETLAND

1 TYNE AND WEAR
2 CLEVELAND
3 WEST YORKSHIRE
4 SOUTH YORKSHIRE
5 GREATER MANCHESTER
6 MERSEYSIDE
7 WEST MIDLANDS
8 BEDFORDSHIRE
9 BERKSHIRE
10 WEST GLAMORGAN
11 MID GLAMORGAN
12 SOUTH GLAMORGAN
13 LANCASHIRE
14 CHESHIRE
15 DERBYSHIRE
16 NOTTINGHAMSHIRE
17 SHROPSHIRE
18 STAFFORDSHIRE
19 WARWICKSHIRE
20 LEICESTERSHIRE
21 NORTHAMPTONSHIRE
22 CAMBRIDGESHIRE
23 AVON
24 GWENT
25 GLOUCESTERSHIRE
26 WILTSHIRE
27 OXFORDSHIRE
28 HAMPSHIRE
29 WEST SUSSEX
30 GREATER LONDON
31 HERTFORDSHIRE
32 BUCKINGHAMSHIRE

WESTERN
ISLES

HIGHLAND

GRAMPIAN

• Aberdeen

TAYSIDE

• Dundee

FIFE

CENTRAL

Edinburgh

Glasgow •

LOTHIAN

STRATHCLYDE

BORDERS

North Sea

• Londonderry

NORTHERN
IRELAND

• Belfast

DUMFRIES &
GALLOWAY

NORTHUMBERLAND

Irish Sea

ISLE
OF MAN

CUMBRIA

Newcastle-on-Tyne
1 • South Shields
• Sunderland

2 • Middlesbrough

NORTH YORKSHIRE

York •

HUMBERSIDE
• Kingston-upon-Hull

• Dublin

IRISH
REPUBLIC

Blackpool •

13 Bradford
Leeds

Huddersfield 3

Blackburn

St. Helens
Liverpool
Birkenhead

6 Bolton• 5
Salford
Manchester •
Stockport •

Sheffield •

4

LINCOLNSHIRE

CLYWD

14

15

16

GWYNEDD

Stoke-on-Trent •

Derby •  Nottingham •

NORFOLK
• Norwich

18

20
Leicester •

POWYS

17

Wolverhampton •

7

Walsall
Birmingham •

21

22

Cambridge •

SUFFOLK

Dudley •

19

Coventry •

• Ipswich

HEREFORD &
WORCESTER

Northampton •

8

DYFED

25

Oxford •

Luton
31

ESSEX

10

24

Newport •

27

32

Basildon •

11

• Bristol

9 • Reading

30 • London

• Southend

Swansea •

12

Cardiff • 23

26

SURREY

KENT

SOMERSET

28

Southampton •

29

EAST
SUSSEX

DEVON

DORSET

• Havant

Portsmouth •

Brighton •

Exeter •

Poole •  •
Bournemouth

ISLE
OF WIGHT

CORNWALL

Plymouth •

• Torbay

0                    120 km

0              80 miles

Map of Britain showing counties and major towns, 1981

# Victorian Britain

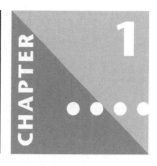

# CHAPTER 1

If the emphasis in our study of twentieth-century Britain is on change, it would be all too easy to present the earlier age as one of stability. This is particularly so because those who direct or affirm change generally see, or at least describe, what came before as static, in need of reform, and thus in some fashion undesirable. This chapter, in contrast, sets out to show the dynamism of late Victorian Britain, and to discuss its rapidly changing economy, society, culture and politics, in order to provide both a background for the remainder of the book, and an explanation of important aspects of the early decades of the twentieth century. It is important to read this chapter because it helps to explain the origins of important trends and problems in the twentieth century, and provides the context for judgements of what came later. It is also necessary to underline the extent to which there was not one Victorian 'age' nor one set of influential beliefs. Indeed, the rich variety of thought in Victorian Britain ensured that an important legacy to the early twentieth century was one of a great diversity in political, social and cultural attitudes. This helped to ensure that the process and pressures of change were understood differently, and that many different strategies to manage change were offered. Indeed the very extent of change in late nineteenth-century Britain encouraged a widespread sense that the country, or many aspects of it, was like an experiment.

## Contents

## Key issues

▶ What was the nature of late Victorian Britain?

▶ What were the principal pressures and developments?

▶ How successfully were the political and social systems coping with change?

▶ What was the importance of Britain's imperial position?

# Introduction

The young Queen Victoria succeeded her uncle William IV on the throne in 1837 against the background of a volatile political situation. Over the previous decade, many of the fundamentals of British political society had been overturned. First to go was the ascendancy of the Established Church (which in England, Wales and

Ireland was the Anglican Church, and in Scotland its Presbyterian counterpart). In 1828, the Test and Corporation Acts that maintained and symbolised Anglican ascendancy by restricting the position of Protestant Nonconformists were repealed. The following year, Catholic Emancipation gave Catholics the vote and repealed the civil disabilities to which they were subject. This rejection of anti-Catholicism as the cement of national identity was a major departure from the public ideology of nearly three centuries.

The Reform Act of 1832 was another major shock. It brought an extension and regularisation of the **franchise** (the right to vote) and a major redistribution of parliamentary seats. In essence, most of the middle class got the vote, but this was more striking because it followed a long period in which the franchise had not been altered and one in which the ability to control seats had been treated as a property right. More radical ideas had been advanced by some reformers over the previous sixty years, especially under the inspiration of the French Revolution of 1789, but these ideas had not been government policy, and indeed had been strongly resisted during Britain's long and arduous conflict with Revolutionary and Napoleonic France in 1793–1815. Conservative notions had been dominant then.

The situation in the 1830s was different and there appeared scant limit to the potential for fresh change. The system of poor relief was completely changed. The Poor Law Amendment Act established the 'workhouse test' as the criterion of public relief, providing an example of the principle of selectivity at work in the field of welfare. In 1835, the nature of urban society was transformed when the Municipal Corporations Act replaced self-selecting oligarchic corporations by elected borough councils, many of which set out to introduce reforms (the Scottish Municipal Corporations Act was in 1833).

Yet, the first three decades of Victoria's reign did not see an equivalent transformation in political society. There was no second Reform Act until 1867 (and in Scotland until 1868), and it is important not to exaggerate the extent to which the 1832 Reform Act changed politics. Undoubtedly, elements of the middle classes were enfranchised, but many felt cheated (an attitude that led to the Anti-Corn Law League campaign) as the old rulers continued to dominate national politics. In a sense, the Municipal Corporations Act was also a consolation prize for the middle classes. The demands for major changes pressed in the late 1830s and 1840s by the Chartists, a popular radical movement, including **universal adult male suffrage** and annual elections, faded with the failure of Chartism in 1848. There was reforming legislation in this period, most significantly Factory Acts and the Public Health Act of 1848, but, in general, there was a low level of state intervention during a period of rapid and massive economic and social change, including industrialisation and urbanisation on a scale never before experienced in history. The direction of government economic policy, as confirmed by the decision of Sir Robert Peel's Conservative government in 1846 to repeal the **Corn Laws**, was firmly set towards the promotion of free trade. The repeal of the Corn Laws led to less expensive food for urban workers, but also affected British agriculture. The spread of the railway linked the country as never before.

A fresh bout of reforming activity started in the late 1860s, and that was the beginning of the late Victorian period, one in which near continual change in society and economics was accompanied by a pace of public activity – by the government and related bodies – that would have seemed frenetic, radical and dangerous in the eighteenth century. Much earlier, especially public health, legislation was permis-

**franchise:** The right to vote in public elections.

**universal adult male suffrage:** Voting rights granted to all men over the legal age of majority.

**Corn Laws:** Laws regulating and restricting corn imports, repealed in 1846.

Box 1.1

## The coming of the railways

The British led the way with steam power. James Watt developed the stationary steam-engine in the eighteenth century, and the locomotive steam-engine followed in the 1820s. Industrialisation supplied the necessary demand, capital and skills. George Stephenson opened the Hetton Railway in 1822, and the Stockton and Darlington Railway followed in 1830. Railways offered new links and cut journey times for both freight and passengers. Large numbers travelled at an unprecedented speed and with increased frequency. 'Space' had been conquered. New sounds and sights contributed to a powerful sense of change, and this was overwhelmingly seen as progress. News and fashions spread round the country. Commuting developed, and London and other cities spread. The railway helped to create suburbs and suburban environments. The shape of towns changed as lines both joined and dissected. Rail travel reflected a social system stratified by wealth. There were three classes with different conditions and fares. On the London to Brighton line, the 3rd class carriages lacked roofs until 1852, and were thus exposed to the weather and the hot ash from the engine.

sive. From the 1880s most was compulsory. The reform process was more insistent because it was pushed by both the major political parties, the Conservatives and the Liberals. Under William Gladstone, Liberal Prime Minister in 1868–74, 1880–5, 1886 and 1892–4, the Whigs were transformed into the more avowedly reformist Liberals. Under Benjamin Disraeli, Conservative Prime Minister in 1868 and 1874–80, Conservatism was effectively redefined as different from and opposed to Liberalism, but not as a creed of reaction. Instead, Disraeli sought to fuse social legislation with a sense of national continuity, and to create a popular Conservatism in the aftermath of the 1867 Reform Act, although he was less determined to align Conservatism with the middle or working classes than some of his successors.

**The repeal of the Corn Laws**
This was designed to help ensure cheap food for the urban population. In this *Punch* cartoon of 1846, Robert Peel, the Prime Minister, stands in the doorway of the baker's, while the Duke of Wellington carries an advertising board.

## Dickens and society

Much of our image of Victorian Britain comes from the novels of Charles Dickens (1812–70), which addressed social conditions and urban society. In his childhood, Dickens had experience of hardship. His father went to the Marshalsea Debtors' Prison, and, at the age of twelve, Dickens began work in a London factory. A committed reformer, especially over capital punishment, housing and prostitution, in his novels he presented the inadequacies of existing institutions. *Nicholas Nickleby*, published in monthly parts in 1838–9, condemned uncaring schools, *Bleak House* (1852–3), the callousness of law, church and society, *Little Dorrit* (1855–7), government bureaucracy and financial fraud.

The consequence was that the two parties competed to woo an expanding electorate and to forward acceptable reform agendas. In office, the Conservatives did not reverse the Liberal attempt to legislate for social improvement. Instead, there were steadily greater attempts to create a legislative framework for reform, the background to the use and perception of the state in the twentieth century. In place of the reliance on self-help and the efforts of individual communities, that had been so important in the mid-nineteenth century, there was a stress on institutional provision and national standards.

Under Gladstone, for example, the 1870 Education Act (the Scottish Education Act followed in 1872) divided the country into school districts under Education Boards, and stipulated a certain level of educational provision. The Endowed Schools Commission established that year redistributed endowments and reformed governing bodies. There were also major developments in other fields. Open competition was introduced in the Civil Service in 1870, an important step in the move from appointments made as a result of patronage towards a stress on merit. The institutionalisation of Easter, Whitsun and Bank Holidays in 1871 provided more opportunities for organised leisure, and also drove home the control of government over the calendar and the organisation of time. The Definition of Time (GMT) Act of 1880 made the use of Greenwich Mean Time compulsory throughout Britain, an important aspect of standardisation that again looked towards the twentieth century. The adoption of the Greenwich Meridian by the rest of the world, especially at the expense of rival American and French meridians, reflected Britain's dominant position in international trade, finance and communications. The introduction of the secret ballot in 1872 made voting less open to coercion. The Corrupt and Illegal Practices Act of 1883 also served to put the conduct of election campaigns on a more secure footing.

Under Disraeli, legislation on factories, public health, and pure food and drugs, systematised and extended the regulation of important aspects of public health and social welfare. The Artisans' Dwellings Act of 1875 made urban renewal possible, although few local authorities took advantage of the legislation. The Prison Act of 1877 established state control over the whole prison system, over local as well as the so-called convict prisons, which were already under the control of central government.

As central and local government became more activist and regulatory, so its control increasingly became a question of policy as much as office-holding. The purpose of politics was far more to gain office in order to introduce particular policies, especially policies of and for change, and this purpose was stated explicitly when seeking public and political support. Again this looked towards the twentieth century. The

**Public health**
Urban crowding exacerbated the impact of epidemic disease and led to concern and action. The picture shows a mass vaccination clinic in London's East End (from *The Graphic*, 8 April 1871).

nature and purpose of power within British society was discussed to a far greater extent than a century earlier. The initial tone of these discussions was rather sombre in nature as fears of revolutionary upheaval abounded. The first signs of organised socialist activity were evident in the 1880s with the establishment of the Social Democratic Federation by Henry Hyndman in 1883. The failure of the expected revolution to occur served to ease the fears which were widely held in late Victorian society and politics concerning the rise of the masses. Their reluctance to engage in revolutionary activity was to continue into the twentieth century.

The Second Reform Act of 1867 offered household suffrage in boroughs and nearly doubled the existing electorate. Women, however, remained excluded from the franchise. Due to the spread of literacy, that owed much to improvements in the education system, and of knowledge about politics through the growing newspaper readership, newly emancipated groups had a national political consciousness. The most effective were the middle class who had gained the vote in 1832 and control over the boroughs in 1835. Prospering from economic expansion, the middle classes expected power and status, and were dubious of established institutions and practices that did not seem reformist or useful. Their views stimulated a demand for, and process of, improvement – economic, civic and moral – that was central to the movement for reform. The Anti-Corn Law League, established under the leadership of Richard Cobden and John Bright in Manchester in 1838, was the first example of the organised power which the middle class was now capable of wielding.

Middle-class pressure for reforming change remained an important feature of British life into and throughout the twentieth century, although by the late nineteenth century this middle-class pressure was abating. In the nineteenth century, as later, it was directed as much against the habits of the poor as against those of **the Establishment**. Immorality was criticised as debasing and unproductive, and thus doubly wrong. This led, for example, to moves to restrict the availability of alcohol, and also to the Contagious Diseases Acts of 1866, 1867 and 1869, under which a harsh system of control was established over prostitutes in garrison and port towns. The

**the Establishment:** The people and organisations in authority who control public life.

**The quest for clean water**
The reappearance of cholera in 1848–9 directed attention to the poor state of the water supply. *Punch*'s comment in 1849 did not capture the full horror of the situation.

"WATER! WATER! EVERYWHERE:
AND NOT A DROP TO DRINK."

prostitutes, rather than their clients, were blamed for venereal disease. Some popular pastimes were treated as disorderly and repressed. Drinking was affected by the 1869 Wine and Beerhouses Act and the 1872 Licensing Act. Attempts were made to curtail gambling.

'Morality' was not only a middle-class cause. Self-improving artisans were also important, especially in expanding and prosperous industrial towns, such as Sunderland, where there was a high percentage of owner-occupiers of property. Similarly, reform agitation was not limited to the propertied. Indeed the developing working-class communities in the expanding towns and cities of Britain were increasingly aware of common interests and keen to press for their furtherance. In the 1870s, for example, textile workers campaigned hard for an eight-hour working day.

As Britain became a more industrial and urban society, it also became a more secular society. Religion lost its central role in everyday life and church attendance began to decline: developments which were to become more marked during the twentieth century. This did not mean that religion had ceased to be a divisive issue in late nineteenth-century Britain. In Wales, for example, the Established status of the Anglican Church in a predominantly Nonconformist country became a particularly potent issue. In such cities as Glasgow and Liverpool, each with their own Protestant and Catholic communities, sectarian tension was never far below the surface. Increasing immigration from Eastern Europe also had a religious impact, as Jewish communities established themselves in the East End of London. As Britain's immigrant population continued to grow during the twentieth century, then the pattern of denominational allegiance was to change even further. Immigration, however, exacerbated prejudice. When in January 1910 Alfred Mond ran as Liberal candidate for Swansea Town, the Conservatives responded with an anti-Semitic campaign.

Before considering how the pace of reform continued and, in part, accelerated, from the 1880s into the twentieth century, it is important to look at the economy and society of late Victorian Britain, for it was pressures within these that reformers sought to address and overcome. Furthermore, unlike in the modern age, when commentators look abroad for trends, solutions and ideas, in Victorian Britain there was a strong and well-deserved, although by no means unanimous, sense that the country was at the cutting edge of modernity, and that it could not be understood by looking abroad. Although this confidence was under pressure from about 1880, especially as a result of economic competition and a degree of cultural uncertainty that has led to the descriptions 'age of anxiety' and 'age of doubt', there was still a mood of national self-confidence which was well captured by the euphoria surrounding the Golden and Diamond Jubilees of Queen Victoria in 1887 and 1897 respectively. This mood was to survive intact until the humbling military defeats experienced in the Boer War (1899–1902) unleashed a wave of intense national introspection.

Britain was the workshop of the world, and was happy to see itself in this light. In 1880–4, the annual average production of coal and lignite in million metric tons was 159 for Britain, and 108 for France, Germany, Belgium and Russia combined, that of pig-iron in 1880, 7.9 for Britain and 5.4 for the rest of Europe, and of steel 1.3 and 1.5; while raw cotton consumption in thousand metric tons in 1880 was 617 for Britain and 503 for the rest of Europe. Increased production interacted with expanding trade. This led to an expansion in merchant shipping, shipbuilding and new docks. In London, the leading commercial and industrial centre in the country and by far the most populous city, the Poplar Docks, opened in 1852, were followed by the Royal Victoria Dock (1855), Millwall Dock (1868), Royal Albert Dock (1880) and Tilbury Docks (1886). Ships bringing goods from all over the world docked in London; most of them were British-owned.

Britain's industrial strength faced challenges, however. The very pace of change required investment in new processes, and international competition was becoming more acute. This was especially so after America had recovered from the Civil War of 1861–5, and after the unification of Germany in 1866–71. Britain's unprecedented economic dominance in about 1870, her near monopoly of manufacturing, was unsustainable. In terms of productivity, in many industries Britain's rivals were catching up with best practice. Many British companies were unable to respond. Established practices were not discarded rapidly enough, and there was considerable caution about investing in new technology. A widespread economic crisis, especially in farming and in some traditional industries, was apparent in Britain in the last quarter of the century, the so-called **Great Depression**. Coal mining, the key activity of the steam age, and the source of power for Britain and of much export wealth, was hit from the 1870s. By the 1880s, one of the leading coalfields, that in County Durham, had passed its peak and miners were leaving the county.

Manufacturing was hit hard from the 1880s, with a squeeze on profits. This was true both of the national economy as a whole and of the centres of heavy industry. In the Sunderland shipyards, there were empty order books and wage cuts in the 1880s. Iron and steel had been central to manufacturing, but this sector was affected by serious bankruptcies. In Gateshead on the Tyne the major ironworks ceased trading: Hawks, Crawshay in 1889 and Abbots in 1909. Elsewhere, the West Cumberland Iron and Steel Company closed in 1891, the Britannia Foundry at Derby in 1910.

Nevertheless, decline in manufacturing industry was relative, and not absolute. Britain was still a leading economy. Her share of world trade had fallen, in particular due to American and German competition, but the volume of trade was now far

**Great Depression:** A period of decline in economic activity that began in the last quarter of the nineteenth century. There was a further serious Depression in the 1930s.

**The industrial landscape – profit, energy and pollution**
This scene of 1885, showing the Stoke pottery kilns, was matched by similar landscapes of industrial activity across the country.

larger. Britain was the largest overseas investor in the world, and able, therefore, to benefit from economic growth elsewhere. She was also the greatest merchant shipper in the world. In addition, Britain was the centre of the world's financial system, and benefited from the expansion of the service sector. This was to remain very important throughout the twentieth century. Global commodity prices, shipping rates and insurance premiums were all set in London, the prime site of what has been termed gentlemanly capitalism. The service sector was crucial to the economic strength of late nineteenth-century Britain, for invisible earnings more than offset the deficit on trade. Thanks to her prominence in submarine telegraphy, Britain was also at the centre of the world's communications. Aside from her major and frequently leading role in the production of traditional goods, such as coal, textiles, steel, iron and ships, Britain was also playing an important part in the development of new sectors: in the growth of production in chemicals, and in new consumer goods, such as motor cars and telephones. However, Britain was slow to move effectively in these fields and much was imported.

In 1902, Arthur Benson's words for 'Land of Hope and Glory', the first of Edward Elgar's 'Pomp and Circumstance' marches, were first heard as part of the Coronation Ode for Edward VII. They promised a steadily 'wider' empire. The Empire was indeed the most extensive and populous in the world, and was still expanding rapidly. It also dominated the production of many important goods. Gold and diamonds came from South Africa, and helped to drive British expansion there. Copper and wheat came from Canada, tin from Malaya, cocoa from Ghana, palm oil from Nigeria, lamb, mutton and wool from Australasia. Imperial products were processed, manufactured and marketed in Britain, and it was from there that the finance for their exploitation and transport came. To a certain extent, however, the existence of the Empire lessened the pressure to improve the industrial base in Britain in order to succeed in more competitive markets, especially in Continental Europe and the USA.

Aggregate figures for British economic growth concealed and reflected a regional geography of great contrasts and variations, again a pattern that persisted during the twentieth century, and one that was true of other industrial countries. As industrialisation gathered pace and became more normal, so did the contrast between industrialised regions and the rest of the country, between, for example, Clydeside and

South-West Scotland. In the industrialised regions, the experience and world of work changed. By the mid-nineteenth century, fewer than 10 per cent of those employed in the Scottish Central Belt counties of Lanark, Midlothian and Renfrew worked in the traditional activities of agriculture, forestry and fishing.

In such areas, the landscape changed. The mining gear of coal and other mines, the slag heaps of mining and industrial waste, and the smoking chimneys of industry, came to dominate visually, while metal beating and the hiss of steam swamped natural sounds, and coal smoke became the prime smell as well as a major restriction on visibility. Paintings such as Myles Foster's *Newcastle upon Tyne from Windmill Hills, Gateshead* (c. 1871–2) showed formerly prominent buildings – the castle keep and the cathedral – now joined by sites of the new industrial world: factory chimneys and the railway bridge. Atmospheric pollution exacerbated respiratory illnesses.

The population of regions experiencing industrial growth rose rapidly, far more so than in other parts of the country. The population of County Durham, a centre of coal mining and heavy industry, rose from 390,997 in 1851 to 1,016,152 in 1891, that of the iron and steel centre of Workington from 6,467 in 1861 to 23,749 in 1891, and that of Newcastle from 28,294 in 1801 to 215,328 in 1901.

Major increases in population were only achieved by migration. The dislocation of extensive migration was part of the pattern of economic growth, essential to provide labour, and yet disruptive for individuals and communities and the source of many difficulties. Migration within Britain was a central feature of the social fabric of Victorian Britain and was, again, a trend that continued into the twentieth century. It contributed to a powerful sense of fluidity, and to the decline of established patterns of social control. Areas with limited economic growth, such as Cornwall and Ireland, produced large numbers of migrants, who were soaked up by growing cities. Glamorganshire and Monmouthshire, the key zone of Welsh mining and industrialisation, had about 20% of the Welsh population in 1801, but 57.5% by 1901, in part because of migration from the more rural areas of Wales, especially from Central Wales, but also from Ireland and South-West England; 11% of Swansea's population in 1901 had been born in South-West England. London, Britain's largest industrial city, drew heavily on East Anglia and the West Country, both areas with limited economic growth, especially that created by industrialisation, and with serious problems in their traditionally important agricultural sector. There was a general flight from the land after about 1870.

Industrial regions that failed to maintain earlier growth rates, for example the Staffordshire coal and iron area, also provided migrants. Staffordshire and Shropshire ironworkers were partly responsible for the expansion of the population in County Durham. Changes in the location of industrial expansion reflected transformation in the economy. Engineering, shipbuilding and chemicals became more prominent, rather than the textiles and metal smelting of earlier decades, although both the latter remained important.

The new society of urbanisation and industrialisation, in turn, created new needs and problems. New living environments had to be created, sustained and improved, including houses for millions, new pastimes, and new systems of control, welfare, education, socialisation and community. This affected all branches of life. For example, the development of urban working-class leisure, away from traditional customs, and towards new mass, commercialised interests, was one response to the new society. Again, this looked forward into the following century. Music-halls and football clubs were founded in large numbers for the working class. This was commercial and institutionalised leisure, a form suited to the large urban masses, and one that was open to regulation, so that it should not challenge the requirements of the established order, though with varying degrees of success. Indeed, the music-halls proved to be valuable agents of social control in late nineteenth-century Britain and were pretty much sanitised by the early twentieth century. By presenting the upper classes as figures of fun rather than hate-figures – 'Champagne Charlie' became the stereotypical society toff – the halls served to ease working-class resentment at their social betters. Professional football was more problematic. Some early twentieth-century critics saw football as an agent for the re-barbarising of society.

Alternative entertainments were scrutinised. Vagrancy laws were used to limit street entertainers, street gamblers and street prostitution, part of the process by which open spaces were controlled. In London, a campaign against street prostitution launched in 1883 came to an end in 1887 amidst public complaints and parliamentary questions about the blackmailing of poor prostitutes, bribery, and harassment through arrests. A fresh campaign was launched in the early 1900s, while in 1906 the Street Betting Act sought to stamp out that practice. The regulations for the parks that were established in towns were another example of the same process, as were the limitations on the opening hours of pubs. It was the public house, however, which provided the main source of entertainment and leisure for the male inhabitants of the newly burgeoning industrial towns. Drink remained central to the lives of ordinary working people – even in those parts of the United Kingdom where the pull of religion was strongest, the 'pub and chapel' culture of South Wales for instance.

More generally, policing expanded. In many areas this led to tension, even conflict, with sections, sometimes large sections, of the working class. These defences of the old 'rough' culture were joined by signs of more politicised working-class protest. One of the most dramatic occurred at the symbolic centre of Empire, Trafalgar Square, on 'Bloody Sunday', 13 November 1887. A meeting called by the Metropolitan Radical Association in protest against the government's failure to tackle unemployment was banned, leading to a violent demonstration involving over 400 arrests and about 200 casualties including three deaths. There had also been riots over electoral reform in 1866–7.

Public space was thus controlled. Private space was also seen as a problem and was increasingly subject to regulation, as part of a process designed to reform society. For example, the Criminal Law Amendment Act of 1885 criminalised all homosexual acts, including those carried out in private, while the Vagrancy Act of 1898 made homosexual importuning a criminal offence.

Industrialisation and population growth had led in the early nineteenth century to a deterioration in the living conditions of the urban working class. They had been affected by overcrowding, and by insanitary conditions, leading to high levels of disease. Cholera, a disease transmitted through drinking water contaminated by sewage, hit hard from the 1830s. The crisis in public health led to action from the 1840s. In 1848, the Public Health Act created a General Board of Health and an administrative structure to improve sanitation, especially water supply. The Act enabled the creation of local Boards of Health. The permissive 1848 Act was followed up by the 1875 Public Health Act, which in practical terms was a far more important piece of legislation.

The health crisis was most serious in cities, but by the 1870s the process of improvement was proceeding rapidly. London had a drainage system completed in

1875 with 82 miles of intercepting sewers that took sewage from earlier sewers that had drained into the Thames, and transported it to new downstream outfall sewage works. Storm-relief sewers followed in the 1880s. On Tyneside, reservoir storage capacity rose to over 3,000 million gallons by the end of the 1880s (compared with 215 million in 1848), and filter beds were installed in 1863. In Huddersfield, sanitary developments, including the improvement in water quality and supply thanks to the 1869, 1876 and 1890 Waterworks Acts, helped cut the impact of infectious diseases.

These developments were necessary in order to cope with the strains of continued growth. The situation remained difficult in many areas. In 1866, 43% of Newcastle's population was still living in dwellings of only one or two rooms; in 1885, 30.6%. Disease continued to be encouraged by the circumstances of urban life. Gastrointestinal disorders linked to inadequate water and sewage systems were responsible for particularly high rates of infant mortality, as in Bradford and the crowded parts of Newcastle. Such circumstances were increasingly thrust into the attention of the rest of the public. The social surveys of Charles Booth in East London in the late 1880s and of Seebohm Rowntree in York in 1899 revealed that over a quarter of their population were living below what they saw as the level of poverty, a level well below late twentieth-century standards. Booth attributed poverty to the role of seasonal and casual labour and the problems of child-rearing and old age without social welfare. The living conditions of the bulk of the population were therefore affected by economic problems and by individual tragedies. The death, injury or unemployment of the principal breadwinner could wreck family life. As mortality figures cut across families, the impact of infections was particularly serious. Aside from disease, public health was also affected by new sources of pollution. Gas works produced coal tar which drained into rivers. Poor urban sanitation, housing and nutrition were widely blamed for the physical weakness of much of the population. There were still serious problems even where jobs were plentiful. In Sunderland the sky was smoke blackened and life took place under a thick layer of coal dust, which was definitely detrimental to health. In 1913, 27 manufacturers in Huddersfield were cautioned over smoke pollution. These difficult urban conditions pressed hardest on the poor. The wealthier sections of the community lived in less crowded areas and generally lived at a distance from polluted industrial zones. Indeed, urban pollution encouraged a move towards suburban villages.

Problems were not restricted to poverty-riddled urban slums. There was also much rural poverty, although it was generally under-reported and is too often overlooked. The most abject poverty was to be found in counties such as Dorset. British farming had survived the initial effect of the repeal of the Corn Laws, because demand was then growing, farming was diversifying, and there were no longer substantial foreign supplies available. It was from the 1870s with the opening of the prairies and the steppes that farming paid the price. Rural poverty was the result of a combination of traditional social inequalities in the countryside with the consequences of a protracted agricultural depression (the Great Agricultural Depression), caused by competition from foreign supplies, especially North American grain, Argentinian beef, Australasian wool, mutton and lamb, and Danish bacon. The technological advances of steamships, refrigerated holds, railways and barbed wire that helped the development of export agriculture in distant areas, much of which was financed by British capital, badly affected British farming.

This crisis hit rural workers hardest, although it also hit hard at the economy of provincial towns dependent on agricultural processing and serving rural hinter-

### Robert, 3rd Marquess of Salisbury (1830–1903)

Conservative Prime Minister 1885–6, 1886–92 and 1895–1902, Salisbury was a member of the great aristocratic house of Cecil. Nevertheless, he understood the need to recruit and maintain middle-class and urban support. Salisbury's opinions and policies were defined in opposition to Gladstone's Liberalism. A supporter of the Church of England and the free market, Salisbury was opposed to Home Rule for Ireland and to diplomatic commitments to European alliances. His interest in foreign policy led to Salisbury also serving as Foreign Secretary in 1885–6, 1887–92 and 1895–1900. Keen on his family, Salisbury was criticised as a nepotist and was indeed succeeded by his nephew Arthur Balfour. Salisbury's last years in office were overshadowed by the difficulties of the Boer War (1899–1902). He failed to control those who wanted war and was a poor war leader.

lands. Robert, 3rd Marquess of Salisbury, Conservative Prime Minister in 1885–6, 1886–92 and 1895–1902, preferred elections at harvest time as agricultural labourers were then least likely to vote. The Agricultural Labourers Union provided a focus for discontent. Landlords were also affected, and many had to cut rents. Arable farmers bore the brunt of a decline in production that was absolute, not relative. They were also hit by recurrent bad weather in the period. Dairying and livestock husbandry expanded, as did specialist agriculture, for example fruit production in East Anglia. Derelict farms could be found in once prosperous areas, such as south Essex. Frequently, the show of landed wealth on the part of landowners resulted not from agricultural profits, but from mineral rights, the development of urban estates, or from marriage with heiresses – especially, towards the close of the century, Americans. There was considerable social tension in some rural areas, including numerous attacks on the police; but migration to the cities or abroad helped to lessen strains. The declining importance of rural Britain had been evident for over a century, but the cumulative effect was still dramatic. The human geography of the country changed, as did the experience of life and the environment of most of the population.

Both rural and urban society were affected by the growth of large-scale organisations, both commercial and of other types. Ownership and production became more concentrated, as in the Northumberland and Durham brewing industry, and with regional banking chains, such as Barclays, which was formed in 1896. The development of public limited companies helped investment by outside interests, and this ensured that national control of businesses became more pronounced. Big retail chains became important. John Sainsbury opened his first dairy in London in 1869, Thomas Lipton his first grocery in Glasgow in 1871. In 1883, Julius Drewe opened the Home and Colonial stores in London; by 1890 there were 107 shops in the company. Regional multiples, such as Hinton's in and around Middlesbrough, also developed.

Politics was also being redefined, as politicians sought to adjust to a wider national and local electorate. The national electorate expanded with the Third Reform Act of 1884, which extended to the counties the household franchise granted to the boroughs in 1867, so that over two-thirds of the adult males in the counties, and about 63% of the entire adult male population, received the vote. In County Durham, for example, the electorate expanded greatly as a result of the miners gaining the vote. The electorate rose from 3.15 million to 5.7 million, although, of these, nearly 750,000 were plural votes. Furthermore, the percentage of adult males who could vote was closer to 40 than 63 because so many people changed address and because a voter needed 18 months' continuous residence. The 1885 Redistribution Act created mainly single-member constituencies and gave boroughs more equitable representation. Women were still denied the vote, although they gained it in local government. The Local Government Act of 1888 created directly elected county councils and county boroughs, and the London County Council. Thanks also to the Local Government Act of 1894, the democratisation of local government entailed elected county and town councils taking over functions formerly performed by the magistrates and the Poor Law Unions.

Such an extension of democracy posed fresh problems to the existing order. As in 1868, the Conservatives in 1885 were defeated in the first election held with the new franchise. Many rural electors voted against their landlords. Democracy challenged the existing social politics of the country.

Yet the Liberal triumph was swiftly overturned. Under Gladstone, the Liberal government supported Home Rule for Ireland, an undoing of the Act of Union of 1800, under which Ireland was joined to Britain and represented in the Westminster Parliament. Home Rule split the Liberals, and created Liberal Unionism, which was opposed to Home Rule. With the support of Liberal Unionists, the Conservatives, under Salisbury and, from 1902, his nephew Arthur Balfour, were in office in 1886–92 and from 1895 to 1905. The Conservatives opposed Home Rule and followed a cautious policy on domestic reform. They benefited from the long-term expansion of the middle classes and from their growing urban strength following the 1885 re-distribution of constituencies. The Conservatives increasingly became an urban and suburban-based party. The transformation of the Tory Party was one of the great success stories of nineteenth-century politics. Given the divisions following the con-troversial repeal of the Corn Laws and the defection of the Peelites, there was a very real chance that the Tories would become little more than a landed rump on the margins of politics. Their transformation into a national party representing significant elements of the new urban middle classes was to be very important for twentieth-century politics. The Conservatives benefited from the perceived radicalism of Gladstonian Liberalism which drove the satiated middle classes (the beneficiaries of the meritocratic reforms of the first Gladstone ministry) into the Conservative camp. Although 'Tory Democracy' had been developed under Disraeli, it was taken further, not least with the foundation of the Primrose League in 1883. This provided a popular dimension to the Conservative political machinery. Salisbury himself, however, was not best placed to create a Tory populism. Two-thirds of his Cabinet were peers, although it did nothing to advance the landed interest other than not passing budgets like the Liberal one of 1894 which had greatly increased death duties. Tariffs (customs duties) were not imposed on imports of food, for fear of affecting the living standards of urban workers. Free trade remained British policy and the centrepiece of British economic ideology.

Imperial expansion helped the Conservatives, who made themselves the un-disputed party of Empire in British politics, but, like the Liberals, they found it difficult to respond coherently to the pressures of a society in which various groups were defining different demands. Growing pressure for more radical political and social policies encouraged political opinion increasingly to coalesce and polarise along social and class lines, although revolutionary sentiment was limited. **Revolutionary Marxism** was effectively checked and marginalised in Britain in the 1880s. The Social

**revolutionary Marxism:** The belief based on Karl Marx's teaching that the working class would rise up and take power from the aristocrats and property owners.

### Karl Marx (1818–83)

Karl Heinrich Marx was a radical German philosopher and economist, who left Germany when the paper he was editing was suppressed. He went to Paris where he met Friedrich Engels, who gave him help and support financially and in his writing and development of the theory of scientific socialism. Marx was convinced that society was class based and that middle-class domination would succumb to that of the working class. The *Communist Manifesto* was published in 1848. In 1849 Marx settled in London where he continued to write. The first volume of *Das Kapital* appeared in 1867, followed by other volumes over the next 16 years.

Democratic Federation (SDF) was the nearest thing to a revolutionary Marxist organisation in England. Its impact was marginal for a variety of reasons, including poor leadership, the unwillingness and failure of the SDF to court and win trade union support, the widespread commitment to reformism (to be seen in the craft unions of the time as well as among the Fabians), based on the belief that the parliamentary system could be made more democratic and therefore more responsive to working-class needs, and a belief that violence was inappropriate and unnecessary in England.

Instead, change was pursued through the political process. Joseph Chamberlain's 'unauthorised' Liberal programme of 1885 called for land reform, and was followed in 1891 by Gladstone's Newcastle programme, which also called for Home Rule, disestablishment of the Church of England in Wales, free education, a reduction in factory work-hours, electoral reform and the reform or abolition of the House of Lords. That year, the Scottish Liberals called for land reform in the Highlands, an eight-hour day for miners, and an extension of the franchise.

Such policies divided the Liberals, making them appear to some as a threat to stability. The landed interest broke from the Liberals, and there was a coalescence of opinion in defence of property and order under the Conservatives, but one with only a fragile basis among the working class. The latter was still largely Liberal, although Socialist organisations were founded: the Social Democratic Federation in 1883, the Fabian Society in 1884, and the Independent Labour Party in 1893. Salisbury sought to reconcile 'Tory Democracy' with traditional Conservative beliefs, while at the same time responding to new problems in a class-based society. This worked better in some areas than others. The West Midlands and Scotland, for example, became more Conservative than Wales, although that owed much to the strength of Liberal Unionism in both areas. Lancashire became more Conservative than North-East England. The Conservatives were able to win elections in 1886, 1895 and 1900.

If politics was developing towards its class-orientated character in the twentieth century, there were also important currents of change in other spheres, not least the weakening of the Established Churches, the rise of trade unions, and continued pressures both from urbanisation and industrialisation and from the economic cycles that affected the latter. Britain was the strongest empire in the world at the start of the twentieth century, but there was doubt and uncertainty alongside optimism and complacency.

# Summary

◆ Victorian Britain was not a static backdrop to the twentieth century. Instead, it was a dynamic and fast-changing society.

◆ The pace of economic change was great and affected all of society. The United Kingdom was the leading economic power in the world in 1860, but its lead was under increasing pressure, and in some respects it had been passed by the USA and Germany by 1900.

◆ Social upheaval was especially acute in the fast-expanding cities which came to dominate the country. Behind long dominant London, other cities, such as Birmingham, Glasgow and Manchester, rose to prominence.

◆ The extension of the franchise created a new mass male electorate that the established parties struggled to come to grips with. There was increasing class tension by the 1890s.

# Questions for discussion

◆ Why did the economy encounter growing problems?

◆ How far were social pressures due to economic expansion or to an already heavily inegalitarian society?

◆ Why was revolution avoided?

◆ How were politics at the close of the nineteenth century different from today?

◆ What did political leadership require in the nineteenth century?

# Further reading

Adelman, Paul, *Gladstone, Disraeli and Later Victorian Politics* (3rd edn, London, 1997).

Barker, R., *Politics, Peoples and Government: Themes in British Political Thought since the Nineteenth Century* (Basingstoke, 1994).

Jenkins, T. A., *The Liberal Ascendancy, 1830–1886* (Basingstoke, 1994).

Machin, Ian, *Disraeli* (London, 1994).

Mason, Tony, *Association Football and English Society, 1863–1915* (Hassocks, 1980).

Roberts, Andrew, *Salisbury: Victorian Titan* (London, 1999).

Rubinstein, W. D., *Britain's Century: A Political and Social History, 1815–1905* (London, 1998).

Searle, G. A., *The Liberal Party: Triumph and Disintegration, 1886–1929* (Basingstoke, 1992).

Steele, David, *Lord Salisbury* (London, 1997).

# The Condition of the People

## Contents

To look at photographs of people in 1900 is to look at people who were very different from us. In part, this is due to fashions, in part to technology: sepia rather than colour photographs. In part, the difference is a matter of changing beliefs, experiences and assumptions. It is also a question of the structures of people's lives, the nature and frequency of birth and death, their health, and the very physical makeup of human beings. These are far from constant and some of the most important changes of the century have occurred not only in the fabric of life, but also in its very nature. Shifts such as the changing age structure of the population and, in particular, the rise of old age, are central not only to the experience of individuals but also to the character of the community.

## Key issues

▶ How has population structure changed during the century?

▶ What are the class and regional dimensions of population structure?

▶ What did the National Health Service achieve?

▶ How did social welfare develop during the century?

## ▮ Demographics

The twentieth century saw a major rise in the British population. Including Northern Ireland, it rose to 58.6 million in 1997 (see census figures in Box 2.1). There is no sign that this increase will end, although the birth rate among long-established resident groups at the close of the century was low. The absolute size of the population in England, Wales and Scotland combined was lower in 1991 than 1981, although by 1997 it had risen above the 1987 level. The overwhelming majority of the population lived in England, which was the most densely populated of the major European countries, far more so than France for example. This density helped to define much of English history, both environmental and socio-political. In the first case, the number of people put pressure on resources, not least the space available for life and for transport. It also ensured that the country could not feed itself, a central feature of its

## Box 2.1

**Census figures, to nearest tenth of a million**

|       | England and Wales | Scotland | Northern Ireland |
|-------|-------------------|----------|------------------|
| 1901  | 35.6              | 4.5      | –                |
| 1911  | 36.1              | 4.8      | –                |
| 1921  | 37.9              | 4.9      | 1.3              |
| 1931  | 40.0              | 4.8      | 1.2              |
| 1951  | 43.8              | 5.1      | 1.4              |
| 1961  | 46.1              | 5.2      | 1.4              |
| 1971  | 48.7              | 5.2      | 1.5              |
| 1981  | 49.1              | 5.1      | 1.5              |
| 1991  | 49.0              | 5.0      | 1.6              |

economy and attitude to trade (see Chapters 3, 9, 11). In the second, the density of population helped to make England more homogenous and less a country of internal spaces than, for example, France or the USA. The situation in Scotland and Wales was different. Nevertheless, in both, the concentration of the population in particular areas – the Central Belt of Scotland, and South Wales, a process that became more marked during the century – ensured that the pressures of high population density were also an issue.

Yet, the population rise was below the general rate of increase in the world population, difficult as that was to measure. As a result, the British were a smaller percentage of the world's population at the close than at the opening of the century. In part, this was an example of a European trend. As a result both of the brutal impact of two world wars centred in Europe, and of a decline in the fertility of couples, the European population dropped behind in relative terms, while improvements in public health and nutrition in the Third World greatly increased the rate of population increase there. Average rates of population growth in Britain as a whole were far lower in the inter-war period, when they fell to below replacement levels, than they had been in the nineteenth century. The number of children in an average family fell from three in 1910 to two in 1940. In addition, because childbearing was concentrated in the early years of marriage, the family-building period for most women fell in length, facilitating their employability or their role in other activities frequently summarised under the heading of voluntarism. It became less common from the 1930s for women to have children after their mid-thirties, and this did not change until the 1990s, when, for a section of the population, later births became more common. The earlier trend, of fewer children and children being born earlier in marriage, had begun in middle-class groups, but, in the inter-war period, spread to the working class. Repeated pregnancy became less common.

Births per thousand people in England and Wales fell from 28.7 in 1900 to 25.1 in 1910. They rose to 25.5 in 1920, partly due to demobilisation, but fell again to 16.3 in 1930 and 14.1 in 1940, before rising to 15.8 in 1950. In terms of decade blocks, the average number of births per thousand fell from 29.87 in the 1890s to 18.33 in the 1920s and 15.7 in the 1950s. This ensured that there was a smaller potential pool of entries to the labour market. Despite a post-war birth-peak or 'baby boom' in 1947, and another in 1966, population growth-rates continued to decline in the 1950s and 1960s, to almost a standstill in the 1970s and early 1980s, before a slight upturn from the mid-1980s.

Birth control became more publicly discussed and available. In place of the somewhat shadowy C. R. Drysdale and Alice Vickery – the leading lights in the British Malthusian League, the only body in Britain advocating the use of artificial contraception – came the more dynamic Marie Stopes, who in 1921 founded the Society for Constructive Birth Control. Artificial contraception then meant mechanical obstacles to conception, especially male sheaths (condoms). The contraceptive pill was not yet available. The principal influences on twentieth-century fertility trends were the growing availability and acceptability of new or improved methods of contraception – including the growing use of the condom in the first half of the century and of the pill, the coil, sterilisation, and the legalisation of abortion in the second half. Underlying the spread of effective contraceptive techniques were various demographic, economic and cultural stimuli. These included lower levels of infant and child mortality; higher real incomes, the growing range of consumer goods and services and the effect these had on spending patterns and expectations for ever-higher standards of life; the increase in the proportion of married women in gainful employment; the growing willingness of the state to provide assistance for ill-health, unemployment and old-age; and increases in the cost of educating and training children to meet the increasingly sophisticated demands of the workplace. Changing cultural values lessened the belief in procreation as the sole purpose of sexual intercourse and promoted a greater sense of individualism which, in turn, freed the individual from the traditional constraints of communal and family control, enhanced freedom of choice and action, and encouraged a greater concern for self-interest, self-respect and self-improvement (see Chapters 4 and 6).

From the 1960s, the ready availability of the contraceptive pill made it easier for women, both married and unmarried, to control their fertility. In 1961, the contraceptive pill was made available on the National Health Service. In 1963, the Brook Advisory Centre for Young People began providing contraceptives to unmarried youngsters, a major shift from the policy of the Family Planning Association. The NHS (Family Planning) Act passed in 1967 made no mention of marriage, and, in response, the Family Planning Association began to advise unmarried women, while the Brook Centres started offering advice to girls under 16. Sexual abstinence, one of the most important contraceptives earlier in the century, especially for unmarried women, became of lesser importance, and it was also unnecessary to resort to *coitus interruptus*. Thanks to the pill and abortion, the number of teenage mothers fell by about a third in 1971–95, although the rate of teenage pregnancies was the highest in Western Europe at the end of the century. The number of 'shotgun marriages' (those entered into because the bride was already pregnant) fell from one in three in 1971 to one in eleven in 1995. Due to the pill and abortion, fewer babies became available for adoption, and, as a consequence, criteria for being accepted as adoptive parents were made more restrictive.

Yet average rates are simply that. They reflect very different experiences that, in part, rose from the expectations of particular socio-economic groups and communities. Analysis of the 1911 *Fertility of Marriage Census* suggested that the character of particular communities was more important for the working class, while the middle and upper classes were more influenced by values and ambitions that stemmed from, and contributed to, a national culture, rather than one rooted in localism.

Local differences often focused on religion, but also on the extent and character of the female role in the workforce.

During the century, emigration also fell, though it was still a major factor in the first quarter of the century. Net emigration, rather than net immigration, was the situation until the 1930s, and then again from the 1950s to the early 1980s. Net immigration was the norm from 1983 to 1990 inclusive, except in 1988. The higher rate of male overseas emigration contributed to the larger number of women in the population, although other factors were also important. These included the higher female survival rates in infancy, childhood and old age, and the losses caused by military service and war. The impact of emigration could be considerable. In 1901–61, 1,388,000 Scots emigrated, a figure that amounted to about two-thirds of the natural increase in population; the equivalent rate in 1871–1901 was about a quarter. This was a reflection of economic problems in Scotland, but one that helped to keep the Scottish population modest.

From the 1930s to the early 1970s, ages at marriage fell and marriage rates rose. From the 1970s, however, marriage rates fell, and there was an increase in the average age of marriage, because marriage in part has been replaced by a growth in co-habitation. Nevertheless, the average conceals a wide variation in practice. Compared with Norway, Sweden and France, there have been many young marriages and this has been linked to the high rate of divorce in Britain. Divorce became much more common after World War Two, especially from the 1960s. The Divorce Reform Act of 1969 matched a powerful demand. This reflected increasing expectations of marital harmony and higher standards for this harmony. The decline in the economic need for marriage became more common, and there was less tolerance than earlier for adultery and wife-beating. Divorce thus replaced stoical or angry acceptance. It was seen as the way out of unhappy and celibate marriages. By 1999, Britain had an annual divorce rate of 3.25 divorces per 1,000 people, up from 2.45 in two decades. This was the highest in the European Union, as was Britain's marriage rate: 6.6 per 1,000 inhabitants (see Chapter 6).

Due, in large part, to divorce, the percentage of single-parent female-headed households rose: from 8.3% of households with children in 1971 to 12.1% in 1980. This is different from one-person households later in life, many of which are due to greater average life expectancy for women, and lower average ages for women at marriage and re-marriage so that women are more likely to outlive their spouses. Death rates for both men and women fell. The annual average rate per 1,000 in the 1890s was 18.21, in the 1950s, 11.63. Infant mortality fell markedly between 1891 and 1921, for both boys and girls, although survival rates were higher among the middle classes, skilled workers, and agricultural labourers (who benefited from the healthier conditions in rural areas), than among unskilled workers and miners. Life expectancy rose to 70 for men and 75 for women in 1979 and 75 for men and almost 80 for women by 1997. As a result, there were (and are) far more widows than widowers. By 1985, about 36% of British people aged 65 or over lived alone. Rising life expectancy and a falling birth rate ensured that the age-pyramid altered. In County Durham, 45.5% of the population in 1911 were under 20, but only 32.3% in 1971, whereas the percentage for those aged over 70 rose from 2 to 7.5. The number of 15- to 19-year-olds in Britain dropped from 4.7 million in 1981 to 3.7 million in 1999.

Although the number of lone parents rose, it was from a low base. The 1995 edition of *Social Trends* revealed that 71% of families still consisted of married couples living with their own children. Despite the increased frequency of stepparents, three-quarters of children grew up in families with both their natural parents. Furthermore, three-quarters of births outside marriage in 1995 were registered by both parents.

It would be all too easy to consider population shifts in Britain in aggregate terms, at the level of the nation, and, indeed, the basic character of change is similar across the country. This is especially true of the experience of ageing and the greatly increased use of contraceptives. However, there are also important variations within Britain. These can be presented in a number of ways, some of them controversial, including attempts to discuss demographics and health in terms of social and ethnic variations. An approach that focuses on regional and local contrasts may appear less controversial, but it can also lead to discussion in the terms already indicated.

Life expectancy was higher among the middle than the working class, always an historical truth: wealth leads to longer life expectancy. Furthermore, in part due to age structure, birth rates were higher among communities based on immigration from 'New Commonwealth' countries, such as India, Pakistan, Bangladesh and Jamaica, than among older-established groups. In addition to differences that can be traced to such contrasts, there was also the great mobility of the population, which much affects demographic structures. The larger percentage of the population above 65, greater disposable wealth on the part of much of the population, and enhanced mobility, combined after 1945 to ensure that a number of towns became especially associated with retirement. This was true, for example, of Worthing, Hove, Eastbourne and Exmouth on the south coast and of Colwyn Bay on that of North Wales. Furthermore, British membership in the European Union was followed in the 1980s by large numbers of international retirement migrants from Britain, especially to Spain. This accentuated the geographical spread of many families, creating problems for support within families. It was mirrored by rural youth depopulation in Wales and rural England.

The old support network which the extended family provided ceased to exist. The family home is now less and less likely to contain grandparents as well as parents and their children. The 'nuclear family' unit became increasingly the norm in post-1945 Britain. The construction of new, out-of-town, housing estates reinforced this trend by making it more difficult for families to keep in regular contact. Families also began to spend less time together. As the package holiday abroad became more popular and affordable, the traditional family day-out at the seaside, visits to such coastal resorts as Blackpool and Southend, ceased to provide opportunities for families to meet.

The complex nature of modern Britain can be appreciated if attention is drawn to the variety of its recent demographic history. Thus, for example, the population stagnation of Scotland was/is not matched in South-East England, where economic growth and immigration both led/lead to high growth figures. Even within a region as small as an individual county, there have often been major contrasts and this is often true of those areas generally presented as unexceptional (see Box 2.2). At the level between an individual county, such as Norfolk, and the UK, there are units in which the contrasts in experience are even greater.

## Scotland in brief

Within Scotland, a country of many diverse regions, there has been a substantial move from the urban areas of the West Central Belt, many of which have suffered

Box 2.2

## The case-study of Norfolk

Norfolk, generally seen as an agricultural county away from the main thrusts of change in the twentieth century, shared in the general decline of death rates. Death rates there decreased from about 22 per 1,000 people per annum in 1851 to 12 per 1,000 in 1951. Birth rates also fell, but in Norfolk, as in many other areas, the relationship between birth and death rates was less important than migration into and out of the county. Agrarian depression and an absence of industrial growth led to sustained and significant emigration in 1851–1951, but, thereafter, there was immigration, both for work and to retire. This, especially the former, was greatly affected by the general state of the economy.

The age structure of the county's population also changed. Whereas, in 1851, 45% of the population were aged under 20, by 1951 this had decreased to 29%, a consequence of the decline of fertility, but also, in part, of the economic depression of the 1930s and the disruption to family life brought by World War Two. In contrast, both the number and percentage of the elderly grew. The population aged 65 and over rose from 9.2% in 1851 to 12.6% in 1951 and about 19.6% in 1990, and, as the total population in the latter period rose from about 550,000 to about 755,000, the number of those who were 65 or over more than doubled.

The more detailed pattern was more complex. Agrarian depression led to a concentration of the population in the towns over the century 1851–1951. The population living in the three largest towns, Norwich, Great Yarmouth and King's Lynn, rose from 29% to 42%. Commuting spread the influence of these towns.

Urban employment became even more crucial after 1951, but greater car ownership increased the separation of work and home. As a consequence, in Norfolk, and many other counties, population growth was often associated with proximity to major roads. This attracted young couples starting or rising in the job market, who then had families. In contrast, areas where there were few new opportunities and that were inconvenient for commuting attracted fewer job-seekers. The demographics of an ageing population was thus accentuated by there being fewer children. This was a particular problem in agrarian areas distant from major towns, such as north Norfolk, and in similar areas elsewhere in the country that were affected by the decline in mining and fishing.

Such shifts were important because aggregate population figures could conceal a changing socio-demographic situation. Thus, for example, the arrival of retirees to 'replace' those who left seeking work could lead to a dramatically different situation, even if there was no net population change.

from industrial decline (see Chapter 12). Glasgow lost 10 per cent of its population in the 1980s. From a lower base, there have been net gains in the Highlands and Islands, the Border region and South-Western Scotland. Within the Central Belt, there has been a move to new towns and suburbs and away from city centres. More generally, the Scottish population has been relatively stagnant, in large part because it has gained little from immigration. Instead, emigration continues to be important. In the 1920s alone, nearly 500,000 Scots left due to a severe depression that affected industry as well as agriculture and fishing. In the period 1900–90 there was only one year (1932–3) in which Scotland gained from migration. Combined with declining birth rates, now lower than those of England and Wales, this has led to a fall in population: 152,000 people in 1976–86. In 1994, there were only 61,656 live births in Scotland, the lowest figure since records began in 1855. The decline of marriage as an institution was such that 31% of these births in 1994 were to unmarried mothers. The population in 1994 was 5,132,400. It is predicted to fall below five million. Writers concerned with Scotland's future were much worried by population trends. Edwin Muir took this up in *Scottish Journey* (1935), as did nationalist writers. Others drew bleak conclusions from the loss of native-born Scots in the face of what they wrongly thought was increasing Irish settlement in the 1930s.

## Other regions

Aside from parts of Scotland, other regions of declining industry also had only modest population growth. This was true of the North, the North-West, and Yorkshire. In contrast, the East Midlands, East Anglia and the South-West had consistent strong

**Box 2.3**

## Population structure: the future

Predicting the future is always tricky, and using demographics is no different. Yet, projections based on current trends suggest that the role of the aged will become more pronounced. The percentage of the population aged over 60 will probably rise from 20 in 1997 to 25 in 2010 and 33 in 2025. The number aged over 65 will probably double in 1997–2027 and the number aged over 100 will probably rise from 300 in 1951 to 34,000 by 2031. As people are having fewer children later, the number of under-fives will probably drop from 3.5 million in 1861 to 1.6 million by 2030, and the percentage of the workforce aged 20–34 from 21 in 1991 to 14 by 2001. In 1996, the number of mothers aged 30–35 outnumbered those aged 20–25 for the first time, while the number of recorded teenage pregnancies was higher than in other European countries. The number of single-person households is likely to continue to rise. As the ratio of youth to age changes, the number of people of working age available to sustain each pensioner will probably fall from four in 1961 to two by 2040. This will increase the pressure for a fundamental reform of the welfare state, particularly in the field of pension provision.

growth. The population of all major cities fell from the post-war peak, with this process being especially marked in the 1970s in Glasgow, Manchester, Liverpool and London. Newcastle's population rose from 267,000 in 1911 to a third of a million in 1961, before falling to 289,000 in 1976, but this fall, like that of major cities elsewhere, owed much to the building of commuter housing outside city boundaries. This shift helped to produce a degree of uniformity in housing densities and thus to reduce the problems of urban overcrowding. Outside London, the population of the South-East rose rapidly. That of Berkshire, for example, more than doubled between 1931 and 1971. Expansion there was concentrated in the east of the county, the part best suited for commuting to London. A new town was founded there at Bracknell to take London overspill. Building started in 1950, and by 1981 the population was 49,000.

The development of Bracknell reflected the pronounced attempt to direct population flow, following World War Two. Planning was seen as a way to tackle housing problems, both substandard housing in the cities and the pent up demand that had been exacerbated by a marked fall in housing during the war. A rise in the marriage rate during the war was also important. Slums were cleared in London, but the creation of new towns led to an increase in long-distance commuting. There was also inner-city blight in London. In population terms, such planning led to a shift in population from London to the South-East.

Thus, in summary, the population of suburban, commuter and southern England has increased more rapidly than that of London, Scotland and northern England. With the exception of London, which attracted many, this was also the trend for immigrants. Thus, whereas in the nineteenth and early twentieth century, Irish immigrants had focused on Lancashire and Scotland, from the 1940s they switched to the Midlands and the South-East, especially London, Birmingham and Coventry. In the 1980s and 1990s, Irish immigrants started to move outwards in such areas as London: for example, to places like Kingsbury in north-west London.

## Immigration

Until the 1950s, immigration was largely from elsewhere in Europe, although there had also been substantial Chinese immigration at the end of the nineteenth and the start of the twentieth century, principally to sea-ports, such as London, Liverpool and Newcastle. Until New Commonwealth immigration from the 1950s, the Irish were the largest incoming group. The two main peaks in Irish immigration were, first, after the potato famine of 1847–8, and, secondly, during and after World War Two. In the early nineteenth century, increased cultivation of the potato had helped the Irish population to increase substantially. However, crop blight in the autumn of 1845 was followed by the complete failure of the 1846 and 1848 crops, and a poor crop in 1847. The resulting malnutrition helped diseases to make inroads, and these, with starvation and, principally, emigration, led to a major fall in the population. This traumatic period seared the consciousness of nineteenth-century Ireland.

Unlike in the nineteenth century, Irish migrants preferred to travel to Britain not the USA. Irish labour was actively recruited to help with wartime needs, and post-war reconstruction led to more immigration. Even after Ireland left the Commonwealth in 1949, Irish citizens enjoyed free access to the British labour market. Until 1971, the largest immigrant minority in Britain came from the Republic of Ireland. That year, those born in Eire were 1.1% of the British population.

Russian and Polish Jews entered Britain in large numbers from the 1880s until the Aliens Act of 1905. There were fresh restrictions on immigration in 1914 and 1919. This followed a long period of no such restrictions and testified to the loss of confidence that affected Britain at the beginning of the twentieth century, although such sweeping generalisations have to be handled with care. Immigration declined in the 1920s and 1930s, and was not a major social or political issue. There was a widespread low-level racism and anti-Semitism, that could at times lead to violence, but which was more commonly a matter of social assumptions and institutional practices.

As with much else, the disruption of World War Two altered the situation. It transformed the international context, providing large numbers of refugees, and also created new demands for labour within Britain, demands that in part reflected the fact that many men were occupied in military service well into the post-war period. Large numbers of Polish refugees arrived after World War Two. These Poles, many of whom were ex-soldiers, were essentially political refugees who did not welcome the prospect of Communist rule. The 1951 census recorded 162,376 as Polish-born. Opposition to them was voiced at the annual convention of the Trades Union Congress in 1946, as well as by the Fascist Union Movement of Sir Oswald Mosley. Immigration in this period was also encouraged in order to cope with labour shortages. Thus Estonians, Latvians, Lithuanians and Ukrainians arrived as European Volunteer Workers. Belgians and Italians also arrived, and until Italian economic growth became more marked from the 1960s, the Italians were an important immigrant community. Many were specifically recruited for the South Wales steelworks and the Bedfordshire brickworks. The Conti ice-cream empire in South Wales is the largest independent producer. These groups underline the need to remember the extent of white immigration after 1945.

Immigration from the Empire brought in Hong Kong Chinese and Cypriots. From the 1950s there was large-scale immigration from the New Commonwealth, although many of the immigrants intended only a limited stay. A temporary labour shortage in unattractive spheres of employment, such as transport, foundry work and nursing, led to an active sponsorship of immigration that accorded with Commonwealth idealism. However, concern about its scale, and growing racial tension, especially over jobs and public housing, led to a redefinition of nationality. The

British Nationality Act of 1948 had guaranteed freedom of entry from the Commonwealth and colonies. This immigration was clearly differentiated from that from elsewhere in the world. The situation changed with the Commonwealth Immigrants Acts of 1962 and 1968, the 1971 Immigration Act, the 1981 British Nationality Act, and the Immigration Act of 1988, which progressively reduced Commonwealth immigration. As a result, Britain had the most restrictive immigrant/refugee legislation in force among the member states of the European Union. These Acts, especially that of 1962, encouraged a rush to 'beat the ban'. The Commonwealth Immigrants Act of 1968 deprived East African Asians with British passports of the automatic right to entry, which they had been promised when Kenya gained its independence from Britain in 1963. By the 1971 census, those born outside Britain amounted to 6.6% of the total population. Increasingly, this ceased to be a measure of the long-term impact on society, because the children of immigrants, born in Britain, had never known any other country. In the 1971 census, 707,110 people were recorded as what would be described as New Commonwealth (see Chapter 6).

The local impact of immigration varied greatly. New Commonwealth migrants concentrated in London, the West Midlands and South Yorkshire. Relatively few went to Scotland, North or Central Wales, Northern Ireland and rural or North-East England, although Glasgow had an important immigrant segment from South Asia. In 1971, the percentage in Bradford was 7.1 and in Birmingham 6.7, but it was only 1.3 in Newcastle. Planning for the New Towns seemed to exclude a mix of ethnicity: Basingstoke and Bracknell have less than 2% of their population from ethnic minorities. Within individual cities, immigrants concentrated in particular areas, influenced by a mixture of opportunity and self-segregation.

Another important legal change arose from entry into the European Economic Community in 1973. Membership entailed and entails free movement for the nationals of member states, and indeed large numbers came to benefit from this in their search for work. However, the issue did not arouse much debate, in large part because the migrants were short-term and because they did not trigger racist tensions.

## Health and disease

There were marked shifts in the health of the nation in the twentieth century, shifts that reflected more than progress in medicine. Developments in public health were also of great importance. In the first half of the century, poor, insanitary and over-crowded housing, and low incomes, limited the decline in infant mortality rates and caused malnutrition among the poor and unemployed. These conditions were seen as sapping the strength of the country. In 1902, half the army recruits from Manchester were rejected due to poor physique. The condition of urban life, especially over-crowding, poor sanitation and atmospheric pollution, was highlighted in the 1904 report of the Interdepartmental Committee on Physical Deterioration on the health and welfare of children. This state of affairs was seen as likely to weaken the country in any future clash with Germany.

**Eugenics movement:** The belief that the nation's stock could be improved by encouraging the healthier, more intelligent people to have children and restricting the reproduction of weaker or 'less desirable' groups.

These concerns helped to drive a variety of pre-war policies and platforms, including the social welfare provisions of the Liberal government that took office in 1905. They were highlighted by the influential **Eugenics movement**, which drew heavily on racist thought, and argued that the poor quality of the urban environ-

ment was sapping the national stock. They supported birth control. The National Efficiency movement was also concerned
about the quality of the workforce. It pressed for an improvement in town living by separating residential from industrial
areas. The latter idea was taken further by the Garden City Association, an increasingly influential pressure group in the 1900s.
This Association, like other reform movements of the period,
drew far more widely than simply upon eugenicist and national
efficiency ideas.

| Box 2.4 |
|---|

**Life expectancy**

| Year of birth | Males | Females |
|---|---|---|
| 1931 | 58.4 | 62.4 |
| 1961 | 67.9 | 73.8 |
| 1981 | 70.8 | 76.8 |
| 1991 | 73.2 | 78.8 |

Despite such policies and platforms, poor housing, low incomes, and crowded hospitals remained a threat to public health.
Overcrowding was a particular problem as it helped encourage the spread of infectious diseases. In 1911, 12.8% of Scotland's houses had only one room. Seven
years later, 45.1% of Scotland's population lived at a housing density of more than
two persons per room. The Royal Commission on Housing in Scotland, established
in 1912, painted a bleak picture five years later of overcrowding, poor sanitation, and
many one-roomed houses. Sewage disposal remained a problem in many areas.
Bristol's sewage was still being discharged into the River Avon, although now downstream from the city, and this remained the case until the 1960s. From 1891 to 1921,
the percentage of Newcastle's population officially overcrowded did not fall below 30;
in 1930, the percentage was still 23. Serious problems with housing and public health
throughout Britain still existed in the 1930s. The Depression brought a high level of
long-term unemployment and poverty to exacerbate the already difficult legacy of
nineteenth-century economic change and social pressures. In Newcastle, an investigation into child health and nutrition in 1933 showed that about 36% of working-
class children were physically unfit and malnourished. Due to poverty, 33% of the
working-class families surveyed could not afford fresh milk. An investigation in the
city in 1936 showed working-class malnutrition that was higher among the unemployed. Post-Second World War social welfare policies, including the construction of new houses and hospitals, helped matters greatly, although they did not end
problems.

Changes both in the legislative framework and in public knowledge affected
health. This became more pronounced in the second half of the twentieth century,
but governments had been active from the nineteenth century. The first Town
Planning Act, passed in 1909, recognised a role for government control and thus
offered a framework for further restrictions on market forces. As in other spheres,
World War One encouraged action. Thus, responding to claims that drug use was
sapping the country, in 1916 the government issued Regulation 40b of the Defence
of the Realm Act, which banned, for the first time, possession of opium or cocaine by
other than 'authorised persons'. The employment of children was greatly limited. In
1907, there were still about 5,000 half-timers under 13 working in Bradford; but
such practices (and jobs) came to an end.

Legislative measures helped improve public health. The Midwives Act of 1902
and the Maternity and Child Welfare Act of 1918, improved infant and maternal
health care and encouraged a sense of public responsibility. The Midwives Act improved the registration and quality of midwives and this has been linked to the fairly
steep decline in infant mortality after the 1900 peak. Awareness of the Clean Air Act of
1956 and other environmental measures, 'safety at work' awareness, and the Health
and Safety at Work Act, as well as a growing understanding of the dangers of work-

### Sir Alexander Fleming (1881–1955)

Alexander Fleming was born in Ayrshire in Scotland, and went to school in Kilmarnock. He worked as a shipping clerk in London before studying medicine and then becoming a surgeon at St Mary's Hospital, Paddington, and a bacteriologist there, being the first person to use anti-typhoid vaccines on people. In 1928 he accidentally discovered a mould which could destroy bacteria – this was penicillin. It was eventually isolated and produced as a drug with the help of Howard Florey and Ernst Chain, with whom Fleming shared the 1945 Nobel Prize.

ing in smoke-filled buildings and with asbestos, all contributed to changes in health, not least to the decline of chest illness. The hazards of drinking to excess and, particularly, of smoking became generally appreciated and were addressed by government action. Lung cancer death rates for men aged 55–64 fell from 326 per 100,000 in the early 1960s to 220 per 100,000 in 1991. The relationship between diet and health was also better appreciated. More generally, health education was improved and become more important.

The pace and impact of medical changes was greater in the twentieth century than ever before. In his novel *When the Sleeper Awakes* (1899), H. G. Wells felt able to look forward 200 years to a world when disease had been vanquished and there was enough food. Britain was in the forefront of medical research and development throughout the century. As general medical knowledge increased enormously, the ability to identify and treat disease increased exponentially. These improvements touched the lives of millions, totally altered the condition of the people, and are arguably far more important than the details of political manoeuvres that tend to play such a major role in historical accounts. Readers should consider the following paragraphs and reflect on whether they themselves, their siblings, friends, neighbours, parents, grandparents, or people they know, have not been affected by at least one of these developments.

Previously fatal illnesses or debilitating diseases and conditions were overcome as a result of new discoveries and their dissemination. Care of the wounded in World War One led to major developments in orthopaedics, blood transfusion and psychiatry, although they did not necessarily translate quickly into civilian practice. Orthopaedics, like reconstructive surgery, struggled to survive as a medical speciality between the wars: blood transfusion was rarely used because there was only the most rudimentary supporting organisation. It was not until World War Two that a comprehensive donor and storage organisation was put in place. Psychological and psychoanalytical developments helped in the understanding of shell-shock.

The impact of diabetes, for example, was greatly lessened by the discovery of insulin in 1922. Its use, from the mid-1920s, enabled young diabetics to live. British scientists, such as the Scot Sir Alexander Fleming (1881–1955), the discoverer of penicillin in 1928, played a major role in the development of antibiotics in the early 1940s. After extensive use in World War Two, penicillin, the first antibiotic, was made available in 1946 as a prescription-only drug. It proved an effective weapon against post-operative infections, septicaemia, pneumonia, meningitis, and endocarditis. Antibiotics were of enormous benefit for dealing with bacterial infections, which, of one kind or another, were a very common cause of death in the first half of the century. Large numbers of children died then, the United Kingdom infant mortality rate being 58 per 1,000 in 1937, while the rate for Newcastle, where overcrowding remained very serious, rose to 91 per 1,000.

Nevertheless, there were also important changes prior to the widespread availability of penicillin. Improvements to the milk supply, through the introduction of milk depots and the provision of free pasteurised milk, helped in the overcoming of summer diarrhoea, which had been a major killer of babies, although both were very uneven prior to 1945. The establishment of antenatal screening in the 1920s was important. So also was the increased distribution in the inter-war years of vitamins, which had been discovered earlier in the century. Infant mortality was linked to socio-economic factors, especially crowding and the quality of the housing stock. Thus, in the borough of Kensington, infant mortality was high in the poor areas in the north, as it also was in the overcrowded parts of Newcastle. The provision of medical services was also important: areas with comprehensive services, such as Stepney and Woolwich, had lower rates of infant mortality than Kensington where there was no universal provision. More generally, much of the population did not benefit fully from inter-war medical advances, which included immunisation against diphtheria and tetanus, improved blood transfusion techniques, the first sulphonamide drugs, and the use of insulin against diabetes and of gamma globulin against measles. Although they were to be outclassed by antibiotics, sulphonamide drugs made a major impact, especially on streptococcal infections. Nevertheless, especially in the 1930s, public health continued under pressure as a result of socio-economic strains.

Tuberculosis had killed one adult in eight at the beginning of the century, including in 1930, at the age of 44, the novelist D. H. Lawrence. Another famous writer, George Orwell (1903–50), had his writing cut short by the disease. Tuberculosis was still serious in the 1930s, especially among the urban poor, although death rates had a steady downward trend from around 1870. Tuberculosis, however, was apparently conquered thanks to the use from the 1950s of an American antibiotic, streptomycin, as well as to better diet, mass radiography, earlier diagnosis and the programme of mass BCG vaccinations of children. In the mid-1950s, deaths from tuberculosis fell dramatically. Antibiotics also helped with other bacterial infections. Some urinary infections and venereal diseases, such as gonorrhoea, could be more readily treated. Some strains of bacteria developed resistance to penicillin, leading to the production of semi-synthetic penicillins – the first, methicillin, in 1960. The sulphonamides also helped cut maternal death rates, as did improvements in blood transfusion. Improved standards of living, especially during and after World War Two, may have contributed to falling maternal mortality.

The pace of change increased after 1945. The common childhood diseases that caused high mortality and high morbidity in children in the early part of the century, such as measles, whooping cough and diphtheria, had been declining since World War One, but were further reduced by the post-war introduction of immunisation programmes for the entire child population. The BCG injection scar on the upper left arm marked out a generational change. It was an aspect of a determined attempt to improve public health by securing the health and welfare of children. Free school milk was introduced in 1945. After World War Two, piped mains water was extended to many rural areas that had hitherto lacked it.

From the 1970s, there was the introduction of limited population screening for the early detection and treatment of other diseases, such as breast and cervical cancer. After a belated realisation that blood transfusion could induce new disease, blood screening hit Hepatitis B in the 1970s. The 1980s saw the increasing development and use of anti-viral agents for the treatment of viral infections: antibiotics had been useless against them.

There was also a revolution in knowledge and treatment of mental illness. Britain played a major role in both. The twentieth century brought recognition of the importance of psychological and mental processes. Diagnosis and treatment both changed. The development from the 1940s of safe and effective drugs helped with major psychoses and depression, dramatically improving the cure rate. Psychopharmacology developed in parallel with psychotherapy. The regulatory framework also developed with the Mental Health Act of 1959. Tranquillisers, however, can be over-prescribed, and become addictive, and this was a particular problem from the 1950s.

The range of surgical treatment greatly increased. The two world wars, especially the second, saw a major improvement in surgical techniques, with, for example, the development of plastic surgery using pig skin grafts. This was one aspect of how war, ironically, could lead to improvements in people's lives. Renal transplants began after World War Two. Transplants had been tried in the nineteenth century, and a successful technique for corneal transplants had been developed. Further attempts were made in the early twentieth century. The technical skills were present, but the basis of rejection was not understood until the 1930s while, in addition, patients were too ill for the operation. These problems were overcome from the 1940s: patients could be kept alive on dialysis and thanks to antibiotics, so that the operation could be carried out.

More generally, a major increase in anaesthetic skills, due to greater knowledge and the introduction of increasingly sophisticated drugs, meant that complex surgical operations could be performed. Once serious operations, such as appendectomies, became routine and minor. To take my immediate family, I had my burst appendix out in 1976 and the peritonitis was dealt with by antibiotics. My then baby daughter had her appendix out in 1990 as part of an operation for an intussusception. Both of us would have died from such conditions earlier.

The range of research and development came to encompass skin grafts and artificial knee joints. There were major advances in the treatment of the heart, and bypass and transplant surgery were completely developed after World War Two. Between the 1950s and the 1980s, the transplantation of human organs was transformed from an experimental, and often fatal, procedure into a routine, and usually highly successful, operation. This was one aspect of the growth of specialised surgery. In the 1950s and 1960s, open heart surgery became possible and major drugs for coronary heart disease were introduced. The first heart transplants in Britain were performed in Harefield Hospital in 1980. These developments responded to the so-called diseases of affluence, especially coronary disease.

The impact of such changes can be seen in changing life expectancy. Average life expectancy for all age-groups persistently rose during the century. The major exception was among those aged between 15 and 44 during the 1980s, and that, in part, reflected their already high life expectancy. Average lifespan increased by an average of two years every decade from the 1960s, rising from 67.8 for men and 73.6 for women in 1961 to 74 and 79 in 1996. Infant mortality fell greatly – by nearly two-

**Hospital care**
The 'Elizabeth' maternity ward at St Bartholomew's Hospital, London, in the 1930s. Improved care from midwives and in hospitals was an important factor in the fall in infant mortality.

thirds between 1971 and 1994. This owed much to improvements in midwifery, in hospital facilities and conditions, and in the ability to deal with premature deliveries. Birth in hospital became the norm: in 1993, only one in every sixty-three births in England and Wales occurred at home. The possibilities of conception extended. In 1978, Louise Brown, the first 'test-tube' baby, was born. This was a success for *in vitro* fertilisation (IVF), in which egg and sperm were mixed in a glass dish, and the embryos created inserted in the womb. By the end of the century about 1,400 IVF babies were being born each year. In 1994, there appeared the first baby born as a result of the use of a frozen embryo.

There were also dramatic changes in the causes of death. Whereas infections were a major cause of death for the entire population in the first half of the century, today infections generally only kill people who are suffering from associated disorders and who are at the extremes of life. Now, later-onset diseases, especially heart disease and cancers, are far more important. Each was responsible for more than a quarter of the deaths in Scotland in 1994.

Not all illnesses were, and are, in retreat. It is difficult to assess the extent to which some illnesses are rising, in part because of reporting issues: especially the extent to which the more thorough collection of statistics leads to a more comprehensive coverage of a problem. This appears to have played a role in rising figures for rape and insurance-related theft in the last quarter of the century. It may also play a role in rising meningitis figures. Nevertheless, there is evidence of a deterioration in some areas of health. Pollution is an issue, pressure on the environment also affecting humans. Possibly as a result of increasing car exhaust emissions, and general pollution, respiratory diseases, such as asthma, have definitely risen. Both the incidence of asthma and subsequent mortality rose, and were combated by asthma clinics, nurses and drugs. Some other respiratory diseases may also be increasing. Eye irritation has become more serious. Allergies and food intolerances are more frequently reported. The massive increase in the importation, treatment and burying of hazardous waste in the 1980s led to concern about possible health implications. Pollutants have been linked to declining sperm counts and hormonal changes among the population, specifically the acquisition of female characteristics by men. Increased use of narcotic drugs from the 1960s led to much physical and psychological damage and to some deaths. Infectious diseases thought to have disappeared in Britain reappeared, in large part due to global travel. Tuberculosis made a comeback from 1987, partly due to refugees and immigrants from countries where it is more common, but also due to HIV infection, homelessness, and the appearance of drug-resistant strains. Malaria has also reappeared. Because of global warming, it is likely that previously rare or absent insects will arrive in Britain, and it is possible that other problems will multiply.

It was not necessary to look abroad for the cause or precipitants of problems. Antibiotic-resistant strains of bacteria appeared. Diseases related to lifestyle remain serious. The frequency of sexually transmitted diseases among teenagers rose markedly in the 1990s. AIDS (Acquired Immune Deficiency Syndrome) developed as a new killer in the 1980s and so far no cure has been found. AIDS has punctured the confident belief and expectation that medical science can cure all ills. There were 138,000 smoking-related deaths in the United Kingdom in 1990. A Department of Health survey in 1993 suggested that half the adult population was clinically over-weight or obese, helping partly to explain high rates of heart disease. This reflected the availability of more and better food and a widespread failure to take sufficient exercise.

There was a powerful social and regional dimension to ill-health and mortality. In 1920, for example, there were an average of 43.3 maternal deaths per 10,000 births in England and Wales, compared with a figure of 61.5 for Scotland. Heart disease was, and is, particularly acute in Scotland, and this may be related to a harsher climate. Blood-pressure rates were especially high in the North of England and the West Midlands. Research has correlated mortality rates with socio-economic indices, and this appears to have been the case throughout the century. Diet was/is class-related and this has helped produce coronary blackspots, such as Glasgow (see Chapter 4). In the course of the century, socio-occupational differentials in mortality have widened, not narrowed. The upper and middle classes benefited more than the working class from a differential decline in death rates. The welfare state created in the 1940s did not end this correlation. The standardised mortality ratios for males aged 20–64 in 1949–53 showed major variations by class. The upper and middle classes were affected by the 'diseases of affluence', such as hypertension, whereas the working class were hit more by diseases of infection such as respiratory tuberculosis and influenza (as shown in Table 2.1), although influenza deaths among the working classes probably disguised a good deal of heart disease that would have been fatal sooner or later.

In part, such class contrasts arose because the social security system offered only minimal standards, designed to prevent destitution rather than provide comfort and security. This reflected the difficult circumstances of post-war Britain, but in the

**Table 2.1** Mortality figures showing ratio of disease to social class

|  | Class | | | | |
|---|---|---|---|---|---|
|  | I | II | III | IV | V |
| Respiratory tuberculosis | 58 | 63 | 102 | 95 | 143 |
| Influenza | 58 | 70 | 97 | 102 | 139 |
| Coronary disease/angina | 147 | 110 | 105 | 79 | 89 |
| Hypertension | 123 | 106 | 103 | 83 | 101 |

1950s, when there was protracted economic growth, successive Conservative governments made scant effort to improve the provision of social welfare. Social security remained low and there was no attempt to introduce a redistributive tax and welfare system. By 1957, Britain was spending a smaller proportion of GDP on social security than other Western European states. In 1981–92, there was a strong correlation between better mortality trends and both more affluent and rural districts, and this was probably the case throughout the century. The Black Report of 1980 showed that the working class had not benefited to the same extent from the National Health Service, vaccination programmes and improvements to the housing stock as the upper and middle classes. Health inequalities appear to have widened during the 1980s, in large part because improvements in the more deprived areas did not match those elsewhere. It is difficult to assess the situation over the century because the geographical units used in official statistics have frequently changed. In the 1950s, for example, the borough of Smethwick was the British borough with the shortest life-expectancy rates, but in the 1960s the borough was absorbed into neighbouring areas and the mortality rates thus appeared to improve. It is unclear whether the situation actually changed in Smethwick. Nevertheless, a British Medical Association report, *Growing Up in Britain* (1999), drew attention to major differences in infant mortality, accidental injury, long-standing illness, height at birth and subsequently, breast-feeding, and diet between the classes. Infant mortality rates were higher than in France, Germany, Japan, Scandinavia and Spain.

Housing quality certainly varied by social group and this had an important impact on health. This was true both of physical health and of the psychological well-being that is so important to it. The affluent were able to buy or rent better quality housing and to live at a lower housing density than the poor. Higher density led to a greater rate of transmission for infectious diseases. This may also have been related to a need to use public transport: crowded buses and trains spread illness, while waiting in the cold and wet was not healthy.

Higher housing density was also linked with psychological factors. It could induce a sense of community, but it also exposed people to levels of noise and rowdyism that were greater than those in more dispersed communities. This was especially so with the tower blocks built from the 1950s. They rapidly became unattractive and unhealthy environments, with litter, graffiti, vandalism and the threat of crime sapping the optimism of their inhabitants (see Chapter 3).

Lower quality housing, whether rented or owned, could be harder to keep warm and, in particular, dry. Damp was a major problem. Although grants for the installation of basic amenities, such as toilets, were available from 1959, much housing continued to pose problems for health. Furthermore, the poor quality of the housing was exacerbated by a shortage of money for heating. This accentuated problems with cold and damp, and thus lessened resistance to disease and made recuperation after accidents and illnesses more difficult. Furthermore, a lack of money was linked to less expenditure on preventive medicine, such as regular dental and optical check-ups. Health was even more of a problem for the large numbers of homeless. These rose, especially in the 1980s. In part, this reflected the decline in the availability of low-cost housing, both public and private, for rent, but other factors were also of importance. These factors included mobility within the country and the run-down of institutional facilities as the policy of 'care in the community' for mentally ill people formerly kept in mental homes was endorsed, but without the necessary resources being made available.

The state of individuals' general health was, and is, important to their ability to survive surgical operations. Partly as a result of improved nutrition, more people survived operations, and increasingly complex operations, but, again, this was linked to social indicators.

## The National Health Service

The British National Health Service (NHS), established by the Labour government in 1948, brought about a fundamental change in the medical provision of the nation. Inspired by egalitarian ideals, building on consideration since 1920 of the extension and development of the National Insurance Scheme, and in reaction to the variations and role of payment in inter-war health provision, Labour brought health provision under state care. This followed the wartime experience when the hospital sector was reorganised under the Emergency Medical Service, creating, among much else, the National Blood Transfusion Service. There had been many hospital beds – 197,000 in England in 1911 (5.5 per 1,000 people) – but there were major regional variations, and access to them had not been determined by need. As a result, there were major variations in medical care. In inter-war London, maternal mortality rates were low in areas which were well provided with hospitals, such as Stepney. More generally, London was relatively overprovided, taking a quarter of all expenditure on centralised health care. Earlier hospital arrangements had in part depended on charity, for the provisions of the National Insurance Act of 1911 related only to general practitioners. For example, to gain admission as an in-patient to the Northampton Infirmary, it was essential to produce a letter of recommendation. This could only be obtained from a subscriber to the Hospital. For every guinea (£1.05p) subscribed, up to five, a subscriber was entitled to one letter for an in-patient and one for an out-patient. The Hospital depended on these annual subscriptions. Churches could gain one in-patient letter for every three guineas contributed by congregations. The Poor Law infirmaries and from 1929 the municipal hospitals offered non-charitable care: and the specialist hospitals had long offered care at a price that artisan and lower middle-class families could well afford. However, the effects of such arrangements varied across the country and, in general, working-class women were particularly poorly served. The 1911 Act did not settle competition between hospitals and GPs for resources and patients.

The NHS did not depend on charitable arrangements, and for a long time was regarded as one of the triumphs of social welfare policy. Its creation reflected demoralisation with the previous state of health care. The old Poor Law hospitals, now municipal hospitals, were run down, in part because of a lack of investment and the effects of World War Two. The state of health care was chaotic, and, at least, under terrible stress. There was a lack of coordination and it was already clear in the 1930s that something needed doing. Most local authorities did not have enough money for the municipal hospitals. For example, they could not buy X-ray machines. In the 1930s, both the municipal and the voluntary hospitals suffered from the impact of the Depression.

The solution was to integrate the voluntary and public (municipal) hospitals and spread resources, and the NHS was one way to do so. It offered a new system through which central government expenditure could be directed and administered. The inherited variety of hospitals was brought under state control that was wielded through the Ministry of Health and new regional hospital boards. The war had shown that a regional system of health care and management could work, and the NHS provided this. The General Practitioner (GP) service was organised on the basis of a capitation fee paid by the government on behalf of every patient registered with a doctor. Health care was provided free at the point of delivery. The new GP arrangements were an extension of the provisions under the 1911 National Insurance Act which had introduced government payments and also control of GPs taking part in the scheme by local Health Committees. Not all GPs joined the NHS, but the number who retained a private practice was small, and the combined impact of high taxation in the 1940s and the availability of free public treatment was important in limiting private health care.

The NHS was flawed from the outset by the problems of nationalised entities, including (frequently inconsistent) political intervention, inflexible national policies, funding problems and poor management and labour relations; and was also harmed by the measures taken to win the consent of interest groups, particularly doctors and dentists. Although capital investment in the hospitals in the first decade of the NHS was considerably less than it had been in the inter-war years, hospitals arguably were overly important in the establishment of priorities. The NHS rapidly encountered problems in dealing with demand for spectacles and dentures and these swiftly became a political issue. Huge demands for both led to massive waiting lists for these between 1948 and 1951. This illustrates the way in which demand always outstripped provision. From the outset, the NHS suffered from rising expectations of care, the greater cost of care that has stemmed from an ageing population, and the rising costs of medical treatment. The subsidised availability of drugs under the NHS, with most prescriptions provided free, was, for example, both socially progressive and expensive. There was also, from the 1970s, declining confidence in the ability of the system to solve problems. In part, this was an aspect of a more widespread decline of faith in modernist, technological solutions. There were also more specific problems with planning and the allocation of resources in the NHS. Confident assumptions about the value of schemes such as the 1962 Hospital Plan, and its ability to provide a comprehensive and effective service, were challenged (see Chapter 7).

The state of the NHS became politically contentious. Waiting lists became an issue, there was insufficient interest in preventive medicine, public health, and possibly, 'alternative medicine', and a series of major reorganisations reflected governmental and public concern. Britain was presented as a strike-wracked and collapsing NHS hospital in Lindsay Anderson's satirical film *Britannia Hospital* (1982). This was a long way from the benign image of the NHS seen in the 'Doctor' series of British films that began with *Doctor in the House* (1954).

The state of the NHS was a major issue in the 1992 and 1997 general elections, and this reflected widespread public unease about the availability of treatment. Other aspects of disquiet were indicated by rising litigation about medical treatment, and also by a growth in private health care. The percentage of the UK population having medical insurance rose from 8.7 in 1986 to 11.3 in 1992, a percentage greater than that of pupils using private education. The growing popularity of private health care has to be seen in the wider context of attempts to impose free-market principles onto the operation of essential public services. During the 1990s, following the 1989 White Paper and the 1990 NHS and Community Care Act, successive Conservative governments strove to create an **internal market** in the NHS and to accompany it with an emphasis upon obtaining value-for-money and cost-effective treatment. Increased bureaucracy was one consequence. More generally, rising demand and

**internal market:** Trade within and between sections of an organisation such as the National Health Service.

greater expectations ensured that the cost of the NHS also rose, from £433 million in 1949 to £26.2 billion in 1989, and £42.3 billion in the fiscal year 1996–7. This substantial increase took place under both Labour and Conservatives. Indeed, government spending on health rose in 1945–98 by an annual average of 4% during Conservative governments and 3.2% under their Labour counterparts. By 1999, health care in Britain was still 85% financed by the state, compared with 14% in Germany. The NHS in 1999 was Western Europe's largest employer with about 1.1 million workers.

Yet the NHS was able to maintain the policy of treatment free at the point of delivery, so that many of the anxieties about the availability and cost of medical treatment that the poor faced earlier in the century ended. To this extent, the broader social aspirations of the NHS were achieved. The attempt at uniform health provision through the NHS led to a fairer geographical and social allocation of resources and skills than existed hitherto. Thus, in North-East England, the traditional concentration of hospital provision in Newcastle was lessened by the construction of new facilities in health districts such as North Tyneside. There was also a positive effort to develop medical education and specialised services spread across the regions, rather than concentrated, as earlier, in a few centres, principally inner London.

At the same time, the centralised planning of health care in the NHS did not respond to local views, and regional differences remained very pronounced. There was a clash between local concern about the disappearance of neighbourhood services and a professional drive for the consolidation of specialised services. For example, by the 1990s, trauma, particularly due to accidents and falls, was the leading cause of death in the age group 0–40. Specialists argued that the distribution of Accident and Emergency Units was inadequate, in large part because it had developed in a fragmented and poorly coordinated fashion, leading to too many poorly-provided centres. The recommended response – fewer but better-supported centres, was medically, but not politically, desirable. The NHS faced the problems of most large concerns, but its ability to cope with them was limited by the particular character of its mission and the extent of political direction and public expectation. There were/ are issues of provision as well as organisation. This is important because medicine is political. This was shown in the direction of research and facilities and the allocation of treatment. For example, gender issues affected provision. Despite high rates of uterine and breast cancer in the 1950s, 1960s and 1970s, research and treatment only attracted major backing from the 1980s. By the 1990s, prostate cancer, which affects men, in turn appeared relatively underrated. Allocation of treatment was and is a serious problem when there is a shortage of facilities or parts, as with renal transplants.

Changes in health care were not simply related to fatal illnesses. Many aspects of people's lives were improved. Pain was increasingly held at bay by more effective and selective painkillers, bringing relief to millions suffering from illnesses such as arthritis and muscular pain. Improvements in dentistry permitted both the better treatment of dental problems and the provision of preventive dentistry. As a result of the latter, the need for fillings fell. Fluoridation was slowly and reluctantly accepted by governments, but the toothpaste companies' addition of fluoride to their products has probably been of greater value in preventing tooth decay than clinical intervention by dentists.

The treatment of eye problems and diseases also improved, and the quality of spectacle lenses rose. Far from being a minor change, this was crucial to the ability of millions to live a full life and to take part in many of the changes outlined in other chapters. Yet such changes cannot be abstracted from their socio-political context. The rising cost of dental and optical treatment in the 1990s, especially the difficulty of obtaining dental treatment on NHS terms, was held responsible for a deterioration in the dental and optical health of sections of the population. This can be discussed in terms both of governmental determination to make people contribute directly to the cost of their health care and of the economics of much of the poorer section of the population, not least the difficulty of saving money.

## Health and contraception

Contraceptive developments dramatically increased the ability of women to control their own fertility. They also played a major role in the emancipation of women, as well as in the 'sexual revolution', the change in general sexual norms from the 1960s (see Chapter 6). At the beginning of the century, women, both single and married, suffered from the generally limited and primitive nature of contraceptive practices. Many women, both single and married, resorted to abortion, which was hazardous to health and treated as a crime. There was an emphasis on maternity, but very much within marriage. Frequent childbirth was exhausting; and many women died giving birth, so that many children were brought up by stepmothers. It was not until the introduction of sulphonamides after 1936 that mortality figures fell substantially. After 1921, when Marie Stopes founded the Society for Constructive Birth Control, it became increasingly acceptable socially for women to control their own fertility, although there was resistance. For example, the National Birthday Trust, founded in 1928, opposed birth control as likely to undermine national and imperial strength. The widespread use of the contraceptive pill from the 1960s and the availability of the pill to all women, whether married or unmarried, gave women far more of an ability to determine their fertility. The pill became a motif of sexual liberation, although the occasional safety scares caused considerable concern. However, many of the changes associated with the 'sexual revolution', such as increasing rates of illegitimacy and abortion, were already under way in the 1950s.

Control over fertility was also linked to the legalisation of abortion by the Abortion Act of 1967, again a measure introduced without discrimination based on marital status. It was followed by a situation close to abortion on demand; although, as access to abortion was controlled by doctors, there were marked regional variations. The number of legal abortions in the UK reached a peak of 184,000 in 1990, a major limitation on population growth. Science not only took away; it also created other opportunities. In the 1990s, the fertility of some of the approximately 20 per cent of couples who are infertile changed thanks to the spread of new techniques, such as *in vitro* fertilisation.

The relationship of the sexual revolution to health and disease was dramatised in the 1980s as a new killer virus, AIDS (Acquired Immune Deficiency Syndrome), spread into the UK, possibly from homosexual milieux in the USA. It was not just homosexuals who were at risk however: infection rates among heterosexuals soon began to rise; drug abuse was another significant channel of transmission for the HIV virus which causes AIDS. The impact of the virus did not really hit home until it claimed the lives of stars in the fields of entertainment and popular music, such as Freddie Mercury. The new disease led to an emphasis on 'safe sex', centring on condoms. The production of the last had changed greatly during the century. Whereas those of the 1930s were supposed to be re-usable and, due to a high risk of breakage, were thick, those of the 1990s were disposable, more sensitive, and marketed with a full understanding of the nuances of a modern consumer society (see Chapter 4).

# Social welfare

The development of national social security and educational provision was important to the condition of the people. Over the course of the century, the indigent and ill were offered a comprehensive safety net. The welfare state that developed became central to government activity and political debate, and came to take a growing percentage of national wealth. At the beginning of the century, less than 3 per cent of the British Gross Domestic Product (GDP) was spent on publicly funded social services. By 1993, nearly a quarter of the then far larger GDP was devoted to education, health and social security. Social security has taken the lion's share of the increase in the welfare budget. For example, health expenditure rose from 4% of GDP in 1950 to 5.2% in 1990. Furthermore, rising public expectations ensured that increases were 'locked in'. A range of services were provided free at the point of delivery to the entire population. Increased expenditure reflected the conviction that the environment in which people grew up and lived was crucial to their welfare.

This seemed an obvious point at the close of the twentieth century, but had been widely debated at its start. There had then been a powerful group of eugenic theorists who were convinced that the central issue was inheritance. They argued that mental and physical social characteristics were inherited and that the possibility of altering these characteristics through environmental improvements, such as better housing and medical care, were limited. This argument, presented with all the conviction of 'scientific' advance, was linked to a discriminatory analysis of society. In essence, most eugenicists argued that unwelcome characteristics were seen among the poor and thus demonstrated their unfitness in a wider sense. To be short and emaciated was seen as innate. Furthermore, as the birth rate had fallen among the middle class, eugenicists raised the fear that the larger size of working-class families would lead to a deterioration in the 'national stock' or 'genetic pool', as the percentage of the poor increased.

Eugenic arguments echoed a number of tendencies and movements. That for National Efficiency pressed for the use of state machinery in order to ensure the morality, temperance and efficiency of the working class. A rhetoric of scientific analysis and control matched a belief in social policing. The environmentalists of the 1870s and 1880s, who had identified slums as a problem, lost ground in the 1890s to advocates of biological causes. Eugenicists argued that degeneration led to a poor urban environment. They focused on the insane, epileptics and those who drank too much. Eugenicists stressed a genetic cause of racial deterioration and were influential until the 1920s. They explained degeneracy in terms of a class of 'the feeble minded'. This analysis was widely accepted, not least because it addressed widespread concerns and could be adapted to a number of political theories. Eugenic arguments were taken up by Fabian Socialists, Social Imperialists, and Liberal economists, although their ideas were also more wide-ranging in their origin. All these movements could agree on a hereditarian understanding of social problems, that social 'degeneracy' was the product of a class of 'feeble minded' that was a biological residium, and all could support state intervention to tackle the problem, although the nature of the action they called for varied.

This analysis was divisive and, in part, reflected the ambivalence that existed in some quarters about the impact of mass society, and more particularly, the nature of a democratic society. The eugenic analysis was also inaccurate. It ignored the impact of environment, and this was realised in the 1904 report of the Interdepartmental Committee on Physical Deterioration, a committee set up in response to concern about the health and strength of army recruits. Unlike the eugenicists, whose remedy was to discourage the poor from having children, the Committee recommended improvements in the conditions of children and mothers. The Committee was unusual in its emphasis on environmental causes as most medical opinion of the period stressed hereditary factors, as, indeed, did many of the environmentalists.

It would be misleading to suggest that the social reform movement was driven simply by a concern with national efficiency and eugenics, and revelations about conditions facing the poor. Pressure groups such as the Garden City movement were connected to a wide range of reforming aims and ideals, whilst the reforms passed by the Liberal government that gained office in 1905 generally drew on the ideology of the New Liberalism, a new religious radicalism, and political calculation.

Legislation responded to such ideas and concerns. Measures such as free school meals (1906), non-contributory old age pensions for those aged seventy and over (1908), labour exchanges (1909), the National Insurance Act (1911), the Education Act of 1918, which designated fourteen as the minimum school-leaving age, and the creation of the Unemployment Assistance Board (1934), were limited, but still an improvement on the earlier situation. As ever, it is difficult to decide whether to put the emphasis on change or on its limitations. The Education (Provision of Meals) Act of 1906 gave permission to levy a compulsory rate in order to provide free school meals, but local authorities did not have to provide these meals until 1914. The regular medical inspection of school children by the School Medical Service, introduced in 1907, did not lead to new living conditions, but did ensure that school clinics became common. Old age pensions were financed by taxes; not state-subsidised contributory pensions. The pensions were low and subject to tests of income and moral probity.

School inspection was valuable in the early diagnosis of conditions such as diabetes. It was intended to reveal hidden disease and to provide the basis for a policy of segregation that was widely seen as important to national health. This policy was modelled on the labour colonies advocated in the 1870s and 1880s. Epileptics, mental defectives and those suffering from tuberculosis were thus categorised. The Mental Deficiency Act of 1913 and the Elementary Education Act of 1914 ensured the segregation of those judged to be mental defectives. This was part of a larger process of surveillance and control (see Chapter 8).

The Liberal government that came to power in 1905 was particularly important in legislating for welfare and state intervention. As Home Secretary (1905–8), Herbert Henry Asquith appointed the first Lady Factory Inspectors, to enforce the provisions of factory legislation regarding women's work. As the President of the Board of Trade (1908–10), Winston Churchill, then a Liberal, keenly committed to the social reform agenda of New Liberalism, sought to develop unemployment insurance, and also to improve wages in the 'sweated' trades where they were low. This led to the Trade Boards Act of 1909, which created Boards to settle minimum wages in these trades. Workers were represented on the Boards. In 1909, Churchill also founded a national system of labour exchanges, designed to help workers obtain jobs in an efficient and undemeaning fashion. Herbert Samuel was responsible for the Children's Act of 1908: legislation extending government responsibility to all children. The Chancellor of the Exchequer, David Lloyd George, became the most notable exponent of the socially progressive New Liberalism of Hobson and Hobhouse.

In 1911, Lloyd George's National Insurance Act provided for unemployment assistance for much of the workforce, and for health insurance for nearly all of it. Medical care, sickness benefit, disablement benefit, and maternity benefit were all stipulated. Those eligible for insurance were to be registered with a doctor, who was to receive a fee per patient, irrespective of the amount of medical attention provided. Employers were to deduct compulsory employee contributions for National Insurance from pay packets, and also to contribute themselves. Despite the role of these contributions, there had been a major extension of government responsibilities. By 1914, £12.5 million was being spent on old age pensions. Philanthropy, mutual aid and voluntary activity, however, all remained important in the practice and policy of social welfare. The old age pension was not intended to be adequate; family support remained necessary. Hospitals were not part of the National Insurance Scheme, although sanatorium treatment against tuberculosis was covered.

State intervention increased during World War One as part of the process of mobilising national resources. Indeed, the health of the population that remained in Britain improved, in part because of better conditions of work such as shorter hours and the introduction of industrial canteens. Government concern with the food supply was also important.

Non-state assistance was emphasised in the 1920s, and both this and public assistance was very much part of a social politics in which middle-class activists sought to mould working-class life, in particular, in their eyes, by improving family life. This aspiration linked voluntary bodies such as the National Society for the Prevention of Cruelty to Children and the Mothers' Union, to their public counterparts, such as juvenile courts (see Chapters 6, 8). Nevertheless, pre-war social welfare was expanded. The 1923 and 1924 Housing Acts were responsible for a subsidy to housebuilders that encouraged the construction of a large number of houses. Whereas the Conservative 1923 Act provided a subsidy of £6 per house to both public and private builders, and then only for two years, the Labour 1924 Act extended the subsidy to 1939 and added another of £9 per house for those built for rent (see Chapter 3). Another Act introduced by Labour, the Unemployment Insurance Act of 1924, extended the provision of unemployment payments, and abolished the means test for this benefit. However, social welfare for unemployment, poverty and ill-health posed a serious problem for both national and local finances. Unemployment benefit had become particularly expensive, as unemployment figures remained above a million. In addition, housing subsidies were cut in 1927 and 1928.

Already inadequate, the system of help proved unequal to the challenge of the Depression of the 1930s. This led to a rapid rise in long-term unemployment and to much hardship (see Chapter 9). Unemployment relief policy became obviously necessary, and with the Unemployment Act of 1934, the notion that the central government must have an effective social policy became well-established. This led towards planning in the 1940–5 wartime coalition government and to the formulation of policy then for what was intended as a post-war welfare state. The Beveridge Report of 1942 called for the use of social insurance to abolish poverty, and pressed the case for child allowances, a national health service and the end to mass un-

## Box 2.5

### Changing shapes

More food helped to lead to a change in shape for the average Briton. Aside from more fat, there was also a build-up in muscles, with people becoming broader, taller and stronger. In the case of women, the average bust size increased by 5cm from 1951 to 1999, while women grew taller by about 12mm and became 3kg heavier each decade, so that a teenage girl in 1999 was an inch taller than her mother, and her mother, in turn, was an inch taller than *her* mother. The shoe size of an average woman in 1951 was a size 4; by 1999 a size 5½. The waist size was 65cm in 1951; in 1999, 72cm.

**Box 2.6**

## Beveridge Report

A key document in the evolution of the Welfare State, the report on Social Insurance and Allied Services drawn up by officials under the chairmanship of Sir William Beveridge bore the imprint of his radical call for a 'comprehensive policy of social progress'. The report advocated a compulsory national insurance scheme designed to provide state-supported security 'from the cradle to the grave', to cover ill-health, unemployment, retirement, and family support. Individuals and employers were to contribute at a flat rate with the balance to be met by the government. Much of this was based on existing principles but Beveridge gave them a fresh lease of life and made it appear possible to use social planning to overcome the effects of disease, unemployment and poverty. The 1946 National Insurance Act incorporated many of Beveridge's ideas.

employment. Although stronger on rhetoric than on precise policy suggestions, the Report helped create a climate of opinion for change (see Box 2.5).

Further developments after World War Two focused on the foundation of the National Health Service in 1948. The creation of the **Welfare State** reflected a conviction that social progress and economic growth were compatible – that, indeed, a major purpose of the latter was to achieve the former. Greater social equality was seen as a crucial aspect of social progress. Stable employment and social security were presented as important goals. This was true throughout the Western world. The economic growth of the period created the necessary resources; and there was a widespread belief that public expenditure was effective. Histories written prior to the mid-1970s tended to adopt an optimistic note about the expansion of publicly provided welfare, although poverty was 'rediscovered' in the 1960s. In practice, many of the social problems of the 1930s ebbed because of post-war economic expansion. This cut unemployment, which did not return to consistently high levels until the 1970s and, even more, the 1980s. Economic growth helped state provision by providing the wealth for higher levels of taxation. This was why, when the economy ceased to grow in the 1970s, many on the right of politics began to argue that Britain could no longer afford a welfare state grounded in universalism. The desirability of targeting resources at the really needy, in order to reduce the escalating welfare bill, in short, of moving from universal provision to 'residualism', proved, however, to be a thorny subject for Labour no less than Conservative governments. By the financial year 1998–9, public spending on social security was £96.7 billion (see Chapters 7, 8, 10).

The Welfare State involved more than expenditure. There was an attempt not only to improve conditions and guard against hardship, but also to extend legal protection to the disadvantaged. This led, for example, to the 1970 Chronically Sick and Disabled Persons Act. The disability movement has campaigned for rights rather than charity, on occasions using direct action. The limited 1995 Disability Discrimination Act did not satisfy its demands.

The legislative framework of social action and the growth of the welfare state lessened the direct role of private philanthropy, but this 'voluntarist' section remained very important, especially in the care of the sick and aged. Charity work continued to be important, even though it was less framed in religious terms than it had been at the start of the century. Furthermore, far from the 'voluntarist' section lacking new initiatives, there was a whole series of important new charities. Some, such as Age Concern and Shelter, helped influence government policy.

**Sir William Beveridge**
Dissension over the nature of post-war society was one of the few issues that challenged the Coalition government's control of the House of Commons during World War Two. The reception of the Beveridge Report led to particular contention in February 1943.

**Welfare State:** The system by which the government provides benefits and services such as health services and pensions for all members of society.

**Box 2.7**

### The cost of the Welfare State

In 1996–7, the current level of government spending was £307 billion. The Welfare State accounted for almost two-thirds:

| | |
|---|---|
| Social Security | 96.6 |
| Health | 42.3 |
| Education | 37.8 |
| Social Services | 9.8 |
| Housing and urban regeneration | 6.4 |
| Employment | 4.0 |
| (Figures in billions) | |

# ■ Education

There were also major changes in education policy. The Education Act of 1902 brought a measure of consistency in England and Wales. The large number of School Boards were replaced by Local Education Authorities, which were given responsibility for overseeing public elementary education. The education authorities of county and county borough councils were made responsible for public secondary education. There was considerable variety in this sector between long-established grammar schools and new local authority secondary schools, but the latter offered some students the prospect of free secondary education. The Liberal government elected in 1906 greatly expanded the number of free secondary-school places. The system was designed to provide education to meet the needs of different groups in society, but this was shot through with social assumptions. In practice, there was a certain amount of social segregation with grammar schools being disproportionately dominated by middle-class children, although in 1913 about 20% of grammar schoolboys were working class. Within this structure, there was a progressive, but slow, expansion in the provision of education. By 1914, about 60% of children in England and Wales remained at school until 14 or older; the percentage in Scotland, where the majority of public secondary schools provided free tuition, was higher. The public provision of state education for girls also increased. By 1914, there were 349 girls' and 237 mixed secondary schools receiving government grants; and the number of girls in secondary-school education in England and Wales increased almost ten-fold between 1900 and 1914.

The close of World War One seemed to offer opportunities for a new society. Universal male suffrage was introduced, women got the vote (although not on the same terms as men for another decade), and a government subsidy for council-house building was promised. Education was part of the process. The 1918 Fisher Education Act raised the school-leaving age from 12 to 14 and planned a further rise to 15. It was assumed that at 14 most people would enter the workforce, but attend 'continuation schools' once weekly until 16. Government subsidies to local education authorities were increased. This, however, was not a comprehensive change. It did not include the numerous church or independent schools, let alone universities, and the Act did not change the curriculum. It offered little scope for science, technology and modern languages. Furthermore, the implementation of the Act was partial. Local authorities frequently acted slowly, employers did not wish to pay for

## R. A. Butler (1902–82)

Richard Austen (Rab) Butler was born in India and educated at Marlborough and Cambridge. He entered Parliament in 1929 as Conservative MP for Saffron Walden, Essex, a position he held until 1965, when he was made a Life Peer. As Minister of Education he was responsible for the Education Act of 1944, which brought in the '11 plus' exam. He was Chairman of the Conservative Party organisation from 1959 to 1961, and was an advocate of the 'middle way' approach in the 1950s. Among the positions he held were: Leader of the House of Commons, 1955–61; Lord Privy Seal, 1955–9; Home Secretary, 1957–62; Deputy Prime Minister, 1962–3; Foreign Secretary, 1963–4; and, after leaving the Commons, Master of Trinity College, Cambridge, until 1978.

workers to go to continuation schools, the 'Geddes Axe' of 1922 ended these schools, and the increase of the leaving age to 15 was postponed indefinitely. An attempt to reach this limit was made under the second Labour government, but blocked in the House of Lords. In 1936, the age was raised to 15 with effect from 1 September 1939, but, with the outbreak of World War Two, this was further postponed. In addition, there was no reform in the curriculum, while education 'policy' was restricted by the independence of local authorities, the determination of religious denominations to resist direction for schools under their influence, and the role of 'independent' (private) schools.

As with much else, World War Two led to plans for post-war social renewal that reflected both concern about pre-war conditions and wartime aspirations. The crucial measure for education was the 'Butler' Education Act of 1944, drawn up by the liberal Conservative R. A. Butler. This increased the school-leaving age to 15 from 1947. It argued that pupils should receive an education relevant to their 'age, abilities and aptitudes', but maintained the tripartite structure of secondary schools: the grammar, secondary modern, and secondary technical. This reflected the Norwood Report of 1943, which claimed that there were three kinds of minds: abstract, mechanical and concrete. The Education Act of 1944 obliged every local education authority to prepare a development plan for educational provision and the Ministry of Education imposed new minimum standards in matters such as school accommodation and size. The minimum school-leaving age was raised to 15, and fees in state-supported secondary schools were abolished. Legislation in 1947 extended the provisions to Scotland and Northern Ireland. The abolition of fee paying in grammar schools would, it was hoped, encourage the entry of children from poorer families. Entry into schools was on the basis of the '11 plus' examination. The most successful went to the grammar schools, the next tranche to secondary technical schools, and the 75 per cent who failed, to secondary modern schools. These drew heavily on working-class pupils. As very few technical schools were built, for the most part a bipartite system operated.

To some critics, this system was unfair and socially discriminatory, and criticism increased from about 1950: already in 1945–7 Ellen Wilkinson, the Minister of Education, had fought strongly for the comprehensive principle. Although popularly acclaimed in 1944, the Butler Education Act was academically reviled by 1956. Most grammar school pupils continued to come from the middle class, but the grammar school system did not satisfy enough of them. In part, this reflected the inability of the grammar schools to expand to cope with the post-war 'baby boom', and, on a longer time scale, the wide variation in grammar school provision across England and Wales. The comprehensive model was tested in the late 1940s and the first purpose-built comprehensive school, Kidbrooke, opened in 1954. Two years later, Anthony Crosland, an able and determined theorist of the Left, published in his *Future of Socialism* a call for egalitarianism through comprehensive education. He vowed to close every grammar school, and when he became the Minister of State for Education he set comprehensivisation in process with Circular 10/65 of 12 July 1965. This obliged local education authorities to draw up plans for replacing the tripartite system. In education, Labour's re-election in 1966 was crucial, for by the time the Conservatives returned to power in 1970 much of the old system had been destroyed. Margaret Thatcher, as Secretary of State for Education, replaced the Crosland circular, but the number of pupils in comprehensives rose through the 1970s and the system became the norm.

It was less clear that changes in the educational system brought the improvements that were sought, a situation repeated with the expansions in the university system in the 1960s and 1990s. The Robbins Report on Higher Education (1963) was followed by state-funded growth. Government support was seen as necessary, not least in order to change the social composition of the student body. The Report had noted that only 29 per cent of UK students came from working-class homes. The 1960s was a crucial decade as it encompassed the founding of new universities such as Essex, Sussex and Warwick, the introduction of distance-learning techniques (via the Open University), an explosion in student numbers, and the emergence of such new subjects of study as sociology.

The school-leaving age was raised to 16 in 1972, but many pupils continued to leave school without necessary literacy and numeracy. Technical skills remained deficient, in part because of the perceived superiority of academic over vocational education (in stark contrast to Germany and Japan). The bulk of the workforce did not measure up to their Continental, Japanese and American counterparts in many categories, and this was blamed on a lower percentage continuing in education to 18 and a smaller role for technical and vocational education. It has been argued both that too much emphasis has been placed on equality and social opportunity and too little on raising standards, and that there has been too great an emphasis on educa-tion, rather than training in skills. These views were aired extensively in the 1980s and 1990s, but it was unclear how best to remedy the problem. The Baker Education Act of 1988 was designed to raise standards by creating a national curriculum. Estab-lished practices in teacher training, school government, and educational supervision were all replaced, but it proved difficult to use schools to address more widespread social issues affecting educational aspiration and performance. These included widespread poverty, poor housing, and low expectations. All remained serious issues affecting the health and education of much of the population.

## ■ Summary

◆ The condition of the people changed in the twentieth century. At the close of the century, they were healthier and living longer than at the outset. Nutrition im-proved considerably, average height increased for both men and women, and the country was affluent and health-conscious enough to emphasise the newly perceived problem of the overweight.

◆ The provision of health care became increasingly controversial after it was brought under the control of central government following the establishment of the National Health Service in 1948. This was crucial to a major expansion in social welfare in the late 1940s, yet, in some respects, the basis of universal social welfare controlled by central government had been laid by the Liberal government in 1906–14.

# Questions for discussion

◆ What were the social implications of changes in population structure?

◆ Why did the creation of the NHS lead to so many political problems?

◆ How important historically were shifts in health?

◆ How much did the changing pattern of the nation's health owe to:

(a) medical advances

(b) social policy

(c) economic growth?

# Further reading

Anderson, M. (ed.), *British Population History: From the Black Death to the Present Day* (Cambridge, 1996).

Behlmer, George K., *Friends of the Family: The English Home and its Guardians, 1850–1940* (Stanford, 1999).

Dorling, Daniel, *A New Social Atlas of Britain* (Chichester, 1995).

Floud, Roderick; Wachter, Kenneth; and Gregory, Annabel, *Height, Health and History: Nutritional Status in the United Kingdom, 1750–1980* (Cambridge, 1900).

Gladstone, David, *The Twentieth-Century Welfare State* (Basingstoke, 1999).

Hirst, David, *Welfare and Society, 1832–1991* (Basingstoke, 1999).

Lees, L., *The Solidarities of Strangers: The English Poor Laws and the People, 1700–1948* (Cambridge, 1998).

Lowe, Rodney, *The Welfare State in Britain since 1945* (2nd edn, Basingstoke, 1998).

McCulloch, Gary, *Failing the Ordinary Child? The Theory and Practice of Working-Class Secondary Education* (Buckingham, 1998).

Macnicol, John, *The Politics of Retirement in Britain, 1878–1948* (Cambridge, 1998).

Marks, Lara V., *Metropolitan Maternity: Maternal and Infant Welfare Services in Early Twentieth Century London* (Rodopi, 1996).

Means, R., and Smith, R., *From Poor Law to Community Care: The Development of Welfare Services for Elderly People, 1939–1971* (2nd edn, Bristol, 1998).

Searle, Geoffrey, *Eugenics and Politics in Britain, 1900–1914* (Leyden, 1976).

Smith, David, *Nutrition in Britain: Science, Scientists and Politics in the Twentieth Century* (London, 1997).

Soloway, Richard, *Demography and Degeneration: Eugenics and the Declining Birthrate in Twentieth-Century Britain* (Chapel Hill, 1995).

Sutherland, Gillian, *Ability, Merit and Measurement: Mental Testing and English Education, 1880–1940* (Oxford, 1984).

Szreter, Simon, *Fertility, Class, and Gender in Britain, 1860–1940* (Cambridge, 1995).

Thomson, Mathew, *The Problem of Mental Deficiency, Eugenics, Democracy and Social Policy in Britain, c.1870–1959* (Oxford, 1998).

Tranter, N. L., *British Population in the Twentieth Century* (Basingstoke, 1996).

Vincent, David, *Poor Citizens: The State and the Poor in Twentieth-Century Britain* (Harlow, 1991).

Webster, Charles, *The National Health Service: A Political History* (Oxford, 1998).

# The Condition of the Country

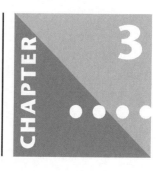

# CHAPTER 3

The condition of the country is as crucial as that of the people, and is also involved with the latter, in terms both of physical and of psychic health. The condition relates to environmental change, not least in the form of major shifts in land use and also pollution. Again, as with the condition of the people, there are important regional and social dimensions. The changing nature of the land focuses a number of issues, including the declining role of the landed interest, and the commodification of land and the environment. These are reflected in abrupt and sweeping alterations, such as the suburbanisation of much of rural Britain.

## Key issues

▶ What have been the major changes in the environment?

▶ Why has rural Britain declined?

▶ How far has the aristocracy declined?

▶ How have townscapes changed?

## Contents

## Environmental change

A growing population, with rapidly rising expectations about its living standards and lifestyle, has been let loose on the environment thanks to greater disposable wealth and technological change, particularly the motor car. The net effect has been an impact on the physical environment greater than in any previous century.

Change is integral to natural processes, as those on parts of the east coast exposed to coastal erosion are only too aware. Furthermore, the environment had been greatly affected by human activity prior to 1900. Rivers had been canalised, swamps drained, woodland cleared. The marshland of the East Anglian Fens, for example, had been progressively drained from the Roman period, with particular activity in the seventeenth century and, again, following the arrival of steam pumps from the 1820s; although the pace of reclamation declined from 1870 until the 1930s.

Yet at no stage has there been such pressure on the environment as in twentieth-century Britain. This was despite the efforts of conservationists and organisations such as the Royal Society for the Protection of Birds (RSPB), founded in 1889, and the National Trust, founded six years later. The RSPB was founded to combat the fashionable millinery trade in exotic plumage which threatened the existence of a number of tropical bird species. Its activities rapidly encompassed the protection of domestic birds of prey. Environmental pressure affected animals, plants and terrains. Other creatures were decimated by human activities. House-building and road-building had a serious impact on the size of the land base while changes in agricultural practice radically altered the way the remaining land was farmed. This impact varied between different parts of the country – house-building, for example, was more of a problem in South-East England than in Lincolnshire. Nevertheless, the general trend was one of cumulative assaults on the environment. The possibility of animals and humans sharing territory diminished. For example, the increased use of the car in the early decades of the century led to the asphalting of former rural tracks. This was environmentally damaging in itself, and also affected the ability of animals to find food there. In the 1990s, between 3,000 and 5,000 barn owls were killed on UK roads each year, joining large numbers of rabbits, hedgehogs, badgers, deer and other animals.

The number and viability of animal species in Britain was hit due to radical changes in forestry, farming and human settlement. Pine martens, members of the weasel family, were reported to have vanished from England in 1994, and to be on the brink of extinction in Wales. Pressure on animal habitats became more insistent during the century, and came to affect all animals. To take a few examples, each of which could be repeated, the numbers of stone curlew seriously declined from the 1960s. The loss of grassland was seen as particularly significant in this case, but changes in grassland management, especially more intensive stocking of pastures and the switch from hay to silage making, which destroys nests, were also very important. For other birds, the number of skylarks fell by about 50% in 1976–98; while that of grey partridge fell by more than half, due in large part to the destruction of nesting sites when hedgerows were grubbed up, and also to the lesser availability of winter stubble for feeding. The falling number of rooks gave cause for concern from the mid-1970s. Loss of habitats and early silage cutting on grassland helped to cut the number of corncrake. Most of the surviving birds were concentrated into a small number of areas. Bitterns were hit by a drastic reduction in wetland habitats. The decline in the population of black grouse was rapid and dramatic. In early Victorian times, the black grouse was common in the New Forest, Hampshire, Wiltshire, Dorset and most counties south of the Thames and was well established in the West Country. A 1924 survey reported that there were only six counties in England and Wales where it had never been recorded. Yet, by the 1990s, there were only remnant populations, probably on the verge of extinction, in the West Country, Derbyshire and North Wales, and Scotland was the only part of Britain where the black grouse was still numerous. Indeed, Scotland was the last remaining stronghold of many other species. On the whole, lowland species were more seriously affected than their upland counterparts by development and agricultural changes, in large part because more upland was protected and because agriculture there was less intensive. Nevertheless, upland species were also affected, in part due to overgrazing as sheep density rose.

The grey partridge is the gamebird that has declined most seriously. Research by the Game Conservatory suggests that its demise was caused by the decline in nesting habitats, the reduction in insect food, and the increase in the level of predation. Pheasants were also affected, but the decline in the indigenous population was partly offset by increasing the number of birds reared artificially and released. The grouse population also declined in the uplands. Not all the damage to bird populations came as a consequence of human action. The RSPB estimated in the 1990s that sparrow-hawks, of which there were 34,000 pairs counted in 1991, ate between 50,000 and 100,000 British songbirds every year.

Other forms of wildlife were also badly affected by human action. The destruction of hedgerows and wetlands ensured that more than 78% of breeding colonies of the pipistrelle bat, the most numerous bat, were lost in 1979–98, while bats as a whole were hit by the increasing use of timber preservatives in the old buildings which they used as breeding sites. The loss of habitats in sand dunes, salt marshes and heath-lands largely wiped out the natterjack toad, and the filling-in of ponds, in which they bred, greatly hit the great-crested newt. Drainage improvements were also respons-ible for the decline in the number of bitterns in the Fens. The brown hare was another species in chronic decline. Reasons included changing agricultural methods, especially 'prairie farming', with its destruction of hedgerows, and an increase in fox predation. Far from being inconsequential, such changes made rarer many sights and sounds that had once characterised the country. Throughout the British Isles, pesticides were used extensively in agriculture. They affected wildlife as well as humans. Thus, the fall in the rook population in Surrey was blamed on chemicals. The diminution (and even disappearance) of the dawn chorus in several parts of the country was a particularly poignant indicator of loss to changes in land-use, as well as pollution and pesticides. The spring became more silent thanks to the massive decline of common garden birds like song thrushes.

Other changes in animal cultures were more varied. Mankind had the capacity to introduce such fur-bearing animals as the muskrat and coypu, and, exceptionally in their cases, the ability to exterminate them, despite their having become feral – the muskrat in the early 1930s and the coypu in the late 1980s. The mink, rabbit (brought by the Normans) and grey squirrel (introduced from North America), however, were examples where it proved impossible to eliminate the species, even locally, once it became established. The ecosystem in the Norfolk Broads altered when coypu escaped from local fur farms, and had an impact on other wildlife. Coypu also damaged the drainage system and destroyed sugar beet. In the New Forest in 1998, 'animal rights' activists deliberately freed mink from fur farms, with unintended consequences for other local wildlife: the mink had a devastating effect on small animals, birds, and farm stock. Four North American mink that escaped from a fur farm on the Isle of Harris in the late 1960s, created a colony of about 12,000 that attacked both rare seabirds and chicken farming. The introduction of the sea eagle led to the loss of sheep on the Isle of Mull in the 1990s. Public concern about the fate of wildlife became more pronounced from the 1960s. It also had a powerful impact in children's literature, with works such as Richard Adams's *Watership Down* (1972).

The process of human pressure on wildlife was not all one-way. The Welsh red kite was brought back from the brink of extinction, the numbers of many species in the 1990s were stable, sparrow-hawks for example, and efforts were made to protect animals. The breeding sites of creatures such as bats and nests of hornets became protected. However, the pressure was almost all one-way. The designation of par-ticular protective areas was generally linked with a deterioration of the situation elsewhere, and was, indeed, commonly a response to it.

Plants were also badly hit. Woods have been cleared. Virtually none of the original virgin forest was left by the end of the Middle Ages. However, the pace of change in the twentieth century was greater than hitherto. Since 1945, 45 per cent of the UK's

Box 3.1

## National Parks

Pressure for national parks led the Labour government in 1929 to establish an inquiry. This recommended a National Parks Authority, but such a body had to wait until the Labour Party regained power after World War Two. The government created a National Parks Commission in 1949, and gave it power to designate national parks in England and Wales. The first, established in 1951, were the Lake District, the Peak District, Snowdonia, and Dartmoor. They were followed by the North York Moors (1952), the Pembrokeshire Coast (1952), Exmoor (1954), the Yorkshire Dales (1954), Northumberland (1956), and the Brecon Beacons (1957). The Commission did not own the parks, but instead had to operate through the county councils. Development pressures on the national parks have been followed by strains arising from leisure demands.

ancient semi-natural forest has been damaged or destroyed. This abrupt disappearance contrasted with the generally stable and conservative management of woodland in previous centuries, with its emphasis on regular cutting or coppicing, although the quality of woodland management declined in the nineteenth century. There are now fewer trees in heavily farmed lowland areas. Not all the decline can be attributed to agricultural change. Dutch Elm disease, for example, hit elms hard in the 1960s. Elsewhere, large plantations of coniferous trees, planted on upland moors and slopes, as in south-west Shropshire, and on infertile lowland areas, such as the Norfolk and Suffolk Breckland, disrupted earlier habitats. Monoculture – large blocks of the same species – has caused the problem. The Flow Country of Caithness is a classic habitat which was devastated by conifer planting.

Hedgerows were grubbed up. The amalgamation of fields and bulldozing of hedges led, from the 1950s, to the replacement, particularly in East Anglia, of the earlier patchwork of small fields surrounded by dense hedges, by large expanses of arable land. Wild plants were affected by the use of more powerful chemical fertilisers and herbicides.

Terrains were also altered. Rivers were deepened and straightened, coastlines altered. Escarpments were cleft to provide routes for motorways, as with the M40 at Stokenchurch in the Chilterns. The M3 was driven through the chalk hills north of Southampton. Estuaries were bridged, and islands linked to the mainland, with both the Skye road bridge and the Channel Tunnel. Such changes not only affected the visual environment, they also affected, or even cut, the customary routes of animals. Similarly, aircraft movements affected birdlife.

The impact of the Industrial Revolution pressed hard on the environmental legacy from the nineteenth century. In 1913, Arthur Sarsfield, a London crime reporter who, under the pseudonym Sax Rohmer, published *The Mystery of Dr Fu Manchu*, described a journey down the Thames, the 'oily glitter of the tide', and 'on the Surrey shore a blue light . . . flicked translucent tongues against the night's curtains . . . a gasworks'. Industrial and mining areas were characterised by sights, sounds and smells of environmental pressure.

The susceptibility of the environment to human pressure was to prove a theme of the century's history. This was due both to economic growth and to decline. By 1957, economic decline in Wales had already left large areas of derelict land: 8,227 hectares of disused spoil-heaps, 3,090 of disused mineral workings and 7,567 of disused buildings and installations. The Aberfan disaster of 1966, in which an unstable spoil-heap engulfed a school in South Wales killing 116 children and 28 adults, indi-

**The legacy of industrialisation**
A vast mound of unstable coal waste slid into the Welsh village of Aberfan in 1966, destroying a school and killing 116 children and 28 adults. This preventable disaster was followed by the removal or grassing over of spoil heaps in mining areas.

cated the price of early industrialisation that was to be paid in the mid-twentieth century. Industrial dereliction was due not only to decline but also to the need for different kinds of sites. In general, industry moved to flat, open land with good access to road links. Earlier locational factors, for example on river and canal links, became less relevant, and traditional multi-storey manufacturing plants were discarded. There was a comparable change in warehousing.

Closed docks provided a large acreage of derelict property. The closure of the London Docks and Surrey Docks in 1970 and of the Royal Docks in 1981, led, after the creation of the London Docklands Development Corporation in 1981, to the regeneration of much of East London, with the building of houses and offices and an improvement in the transport system. Elsewhere in the country, for example Liverpool and Newcastle, derelict dockland was also redeveloped. Some of the derelict industrial sites of the 1960s which were not reclaimed, for example Iron-bridge and Wigan Pier, became the industrial museums and heritage centres of the 1980s and 1990s.

Industrial pressure on the environment increased after World War Two, in part due to new technologies and processes. This was particularly true of nuclear power and of developments in the chemical industry. Aside from problems arising from what was permitted, there was also a new range of accidents. Thus, in 1957, a fire in the poorly-designed nuclear pile at the nuclear reactor at Windscale produced radioactive fall-out. Cumbria was badly affected in 1986 by the effects of radioactive fall-out from the nuclear reactor that exploded at Chernobyl in the Ukraine. In 1975, a serious explosion at a chemical plant at Flixborough threatened nearby urban areas. Oil-tanker accidents produced serious coastal pollution, particularly from the *Torrey Canyon* in 1967, the *Braer* in 1993, and the *Sea Empress* in 1995.

More generally, economic growth, greater affluence and more people put pressure on the environment. Coastal waters were heavily polluted by sewerage outflows. Industrial pollution was responsible for 'acid rain', which damaged some of the country's woodland and hit both rivers and lakes. Pollution caused by 'high-stack emissions' had the capacity to affect distant environments both in the country of origin, particularly in the uplands, and in other countries also. Lead emissions from traffic seriously affected air quality.

There were also improvements. The toxicity of rivers, such as the Mersey, the Thames and the Tyne, decreased, permitting the return to them of species of fish and shore wildlife. Concentrations of heavy metal pollutants declined. In the case of the Tyne, the Tyne Interceptor Sewer intercepted sewers discharging untreated sewage into the river and the sea, and instead took the sewage to a new treatment works at Howdon, whence the sludge was dumped off the coast. Cities such as Sheffield enjoyed far more sunshine hours from the clearer atmosphere after clean-air legislation and the declaration of smokeless zones. However, in the 1990s, their inhabitants started to notice a decline due to greater emissions from car exhausts. This was caused by an increase in the volume of traffic, since car engines were becoming cleaner.

Environmental pressure took many forms in the twentieth century. It affected, for example, water availability and purity, and noise, as well as land quality. Increased use of water, thanks, in part, to the use of hosepipes for washing cars and watering gardens, more toilets, baths and showers, and machines such as washing machines and dishwashers, placed great demands on water reserves, and led to the depletion of natural aquifers and to restrictions on water use. In 1990, hosepipe bans affected 20 million customers. Greater demands for water exacerbated droughts such as that of 1995.

Demand for water led to the drowning of many picturesque upland valleys, such as the North Tyne, the Durham Derwent and several in Wales, for reservoirs. Newcastle, for example, was provided with water from the Catcleugh Reservoir in Redesdale completed in 1905 and from the Kielder Reservoir on the North Tyne completed at a cost of £150 million in 1982 and filled in 1983. Valley drowning was a controversial policy, although the areas drowned were usually ones of relatively low-intensity agricultural use and dispersed settlement. Water quality (purity) was affected by the large-scale adoption of detergents after 1945. This was a problem which, when once recognised for what it was, the industry itself went a long way to resolving. Water quality was also affected by agricultural change. The marked increase in nitrogen levels was the result not only of the increased leaching of artificial fertiliser run-off from agriculture, but also of the ploughing up campaign of World War Two.

More material goods meant a greater use of energy, despite increases in energy efficiency. In 1990, 158 million tons of carbon dioxide was dispersed into the environment above Britain. Furthermore, the consumer society produced greater and greater quantities of rubbish, much of it non bio-degradable and some of it toxic. By 1999 up to 76 million tonnes of commercial waste and up to 29 million tonnes of industrial waste were being produced annually. About 20 million tonnes of household waste were also being produced, with the figure growing at an annual rate of 3%. Only about 8% of the household waste was recycled, although the percentage for the other types was higher. Kitchen and garden waste, and newspapers and magazines were the largest category of household waste, but other categories also posed major demands. In Devon alone by 1999, 80,000 disposable nappies were being buried each day. Rubbish disposal increasingly became a problem for both local government and business, not least because of greater public sensitivity about the means and locations of dumping. Finding suitable landfill sites became a serious problem. Noise and light pollution also became more serious and more widespread. The Countryside Commission's map of tranquil areas showed that an area the size of five Kents was lost to tranquillity in England between the early 1960s and the early 1990s.

Thus, the unprecedented rise in average real earnings – over two and a half times between 1945 and 1995 – had a serious impact on the environment. Economic growth also created some of the resources to tackle environmental problems, as well as the affluence to encourage many to argue that growth should not come at the expense of environmental considerations.

# A changing landscape

## World War One and rural society

One of the major changes over the twentieth century was the decline of the traditional rural world. Rural Britain is now like a skeleton, without its people, a skeleton being clothed increasingly by commuters who live there but work elsewhere. Having recovered from the Great Depression of the last quarter of the nineteenth century, which had led the Duke of Bedford in 1897 to write about his 'ruined' estate, agriculture was pushed forward in World War One as German submarines attacked shipping. Food supplies became a matter for government action and public concern. With the Food Production Act of 1917, the government imposed a policy of expanding tillage (land that was ploughed). It was more efficient to feed people directly from the land, rather than indirectly via meat and milk. This policy started in 1917 after the Germans began unrestricted submarine warfare, but had only a limited effect across much of the country, because the war ended in 1918. County Agricultural Executive Committees oversaw a 30 per cent rise in national cereal production as much grassland was ploughed up (meat and milk production fell). The price of grain was guaranteed. In part, however, the rise in output in 1917 and 1918 was a recovery after a major decline in food production in 1916 and the calorific value of the food produced was similar to that in 1914. Furthermore, despite the attempts of the Board of Agriculture to claim the credit, the recovery owed much to favourable weather. The war brought great prosperity to the farmers, and for a brief period it shielded them from the effects of foreign competition. This prosperity proved short-lived.

## The decline of rural Britain

Agriculture was hit again in the 1920s and early 1930s as it was exposed to the full force of international competition. This was particularly a problem for cereal farmers, but less so for dairy farming. The government stopped subsidising grain prices in 1921. Dairy farmers and livestock producers encountered problems, particularly when prices fell dramatically in 1932, but, on the whole, did better than arable farmers. This relative shift had a geographical component, for arable farming was more important on the drier soils of eastern Britain than in the wetter west. In Berkshire, acreage devoted to wheat fell from 40,000 in 1918 to less than 28,000 by 1930.

Agricultural problems led to demonstrations, pressure on government, and literary comment. In John Galsworthy's novel *A Modern Comedy* (1929), part of *The Forsyte Saga*, Sir Lawrence Mont, a landowner, leaves Snooks' Club in London meditating: '. . . how the devil was this definite community, the English nation, to exist, when all its land was going out of cultivation, and all its ships and docks in danger of destruction by aeroplanes? He had listened that hour past for a single mention of the land. Not one! It was not practical politics!' *Farmer's Glory* (1932), by the

Wiltshire farmer A. G. Street, was a more personal account of problems and decline. Lord Beaverbrook, the owner of the *Daily Express*, launched an Agriculture Party in 1931, but it had little impact. Nevertheless, the government introduced a measure of agricultural protectionism in the 1930s (see Chapter 9).

In 1921–39, the number of agricultural workers in Britain fell by a quarter, and the pace quickened after World War Two, although, during that conflict, there was again a massive increase in arable farming. After the war, the state was committed to ensuring stability for agriculture, but mechanisation led to a major fall in the work-force. The number of agricultural workers declined much more rapidly than the number of farmers. The latter exhibited a high degree of occupational and agricultural immobility. There have been other important shifts. Horses were superseded by tractors, and local mills, both windmills and watermills, fell into disuse as they were superseded by electricity. Hand-milking was replaced by machines. In Berkshire between 1942 and 1950, the number of tractors doubled to 3,800, while milking machines increased five-fold to 700, and combine harvesters four-fold to 248.

The decline in manual work was followed by a fall in the number of farm workers. By the early 1970s, only 2.5% of the UK's workforce was employed in agriculture. Agriculture continued to shed workers thereafter, and became increasingly a solitary activity. It also became a more stressful one – the number of suicides rose in the 1980s and 1990s as financial and other worries, in what was always a poorly paid and dangerous life, mounted. The increase in the level of suicides also reflected changes in working practices and the increase in the level of bureaucracy. The impact on the landscape of a falling workforce included deserted farms and abandoned farm buildings. The bothies in which many male Scottish farm workers lived in claustrophobic and insanitary conditions, disappeared in the 1960s. The old countryside largely crumbled away.

Other non-urban activities, such as forestry, mining and quarrying, also either declined or dramatically cut their workforces. These changes led, especially after World War Two, to the depopulation of many rural regions, especially remote upland areas, such as Mid-Wales, and also those beyond commuting distance from towns, for example much of Cornwall and the Lincolnshire Wolds. The Rural Development Council divided rural areas into two main types. The first are accessible, that is areas close to urban centres. In these areas, the population expanded rapidly in the 1980s and 1990s, and economic development was also quite rapid. The second were the remote areas, where the problems of economic decline and stagnation were widespread. Rural depopulation was part of a reversal of the earlier, long-term extension of the pattern and density of population that had been the principal means of the human impact on the landscape.

The rural world of 1900 was in many respects the result of the major changes of the period 1500–1900. Change is and was constant, but not equally fast over time. The agricultural depression of the late nineteenth century hit arable farming particularly hard on the heavier soils such as Essex (30 per cent of the arable area of Essex was officially 'derelict'), and more generally, routine tasks such as hedge-laying were badly neglected. Many fields were already chronically neglected or even derelict, and occupied by thistles and dandelions. Yet, in terms of the sense of place and identity of the British population of the twentieth century, the past seemed more fixed. The countryside was believed to represent eternal values and traditions. Attractive images of a countryside of apparently timeless appeal and values were used in recruiting posters for World War One and in railway posters between the wars. The notion of a quintessential English landscape was especially strong in the inter-war period. For example, in the 1920s, Stanley Baldwin, Conservative Prime Minister in 1923–4, 1924–9, and 1935–7, frequently used rural imagery as an important way to address the issue of the national character and to ease the strains which were dividing contemporary industrial society (see Chapter 9). One of the most popular novelists of the period, John Dickson Carr (1905–77), the master of the locked-room mystery, began *Hag's Nook* (1933) with an assertion of the landscape as a product and safeguard of eternal values. He eulogised what was perceived as the rural idyll,

There is something spectral about the deep and drowsy beauty of the English countryside; in the lush dark grass, the evergreens, the grey church-spire and the meandering white road. To an American, who remembers his own brisk concrete highways clogged with red filling-stations and the fumes of traffic, it is particularly pleasant. It suggests a place where people really can walk without seeming incongruous, even in the middle of the road . . . a feeling which can haunt the traveller only in the British Isles. A feeling that the earth is old and enchanted; a sense of reality in all the flashing images which are conjured up by that one word 'merrie'. For France changes, like a fashion, and seems no older than last season's hat. In Germany even the legends have a bustling clockwork freshness, like a walking toy from Nuremberg. But this English earth seems (incredibly) even older than its ivy-bearded towers. The bells at twilight seem to be bells across the centuries; there is a great stillness, through which ghosts step, and Robin Hood has not strayed from it even yet.

Such a rhapsody seems very dated, even embarrassing to modern tastes, but it was typical, not least in its description of the British Isles in terms of the English countryside (see Chapter 12). The growing middle class sought to remind themselves of it through their frequent weekend visits back to the countryside, and also to reproduce it in their suburban gardens. Indeed the great expansion of suburbia was, in part, a quest for garden space and for a semi-rural image that alas devastated the countryside. The rural world was presented as benign in, for example, Vaughan Williams's music or children's fiction, such as A. A. Milne's *Winnie-the-Pooh* (1926) and *The House at Pooh Corner* (1928) (see Chapter 15).

The scale of change, especially after World War Two and from the 1960s, therefore, appeared disturbing. This was especially so in areas of rural depopulation. Change there was a matter not only of a fall in population, but also of a collapse of the rural infrastructure. Rural schools, shops, pubs and post offices closed, rural bus and train services were cut or ended (see Chapter 5). Once crucial to a sense of community, order, hierarchy and place, rural churches were increasingly declared redundant or demolished from 1950. In the Withern group of parishes in Lincolnshire, there were thirteen parish churches in the Middle Ages, eleven in 1900, and only five in 1993. The situation was even worse than these figures may suggest. Many churches no longer had their own vicars but frequently shared with another parish.

Alongside depopulation, there was a significant extent of rural re-population, certainly compared with most European nations. Much of this was caused by commuters seeking an urban way of life in a more rural setting. The countryside and coast were also particularly attractive to those who had retired, and that sector of the population increased greatly. Thanks in large part to commuting and retirement, the countryside became, for many of its inhabitants, a place of residence and leisure, rather than of work. Commuters and the retired came to dominate many villages and hamlets. This reflected both the appeal of an image of the countryside, and a shift in the nature of rural life. The consequence was an effective erosion of any significant boundary between rural and urban society in large parts of the country.

This change was not new. The railway had brought the countryside closer to the town, and from the late nineteenth century rural Britain had increasingly been used for urban purposes. In part, this was a matter of direct services to urban areas, as with reservoirs, asylums and sanatoria. Thus the mental hospital for Gateshead, St Mary's, was built in the Northumberland countryside. The first masonry dam, at Vyrnwy in central Wales, built between 1881 and 1892, provided Liverpool with water. Leisure uses also became important. Upland areas were organised for hunting and shooting, both of which also still survived in lowland Britain. Upland areas were also used for walking, while new patterns of middle-class leisure in the form of golf courses spread across much of lowland Britain. The latter trend remained very important in the early twentieth century, as politicians and celebrities took up the game. The increased use of cars encouraged the use of rural golf courses. This was a major aspect of the 'pretend countryside' that was developed for recreation.

Urban attitudes were increasingly introduced into rural areas in the twentieth century. The intensification of livestock production made the problem of smells and noise more acute. Newcomers to the countryside had fixed and sanitised expectations. These attitudes led to complaints about the animal smells and noise stemming from intensive livestock production, as well as the noise produced by cockerels, and also about the hunting for sport of wild animals, principally foxes and stags, complaints that became especially strong from the 1980s. In much of rural England, housing became scarce and expensive as a result of purchase by commuters and by buyers of second homes, while the problems of the agrarian economy led to a large number of rural households living below the poverty line. During the 1960s and 1980s, the fact that there were so many second homes in Wales owned by English town dwellers led to a spate of cottage burning by militant nationalists.

## The decline of the landowner

At the other end of the social scale, farmers and landowners were helped by boosts to national food production during the two world wars. They were also helped by state subsidies for agriculture under the 1947 Agriculture Act and by the move to a more expensive food policy following Britain's entry into the European Union in 1973. However, there were also major blows, especially as a result of taxation and death duties. The 'People's Budget' announced by Lloyd George in 1909 included new taxes for the wealthy: land taxes, supertax and increased death duties (see Chapter 9).

The burden of taxation was not the only blow to the world of rural grandees. Many heirs to estates died in World War One and the conflict was followed by massive land sales which broke the traditional landlord–tenant relationship. It has been estimated that a quarter of the land in England and Wales changed hands in 1914–27. For example, the Lincolnshire estate of the Earls of Yarborough, 60,000 acres in 1885, fell to about half after land sales in 1919, 1925, 1933, 1944 and 1948, although their links with tenants in north Lincolnshire remain close and extensive today. Another aristocratic Lincolnshire family, the Brownlows, sold most of their Ashridge estate in the Home Counties in the 1920s, their Shropshire estate after World War Two, and the remaining Lincolnshire estates after the death of the 6th Baron Brownlow in 1978.

The growth of owner-occupation of farmland ensured that the tenurial relationship upon which landowner control had rested became less important: the influence of landowners in the politics of agriculture was replaced by that of farmers. The

### David Lloyd George (1863–1945)

David Lloyd George was born in Manchester but grew up in Wales after his father died when he was two years old. He became a solicitor, and was elected as Liberal MP for Caernarvon in 1890. As Chancellor of the Exchequer (1908–15) he introduced many reforms, including the first old age pensions and the National Insurance Act, 1911. His 'people's budget' of 1909 led to a crisis and the Parliament Act of 1911. During the First World War he was Minister of Munitions (1915–16) and then Secretary of State for War (1916) and coalition Prime Minister (1916–22), and played an important part in the subsequent peace negotiations. In 1921 he negotiated with Irish nationalists to create the Irish Free State, but this was unpopular with many. A rebellion by the majority of his Conservative coalition partners led to his resignation in 1922, and thereafter he never held office. He remained in Parliament until 1945, and was made an earl shortly before his death.

dominance of much of rural England by the aristocratic estate became a thing of the past. Legislation passed in 1923 gave tenant farmers greater freedom of cropping. Landlords were adversely affected by the agricultural depression of the 1870s which resumed after World War One. Rents had to be cut and more farms had to be taken in hand. Aside from owner-occupation, there was also a growth of institutional landownership.

Taxation and the disappearance of the vast labour force of cheap servants hit country-house life. Many country houses were demolished or institutionalised. Over 1,200 were destroyed or abandoned in 1918–75. Many others were transferred to the National Trust, became reliant on paying visitors, or became schools or other institutions. National agencies, such as the National Trust, took over from private landowners in preserving and maintaining houses and estates.

In so far as new country houses were built, they were not for landed families, but essentially for rich businessmen or foreigners, who intended to play no role in local government and politics, and did not wish to build up extensive landholdings. Some families maintained control of their estates, but often the estates had shrunk, and in any case, they were little more than remnants of their former glory. More than half of the great estates in the East Riding of Yorkshire sold much or all of their land.

### Box 3.2

### The National Trust as a non-government organisation (NGO)

Founded in 1895 to care for land or buildings of beauty or historic interest, the Trust by 1998 owned 603,000 acres, making it the largest private landowner in England. It is one of the largest owners of farmland. It also had more members than any political party, in 1998 over 2½ million. Visiting Trust properties became a part of the lives of millions, whether walking across magnificent scenery or going for tea (and visiting the accompanying stately homes). The Trust reflected the character of British society with its reliance on voluntarism and its dependence on government tax policies. It is of considerable interest as an NGO. Such bodies are of great importance in British society, and may become more so as the state and its government are transformed, in large part losing functions to European bodies and maybe disintegrating as the United Kingdom is dissolved. NGOs may end up within a European super-state as the prime representatives of national identity and continuity.

Those who failed to keep pace with the changes faced aristocratic impoverishment. The aristocracy also lost their town houses. The Earl of Powis gave up his (45 Berkeley Square) in 1937. Town houses were demolished or converted to institutional use, the American Embassy on Grosvenor Square rising from the ruins of the London town house of the Dukes of Westminster. The present Duke, Gerald Grosvenor, rebuilt the family ancestral home in Cheshire and developed Grosvenor Estates into a multi-million pound business. The aristocracy declined, but 'old money' continued to make its presence felt. The successful aristocracy sold their land and moved into new activities, especially the City and business where they were able to exploit the 'Old Boys network'.

In Scotland, some traditional landholding patterns survived, especially in the Highlands, where the issue of 'who owns Scotland' has for long been controversial. The Dukes of Buccleuch, the Grants, and the Camerons of Lochiel continued to own major estates, but the number, extent and role of such estates were far less than in the past. The position of Anglo-Irish landowners collapsed due to land reform and civil violence in the first quarter of the century. Throughout the British Isles, the land-owners who managed best were those whose land was built on, or who had other sources of revenue, such as stocks and shares or urban property.

## World War Two and rural society

The ruined or destroyed country house was symptomatic of more than a changed pattern of land-use. It also reflected a different world. This gathered pace after World War Two, especially as traditional buffers to change, such as inherited wealth and geographical remoteness, weakened. World War Two had offered agriculture opportunities, but taxation also rose significantly in the 1940s. The war led to a marked revival in agriculture. The cost of imports encouraged an emphasis on domestic production of arable crops, as did German submarine attacks. In World War Two, unlike World War One, the policy of encouraging tillage was imposed as soon as the war began. Farmers were also provided with labour, especially young women from the Land Army, and machinery. Tillage rose greatly: by 1945 it was 55% more than the 1935–9 average. This rise varied geographically, and was greatest in Wales and the East Midlands. In Berkshire, wheat acreage doubled to 66,000 acres and barley also rose. It was World War Two that established modern agriculture as we know it today. The net effect was a cut in food imports, although about 60% of the nation's food was still imported. Large-scale evacuation of mothers and children from the cities in response to the threat of German air attack, led to more people seeing 'the land' and having to adapt to living in rural society.

## The post-war landscape

The pace of change continued after the war, not least with the decline in the agricultural workforce and in the number of rural craftsmen. The countryside became a site for residence and leisure, and, as a result, the nature of rural life and experience changed. In particular, it ceased to be largely co-terminous with agriculture. There became, in effect, two rural histories, that of life outside the towns and that of agriculture. Three-quarters of the UK space continued to be used for farming and forestry. They no longer provided large numbers of jobs but they continued to constitute places of work.

Agricultural support during World War Two was maintained thereafter with state subsidies for agriculture under the 1947 Agriculture Act. This Act was of pivotal importance in putting such unprecedented support on a peacetime and, by implication, permanent footing. It paved the way for agricultural expansion. The agricultural subsidies that followed World War Two and later Britain's accession to the European Economic Community (now European Union) in 1973 helped encourage and finance an intensification of agricultural production. This led to the application of more fertilisers, and the amalgamation of fields and farms in order to improve access for machinery, especially combine harvesters, which became more effective from the 1940s. Investment per worker rose. A 'chemical revolution' occurred in the 1950s and 1960s, in the form of new fertilisers and pesticide compounds. By 1969, about 9 million acres were being sprayed with hormone weedkillers, available since the early 1950s, which prevented weeds from seeding. The loss of arable weeds hit wildlife. Pesticides gave farmers greater flexibility in selecting crops and rotations. New crops made an impact, not least visually. This was especially true of maize, of the striking yellow colour of oil-seed rape, especially from the 1970s, and, in the 1990s, of the pale blue of European Union-subsidised flax.

'Factory farming' became controversial, particularly the treatment of 'battery hens'. When a government minister – Edwina Currie – claimed in 1988 that much of Britain's egg production was contaminated by salmonella it created an outcry. In the 1990s, a crisis over bovine spongiform encephalitis (BSE) in the cattle herd drew attention to the consequences of agricultural practices for animal and human health. A controversy in 1999 over genetically modified crops reflected fear about the impact of science, although the genetic modification of the raw materials of farming and forestry was nothing new. Debate as to the merits of individual agricultural systems or practices was conflated with the question as to how far it was desirable, let alone feasible, to make or resist significant changes in the nature of agriculture (see Chapter 4).

The conquest of nature became ever more comprehensive and insistent. This also increased vulnerability to environmental variations. For example, large-scale land drainage and major changes in the use of low-lying areas left more land vulnerable to flooding. This was a problem throughout Britain. Variations in flood frequency and magnitude in areas like the Yorkshire Ouse catchment were in large part due to atmospheric changes, but land-use alterations were also important. The ploughing of downland affected drainage. Improved systems of drainage enabled the water to get away quicker but low lying land was more prone to flooding when rivers overflowed.

Environmental pressure owed much to the rural economy, not least the opportunities and problems created by change in the regulatory regime. In addition to subsidies, there was also government pressure over rural land-use. Furthermore, systems of control changed. For example, in 1994, the statutory Milk Marketing Board for England and Wales was abolished. This changed the regulation of the dairy industry from a state-controlled producer corporatism to control by retailers.

In the 1990s, British agriculture was severely hit by a number of crises. Aside from specific problems, such as BSE or the decline in the productivity of pig farming caused by economic problems in Far Eastern markets, there was also a more general crisis of confidence in farming. This owed much to the strength of sterling, which made food imports competitive and hit British agricultural exports. There was also concern arising from the European Union's attempts to cut agricultural subsidies.

These subsidies had disguised the real economics of British farming and, in particular, its limited international competitiveness. Pressures on farming affected the rest of the rural economy, as well as that of small towns. They also encouraged an exploitation of agricultural opportunities that put further pressure on the environment.

## ■ Changing townscapes

From the outset of the period, Britain was heavily urbanised. In 1901, 78% of the population lived in communities of more than 2,500 people and nearly 44% in the 23 towns with more than 100,000. Urban areas were growing rapidly, in part thanks to the expansion of rail, tram and bus services. Lower fares were offered in order to encourage workers, as well as the middle class, to commute. Tram systems were frequently run by town councils and, from the 1890s, they subsidised fares in order to encourage people to move away from crowded residential areas in city centres. In Bradford, Leeds and Sheffield, tramways were built into open country in order to encourage development. The fastest growing urban areas in 1891–1901 were suburban: Walthamstow and West Ham near London, King's Norton and Northfield near Birmingham. North of Newcastle, there was expansion in Jesmond and Gosforth. In total, half a million acres of agricultural land were built over between 1893 and 1903 (see Chapter 5).

The British townscape changed considerably during the twentieth century and, as with the countryside, there was both great variety in the change and an ever increasing pace of transformation. As with the countryside, environmental change and pressures were linked to the impact of technology, but also to social processes and economic shifts.

The terms 'process' and 'shift' are overly benign or neutral words when used to describe some of the harsh and difficult changes that occurred. People not only moved off the land, but also migrated away from declining industrial regions. Areas that were collectively the nineteenth-century 'workshop of the world' became industrial museums and regions of social dereliction, designated as problems requiring regional assistance, as under the Special Areas Act (1934), which in fact provided only limited assistance. During the slump of the 1930s, the urban fabric in depressed industrial regions was devastated, as communities were squeezed and businesses shut. Unemployment in Sunderland rose to 75 per cent of shipbuilders and half of the working population, and was associated with hardship and higher rates of ill-health. Jarrow, another shipbuilding town in North-East England, also had unemployment levels of over 70 per cent, following the closure of Palmers Yard, the main employer in the town – a plight clearly described in *The Town that was Murdered* (1939), by the MP Ellen Wilkinson (see Chapter 11).

People moved from such towns to areas of greater economic opportunity, mostly in the Midlands and South-East England. Scottish coal-miners moved to Nottinghamshire, and others migrated to the new steel town of Corby in Northamptonshire. Internal migrants left fossilised townscapes and helped create sprawling suburbs where they moved. In addition, especially after World War Two, crowded inner-city areas lost people as slums were torn down. Instead, people moved to new developments on 'green-field' sites in the countryside, or on the edge of older settlements. Some of the former were New Towns, the first 'garden city' being Letchworth, founded in 1903, although not all greenfield developments were New Towns: for example, Kirkby. The 'garden city' movement pressed the social and health value of building at lower densities and with a plentiful provision of green spaces (see Chapter 2).

Expansion on the edge of older settlements led to suburban sprawl, the suburbia where a far greater percentage now came to live. Land, and therefore mortgages and rents, were cheaper there. This was especially the case around major cities, particularly London, which expanded greatly in the 1920s and 1930s, the city springing forward, for example from Hampstead to Edgware. London became Greater London. Between 1921 and 1937, the population of inner London fell by nearly half a million, but that of Greater London grew by about 1½ million to a total of about 8 ½ million, about a fifth of the nation's population. Elsewhere **suburbia** spread. In the inter-war period this was mainly ribbon development along arterial roads and railways, creating new suburbs, such as Kenton to the north of Newcastle. V. F. Soothill, the Medical Officer for Norwich, wrote, in 1935, of the spread of suburbia as a 'quiet social revolution'. It reflected the desire for a life away from factory chimneys and inner-city crowding, a desire catered to in the posters advocating life in the new suburbs. The novelist D. H. Lawrence more critically referred to 'little red rat-traps', while the poet John Betjeman described Swindon's houses as 'brick-built breeding boxes of new souls': Swindon was designated an overspill town in 1952. In his *England and the Octopus*, the architect Clough Williams-Ellis berated builders and planners for their destruction of the countryside and what he called 'the common background of beauty'.

Suburbia certainly reflected sameness and national standardisation. Indeed, a predictability of product helped to make the new housing sell. The houses were mass produced and had standardised parts. They also looked similar. In part this was because of the dominance of brick as the building material and the dominance of much brickmaking, especially in the growing south-east of England, by the Fletton process using the Jurassic clays of the East Midlands, whose high carbon content cut the cost of firing. Brickmaking developed as a massive industry between Bedford and Bletchley and also near Whittlesey on the Cambridgeshire–Huntingdonshire border, feeding the new suburbia. Bricks, and other products for the housing market, such as prefabricated doors and windows, could be moved not only by rail, but also by the new expanding road system. Inter-war London provided more than one-third of the population increase of the whole of England and Wales. Suburban culture became increasingly defined and important.

A larger proportion of land was converted to building development between the wars than since that period, although it is possible that official statistics significantly underestimate the amount of agricultural land lost since 1945. Much new building was by private enterprise, often by speculative builders, such as John Laing and Richard Costain. They were largely responsible for the plentiful supply of inexpensive houses by the mid-1920s. The ability to borrow at low rates of interest from building societies was important. In the mid-1920s houses cost between £400 and £1,000.

However, council-house building was also important: between 1919 and 1939 there were a total of 4,105,507 new units in England

**suburbia:** The areas on the outskirts of towns and cities where most people live and from where they travel to work or to shop.

---

**Box 3.3**

## House-building by the public and private sector

In thousands (to nearest thousand)

| | Public (local authority) | Private |
|---|---|---|
| 1945–9 | 432 | 126 |
| 1950–4 | 913 | 229 |
| 1955–9 | 689 | 623 |
| 1960–4 | 546 | 879 |
| 1965–9 | 761 | 994 |
| 1970–4 | 524 | 885 |
| 1975–9 | 542 | 747 |
| 1980–5 | 226 | 736 |
| 1986–90 | 156* | 904 |

Highest figure underlined
*Includes construction by Housing Associations

Box 3.4

### Types of housing tenure in England and Wales

|      | Owner-occupiers | Rented from local authority | Rented from private landlords |
|------|-----------------|-----------------------------|-------------------------------|
| 1914 | 10              | 1                           | <u>80</u>                     |
| 1939 | 31              | 14                          | 23                            |
| 1966 | <u>47</u>       | 26                          | 15                            |
| 1970 | <u>50</u>       | 30                          | 9                             |
| 1977 | <u>54</u>       | 32                          | 8                             |
| 1985 | <u>62</u>       | 27                          | –                             |
| 1990 | <u>67</u>       | 24                          | 7                             |

To nearest percentage
Other categories not included so figures do not add up to 100
Highest category underlined

and Wales; 2,969,050 of them were privately-built and 1,136,457 local-authority units. Treasury loans for local-authority building had been available from 1866, but most local authorities had been reluctant to incur debts. From 1919, however, as a consequence of Addison's two Housing Acts, grants replaced loans, and council-house building expanded. This was designed to give bricks and mortar to Lloyd George's promise of 'Homes fit for Heroes' at the end of World War One. Following many of the recommendations made in the Tudor Walters Report of 1918, the Housing and Town Planning Act of 1919 sought to provide lower-density housing for the working class. Minimum room sizes were decreed, as was the inclusion of internal bathrooms. The Acts were hit by the financial crisis of 1921–2, but they still led to much construction, as did Neville Chamberlain's Housing Act of 1923 and the Wheatley Act of 1924 (see Chapter 9). Large new estates included Longbridge near Birmingham, Wythenshawe near Manchester, and Speke near Liverpool. The London County Council's Becontree estate, begun in 1921 and finished in 1932, occupied 277 acres and consisted of about 26,000 houses. It housed 120,000 people. Not all the new estates were successes. Blackhill, built by Glasgow Corporation, was an example of what could go wrong when funds were short and little care was given to location. Council housing was increasingly important because the private rental sector had declined, in part because private landlordship had become less profitable, and there was therefore less private investment in the building of new properties for rent.

The process of council-house building was only halted by World War Two. Thereafter, it revived, driven on by wartime damage to the housing stock, a low rate of wartime construction, expectations of a better life after the war, and a rise in the birth rate. A shortage of resources in the post-war economy, and the priority given to industrial reconstruction, ensured that, although the Attlee governments (1945–51) built many houses, the number – under 200,000 per year in 1949–51 – was inadequate. The urgent need for housing led to the mass construction of 'prefabs' – prefabricated bungalows intended as temporary homes. Many were still inhabited as late as the 1970s.

In the late 1940s, by necessity, many families remained with their parents long after they wished to move. The Conservatives saw this as an opportunity, and, in the election of 1951, made much of a promise to build 300,000 units a year. Once elected, Churchill repackaged the previous Ministry of Town and Country Planning that had become the Ministry of Local Government and Planning, to create the Ministry of Housing and Local Government, and appointed to it one of his protégés, Harold Macmillan. Helped by a higher allocation of government resources and a cutting of the building standards for council houses, Macmillan achieved his target in 1953. There was extensive rehousing in the 1950s. Then, for example, Londoners from the East End were rehoused in new council-housing estates at Debden, Hainault and Harold Hill.

Concern about the rate of the spread of suburbia and the threat to the environment, combined with a growing willingness to accept government control, led to the passage of legislation. The Housing, Town Planning Act of 1909 was the first piece of British legislation to use the term 'town planning'. John Burns, the President of the Local Government Board, introduced the legislation in 1908 by telling Parliament that it set out to 'provide a domestic condition for the people in which their physical health, their morals, their character and their whole social condition can be improved . . . to secure the home healthy'. The Greater London Planning Committee was established in 1927, and another Town and Country Planning Act followed in 1932. The Restriction of Ribbon Development Act of 1935 attempted to prevent unsightly and uncontrolled development along new or improved roads. It was an admission of a serious problem. The Green Belt (London and Home Counties) Act of 1938 arose from a local government initiative. It provides an excellent example of local government pioneering – acting as laboratories, whose experiences provided guidance as to what might later be generalised by central government. The Act was followed by the 1940 report of the Barlow Commission proposing more state control over development, particularly in the London area, and the Scott Report of 1942 which advocated planning for the countryside to protect prime agricultural land and areas of natural beauty. In 1943, the Ministry of Housing and Local Government was created. This provided a context for a national planning policy; hitherto each local authority had done what seemed appropriate under the general guidance of the Ministry of Health. Professor Patrick Abercrombie, a leading town planner, was appointed to draw up plans for London, and in 1943 the County of London Plan was published. The following year, Abercrombie's Greater London Plan looked at the wider regional situation, putting the London County Council (LCC) in a planner's framework. This plan suggested moving housing and jobs away from London to New Towns built on greenfield sites around the capital.

A belief in planning was taken forward with the Town and Country Planning Acts of 1944 and 1947 and the New Towns Act of 1946. Under the 1947 Act, local authorities were required to take comprehensive views of land-use. New Towns were designed to complement Green Belts. London was to be contained with a Green Belt and New Towns were to be built outside the Belt. The first, Stevenage, was designated in November 1946. Within three years, another seven were designated for London overspill: Harlow, Hemel Hempstead, Crawley, Bracknell, Basildon, Hatfield and Welwyn Garden City. The London Green Belt was finally secured with an Act of 1959. There were other New Towns elsewhere in the country, for example Cumbernauld for the Glasgow 'overspill' of population and Skelmersdale for Liverpool. The other Scottish New Towns were East Kilbride, Glenrothes, Livingston and Irvine. Thanks to its Green Belt, London did not leap forward from Edgware to Elstree. Nevertheless, as much development simply passed the Green Belt, it created new pressures further afield, for example in South-East England around Ipswich and

Reading. The process is still continuing, although new housing is overwhelmingly built by the private sector. The fastest growing urban areas in the 1980s and 1990s were Swindon and Taunton. In July 1992, the government indicated that it expected 855,000 new houses to be built in South-East England between 1991 and 2006 (see Chapter 2).

This expansion poses a problem both for the rural environment and for the existing urban structure. Many new or greatly expanded towns, for example Crawley, Basingstoke and Peterlee, translated old social problems to new sites. In Basingstoke in 1999, the 'deprivation index' of the Office of Population, Census and Surveys remained highest in Popley, the housing estate built in the 1960s to accommodate London overspill. New towns also exacerbated old social problems by destroying the 'old communities'. This was part of a more general process of change. The 'Greenwood' Housing Act of 1930 had given local authorities powers to clear or improve slum (crowded and substandard housing) areas. Passed by the Labour government, it provided the local authorities with subsidies related to the numbers rehoused and the cost of slum clearance, and obliged them to produce five-year plans. The terms of the subsidies were renewed with an Act passed by the National Government in 1933. Thus, the responsibility of the central government for the availability and quality of housing was clearly established in the inter-war period. Much was achieved in the 1920s and 1930s, in part thanks to the ready availability of labour and materials, and low interest rates in the 1930s. In 1931–9, local authorities built over 700,000 houses and cleared 250,000 slum properties. After 1945, slums were swept aside and their inhabitants moved into new council-housing estates, as part of an effort to build a 'New Jerusalem'. The effects of this policy are a matter of controversy. It is unclear how far problems apparent during the 1960s and thereafter were an issue in the late 1940s and 1950s when there was a greater desire simply for new housing. In particular, it is difficult to recover the attitudes of the 1950s. The buildings of this period, many of which were fairly generous with space, should be distinguished from the system-built tower blocks largely built in the 1960s. Many of the new houses provided people with their first bathrooms and inside toilets. There is considerable evidence to suggest that the problems of poorly-built estates were much more apparent in the 1960s, and that earlier developments were often better built and more popular.

Nevertheless, a critical view dominated subsequent discussion. Aside from the social disruption of the move to new locations, many of the new neighbourhoods were poorly planned and unpopular with their occupants. They tended to lack community amenities, such as pubs and neighbourhood shops. Families were separated from relatives, hitting the support systems crucial for childcare and for looking after the elderly. On the new housing estates, there was a decline in the three-generation extended family and a move towards the 'nuclear family'. Such families 'privatised' from their traditional communities and close knit relationships. Shared roles between husband and wife replaced segregated roles. Grandparents were more socially and geographically isolated as a result of these changes.

Concern about urban sprawl encouraged higher-density housing after World War Two. Alongside architectural and planning fashions, and land prices, this contributed to high-rise development. Prefabricated methods of construction ensured that multi-storey blocks of flats could be built rapidly and inexpensively, and local councils, such as Glasgow, Liverpool and Newcastle in the 1950s and 1960s, took pride in their number, size and visibility. Glasgow Corporation began to rebuild the Gorbals as a high-rise district in 1951. By the early 1970s, one home in every three being built in Scotland was in a block of six storeys or more. Extolled at the time, and illustrated alongside castles and cathedrals in guidebooks of the 1960s, municipal multi-storey flats were subsequently attacked as of poor quality, ugly, out of keeping with the existing urban fabric, lacking in community feeling, and breeders of alienation and crime. Frequent heating and ventilation problems caused condensation, lifts often broke down, vandalism became a serious problem, and the morale of tenants in tower blocks fell. The lack of gardens may also have affected many of the inhabitants. In place of individual gardens, there were unfenced green spaces for which none of the residents had responsibility and which were apt to be desolate. New estates, such as Park Hill in Sheffield, an estate of concrete inner-city tower blocks built in 1957, were designed as entire communities with elevated walkways called streets in the sky. Most, however, were failures, not only because they were poorly built, but also because they did not contribute to social cohesion. Kirkby on Merseyside, for example, was associated with unemployment, crime and vandalism. Part of the Ronan Point tower block in Newham, London, collapsed after a gas explosion in 1968. By the 1970s, Park Hill was, in part, like a concrete slum, and other nearby blocks were demolished. The decision of English Heritage in 1998 to list Park Hill as an architectural masterpiece, at the same time as five blocks on the Alton Estate in Roehampton, London, was widely deplored by the tenants. Elsewhere, there were many demolitions, not only of high-rise estates but also of low-rise, deck-access blocks, such as the Chalkhill area in Brent, London, demolished in 1998–9.

Alongside much unattractive and poor-quality municipal housing in the 1960s, there was also a brutal rebuilding of many city centres, for example, Birmingham, Gateshead, Manchester, Newcastle and Plymouth. Professional planners played a major role in this process, which sought both to cope with traffic congestion and to provide modern images for cities.

The role of government in planning is a reminder that changes in the environment cannot be divorced from politics. In general, successive governments paid limited attention to the issue until after World War Two. During wartime, other issues came to the fore, and in peacetime there was a general lack of interest in the state of the physical environment and a sense that it was inappropriate for government to intervene too closely. There was, however, important intervention in landlord–tenant relations. Following the 1915 Rent and Mortgage Interest Restrictions (War) Act, which owed something to the Clydeside rent strikes of that year, tenants' rights became more secure, private landlordship less profitable, and renting from local authorities – 'council housing' – more important. It was not until the Rent Act of 1965, however, that rent control was established on a secure legislative footing.

Urban planning changed after World War Two, although environmental interests did not rise to great prominence until the 1960s. Nevertheless, Green Belt and Clean Air legislation represented major advances in the principle of national responsibility and the practice of governmental intervention. The establishment of Areas of Outstanding Natural Beauty under the 1949 Countryside Act, and of National Parks in England and Wales from 1951 was important (see Box 3.1). However, despite greater interest in planning from the 1940s, such moves were not part of a coherent strategy, and the Clean Air Act of 1956, in particular, was a response to a specific crisis created by a very bad London smog of 1952, which killed more than 4,000 people. The Act made the individual responsible for the measures needed, namely the trouble and cost of converting from one type of fuel to another. This, in turn, was made possible by the fact that (as never before) the means for such conversions were now readily to hand. The first smokeless-zone legislation was introduced in the Manchester Corporation Act of 1946 and the first smokeless zone was established (in Coventry) in 1951. London was declared a smokeless zone in 1955. However, about 750 Londoners died in another smog in 1962. Another Clean Air Act followed in 1968. Following the designation of most of London as a 'smokeless zone' the same was applied to other cities. Smoke emissions in Newcastle were controlled from 1958.

Economic change pressed hard on the urban environment. Growth created serious problems, but so also did decay. This left derelict premises and helped to undermine the quality of surrounding areas. When demolished, many industrial sites left serious pollution problems, as well as much ugliness. The rate of industrial decline was considerable. For example, by the 1980s, more than half the 2,400 cotton mills built in the Greater Manchester area between the late eighteenth century and 1930 had been demolished, including more than three-quarters of those built within the city boundaries.

Greater public awareness of environmental degradation and the fashionability of environmental concern led, from the 1960s, to more consistent and insistent government intervention. The Countryside Commission was founded in 1968 (a year after the Scottish Countryside Commission), as a revamping of the National Parks Commission created in 1949, and a further Town and Country Planning Act passed the following year. The Department of the Environment was established in 1970. Various restrictions on land-use were introduced in 1968. Conservation areas in towns were designated as were scheduled ancient monuments. More money was spent on maintaining environmental standards, most obviously with payments – about £900 million in 1994 – under the Agriculture Act of 1986 to farmers to 'set aside' land from farming or to adopt less intensive farming methods and introduce environmental improvements.

This Act made it possible for the first time for Agriculture Ministers to use the agricultural budget for purposes other than the furtherance of agricultural production, namely for agric-environmental schemes and the diversification of the rural economy generally. Paying farmers to 'set aside' was initially voluntary before being made compulsory. The Wildlife and Countryside Act of 1981 established Sites of Special Scientific Interest, which were partly protected from 'damaging agricultural operations'. The pressure for development increasingly clashed with environmental concerns, leading to flash points, for example new road schemes, over which governments had to take a view. The long proposed Newbury bypass, which finally opened in November 1998, provides but one example of this.

By the end of the century, the environment was more clearly a political issue than it had been at the outset. The *Ecologist* magazine was founded in 1969. What in 1987 became the Green Party was founded in 1975, and in 1989 it won 15 per cent of the vote in the elections to the European Parliament (which, given the first-past-the-post system, was not enough to win it any seats). This was exceptional, but environmental consciousness and activism became more pronounced. Friends of the Earth and Greenpeace enjoyed much support in the 1990s, while the mainstream political parties presented themselves, with different degrees of success, as being the 'pro-environment party'.

The relationship between town and countryside was more than a matter of planning how to manage growth. It was also bound up with images of identity and assumptions about psychic health. In general, the city, certainly in England (but far less so in Scotland), was conceptualised as the source of challenge to national values, and national identity, certainly prior to World War Two, was presented in terms of rural images and a benign view of rural values (see Chapters 12, 15). The city was associated with the (numerous) ethnic, behavioural and social groups seen as threatening traditional assumptions, for example militant working-class elements, the Irish, Jews, New Women and homosexuals. Conversely, it had much to offer these groups including anonymity, mobility and collectivity.

# Summary

◆ The environment changed greatly in the twentieth century and this was true both of the rural and of the urban economy.

◆ The pace of change accelerated from the 1950s, although it had been constant from before the century began.

◆ Affluence and technology were the two major motors of environmental change. They combined in the motor car. Lower-density housing was also of great importance.

◆ Concern about the environment became more widespread from the 1960s, although it had become an important aspect of public consciousness from the late nineteenth century. Then the focus was largely on the threat supposedly posed by expanding cities. In the 1960s, environmentalism focused more on the consequences of industrialisation and the consumer culture.

◆ By the 1990s, much environmental concern was directed to the 'industrial' nature of agriculture.

# Questions for discussion

◆ Was there a rural interest in twentieth-century Britain?

◆ How did attitudes towards the countryside change in the twentieth century?

◆ How did planning affect the issue?

◆ How far do notions of town and country affect your understanding of identity, whether of England or Scotland, Wales or Northern Ireland, Britain or the United Kingdom?

◆ What was the importance of the countryside for British culture in the twentieth century? (See also Chapter 1.)

◆ How far was housing policy affected by its position at the intersection of welfare and environmental policies and practices? (See also Chapter 2.)

◆ How far has agriculture suffered from the problems of the rest of the economy? (See also Chapter 11.)

# Further reading

Beard, Madeline, *English Landed Society in the Twentieth Century* (London, 1989).

Burnett, J., *A Social History of Housing, 1815–1970* (London, 1978).

Esher, L. A., *Broken Wave: The Rebuilding of England, 1940–1980* (London, 1981).

Martin, John, *The Development of Modern Agriculture: British Farming since 1931* (Basingstoke, 1999).

O'Connor, R. J., and Shrubb, M., *Farming and Birds* (Cambridge, 1986).

Swenarton, M., *Homes Fit for Heroes: The Politics and Architecture of Early State Housing in Britain* (London, 1981).

Thompson, F. M. L. (ed.), *The Rise of Suburbia* (Leicester, 1982).

# Technology, Science and the World of Goods

# CHAPTER 4

Technology and science had a sweeping impact in the twentieth century. The nineteenth century had brought major changes, but the twentieth witnessed revolutionary transformations in theoretical and applied science and technology in most fields, whether transport, the generation and distribution of power, medicine, contraception, cloning, agricultural yields, or the accumulation, storing and manipulation of information. The wealth was created and the means provided that would make it feasible to suggest that humanity's lot on earth could be substantially improved. Yet, at the same time, disquiet about the pace of technological change, and the process and consequences of scientific advance, increased markedly, especially with the 'Ban the Bomb' movement of the 1950s, and more generally from the 1960s as the environmental movement became more vocal and popular. Anxiety about technology was linked to a wider questioning of the rationale of economic growth, although it was the case that such growth was required in order to fund policies of environmental rehabilitation.

## Contents

## Key issues

▶ How important was a sense of change?

▶ What were the major effects of technological development?

▶ What was purchased?

▶ How far can eating habits serve to indicate a changing society and consumer culture?

▶ What did consumerism amount to?

## New technology

Technology had become a freed genie in the nineteenth century. It led to a great pace of change, one of the key words for any study of modern Britain. In the late nineteenth century, railway and telegraphy were succeeded by motor car and telephone, electricity and wireless. The growth of the genre of 'scientific romance' testified to the seemingly inexorable advance of human potential through technology and its impact on the collective imagination. In *The Coming Race* (1871) by Sir Edward

THE COMING FORCE—MR. PUNCH'S DREAM.

**Hope for the future: electricity sweeping all before it**
John Tenniel's *Punch* cartoon (6 December 1882) both satirises the enthusiasts and captured their sense of excitement of new frontiers. An earlier coal-based world of fog, chimney sweeps and coalmen succumbs.

Bulwer Lytton (one of the leading men of letters of his age and a former Conservative Secretary for the Colonies), a mining engineer encountered at the centre of the earth a people who controlled 'Vril', a kinetic energy offering limitless powers. The novel is largely forgotten, other than through the name of the drink Bo[vine]vril.

Science fiction played a greater role in the work of H. G. Wells (1866–1946), who had studied under Charles Darwin's supporter T. H. Huxley. Humanity's destiny in time and space was a central question for Wells, reflecting in part the intellectual expansion and excitement offered by the evolutionary theory outlined by Darwin in his *On the Origin of Species*, and by interest in manned flight. Wells's first major novel, *The Time Machine* (1895), was followed by *The War of the Worlds* (1898), an account of a Martian invasion of England.

Developments were less lurid than those outlined by Wells, but they still changed many aspects of human experience and did so in a readily apparent fashion. For example, the capacity of humans to find new ways to provide heat and light, industrial production, and transport was demonstrated throughout the period as the age of coal passed. At the outset of the twentieth century, power, heat and light were all dependent on coal, and the associated sights, smells, sounds and tasks made up much of the structure of the national economy and much of the fabric of life. By the end of the century, natural gas was more important as a power source, and this had brought associated changes to both the economy and the fabric of life. The first demonstration of electric lighting, in Birmingham, was in 1882; the Birmingham Electric Supply Ltd. following seven years later. The electric lighting industry developed and spread rapidly: the installed capacity in the local-authority sector in Scotland alone rose from 6,332 kilowatts in 1896 to 84,936 in 1910. Electricity was also regarded as a means to improve the social environment. It was cleaner than coal. In a less elevated manner, the cinematograph was introduced to London in 1896 by

Louis Lumière. The same year, Guglielmo Marconi arrived in London to try to interest the Admiralty in radio.

The pace of change also affected transport. The first original, full-size British petrol motor was produced in 1895, the first British-made motor car the following year. The first successful powered flight, by the American Wright brothers in 1903, led the press baron Lord Northcliffe to remark that 'England is no longer an island'. Blériot flew across the Channel in 1909. Air power changed Britain's fundamental geopolitical character. It was no longer defensible by sea alone. In January 1904, Leo Amery emphasised the onward rush of technology when he told the Royal Geographical Society that sea and rail links and power would be supplemented by air, and then:

a great deal of this geographical distribution must lose its importance, and the successful powers will be those who have the greatest industrial basis. It will not matter whether they are in the centre of a continent or on an island; those people who have the industrial power and the power of invention and of science will be able to defeat all others.

This shift was not welcome to the government. It feared any development that would lessen the value of British sea power. The War Office made less effort than its French and German counterparts to develop air power. As a consequence, the industry made only slow progress, especially in the manufacture of engines. By 1911, nevertheless, there was an aerodrome – Northolt – in London's suburbs.

As with much else, change was greatly accelerated thanks to World War One (1914–18). The use of aeroplanes for combat led to considerable investment in their development and in 1919 a converted British Vickers 'Vimy' bomber was the first aeroplane to cross the Atlantic non-stop. A system of long-distance passenger services developed by Imperial Airways linked the British Empire by the mid-1930s, and in the 1950s the British developed passenger jet services with the Comet, the world's first jet-propelled airliner: the Comet had its maiden flight in 1949, and carried its first fare-paying passengers in 1952, but it was to be the American Boeing 707 that became the major passenger airliner. The military potential of air power undermined Britain's confidence in its ability to defend itself from enemy attack in the 1930s. Stanley Baldwin remarked in 1932 that 'the bomber will always get through'. It was an outlook which played some part in the decision to pursue a policy of appeasement against Nazi Germany.

Northcliffe's sense of transformation was to be echoed throughout the twentieth century. For an elderly person at its close, and they were a growing percentage of the population, it was not only the individual major technological innovations of their lifetime, whether atomic energy or contraceptive pill, television or microchip, jet engine or computer, bio-technology or artificial hip, that were of importance in affecting, directly or indirectly, insistently or episodically, their life. It was also the cumulative impact of change. The past ceased to be a recoverable world, a source of reference, value and values for lives that changed very little, and became, instead, a world that was truly lost, a distorted theme-park for nostalgia, regret or curiosity.

The science and technology that transformed Britain and the British were global. Indeed, the openness of Britain to trade and foreign influence ensured that technological developments made a greater impact than in more self-sufficient societies. American inventions were of particular importance and access to them was eased by the openness of Britain to foreign investment.

A history of science and technology in twentieth-century Britain would, therefore, in large part be their global history. That does not make developments such as the impact of the use of plastic in many industrial processes less important or less noteworthy in a history of Britain. Nevertheless, there were distinctive points of note. British scientists and institutions did make a considerable contribution, as measured, for example, by the number of Nobel Prizes. One prizewinner, Ernest Rutherford, a New Zealand physicist who discovered the nucleus of the atom, highlights the role of British institutions. He was Director of the Cavendish Laboratory in Cambridge from 1918 until 1937, a formative period in the development of British physics and one closely linked with the Cavendish.

British scientists did not only make major contributions in nuclear and astrophysics. In molecular biology, a 'new biology' of the 1950s, scientists in Britain played a crucial role in the discovery of DNA, the very stuff of life. The crucial breakthroughs were made in 1951–3 by Francis Crick, Rosalind Franklin, James Watson and Maurice Wilkins, and in 1962 Watson, Crick and Wilkins won a Nobel Prize for their work; Franklin was already dead. In medicine, Alexander Fleming, Professor of Bacteriology in London, 1928–48, discovered penicillin in 1928. Medical research was affected, but not prevented, by legislation and regulation. Technological advances solved technical issues, but, in turn, created ethical and legal problems. The Human Tissue Act of 1961 specified the ways in which organs could be taken from the body for research, teaching and transplantation. It reflected the scientific optimism of the 1950s. In 1989, it was necessary to pass another Act, the Human Transplant Act, because the provisions of the 1961 Act related only to dead humans; by 1989 organs could be transplanted from live people. It is possible that future legislation will address the issue of whether it will be necessary to contract out from being eligible, once dead, to have one's organs transplanted, rather than contracting in, as at present. In the field of computing, Alan Turing's theoretical work in the 1930s and 1940s helped pave the way for the Manchester Mk 1, the first all-electronic computer to function. Designed in Manchester University's Computer Laboratory, it first went into action on 21 June 1948.

## Science and society

Some scientists grasped the public imagination. In the 1990s, Stephen Hawking's explanation of time and the universe proved a best seller. Most, however, seemed remote. Whereas the scientist had been a heroic figure in the nineteenth century, in the twentieth his or her knowledge seemed incomprehensible, even though television programmes such as the long-running *Tomorrow's World* sought to bring the latest innovations to a wider audience. Thus, in an age when science made an ever greater impact, it was understood by only a minority. The numbers of students taking science at university was repeatedly less than that for 'arts' subjects.

Concern about the divorce of scientists from the rest of society led in the 1950s to a debate about the 'Two Cultures', an idea advanced in 1956 by C. P. Snow, an influential scientist and man of letters. The Labour government that came to power in 1964 sought to identify itself with Science (Snow was given a life peerage and became a member of the government). Labour's leader, Harold Wilson, presented himself and his party as more closely linked to science and technology than the Conservatives. On 1 October 1963, he had promised the Labour Party Conference at Scarborough to harness the 'white heat' of the technological revolution for the future of the country. Wilson saw scientific socialism as a commitment to modernisation. In office, in

**Applied technology: new power sources**
Calder Hall, Britain's first nuclear power station and the first in the world to supply substantial quantities of electricity to a national system, opened on 17 October 1956. Initial optimism and expansion of the nuclear power industry was replaced by environmental concerns and by anxiety about long-term problems of processing and storing nuclear waste.

1964, Wilson founded a Ministry of Technology and renamed the Department of Education as Education and Science.

The 1960s, indeed, saw a continuation of a bout of applied scientific advance that since World War Two had witnessed major developments, including the production of the British atomic (1952) and hydrogen (1957) bombs and the creation of a nuclear power industry. More generally, the British proved responsive to technological developments elsewhere, although there was a measure of reluctance, seen both in trade union hostility to new industrial practices, and in a growing romanticisation of the past. This affected even activities at the cutting edge of change, such as pop music. In 1966, the pop hero Bob Dylan played the Manchester Free Hall with a powerful amplifying system for his backing band flown in specially from Los Angeles. The audience, expecting to hear the lyrics, responded with slow handclaps, boos and a shout of 'Judas'.

## Science and national decline

Martin Wiener concluded, in a highly influential book, first published in 1981, that there was a link between English culture and the decline of the industrial spirit in Britain. The British, he argued, or at least much of their Establishment elite, had never really accepted industrialisation and the philosophy of industrialism. For them, Britain was always 'a green and pleasant land', rather than 'the workshop of the world'. Economic growth became synonymous with the harsh realities of factory-based production, the degradation of urban life, environmental pressures and the destruction of the countryside, rather than with its more positive consequences. As a result, Wiener argued, Britain experienced an economically damaging process of 'psychological and intellectual de-industrialisation'.

This has been a controversial thesis, but it is certainly true that scientific researchers frequently complained about receiving less support than their counterparts in the USA or Germany. John Logie Baird (1888–1946), who in 1926 gave the first public demonstration of television in London, suffered from a lack of state support. However, there was still considerable expenditure on research. For example, in the 1890s and 1900s concern about Britain's relative position led to much more government expenditure on the universities, and also to the creation of important new institutions, especially Imperial College, London, the National Physical Laboratory, and the Medical Research Council. Government did not adopt a *laissez-faire* attitude. Scientists thus gained career support, although later than in Germany and the USA.

Nevertheless, despite successes, during the century as a whole the synergy or profitable interaction of science, technology and industry that characterised the American, German and Japanese economies proved elusive. Thus, in electronics and information technology the British dropped behind and became dependent on foreign advances. It was during the 1960s that the effects of the 'brain drain' were first seen; many British scientists moved to the USA to take advantage of the higher salaries and better working conditions there. Sir Christopher Cockerell, the inventor of what he called the 'hovercraft', complained about the way in which his invention was handled by the Government's National Research Development Corporation, and claimed that it was an example of the failure of the British to benefit from advances in design and engineering. Certainly, his invention – the world's first practical hovercraft was launched in 1959 – did not lead to the anticipated results. For many, it symbolised the problems of applied science in Britain.

In the same period, the British lost their position in atomic power. Changes in weapons technology during the 1950s made Britain dependent upon the USA for its nuclear deterrent. At Nassau in December 1962, Britain purchased the Polaris missile system from the Americans. Its replacement some thirty years later, Trident, was also American developed. The Treasury had been reluctant to support the continued development of a nuclear delivery system when one could be obtained from the Americans. Limited economic growth could only finance so much high-cost military research, and it was necessary to choose between possible commitments. France took over from Britain the leadership in the use of atomic power for electricity generation in Western Europe. The most spectacular failure among Britain's attempts to remain a leader in the field of high-technology application was the Anglo-French supersonic aircraft project in the 1960s. Spiralling research and development costs made Concorde the most expensive aircraft ever built.

Despite Margaret Thatcher's enthusiasm for science, scientists complained about a lack of funding in the 1980s and 1990s, but the problem, instead, seemed to be a failure to concentrate on readily exploitable work. This was compounded by a lack of interest in developing a research base on the part of many companies, which was a problem that certainly hampered the work of the Ministry of Technology in the 1960s. The public did not identify with British science, and they were not given much incentive to do so by successive governments.

Furthermore, there was considerable disquiet over scientific and technological developments. Disastrous side-effects, such as the birth defects from the drug thalidomide in the 1960s, and unexpected consequences, as from asbestos, fuelled public alarm, and in 1999 this led to a panic about genetically modified crops. Biotechnology was regarded as a threat to human health and the physical environment, rather than an opportunity to continue earlier advances in enhancing the productivity of crops. In 1999, there was also controversy over access to pornography on the internet, and over the alleged effects of the use of mobile phones on users' brains, both apparently side-effects of the developments in information technology and access that were so important in the 1990s.

The end result was a failure to reproduce the sense of achievement that had characterised the Victorian age and, combined with serious economic problems, the transformation of parts of British industry from a show-case into a museum-piece. Nevertheless, much was achieved. In 1997 Dolly appeared, the first cloned animal: the nucleus of an adult sheep cell was transferred to an egg cell from which the nucleus had been removed, and the egg developed to become a mature sheep. This would have seemed a fantasy a century earlier.

# The world of goods

The twentieth century was an age of hitherto unprecedented consumption, again a trend found throughout the Western world. There was of course a larger number of people than ever before; but, in addition, people were wealthier than ever before, and able and willing to spend more. This was true of the overwhelming majority of the population. Furthermore, consumerism, the cult of purchasing, became a major part of Britain's cultural, economic and social life. 'Auto-production' – the production of goods for one's own consumption – became rare. In addition, such production was now largely a matter of fashion, not need. This was seen in bread, beer and wine making in the last quarter of the century. To make them at home became fashionable, but for sections of the middle class rather than for the poor, who tended to buy processed food and drink, and were thus almost totally dependent on shops.

## A more affluent society

The rise in the wealth of British society more than exceeded the growth of population. Furthermore, although many remained poor, increases in income and wealth were widely spread. This was increasingly so in the second half of the century. In the first half, the two world wars (1914–18, and 1939–45) had brought much destruction, economic activity had been greatly disrupted, earning careers had been interrupted, and taxation had shot up. It had been difficult then to accumulate capital. Furthermore, more generally, the concentration of wealth and reasonable incomes within a relatively small stratum of society had limited consumption by the bulk of the population. Nevertheless, the 1930s had witnessed a 'new domesticity', with the use of advertising to promote consumerism, especially the purchase of 'white' goods, such as washing machines.

The position was different after 1945. Britain did not engage in another major war, and, with considerably lower rates of peacetime unemployment until the early 1980s, and the end of conscription in 1963, most men were able to enjoy a longer period of employment, although the impact of this was lessened by the raising of the school-leaving age and the increased frequency of continuing in further education. The rise in real wages was more important than any change in the number of years of employment. Furthermore, young workers were increasingly paid a higher percentage of the average wage. This change in the average income gradient ensured that youth was a more important market and setter of trends.

Prolonged economic growth from 1945 increased the national wealth. **Redistributive taxation** and **benefit policies** helped further to spread income. This was accentuated by the growing number of women who spent much of their adult life in the labour force. The percentage of women who stopped work on marriage or, permanently, on having children, fell substantially. This made a major impact on family incomes.

**redistributive taxation:** The system whereby wealthier people pay higher taxes, which are used to provide benefits for the poor or disadvantaged.

**benefit policies:** Policies for the government provision of pensions and allowances.

These trends had been apparent during the inter-war period, but were accentuated and more common after 1945. In addition, the cost of many staples as a percentage of average income fell. Whereas in 1971, food took one-fifth of the average family budget, in 1993 it took one-ninth. This freed **disposable income** for other forms of expenditure. New patterns of spending, including a relative shift from essentials to what had been considered luxuries, first emerged in the 1950s.

Much of this expenditure was on goods, although other sections of expenditure that increased greatly included leisure, especially drink, sport and holidays. In 1979, 10.25 million people took a holiday abroad; in 1996, 23.25 million. By 1996, 95% of households had a telephone, compared with 42% in 1972. For washing machines the percentages were 90 and 66. By the end of 1979, only 230,000 homes had a video recorder, but by the 1990s 73% of British households owned video recorders and 62% microwave cookers. By 1996, nearly 90% of households had a deep freezer, compared with 45% in 1979, 20% had a dishwasher (then 4%), and more than half had tumble driers (20%). There were also new goods. CD players did not arrive until the 1980s. They were followed by computer games and mobile phones. More things encouraged more crime, which began to rise in the late 1950s.

This world of things was very different from that which existed at the start of the century. First, the range of products then had been much more dramatically limited, in large part because the basic materials, such as wood, tinware, ironware and ceramics, were far less flexible than the world of plastics that became important in the second half of the century. New materials and new uses for already exploited materials were important to both corporate and individual image. In Edmund Crispin's novel *Love Lies Bleeding* (1948), the Boyce family is described as 'worldly. The parents are of the expensive, cocktail-party-and-chromium kind.' Secondly, there was no equivalent to the miniaturisation of parts that was so important in the second half of the century. As a result, many techniques and appliances could not then be converted to household use.

Thirdly, the network of energy provision at the beginning of the century was far more limited and inflexible than was later to be the case. Although electricity was in use, it was not available for most people, and coal still played a major role as the direct source of energy. The widespread use of labour-saving devices, such as vacuum cleaners, depended on a reliable electricity supply. There was also no equivalent to the intellectual energy that was to be made available by computers. Again, initially, in the absence of miniaturisation, this was an industrial product, of great scale and cost, but, from the late 1970s, it became widely available as a household tool, consumer symbol and guide for **consumerism**: goods and services were advertised and made available through household computers, particularly with the development of the internet.

It would be misleading to present the first half of the century as static. In some fields, such as car and wireless (radio) ownership, there was massive growth. By 1914, there were 132,000 private car registrations. National private ownership of cars increased more than ten-fold in the 1920s and 1930s, over 300,000 new cars were being registered annually by 1937, and there were nearly 2 million cars by September 1938. More generally, despite the Depression, for most of those in work, the 1930s was a decade of improved housing, wider consumer choice and a better quality of life. Nevertheless, the distribution of wealth was such that many goods or things, were only enjoyed by a minority of the population. This was true, for example, of cars and telephones. Others, such as wireless sets, were more widely distributed.

**disposable income:** The money people have left to spend as they like after tax deductions.

**consumerism:** The focus on the role in society particularly of manufactured goods, and the processes of buying and selling.

**The department store: Selfridge's, Oxford Street, London (December 1939)**
An important development of the nineteenth century, the department store remained pre-eminent until affected by the increased popularity of car-borne shopping from the 1950s. Hit by chain stores, department stores nevertheless enjoyed a revival from the 1980s as anchor shops in out-of-town hypermarkets.

The same contrast was true of the recessions at the beginning of the 1980s and the 1990s. Alongside high unemployment, and serious social strains, manifested in rising crime rates and urban riots, many of those in work had high living standards. Average British disposable income rose by 37% between 1982 and 1992, a trend that helped to keep the Conservatives in power, although it did not save them in the 1997 election. Thanks, in part, to the policies of the Conservative governments of 1979–97, average income differentials also rose. The real income of the bottom 10% in Britain increased by 10 per cent in 1973–91, but the top 10% gained by 55%. This led to criticism, but, in terms of aggregate demand, the rise in the real income of the bottom 10% was important, and had an impact on total consumption and on changing assumptions about living standards.

Yet it is also important to note wider aspects of the down-side of consumerism. Undoubtedly, people had and have more material possessions than ever before, especially as teenage and child markets are exploited, but it is worth noting problems created by the peer pressure for consumer conformity (and related exclusion of those unable to participate), the extension of adult 'tastes' onto teens and pre-teens, and what can be seen as the reverse infantilising of adults in their twenties and even thirties. Furthermore, British consumerism is an aspect of a global economy in which Third-World workers and resources are in some eyes exploited.

# The British diet

## Food

The role of greater wealth and of consumerism in the twentieth century was reflected in the greater commodification of food and the fashionability of particular foods. In the first half of the century there were only modest changes, certainly nothing to compare with the Victorian impact of transoceanic products brought in refrigerated ship-holds. The national diet changed relatively little in the early twentieth century, and other aspects of eating, such as outlets and meal times, were also fairly constant.

The nutritional value of the diet was limited. Soggy vegetables and meals heavy in carbohydrate predominated in most homes and restaurants. They offered little fresh fruit. There was a high consumption of sugar in hot drinks, desserts and confectionery. Dairy products were also important in the diet, and butter and lard were used for cooking. The poor ate a lot of cold food – bread, cold meat and cheese. Potatoes were also very important to their diet. Traditional dishes retained great popularity, in part, possibly, because there were few alternatives. In 1928, Harry Ramsden started serving fish and chips from a wooden hut at White Cross near Leeds. Three years later, thanks in large part to road-borne eaters, he was able to replace the hut with the most luxurious fish and chip restaurant hitherto built.

Wartime and post-war economic problems, especially the strains of sterling, limited purchasing power, and the continuation of rationing ensured that there was only limited change in the national diet in the 1940s and 1950s. Sugar rationing did not end until 1953, food rationing until 1954. Since the 1960s, however, the national diet has been increasingly affected by new ingredients and by dishes introduced from foreign countries. Chinese, Indian and Italian meals came to dominate the restaurant trade. By 1998, there were over 8,000 Indian restaurants. In the 1970s, takeaway food was overwhelmingly either fish and chips, or what was provided by the Wimpy chain. There were only 38 branches of McDonald's in Britain in 1979, but, by the 1990s, American hamburger chains were ubiquitous. McDonald's, with over 750 branches in 1997, continued to expand. Kentucky Fried Chicken was another American fast-food chain successfully translated to Britain. Thai restaurants followed where Indian and Chinese had led. In a few spheres, 'British' food was resilient. Harry Ramsden's, for example, was profitable enough to be floated on the stock market in 1989, and to open new branches world-wide. Its most luxurious restaurant was at Blackpool. However, in general, 'British' cooking came to mean curries, as much as steak and kidney pies or fish and chips. In homes, traditional breakfast dishes, such as bacon and eggs or kippers, became far less common.

Supermarkets increasingly stocked foreign dishes. In the 1990s there was growing consumption of Continental-style breads, a marked contrast to the dominance of sliced white bread in the 1960s and 1970s. There has also been a widening in the range of fruit available. Avocados, passion fruit, star fruit, kiwi fruit and mangoes, largely unknown in Britain in the 1960s, became widely available in supermarkets. The one area where supermarket produce was challenged effectively in the 1990s was health foods. More specialist, independent outlets developed, providing such items as herbal teas, alongside a wide range of vitamin pills and other dietary supplements.

The shift towards new foodstuffs reflected more than greater purchasing power and increased trade. In addition, there was a willingness to try new dishes and also far more information about how to prepare them. The cookbooks of the last hundred years provide an interesting guide to attitudes and practices. Whereas at the beginning of the century, such Victorian staples as Mrs Beaton were reprinted with no hint of a changing world, by the 1980s cookbooks had themselves become a consumer product. Lavishly published, with full-colour photography and printing, they catered for households that were no longer prepared to accept inherited recipes or one biblical cookbook. Instead, consumers purchased several cookbooks, and some of the more popular ones focused on the food of foreign, even exotic, areas such as Provence and India. Cookery programmes also became very important on television. Fanny Craddock, the somewhat conventional television cook of the 1960s, was succeeded by a more enterprising host of celebrities, and, by the 1990s, there were several cookery programmes on television hosted by well-known figures such as Delia Smith, or, with the accent more on the entertainment angle, Ainsley Harriett or the Two Fat Ladies. Their impact increased as a result of the ability and willingness of supermarkets to stock a wider range of ingredients, and to do so throughout the year.

Technology also played a major role. The increased consumption of convenience foods, generally stored in deep freezers and reheated rapidly by microwave cookers, has provided a major market for new dishes and meals for one or two. Refrigeration transformed eating habits by making it possible to preserve foodstuffs. The changing diet interacted with concern about healthy eating, to lead to a shift in the consumption of various types of food. Red meat, such as beef, mutton and lamb, became less popular, in favour of chicken, and the consumption of fats, such as butter and cheese, dropped, in favour of low-fat spreads. The consumption of eggs also fell. Grilling became more common than frying, while the consumption of wholemeal bread rose. Assumptions about 'appropriate' food were linked to gender stereotypes, as with the claim (or boast) in the late 1970s that 'real men don't eat quiche'. In general, the traditional diet which had been formed largely in accordance with the needs of men, became less widespread, both for men and for women. Thus, the consumption of calories fell, while vegetarianism became more common. The increased popularity of vegetarianism did much to make the publication of cookbooks a growth industry. A range of enticing recipes for meat-free meals was pioneered and sold on the back of endorsements from celebrities such as Linda McCartney.

Although this account is true of the United Kingdom as a whole, there are also important geographical and social variations. Thus, consumption of fresh fruit and vegetables, and fresh (as opposed to fried) fish, is higher among affluent groups, while the poor tend to have less variety and fewer fresh ingredients in their diet. The 1999 British Medical Association report *Growing Up in Britain* revealed that poor children were far less likely to drink fruit juice and eat fresh fruit and vegetables. These social contrasts were linked to regional images, for example the 'pie and pint' male food culture in Northern cities. The overall difference between Scotland and England was significant. The Scots consumed more salt, sweet things and animal fats and less salads, green vegetables and wholemeal bread. Thus, for example, more sausage rolls, meat, butter and chocolate were/are eaten per head in Scotland, while the bread was/is saltier. As the epitome of the less-than-healthy Scottish diet, there were reports of chip-shops selling 'deep-fried Mars Bars'.

# Drink

Changes have not been restricted to food. Foreign alcoholic drinks, and foreign types and brands of beer became more important. This process also reflected technological and retail shifts, most obviously the growing sale of canned beers and the development of supermarket sales of alcohol. The shifting pattern of alcohol consumption reflected social, gender and age shifts. The stereotypical view of drinking at the beginning of the century, with the male working class drinking beer, in some agricultural areas, cider, and in Scotland beer and whisky, and the middle and upper class drinking wine and a narrow range of spirits, especially whisky, is substantially correct. The situation changed slowly after World War Two, with a wider drinking public for wine, but, again, the pace of change did not increase until the 1960s.

Female drinking rose and encouraged major shifts in the market. As far as spirits were concerned, whisky and brandy became less important, and the white spirits – gin and, to a lesser extent, vodka – more so. Wine consumption rose, especially that of lighter white wines. From the 1980s, it became easier to buy wine in pubs.

The greater importance of young drinkers affected sales of beer. Bitter and stout, the traditional drinks of working-class men, became less important and lagers more important. Traditional cask-conditioned or real ales enjoyed a revival from the 1980s. The prevalence of young drinkers also influenced the way in which drink was sold. Bottled beers became increasingly commonplace, particularly in night clubs. However, sales of whisky continued to be important in Scotland; 45 per cent of Scottish pub orders in the 1970s were for spirits. Bitter was less common in Scotland. Instead, 'heavy' or beers rated by duty was drunk.

The pace of change remained high. The 1970s and 1980s saw a further shift in the wine industry, with the rise of sales of white wine from the USA, Australia, New Zealand, Chile, Argentina and, especially after the fall of the apartheid system, South Africa. Although less markedly, red wine purchases from these areas also rose. The dominance of wine sales by French and German producers slackened. Wine growing revived in Britain. In 1951, 1.5 acres of vines were planted at Hambledon in Hampshire. By 1973, there were 200 acres under vines in the country, by 1998 about 2,350.

This was not simply a matter of new and different products. The forms in which drinks were delivered changed, largely in order to maintain consistent qualities for bulk provision, a characteristic need of modern capitalism. Pressurised pumps were used to deliver beer in pubs. Wine boxes were designed to enable drinkers to drink less (or more) than one bottle without spoiling the rest. Wine bars became popular from the 1970s. The popularity of wine bars forced the traditional public house to change its image in order to win back customers. Pubs ceased to be male-orientated, domino-playing, crisp-eating places to visit. Instead, the need to attract younger people led to the emergence of the 'theme pub' serving a wide range of beers and spirits, to the sound of the latest chart hits. Pubs increasingly served food in a quest to make them more family-friendly. The advent of beer gardens also allowed children to accompany their parents to the pub. The possibility of near all-day drinking, with the liberalisation of licensing hours, first in Scotland after the report of the Clayson Committee in 1973, and then in England and Wales, represented a significant social change. Pubs in the 1990s opened at 11a.m. and closed at 11p.m. (with clubs open until at least 2a.m.).

Coffee drinking also changed radically. In place of a situation in which there were few alternatives to 'instant', filter coffee had quickly evolved from the bland espresso of 1960s coffee bars to the ubiquitous cafetiere of the 1990s. Tea had been the overwhelmingly dominant hot drink, but its relative decline was part of a major shift in the consumption of non-alcoholic drinks. This was a matter not only of the rise of coffee, which had been drunk in Britain for centuries, but also of decaffeinated hot drinks. The range of cold drinks also altered, with the increased consumption of bottled water and of a wide range of fruit juices. These shifts all became pronounced from the 1980s. Even conventional products changed. Thus, in 1980, the range of speciality teas available in supermarkets or cafés was limited, principally to Darjeeling. Earl Grey was a minority choice. Most people drank tea with milk and the majority also took sugar. In contrast, by 1999 the readily-available range had expanded greatly to include Chinese and Japanese green teas, as well as fruit teas. Furthermore, the use of milk and, in particular, sugar in tea had become less widespread.

**Box 4.1**

## Victorian chains

The development of big retail chains was a feature of the late Victorian period and a product of the increased importance and possibilities of advertising, bulk purchase, and warehousing. John Sainsbury opened his first dairy in London in 1869 and by 1900 the company had 47 provision stores. Thomas Lipton opened his first grocery in Glasgow in 1871 and by 1914 had 500 shops. In 1883, Julius Drewe and his partner opened the Home and Colonial Stores in the Edgware Road in London. By 1906, there were over 500 shops in the company. In 1894 Marks and Spencer was founded. Such chains affected tastes. Drewe encouraged the drinking of Indian, not Chinese, tea. Other influential chains included the chemists Boots, and the newsagents W. H. Smith. They rapidly became national institutions.

**Box 4.2**

## The Co-op

A product of nineteenth-century idealism, the Co-op was a 'mutual' system in which members established shops and drew dividends based on what they spent. It became crucial to urban working-class shopping in the Victorian period, and, as a force for working-class empowerment, had links with the Labour Party. The Co-op opened Britain's first self-service supermarket – in Southsea – in 1947. It was very innovative, and crucial to shopping until the 1960s but was then hit by the development of national supermarket chains based on American models.

# Shopping

More generally, the nature of the retail world changed in the second half of the century. High streets became more uniform and outlets were increasingly reliant on a relatively small number of suppliers. Supermarkets were responsible for the decline in independent retail activity, although earlier chains had also played a major role. The abolition of resale price maintenance (RPM) in 1964 by Edward Heath, when he was President of the Board of Trade, was the key moment in the shaping of modern British retailing. RPM had obliged shops to sell goods at standard prices set by suppliers, and thus prevented the search for more business through undercutting. This helped small independent shopkeepers in their resistance to multiples. Once RPM was abolished, it became easier for supermarkets benefiting from economies of scale, such as mass purchasing, to offer pricing structures that drove competitors out of business. A form of RPM continued for books and medicines, and that was important to the survival of small bookshops and chemists, but the situation in these spheres similarly changed in the 1990s.

The rise of the supermarket in the 1950s, and the hypermarket, mainly out of town, in the 1980s, led to new shopping patterns. By 1992, 16 per cent of the total shopping space in Britain was made up of shopping centres, such as Brent Cross in north London, Lakeside Thurrock in Essex, the Glades in Bromley, south London, Meadowhall in Sheffield, and the Metro Centre in Gateshead. The last was applauded by Mrs Thatcher, and its development made the fortune of John Hall, enabling him to become the leading entrepreneur of North-East England and to transform the fortunes of Newcastle United football team; the way to wealth was through selling, not making. Despite anxiety about the impact of such shopping centres, both on shopping elsewhere, especially on town-centre and high-street shopping, and on traffic patterns, other centres were developed and planned. When one opened at Cribbs Causeway north of Bristol, there was a definite impact on retail activity in the city centre and on local traffic patterns. The Bristol branch of John Lewis moved out to the new shopping centre, part of the pattern in which department stores sought to survive by taking advantage of new developments. Paisley's 900,000 square foot Braehead development claimed in 1999 to be the biggest in Europe. The Bluewater centre in Kent's London suburbia, opened in 1999, also claimed to be the largest retail development in Europe: it created nearly 7,000 jobs.

Such shopping centres were the moulders of taste and provided spheres of spending activity at the centre of the consumer society. Almost all of their customers came by car, abandoning traditional high-street shopping, with its gentler pace and more individual service. Mobility thus brought access to wider shopping opportunities, but the net effect was less beneficial, as many shops on high streets closed. By 1999, 88 per cent of all the food purchased in Britain was bought from big shopping chains. Dunmow in Essex was a good example of the 'doughnut' effect. Following the opening of Tesco on the outskirts at the beginning of the 1990s, the High Street became almost entirely charity shops, where once were grocers, newsagents, ironmongers, butchers, bakers and greengrocers. The pattern was similar in many other high streets, with just the occasional boutique and antique shop providing opportunities for old-style shopping; although, especially outside the cities and poorer suburbs, most high streets still offer a range of shops. The fate of local shops was linked to that of local economies. Far from purchasing from local suppliers, superstores bought their food only from very large producers and it was moved by lorry from central warehouse sites. This hit local wholesalers, thus reducing the availability of fresh food for local shops.

The fate of high-street shopping became the focus of planning disputes, especially from the 1980s, and, also, was increasingly important in contested senses of local identity. In Leominster, for example, in 1996, the town launched a shopper 'loyalty card' as part of a 'fightback' against a Safeway out-of-town superstore and its loyalty scheme. City centres sought to avoid the decline of high-street shopping by constructing glazed-over shopping precincts, such as St Enoch Centre and Princes Square in Glasgow, and Eldon Square in Newcastle. These developments kept shoppers in the city centre, but frequently had a detrimental impact on shopping outside the precinct: Eldon Square, opened in the 1970s, hit Pilgrim, Clayton and Grainger Streets.

Supermarkets and superstores played a major role in the 1990s in introducing Sunday shopping and round-the-clock stores. Alongside the liberalisation of drinking laws in the 1990s, the last was an aspect of the emergence of the 24-hour city. Leeds as much as London marketed itself in these terms in the late 1990s.

The supply of food, an essential of life, is a major indicator of the nature of the world of goods. So also is the provision of more expensive items and others that are purchased episodically. The role of the latter in the consumer economy increased not simply because of greater disposable wealth, but also because a habit of disposability came to be important. So also did fashion, with its attendant replacement of goods, even when they were still functional. This had always been the case with wealthier groups in society, but it became common throughout society. Women's clothes and shoes led the way, with fashions, such as the mini-skirt of the 1960s, and the maxi-skirt or platform heels of the 1970s, affecting all regions and classes. The effect was then translated into men's and children's clothes. Aspiration and identity were focused on image, the entire process expressed through expenditure on consumer goods and mediated by the growth in fashion reporting. This was encouraged by the spread of colour photography, both in magazines and in newspaper supplements.

A good example of the non-necessary product becoming a staple good was provided by toiletries and cosmetics. In the first half of the century, toiletries meant soap

**Box 4.3**

## Shifting fashions

Changing fashions in dress have in part reflected social shifts. At the same time as the suffragette movement prior to World War One, Edwardian elegance gave place to less restrictive forms of female dress, including higher hemlines and the end of tightly-laced corsets. The war accentuated the change, leading to shorter, wider skirts. Trousers also became acceptable for women. The emphasis on ease of movement persisted in the 1920s, encouraging unshaped dresses and short hair. There were also more comfortable clothes for men, including easy fitting jackets and wide trousers (Oxford Bags). World War Two led to clothes rationing and the utility scheme that dictated the design and production of clothes.

The post-war reaction against austerity led in 1947 to what was seen as the femininity of the 'New Look': long as opposed to short skirts, softly-rounded shoulders instead of boxy suits, and high-heeled, rather than sensible shoes. Clothes rationing ended in 1949. The 1960s brought a newly active and affluent youth culture, with bolder colours and shapes of clothes. Carnaby Street in London became famous for trend-setting boutiques that appealed, in particular, to the young. Styles have changed since, for example skirt and hair length have moved up and down, but the common theme is fashion appeal, not durability.

for most of the population, but the use of other products – conditioners, moisturisers, lotions – spread greatly from the 1960s. Furthermore, this was followed by a great expansion in the range of male toiletries. The production and sale of cosmetics and toiletries became far more important in terms of turnover, employment and profitability, and the leading products and stores in the field became household names. From the 1980s, the Body Shop (a chain opened in 1976), with its bright colours, fragrances and novel products, and 'eco-friendly' image, came to play a role on most high streets. Established providers in the field, such as Boots, came to offer similar products. The battle for customers became so intense that advertising campaigns would stress how environmentally friendly a company's products were, which itself was a response to the animal rights 'lobby'.

Furthermore, once started, the pace of innovation increased and the product range interacted with developments in other fields of society. In the 1990s, both the Body Shop and Boots offered ranges of toiletries and products linked to aromatherapy, a fashionable alternative medicine designed, in particular, to combat stress. This represented a different pattern of demand from that at the beginning of the century.

Shopping was transformed by credit cards, which made it easier to anticipate income and accumulate debt. Plastic rather than cash purchases became the norm from the 1980s, although a large section of the population lacked such credit and many indeed remained without bank accounts. Thus the mechanics of consumerism reflected and underwrote social divisions. The widespread shift to credit cards would not have been possible without the development of new cash registers and electronic transfers (which also transformed the financial and banking world in general). Social divisions were also seen in another area in which shopping became more pronounced, house purchase. The marked rise in the percentage of the population who lived in owner-occupied housing in the 1980s was linked to a more active and prominent housing market, and one that estate agents sought to mould with 'high-pressure' salesmanship. Those who lived in publicly-rented accommodation did not take part in this change.

The growth of advertising and the advertising industry also transformed the world of shopping. Traditional methods of advertising – on bill boards, on the sides of buses, in shop windows, and via 'sandwich men' – were supplemented by more novel methods. With the advent of commercial television in 1955, the advertising of products was given a whole new dimension, and another followed in the 1990s with advances in computer technology. Home-based shopping using mail order had begun in the 1860s, growing out of artisan watch clubs. Mail order had a fresh lease of life after World War Two. This owed much to John Moores, who founded Little-woods Pools and launched a Littlewoods catalogue which was based upon a network of local agents or direct purchasers. The internet came to transform the nature of home shopping in the 1990s. Advertising focused on the national market and helped make products and activities national. This was true not only of foodstuffs but also of the fame of hitherto local or regional groups or products, such as football teams. National advertising both encouraged and helped to focus consumerism.

# Work

Consumerism – the world of goods – was more than a product of social trends. It also helped to drive the economy. This was increasingly the case during the twentieth century. The percentage of goods manufactured in Britain for sale to British consumers, rather than sold to manufacturers or institutions, or exported, rose. Furthermore, changing consumer demand interacted with the pace of technology to force shifts in manufacturing, and, indeed, agriculture. This was seen in the decline of 'smoke-stack' industries, the traditional heavy manufacturing sector. The size and economic importance of the coal, heavy engineering, shipbuilding and steel industries all declined. Instead, there was a rise, from the 1930s, in the production and sale of 'white goods', consumer durables, such as washing machines, and later, from the 1970s, of personal electronic goods. This was linked to a shift in the workforce within a world in which jobs for life were increasingly things of the past. Much of the new work placed little stress on manual strength or traditional skills. Instead, there was an emphasis on manual dexterity and on an ability to acquire new skills, both of which were important in electronics. This shift played a marked role in the rise of female industrial employment. More generally, there was also a shift in work patterns. The demand for consumer goods was such that it led to continuous production in many industries. Shift work fundamentally altered the nature of the working week. The rise in female industrial employment also played a part in the trend towards part-time employment and even job-sharing in the 1980s and 1990s.

Employment was also provided by the expansion of shopping, which by the late 1990s was available round the clock in or near most major urban centres. Furthermore, Sunday opening had become the norm. Shopping was increasingly a weekend recreational activity. The expansion of shopping hours increased the labour demands of retailing (selling to the public). The role of retail within the labour market also became more important because the spread of labour-saving technologies and practices reduced the jobs available in manufacturing. The prominent role of women in retailing also contributed to the importance of part-time jobs.

Nevertheless, by the late 1990s, women were also affected by a pronounced trend against older workers. By then, male employment rates started to fall sharply at the age of 50. By 1999, about a quarter of British men had stopped working by their 55th birthday, against only a tenth twenty years earlier. For men aged 60, nearly half were

## Box 4.4

### Female retail employment

Jobs in retailing, December 1998, in thousands

| | |
|---|---|
| Female part-time | 1108.2 |
| Male part-time | 295.3 |
| Female full-time | 560.4 |
| Male full-time | 509.4 |
| Total | 2473.3 |

## Margaret Thatcher (1925– )

Margaret Hilda Roberts was born and grew up in Grantham, Lincolnshire, where her father was a grocer, part-time lay preacher and, later, mayor. She read chemistry at Oxford. In 1951 she married Denis Thatcher and began to study law; in 1953 she gave birth to twins and was called to the bar, specialising in tax law. She was elected Conservative MP for Finchley in 1959. As Secretary of State for Education and Science (1970–4) she was best remembered for ending free school milk. In 1979 she became the first British woman Prime Minister, becoming known as the 'Iron Lady' for her firm handling of foreign affairs, especially during the Falklands War, and was re-elected with big majorities in 1983 and 1987. Her financial policies – tight control of public expenditure, sale of shares in public companies – became known as Thatcherism; however, her insistence on the unpopular 'poll tax' and her opposition to further integration with Europe led to her leadership being challenged and in 1990 the longest serving Prime Minister of the twentieth century was forced to resign. She left Parliament in 1992 and was made a Baroness.

out of the labour force. For women above 55, a slightly smaller percentage were at work, compared with the situation in 1979, although, over much of the age range, female participation rates were far higher. Ageism, a sense that those in their fifties were out-of-touch and less vigorous, increasingly affected the labour market in the 1990s.

Changes in technology and the economy very much affected the world of goods. The rise of electronics led to a marked fall in the centrality of paper products and records, and in the need for cash transactions. This had effects in many fields. For example, in 1956 premium bonds were introduced in order to raise money for the government. The winning numbers were selected not by calculations on paper, but by ERNIE: Electronic Random Number Indicator Equipment. The proliferation of credit card companies and cheque guarantee cards was another consequence. Credit cards facilitated telephone purchases and therefore helped to limit the importance of face-to-face commercial transactions in the 1990s. Purchasing was increasingly divorced from shops and other retail premises. The same shift affected other branches of the economy. Telephone banking was introduced in 1989 and was followed, in the late 1990s, by internet banking. Both hit the role of the high-street bank. By 1999, 42 per cent of UK workers were estimated to use the internet in what was increasingly a knowledge economy with information a key product and 'messaging' a major form of work.

## Conclusions

The world of goods was thus more than the consequence of consumer preferences. It was also more than the end product or residue of the economy. Instead, what has been termed material culture was important as a focus of wider social currents and economic practices. In one respect, this world of goods was an intermediary, an aspect of demand as well as supply – demand, for example, for particular labour skills or industrial products.

The world of goods was, and is, also interesting as an aspect and indicator of what is generally termed culture. Thus, the images associated with desirable goods in the 1930s were the style of that society. They were propagated through advertising and through women's magazines, both of which expanded in the period. This relationship was accentuated by the growth of industrial design as a distinct practice and subject, especially from the 1960s, when the value of new design, as a device to improve sales and enhance the image of a good or service, was widely recognised. Furthermore, there was greater interest in the world of advertising. Already important from the eighteenth century, advertising became far more so in the twentieth, not least thanks to the widespread availability of newspapers and television. From this, came the role of design consultants. Initially important only in sections of the economy, such consultants and their advice became more sought after, and, indeed, newsworthy from the 1980s. This affected other branches of life, including eventually politics. Margaret Thatcher, Prime Minister 1979–90, was interested in the advice of such consultants, making use of Saatchi and Saatchi at election time. The impact of image consultants reached new heights with the successful Labour general election campaign of 1997, with the emphasis upon focus groups and media manipulation. 'Spin-doctoring' entered the vocabulary. The conflation of politics and society through the focus of consumerism led the devices of marketing and market research to encompass policies and votes. Politics had fully entered the world of goods.

## ■ Summary

◆ The lives of everyone were affected by scientific developments in the twentieth century; far more so than in any previous century.

◆ Many important scientific advances were made in Britain, and the British played a disproportionately large role in the 'scientific revolution' of the twentieth century. Nevertheless, this role was far smaller than that of the Americans. Furthermore, the British did not prove adept at achieving the maximum profit from their scientific advances: they proved more successful at 'pure' than at 'applied' research.

◆ A combination of entrepreneurialism, consumerism, and advanced technology helped turn scientific advances rapidly into readily obtained production in the world of goods.

◆ The basic fabric of life, for example food, changed dramatically during the century, particularly in the decades of widespread affluence from the 1950s.

◆ Consumerism and advertising affected the full range of social and political activities, ensuring that image became more crucial to both identity and success.

## ■ Questions for discussion

◆ Why didn't Britain lead in the Scientific Revolution of the twentieth century?

◆ What is the most important scientific development of the twentieth century?

◆ In what ways does technology affect ordinary peoples' lives?

◆ How did consumerism change during the century?

◆ What was its impact on social behaviour and structure?

◆ Has politics become a commodity?

# Further reading

Alter, Peter, *The Reluctant Patron: Science and the State in Britain, 1850–1920* (Oxford, 1987).

Edgerton, David, *Science, Technology, and the British Industrial 'Decline', 1870–1970* (Cambridge, 1996).

Gollin, A., *The Impact of Air Power on the British People and their Government, 1909–1914* (London, 1989).

Lancaster, B., *The Development Store: A Social History* (Leicester, 1995).

Lancaster, B., and Maguire, P. (eds), *Towards the Cooperative Commonwealth* (Manchester, 1996).

Wiener, Martin J., *English Culture and the Decline of the Industrial Spirit, 1850–1980* (2nd edn, London, 1985).

# Getting Around: People, Messages and Images

## Contents

The twentieth was a far more fluid century than its predecessor. There had been massive changes in the nineteenth, but they had not extended to the reconfiguration of society and social attitudes that characterised the twentieth. This fluidity is one of the major themes of this book and will be variously approached in different chapters. This chapter concentrates first on the actual processes of getting around, the mobility of people and goods and the transmission of news, ideas, and images. It then continues by considering some of the implications. The changes in transportation are truly staggering. Someone born around the turn of the century was born in a world in which people had not flown (other than in balloons), and in which there was no radio or television. If they lived to seventy, they would have seen men on the moon on their television sets.

## Key issues

▶ What were the major shifts in transport during the century?

▶ Why did the role of trains decline?

▶ What was the impact of the rise of the car?

▶ How far did radio and television affect society?

▶ What was the importance of the collapse of the BBC's monopoly in radio and television?

## The rise of personal mobility

Like much else in British history in this period, shifts in transport patterns and use were not unique to Britain. Indeed, much in British communications in the twentieth century – methods, attitudes and models – derived from the USA, especially after World War One, and more particularly, from the 1950s. That, however, did not make the shifts any less important to the British.

### The rise of the car

The statistics and impact of the rise of the car were awesome, as was the speed of change. New developments and steadily larger statistics succeeded each other rapidly.

## Road bridges

The Victorians used first cast and wrought iron and then steel to bridge the rivers and estuaries that constrained the rail system, culminating with the second Tay Bridge and the Forth Bridge, completed in 1887 and 1890 respectively. In the twentieth century, the stress was on steel and concrete and the road system. In the 1960s, the Forth and Severn were bridged on the suspension principle. The Humber Bridge built in 1972–80 was the longest single-span bridge in the world, with an overall length of nearly 2,220 metres (about $1\frac{1}{2}$ miles), and 1,410 metres (4,626 feet) between the towers. Due to its length, the two supporting towers had to be set out of alignment by 36mm ($1\frac{1}{2}$ inches) to allow for the curvature of the earth. The Humber Bridge helped make the new county of Humberside a more viable unit. The record length of the bridge was only beaten in 1998: by the Akashi–Kaikyo bridge in Japan.

In 1896, Parliament repealed the legislation that had required cars to follow a man carrying a red flag, and instead allowed them to drive at up to 14 mph, 20 mph from 1903, until 1930, when all speed limits were abolished. The first original, full-size British petrol motor was produced in 1895; the first commercial motor company was established at Coventry in 1896; motor buses were introduced in 1898. The Motor Car Act of 1903 extended the rights of the motorist, the motor bus was introduced in London in 1905, and four years later the National Road Board was founded to lend energy and cohesion to road construction. Motor transport led to the upgrading of existing routes so that they could provide all-weather surfaces. Victorian by-roads had frequently been poorly surfaced. The widespread tarring of roads from the early 1900s was a major visual and environmental change. This process was largely complete by 1939, the country bisected by black lines.

By 1914, there were 132,000 private car registrations. There were also 124,000 motorcycle registrations and 51,167 buses and taxis on the road. Motor buses were more flexible and often quicker than electric trams, the use of which had greatly expanded in the 1890s and 1900s. The first electric trams in Newcastle ran in 1901, replacing the earlier horse tram network. By 1904, electric trams were running on most of the main roads in Newcastle, and new lines continued to be laid until 1928. Unlike trams, which ran on steel tracks and required a power supply, and trolley-buses, which also relied on an overhead power supply but did not run on tracks, buses required no route infrastructure and could respond rapidly to changes in demand.

Cars ensured that bicycling, which had boomed following the development of the safety bicycle in 1885, descended the social and age scales. A new world of speed and personal mobility, with its own particular infrastructure, was being created. Cars were still a luxury, and the *Autocar* estimated in 1936 that 60% of Britons could not afford to run a car, even if one were given to them free. Nevertheless, every innovation contributed to a sense of change that was possibly the most important solvent of the old order.

## Railway history

Increased car use at the turn of the century did not prevent a spread of the rail network in some areas, especially of light railways, nor the continued importance of coastal shipping. In *The House with the Green Shutters* (1901), George Brown's

**Pollution**
The train exacerbated the environmental problems of urban and industrial Britain. This lithograph (*c.* 1845) shows a train crossing the Stockport Viaduct on the London and North Western Railway. The viaduct dominates a scene that includes smoking chimneys and the pollution of the river banks.

critical novel about his native Ayrshire, carting is ruined by the railway. Canals also played a continued role. In 1911, Cadbury's even established a new factory at Knighton on the Shropshire Union Canal. It produced condensed milk, which was moved to the Cadbury works at Bourneville by canal. However, canal traffic declined. Damaging long-term competition from rail was supplemented by road. In Berkshire, commercial traffic on the Wilts and Berks Canal stopped in 1906, the canal closed in 1914, and on the Kennet and Avon Canal traffic had all but ceased by 1939.

The rise in commuting as the urban areas expanded at a rapid rate encouraged a demand for suburban rail services, and many of these were electrified. In Newcastle, this began in 1903 and annual passenger numbers on the Tyneside loop rose from six million in 1903 to nearly nine and a half a decade later. The London underground railway system became a widespread overground to the west, north and east of London; and, to a limited extent, also to the south of the Thames. The 'sub-surface' lines (as opposed to the 'tube' – the bored tunnels) were already well into the country by 1914. The first 'tube' extension into green-fields areas was the Northern Line extension from Hampstead to Edgware in 1923–4. It was followed by the Metropolitan (later Bakerloo) to Stanmore in 1932, the Piccadilly to Cockfosters in 1933, and then the Northern to Barnet. South of the Thames, the Northern Line reached Morden in 1926: the 17-mile tunnel between East Finchley and Morden was, at the time of its construction, the longest continuous tunnel in the world. The London Passenger Transport Board was formed in 1933 by bringing together Underground lines, tramways and buses. A major change came with the government-backed 'New Works Programme' of 1935–40, which saw substantial lengths of ex-Great Western Railway (GWR) and ex-London and North Eastern (LNER) track handed over to London Transport; thus the Central Line reached to Ongar in Essex.

The railways had often pioneered feeder bus services, and invested heavily in them after 1928. This was legally dubious, but it was allowed under the Road Transport Act of 1930; an example was LNER investment in United. However, from the 1920s, competition from road transport became serious for the railways. Buses were more flexible. They could go through villages, and deliver people directly to and from centres. Also, bus companies were more willing to run late-night services, especially on Saturdays. This scooped the cinema and pub crowds. Cars, buses and trams hit suburban train services, leading, for example, to their removal in Aberdeen and, to a considerable extent, in Edinburgh.

The fall in the cost of motoring hit the railways, although some of their problems

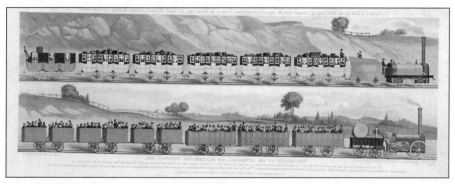

**The new world of transport: travelling on the Liverpool and Manchester Railway (1831)**
First-class carriages were drawn by *Jupiter*, second- and third-class carriages by *North Star*.
Passengers had to put up with choking smoke and hot sparks.

were due to over-ambitious expansion in the nineteenth century, and others to a lack of investment during World War One, and to inter-war economic problems, especially in their traditional freight markets of coal, metallurgy and heavy engineering. The General Strike of 1926 proved that the nation could live without railways, and a lot of the lost high-value traffic never returned after the strike. In the inter-war period, 240 miles of track and 350 stations were closed completely and another 1,000 miles and 380 stations were closed to passenger traffic. Among the 'Big Four' railway companies compulsorily created in 1923 by the amalgamation of more than 120 companies, the Southern Railway (SR) was alone in paying a regular dividend to shareholders before 1948. This was the only company that electrified on a large scale and that did not serve depressed industrial areas: instead, it catered to London's massive expansion south of the Thames. The inter-war railways continued to compete, but suffered from under-investment, over-capacity and a massive wages bill. They were also affected by the impact of the Depression, especially as it hit hard at their traditional freight goods, particularly coal. In contrast, the newer consumer industries tended to have lower freight needs, many of which were met by road transport. The 1933 Road and Rail Traffic Act provided inadequate assistance for the railways. Price increases in 1937 hit rail freight.

The rail system, however, should not be written off before World War Two. The reorganisation of 1923 led to a measure of rationalisation. Standardisation of locomotives and rolling stock cut maintenance costs and helped efficiency. There was a big increase in maximum speeds in the 1930s, especially with the LNER's *Silver Jubilee* and *Coronation* trains. The *Mallard* set the world steam record of 126 mph in 1938. There was a freight revolution, thanks to the gradual introduction of containers and mechanised marshalling yards, such as Whitemoor. In addition, an attempt was made to project a modern image. LNER used Gills Sans lettering, which was invented for it, on publicity. Much building on the rail network used modern architectural techniques, for example Surbiton station and SR 'glasshouse'-style signalboxes. More generally, there was a lot of streamlining.

In the early decades of the century, both rail and road helped to structure the country. Aside from infrastructural projects that cut journey times, and thus brought places nearer, there were also important shifts in perception. Thus, for example, the advertising campaigns of rail and petrol companies encouraged particular demands. The GWR invented the Cornish Riviera and promotional packages

Box 5.2

## The decline of rail

| | Railway track open in miles (to nearest hundred) | Freight in million tonnes | Passengers in million |
|---|---|---|---|
| 1945 | 19,900 | 266 | 1,056 |
| 1950 | 19,500 | 281 | 704 |
| 1955 | 19,100 | 274 | 730 |
| 1960 | 18,400 | 248 | 721 |
| 1965 | 15,000 | 228 | 581 |
| 1970 | 11,800 | not available | 824 |
| 1977 | 11,200 | 156 | 702 |
| 1985 | 10,400 | 122 | 697 |
| 1993 | 10,000 | 32 | 745 |

Source: C. Cook and J. Stevenson, *Britain Since 1945* (London, 1996), p. 172.

fed off posters and guidebooks. Such campaigns were important not only to the economy of particular areas, but also in creating images of them. Cornwall was seen as a land of romance, rather than of difficult upland farming, and the railway presented itself as bringing nearer a land with different values.

Air travel also developed. The first across the Atlantic non-stop – John Alcock and Arthur Whitten Brown in 1919 – were British. By the end of the 1920s, about 20 aeroplanes daily were leaving London's airport, Croydon aerodrome, which had been opened in 1921. Imperial Airways developed long-distance air travel. From 1930, the journey to Australia took two weeks. Planes held 16 passengers and stopped each evening for refuelling and for passengers to stay in luxury hotels. The model was clearly leisurely sea travel rather than swift air travel.

The rail system was badly hit by World War Two, and the immediate post-war situation was even more serious. A government-imposed ban on fare and freight price increases led to a serious fall in net earnings in 1945–7. Nationalised by the Labour government in 1948, the railways were placed under the British Transport Commission, which was also made responsible both for London Transport and for a large amount of road transport. The Commission was supposed to integrate the transport system and rebuild it after wartime damage and lack of investment. However, such integration was not pursued, not least because road haulage was denationalised in 1953.

The railways lost money from 1953; quite how much was lost would depend on which accounting convention is used. This undercut the positive changes that did occur as a consequence of the Railway Modernisation Plan of 1955. Steam was replaced by diesel and electricity. The West Coast Main Line from London, via Birmingham and Crewe, to Liverpool, Manchester and Glasgow, was electrified between 1959 and 1974. Nevertheless, there was no investment to match that being spent on roads.

The Beeching report of 1963 by Dr Richard Beeching, the Chairman of British Rail, led to dramatic cuts in the network. The report had positive aspects. It urged a concentration on fast inter-city services, and bulk freight flows, for example to power stations, and foresaw the container revolution before anyone else did. Beeching, however, was specifically excluded from considering the social and economic consequences of rail closures by his brief from the Minister of Transport. There was a sub-text of regret in the *Report* about this. Beeching's remit was simply to make the railways pay their way. Freight and passenger services were greatly curtailed, the workforce cut, lines were taken up, and many stations became unmanned halts, or were converted to other uses. Cross-country lines, such as the Somerset and Dorset (Bath to Bournemouth) and Oxford to Cambridge, were shut, as well as numerous branches. Railway buildings became homes, offices, workshops and shops. Berkshire, for example, had several major lines running through it. After the Beeching Report, however, many branch lines were cut. The Abingdon and Faringdon branches both closed to passengers in 1963, while in 1964 the Didcot to Newbury line was shut (the last link in a connection to Winchester shut in 1961). Another short branch in Berkshire, the one to Wallingford, closed in 1981; the longer branch to Lambourn had closed in 1973. With the rise of leisure activities, several former railway track-beds, such as that between Consett and Sunderland, two power-houses of industry in North-East England, were turned into footpaths or cycleways.

In 1991, Britain spent less per head on rail improvements than any other country in the European Union apart from Greece and Ireland, neither of which had a substantial network. British Rail was privatised by the Conservatives in 1993, but complaints about late-running or even cancelled services continued: in 1998, one journey in ten was either cancelled or seriously delayed.

The rail system, however, remained important, especially in travel between the major cities and in commuting into them. From the 1960s, the London Underground expanded greatly within London. The Victoria Line, opened in 1968–9, the first automatic underground railway in the world, was followed by the Jubilee Line completed in 1979, the Piccadilly extension to Heathrow opened in 1977, and the Jubilee extension to Greenwich in 1999. The Docklands Light Railway was opened in 1987. Sections of the Newcastle Metro were opened from 1980.

The national train system avoided the dramatic cuts proposed in the Serpell Report of 1983. This would have reduced the system to 1,600 miles, essentially a few major routes. Instead, the system stabilised at about 11,000 miles, just over half the inter-war mileage. Furthermore, there were important improvements. The InterCity 125, a high-speed diesel train capable of travelling at 125 mph, was introduced in 1976 on the Paddington to Bristol and South Wales routes, and then spread to other non-electrified main lines. The tilting Advanced Passenger Train did not prove a success, but, on the East Coast Main Line from London to Edinburgh, fully electrified 225s, capable of travelling at 225 km per hour (140 mph), were introduced in 1991. Journey times from London to cities such as Newcastle were considerably less than they had been in the days of steam. The Channel Tunnel was opened to rail travel in 1992. Commuting to work by rail, however, continued to be important, especially for those inhabitants of the London suburbs who worked in the City and those who travelled daily from the 'Home Counties' to London to work. Nevertheless, although passenger and freight traffic on major rail routes rose in the 1990s, car travel rose far more.

Paradoxically, the relative decline of rail travel did not end its grip on the popular imagination, although that focused on the now-discarded system of steam trains, and, with the decline of locomotive-hauled trains, the adulation given the 'classic' diesel types. Preservation groups and other enthusiasts re-opened a few lines and stations, while the storybook character 'Thomas the Tank Engine' became, especially from the 1980s, a figure of great popularity for young children, and some adults.

# Car history

'The sound of horns and motors', referred to in T. S. Eliot's poem *The Waste Land* (1922), became more insistent, and created a national mass culture. There were half a million road goods vehicles, nearly 2 million cars, and 53,000 buses and coaches by September 1938. The number of cars had risen from 110,000 in 1919, and, by 1939, estimated expenditure on private road transport was £135 million a year. Motoring was encouraged by a fall in its cost, especially in the 1930s. Far more money was being put into developing the road system than was being spent on the rail infrastructure. Major road bridges, such as the Tyne Bridge built in 1928, matched rail counterparts. Local government was especially active in roadbuilding. Within towns, buses competed actively with trams. The latter could carry more passengers, and in 1930, the London County Council introduced 'Felthams', comfortable and quick trams, but the greater flexibility of buses ensured that London was soon planning to close its tram routes by 1941. The new roads led to new smells and sounds, and affected the visual context of life, both in towns and in the countryside. Roads created new demands for road signs, lamp posts, manhole covers and traffic lights. Roads led to new boundaries and commands, to zebra crossings and belisha beacons, the latter named after a Minister of Transport, Hore-Belisha. His period in office (1934–7) also saw the introduction of driving tests, urban speed limits and one-way systems.

Increased use of the car and the construction of more roads interacted. There was a long history of attempts to improve traffic flows. In the nineteenth century, there were attempts within cities, for example by the Metropolitan Board of Works. Further improvements followed in the early twentieth century, for example the Rotherhithe Tunnel. Major roads that had been overshadowed during the age of rail, such as the London–Brighton route via Crawley, revived in importance. Greater traffic flow led to pressures to improve roads. The Trunk Roads Programme was devised in 1929, both to provide employment and to ensure that road improvement schemes were pressed forward. The government agreed to provide much of the cost. Nevertheless, there was no centralised planning or overruling of local views and property rights akin to that of the German autobahns in the 1930s. In the 1920s and 1930s, arterial roads were constructed, for example the Great West Road and the East Lancashire Road. Trunk roads with dual carriageways became more common from the 1930s. Improvements to infrastructure included in 1934 what was then the longest under-water tunnel in the world, the road link under the Mersey between Liverpool and Birkenhead. Although there were no motorways, new arterial roads, such as the Southend Arterial Road, were effective long-distance routes. Sir Charles Bressey, the Ministry of Transport engineer, investigated traffic problems in central London in 1936. He proposed a programme of massive roadbuilding, including large round-abouts and big flyovers.

After a fall in car ownership during the Second World War, when national and personal resources were perforce concentrated on war, its rise accelerated rapidly, especially after petrol rationing ended in May 1950. Car ownership doubled between 1949 and 1957 and trebled between 1949 and 1961. In terms of thousand million passenger-kilometres, private road transport shot up from 76 in 1954 to 350 in 1974, and this was an increase from 39 to 79 per cent of the total passenger-kilometres covered. This gain was made at the expense of bus, coach and rail transport. The percentage of goods traffic moved by road rose from 37 in 1952 to 58.3 in 1964. Lorries benefited from the programme of major roadbuilding. A motorway system was

## Box 5.3

### Car ownership

| | Private car ownership in millions |
|---|---|
| 1914 | 0.13 |
| 1919 | 0.11 |
| 1939 | 2.03 |
| 1945 | 1.49 |
| 1950 | 2.26 |
| 1955 | 3.53 |
| 1960 | 5.53 |
| 1965 | 8.92 |
| 1970 | 11.52 |
| 1978 | 14.07 |
| 1985 | 16.45 |
| 1992 | 20.70 |

created, beginning with the M6 Preston bypass, opened in December 1958 by the Prime Minister, Harold Macmillan. The M1 was punched through the Midlands from Watford to Birmingham in 1959. National life was changed as road transport led to the development of particular cultures, such as caravanning, with their own conventions and hierarchies.

Trams were finally replaced by diesel-engined buses. Many cities, such as Glasgow, Leeds and Liverpool, were still investing strongly in tram systems in the late 1940s, but in the 1950s they were swiftly discarded. Newcastle's last tram ran in 1950, Gateshead's in 1951, London's in 1952, and by 1960 the sole surviving electric tramway in England was essentially a tourist attraction between Blackpool and Fleet-wood. Aberdeen's last trams ran in 1958, and by 1962 even the expensive Glasgow system, the last in Scotland, had ceased. London's last trolleybus followed in 1962, and in 1963, Newcastle Corporation decided to replace trolleybuses by motor buses. The cost of electricity and the maintenance costs of the wires hit trolleybuses, while motor buses benefited from greater manoeuvrability and lower petrol prices. The rise and fall of the trams and the trolleybuses is a reminder of the rapidity of change in communications. They were accompanied by different sounds, sights and other experiences. In the 1990s, however, there was a small-scale revival of trams in Manchester and Sheffield and, later, Wolverhampton. They were now seen as a viable alternative to buses.

There were 12.2 million cars in Britain in 1970, over 20 million in 1995, a rise far greater than that in population. Car ownership rose from 224 per 1,000 people in 1971 to 380 per 1,000 in 1994. Two-car families became more common. Although the OPEC price rise of petrol in 1973 increased the cost of driving, and it was always greater than in the USA, pre-tax British petrol prices were then held down both by the discovery of oil under the North Sea and by a major fall in the world price of petrol in the 1980s and 1990s. People not only bought cars. They also used them for work and leisure. Commuting increased. Only 42% of those who worked in Newcastle in 1971 lived in the city. Most of the rest commuted by car. The same was also true of the increases of commuting in 1981–91: by 7% into London, 18% into Birmingham and 29% into Manchester.

Motorways linked urban areas and were joined to create a network. Increased road usage, however, meant that it became progressively necessary to supplement existing roads. The Oxford to Birmingham section of the M40, opened in January 1991, was designed to supplement the overstrained M1 as a route between London and the Midlands. The M25 around London became the busiest route in the country, and because of frequent traffic jams there were soon plans to add more lanes. By 1996, there were nearly 2,000 miles of motorway in the country. Major bridges were also built for road traffic. When opened in 1981, the Humber Bridge was the longest single-span bridge in the world. In 1997, a second road bridge was opened across the Severn.

Greater road usage did more than affect the motorway network. At the neigh-bourhood level, major routes became obstacles, as high streets were turned into through routes. This encouraged the building of new through routes unrelated to existing neighbourhoods, as in Glasgow in the 1970s, or the East Central Motorway in Newcastle in the early 1970s and the Western Bypass in Newcastle in 1990. Such roads, for example the West Way in London, caused destruction and blight. Those neighbourhoods that were not thus bisected were still affected by the car. Side streets became 'rat runs', quick shortcuts linking busier roads, and the sides of all roads filled up with parked cars. Parking space came to take a greater percentage of city space, and the problems of parking became a major topic of conversation. Every town soon required its bypass – Kingston's was opened in 1934, Exeter's in 1938 – but bypasses, such as that of Newbury, were soon unable to cope with the pressure. From the 1960s, every town also required the multi-storey carparks which came to disfigure many townscapes, including those of historic towns such as Bath. Park and ride schemes were introduced, especially from the 1980s, in an effort to reduce traffic flows. Pedestrianisation of city and town centres also became important.

Road transport was increasingly dominated by cars, not by public transport in buses and coaches. The latter were important in the first half of the century, but lost market share in the second, as most travellers came to put a greater premium on flexibility and had the affluence to translate this into car purchase. In 1986, as a result of the Transport Act of the previous year, deregulation of local bus services occurred outside London. Intended to encourage competition, this was followed by a fall in operating costs, but not by a return to the bus. Bus privatisation was to be followed by that of the rail system.

Freight travel was dominated by lorries. They were flexible, but less appropriate for bulky goods such as coal and gravel, although the movement of these was now less important to the economy. Canals fell into disrepair or were used primarily for leisure, mainly holidays. Coastal shipping also declined, although, as late as the 1970s, it was the least expensive way to move coal, and was used, for example, to ship it from the North-East to the gasworks and power stations in the Thames estuary.

## The impact of the car

The car led to many problems. Car exhaust emissions led to environmental pollution. The Royal Commission on Environmental Pollution that reported in 1994 pressed for a switch from roads to railways. In addition, many people were killed or injured by cars. In 1962, 4,287 children under ten were killed on the roads, and in 1979, 6,352 people were killed, and in 1994, 3,650 people. By the early 1990s, 45,000 children were being hurt on the roads every year and among those aged 5–15, two-thirds of deaths were the result of road accidents. Alarmist, and frequently lurid, reports about the far lower murder figures (499 in 1992) fed popular concern about crime. In contrast, deaths and injuries due to cars aroused less public interest and concern and were treated as a fact of life, in contrast to rail and air accidents. However, high-profile 'don't drink and drive' campaigns at Christmas served to focus public attention on road deaths and accidents. Fear of accidents (and rising car use) ensured that by 1998 cyclists were cycling only a fifth of the total mileage covered forty years earlier.

Greater personal mobility for the bulk, but by no means all, of the population, especially from the 1960s, enabled, and was a necessary consequence of, lower-density housing and declining subsidies for public transport. This was linked to changes in employment patterns. In place of factories or mines that had large labour forces, most modern industrial concerns are capital intensive and employ less labour. They are often located away from the central areas of cities on flat and relatively open sites with good road links. This is true of business, science and shopping 'parks'. In contrast, the 1930s schemes, such as Slough, Park Royal and Team Valley, Gateshead, had had railside locations, as well as road links.

Related changes in location have also been of great importance in such areas as

**Consumerism and the car**
A *Picture Post* advertisement from 19 June 1954, showing a Hillman Minx convertible for sale at £510 plus tax. Large numbers of cars were sold in the 1950s, contributing to the consumerism associated with the Conservative governments of 1951–64.

education, health, shopping and retirement. In 1971, 14 per cent of junior school children were driven to school, in 1990, 64 per cent. The percentage walking or going by bus fell markedly, an aspect of the declining use of 'public space' and one related to the increase in obesity and unfitness among children. The availability of cars interacted with fears about children being out by themselves. Reductions in government subsidies for school transport were also important.

Cars also greatly influenced the layout of residential areas. The cul-de-sac was created as a way to restrict traffic flows through zones (areas) where people lived, while at the same time providing access to the road system. Cul-de-sacs were an aspect of the organisation of roads in a hierarchy based on traffic flow.

Cars also affected the development of leisure. 'Days out' and the Sunday afternoon drive changed the nature of leisure (and especially of 'the day of rest'). Cars also became a method of taking holidays, not least in caravanning. Motorcycles were also used for the same purpose.

Cars were a democratising mechanism, making work and leisure more accessible. Greater mobility for most, but not all, of the population, however, exacerbated social segregation. Car ownership brought a sense, maybe an illusion, of freedom, and an access to opportunities and options for many, but not all. The division of the population into communities defined by differing levels of wealth, expectations, opportunity and age was scarcely novel. Indeed, in most towns, for example Edinburgh, London and Newcastle, it had developed greatly from the eighteenth century. However, it became more pronounced during the twentieth century, and an obvious aspect of what was termed the 'underclass', in both town and countryside, was their relative lack of mobility. This was doubly important because of links between cars, status and notions of masculinity.

Aside from ground transport, journeys by air also developed. They supplanted ocean liners as the major way to travel to Australasia, North America and South Africa. With the introduction of jet passenger aircraft in the 1950s – the first, the DH106 Comet, was British and went into commercial service in 1952 – increasing numbers travelled by air, particularly as the package holiday abroad, to such destinations as Spain, became more popular (see Chapter 4).

# The transmission of sound and image

What had been, for most, fantasy or science fiction in the nineteenth century, became reality in the twentieth (see Chapter 4). Radio and television came to play a major role in society, and became important to government and the economy. Marconi's first broadcast, in 1896, represented the birth of broadcasting. This was soon brought under state supervision. Under the Wireless Telegraphy Act of 1904, all transmitters and receivers had to be licensed by the Post Office. The potential security risk led to the impounding of equipment during World War One, but, thanks to extensive military use, radio technology rapidly developed. The military aspect of radio use led to continued restrictions on civilian broadcasting in the immediate post-war years, but restrictions were lifted in 1921. This created the possibility of a competitive system as in the USA. Instead, the corporatism and belief in regulation that characterised much of British society and industry after World War One led to the formation of a publicly-owned monopoly.

Public radio broadcasts began in England in 1922, and in Scotland the following year. The British Broadcasting Corporation, a monopoly acting in the 'national interest', and financed by licence fees paid by radio owners, initially 10 shillings (50p), was established in 1926. The radio became very popular. Whereas licences were held by 10% of British households in 1924, by 1939 the percentage was 71, and reception had improved as crystal sets were replaced in the 1930s by valve sets. The BBC began television services in 1936. Commercial television companies, financed by advertising, were not established in Britain until 1955, and the first national commercial radio station, Classic FM, was not founded until 1992 (although 'pirate' radio stations such as Radio Caroline and Radio Luxemburg had a loyal following in the 1960s and early 1970s).

Under Sir John Reith, the first General Manager (1922–6) and then Director General (1927–38), the BBC enjoyed reasonably close relations with government, and it was shaped as a public institution with a social and cultural mission to enlighten as well as entertain. Reith was opposed to commercial control and put a

## Box 5.4

### British Broadcasting Corporation

Founded as the British Broadcasting Company in 1922, this rapidly became a national institution. For long a monopoly, it helped set the tone for first radio and then television, but this led to much criticism. The BBC was variously seen as conservative and an expensive monopoly. Independent, in theory, of government control, the BBC has been affected by its reliance on the licence fee, while the Board of Governors are government appointees. The BBC became more liberal in the 1960s and found itself vulnerable to Thatcherite criticism in the 1980s. It is unclear how far it will respond successfully to new technology, particularly the competition of cable, satellite, and interactive media.

major emphasis on moral improvement and broadcasting standards, both of which he linked. During the General Strike of 1926, the BBC's role within the media establishment was strengthened. The BBC also became important as a consolidator of national identity and supporter of the *status quo*. Nevertheless, some BBC programmes, such as *Men Without Work*, challenged cosy assumptions. So also did a few films, such as, eventually in 1941, the film of Walter Greenwood's account of the harshness of unemployment, his novel *Love on the Dole* (1933), although the earlier proposal in 1936 to film it was rejected. The British Board of Film Censors encouraged caution in the film industry (see Chapter 15).

Before criticising the media, it is worth noting that there is little sign that audiences sought complexity or unsettling notions. This was underlined during World War Two when the propagandist role of the media was welcome. Reith was, briefly, Minister of Information in 1940. During the war, the radio with its greater capacity for immediacy and its access to government, not the press, became the main source of news. This helped make the BBC central to national identity. It did so as a source of radio: television was suspended during the war and not relaunched until 1946. BBC television began broadcasting in Scotland in 1952.

Television ownership shot up in the 1950s, a response both to the end of post-war austerity and to the foundation of the commercial companies. The numbers of those with regular access to a set rose from 38 per cent of the population in 1955 to 75 per cent in 1959. By then most of the country could receive BBC and ITV. ITV had been set up as a result of the Television Act of 1954, but commercial television was not unregulated. Instead, an Independent Broadcasting Authority was also established to control the system. This was a dramatic change from the situation in 1949 when the Broadcasting Committee rejected any end to the BBC's monopoly and any advertising. Commercial television transmissions began in 1955. BBC2 followed in 1964, and in 1969 colour television became fully operational on all three channels. Channel 4 followed in 1982.

As with the rise of the car, television hit another 'public space', in this case the cinema. This had made a major impact in the first half of the century. In 1914, Manchester had 111 premises licensed to show films. Even the more rural, and less affluent, Lincolnshire, had 14 cinemas in 1913. During World War One, the War Office created a Cinematograph Committee. Newsreels, such as *Battle of the Somme*, followed the course of the war. Others, such as *Life of Lloyd George*, sought a political impact. After the war, silent films were followed by the 'talkies', a revolution in the impact and potential of cinema. The first British sound production, Alfred Hitchcock's *Blackmail* (1929), was a considerable success. Large numbers of cinemas were constructed, distribution chains were organised, and going to the 'flicks' became an activity that spanned classes, not least because the cinema provided escapism. This was a product both of Americanisation and of the 'sing as we go' feel of many British films. In 1934, out of a population of 46 million, 18.5 million went to the cinema on a weekly basis. Despite their relatively low population, Suffolk had 40 cinemas in 1937, and Lincolnshire 58, and there were close to 5,000 cinemas throughout the 1930s. Birmingham alone had 110 by 1939. Furthermore, many cinemas were far larger than the pre-war cinemas, many of

**Box 5.5**

### Cinema statistics

|  | Number of screens in UK to nearest ten | Weekly attendance in millions |
|---|---|---|
| 1945 | 4,720 | 20.5 |
| 1950 | 4,580 | 26.8 |
| 1955 | 4,480 | 22.7 |
| 1960 | 3,030 | 9.6 |
| 1965 | 1,970 | 6.3 |
| 1970 | 1,530 | 3.7 |
| 1975 | 1,530 | 2.2 |
| 1980 | 1,590 | 2.0 |
| 1985 | 1,230 | 1.4 |
| 1990 | 1,560 | 1.9 |

Source: C. Cook and J. Stevenson, *Britain Since 1945* (London, 1996), pp. 134–5.

which had been converted shops. Enormous cinemas were thrown up in new London suburbs, such as Gants Hill, Becontree Heath and Hendon, for example the Granada at Tooting (1931), and also elsewhere, for example the vast Ritz at Gosport. Some cinemas, such as the Ilford Hippodrome and the Rex at Stratford, were converted theatres.

The cinema was especially popular in working-class areas and more popular with women than married men, although the very poor could not afford it. It offered an equivalent to male patronage of the pub and the (working men's) club. Youths were also more likely to attend the cinema than their elders. The cinema became more popular with the middle class from the late 1920s and this was linked to investment in large and luxurious cinemas in middle-class suburbs. Aside from acting as foci within towns, including new suburban areas, cinemas also gave a new vitality to the appeal of towns to their rural hinterlands. Country dwellers went to urban cinemas, such as the Grand in Banbury, to see the wider world, both through films and in newsreels.

The impact of the cinema was a cause of controversy. Commentators had little doubt that seeing moving images of very different lives could lead to a rethinking of assumptions that might itself be subversive. Some conservative commentators were worried about the effect on social and moral values, especially the last. The depiction of independent women gave particular rise for concern. Conversely, other commentators suggested that the potential of cinema as a form of mass instruction and entertainment had been subordinated in order to produce messages and images that would support the existing social order and encourage enthusiasm, compliance or apathy. Aside from the politics of film, it is clear that the cinema influenced fashions, especially in clothes, hairstyles, manners and language. This impact was taken further by the extensive coverage of films and film stars in other media and their use in advertisements. Cinema greatly aided exposure to American culture (see Chapter 14).

From the 1950s, the cinema was hit by television. By 1966, over half of the cinemas in the North-West of England had closed, although in the 1990s there was to be a significant resurgence of cinemas with multiplexes. Cinema admissions in Britain fell from a post-war peak of 31.4 million weekly attendances in 1946 to one million in 1984, before rising to two million in 1992. However, to a great extent, the cinema had been supplemented by television or became an adjunct to it, through the use of video and, more recently, due to the fact that both the BBC and Channel Four became engaged in film production. Newspapers were also hit by television.

By 1992, 93 per cent of British households had televisions, and in 1994 the percentage rose to 99, with 96 per cent having colour television. In the 1990s, the number of regular terrestrial television channels rose to five. This was supplemented for many, first by satellite transmissions, which began in 1989, and then by cable television. The receiving dishes of satellite television altered the appearance of many houses, as television aerials had earlier done. By 1992, over a million Sky Television dishes had been sold in Britain. Furthermore, over 50 per cent of British households had video recorders, giving them even greater control over what they watched, although critics would claim that this control is an illusion. Technology had also helped radio, with the impact of the transistor.

## The impact of television

Television had a major impact on the economy, society and culture. As far as the first was concerned, the manufacture of television sets was a major industry. This followed on from the earlier impact of first the telegraph and then radio. The detailed impact could be considerable. For example, the development of industries in towns that had not hitherto been major centres of industry was particularly associated with electrical engineering. The Marconi Wireless Telegraph Company opened its first factory in Chelmsford in 1893 and moved to a new site there in 1912. The Japanese Sony Corporation alone manufactured 6 million television sets at Bridgend in South Wales in 1973–93, and in 1993 opened a new colour television factory at Pencoed in Mid-Glamorgan. Aside from the manufacture of televisions and furniture accessories, such as stands, there was also a range of associated activities, such as the production of guides to programmes: *Radio Times* and *TV Times* were two of the top-selling journals. This encouraged the weekend press, broadsheet as well as tabloid, to publish their own television supplements for the week ahead (the major national dailies had long contained programme listings).

From the 1950s, television succeeded radio as a central determinant of the leisure time of many, a moulder of opinions and fashions, a source of conversation and controversy, a cause of noise, an occasion of family cohesion or dispute, a major feature of the household. A force for change, a great contributor to the making of the 'consumer society' and a 'window on the world', which demanded the right to enter everywhere and report anything, television also became, increasingly, a reflector of popular taste. As such, it was criticised heavily from the 1960s with Mary White-house and others raising concerns about decency. Series such as *Play for Today* offered hard-hitting social comment.

Radio had earlier helped to provide common experiences: royal Christmas messages from 1932, King Edward VIII's abdication speech in 1936, and the war speeches of Churchill, heard by millions, as those of Lloyd George in the First World War could not be. In W. H. Auden and Christopher Isherwood's play *The Ascent of F6* (1936), the general public, in the persons of Mr and Mrs A, keep in touch with the distant mountain ascent through the radio.

Television came to fulfil the same function of providing common experience, offering much of the nation common visual images and messages. This really began with the coronation service for Elizabeth II in 1953, which was a cause of many households purchasing sets or watching for the first time. The Queen's first televised Christmas broadcast followed in 1957, and the wedding of Princess Margaret in 1960.

Thanks to television, the royals almost became members of viewers' extended families, treated with the fascination commonly devoted to the stars of soap opera. The *Royal Family* documentary of 1969 exposed monarchy to the close domestic scrutiny of television. Indeed, both the 'New Elizabethan Age of optimism', heralded in 1952 and reaching a peak in June 1953, and discontents in the 1990s about the position and behaviour of the Royal family, owed much to the media. Much of the population watched the wedding of Prince Charles and Diana Spencer on television in 1981, and, again, the latter's funeral in 1997 (see Chapter 8).

Television was central to much else, including the trend-setting and advertising that was, and is, so crucial to the consumer society, and the course and conduct of election campaigns. Harold Wilson, Labour Prime Minister 1964–70 and 1974–6, recognised the growing importance of television and deliberately created a televisual image. He used his pipe as a symbol of stability. Baldwin, earlier, had made very successful use of the radio. Thatcher received a 'make-over' to make her image more television-friendly. Conversely, politicians who were 'un-televisual', such as Alec

### Elizabeth II (1926– )

Elizabeth was the eldest daughter of Prince Albert, the Duke of York, George V's second son who came to the throne in 1936 after his brother's abdication, and Lady Elizabeth Bowes-Lyon. In 1947 Elizabeth married her third cousin Philip Mountbatten, who became the Duke of Edinburgh. They had three sons and a daughter. When her father died in 1952 she became Queen of the United Kingdom and Commonwealth. She was crowned in 1953 and then embarked on a world tour. As Queen her duties include opening Parliament and holding meetings of the Privy Council, awarding honours and decorations, and receiving visiting heads of state. Her private interests include horse racing. Her jubilee in 1977 was greeted with celebrations and street parties but in the 1990s the image of the royal family suffered, following several divorces. Efforts have been made to modernise the monarchy, particularly following overwhelming public reaction to the death of the Princess of Wales.

Douglas-Home, suffered. Parliament was televised from the 1990s, the House of Lords before the House of Commons, and much of public politics from the 1970s became a matter of sound bites aimed to catch the evening news bulletins.

More generally, television increasingly set the idioms and vocabulary of public and private life, as radio had earlier done. For example, on 14 July 1989, the Prime Minister, Thatcher, was attacked by Denis Healey of the Labour Party for adding 'the diplomacy of Alf Garnett to the economics of Arthur Daley'. This attack was based on the assumption that listeners would understand the reference to prominent television characters. It was also an aspect of the blurring between image and reality that radio and television offered, as also with the use of reconstructions. The impact of television was seen in the naming of children after television stars.

Television was also important to other media. It helped set fashions in popular music. Stars were created. The singer Marion Ryan, who appeared in more than 200 episodes of *Spot the Tune* in 1956–62, owed her fame essentially to this screen opportunity. The pop music boom of the late 1950s and 1960s particularly depended on television and, in turn, attracted viewers. The BBC's *Six-Five Special* (1957) was followed by ITV's *Oh Boy!* (1958), and in 1962 by *Pick of the Pops* on BBC radio. *Top of the Pops*, which first started on BBC television in 1963, was especially important. The first record played on the programme, *I Only Want to Be With You*, was the first solo hit of one of the leading singers of the decade, Dusty Springfield. Radio also played a major role in setting music fashions (see Chapter 15).

The shift from radio to television as the main source of home entertainment was important in a wider cultural sense. Some radio programmes remained popular, and the impact of Radio 4 programmes covering news and current affairs remained strong. The enduring appeal of *The Archers* showed that radio could still capture the imagination of the public. Yet television established itself as the authentic chronicler of everyday life. Through programmes such as *Coronation Street* and, more recently, *EastEnders*, viewers experienced life as they lived it. A tradition of high-quality drama, from Jane Austen to Evelyn Waugh, Dennis Potter to Lynda La Plante, gave British television an international reputation for viewing excellence. Yet, the import of soap operas from the USA and then Australia, with the proliferation of game shows, many of which had American origins, led to accusations of 'dumbing down'. Nevertheless, at its best, television could, and can, still unite the nation in a way which no other means of mass communication could. The real national theatre was to be found, in the opinion of the pre-eminent television dramatist of his time, Dennis Potter (1933–95), in the corner of the sitting room, rather than on the banks of the River Thames, the site of the National Theatre (see Chapter 15). As far as 'dumbing down' was concerned, characters such as Del Boy and Rodney in *Only Fools and Horses* had merely replaced earlier favourites such as Eric and Ernie. Assessing the multiple impact of television is very important, and there is something of a contradiction between the way in which it has led to a more homogenous 'culture', while also, in recent years, leading to compartmentalisation and isolation within the family, especially as more children possess bedroom sets.

## A wired world

By the 1990s' television screens were increasingly understood or used in conjunction with computerised information systems. This was part of a major change in the communication of messages that went back to the nineteenth century: the telegraph represented the first divorce between transport and communication. Telephone ownership had already risen to a high level. Fax machines and mobile phones became important from the 1980s, and the latter were the fashionable Christmas present in 1994. They became the fastest selling consumer good of the century in the United Kingdom. In addition, the growing numbers of company and personal computers facilitated the use of electronic mail and access to the internet (see Chapter 4).

Thanks to computers and electronic mail, more messages were sent and more information stored in the 1990s than ever before. Indeed, the overload, management, and accessibility of information became major problems for both institutions and individuals. It also became a problem for the government, as calls for freedom-of-information legislation became more vocal. The Blair government promised to introduce a Freedom of Information Act, but it is likely to lack the scope of similar legislation in the USA.

## ■ Consumerism, crime and technology

Moving around was important to the world of ideas, the world of work, the fabric, structures and content of society. The consequences have been varied and sometimes unexpected. The spread in the 1930s of large numbers of affordable cars with reliable self-starter motors, so that it was not necessary to crank up the motor by hand, led to a wave of 'smash and grab' raids, as the criminal fraternity took advantage of the new technology. Greater mobility changed the pattern of crime. In response, London's Metropolitan Police experimented with mounting ship's radios in cars, and was able to develop a fleet of Wolseley cars thus equipped with which to launch an effective response. The 1970s was to see computer fraud, but also the use of computerised information and of sophisticated forensic techniques by the police.

The car had other effects in crime and politics. Traffic offences brought middle-class individuals into contact with the police and the courts. One of the original purposes of the AA (Automobile Association) was to warn members of speed traps. Driving helped change perceptions of the police. 'Flying pickets' (mobile groups of trade unionists) used cars to spread strike action, as in the 'Winter of Discontent' strikes of 1978–9 and the miners' strike of 1984–5 (see Chapter 10). 'Road rage' became a problem in the 1990s. Consumerism and technology was also fused with the National Lottery, which came into being by law in 1994. Similarly, the emphasis on mobility led to the development of mobile versions of consumer technological products, such as transistor radios, mobile phones, and mobile CD players.

Another form of mobility, that combined consumerism and technology, was offered by the domestic video cassette recorder (VCR). This permitted the viewing of programmes when wanted. The time shift offered by the VCR combined with mobile television controls to change the relationship between viewer and television programmer, a shift that challenged advertising strategies: viewers could fast-forward or skip channels to avoid advertisements. Thus the movement of images and ideas provided opportunities as well as problems for individuals, companies and institutions.

## ◼ Summary

◆ Greater mobility was important both in its own right, and as a facilitator or enabler of other wide-ranging changes. That is a functional interpretation, and a valid one. But, in addition, greater mobility was important as a source of motifs and icons that gave form to an increasingly fluid society. Car and television are arguably the two major icons of the twentieth century: the internet, of the next?

◆ Greater mobility was closely related to the consumerism discussed in Chapter 4. The world of things was increasingly a matter of means for movement, of people, images, words and ideas. 'We move, therefore we are' seemed to express the values of a society that was less reverential of the past. This was an increasingly important aspect of the popular culture.

◆ The marked increase in disposable wealth from the 1950s encouraged a social emulation in which gaining cars and televisions became important to status. This was part of a reconfiguration of society in which the prosperous many were different from a smaller and poorer underclass (see also Chapter 6).

## ◼ Questions for discussion

◆ How far was the decline of rail traffic linked to wider shifts in the British economy? (See also Chapter 11.)

◆ Why has the car had such an impact on British society? (See also Chapter 3.)

◆ Was the car an aspect of the Americanisation of British society? (See also Chapter 14.)

◆ Did television diminish diversity within society? (See also Chapter 6.)

◆ Is it appropriate to have state regulation of radio and television and, if so, how should it be carried out?

## ◼ Further reading

Negrine, Ralph, *Television and the Press since 1945* (Manchester, 1998).

Curran, J., and Seaton, J., *Power without Responsibility: The Press and Broadcasting in Britain* (4th edn, London, 1991).

Goldie, G. W., *Facing the Nation: Television and Politics, 1936–75* (London, 1977).

Pegg, Mark, *Broadcasting and Society, 1918–1939* (Beckenham, 1983).

Richards, J., *The Age of the Dream Palace: Cinema and Society in Britain, 1930–1939* (London, 1984).

# Social Structures

The nature of the society in which we live is often hard to grasp, not least because much, especially social attitudes, is taken for granted and, otherwise, hidden from view. The categories that are employed to dissect and describe social structure and attitudes are often ambiguous and/or inadequate to the task of assessing the complexity of modern society. It is unclear how best to describe people. Are they primarily motivated by their economic position, ethnic group, parental background, personal assumptions, or by peer-group pressures? How much does any one of these flow from the others? Do terms like 'class' mean much for the bulk of the population, and, if so, what do they mean? Do they describe a situation or do they describe and explain it? How far is it possible to include an explanation of change in any description of society?

Yet, despite these problems, it is necessary to assess social structures in order to understand the nature and dynamics of society. There has been considerable emphasis recently on the irrelevance of traditional classes, but, even though the numerical balance between working and middle classes has clearly changed, there is a danger of ignoring the persistence of class differences. Furthermore, class acts as an important prism for refracting views and identities.

## Key issues

▶ How is society structured?

▶ How has this changed during the century?

▶ How far are there regional differences?

▶ How are social structures and practice affected by issues of gender and race, and how have these changed during the century?

▶ What is the importance of social differences?

▶ What was the impact of the world wars on the social system?

## Class

Class-based analyses of society have been the most important this century. A class is essentially a large group of people who share a similar social and economic position.

Much of the basis of class analysis derived from Marxism. Karl Marx claimed in the *Communist Manifesto* (1848) that 'the history of all hitherto existing societies is the history of class struggle'. His analysis was influential among many commentators who were not strictly Marxists and, indeed, among many who rejected Marxism. In Marx's analysis, class is linked to economic power, which is defined by the individual's relationship to the means of production, society being understood as an engine for the production of goods and for the distribution of tasks and benefits. Society is divided between two groups, the proletariat, or 'workers', who live off the sale of their labour power, and the bourgeoisie or property owners, who buy that labour power. These groups are assumed to be in a conflict to benefit from and control the fruits of their labour power, and society itself is the sphere for this conflict and is shaped by it.

Non-Marxist analyses are less dominated by the notion of conflict and keener to present social structures as more complex, although Marx himself was explicit about complexity in his historical works. Income and status (in part market position) differences between occupational groups dominate such analyses. The Victorians employed such an occupational classification, and it was continued in many subsequent surveys, as in the 1911 *Fertility of Marriage Census*. Occupational classifications centre on a difference between the 'middle' class, white-collar (non-manual) workers, and the 'working' class, 'blue-collar' (manual) workers. These differences have been further refined by consumer analysts concerned to dissect society for marketing purposes and by government surveys, to produce a system in which society is essentially divided between professionals (class A), managers (B), clerical workers (C1), skilled manual workers (C2), semi-skilled and unskilled workers (D), and those who are unemployed or unable to work (E). The latter classification gained considerable public attention in the last quarter of the century, sufficiently so for people to understand what was meant by saying that support from C2s was crucial to Thatcher's electoral success in 1979, 1983 and 1987.

Occupational classification is weakened by a focus on male, not female occupations. There is also a problem if the particular characteristics of youth society are ignored. For long, it was argued that a distinct youth culture did not emerge until the 1950s and 1960s, but, more recently, attention has been focused on the distinct attitudes and interests of young wage earners in the inter-war period. Far from being structured by apprenticeship or (as in many Continental states) military service, these youths enjoyed considerable independence, as well as the vote. With relatively low rates of juvenile unemployment, particularly in the 1920s, the young were able to choose jobs and did not need to be deferential at work. They also had their own leisure choices, especially the cinema and dance halls. A stress on the distinctive lifestyles of youth, and particularly on youth independence, underlines the fluidity of social life. To be 'working' or 'middle' class meant very different things at different stages of life, and this undermined any notion of class coherence, let alone unity.

Before turning back to more general analytical points, it is necessary to provide a brief chronological coverage of major shifts in social structure this century. It is worth bearing in mind throughout this discussion that the structure has never been as rigid as much of the discussion might suggest, that there has been (and is) much fluidity in the concept of social status, that notions of social organisation, hierarchy and dynamics vary, and that the position of individuals and groups, and the cohesion of the latter, involve and reflect much besides social status. Both religion and ethnicity, for example, can be very important. Ethnicity has become more important,

Box 6.1

## The Media and social fluidity

The Media did more than record social currents and shifts. They also helped to shape them. Television was more successful in setting the tone of British society than more historic institutions, such as the monarchy and the Established Churches. Television, for example, encouraged a permissiveness in language and behaviour by making such conduct appear normal. By the mid-1990s, most television and radio 'soaps' supposedly depicting normal life seemed to have their quota of one-parent families, abused children, and sympathetically-presented homosexuals. A sense of social fluidity was also captured by cartoonists. One of the best, Mark Boxer, had a braying upper-class woman declare in the *Guardian* on 1 June 1983, 'Nonsense, nanny. We're *thrilled* Emma's fiancé is self-made', and another on 3 October 1983, 'We couldn't afford to give Fiona a season; but luckily she is in a soft porn movie'. On 27 July 1983, a woman in a Boxer cartoon addressed her partner, 'Will you get out of bed; I want you to be one of the 8 per cent who propose on their knees', an ironic comment on the prevalence of pre-marital sex.

not least because, in the late 1960s and early 1970s, integration and assimilation were rejected as an ideal in favour of an ideal of 'multi-culturalism'.

Simply focusing on social structure, shows that the twentieth century saw the continuation of powerful inegalitarian tendencies, not simply in terms of wealth, both capital and income, but also with regard to assumptions. This was, and is, true not only of assumptions of particular groups about themselves, but also of their assumptions about others. Yet, there has also been a decline in the traditional upper class, and a broadening of the middle class, such that the structure of society is increasingly one in which a large portion is comfortably off, and the essential divide is between this broader middle class and those who are poor, sufficiently so for them to be eligible for regular social welfare payments. Longitudinal surveys of babies born in 1946 and 1958 showed how social class was linked to life chances (see also Chapter 2).

Society, however, is far more complex in its dynamics than a structural account might suggest. In place of an account that presents identities and choices as determined, or at least heavily influenced, by social 'structures', it is possible to emphasise the role of human agency. Such an emphasis, with its stress on the role of human decisions and on concepts and ideologies, leads to a less clear-cut and more complex, not to say indistinct or 'messy' situation, especially if the individual, rather than the collective, is seen as the basic unit of decision-making. Patterns become less apparent and processes of causation less easy to define.

Other problems arise from different understandings of the nature of social organisation. Class was traditionally seen in relatively simplistic terms and with reference to factors of production. In the post-war world, however, analyses of class became more complex for a number of reasons.

At the 'micro' level, families increasingly contained individuals who were in different social groups. It was also clear that attitudes towards social mobility varied greatly, both between individuals and within social groups. Furthermore, the growing emphasis on self-identification as a major source of social location in the second half of the century necessarily limited both broad-brush approaches and 'realist' analyses based on measurable criteria, whether related to the means of production, income, or other factors.

Social location through self-identification involved a number of factors, including not only age, religion and ethnicity, but also lifestyle. Thus, for example, there has been important work on leisure activities that has traced the social configurations of organised sport. This, however, has to be handled with care. Football may have emerged as a working-class game, but its following is not socially exclusive. Furthermore, there was and is a regional dimension to the social location of sport and other leisure activities. For example, golf in England tended and tends to be more exclusive than is the case in Scotland. Similarly, rugby had and has a more popular following in some towns than football. Nevertheless, sport and related activities did reflect, and, in part, create, social differences, and thus a sense of social location. Football pools and greyhound racing, both introduced in the 1920s, were popular with the working class, while the authorities were more hostile.

Another factor stressed in the 1990s relates to the idea of 'sectoral cleavages'. From this perspective, it is the sector of the economy which an individual works in, private or public, which is the key criterion of self-identification. The private and public sectors are presented as having different cultures and contrasting attitudes towards individual development. Sectoral cleavages can also emerge from patterns of consumption, that is, whether someone consumes goods and services from the public sector or the private sector. The practical implications of such sectoral cleavages have been particularly important in the field of electoral behaviour. Individuals employed in the public sector are relatively more likely to vote Labour than their private-sector counterparts, even when their occupations would be deemed middle class. Alternatively, individuals who rely upon private-sector provision, who are 'owner-occupiers' for instance, are more likely to vote Conservative, irrespective of their class background. In turn, the existence of sectoral cleavages helps to explain the Labour Party's run of electoral defeats in the 1980s. The **privatisation** policies of successive Thatcher governments served to undermine Labour's support base, that is, the public sector.

As so often with history, what did not happen is as important as what did. The social structure did not have to cope with the consequences of major changes stemming from defeat and occupation in war, or massive inflation, as in Germany in the 1920s, or the existence of a government pledged to social revolution. These fates were possibly closer than many appreciate, the resulting anxieties and hopes providing part of the flavour of twentieth-century politics, especially in the inter-war period, but they were avoided. Most crucial here was the dominance of the Labour Party by politicians who wanted social progress, not revolution, and their attempt to direct, not destroy, capitalism. This emphasis reflected the underlying moral imperative to British Socialism. It has always existed as a philosophy of improvement, rather than a doctrine of confrontation, although the latter alternative was only defeated after serious conflicts within the organisation. The Labour Party was created by men who believed in the words of the Bible (as well as Dickens and Ruskin), rather than the works of Karl Marx: brotherhood, not class-war. In 1924 and 1929–31, the desire by minority Labour governments to humanise capitalism can in part be attributed to a weak parliamentary position, but the crucial factor was a determination to work within the constitution. In 1945–51, the Attlee governments tempered Socialism with the immediate need to rebuild the economy, and with its fears about Communism. These political choices all affected social structures. An attempt to work with capitalism was clearly seen in the Labour majority governments of 1964–70 (through planning) , 1974–9 (through the 'Social contract') and, most explicitly, since May 1997 (through the open praise of the market).

**privatisation:** The transfer of government-owned industries to private ownership through the selling of shares on the stock market.

Yet the Labour Party was not alone in lessening social division. In politics, 'one nation' and populist Conservatives were both important, while more widely in society a whole range of institutions and practices helped to link people of different backgrounds and to lessen social tensions. These included churches and sport, patriotic groups and youth bodies such as the Boy Scouts. The last is claimed to have included 34 per cent of all males born between 1901 and 1920. It sought to lessen class division. Clearly such bodies and practices were not free of tension and could themselves be the sites, and even cause, of social division and even antagonism. Nevertheless the determined effort of many such institutions to offer a different basis for identity and activity to that of class division was important. Furthermore, they affected the political world. Many prominent Labour figures, such as Arthur Henderson, were committed Christians.

## Before World War One

Britain was still a very hierarchical society at the start of the century. In 1914, King George V (reign 1910–36) summoned 'My loyal subjects' to take part in World War One. Society was scarcely egalitarian. Wealth was distributed very unevenly. In 1880, over half of the fertile county of Norfolk was owned by landowners with more than 1,000 acres, while all those with estates there of more than 15,000 acres were members of the aristocracy, with the Earl of Leicester alone owning 43,000. In 1874, the Duke of Buccleuch owned 37% of the land in both Selkirk and Dumfries and 25% in Roxburghshire.

New institutions and developments were moulded to take note of existing social divisions. Rail passengers were classified by class and each had different conditions. Third-class passengers were not permitted on Great Western Railway expresses until 1882. The composition of the new county councils reflected social patterns. The first elections led in 1889 to the Duke of Richmond and Lord Monk Bretton becoming chairmen of the West and East Sussex county councils respectively.

Yet the structure of society was being affected by the rise of individual and collective merit as a defining characteristic of precedence, at the expense of hereditary. Greatly expanded institutions with a meritocratic ethos – the civil service, the professions, the universities, the public schools, the army and the navy – were all very significant in the creation of a new social and cultural establishment to replace the aristocracy. A sense of flux was captured in the House of Commons on 17 October 1899 when the Irish nationalist MP William Redmond attacked Joseph Chamberlain, the Colonial Secretary, as 'a man who in turn has been everything by degree . . . the man who, under the power of an overwhelming ambition – an ambition seldom coming to gentlemen, but to people of that class who aspire to mix with them'. After Robert, 3rd Marquess of Salisbury, and his nephew Arthur Balfour, had led the Conservatives, the Party turned to Bonar Law, Baldwin and Neville Chamberlain, three middle-class figures.

The tension between established and new social forces became stronger in the 1900s, as a result both of the rise of the Liberals to power in 1905 and of the growing prominence of the Labour Party, which from 1903 had an electoral pact with the Liberals, which some prominent Liberals, especially the dynamic David Lloyd George, President of the Board of Trade 1905–8 and Chancellor of the Exchequer 1908–15, were determined to use, as well as to gain office, in order to undermine the power and possessions of the old landed elite, and to woo Labour and the trade unions. Lloyd

### George V (1865–1936)

The second son of Edward VII was born in Marlborough House in London. He began his career in the Navy in 1877. When his older brother the Duke of Clarence died in 1892, George left the Navy and in 1893 married Mary of Teck, with whom he had five sons and a daughter. He became Prince of Wales in 1901. On his father's death in 1910 he became King of the United Kingdom and Emperor of India. In 1917, when Britain was at war with Germany, he changed the family name from the German-sounding Saxe-Coburg to Windsor. He was a popular king who enjoyed speaking to his people on the 'wireless', starting the annual Christmas Day broadcasts in 1932. His jubilee was celebrated enthusiastically in 1935.

George wished to move the Liberals to the left, and in 1909 announced a People's Budget, introducing new taxes for the wealthy: land taxes, supertax and increased death duties. He declared in a speech at Newcastle, not a town where the aristocracy were popular, that 'a fully equipped duke costs as much to keep up as two Dreadnoughts [battleships]', and that the House of Lords comprised 'five hundred men, ordinary men, chosen accidentally from among the unemployed'. His Liberal predecessors had never been so critical. Gladstone himself backed the 'classes' against the 'masses' and John Bright could be even more critical.

Lloyd George's was the language of class conflict, although it was not government policy. Whereas Disraeli, an outsider, had acquired a country estate in 1848, the Liberal Herbert Asquith, a barrister, was in 1908 the first Prime Minister not to have his own country house, although he was to end up with one, and an earldom. Asquith was more hesitant than his predecessors about accepting the claims of hereditary aristocrats to high office, although most of his Cabinet came from the old upper classes. Andrew Bonar Law, Asquith's opponent as Conservative leader in 1911–21 and 1922–3, came from a background in iron and banking, lacked a country house, was clearly middle class, and was described by Asquith as a 'gilded tradesman'.

The political struggle over the aristocracy that led, with the Parliament Act of 1911, to the removal of the veto power of the House of Lords over Commons' legislation

### Box 6.2

### The novelist's eye

Novels can be a good way to recover atmosphere and record change. Aldous Huxley's *Antic Hay* (1923) depicted a new London society of jazz clubs, drug-taking and birth control. Social values had been challenged by World War One. Huxley also noted the pressures of a harsh economic system, social snobbery and exploitative gender relations. In the book, Porteous was supported by 'the weariness and the pallor of a wife who worked beyond her strength', and had 'ill-dressed and none too well-fed children'. Gumbril Senior lived 'in a decaying quarter' near Paddington: 'The houses, which a few years ago had all been occupied by respectable families, were now split up into squalid little maisonettes, and from the neighbouring slums, which along with most other unpleasant things the old bourgeois families had been able to ignore, invading bands of children came to sport on the once-sacred pavements.'

focused and exacerbated social tension. So also did the strike wave of 1910–12 (nearly 41 million working days were lost through strike action in 1912 alone). Although strikes arose from particular disputes in individual industries, they also benefited from a growing sense of class consciousness felt by the working class, which was reinforced by the coercive response to the strikes. This encouraged the growth of the Labour Party, the attraction of the radical programme of 'New Liberalism', and Liberal–Labour cooperation. The growing Socialism of the unions was a victory for the more militant elements among the working population, their militancy in part stemming from immersion in the doctrines of syndicalism, although the last was limited geographically and occupationally.

Yet, there were also important divisions within social classes. Ethnic, religious, regional and occupational divisions were as important as class issues. In 1914, over 75% of the working population were not members of trade unions, and divisions existed within the workforce, between skilled and unskilled, between Protestants and Irish immigrants, and between and within regional economies. Thus, in the cotton finishing industry, elite foremen engravers had little in common with poorly paid bleachers (see also Chapter 9).

# Women's role

Gender divisions also played a growing and more prominent role in social politics. Successive extensions of the franchise in the nineteenth century did not bring the vote to women, although they were socially less dependent than is generally assumed and than their legal situation might suggest. Their control of the family budget gave women a degree of authority in the house which their husbands were denied in the workplace. Women also wielded consumer power. Women from the upper and middle classes came to have more opportunities in the late nineteenth century. This was particularly so in education. Higher education was open to women, although they were not permitted to take degrees in either Cambridge or Oxford. At Aberdeen University it was formally agreed in 1892 that women be admitted to all faculties, but they still suffered discrimination. Women were not offered equivalent teaching in medicine and there was unequal access to the Bursary competition. Women students took no positions of influence and the student newspaper, *Alma Mater*, was hostile, presenting women students as unfeminine, or flighty and foolish.

Most women lacked such opportunities. Women generally moved into the low-skill, low-pay 'sweated' sector as they were denied access to the new technologies. Female factory workers were generally worse treated than men in pay, training and opportunities, a practice in which the trade unions (essentially male organisations) cooperated with the management. Definitions of skills, which affected pay, were controlled by men and favoured them; skilled women were poorly recognised. In J. M. Barrie's comedy *What Every Woman Knows* (1908), John Shand, the railwayman turned MP, owes his success as a debater to his wife Maggie, who has transformed his boring speeches when she typed them up.

More generally, women were affected by the processes of change, but modern standards of equality were still a long way off. The notion of 'separate spheres' was well established. Women's special role was defined as that of home and family. This was both employed to justify the exclusion of women from other spheres and served to make the large number of women who had to work appear as unsatisfactory.

Box 6.3

## The suffragette call

In a speech of 24 March 1908, Emmeline Pankhurst of the Women's Social and Political Union declared 'Men politicians are in the habit of talking to women as if there were no laws that affect women. "The fact is," they say, "the home is the place for women. Their interests are the rearing and training of children. . . . Politics have nothing to do with these things, and therefore politics do not concern women." Yet the laws decide how women are to live in marriage, how their children are to be trained and educated, and what the future of their children is to be. All that is decided by Act of Parliament. . . . I was in Herefordshire . . . an unmarried mother was brought before the bench of magistrates charged with having neglected her illegitimate child. She was a domestic servant. The magistrates . . . did not ask what wages the mother got; they did not ask who the father was or whether he contributed to the support of the child . . . if women had had some share in the making of laws, don't you think they would have found a way of making all fathers of such children equally responsible with the mothers for the welfare of those children?'

Furthermore, the concept of 'separate spheres' did not do justice to the complexities of gender relationships.

Gender relations had been affected by the declining influence of religion and the rise of scientists to become the new authorities. Older ideas of the intellectual superiority of men over women were given new authority by claims that the greater brain size of men proved the point. Medicine presented women as hormonally unstable. The natural differences between men and women were stressed in order to make women appear unsuitable for public positions. Seen as potentially hysterical, women appeared to some commentators as unsuited for the vote. Furthermore, ideologies of race and Empire helped shape the dominant constructions of masculinity, and these ideologies did not award women a commanding role.

In the years before World War One, there was growing pressure for votes for women from a vociferous, although largely middle-class, suffragette movement. Women ratepayers had had the vote for local government since 1869 and were able to stand for urban and rural district councils from 1895 and for town and county councils from 1907, but they lacked the same role in national politics. The militant tactics of the Women's Social and Political Union, founded by Emmeline Pankhurst in 1903, were designed to force public attention, although democratic, non-violent tactics were advocated by other feminist leaders, such as Millicent Fawcett, the leader of the National Union of Women's Suffrage Societies. Labour, which was associated

Box 6.4

## Suffragette militancy

Emmeline Pankhurst and the Women's Social and Political Union (WSPU) were unconvinced that women would gain the vote through persuasion and lobbying. Instead, they sought to shame the Establishment and to gain prominence by violent gestures. From 1905, Cabinet Ministers' speeches were heckled, and in 1909 window breaking began. Suffrage Bills in 1910 and 1911 led to a lull, but their failure due to a lack of government support led to a fresh upsurge of violence, including destruction of the mail in 1912, arson in 1913 and the death of Emily Davidson under the hooves of the King's horse in the 1913 Derby. These policies did not win political support and, instead, seemed to have rebounded to the favour of the less militant National Union of Women's Suffrage Societies.

**Suffragette agitation**
Emmeline Pankhurst (1858–1928), the
founder of the radical Women's Social
and Political Union in 1903, advocated
militant tactics in order to gain publicity.
As well as embarrassing ministers, she
was often imprisoned.

with most of the leaders of the movement, officially endorsed women's suffrage in
1912. Several prominent Liberals, including Asquith and Churchill, were more
hostile, and the progressive character of Liberalism was in part undermined by its
position on women's suffrage. The following year, women comprised over 40 per
cent of the membership of the influential left-wing Fabian Society. Suffragette
activism paralleled, and in some cases was related to, trade union activism.

Less dramatically, but also indicative of pressure from women for a different
society, the Co-operative Women's Guild, founded in 1884, campaigned for rights
for women workers, and in the early twentieth century pressed for divorce reform,
pensions, and better schools. The Women's Labour League, founded in 1906, campaigned for child care, free school meals, and for improvements in midwifery and
nursery care to cut infant mortality, and for improvements to the Poor Law and the
condition of sweated labour, although the last proved very divisive. The League was
affiliated to the Labour Party, and came to support women's suffrage. In 1918, it was
replaced by the Labour Party Women's Organisation.

# 1914–45

## World War One, 1914–18

What was termed the Great War helped transform society, not least because there
had been no equivalent for a century, and the British had had no experience of
conscription. The war brought universal male military service, with conscription
(although not in Ireland) in 1916, and was a major force for social change. Millions

of men served without resistance, although there were to be a number of conscientious objectors by the end of the war. Habits of mass mobilisation acquired prior to the war, thanks to industrial labour, trade unions, and the organisation of democratic politics, contributed to this willingness to accept discipline and order, as also did passive acceptance of the social order. In addition, many wanted to fight: the initial rush to enlist in August 1914, admittedly when the expectation was that the war would be 'over by Christmas', was indicative of this. A sense of adventure was important. The creation and deployment of a mass volunteer army in 1914–16 was a formidable administrative achievement and also a testimony to the nature of public culture. Furthermore, despite the strains of the war, there was no level of radicalism in the army comparable to the French and Russian armies in 1917. In 1916, Robert Blatchford, a patriotic ex-serviceman, attacked summary punishments in the army in articles in the *Sunday Chronicle* and the *Illustrated Sunday Herald*. There was no widespread resonance within the armed forces.

The social order was itself affected by higher inflation, greater taxation, an extension of state control, and the spread of trade unionism and female employment. New roles, many in industry, were performed by women. For example, large numbers of women workers were recruited by Lloyd George's Ministry of Munitions in 1915. The female percentage of trade unionists rose from 7.8 in 1900 to 17 in 1918. Women received higher wages, although they remained lower than men's, and in factories women were controlled by male foremen. Whereas only 72 army sisters had been employed in British military hospitals in 1898, a total of 32,000 women served as military nurses in 1914–19 and women had a place in the command structure, and were able to give orders to male ward orderlies. There was an important change in attitudes, such that in 1918 it was possible to extend the vote to women of 30 and over, as long as they were householders, wives of householders, occupants of property worth £5 annually, or graduates of British universities; for men the age was changed to 21, although there were no such restrictions, and younger men in the forces could also vote. Conscription appeared to require democracy: total war and universal participation walked hand-in-hand. It has been suggested that women's war work gained women the vote, but it has also been argued that (some) women got the vote because the 'political class' of 1916–18 was terrified by the prospect of universal male suffrage. That, they knew, would have to come. Thus, enfranchising women in their maturity was seen as a defensive step to lessen the impact of the proletarian vote. The women who did war work were predominantly propertyless and under 30.

The changing position of women was not simply restricted to work and the vote. Some women rejected the human cost of the war and launched the Women's Peace Crusade. New opportunities were related to increased mobility and independence. This included a decline in control and influence over young women by their elders, male and female. As a consequence, there was a new sexual climate. Chaperonage became less comprehensive and effective, and styles of courtship became freer. The percentage of illegitimate births rose to six in 1918. Furthermore, there was a greater interest in the informed public discussion of sex. The British Society for the Study of Sex Psychology was founded in 1914, and Marie Stopes's influential *Married Love* was published in 1918. There was an emphasis on mutual desire as a basis for sex. At the very least, Victorian codes were challenged. Alongside this, it is important to point out the persistence of class-based attitudes and practices. These were seen, for example, in recruitment and promotion within the armed forces and also in civilian war work.

## Inter-war years

Post-war demobilisation and the absence of a Communist revolution, as had affected Russia in 1917, ensured that the end of war was followed by an attempt to return to pre-war normality. In some respects this was successful, as is suggested by the subsequent avoidance of any breakdown in political order, although there was a very tense situation at the end of the war. The relative stability of inter-war Britain, all the more remarkable given the continuous existence of unemployment levels in excess of one million, owed much to the legacy of the Great War itself. For those who survived and those who remained at home, the war acted as an integrating experience. Unlike in defeated Germany, the army became part of post-war society in Britain as soldiers and civilians united in shared remembrance. The construction of the Cenotaph in Whitehall bore eloquent testimony to the nation's desire to remember its own. The determination never to forget the sacrifice which the 'lost generation' had made gave rise to a particular national outlook in the inter-war period. Those who had died between 1914 and 1918 were owed a Britain that would subdue conflict in the interests of community. Under these circumstances, it would be to betray the dead if matters were pushed to extremes. Nowhere was the link between conflict and betrayal seen more clearly than in the relative passivity surrounding the General Strike in May 1926.

Nevertheless, social attitudes did not return to the pre-war mould, while 1918–21 was a dangerous period for the British state. As already suggested, it would be inaccurate to suggest any pre-war rigidity, but, allowing for that, society was less deferential in the 1920s than hitherto. There was more of a cult of youth and novelty. Yet new practices did not necessarily lead to radicalism. After achieving equal suffrage in 1928 (when they reached the age of 21), women comprised a majority of the electorate, but they were not a united bloc with a shared interest and sense of identity. Having won the vote, the women's movement lost a measure of unity. Instead, aside from the customary divisions that affected men, on social, ethnic, religious and ideological lines, there were also specific differences between, for example, housewives and employed women, married and unmarried, older and younger, feminists and non-feminists, and these categories clashed, not coincided. Women continued to suffer discrimination in most fields. This related to the jobs they were expected to do and the tasks allocated to them in these jobs. Thus, women police were introduced during World War One, but, for long, they were essentially required to deal with women and children. No attempt to integrate them across a wide range of policing was made until the 1960s. Many women workers were 'sweated' workers. Furthermore, the new ideology of domesticity that emerged in the inter-war period affected attitudes towards women workers. Women played a more passive role in the labour force in the inter-war period than they had done in World War One.

The Conservatives benefited far more from votes for women than their opponents; indeed, throughout the 1920s and 1930s Conservative propaganda skilfully emphasised the threat which 'Socialist' Labour allegedly posed to the family. In 1929, the Conservatives claimed a million female Party members, about four times the Labour amount. These members provided the basis for Party organisation, women being particularly important in the Primrose League. Women voted Conservative far more than Labour. In part, the latter suffered from the strong anti-feminism of the trade union movement and from the Party's failure to cultivate female voters, although the first woman Cabinet minister, Margaret Bondfield, Minister of Labour

1929–31, was both a Labour MP and an active trade unionist: she had become Assistant Secretary of the National Union of Shop Assistants in 1898, and was Chair of the TUC General Council in 1923. Some feminists were seen by Labour as overly radical in their feminism. Selina Cooper was turned down as a municipal candidate in 1919, and expelled from the Labour Party in 1941. Opinion polls suggest that if men alone had had the vote, Labour would have been in power throughout the period 1945 to 1979.

The National Federation of Women's Institutes was another body that was very successful with women. Founded in Canada in 1897, it was established in Britain in 1915 and became Britain's largest women's voluntary organisation. Yet, voting Conservative and joining the Women's Institute in large numbers did not delimit women's activism. The women's movement in the 1920s continued to be active, pressing for franchise extension, as well as to remove bars on female activity and to ensure equality throughout society. Under the leadership of Eleanor Rathbone, the National Union of Societies for Equal Citizenship sought by parliamentary lobbying, not the Pankhursts' militant tactics, to gain legislative goals, such as welfare benefits for married women. Women were allowed to enter the legal profession and become JPs in 1918, and were given the vote on the same basis as men in 1928, and the divorce law was liberalised in 1923 and 1937. The Matrimonial Causes Act of 1937 was the brainchild of A. P. Herbert, who was shocked at the inequality of women in divorce cases. The Act allowed women to divorce men on the grounds of desertion for three years or more; and on grounds of insanity, cruelty, adultery, rape and sodomy. Alongside attacks on birth control (and abortion) for evading motherhood, birth control was also presented more sympathetically, as in the film *Maisie's Marriage* (1923). An emphasis on the diversity of the female experience in this period helps explain why feminism was not focused on one cause, why many women were not feminists, and why activists were not only involved with causes such as trade union activity, abortion law reform, and pacifism.

The extent to which radical ideas affected social structures is unclear. Indeed, economic developments appeared more important. Sustained growth in the 1920s and the expansion of new industries, such as car making and electronics, in the inter-war period encouraged an important growth in the skilled labour force, much of it in parts of the country that had not earlier been important industrial zones, for example the car industry in Oxford. The growth rate in gross national product per head was about 1.5% in the 1920s compared with 0.4% in 1900–13. This reflected the expansion of high-productivity consumer industries, although it also owed much to recovery after wartime disruption. The division within the labour force could be seen in different responses to politics and trade unionism, for example very varied levels of support for the General Strike of 1926. The response for the latter was solid in London, most coalfield towns, and a number of other cities, including Birmingham, Hull, Liverpool, Norwich and Plymouth. The response was far weaker across much of southern England, including Portsmouth and Southampton.

A differential regional economic basis to social experience could also be seen with the Depression of the 1930s. The Slump was very pronounced in mining and heavy manufacturing areas, both of which were dependent on exports and thus affected by the downturn in the world economy, for example South Wales, North-East England and Clydeside. The shipyards on the Tyne launched 238,000 tons of shipping in 1913, but fewer than 7,000 in 1933. That was the basis of the Jarrow March of unemployed shipworkers to London in 1936, for unemployment rose greatly, to 3.4

million in 1932, about 17% of the labour force; 2.6 million jobs were created in 1933–8, but 2.2 million people were unemployed in 1938, because the numbers looking for work rose by 1.4 million, a consequence of a large expansion of the potential labour force due to the relatively high pre-war birth rate and the absence of any war in this period. Unskilled workers were particularly hard hit by unemployment, and managers and professionals far less so. The unskilled were also hit hardest by short-time working. More than a quarter of the Scottish labour force was out of work in 1931–3, as were about one-third of Derbyshire's miners. Welsh unemployment rose to 37.5% in 1932 and was over 40% in the mining and industrial heartland of Glamorgan and Monmouthshire.

In other areas, there was more prosperity. Thanks to the Morris car works at Cowley, Oxford had only 5% unemployment in 1934. The Great West Road out of London became the site of a series of spacious factories that, with their use of electricity, were very distant from the smoke-shrouded metal-bashing works of heavy industry. Aside from large-scale factories, such as those manufacturing Smiths crisps, Gillette razors and Curry's cycles, and the Hoover factory (all consumer industries), there was a host of smaller works on the Park Royal estate, and comparable development along the North Circular Road at Colindale and Cricklewood, and also in the Lea Valley to the north-east of London. An instructive contrast from 1936 was that between the unemployed workers of Palmer's shipyard at Jarrow on the Tyne, who drew attention to their plight with a march on London, and the new Carreras cigarette factory opened at Mornington Crescent in London and employing 2,600 workers. This contrast ensured that it continued to be unhelpful to think of a common working- (or middle-)class experience, and this obviously inhibited the development of class consciousness.

The expanding world of material goods reflected and sustained social contrasts, both between the middle and working class and within the latter. The spread of household electricity was especially important. The housing boom of the period meant that there were many houses which had to be equipped and decorated. The percentage of homes wired for electricity rose from 31.8 in 1932 to 65.4 in 1938, and this had an impact on electricity consumption and the purchase of electric cookers, irons, fridges, water heaters and vacuum cleaners. Such expenditure reflected, and helped to define, social differences. Whereas radios, vacuum cleaners and electric irons were widely owned, in part thanks to hire purchase, electric fridges, cookers and washing machines were largely restricted to the middle class, and were linked to an aspect of the major social divide between those who employed others and the employed, in this case, the replacement of full-time domestic servants by occasional daily help; although this meant that many middle-class housewives worked harder.

Social differences had a regional component, with ownership of electric goods, as well as of cars and telephones, and electricity consumption, higher in the South-East than in poorer areas, such as South Wales. Whether defined in terms of income or occupation, the middle class was proportionately far more important in London and the South-East than in any other region.

For the middle class, the inter-war period meant mobility, the mobility of the car, and movement to suburbia. Their values dominated society in the 1930s, whether with the popularity of suburban gardening (not the allotments of the working class), or the success of the Conservative Party, or the tone and content of the radio under the BBC, or the success of the Burton's clothing chain. This did not mean, however, that there were not other aspirations and models. However, the most important, the self-improving, often Nonconformist, skilled working class of northern industrial cities, took a battering in the 1930s (see also Chapters 12, 15). A reconceptualisation of middle-class attitudes was to be important to a new social politics in the 1940s.

# World War Two, 1939–45

Society was nationalised again, for a second world war. This nationalisation was more insistent, and came earlier in the conflict, than that in World War One, and its effects were more long-lasting. The experience of state intervention in World War One ensured that it was more effective in World War Two. War boosted the role of the state within society, and as a model for social organisation and attitudes. It was necessary to produce formidable quantities of equipment, to raise, train, clothe and equip large numbers of men, to fill their places in the workforce, and to increase the scale and flexibility of the economy. Free trade and hitherto largely unregulated industrial production were both brought under direction. The production of consumer goods was cut in order to free labour and other resources for wartime goals.

Conscription of men began in 1939 and of women in 1942. Conscription of men not only occurred earlier in the conflict than in World War One but also without the political controversy that had then characterised the issue. Many who did not serve in the armed forces in World War Two joined other military or semi-military organisations, for example becoming air-raid wardens. At its peak, the Home Guard was 1,793,000 strong. At work, overtime was made compulsory, and more married women were recruited than in World War One. The war affected all sections of society. In response to the threat of German bombing, there were mass evacuations of children from the major cities (690,000 alone from London) at the outset of the war. This was the biggest state-directed move of civilians in British history, and the cause of much disruption. Some wealthy families sent women and children overseas, mostly to North America, but this option was not available to the bulk of the population.

Bombing, evacuation, rationing, and single parenting all brought much disruption. Social mores were also affected. There was more freedom for women, because far more were employed, frequently away from home; because of an absence of partners; and, in part, because of different attitudes. In June 1943, for example, the Mass-Observation Survey, reporting on female behaviour in some London pubs, found: 'a free and easy atmosphere in which it was very easy and usual to pick up with a member of the opposite sex'. The films *Waterloo Road* (1944) and *Brief Encounter* (1945) suggested that the war was offering new possibilities for relationships between the sexes, even at the cost of marriages. A 1944 report, 'Women at Work', from the government's Wartime Social Survey, produced evidence from questionnaires that war work was popular for women, first for the pay and secondly for friendship.

The war was not only a 'total war'; the people were also told it was one. State control over the means of propaganda ensured that the greater access of the public to news, through mass literacy and the ownership of radios, helped to create national views largely in accordance with government intentions. The BBC played a major role in supporting the war effort, not least by successfully reaching outside the middle class and encouraging a sense of common experience and purpose. Radio comedy presented working-class life as in no way inferior, and wartime films were notable for their gritty realism and 'bull-dog spirit'. Cinema newsreels were also important in creating an image of a 'people's war', as were films such as *Dawn Guard* and *Millions Like Us*.

### John Maynard Keynes (1883–1946)

John Maynard Keynes was an innovative and influential Cambridge economist who pressed the case for economic management by the state in order to tackle unemployment. Rejecting the so-called classical economists, Keynes pressed for deficit financing to stimulate growth, rather than balanced budgets. His book *The General Theory of Employment, Interest and Money* (1936) became very influential from the 1940s. From the mid-1970s there was a reaction against Keynesian thought which reached its height with the monetarism of the early 1980s.

The war encouraged an inclusive notion of nationhood. A language of inclusiveness and sharing, and a stress on the home 'front', made social distinctions seem unacceptable. Rationing rested on a theory of equality. Farmers' journals, such as *Farmers Weekly*, praised wartime control, and there was little printed criticism of alleged abuses by the War Agricultural Executive Committees and their failure to allow their decisions to be subject to independent tribunals. Although the extent to which, during the war, the classes mingled, for example in work, should not be exaggerated, such mingling was stressed as a desirable goal and was more extensive than before the war, not least because of the amount of time which was spent in air-raid shelters. Wartime aspirations were focused by the Beveridge Report, an official report of December 1942, that called for the use of social insurance to abolish poverty and pressed the case for child allowances, a national health service and the end of mass unemployment. This formula for post war reconstruction encouraged the sense that the war had to lead to change. The Butler Education Act (see Chapter 2) followed in 1944, as did an *Employment Policy* White Paper that called for government action on Keynesian lines to help maintain employment. It was argued that the people should be rewarded: a people's war should be followed by a people's peace. The 1945 election, held within a short time of the defeat of Germany, was nevertheless a strange affair. The outcome was the first majority Labour government, but the electorate appears to have been primarily motivated by the desire to keep the Conservatives out. Labour's huge majority owed more to the unattractiveness of its opponents than it did to its own positive appeal (see Chapters 9, 10).

The extent to which there was a consensual and disciplined society in the 1940s has been questioned. By its very nature, such an issue is difficult to determine, but it is important because it affects any assessment both of the significance of the 1945 election and of the extent to which the new government was able to shape society. In particular, the notion that the war created an opportunity for a radical social and economic transformation that was not adequately grasped depends, in part, on the understanding of social attitudes in the period. There was certainly opposition to government policies. This came, for example, from widespread participation in the 'black market', a means to evade rationing. In rural Britain, farmers' groups resisted government direction. The Farmers and Smallholders Association opposed the War Agricultural Executive Committees (WAECs) and their power to evict farmers without review by an independent tribunal. Other groups that criticised the government included the Cheap Food League, the Council for the Reduction of Taxation, the Independent Livestock Producers Association, and the Essex Countrymen's and Gentlemen's Association. The Dispossessed Farmers and Sympathisers Association formed in 1943, which became the Farmers Rights Association, had a peak membership of 5,000–6,000 farmers and criticised the WAECs. The President of the Association, Sir Walter Blount, a Worcestershire landowner, had had land taken over by the local WAEC on the ground that it was poorly farmed. The Association was backed by two MPs. Such groups may well have reflected a more widespread hostility to regulation and regimentation, a view that undermines any stress on a united society.

# ◼ Collectivism, 1945–65

World War One had been followed by politics much as before; the 'land fit for heroes' was never delivered, and many wartime gains, especially women's, were lost. World War Two, in contrast, was followed, as noted above, by the first Labour government with a parliamentary majority, and by the policies and politics of planning, economic control and social engineering. This had major implications, not simply for the position of social groups, but also for the language of public identity and for social attitudes. The extent to which the planned wartime economy demobilised after the war was lessened by nationalisations, by the continuation of high rates of taxation (to finance the emerging welfare state), and by the continued major role of the state in the economy, including, until 1948, the allocation of raw materials. The Labour governments of 1945–51 sought to use planning to ensure full employment and growth, and thus to achieve social welfare and also demonstrate the value of state control. The welfare state (see Chapter 2) was seen as an aspect of the continued process of state control over society and economy, while nationalisation of much of the economy consolidated the trend towards national control, planning, products, conditions, pricing and wage settlements, seen by many as the path towards **collectivism**.

Some of the Labour agenda was reversed under the Conservatives in 1951–64, and the greater prosperity of that period with its stress on the consumer and on consumption was different in tone from the 1940s. Nevertheless, there were important continuities in government policies and social attitudes. What differences there were, were largely matters of emphasis rather than differences over principle. Labour supported more nationalisation, the Conservatives less. The Conservatives argued for a more selective approach towards welfare provision, Labour remained wedded to **universalism**. There was broad agreement between the two main parties over the fundamentals of social and economic policy, the existence of the welfare state, and a mixed economy of public and private concerns. This broad agreement over essentials made the period 1951–64 the high-water mark of the so-called 'post-war consensus' (see Chapter 10).

Collectivism also had a moral dimension. Public morals and popular culture had for long been policed. This policing was accentuated in the mid-twentieth century, both because fears of subversion and the disruptive consequences of **individualism** influenced attitudes to practices that were not in the accepted social mainstream, and because the emphasis on the collective effort and provision led to a hostile attitude towards those who did not accept norms. Not filling in forms or not having

**collectivism:** Belief that agricultural or industrial units should be collectively owned, with the owners sharing the work and the profits.

**universalism:** The belief that no one should be excluded from the provisions of the welfare state.

**individualism:** The belief that all people have individual rights and freedoms within society.

a fixed address was a defiance of bureaucracy, but there was also a moral policing that criminalised habits judged unacceptable, such as drug-taking. Abortion, homosexuality, prostitution and suicide were criminal offences, and consenting adults had therefore no privacy. As a result of legislation such as the Offences Against the Person Act of 1861 and the Infant Life Preservation Act of 1929, abortion was a crime that led to prosecution, and early campaigners for publicly available contraception were also prosecuted. In 1960, the House of Commons rejected the recommendations of the Wolfenden Commission for the liberalisation of the laws on homosexuality.

Restrictive divorce laws affected marriage, child care and sexuality. Censorship affected what could be read, seen and listened to. Literary merit was no defence against charges of pornography, as Penguin Books was to discover when it re-published an edition of *Lady Chatterley's Lover* in 1960 (see Chapter 15). The leisure activities of the many were regulated, whether drinking, gambling or watching television. There were permitted hours for drinking in pubs, and, in the case of gambling, no off-course cash betting. Such restrictions made criminals out of the large numbers who broke them. Corporal punishment (beating with the cane, slipper or, in Scotland, tawse) remained common in schools. Young men were brought under the sway of the state through conscription. Continued after World War Two, this was not phased out until 1957–63. The first of the 'Carry On' films, *Carry On Sergeant* (1958), focused on this universal obligation. Although capital punishment – hanging – was only imposed for murder, the ability of the legal system to deliver such a verdict contributed to the sense of a powerful state, with moral codes that it was determined to enforce. Some of this legislation would strike modern observers as reasonable, for example the 1908 Punishment of Incest Act and the attack on child pornography in the 1958 Children and Young Persons (Harmful Publications) Act, but a lot is very much that of a 'different world'. Attempts to end capital punishment were unsuccessful. The House of Lords rejected abolition in July 1956.

## ▮ Individualism after 1966

The situation changed fundamentally in the 1960s, with a stress on the individual, and on his or her ability to construct their particular world. The outcome of the *Lady Chatterley* trial, with Penguin Books acquitted of the charge of obscenity, indicated that the new decade would be a decade of change. This change rapidly followed from 1963, gathering pace thereafter. This was a period in which fashions, such as the mini-skirt and popular music, both stressed novelty. Songs and films, such as *Tom Jones* (1963) and *Darling* (1965), featured sexual independence. Hedonism focused on free will, self-fulfilment and consumerism. The last was the motor of economic consumption and growth. The net effect was a more multifaceted public construction of individual identities. This stress on individual identities did not lend itself to a classification of identity, interest and activity in terms of traditional social categories, especially class. It would, however, be misleading to ignore pressures for change in the 1950s. Indeed, images of sex played a much greater role in life in the late 1950s, not least in newspapers, novels and films, than they had done a decade earlier.

The current of change was not restricted to Britain. Youth culture, feminism, drugs, and sexual liberation were international themes, as, more generally, was anti-authoritarianism. Novel gender and youth expectations and roles commanded attention. There was also legislative action. The death penalty was abolished and racial discrimination declared illegal in 1965, while abortion was legalised in 1967 by the Abortion Act. Homosexual acts between consenting adults were legalised in 1967 by the Sexual Offences Act; although in Scotland not until 1981. Furthermore, as the age of consent for homosexual sex remained higher than for heterosexual sex, homosexuality was only partially decriminalised. The Divorce Reform Act of 1969 and the Equal Pay Act of 1970 sought to improve the position of women, although the latter excluded the large number of female part-time workers.

The hedonism and self-centredness of the Permissive Society was attacked by some critics, for example Malcolm Bradbury in his satire *The History Man* (1975), but their impact was limited. Campaigners against pornography and changing public standards, for example Lord Longford and Mary Whitehouse, were cold-shouldered or lampooned by the media, and did not succeed in winning government support. In the 1980s and early 1990s, there were attempts to reverse the libertarian trend with talk of 'family values', but the movement had scant success and even its political sponsors, the Conservative government, made only a limited effort.

# Gender

Outside the control of government, there was a whole series of social changes from the 1960s, frequently involving the breaking of past taboos. The most important related to women, and in the late 1960s, women's liberation arose as a second wave of feminism. The first British women's rights group was formed in Hull in 1968. As with other movements lacking a centralising structure, the 'women's liberation' movement was a diverse one. What was termed 'consciousness raising' was, however, a feature of much of this diversity. Conventional assumptions were widely attacked. Thus, nuclear families, the authoritarian role of men within households, and sexual subservience were all criticised. Demands for the recognition of an independent sexuality focused on heterosexual activity with an assertion of women's rights to enjoy sex, to have it before marriage without incurring criticism, and to control contraception and, thus, their own fertility. There was also pressure for more radical options. Lesbianism was affirmed, and connections opened with the gay men's movement. The 1970 national conference of the Women's Liberation Movement agreed four main demands: equal education and opportunity, equal pay, free and automatically available contraception and abortion, and widespread nursery provision. An end to discrimination against lesbians followed in 1974, as did legal and financial independence for women.

There was powerful pressure for legal change. The Abortion Act of 1967 was followed by a situation close to abortion on demand. Doctors lost their ability to control the process. The Sex Discrimination Act of 1976 had considerable impact on the treatment and employment of women. The police were encouraged to take a firmer line against wife-beating and child abuse. Aside from demands for legal changes, feminism led to pressure for changes in lifestyles and for social arrangements that put women's needs and expectations in a more central position.

Jobs and lifestyle became more important as aspirations for women, complementing, rather than replacing, home and family. The number of married women entering the job market escalated from the 1960s, and more women returned to work after having children. The percentage of working women who were married rose from 14 in 1911 to 43 in 1951 and 59 in 1970. This enormous growth in female employment, and in long-term employment at that, owed something to the full-employment policies followed from the 1940s to the 1970s. Whereas previously most women had given up work when they married, older married women entered the labour force in large numbers from the 1940s. However, as unemployment rose in the 1970s, competition with men for jobs increased.

The range of female activities expanded. The Women's Rugby Football Union was formed in 1983; the first Briton in space was Helen Sharman; in 1987, Elizabeth II amended the statutes of the most distinguished of British chivalric orders, the Order of the Garter, to permit the admission of women on terms equal to those of the Knights Companion of the Order. After considerable controversy, the first women were ordained priests in the Church of England in 1994; although the relevant dates for Nonconformist ministers and those in the Church of Scotland (1968) were earlier.

In 1975, Margaret Thatcher became the first British woman party leader, and in 1979 the first British woman Prime Minister. Her rise showed that there was no ceiling of opportunity for women. Thatcher had said that a woman would never be Prime Minister, but her determination and success proved that a woman was easily capable of the job. Conversely, other women reacted to Thatcher's policies, specifically her support for the deployment of American Cruise Missiles in Britain, by picketing the American base at Greenham Common with a women-only camp that offered a counter culture, not least to Thatcher. Thatcher's success was not matched by many other women. From 1918 to 1997 only seven of the 248 Welsh MPs were women. In the election of 1992, 18.3% of candidates and 9.2% of the MPs elected were women, a percentage lower than that in Scandinavia and Germany and higher than France. The election of 1997 led to a far more prominent role for female politicians. In large part, this was due to Labour's victory. The change in the Labour Party selection process helped lead to the election of 101 women Labour MPs. The new Labour government included five women Cabinet members and two women ministers specifically to ensure that policies were beneficial to women. The Scottish Parliament elected in 1999 had 50 female MPs and 79 male MPs.

Changes in the position of women cannot, however, be separated from other social questions. Women's identity and experience have shifted within social, economic and political contexts that have themselves altered. These contexts, whether national or local, have not been primarily structured by gender issues. For example, the economic shift from manufacturing to service industries created more opportunities for salaried work for women.

Class, generation issues, ethnic background, and political views have all been important in influencing the position and experience of women. For example, while the number of full-time male undergraduates at universities increased by 20% between 1970 and 1989, the number of women increased by 30%. This helped rectify an earlier imbalance against women. But there was also a class dimension. The greater number of women were overwhelmingly from the middle class. Among both women and men there were, especially, few students from the lowest social group: the unskilled working class. The same class dynamics was true in other fields. In golf clubs, for example, women golfers first gained entry, generally with associate membership, and then, in many cases, became full members, but the social composition remained skewed towards the middle class.

The value of increased female participation in all forms of activity is in no way lessened by this class dimension, but it has to be borne in mind. Dealing with gender inequalities does not necessarily help with the more general problems of class differences. 'Positive discrimination' in favour of hiring and promoting women in recent years has worked most to the benefit of middle-class women. As men and women tend to marry those of a similar background, especially in terms of educational attainment, a practice that can be described as endogamy (marriage within the class), the net effect of greater opportunities for women may well be a strengthening of class differences, rather than their breakdown. There are not many refuse collectors (generally dustmen) who have headmistresses as partners. Because men have usually played only a minor role in full-time child care, greater opportunities for middle-class women can be linked directly to an expansion in the number of paid domestic workers, especially child-minders. These are overwhelmingly women and most receive low salaries. There was a difference between a middle-class feminism that complained about exclusion from the middle-class workplace and a working-class counterpart that was concerned about the conditions of work (and life).

Gender was, and is, an issue for men as well as women. The loss of Empire and the end of conscription affected notions of masculinity and also gendered constructions of citizenship. Less emphasis was placed on what had been seen as masculine values, and some of these values were questioned, indeed mocked. This was part of a process of change in the images of masculinity. The decline of manual work and the growing importance of women workers also contributed to the same sense of changing, indeed, in some contexts, imperilled, masculinity. Different attitudes to homosexuality contributed powerfully to this sense.

# Race

As well as gender, ethnicity was an increasingly important theme from the 1960s. The Race Relations Act of 1965 was an attempt to include immigrants within the nation without any demand that they assimilate. The Act made it illegal to discriminate in public places, and established the Race Relations Board to tackle complaints. Housing and employment, both major spheres of serious discrimination, were excluded until the Second Race Relations Act of 1968. The latter Act also gave the Race Relations Board the ability to initiate proceedings. A third Act followed in 1976. It replaced the Race Relations Board, and the Community Relations Commission established under the Second Act to improve race relations, with the Commission for Racial Equality. This was designed to deal with general problems of discrimination, as well as individual cases. The Act also extended the provisions of the first Act against racial incitement by removing the need to prove that the accused sought to cause hatred. This legislation failed to convince many immigrants that they were not the victims of a racialist system, but it marked a major advance on the earlier situation when no such legal protection existed.

The Race Relations Acts were very different from the exclusionist arguments of the racists of the period, typified by Enoch Powell's notorious 'rivers of blood' speech of April 1968. Yet, many immigrants rapidly showed that they had no intention of being typecast and organised with reference simply to existing divisions within society. Although a much debated concept, **multi-culturalism** has given the process of self-identification within contemporary British society another dimension.

**multi-culturalism:** The ability of people from different religions and ethnic groups to take a full part in society side by side without cultural conflict.

**capitalism:** The system whereby property and the means of production are privately owned, and regulated by market forces rather than by government intervention.

The existence of ethnic divides cut across attempts to explain social structure simply in occupational terms. These divides were a matter of identity and identification, the latter an aspect of the discrimination that helped to account for higher rates of unemployment among young blacks and Asians in the 1980s and 1990s. There was also discrimination in housing, for example in East London and Liverpool, and, allegedly, in policing. Despite the passing of the Race Relations Acts, race relations in Britain continue to be a high-profile and contentious issue, as seen by the riots in largely black areas such as Brixton in the 1980s, the Stephen Lawrence case in the 1990s, together with recent conflicts between Moslems and Sikhs.

## ■ Capitalism and youth society

**Capitalism** has been another force shaping the democratisation of society and the practice of class, for, at the same time that the differing wealth and income of individuals ensures that their purchasing power varies, each is a consumer able to make his or her own purchasing decisions. This has always been true, but the marked rise in labour participation rates and in real incomes in the 1980s and 1990s left most of the population with more disposable wealth. They were therefore able to define themselves through spending, very much part of a 'we spend, therefore we are' culture.

This element of choice, and the need to shape and cater for it, have combined to ensure a whole range of social shifts. One of the most striking has been the emergence of the youth consumer, and the development of cultural and consumer fashions that reflect the dynamism and volatility of this section of the market. It is easy, when discussing youth, to focus on rock, pop and the drug culture transmitted via the Beatles and the Sex Pistols, psychedelia and punk, or to note the rise of specialised categories, such as the appeal of the all-female Spice Girls pop group as a role model for young girls in the late 1990s, or of militant action, such as the radical anti-Vietnam War demonstrators of 1968.

More important was, and is, the impact on social structure and attitudes of the widespread wish and ability of youth first to create an adolescent identity – not to be younger copies of their elders – and secondly, and more specifically, to reject the opinions of their parents; pop culture is only one manifestation of this, but it has been a particularly important manifestation ever since the 'generation gap' began to emerge in the 1950s. Pop culture reflected, in part, a desire to focus the aspirations of youth on young adults, rather than on parents. This was clearly seen in the 1960s, when the hairstyles and clothes of young performers, such as the Beatles, were widely copied. In the mid-1960s, many teenage girls copied the beehive blonde hairstyle and dark 'panda' eye makeup of the singer Dusty Springfield, who, herself, was in her mid-twenties. An emphasis on personal gratification and a decline in traditional norms led to a great increase in sexual activity among teenagers. Whereas surveys suggest that at the close of the 1950s the average age at which people began having sex was 20 for men and 21 for women, by the close of the 1990s it was 17 and, despite the ready availability of contraception, there were nearly 90,000 teenage conceptions a year, although due to abortion the number of live births was actually around 56,000, a rate of more than 20 per 1,000 girls aged 15 to 19.

The newly energetic, demanding and distinctive youth culture of the 1960s drew on new technology. Designers, such as Mary Quant, deliberately sought to appeal to a mass young clientele. Artificial fabrics were pursued more actively, leading to the use of modern plastics such as PVC (polyvinyl chlorides). The colours and shapes of clothes became bolder, as did jewellery. Trousers became more acceptable for women. Many dressed like men, in denim jeans, and with similar hairstyles. Others wore mini-skirts that would have been regarded as totally unacceptable by their parents. Fashions changed rapidly, reflecting the mass market of modern consumer society and the concern of youth culture with youth. The dominant theme was fashion appeal, not durability, nor other utilitarian goals. From another perspective, in keeping with much of modern society, consumerism had become the utilitarian end.

The willingness to try different foods, to holiday in different places, to move away from parental religious preferences, to go on to higher education, or to purchase property, were all part of the same process. So, also, possibly, were the subcultures of youth violence that attracted considerable attention in the late 1950s and early 1960s and, again, becoming associated with football hooliganism, in the 1980s and 1990s. The willingness and determination of the young to redefine themselves, frequently in opposition to their parents, has greatly affected society. It is probably the most important means of social change, more so than alterations in attitude and income by individuals later in life or in 'adulthood'. Social and geographical mobility increasingly focuses on higher education, as above half the population now undertakes some form of further education and, thereafter, most do not return to become copies of their parents.

# Social trends at the end of the century

## The growth of the middle class

The relationship between economic developments and changes in society, with the particular focus on the transition period of youth can be particularly seen in the major expansion of the middle class that has been such a marked feature of the last three decades of the twentieth century. In 1900, 75% of the labour force were manual workers. By 1974, the percentage had fallen to 47, by 1991 to 36. The manufacturing base has declined and the nature of much of the work in it has become more skilled, while the service sector has grown. This transition was true even of heavy manufacturing towns. In 1901, 15.2% of the inhabitants of Newcastle were employed in shipbuilding and engineering, but over the century manufacturing industry became less important in the city and the region. In the late 1970s, the largest employers in Newcastle were the City Council, the Department of Health and Social Security, the Area Health Authority and the University.

The shift to services affected both male and female workers. Women outnumbered men in the service sector, especially in health, shops and catering. Female employment in traditional manufacturing sectors such as textiles, declined, while 'white blouse' jobs, such as banking, teaching, and office work, grew in importance. For men, white collar has replaced blue collar. Average incomes for those in work have risen appreciably, ensuring that, whether they think of themselves as working class or not, much of the working population can afford a lifestyle associated with middle-class occupations.

This change has affected many of the collectivist responses that carried class meanings, especially political and trade-union affiliation. The decline of the working class hit the Labour Party, and, in order to gain power in 1997, its leader, Tony Blair, deliberately set out to reposition the party as 'New Labour', as a means to win over the middle class (see Chapter 10). Trade union membership fell: the Trades Union Congress had more than 12 million members in 1979, fewer than 8 million in 1992. Rising home ownership was another aspect of social change as a characteristic of the working class had been that they lacked property. By the late 1980s three-quarters of trade unionists owned their home (see Chapter 4). The overwhelming majority also had bank or building society accounts, and many became shareholders, either thanks to the privatisations of state companies in the 1980s or due to the floating of building societies as public companies on the stock market in the late 1990s. These social changes affected traditional working-class culture. Thus, working men's clubs lost members in the 1990s, under the pressure of more social mobility, increased leisure activities, and their failure to offer much to women or the young.

The combination of changes hitherto discussed for the last third of the century not only remoulded social structures. They also radically altered the understanding of class. Both middle- and working-class assumptions about behaviour – their own and that of others, and how it placed people socially and exemplified (different) values – were challenged. In Daisy Ashford's *The Young Visiters*, a work written in the early 1890s and eventually published in 1919, Mr Salteena, the unsuccessful suitor of Ethel Monticue, is put down as 'not quite a gentleman'. In response, he goes to stay with the earl of Clincham in order to learn how to behave like one.

Such a world still had a powerful grip in the 1950s, as captured so convincingly by John Osborne in his play *Look Back in Anger* (1956). In Osborne's play, what made the central character, the anti-hero Jimmy Porter, so angry was the limits to social mobility in class-ridden Britain. Despite his university education, Jimmy would never be able to escape his working-class background. That was why he chose to run a stall, rather than accept a form of employment which his educational qualifications would allow him to undertake. This was a world which lost its power to unleash such scathing anger. To move from the 1950s to the 1960s is to move from the world of Jimmy Porter to the world of Alfie. For Alfie, played memorably by Michael Caine in the 1966 film, women, clothes and cars were commodities which proved that one could get on in the world without the privileges of birth and education. Alfie's determination to enjoy life to the full gave him no time to be angry.

## The prosperous and the underclass

The structure of society is now, in so far as economic factors take precedence, essentially defined by a prosperity that encompasses the majority. Its basic lineaments for the foreseeable future are of a capitalist, consumerist, individualist, mobile, predominantly secular and urban, property-owning democracy. This was very much a national picture. Compared with earlier in the century, national broadcasting, state education and employment, nationwide companies, unions, products and pastimes, have all brought a *measure* of convergence that can be seen in the decline of dialect and of distinctive regional practices such as cooking. There were variations to the basic lineaments just sketched. For example, massive feudal landownership has remained important in Scotland outside the Central Belt right up to the present day, but most people, both in Scotland and elsewhere, no longer lived in such a context.

More generally, the decline of the aristocracy robbed the upper class of symbols of difference. Instead, the wealthy professionals who have benefited from the expansion of the City of London and mostly live in South-East England were/are able to present themselves as middle class and thus apparently lessen the presence of class division; although there were still major differences in opportunity between social groups.

There is also, however, what was increasingly termed in the 1990s the underclass. Large numbers of beggars appeared on the streets, especially in London. The closure of mental hospitals created problems, as the alternative policy of 'care in the community' proved inadequate. Cases of tuberculosis among the homeless rose, as did the number of homeless themselves: parts of London rapidly became a 'cardboard city', as the number of inhabitants who slept rough, usually teenagers who had left home to look for work or to escape parental pressure, increased. The percentage of 16- to 17-year-olds neither in work nor in full-time education doubled from 5% to 10% in 1989–96. Over 20% of 18–25-year-olds had not registered to vote in 1992. 'Travellers' posed difficulties for local authorities. Poverty and despair were also present in run-down industrial areas, for example Sheffield as captured in the film *The Full Monty* (1997).

The so-called underclass was not a new problem. There are parallels between late twentieth-century ideas of the underclass and late nineteenth-century notions of the residuum. Concern over poverty had led to rising levels of income support that, by 1970, were providing for nearly 8% of the population. Some of the 'underclass', however, were not catered for by such support. In 1997, the new Labour government of Tony Blair made the ending of social exclusion its prime domestic policy objective. One of Blair's first acts as Prime Minister was to visit the Aylesbury Housing Estate in Southwark, South London, on 2 June 1997. A new, Cabinet Office-based, Social Exclusion Unit was established. Both the Major and the Blair governments sought to deal with the problem of young people sleeping rough. However, by defining citizenship in terms of participation in the labour market, for example through its 'welfare to work' scheme, it was unclear whether the Blair government would be able to find an answer to the age-old problem of poverty. Rather, the problem was posed, and answered (or possibly marginalised), in a different form.

## Classification

The question of classification thus arises for the 1980s and 1990s. Should the basic typology be of a broad propertied stratum and a disadvantaged underclass, or is it more appropriate to highlight contrasts among the propertied? While it is true that the working class as a whole ate less well, had poorer health and housing, more children, lower expectations, and less access to higher education than the middle class, how far was this because those termed the underclass were included in the working class for purposes of analysis? A different typology was offered by Will Hutton in his very influential left-wing critique of Conservative Britain, *The State We're In* (1995). Hutton suggested that Britain is a 20:40:40 society; 20% of the population are seen as rich and without fears; 40% have enjoyed none or little of the great economic growth of the 1980s – they are casual or poorly-paid workers, single mothers and the long-term unemployed; the other 40%, although relatively affluent when in work, live in fear of unemployment and house forfeitures. Indeed, many of the middle class experienced periods of unemployment and hardship in the recessions

**monetarism:** The belief that the economy can be regulated by the control of the money supply.

**deregulation:** The lifting of government restrictions, in order to encourage competition.

**full employment:** The belief that everyone who is able to work should be able to find a job – it will never be 100 per cent because there will always be some people moving between jobs.

of the early 1980s and early 1990s. Hutton's book is very much a critique of Thatcherism, but, more than that, it is also a critique of the social consequences of longer-run Conservatism, and of Conservative control of financial and political institutions. Hutton argues that, since the nineteenth century, too much has been invested in quick returns (the shareholder over the waged worker; dividends over wages) at the expense of long-term investment. He sees this as the reason for economic malaise, as well as the dynamic underlying social divisions.

In addition, the question of classification and analysis confronts the difficulty that society was/is not static. Economic shifts and government policy have greatly contributed to this volatility. Until the 1970s, there was a strong labour market for skilled and semi-skilled workers and many jobs for the unskilled, but extensive de-industrialisation since has reduced opportunities for unskilled labour. The real income of the bottom 10% increased by 10% in 1973–91, although the top 10% gained 55%, a reflection of the strong demand for educated labour. The bottom tenth of manual workers earned only 64% of average income in 1991. Thus the differentiation within the workforce linked to skills rose greatly. Differences in disposable wealth were related to other financial indices, such as savings and house prices. In 1999, it was claimed that half the adult population had less than £200 in savings. Differences in disposable wealth were also linked to variations in consumption patterns, such as car ownership and tourism. Some of these variations were a matter not only of quality of life, but also of life safety indices. This was true not so much of health insurance, as of the ability to keep homes warm, which is especially important for the elderly, and other comparable indices.

The impact of the Conservative policies of **monetarism, deregulation**, privatisation, and the abandonment of the goal of **full employment** in the 1980s and 1990s, exacerbated economic strains and the accompanying social differences. For example, council-house sales under the 'Right to Buy' legislation of the 1980 Housing Act were widespread, but skewed. The better housing in the wealthier areas sold, while the public sector increasingly became 'sink housing', rented by those who suffered relative deprivation. Thus, in Newcastle, there were above average sales of council houses in the western and northern estates, and below average sales of those along the river and in the east. Other cities had similar trends.

Even if agreed criteria for classification exist, there are still problems with accumulating and assessing the necessary information for analysis. Frequent surveys and the massive amount of information available to government bodies and private-sector marketing agencies ensured that more data was, and is, available in, and for, the twentieth century than for any previous age. The significance of what was measured, however, was, and is, a matter for profound disagreement, as indicated, for example, by the bitter controversy in the 1990s about the impact of single parenthood. These issues are likely to become more complex due to the process of convergence within the European Union. It is increasingly likely that Union-wide criteria are advanced and/or adopted and that the British will have to become used to being classified in this fashion. For example, the British rates of property and pension ownership are very high by European standards, and a class analysis based heavily on these would put many into the middle class who might not be used, or even wish, to see themselves in that light. That then raises the question of how far self-image is crucial to social identification, and, thus, classification. As television is central to the process by which many today identify themselves and learn how to articulate their identification, it is possible that commentators should search there, at what we watch, who watches what, and how often, for social classification.

## Summary

◆ Social classification is always a vexed problem. A class-based analysis that focuses on income and/or occupation has to confront other ways in which people identify themselves. Some of these ways can be accommodated in such an analysis, but frequently such an approach is unconvincing.

◆ During the century the working class had declined proportionately and numerically as the middle class greatly expanded. This process was particularly important in the second half of the century. It was linked to major changes in the economy, especially the expansion of the service sector.

◆ Gender has been one of the major themes of the century. Earlier notions and practices of gender order, relationships and control, all of which privileged male views, were strongly challenged from the outset of the century. Gender became more important as an issue from the 1960s, but gender does not necessarily subvert class-based analyses, especially because of differential opportunities for women of different backgrounds.

◆ The rise of youth culture increased social fluidity and is important to our understanding of change. Youth had more purchasing power and self-consciousness, and was less willing to consider itself as proto-adulthood.

◆ In the 1980s and 1990s, the basic distinction appears to be between the propertied and the underclass. The former encompasses much of the working class, and thus throws into focus the deficiencies of the classic class-based analysis. Possibly a new one is required.

## Questions for discussion

◆ What is the relationship between shifts in society and changes in methods of social classification?

◆ How useful is a class-based analysis for considering British society in the twentieth century?

◆ What was the impact of female emancipation?

◆ How has 'youth culture' become distinctive and how has it transformed society?

◆ What were the consequences of social changes for British politics? (See also Chapters 8–10.)

◆ What were the consequences of social changes for British culture? (See also Chapter 15.)

◆ What were the consequences of social changes for religious observance, and both egalitarian and libertarian ideas? (See also Chapter 7.)

## ■ Further reading

Benson, John, *The Working Classes in Britain, 1850–1939* (London, 1989).

Bock, G., and Thane, P., *Maternity and Gender Policies: Women and the Rise of the European Welfare States, 1880s–1950s* (London, 1991).

Bourke, Joanna, *Working-Class Cultures in Britain, 1890–1960: Gender, Class and Ethnicity* (London, 1994).

Braybon, Gail, and Summerfield, Penny, *Out of the Cage: Women's Experiences in Two World Wars* (London, 1987).

Briggs, Asa, *A Social History of England* (3rd edn, London, 1999).

Bruley, Sue, *Women in Britain since 1900* (London, 1999).

Cannadine, David, *The Decline and Fall of the British Aristocracy* (New Haven, 1990).

Hall, Lesley, *Sex, Gender and Social Change in Britain since 1880* (London, 2000).

Hargreaves, John, *Sport, Power and Culture: A Social and Historical Analysis of Popular Sports in Britain* (Cambridge, 1986).

Harrison, Brian, *Prudent Revolutionaries: Portraits of British Feminists between the Wars* (Oxford, 1987).

Hirst, David, *Welfare and Society, 1832–1991* (London, 1999).

Holt, Richard, *Sport and the British: A Modern History* (Oxford, 1989).

Hutton, Will, *The State We're In* (London, 1995).

Law, Cheryl, *Suffrage and Power: The Women's Movement, 1918–1928* (London, 1999).

Marwick, A., *British Society since 1945* (London, 1982).

Mason, Tony, *Sport in Britain* (London, 1988).

Miles, Andrew, *Social Mobility in Nineteenth- and Early Twentieth-Century England* (London, 1999).

Nicholas, Siân, *The Echo of War: Home Front Propaganda and the Wartime BBC, 1939–45* (Manchester, 1996).

Perkin, Harold, *The Rise of Professional Society: England since 1880* (London, 1989).

Pugh, Martin, *Women and the Women's Movement in Britain, 1914–1959* (London, 1992).

Rose, Nikolas, *The Psychological Complex: Psychology, Politics and Society in England, 1869–1939* (London, 1985).

Stevenson, John, *British Society, 1914–45* (London, 1984).

Taylor, P. M. (ed.), *Britain and the Cinema in the Second World War* (London, 1988).

Thom, Deborah, *Nice Girls and Rude Girl: Women Workers in World War One* (London, 1999).

Thompson, F. M. L. (ed.), *The Cambridge Social History of Britain, 1750–1950*, 3 vols (Cambridge, 1990).

# Beliefs and Ideologies

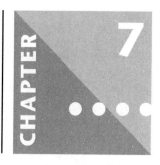

# CHAPTER 7

'Man does not live by bread alone.' Quite. Beliefs and ideologies are important, but there is a terrible tendency to neglect them, either by treating them as essentially a response to socio-economic conditions and pressures, or by assuming that they have been roughly similar throughout the twentieth century. This chapter questions both assumptions and seeks to probe the world of belief.

## Key issues

▶ How has the religious life of the country changed?

▶ Why have the Established Churches declined?

▶ What has been the impact of religion?

▶ What have been the dominant secular (non-religious) ideologies?

▶ Why has Britain not had a Christian Democratic party?

▶ How influential has Socialism been?

## Victorian background

The background to the twentieth century was far from static. Indeed, it is arguable that there were fewer changes in British religion in the seventy-five years from 1900 than in the previous seventy-five. As Britain became a more industrial and urban society, it also became a more secular society, although industrialisation was also linked to religious revival in some areas. Religion lost its central role in everyday life, and church attendance began to decline: developments which were to become more marked during the twentieth century.

The 1820s had seen the dismantling of much of the legal privilege of Establishment (official status as the state church) for the Anglican Church in England, Wales and Ireland and the Presbyterian Church in Scotland (the Church of Scotland). The repeal of the Test and Corporation Acts in 1828, and Catholic Emancipation the following year, were not the last blows. Instead, as with the First Reform Act, they were followed by a series of challenges. The political, religious, intellectual, and educational authority of the Established Churches came under pressure. The challenge came from a number of directions, from social and economic change, from other faiths, and from government. The first led to major population moves, particularly the expansion of industrial cities, that tested the existing ecclesiastical structure. In many cases, there were insufficient church buildings, or the mission of the churches did not strike a response with people who were adapting to a rapidly altering society. Nevertheless, there was also a powerful movement of Church reform from the 1830s. Committed clerics sought to make Christian teaching more accessible. 'Slum priests' took the Church's message to the urban poor. Anglican Church interiors were rebuilt in order to replace box pews, which belonged to families, with rows of identical, open pews, most of which were rent-free and open to all. The Church of England's control of the public schools helped extend its influence.

The Church of England encountered particular difficulties in those parts of the country that were developing fastest. The rise of Dissent (Protestant Nonconformity) between 1790 and 1850 was a problem, especially in Wales and northern England. The re-emergence of 'public' Catholicism, with the re-establishment of the Catholic hierarchy in England in 1850, and in Scotland in 1878, caused tension. This was accentuated by massive Irish immigration in 1845–8, the years of the potato famine. Between 1850 and 1910, 1,173 Catholic churches were opened in England and Wales, the largest number in London and Lancashire. Not only did variants of Anglicanism become 'respectable' as Nonconformity gained ground, but 'unbelief' also gained respectability through the development of Darwinism.

The changing role of government also challenged the Established Churches. The role of the parish in education and social welfare declined in favour of new government agencies. Municipal and county government was better able than the churches to channel and implement the aspirations of society for reform and control.

## Religion and politics

There was also criticism of the very idea of an Established Church, and this became an important political issue and a cause of division between the political parties. Church issues were linked to the control and funding of education, matters of great contention. Liberals pressed for disestablishment from the 1860s. The Church of Ireland was disestablished by Gladstone in 1869, and in Wales there were bitter political disputes over disestablishment throughout the rest of the century and beyond. Welsh Liberals were also strongly opposed to Church schools, especially to measures to provide public assistance to them. The 1902 Act compelling finance from the rates for Church schools, passed by a Conservative government, led to the 'Welsh Revolt', as County Councils refused to implement it. Opposition was not limited to Wales. By the time the Conservative government fell in late 1905, there had been 65,000 prosecutions for non-payment. Much bitterness was caused by the hundred imprisonments and the 3,000 property auctions to pay the rates; and the entire episode indicated the depth of anger that disputes linked to religion could generate. They were not restricted to Ireland. A Liberal government finally pushed through Welsh disestablishment in 1914, although, with the intervention of war, it was not implemented until 1920, by which time the issue had lost its potency in Wales. No fewer than 217 Bills on religious subjects were introduced in Parliament between 1880 and 1913.

At this point Britain was still very much a Christian country, although, since Catholic Emancipation in 1829, it had ceased to be a confessional state (unlike the

Republic of Ireland, once independent, which was to remain one until the 1980s). Although Jewish immigration became important in the late nineteenth century, leading to an upsurge in anti-Semitism, the vast bulk of the population remained Christian, and most subscribed at the very least to the formal requirements of Christian living. The major Christian sects still had much life in them. They were energetically building new churches in an effort to reach out to new congregations. Furthermore, there was extensive improvement to existing buildings. Far more effort was devoted to training clerics than had been the case in the eighteenth century. Attention was also devoted to organisation. New dioceses were created. Chelmsford was selected in 1913 for the new cathedral for Essex. Derby became a diocese in 1914, and Portsmouth as late as 1926.

The Established Churches remained close to the Establishment, although there could be tensions between radically minded Anglicans from the social elite, and the Conservative Party, with Socialists such as Conrad Noel and Hewlett Johnson ('the Red Dean of Canterbury', 1931–63) becoming well-known to the public. Some leading Conservatives were prominent Anglicans, mostly High Church, and, indeed, Churchill's nickname for Lord Halifax was 'The Holy Fox'. After the General Strike of 1926, the Party Conference helped push Baldwin into passing the anti-trade-union Trades Disputes Act of 1927. The Conservatives did not take kindly to Randall Davidson, Archbishop of Canterbury 1903–28, who joined with the Free Church leaders in order to seek reconciliation, not the victimisation of workers who had fallen foul of management. Furthermore, although Nonconformity was important to Liberalism and Labour, it would be misleading to ignore the number of Anglicans among both movements. George Lansbury, Labour leader 1932–5, was a devout Anglican. Christian Socialism was an important strand in Labour thought. There was no equivalent in Britain to the stress on common Catholic values that characterised inter-war elections in Eire.

# The decline of religion

At the end of the twentieth century, most Britons saw themselves as Christians, but, for many, their religion was not central to their life. The Church of England was hit by a strong current of secularism and scepticism in society. As it sought to minister to all, rather than simply the committed, the Church of England was more affected by general developments in society, although the Church of Scotland was not hit to the same extent by the same problems. Instead, its share of Scotland's population remained roughly constant, showing, if anything, a slight rise between 1900 and the mid-1920s. The (Anglican) Church of Wales, which had been disestablished in 1920, also saw its number of communicants rise in the inter-war period.

During World War One, widespread disruption affected established practices, including church-going, throughout Britain, and the war sapped confidence in the divine purpose, but there seems to have been a recovery in at least nominal church attendance thereafter. In the inter-war years, however, the Established Churches continued to find it difficult to reach out successfully to the bulk of the industrial working class. Much of this group was indifferent to, or alienated from, all churches. The Catholics were most successful. Their number rose from 2.2 million in 1910 to 3.0 million in 1940. In contrast, in the inter-war period, the numbers of Methodists, Baptists, Congregationalists, and Welsh Presbyterians all fell, as did the number of

Scottish Episcopalians after a peak in membership in about 1920. The Church of England had scant change in membership, but, given the rise of population, this was an important proportional decline.

The most influential clergyman of the inter-war years, William Temple, Bishop of Manchester 1921–9, Archbishop of York 1929–42, and of Canterbury 1942–4, sought to reverse the decline of organised religion, and to make England an Anglican nation again, and thus justify the Church of England's claim to speak for it. Temple offered a synthesis of Christianity with modern culture in works such as *Mens Creatrix* (1917), *Christus Veritas* (1924), and *Christianity and Social Order* (1942). At times, Temple, who viewed welfare as representing Christian social values, was seen as left-wing, but it was a label he would have denied. Although he strengthened the Church, Temple failed to give England a more clearly Christian character. Furthermore, Temple's inspiration of the already developing role of the Church as a voice of social criticism and concern led to it being seen increasingly in a secular light. This was despite major efforts to keep religion central to society and to public life.

Church-based societies became less important, both for the young and for their elders. Poverty helped lead many to question Church teachings; although many of the poor did find meaning and support in faith. Religious ideas were important in popular moral codes, and in public traditions, even for those who lacked faith. The Established Churches were more successful in catering to a middle-class constituency, not least because of the important role they left for middle-class socialising and female 'voluntarism' (voluntary service).

This contrast remained apparent after World War Two. During World War Two, there was a fall in denominational membership, especially of the Church of England. The 1950s, however, were not a period of obvious crisis. Church attendance ebbed, for both the Church of England and the Methodists, but not greatly, and the Catholic Church and the Church of Scotland remained strong. Elizabeth II's coronation in 1953 was very much an Anglican ceremonial, and there were signs of vitality, including the building of a new Coventry cathedral, the construction of churches in New Towns and other newly-built neighbourhoods, and the popularity of Billy Graham's evangelical missions and of the theological writings of C. S. Lewis, such as *The Screwtape Letters* (1942) and his spiritual autobiography, *Surprised by Joy* (1955).

From the 1960s, the Established Churches were hit by the general social currents particular to that period, especially the decline of deference, patriarchal authority, social paternalism, the nuclear family, and respect for age. Divorce reform had prefigured this shift, for the Matrimonial Causes Act of 1937 had loosened matrimonial ties and sought to make men and women equal. The permissive 'social' legislation of the 1960s and later, such as the decriminalisation of homosexual acts between consenting adults in England and Wales with the Sexual Offences Act of 1967, changes in divorce legislation, and the granting of equal rights to illegitimate children, flew in the face of Church teachings, and left the Church confused and apparently lacking in 'relevance'. This was especially serious for an age that placed more of an emphasis on present-mindedness than on continuity with historical roots and teachings. Belief in orthodox Christian theology, especially on the nature of Jesus, and in the after-life, the last judgement, and the existence of hell, lessened. Absolute and relative numbers of believers fell rapidly, especially for the Church of England, the Church of Scotland, and the Methodists. The issue of relevance was raised in 1963 in *Honest to God*, a widely-read book by John Robinson, Anglican Bishop of Woolwich, that sought to address the inability of the Church to cater for many, especially in run-down urban areas, by pressing the need for a determination to respond that would include a new liturgy. Cranmer's Prayerbook English was criticised as antiquated, and was replaced by a series of new liturgies.

The Church of England did manage to reassert its moral authority, and its continued allegiance to some sort of social gospel, albeit momentarily, during the 1980s. The report it published in 1985 on the problems facing the inner cities, *Faith in the City*, made a considerable impact. Government policies were lambasted for laying waste to the cities. However, the response of the Thatcher government to the report, dismissing its supposed 'Marxist' leanings, highlighted the difficulties which the Established Churches had in finding a role in an increasingly secular society. The roots of Thatcherism in part lay in a Nonconformity that was hostile to an Anglicanism which was perceived as too strongly connected to 'consensus politics'. Thatcher saw the Church as wedded to consensus and conciliation. Her call for 'Victorian values' did not extend to a leading role for clerics, many of whom were disenchanted by what they saw as an excessive stress on individualism and economic gain. This gap between Church and State was not, however, restricted to the Conservatives. It was found across the political spectrum and also reflected general social values. Furthermore, the public perception of the Church, as captured on television or in plays such as David Hare's *Racing Demon* (1990), was frequently critical. The Church of England certainly could not readily generate respect. Instead, it appeared divided and unsure of itself. Christianity was also satirised, as in the film *Monty Python's Life of Brian* (1979).

The Established Churches also had to confront challenges from within the world of religion. They were affected by other Christian churches, by traditional non-Christian faiths, and by new cults. In the first case, the greater success of the Catholic Church in retaining the loyalty of its flock and its greater religiosity, at least as measured by church attendance, was a particular reproach in the 1980s and 1990s, although the Catholic Church's hold over many of its communicants was lessened by widespread hostility towards the ban on artificial methods of contraception in the 1968 papal encyclical *Humanae Vitae*. Furthermore, much of the Catholic clergy proved unresponsive to lay initiatives. Hopes of ecumenical rapprochement with the Catholic Church were chilled by the attitude of Pope John Paul II, who treated the Church of England as very much a lesser creed, while the decision to ordain women to the priesthood in the Church of England in 1992 (implemented in 1994) led some traditionalist Anglicans to join the Catholic Church, which rejected female ordination.

The attitude of the traditionalists reflected longstanding tensions within the Church of England, and the difficulty of accommodating differences in a society increasingly ready to reject such accommodation. Liberal Anglican theologians fell foul both of Evangelical and of High-Church Anglicans. In reality, this liberal tradition is one that dates back (at least) three centuries, and emerges from time to time. In 1984, one such theologian, David Jenkins, became Bishop of Durham. His unorthodox views on the Virgin birth and the bodily resurrection of Jesus caused great controversy. When, that year, York Minster, where he had been consecrated, was struck by lightning, this was seen by some Evangelical critics as divine judgement. It was not only the Church of England that was in serious difficulties. The Nonconformist churches were also affected by a decline in faith. The number of Baptists for example, fell from 300,000 in 1970 to 230,000 in 1992, and the number of young believers was particularly hit.

The Established Churches were also challenged by the rise of 'fundamentalist'

Christianity, inspired from America. This focused on a direct relationship between God and worshipper, without any necessary intervention by clerics and without much, if any, role for the sacraments. Certain aspects of this Christianity, especially its charismatic quality, epitomised by the American evangelical Billy Graham, appealed to some Anglicans, creating tensions within the Church of England. The Christian tradition also became more diverse, as a consequence of the participatory character of worship introduced by immigrants from the West Indies. In addition, non-Trinitarian religions (that do not regard Jesus as the Son of God), such as the Christadelphians and Jehovah's Witnesses, grew in popularity in the 1980s and 1990s. The long-established Mormons had 90,000 members in Britain in 1970 and 150,000 in 1992.

Traditional non-Christian faiths had less of an appeal to Christians. Instead, they essentially catered for immigrant groups and their descendants: their logic was ethnic and exclusive. This was true of Jews, Muslims and Sikhs, particularly the first and the last. Judaism was seen as a religion for those who were ethnically Jewish. All three were also affected by the increasingly sceptical and secular nature of society. Islam, however, benefited greatly from its strong presence in large communities of Muslims and from fresh currents of immigration. Although these faiths converted very few Christians, and, indeed, apart from Muslims, did not seek to do so, they greatly challenged the Christian churches, because they claimed that Britain was a multi-cultural society, and that Christianity, therefore, should not enjoy what were presented as special privileges. Initially, such claims were not pushed. Indeed, the first major such group, the Jews, were essentially concerned to achieve a safe position, and to lessen or avoid anti-Semitism, rather than to challenge the Christian nature of society. The number of Jews rose from about 300,000 in 1920 to about 450,000 in the 1960s, before falling, largely due to intermarriage, to about 350,000 in 1988 and maybe 300,000 in 1993.

The situation changed greatly in the 1980s as multi-culturalism was pushed actively, especially on behalf of Islam. The alleged blasphemy of Salman Rushdie's novel *The Satanic Verses* (1988) created an important controversy in 1989, because Islamic figures were outraged that Christianity, but not Islam, enjoyed protection under the blasphemy laws; not, though, that the churches had much recourse to them. There were numerous demonstrations against the book in 1989, and in 1992 the controversy led to the first meeting of the (self-selected) Muslim Parliament of Great Britain. Having been 250,000 strong in 1970 and 400,000 in 1975, the number of Muslims in the country doubled between 1980 and 1995, rising to 1.2 million. In 1993, there were also 0.3 million Sikhs and 0.32 million Hindus, although the number of those in ethnic communities was not necessarily a measure of religious practice. The first Hindu temple in London was opened as late as 1962. At Neasden in north London, the largest Hindu temple outside India opened in 1997. These figures represented a very rapid increase. There had been only about 50,000 Hindus in Britain in 1970 and only about 75,000 Sikhs. Thus, whereas, in 1970, Jews had outnumbered Hindus, Muslims and Sikhs combined by about 450,000 to 375,000, by 1975 the figures had already changed to 450,000 to 615,000, and by 1993, they were closer to 300,000 to 1,620,000. This very much altered the content and perception of the non-Christian religious life of Britain.

The challenge to Christianity from cults was very different in character. It was not new. Spiritualism, for example, had been popular in the late Victorian period and enjoyed a marked revival in popularity and prestige during World War One. Both 'new age' religions and Buddhism appealed from the 1960s to many who would otherwise have been active Christians. They proved better able than the churches to capture the enthusiasm of many who wished to believe amidst a material world where faith had become just another commodity. The popularity of cults was also a reflection of the atomisation of a society that now placed a premium on individualism and on personal responses. Such a society was peculiarly unsuited to the coherence and historical basis of doctrine, liturgy, practice and organisation that was characteristic of the churches.

This begs the question of whether the earlier decline of religious practice and belief had not itself permitted the development of just such a society, rather than the society causing a decline. In part, it is necessary to stress the diversity of the 1960s and subsequent decades, and to note our limited knowledge and understanding of popular religion and what is termed folk belief. It is unclear, for example, how best to understand the popularity of astrology, and in particular, how far this was an aspect of a magical or non-Christian religious worldview. Christianity did not collapse; it declined, and there were still many committed Christians, as well as a large number of conforming non-believers.

By the 1990s, only one in seven Britons was an active member of a Christian church, although more claimed to be believers: generally over two-thirds. Both for most believers and for the less or non-religious, faith became less important not only to the fabric of life but also to many of the turning points of individual lives, especially dying and death. Events such as marriage ceremonies and baptisms became less important as occasions for displays of family and social cohesion. This was due to the simple fact that more couples were choosing to live together and more parents were choosing not to have their children baptised. A disproportionately high percentage of those who attended church were women, middle-aged, and middle class. Furthermore, it is difficult to blame the Church of England without noting that religious observance also declined throughout the western Christian world outside the United States. In Eire (the Republic of Ireland), there were legal and political battles over divorce, homosexuality, abortion and contraception as the authority of the Church was contested.

Yet, the decline was certainly stronger in England than in Northern Ireland or Eire, Scotland, or the USA. In the late 1990s, 10% of the English population had been in a church in the previous month, but the percentages for Scotland and Northern Ireland were 16 and 52 respectively. In terms both of levels of faith and of church attendance, 35% of the Scottish population were church members. In Northern Ireland, communities were and are more tight-knit and religion is a

## Box 7.1

### Future societies

Part of the debate over ideologies was fought out through competing visions of the future. One of the most powerful, a warning about the dangers of the cult of technological progress without a moral framework, was provided by Aldous Huxley's novel *Brave New World* (1932): ' "Stability," said the Controller, "Stability. No civilization without social stability. No social stability without individual stability . . . Hence all this." With a wave of his hand he indicated . . . the huge buildings of the Conditioning Centre . . . "Fortunate boys . . . No pains have been spared to make your lives emotionally easy – to preserve you, so far as that is possible, from having emotions at all." '

**secular ideologies:** Belief
systems and philosophies that
are not based on religion.

crucial expression of community identity. This is not true of England, but religious observance is also less pronounced in England than in other societies where it is less important for community identity.

This has been the case now for several decades, and is likely to continue to be so in the next century. The change can be perceived in different ways. It can be argued that secularism is a sign of an advanced society or, alternatively, or in addition, that it is a cause of an atomisation of social mores and practices that has destructive consequences. Good or bad, it is worth reiterating that the secularisation of society was one of the major trends from the 1960s. The failure in the 1990s of the 'Keep Sunday Special' campaign, heavily backed by the Established Churches, to prevent shops from opening on the sabbath, confirmed this general trend.

# Secular Ideologies

The debate over the decline of religious commitment interacts with the question as to how far **secular ideologies** have provided a sense of identity, value and purpose to individuals and the community. Like all important questions about modern society, this is one that can be answered differently by commentators, and indeed, and as valuably, by readers. It is therefore terribly tempting to avoid such a controversial issue, in favour of the safer pastures of the succession of ministries or such like topics. However, to do so would be both to neglect an important topic and, more generally, to slight much of the value of history, namely the extent to which it can lead us to ask informed questions of our present world and to see ourselves in the continuum of past, present and future.

## Reform

Secular ideologies this century have tended to depend on the notion of progress and the improvability of mankind, and have thus rejected the Christian lapsarian view of mankind. Although they have varied in their political, economic, social and cultural analyses and prescriptions, such ideologies have shared a belief that it is possible and necessary to improve the lot of humanity, or at least life in Britain, and that such a goal gives meaning to politics and society. In short, reform has been seen as a goal in itself, and progress has been seen as being attainable. Evolutionary change was held to be the hallmark of the British political system, as exemplified by the staggered process of franchise reform in the nineteenth century, and social welfare reform in the twentieth. There has been only limited support for continuity and stability, as opposed to reform, as public goals; and for an institution or government to pledge itself to inaction has been unthinkable. This reflects the major role of the state in the economy and in social welfare, but far more has been, and is, involved. Commitment to change rested on powerful ideological currents, rather than on prudential considerations, although these were clearly important as well, as in any political system which allows governments to be voted in and out of office at regular intervals. This was seen very clearly in 1945–51, 1970–4 and 1979–90 when the Labour governments of Clement Attlee and the Conservative governments of Edward Heath and Margaret Thatcher, although very different in political outlook, were all pledged to change. Thus reform, as means and goal, has been the foremost secular ideology of the century and there is no sign that this will change.

### Edward Heath (1916–   )

Edward Heath was born in Broadstairs and educated at Chatham House School in Ramsgate and then at Balliol College, Oxford. He was Conservative MP for Bexley from 1950 to 1974, for Sidcup in 1974–83, and for Old Bexley and Sidcup from 1983. He served as Minister of Labour (1959–60), Lord Privy Seal (1960–3) and Secretary of State for Industry and President of the Board of Trade (1963–4), and played a large part in early negotiations for entry to the European Common Market. He was elected as Party leader in 1965 (the first to be chosen by ballot) and became Prime Minister in 1970, negotiating successfully for Britain to join in Europe in 1973. His government was challenged by miners' strikes which led to the 'three-day week' in 1972. In 1974, after two election defeats, he was replaced as leader by Margaret Thatcher, but continued to let his opposition to her policies be known. Outside Parliament he was well known for his love of yachting and of music.

The only thing that will change in the future is the nature of the reforms which are made. Constitutional issues have come to the fore in recent years, not least because of devolution in Scotland and Wales. Britain's membership of the European Union also had important constitutional implications given the momentum of economic and monetary union.

Reform, however, has meant very different attitudes and policies. It has focused both on improving and on abandoning the past. This was true not only of domestic policies but also of those abroad, both in the Empire and in foreign policy. 'Reform' could entail the development of Empire, but also its dissolution. A sense of contradictory pressures was captured in the House of Commons on 17 October 1899 when the Irish nationalist MP William Redmond attacked the government for going to war with the Boers: 'in this country there are thousands of people in the direst poverty, but you have not a million to help them, not a farthing, but you may spend fifty millions in subjugating a people who have injured England'. Empire, however, was a widely (although not universally) powerful ideology. When, on 15 May 1900, the news arrived that the Boer siege of Mafeking had been raised, there was widespread joy, including the ringing of church bells, railway engines blowing their whistles, and scenes of patriotic euphoria in music-halls. Imperialism was linked to racialism, specifically a belief that an Anglo-Saxon race existed and was superior to other races. Kipling's poem 'The White Man's Burden' explained the need to fight 'the savage wars of peace' on behalf of civilisation.

Yet, beginning in the late 1940s, and proceeding rapidly in the late 1950s and early 1960s, Britain divested itself of the majority of its colonial possessions. The process of decolonisation was all the more remarkable in Britain's case because it was not, by and large, accompanied by any of the stresses and strains which bedevilled the French retreat from Empire. Britain presented its own retreat from Empire as the logical outcome of its philosophy of Empire, that is that the purpose of imperial rule was to prepare the territories ruled for eventual self-government.

'Reform' can mean both more and less government intervention, and this helped to contribute to controversy. Like 'freedom' and 'liberty', reform was a value-laden term. The general thrust during the century was for more intervention. Tariff reform was supported from the 1900s as a means to strengthen both Empire and economy and to fund social reform. Tariffs were seen as a way to protect producers and to create an alliance of capital and labour. With its stress on the role of the state, tariff

neo-liberalism: A renewed
interest in liberal principles
regarding social and political
affairs.

reform represented an abandonment of the Conservatism associated with Salisbury, but it was designed to defend the existing distribution of power.

The proponents of tariff reform pressed for the replacement of free trade by government control. This was unsuccessful until 1932, but World War One led to a new emphasis on planning and the mobilisation of national resources. In the 1930s, there was a widespread sense that government had to act in response to the Depression, and there was a wave of what was later termed 'middle opinion', which began to champion the ideas that would later underpin the post-war consensus. For example, in 1931 the pressure group Political and Economic Planning was formed to promote planning and a more interventionist style of economic management. However, there was far less intervention in the economy than critics thought appropriate.

From 1945, the policies of successive Labour governments further strengthened this identification of reform with government action. Labour thinkers in the 1930s had elaborated ideas of corporatist Socialism that were implemented by the 1945–51 Attlee governments. Planning reflected a strong current of collectivism. Self-help had gone, as well as the *laissez-faire* state. The memory of widespread unemployment in the 1930s encouraged government action. Furthermore, 'welfare' in part represented the triumph of human agencies in society over spiritual responses to life.

Until the advance of **neo-liberalism** in the late 1970s, state intervention in the economy was conventionally seen in terms of reform. Although particularly associated with Labour, it was also supported by Conservative governments, as with the establishment of the Central Electricity Board (1926), the British Broadcasting Corporation (1926), the London Passenger Transport Board (1933), and the British Overseas Airways Corporation (1939). Furthermore, there was also considerable regulation in other sections of the economy, for example the rail system. In 1938, coal royalties were nationalised as from 1942. This did not represent some lack of confidence in capitalism by Conservative governments, but, rather, a pragmatic willingness to consider a range of options for the organisation of sections of the economy, and a belief that public ownership could be a positive step. Competition was not seen as a goal in itself. Instead, public ownership was viewed as a potentially effective form of management, as with the creation from 1933 of the National Grid by the Central Electricity Board.

These policies were developed by the Labour governments of 1945–51; although in the case of the nationalization of the steel industry there was less obvious need for state control, the issue was more contentious, and the industry was denationalised in 1953. Nevertheless, most of the Labour nationalizations were not reversed by the Conservative governments of 1951–64, and in the early 1960s the Macmillan ministry sought to develop economic planning. Yet, from the late 1960s, there was also a tendency among Conservatives to argue that reform should be achieved at the expense of government. This drew on several strands of thought, including traditional liberalism, individualism, libertarianism and neo-liberalism.

The neo-liberal view of reform first came to prominence in the 1960s as the planning experiments of both Conservative and, especially, Labour governments failed to revitalise Britain's flagging economic fortunes. The first concerted effort to reduce the scope of government action in post-war Britain took place under the Conservative government of Edward Heath in 1970–2. Heath wanted to remould the contours of British society in line with the competitive features of 'Selsdon Man' (see Chapter 10). A more sustained assault was mounted by the three successive Conservative governments which Margaret Thatcher led between 1979 and 1990. They sought to roll back the state in the interests of free-market participation and competition. Thatcher was committed to the view that the independence of the free market was constructive. Like the tariff reformers, Thatcher advocated radical prescriptions for conservative purposes, in the sense of maintaining the social system, but she was more disenchanted with the nature and role of the British state than earlier Conservatives.

**egalitarianism:** The belief that all people should have equal shares in society's rights, benefits and duties.

# Egalitarianism

Second, as a powerful secular ideology, has been **egalitarianism**. A belief that people are equal and should be treated equally has classically been associated with the left and was indeed pushed hard both by radical Liberals and by Labour. It lay behind the National Health Service (NHS). This was both an assertion of the importance of equality within the community and a device to achieve it. Whereas the National Insurance Scheme of 1911 had been intended to help transfer income over the lifetime of an individual in order to provide for health care, the National Health Service offered state provision paid for by state-imposed charges on the wealthier part of the community (taxation). Family allowances were introduced in 1945, paid from the outset to mothers, not fathers. The creation of the NHS was a good example of Labour's success in adapting Socialist ideology to the British political and governmental system.

The radical tradition was adapted by the Labour Party in the early decades of the century. This Lib–Lab continuity was important in developing anti-Conservative identities in many communities: 'New Liberalism' was very much directed against pre-war Conservatism, although it was also seen as an alternative to Socialism. Both New Liberalism and Labour were the product of a variety of ideological drives. These included Christian Socialism, Fabianism, a belief in planning, and Marxism, or, at least, diluted Marxisant ideas. These drives interacted and clashed, and both were affected by the pressures of political tactics, especially the difficulties of government. These differences and difficulties helped to divide the Labour Party, both in and out of office. There were particularly serious splits in 1931, the 1950s, and the 1980s; but serious divisions can also be traced in other periods, such as the 1960s and 1970s. These divisions interacted with personality differences, the quest for power by particular individuals, and the vexed question of relations with the trade union movement.

In ideological terms, the relationship between Socialism and capitalism was an acute issue, more particularly the problems of how far it was possible to intervene to ensure egalitarianism, and, especially from the 1950s, how to make Socialism relevant in a period of general, but unequal, growth and affluence. Emotionally, this debate was linked to accusations that 'moderate' or 'right-wing' Labour governments had betrayed Socialism and the working class.

This charge was flung at all Labour governments. The Bevanites (supporters of Aneurin Bevan on the left wing of the Labour Party) criticised Attlee on this score in the early 1950s, and, after Labour's electoral defeat in 1970, Tony Benn attacked Harold Wilson on the same head. This argument, repeated after their 1979 defeat, encouraged Labour to move to the left in opposition in the early 1980s, only to discover that it did not bring victory: instead, the 1983 election, fought on a clearly left-wing manifesto, was a disaster for Labour. As a consequence of the thesis of betrayal and failure, the achievements of the Wilson years were ignored and their ideology

### Aneurin Bevan (1897–1960)

'Nye' Bevan, a miner's son, was born in Tredegar, Monmouthshire, into a large family and left school at 13 to begin work in the pits. An active trade unionist, he led the Welsh miners in the General Strike in 1926. He was elected as Independent Labour MP for Ebbw Vale in 1929, and joined the more moderate Labour Party in 1931. In 1934 he married Jenny (later Baroness) Lee, who was herself a Labour MP (1929–31, 1945–70). From 1940 to 1945 he edited the left-wing weekly *Tribune*. As Minister of Health (1945–51) he introduced the National Health Service in 1948, but in 1951, having been made Minister of Labour, he resigned over proposed health service charges. He became Shadow Foreign Secretary in 1956, opposing unilateral nuclear disarmament at the Party Conference in 1957, and was deputy leader from 1959 to 1960.

and attitudes were deleted from the Labour record. Thus, Blair has ignored the extent to which his attitudes had been prefigured by Labour in the 1960s, while his Labour critics were misleadingly able to present his policies as if they were simply Thatcherite (see Chapter 10).

Undoubtedly there has been a rhetoric of egalitarianism to be found in the Labour Party for much of the twentieth century, but it has proved difficult to turn that into reality. Indeed, it can be argued that Labour has been characterised as much by a commitment to inequality based on ideas of meritocracy and market economics and tempered by a social conscience for the deserving poor. Major reforms in the provision of health in the late 1940s and education in the 1960s were compromised from the outset. There was a powerful and persistent Gladstonian belief in equality of opportunity running through the twentieth century (shared by Thatcher and Blair), one that justified inequality in the name of meritocracy, and argued that meritocracy would lessen the social costs of inequality.

Egalitarianism as a goal or rhetoric was not restricted to Labour. It was adopted by the Churches, and also had a wider purchase in the political world. Conservative populists have been less important in this sphere than 'One Nation' Conservative paternalists. The latter have been inspired by a number of views, including a sense that a nation has an organic character (is like a body), and therefore, that the health of one is the health of all. Other Conservatives have stressed the need for opportunity for all, and argued that, although it is normal for people to enjoy different levels of material success, it is important for all to have access to opportunity. This view led to a 'Social Darwinism' in which the possibility of social mobility was seen as providing judgement on and excuse for very different levels of material success. Such attitudes were especially strong during the Thatcher governments.

The varied, and interacting, strains of Conservative thought reflected the difficulty of defining a cohesive and attractive Conservatism in a rapidly changing world. The impact of two world wars, the loss of Ireland and Empire, mass democracy, democratisation, female emancipation, social change, rising affluence, all posed problems of identity and adaptability, and led to uncertainty on the part of Conservative thinkers and strategists. Nevertheless, on the whole, Conservatives have stood for less government intervention and expenditure, and lower taxes than their opponents. This helped bring them victory in elections such as 1931, 1959, 1979, 1983, 1987 and 1992.

The commitment of the Right to egalitarianism has been more varied than that of the Left, and, in some cases, has been ambivalent, but what is striking is that, in the first forty-five years of the century, there was no strong British equivalent to the Right in large parts of the Continent. Instead, the Conservatives have articulated an inclusive notion of community, rather than a policy of simple class interest or a reactionary opposition to change. Although there was alarmist talk, for example of fighting to keep Ulster in the Union in 1912–14, or Bonar Law's idea in 1919 that 'Friends of the Public' should be armed in England, the Conservatives accepted change without any such action. Furthermore, Conservative participation in coalition governments in 1915–22 and 1931–45 helped to lessen a sense of internal conflict. Indeed, the role of such governments, alongside less formal electoral and parliamentary pacts, testified both to a determination to make the political system work and to a widespread search for agreement and compromise that could create a powerful consensus. Their appeal as the 'national party' in British politics enabled the Conservatives to survive and prosper in a class-based society.

A similar, but different, contrast between Continental Conservatism and the British version has been seen since 1945. On the Continent, the nationalist, traditional Right was discredited by World War Two, tainted by collaboration, or, in Eastern Europe (bar Greece), brutally suppressed by the Communists. Instead, Christian Democracy emerged as a powerful force, especially in West Germany and Italy, but also in the Benelux countries. It had much in common with 'One Nation' Conservatism, but very little with the more radical Conservatism that emerged with Thatcher, even more so as Euro-scepticism took hold of the Conservative Party under John Major (1990–7). Indeed, the anti-corporatist and anti-collectivist rhetoric, attitudes and policies of the Conservative Party ensured that in the 1980s British Conservatism looked more to the USA than to the Continent, a trend which continued under William Hague, who became leader in 1997. Although less consistent and constant, and more ready to compromise in office than she claimed, Thatcher pressed a 'conviction politics' of neo-liberal free-market policies combined with anti-statist rhetoric. Elements of these policies and rhetoric had been present within the Conservative Party earlier, some such as monetarism from the 1950s, but they did not prevail until after Heath was replaced as party leader by Thatcher in 1975 (see Chapter 10).

A focus on Conservative thought takes us to the heart of a major contrast within egalitarianism. On the Left, this has been seen as a goal and policy in social terms, with society understood as an adjunct of, and in many respects a consequence of, state policy. On the Right, in contrast, egalitarianism has been seen as a matter of individual rights and opportunities, shared by all. The role of society and the state in Conservative thinking lessened dramatically from the mid-1970s. Thatcher believed in the market and the right of the individual to spend her/his money as s/he sees fit. In the 1980s and 1990s, the growth of private education and private health treatment increased social inequalities. Thatcher famously voiced her scepticism about the very notion of society. A classic example of 1980s policymaking in this respect was the end of the 'closed shop' – compelling employees to belong to, and thus be represented by, a trade union. Instead, individual workers were encouraged to make their own mind up. State monopolies were broken under Thatcher and the idea of state monopoly was attacked. This was true both on the 'macro' level and at the level of local communities. For example, the extension of compulsory competitive tendering to a wide range of local government services in 1988 was designed to challenge the

**libertarianism:** The belief that people should be free to express their religious or political ideas.

role of council workers, and their unions. In many localities it led to the entrance of private-sector contractors into public-service work, for example refuse collection. Established boundaries between public and private sectors were challenged. Similarly, in 1991, the Conservatives attempted to create a quasi-market within the NHS, allowing 'purchasers', principally District Health Authorities and GP surgeries, to select 'providers', principally hospital services.

Thatcherism was successful in winning extensive, but far from universal, support, because it struck a chord with wider social and ideological movements. One of the most important was a disillusionment with planning. This was seen very much in a hostility to post-war urban rebuilding, specifically to its unwillingness to heed local wishes. Thatcher's refusal to allow local authorities to use the proceeds of council-house sales in order to embark on new building projects reflected this concern about planning.

'Corporatism' – the amalgamation of people into blocs, who were then seen as representing them – was, at the same time, the division of society into such blocs. Hostility to such corporatism can be seen as egalitarian – as treating people equally, whatever their apparent affiliation. It can more appropriately be regarded as libertarian.

## Libertarianism

**Libertarianism** has been a powerful ideological current in twentieth-century Britain. 'Allowing people to do their own thing' was not an invention of the 1960s. Indeed, similar demands had been voiced at the time of the *fin de siècle* movement of the 1890s, most famous today for Oscar Wilde, and again, by those championing women's emancipation in the early decades of the twentieth century. The notion that women did not need to behave in accordance with the dominant behaviour pattern for them was designed to be liberating. The fictional Bertram Wooster, no friend to modernity, was concerned in P. G. Wodehouse's novel *Right Ho, Jeeves* (1934) that his wan friend Gussie Fink-Nottle would have little luck wooing his beloved, 'Especially if the girl he had earmarked was one of these tough modern things, all lipstick and cool, hard, sardonic eyes, as she probably was.' In the 1920s, 'Bohemianism' – a challenge to conventional lifestyles – was championed by many commentators, not least the writers of the Bloomsbury Circle, such as Virginia Woolf.

The Depression of the 1930s, World War Two, the austerity and corporatism of the post-war Labour governments, and the conformism of their Conservative successors, lessened the impact of such ideas. They were given scant voice on radio or television. Libertarianism became more powerful in the 1960s, first as an aspect of lifestyles that were uneasily contained within existing social structures, and eventually as an anti-authoritarian individualism that was championed by Thatcher and which helped in the overthrow of collectivist notions in the 1980s.

Libertarianism was the cult of self, and was linked with a wholesale transformation in the language of politics and society away from duties and responsibilities and towards rights. This had a number of manifestations in the 1990s, including the 'charters' proclaimed by the Conservative governments of John Major (1990–7) that laid out rights, for example for patients in the National Health Service and users of other public services. The growing emphasis, in education and in later life, on personal (self-) development was another aspect of the same tendency. It is a trend which may well continue into the next century, given the Blair government's commitment to 'education, education, education'. Yet, many were only poorly catered for by the fashionable ideas of the 1980s and 1990s. The '**trickle-down**' thesis of prosperity, that suggested that all would benefit from liberalisation and could be free, proved deceptive.

## Capitalism, Communism and Socialism

Libertarianism was related to another powerful ideology in twentieth-century Britain: capitalism. Other options were offered. Radical Socialist ideas were advanced in the first quarter of the century and, with less energy, also thereafter. These ideas were very varied and reflected a number of traditions. For example, James Connolly (1868–1916), Edinburgh-born from Irish immigrant stock, sought to unite the working class throughout the British Isles on radical Socialist lines, but found that there was only a limited working-class consciousness. His attempt in 1913 to win British support for locked-out Dublin workers was as unsuccessful as his subsequent search for a Socialist dimension for Irish nationalism.

The Labour Party constitution approved in 1918 committed the movement, in Clause IV, 'to reserve for the producers by hand or brain the full fruits of their industry . . . upon the basis of the common ownership of the means of production and the best attainment system of popular administration and control of each industry or service'. This, however, was not the policy of the minority Labour governments of 1924 and 1929–31, while, more generally, the National Executive Committee was dominated by trade unions whose leadership was on the whole less radical. **Communism** enjoyed a following after World War One, but it was far weaker than a Labour movement determined to contain militancy.

More powerfully, the post-World War Two planned society and economy left scant room for free-market capitalism, and this remained true thereafter of the attitudes of the Labour Left, and, indeed, of the policies advocated at the time by the Labour Party. An anti-capitalist Socialism might have worked had society remained as regimented as it was in the 1940s, a time when the gentlemen in Whitehall were generally regarded as really knowing best. Had television remained a state monopoly without advertisements, then challenging images of prosperity would have been suppressed, while if the very high rates of personal taxation had been sustained, then it would have been difficult for many to avoid the norms of a planned society.

In Britain, however, a combination of demands for economic, social and political freedoms destroyed this prospectus. This was not simply a success for the Conservatives. More significantly, in the late 1940s and 1950s, powerful forces within the Labour Party thwarted the implications of Socialism by stressing the need to pursue equality within the framework of a mixed economy.

The Communist Party of Great Britain was founded in 1920, but Communism was discredited from the 1930s by its association with Soviet tyranny. The Stalinist purges horrified many, but not all, on the British Left. In *The Road to Wigan Pier* (1937), George Orwell referred to 'the stupid cult of Russia'. Communist membership rose to 11,500 in late 1926, in the aftermath of the General Strike, as miners joined, but then fell to below 3,000 in 1930, the year in which the *Daily Worker* was launched, before rising to 5,500 in 1933 and 18,000 in December 1938. Hopes that membership would reach 100,000 were fruitless. Numbers in France and Germany were far higher. Alliance with the Soviet Union in 1941–5 helped Communism in Britain, but post-war Soviet expansionism swiftly tempered this (see Chapter 9).

**trickle-down:** The benefits that come to poorer sections of society as a result of more successful people having, and spending, money.

**Communism:** A political system based on the teachings of Marx, in which the workers control the means of production.

Before, during and after World War Two, there were attempts on the Left to define an ideology that was clearly divorced from Communism, but which advanced policies that could be seen as left-wing. This attempt to promote a democratic Socialism appropriate for a property-loving democracy, ensured that the Labour Party had to respond to social trends. In 1956, Anthony Crosland's influential *The Future of Socialism* proposed a more equitable society but within the framework of a mixed economy, instead of increased public ownership. That year, the Soviet invasion of Hungary hit the left hard, leading to the departure of many intellectuals from the Communist Party. With the Suez Crisis of the same year (see Chapter 13), this helped lead to the emergence of the *Universities and Left Review* (1957) and to the publication in 1958 of *Conviction*, a set of essays which were important as a focus for debate on Socialist policy. The publishers presented *Conviction* as an attempt to chart a new course for the left, going beyond the limitations of post-war welfare and reform. The case for a more democratic and less class-bound culture was pressed, and the relationship between class and educational opportunity proved.

In office for most of the period 1964–79, Labour extended public ownership, for example by nationalising the steel industry, but did not go as far as many of its left-wing supporters wished. For example, calls in 1967 for the public ownership of the building industry were ignored.

## Stability

The relationship between the Left and capitalism has remained uneasy, but a characteristic of British society is that capital ownership is widely distributed, not through the direct ownership of shares, but through their indirect ownership, in pension funds, and as a consequence of property ownership. Without being facetious, the last can be seen as one of the prime ideological commitments of the British, especially the English, for home ownership is higher in England than in Scotland. The desire to own property and the attempt to improve it, in particular by DIY (Do It Yourself) work, appear to focus aspirations far more than do wider political movements. From the 1930s, the availability of mortgages on low rates of interest and with long repayment periods helped property owning, and this was encouraged by tax relief on mortgages. With television, DIY was the main leisure pursuit of men, according to polls in the 1970s, 1980s and 1990s. Very substantial sums were spent on DIY work. Changes in the product range from the leading manufacturer, Black and Decker, for example the introduction of the Workmate portable work bench in 1979, were of great importance.

The public desire to own property helped ensure that home ownership was treated more favourably than renting in taxation. Until 1974, all interest on loans for buying or improving a house qualified for tax relief. Under the 1974 Finance Act, a loan ceiling of £25,000 for tax relief was introduced and in 1983 this was raised to £30,000, but from 1988 this was restricted and in 2000 it was withdrawn. Even so, the cost in the 1993–4 tax year was £4.3 billion.

More generally, it is necessary to put politics and what is often termed ideology in the context appropriate for a democracy, namely popular participation. Repeatedly, throughout the twentieth century, it is notable how active participation in the political process has been limited. A higher percentage of the electorate vote in national elections than in the USA, but it is striking to contrast party membership with the larger membership of organisations such as the National Trust. This is not only true of recent decades, but has been the case throughout the twentieth century. A lack of active supporters did not only affect the mainstream political parties. In the 1930s, when the combined total membership of the Communists and the Fascists reached a highpoint, it never exceeded 70,000. Far more Cambridge undergraduates of the 1930s were interested in sport than in the Communist activism that subsequently attracted press attention. The climate of the times encouraged a number of individuals to become Soviet spies, of whom the best known are Anthony Blunt, Guy Burgess, Kim Philby, Donald MacLean and John Cairncross, but, for most people, the choice was not between Communism and Fascism; and most people, both then and subsequently, were unwilling to push their own views and interests to the point of taking direct action against government and in breach of the law.

This reflected a more general commitment to stability that was a feature of British politics. Outside Northern Ireland, the number of those willing to defy parliamentary government was limited and they lacked effective organisation. Within the political system, governments instinctively sought to avoid pressing the bounds of what was acceptable, and when this skill appeared lost, as with Thatcher and the Poll Tax, they lost support. As a consequence, until the late 1990s there was a hesitation about constitutional reform, and a desire to seek widespread support at moments of crisis. This led to backing for broad-based coalition governments. Although unsuccessful, in 1910 the Conservatives and Liberals held talks for five months to try to settle the constitutional crisis created by the House of Lords' opposition to the Liberal government, and Lloyd George proposed a government of national unity. One indeed followed in 1915, under the pressure of political tensions and the need for national mobilisation during World War One. In the meanwhile, Lloyd George had suggested a Liberal–Labour coalition in 1911 and 1912, only to have it rejected by the Labour leadership, which was aware of activist criticism of the existing cooperation between the two. In response to the tri-party politics of 1922–31, there was widespread support not for overthrowing parliamentary politics, but for a National Government. In 1940, Labour, in turn, proved willing to back a coalition government.

Minority parties found it difficult to win support, and this was not only due to the first-past-the-post system. On the Right, the racist Union Movement, formed by Sir Oswald Mosley in 1948, fought five seats, one in 1959 and four in 1966. In 1966, their average vote was only 3.7%. The League of Empire Loyalists put up candidates for four seats in 1957–64, but all lost their deposits. Their supporters joined the National Front, founded in 1967, but its average vote in the ten constituencies it contested in the general election in 1970 was only 3.6%; and in February 1974 the average was 3.3% for 54 constituencies. By 1983, this had dropped to just over 1% for 58 constituencies, and in 1987 the party did not take part in the general election. The Referendum Party, a predominantly right-wing attack on the European Union, failed to make much of an impact in the 1997 general election.

On the Left, the Independent Labour Party (ILP) no longer enjoyed the modest success it had had in the 1930s. Candidates stood in the 1950, 1951, 1955, 1959 and 1970 general elections, but all lost their deposits. In 1975, the ILP rejoined Labour. Communist support fell. In 1950, the Party lost the two seats they had gained at the 1945 election; and 97 out of their 100 candidates forfeited their deposits. In October 1974, the Party polled only 11,606 votes. The hardcore who refused in 1991 to accept the reconfiguration of the Party into Democratic Left put up four candidates in 1992, only for them to win an average of 150 votes. The Workers' Revolutionary

Party put up 101 candidates for parliamentary elections in 1974–83; all lost their deposits. The Socialist Workers' Party, formed in 1976, had about 3,000 members at its height, but had no impact on the mainstream.

This politics had its cultural counterpart. For example, the British films, news-reels and television of the 1930s offered an optimistic emphasis on social cohesion and patriotism. D. C. Thomson, and Mills and Boon, two of the most successful publishers of popular fiction, actively disseminated conservative social and moral standards: sexual energy was contained, while radicalism, social strain and moral questioning were ignored. This emphasis was less pronounced after World War Two, especially from the 1960s. Thus, the *Spitting Image* television series of the 1980s and the 'Alternative' comics of the 1990s savaged Conservative politicians, policies and attitudes. Nevertheless, the social bite of such works was less strong than its political counterpart; while the vast majority of non-documentary television pro-grammes, whether 'sit-coms' or 'soaps', did not challenge, let alone push hard at, such issues as different social opportunities. Such points need to be borne in mind before attempting to present the history of the century in adversarial political terms.

## ■ Summary

◆ Religion has declined in importance during the century. The twentieth has been more secular than any previous century. People are less religious, pious and de-vout, and those who are religious are more willing to choose how they follow their faith. The Church of England has been especially badly affected. It has become less important to public and private morality.

◆ New immigrant groups have ensured a more varied religious scene. Islam has been especially important among the immigrant population. Thus a multi-ethnic society has also been a multi-religious culture.

◆ Rather than thinking of ideologies primarily in terms of party politics, it is best to consider wider currents, such as egalitarianism.

◆ Individualism and capitalism have been powerful in secular thought. Libertarian-ism became stronger from the 1960s, and, through its links with capitalism, became the dominant secular ideology. This was part of a wider challenge to communal values, attitudes and discipline from individualism.

◆ There has been a variety of beliefs within the main political parties for much of the century.

## ■ Questions for discussion

◆ What was the impact of the decline of religious commitment on the part of the bulk of the population?

◆ How has Islam affected British society?

◆ What were the dominant ideas in society and social policy? (See also Chapters 8–11.)

◆ How much difference do ideologies make to government policies and public attitudes? (See also Chapters 8–11.)

# ■ Further reading

Alderman, Geoffrey, *Modern British Jewry* (Oxford, 1992).

Barker, R., *Politics, Peoples and Governmen: Themes in British Political Thought since the Nineteenth Century* (London, 1994).

Davie, Grace, *Religion in Britain since 1945* (Oxford, 1994).

Gladstone, David, *The Twentieth-Century Welfare State* (London, 1999).

Kent, John, *William Temple* (Cambridge, 1992).

Laybourn, Keith, *The Evolution of British Social Policy and the Welfare State, c.1800–1993* (Keele, 1995).

McLeod, Hugh, *Religion and Society in England, 1850–1914* (London, 1996).

McLeod, Hugh, *Piety and Poverty: Working-Class Religion in Berlin, London and New York 1870–1914* (London, 1996).

McRoberts, David (ed.), *Modern Scottish Catholicism* (Glasgow, 1978).

Thompson, Noel, *Political Economy and the Labour Party: The Economics of Democratic Socialism, 1884–1995* (London, 1996).

# CHAPTER 8

# Democratisation and the Constitution

## Contents

Change describes the mood and method of twentieth-century Britain, but if any one word captures the content and impact of social and political change it is democratisation, the process of becoming responsive to the popular will or to aspects and impressions thereof. Throughout the twentieth century, Britain was a democracy, although, until 1918, when universal male suffrage and a substantial measure of female suffrage were introduced, it was a limited democracy and in 1914 one of the least democratic states in Western Europe. The continuity of political institutions and democratic practices might seem obvious, but it actually distinguishes Britain from most of Europe and most of the world. The next part of the book is devoted to this political history, and at every stage we are searching for the key features of British political history. There is a division into three chapters. Chapters 9 and 10 offer essentially a narrative, and so it is there that readers will find elections, political parties, and ministries discussed in a chronological fashion. This earlier chapter looks at more long-term issues and questions, in its attempt to understand the nature of political power, the character of government and governance, and the world of politics.

## Key issues

▶ What is democratisation and how has it been important to Britain in the twentieth century?

▶ What is the British constitution?

▶ What has been the role of Parliament?

▶ How much power have Prime Ministers had?

▶ How has Cabinet government developed?

▶ What has been the role of local government?

▶ How has the practice of politics been affected by the major changes of the twentieth century?

# Democracy and democratisation

The struggle for **democracy** is generally thought of in terms of gaining parliamentary government and the vote. At the beginning of the twentieth century in the United Kingdom, about a third of adult males and all women lacked the vote. As far as UK men were concerned, this was a history finished in 1918, and for women in 1928, although the double votes made possible by the business and university franchise were only abolished by the Representation of the People Act of 1948. Furthermore, there was no political struggle over voter registration akin to that in the USA, especially over the Black vote.

The extensions of the franchise in 1918 and 1928 were important. Irrespective of the advantages that they brought to particular parties, the sheer size of the electorate – up from 8 million in 1914 to nearly 29 million in 1929 – forced changes in political attitudes and in methods of electioneering. The Conservatives responded by efforts to create a mass base through organisations such as the Women's Unionist Organisation and the Junior Imperial League. Important organisational changes in popular politics began to take place in the late nineteenth century in the aftermath of the 1867 Reform Act. The Conservative Party established the Primrose League in 1883 for instance. Mass democracy, however, required not only a new organisation, but also a new ideology. The new ideology, however, was not to come until the twentieth century.

The larger electorate encouraged populism, not that this factor had been lacking prior to 1918. The popular press was truly born when Alfred Harmsworth (Viscount Northcliffe) founded the *Daily Mail* in 1896. This was important in bringing a marked increase in the availability of news. During the Boer War (1899–1902), images of the conflict were made available. The Warwick Trading Company and the British Mutograph and Biograph Company fiercely competed in the development of 'topicals', the predecessors of newsreels. The rise of Labour also contributed to populism, for Labour had an explicitly democratic political language, while many of its activists came from the trade unions and the cooperative movements. Yet, popular Unionism and Conservatism were also important.

In addition to democracy, it is helpful to think in terms of **democratisation**. This relates to a responsiveness to the popular will, a concept that is difficult to judge, but no less important for that. It can be argued that democracy – the extension of the

**democracy:** Government by freely elected representatives of the people.

**democratisation:** The process by which institutions and practices become more accountable to the public.

---

### Box 8.1

## The growth of the electorate

Successive Representation of the People Acts greatly increased the electorate. The 1918 Act nearly trebled the electorate, by giving the vote to all men over 21 and to all women over 30 who were ratepayers or wives of ratepayers. The 1928 Act gave women equality with men. The 1948 Act abolished plural voting: the university vote by which MAs could vote for university seats, as well as in the constituency where they lived, and the business vote by which businessmen could vote where they had businesses and where they lived. The six months' residence qualification for voters was also abolished. Permanent Boundary Commissioners were established to report on the distribution of seats. The 1969 Act cut the voting age to 18, while the 1985 and 1989 Acts extended the vote to ex-patriates (those living abroad).

franchise – was, and is, incomplete without democratisation. Indeed, it can be suggested that democracy created a new means for validating a power structure and social system that was essentially impervious to democratic pressures. This situation was fought with democratisation. The latter entailed both a reconceptualisation of the state, so that it represented, at least in theory, the organised will of the people, and the use of the state to try to change society.

That democracy would entail such changes led to a powerful reassertion of elitism among certain intellectuals in the late nineteenth century. W. H. Mallock established himself as the most cogent exponent of elite theory with his basic contention that there was a link between aristocracy and evolution. There was indeed an ambivalence towards the democratisation of society, one that had different sources and took different forms. Few were as critical of democracy as the Earl of Halifax (1881–1959), an Old Etonian who, aside from serving as Foreign Secretary (1938–40), was also Viceroy of India (1926–31) and, later, Chancellor of Oxford University. He wrote to his father, 'what a bore democracy is to those who have to work it. . . . I think it is a great pity that Simon de Montfort . . . ever invented our parliamentary system.' Social snobbery was satirised in the person of Lady Bracknell in Oscar Wilde's play *The Importance of Being Earnest* (1895):

*Lady Bracknell:*   The whole theory of modern education is radically unsound. Fortunately in England, at any rate, education produces no effect whatsoever. If it did, it would prove a serious danger to the upper classes, and probably lead to acts of violence in Grosvenor Square. . . . You have, of course, no sympathy of any kind with the Radical Party?

*Jack:*   Oh! I don't want to put the asses against the classes.

There was also considerable upper-class hostility to and suspicion of popular pastimes, such as football. Many senior Conservatives were concerned about the expansion of the franchise in 1918 and 1928. Such attitudes were shared by members of the social elite who were further to the Right, in some cases crypto-Fascists, such as the Duke of Northumberland, chairman of the *Morning Post*, a conservative newspaper, and Lady Houston, editor of the *Saturday Review*. H. A. Gwynne, editor of the *Morning Post* (1910–37) and President of the Institute of Journalists (1929–30), hated democracy and regarded the First Reform Act as the greatest error in modern British history: 'When we handed over the pistol to our masters in 1832 we let ourselves in for all the evils that pursued us.' Lady Bathurst, the paper's owner from 1908 to 1924, stated in 1918 that 'democracy is idiotic'.

Yet such views did not prevail. Gwynne noted in 1918 that major politicians were disinclined to talk to him. Fascism was marginal in the 1920s (see Chapter 9). The National Government (1931–40) was not a Fascist, or even authoritarian, exercise, and in 1940 the populist Churchill, not Halifax, became Prime Minister. Popular views were regarded as important in the 1930s: mass-observation and the Documentary Film Movement sought to express the voice of the 'people', and to raise its status by promoting a more democratic idea of citizenship. The popular press of the day contributed less self-consciously to the same end.

Hostility to democratic accountability was also, and more effectively, demonstrated, albeit in an implicit, not overt, manner, by the unwillingness of often self-defining elites, such as the judiciary or town planners, to accept popular beliefs and pastimes as worthy of value and attention, and their conviction that they were best placed to manage society and define social values. Paternalism was a powerful attitude in what were to be termed by the novelist and scientific bureaucrat

### Sir Winston Churchill (1874–1965)

Winston Churchill was born in Blenheim Palace, Oxfordshire, and educated at Harrow and Sandhurst. He joined the army, serving in India and Sudan, and then went to South Africa as a newspaper correspondent. He was elected as Conservative MP for Oldham in 1900 but joined the Liberals a few years later. His posts included Home Secretary (1910–11), First Lord of the Admiralty (1911–15) and Chancellor of the Exchequer (1924–9). He lost his seat in 1922 but was re-elected in 1924 as a Constitutionalist, and then as a Conservative for Epping and then Woodford, a seat he held until 1964. He was called on to form a coalition government in 1940, serving as both Minister of Defence and Prime Minister, and is best known for the stirring speeches he made during the war, urging the Allies to continue the struggle against the Nazis. After the war he became concerned about Soviet expansion and spoke of the 'iron curtain' descending across Europe. He remained an MP until he was 90, as well as writing a 6-volume history of *The Second World War* and a 4-volume *History of the English-Speaking Peoples*.

C. P. Snow 'the corridors of power', the title of his novel published in 1964. The extension of the scope of government during the twentieth century exacerbated this tendency, because much of it entailed social policing. Behaviour deemed anti-social in the spheres of education, health, housing, personal conduct, and law and order all became a matter for scrutiny, admonition and, in some cases, control by the agencies of the state. Thus, in 1915, Lloyd George attacked the drink trade as part of his programme for national mobilisation (see Chapters 2, 7).

In many cases, there was a class dimension; namely middle-class control over the working class. A good example was the Street Betting Act of 1906, which banned all cash-betting other than on a recognised race course. This prohibition of off-course cash-betting hit the working class. The acceptance of credit-betting was of limited value, as only the credit-worthy could practise it. The legislation reflected the lobbying of the National Anti-Gambling League, a middle-class lobby group, albeit one supported by Labour politicians such as Ramsay MacDonald, who opposed what they saw as a threat to working-class livelihoods. The Act was widely ignored, because working-class communities did not regard betting as criminal or wrong. Communal networks ensured that illegal betting continued, and the same remains the case today, although the law has changed. In 1923, police witnesses told a parliamentary committee that the 1906 Act was unworkable, but the law was not changed.

This was by no means the limit of social policing. Subsequently, the BBC was constructed in terms of middle-class morality, at least of the improving, not the gin and tonic, variety (see Chapter 5). Similarly, the film industry of the 1920s offered middle-class attitudes and values. These may well have limited creativity in the British cinema, as well as encouraging the audiences' preference for American films. Facets of popular culture, such as gangster films in the 1930s, horror comics in the 1940s and 1950s, and video nasties in the 1990s, were blamed for crime.

Pressure on unmarried mothers to hand over babies for adoption frequently had a class dimension, although it is necessary to avoid suggesting that behaviour and attitudes necessarily corresponded to class lines. The expansion of government agencies and extension of state control brought income and status to those who ran or benefited from government. This had a powerful class component, and was linked to the prestige of 'white-collar' over 'blue-collar' occupations.

More generally, middle-class social and cultural condescension could be linked to contempt for popular views on such matters as capital punishment and immigration. Thanks to the growth of state power, the twentieth was the century in which the frequently-discerned rise of the middle class reached its apogee (see Chapter 6). This was little challenged by Labour, in large part because the Labour Party came to be dominated by the public-sector middle class. From the outset, many Labour leaders had lived in the suburbs, not in working-class districts. Prior to 1914, Labour leaders had shown only limited interest in extending the franchise to include all adult males. Instead, they had sought to focus on the 'education' of those who already had the vote, but, who in their terms, did not use it 'rationally'. Furthermore, a reforming zeal and, at least public, Puritan morality characterised many Labour politicians. This led Labour governments to raise taxes on drink and tobacco, and in 1948 to introduce a tax on greyhound race-track totalisators and football pools, even though these taxes were regressive, meaning that the poor, relatively speaking, paid more. Labour both spoke for the people *and* sought to change them.

In contrast, the Conservative Party was dominated by the private-sector middle class: landed gentlemen were replaced by professionals and businessmen, and this was more than a case of younger sons succeeding. The former Labour Chancellor of the Exchequer Denis Healey quipped that by the 1980s, estate owners had been replaced by estate agents as the driving force in the Conservative Party. There was a broadening of the social composition of the Conservative Party. Whereas in 1945, 80 per cent of the Party's MPs had been educated in public schools, the percentage in 1992 was 50. The Maxwell Fyfe Committee Report adopted by the Party conference in 1948 made the process of selecting candidates more democratic. Whereas previous Conservative Party leaders had 'emerged' through private negotiations between those at the top, Edward Heath was elected leader in 1965. He did not come from the social elite, but was a 'grammar school boy', and his election reflected the fact that the Conservative Party realised it needed to challenge the meritocratic appeal of Labour's Harold Wilson. Heath, in turn, fell as a result of a leadership election held in 1975, while his successor, Margaret Thatcher, fell the same way in 1990 (see Chapter 10).

Similarly, there was a social broadening in the hero-class of comfortable society, whether real heroes, or those of fiction. In the inter-war period, aristocrats had been important in detective novels: Dorothy L. Sayers's Lord Peter Wimsey and Margery Allingham's Albert Campion. The cast was very different later in the century. The age of 'clubland heroes' passed when Ian Fleming's James Bond was represented for the screen, from *Dr No* (1962), by Sean Connery, as a charismatic figure free of class constraints (and with a Scottish accent), rather than the Old Etonian Fleming's choice, the public-school-educated David Niven, as an English gentleman.

Heath was elected leader by the Conservative MPs. The idea of a leader chosen by a ballot of Party members, rather than by their representatives, was not introduced until the 1980s, and then by the Social Democrats, a non-governing party. Labour did not lessen the role of trade union bloc votes in its decision-making processes until the 1990s.

Most institutions, whatever their rationale, and irrespective of their being in the public or the private sector, resisted unwelcome pressures. This was a particular problem in the state sector as the 'providers' or employees, such as teachers, academics, doctors and nurses, sought to define what was appropriate for their institutions and to control them. From the Labour Left, Aneurin Bevan warned in 1952 that 'the boards of our nationalised industries, in their present form, are a new and potentially dangerous problem, both constitutionally and socially. We have still to ensure that they are taking us towards democratic Socialism, not towards the managerial society' (*In Place of Fear*).

Yet the problem was far more widespread. It affected sport for example. Football authorities and individual clubs tended to keep supporters at a distance. They did not accept that supporters' clubs could be part of the organisation. This was true of clubs with such mass followings as Liverpool. Democratisation entailed an attempt to make these institutions more responsive to those they were supposed to cater for.

# A democratising history

In *Major Barbara* (1905), written by the radical playwright George Bernard Shaw (see Chapter 15), the armaments manufacturer Andrew Undershaft declares 'Your pious mob fills up ballot papers and imagines it is governing its master; but the ballot paper that really governs is the paper that has a bullet wrapped in it. . . . When you vote, you only change the names of the cabinet. When you shoot, you pull down governments, inaugurate new epochs, abolish old orders and set up new.' The Labour Party, the major party of the Left for most of the century, was opposed to revolution and determined to maintain the parliamentary system. Furthermore, Labour was able to take over from the Liberals on the Left without having to resort to violence. The split that occurred in the Liberal Party after Lloyd George succeeded Asquith as prime minister of the wartime coalition government in December 1916 helped ensure that it did not have to. Shaw himself wrote, in the 1908 preface to *Fabian Essays in Socialism*: 'The Fabian knows that property does not hesitate to shoot, and that now, as always, the unsuccessful revolutionist may expect calumny, perjury, cruelty, judicial and military massacre without mercy. And the Fabian does not intend to get thus handled if he can help it. If there is to be any shooting, he intends to be at the state end of the gun. And he knows that it will take him a good many years to get there'. The authoritarian strain in Fabianism was later manifested in the Webbs' praise for Stalin and the Soviet Union. However, once the Fabians were at the 'state end of the gun', they did not use it. Indeed, their whole outlook, based upon notions of permeation and propagation, militated against its use. Instead, the degree to which change was effected without violence is striking. The number of those who took part in violent demonstrations during the century was small, and such action rarely won majority support.

The absence of violent change also ensured that many important shifts passed without crucial turning points. This was true, for example, of the widespread ending of personal service. Servants had been central to the support of middle- and upper-class life at the beginning of the century, and in 1911, 11.1% of the female population of England and Wales were in domestic service. By mid-century, however, servants were only a small minority of the population. Furthermore, a life 'in service' became very uncommon. This was important to the theme of democratisation, because the ready availability of servants had affected attitudes, and greatly tempered egalitarian assumptions, as indeed had conscription in which the majority of those conscripted only served as ordinary rankers. There was conscription in 1916–19 and 1939–63.

The notion of social reversal was treated humorously in J. M. Barrie's successful comedy *The Admirable Crichton* (1902), in which the first-rate butler takes charge when Lord Loam's household is shipwrecked. Loam becomes a labourer. Rescued in the last Act, Crichton returns to his role as butler, although an exchange with Loam's elder daughter glances at the subversive implications: 'You are the best man among us,' Lady Mary says to Crichton, earning the reply 'On an island, my lady perhaps; but in England, no.' Lady Mary observes, 'Then there is something wrong with England.' The electoral system was to see no such return. Both it and the Victorian Poor Law system of public welfare were transformed without violence. Thus, for example, it proved possible to introduce old age pensions, National Insurance, and universal male suffrage without any serious political storm, let alone widespread public agitation. This helped to lessen the potential radicalism represented by the growth of the trade union movement and of the Labour Party. The collapse into crisis that was widely feared in the inter-war period and again in the late 1940s and 1970s did not occur.

Had it done so, then it is possible that any discussion of the structure of government in twentieth-century Britain would have had to place greater weight on the role of force, and thus on how the forces at the disposal of government were controlled. This has been important on several occasions. Pre-World War One labour disputes led to the deployment of police and troops, and this recurred in the inter-war period. The police forcefully dispersed unofficial strikers in George Square in central Glasgow on 'Bloody Friday', 31 January 1919, and also ended riots on the part of striking miners at Harworth in Nottinghamshire in 1936–7. In Glasgow in 1919, 12,000 troops were deployed, as were tanks, and the Scottish Secretary talked of a 'Bolshevist uprising'. There were extensive troop movements at the time of the General Strike in 1926, although no use of force. Industrial disputes after World War Two again led to the use of police and, to a far lesser extent, troops, as with the deployment of large numbers of police in the East Midlands during the 1984–5 miners' strike. Nearly 12,000 miners were arrested during the strike. The tradition of non-violent policing in Britain was matched by a willingness to be firm. In Northern Ireland, there was a greater readiness to use force, as shown by the B Specials in the 1960s. Furthermore, the 'Troubles' in Northern Ireland (see Chapter 12) led to the development of new tactics of crowd control, which were then employed in Britain during the inner-city disturbances of the 1980s. More generally, the ability of the police and courts to arrest and imprison or fine large numbers of those who have broken the law has been an important support of the system. The daily average prison population in England and Wales rose from 200,000 in 1950 to 390,000 in 1970 and 486,000 in 1988.

The role of the police in defeating the 1984–5 miners' strike focuses attention on the attitude towards the use of force in domestic disputes, of government, the army, the police, law-breakers and whatever is meant by 'public opinion'. In general, both the police and the armed forces have remained under the control of the state. There have been strikes, such as the Liverpool and London police strikes in 1918–19, and the Invergordon naval mutiny of 1931, but they were few and short-lived. Potentially the most serious incident occurred in March 1914. In the 'Curragh Mutiny', Brigadier-General Hubert Gough and 59 other officers of the 3rd Cavalry Regiment stationed near Kildare at the Curragh Barracks resigned their commissions rather than impose Home Rule. No orders had as yet been given, so there was no 'mutiny'. The potential crisis was defused when the War Office promised that they would not be ordered to do so and refused to accept the resignations. There was no Cabinet authorisation for this assurance, given by the Secretary of War and the Chief of the

## Naval mutiny

The armed forces had followed governmental wishes after difficulties within the ranks following World War One about delayed demobilisation and intervention in the Russian Civil War. Nevertheless, military loyalty was a sensitive issue and in 1924 there was a serious political controversy when John Campbell, editor of the *British Worker*, published a piece pressing soldiers never to shoot at strikers. The Labour government's hesitation about prosecution led to a vote of no confidence in the Commons. In September 1931, pay cuts imposed by the National Government led to the Invergordon Mutiny, in which sailors of fifteen warships of the British Atlantic fleet, based at Invergordon in the Cromarty Firth, refused to go on duty. The Admiralty's willingness to revise the cuts ended the crisis in the fleet, but the whole episode helped cause a run on sterling in the foreign-exchange markets. The government had to come off the Gold Standard on 20 September.

Imperial General Staff, and they were both obliged to resign. The Prime Minister, Asquith, repudiated the assurance. The crisis was part of a breakdown of constitutional and political assumptions in the early 1910s. Bonar Law's call, as leader of the opposition, on Ulster to resist Home Rule by force was very serious in this context. The outbreak of World War One dramatically shifted attention away from Ireland, and Home Rule was shelved. The possible consequences of the Curragh Mutiny are thus unclear, but it suggested that the government would have encountered problems in using the army to impose an unwelcome solution on Ulster. This might well have divided and politicised the armed forces. In contrast, the army was willing to act against strikers in 1910–11.

No comparable crisis was to occur. The professionalism of the armed forces and the limited nature of peacetime conscription in Britain (it ended in 1919 and 1963) were important factors in maintaining government; and also made it easier for the government to use troops in Northern Ireland from 1969.

It is possible to present a benign account of the role of the military, to note its non-interference in civilian politics even in periods of real or apparent political and economic crisis, such as 1910, 1926, 1931 and 1975–6, and to draw attention to the major effort made by the military to adopt norms similar to those prevailing more generally in society. Thus, the social composition of the officer ranks is now far less dominated by the upper class than at the start of the century, while, as with the police, recruitment from ethnic minorities has been encouraged.

A less positive interpretation could also be advanced. First, it can be argued that the military have made insufficient efforts to adopt general social norms. Secondly, it has been suggested that the social structure and 'politics' of the military, and its general assumptions, have had detrimental consequences in war and peace. For example, many of the generals of World War One, such as Field Marshal Haig, had a conviction of the value of the attack that in part arose from their social and cultural attitudes. Similarly, the Admiralty's unwillingness to adopt A. J. Pollen's advanced gunnery system in the 1910s has been attributed to political and religious dislike for Pollen, as well as a more general distaste for the technical values presented by Pollen's automated system with its use of analogue computers. This challenged the role of gunnery officers and the nature of service cohesion and identity. Thirdly, it is possible that the currency of militaristic attitudes played a role in the continued commitment to imperialism in the first half of the century, although this commitment did not rest on the military alone. Since World War Two, Britain has also spent a higher percentage of government expenditure on 'defence', i.e. the military, than other Western European states, and this can be traced not only to the ambitions of politicians anxious to act on the world stage but also to the role of the military.

Much of the history of twentieth-century Britain can be presented in terms of the tensions created by democratising: the working out of the implications of democracy in a society that had rising expectations. These were not only narrowly material, but also wider. This was especially true as regards what might be termed social politics, namely the workings of society, understood not as operating in accordance with some immutable objective code, but as reflecting the distribution and nature of power within society. Education policy provided an example of this (see Chapter 2). What could be presented as privileged and elitist was marginalised, although the eventual situation was far more complex. The state educational system became 'comprehensive' at the level of individual schools. In the 1950s, and especially from 1965, the streaming of children by ability into different schools after examination at the age of 11 (12 in Scotland) was abandoned. Grammar and secondary-modern schools were replaced by comprehensive schools, a policy actively supported by the 1964–70 Labour governments. Wider access to opportunities also led to the foundation of the Open University in 1969. This was actively backed by Harold Wilson in order to help mature students without formal academic qualifications study to degree level employing distance-learning methods. By making it unnecessary to give up full-time employment, the Open University dramatically increased the opportunities for further education. In 1964, Wilson had declared 'We intend to pay just as much attention to the needs of the apprentice at the tech as we do to the needs of the undergraduate at Oxford and Cambridge. Because our future depends just as much on the one as on the other' (*The New Britain: Labour's Plan*).

In social welfare, as in education, there was a shift from the situation in the first two decades of the century, when both non-government charity and state provision were presented in a philanthropic, patronising and top-down manner, to an increasingly democratic and inclusive notion, in which rights played a greater role. The publication of the Beveridge Report in December 1942 marked the beginning of this new conception of welfare provision. This was linked, in part, to the decline of the habit of viewing the bulk of the population as a problem, or as entitled to little, and the fall in the habit of analysis in terms of eugenics, with its tendency to distinguish between sections of the population. The tensions created by democratisation were most marked in the field of welfare. In a society of rising expectations, which society expected government action to meet, economic performance became central. Without economic growth, it would be impossible to finance the welfare state. Much of post-war British history could be discussed in terms of the tension between social priorities and economic needs at a time of relative industrial decline, and also with regard to concomitant pressures for the reconceptualisation and redefinition of welfare needs (see Chapter 2).

Wider access was literally an issue in debates about the right to roam. These rights were limited by landowners and asserted by campaigners keen to prevent the public from being shut out from much of the country. Parliament has had to legislate uneasy truces. The Right of Way Act of 1932 established that to assert a right of way it was necessary to prove that the route had been used by the public for the previous twenty years, a provision which has subsequently proved to be the cause of confrontations between farmers and ramblers. The obverse of wider access, exclusive practices, also created controversy. This was seen in attacks on private institutions, especially fee-paying 'public' schools, but also fee-paying private wards in NHS hospitals.

The issue of exclusion was addressed not only from the perspective of fairness, but also with reference to the supposed effects of such practices on society as a whole. Thus, for example, there was protracted controversy about traditional aspects of public-school life, including single-sex education, boarding, the cult of sport, and religious pontification. Attacks included Kipling's *Stalky and Co.* (1899), Alec Waugh's *Loom of Youth* (1917), and Orwell's essay 'Such, Such Were the Joys'. These were based on their authors' experiences, respectively, of the United Services College, Sherborne and St Cyprian's Preparatory School, and Cyril Connolly mounted his attack in *Enemies of Promise* (1938). In turn, a whole series of writers, many, such as 'Frank Richards', not ex-public schoolboys, wrote extensively in support of the public schools and their culture with its emphasis on playing the game, a sense of gentlemanly duty in a fair world in which all will be for the best. These values were also propagated in children's magazines, such as *The Gem* and *The Magnet*. Most of their readers were not from the prosperous sections of society, but they were encouraged to subscribe to values that were fundamentally those of hierarchy and deference (see Chapter 7).

Yet, these values came under increasing attack not only from radical writers in the first half of the century but also, after 1945, from inclusive governmental practices stemming from universal provision in crucial fields such as education, health and military service, and from a sense that such values were traditional and thus redundant. This attitude came to play a greater role throughout society. More generally, there was a reaction against deference and hierarchy that affected all organisations and careers, and also relations between people and organisations such as the police. A willingness to question the police became more pronounced from the 1960s. More widely, pressure groups challenged existing arrangements and sought to stir up and/or direct public demand for change (see Chapter 7).

It would be naive to suggest that pressures within society were simply in one direction, namely towards a readily-apparent democratisation. Had that been true, as is sometimes implied in simplistic accounts of the century, then the history of Britain should have been different. Instead, British society, government and culture are nowhere near as democratic as their American counterparts. In America, elections are far more numerous, and many public offices, for example judges, are filled by elected candidates. In Britain, by contrast, the 1980s and early 1990s arguably saw a de-democratisation, at least in the shape of a rise in the power of quangos (government-appointed bodies). In the mid–1990s, it was estimated that Wales had more Quangocrats – unelected officials – than it had local councillors.

The process of democratisation, anyway, is a complex one, because as any consideration of British society reveals, structures, attitudes and changes were, and are, far from simple and it is not always clear how far particular shifts can be described as democratising in nature. Indeed, the greater possibility provided by a democratising society for the expression of views was such that this very complexity was enhanced. The relationship between democracy and democratisation was similar to that between literacy and the expression of views. Mass literacy had been ensured in Victorian Britain, but it took time before this led to a widespread receptivity to, understanding of, and voicing of coherent opinions in a form other than the most transient. Thus, far from suggesting that democratisation implied one social agenda or political programme, its importance lies in the degree to which it gave vitality to democracy, translating it, in particular, from politics to society. Yet, at the same time, democratisation tended, in its focus on customers/voters/members, and its emphasis on rights not responsibilities, to make it harder for institutions to operate.

All institutions, including the highest in the land, were affected by public scrutiny and demands. In 1992, for example, Windsor Castle suffered a serious fire that caused major damage to the state apartments. It was initially suggested that the cost of the repairs be met from public funds, but this led to an outcry on a scale that would have been inconceivable when Queen Elizabeth II came to the throne in 1952. Similarly, *Britannia*, the royal 'yacht', in practice a large ship, was not replaced when it ended service in 1997. In November 1992, the Queen felt it appropriate to decide to pay income tax on her private income.

The Church of England was widely satirised from the 1960s, as was the upper class. Far from being presented as leaders and role-models, the upper class was seen as farcical, parasitical or dangerous, as in Peter Barnes's successful play *The Ruling Class* (1968) and Steven Berkoff's play *Decadence* (1981). Such attacks were more bitter than the satires of the 1950s, such as *Carlton-Browne of the FO* [Foreign Office], an Ealing film comedy of 1958. The automatic assumption of power and authority by members of the upper class lessened markedly. For example, landowners became less important than farmers in voicing the opinions of the agricultural interest and influencing government because, from the 1930s, the latter turned to the National Farmers Union for advice and leadership. Government bodies were also subject to greater scrutiny. A Police Complaints Board was established in 1979, and, in 1984, the independent Police Complaints Authority followed.

In the financial sector, the power of established practices and the City Establishment was challenged, leading to changes in the practice of corporate finance and also more effort to appeal to shareholders. A series of contentious takeovers registered the shift. In 1958, the successful contested takeover of British Aluminium saw S. G. Warburg, a banking house then outside the City Establishment, outmanoeuvre the latter, not least by writing to shareholders over the heads of their boards and talking to the press.

A powerful pressure against democratisation, however, was provided by globalisation, specifically the rise of multinationals in the economy and their extension into the service sector. This was very much seen in the media. A new generation of foreign ownership began in the 1970s with Rupert Murdoch's purchase of the *Sun* newspaper, and developed subsequently with the role of private ownership in satellite and cable television. This was dramatised in the 1990s when private companies purchased the right to broadcast sporting events, emphasising the degree to which the BBC had lost its pre-eminence as the focuser of national memories and images. Instead, these events were open only to those who could pay; although, to strike a more positive note, there was now more choice among providers. Globalisation also posed a potential challenge to national identity.

The privatisations of the 1980s and 1990s also opened new fields for foreign ownership. French companies came to play a major role in the water industry and American companies in the electricity supply industry. With their foreign bases and ownerships, such concerns were in part removed from British opinion. Nevertheless, the breakdown of monopoly provision and the emphasis on customers in an age of fast-changing consumer preferences ensured a degree of responsiveness.

In the 1990s, democratisation contributed to a stress on the importance of individual customers, which affected not only business, but also administration in general, with an emphasis on responsiveness to customers in both government and the public sector, for example in the NHS. This administrative pressure was linked to a so-called 'quality revolution'; and to an improvement in the management of both the public and the private sector. A major problem of the 1960s and 1970s, this was partly resolved by better training and education. Democratisation was about far more than administrative responses. It proposed and arose from a notion of 'politics for the people', and thus this section serves as a bridge from a section on society to another on politics.

# The British constitution

In the late 1990s, Britain entered a period of constitutional flux, one that was presented by its supporters as deliberate reform. This was surprising because, although the constitution had changed significantly earlier in the century, there had always been major efforts to assert its essential continuity. Furthermore, compared with constitutional change elsewhere in Europe, the extent and pace in Britain had been modest. There was, for example, no equivalent to the fall of the Third Republic in France in 1940 and the creation of the Fourth (1946) and Fifth (1958) Republics. There had been no major discontinuities produced by war, as in Russia, Germany and Italy, nor the need to consider how best to integrate another state, as in Germany with the collapse of East Germany.

The process of constitutional change in Britain is made more complex because of the nature of Britain's constitution as 'unwritten'. This does not mean that there are not laws affecting political practices, but rather that conventions, customs and traditions have, on the whole, played a major role; although that role itself is not a fixed one. The nature of the Royal Prerogative, and also of ministerial responsibility to Parliament and to the courts, are largely based on convention. For example, considerable uncertainty has surrounded the issue of who should be asked first to try to form a government if a general election has left no overall majority. Should it be the outgoing government or the party with the largest number of MPs? This was a major issue after the February 1974 election, when Heath and the Conservatives tried to hang on to power, and has been mentioned on other occasions since, for example at the time of the 1992 election. As far as ministerial responsibility is concerned, it is unclear how far this is individual or collective. It is also unclear what precisely should lead to resignation. This again was a controversial issue during the 1990s.

The role of political parties has also been a matter essentially of convention, as indeed has been their internal dynamics. This has caused much instability during the century, especially during periods of dissension over leadership and policy. The situation has been particularly unclear during coalition ministries and 'national' governments. Thus, the position of Lloyd George as the Liberal leader of a predominantly Conservative ministry, and the respective roles of the Conservative leadership and MPs, caused much disagreement in 1922.

The British constitution altered during the twentieth century in response to statute law – law made by Parliament; common law – law as interpreted in the courts; the shifting nature of conventions; and, in the last decades of the century, the positions and demands of European bodies, both governmental and legal, in the latter case the European Convention on Human Rights. Parliament sought to control this process. In the absence of a written constitution, Parliament has made and unmade laws, often at a furious pace. Increasingly in the 1990s the courts have sought to moderate this process, and, indeed, the entire conduct of government, not least through the extension of the theory and practice of judicial review.

The sovereignty of Parliament – the authority of Parliament to make, change and repeal the law – has been an ongoing process. Parliaments are not able to bind their successors. Furthermore, this sovereignty extends to the electoral process. Parliament has changed the composition of the body electing it, and frequency with which its members have to face election.

These rights, and their use, led to claims that the constitution was in fact that of an 'elective dictatorship', a charge made by the Tory jurist Lord Hailsham in 1976 (when Labour was in power). This claim focused not only on the powers of Parliament but also on the degree to which they have been used throughout the century to forward the views of the government without any real prospect of effective hindrance. The government has been that of the majority party (or parties) in the House of Commons; and the possibility of this power being contested within Parliament was largely ended by the Parliament Acts passed by Liberal and Labour governments – in 1911 and 1949 respectively. The first reduced the delaying power of the House of Lords to two years and the second reduced it to one. The Labour government elected in 1997 set out to introduce major changes that would further lessen the ability of the Lords to delay government business.

Outside Parliament, this power to forward the views of government was used to remove the rights and liberties of others – both individuals and institutions; leading to the claim, increasingly voiced from the 1970s, that there was no real freedom in Britain. In part, that claim was politically partisan – directed against Labour in 1974–9, the Conservatives in 1979–97, and Labour thereafter. In part, however, it reflected a marked shift in the character of politics, in terms both of government policy and of popular response. In the first, both major political parties followed more radical and less consensual policies in office, and, in the second, the decline of deference in society led to a hostility towards what was seen as authoritarian political practice.

Britain's membership of the European Union poses a threat to parliamentary sovereignty, because, in signing the Treaty of Rome in 1973, Britain accepted that European law takes precedence over national law. The increased recognition of this reality, as economic and monetary union gathered momentum in the 1990s, served to transform the question of Britain's relationship with Europe into the burning political issue (see Chapters 10, 13).

## The monarchy

In 1867, in his influential *The English Constitution*, Walter Bagehot distinguished the 'efficient' parts of the constitution from what he termed the 'dignified' parts, namely the monarchy and the House of Lords. This was a misunderstanding, because the monarchy and the House of Lords retained considerable power in the late nineteenth century. Nevertheless, Bagehot's distinction was valid and became more so during the twentieth century. Monarchs have not been without influence, but they have known how to adapt. Edward VII (reigned 1901–10) was a devotee of aristocratic society who could cope with New Liberalism. He refused to threaten to create sufficient Liberal peers to push through the Parliament Bill. George V (reigned 1910–36) was more accommodating, and was willing to threaten to create sufficient

### Edward VII (1841–1910)

Edward Albert was born in Buckingham Palace, the eldest son of Queen Victoria and Prince Albert, and spent 60 years as Prince of Wales before succeeding to the throne in 1901. Although he took his seat in the House of Lords in 1861 after his father's death, he took little part in affairs of state, preferring the life of fashionable society, where he was a charming and popular figure, with several mistresses. As King he promoted international relations, with Continental tours, and fostered the Entente Cordiale with France in 1904. In 1863 he married a Danish princess, Alexandra, with whom he had six children, of whom the second, George, succeeded him as George V.

peers to make the House of Lords give way in its clash with the government in 1910–11. In 1913, he ignored the advice of Lord Esher to dismiss the Liberal government. George V proved more effective as a wartime symbol than the Prince Regent, later George IV, had been during the Napoleonic War. War with Germany led to a change in the name of the dynasty. In place of Saxe-Coburg-Gotha, inherited from Queen Victoria's husband Albert, the name of Windsor was adopted in 1917. After the war, George V adapted to Labour governments and was rewarded with the support of his Labour Prime Minister, Ramsay MacDonald, and other prominent Labour ministers. He played an important role in the 1931 political crisis, encouraging the formation of a broadly-based National Government under MacDonald. Although a traditionalist, George V accommodated himself to change, not only to Labour governments, but also to a more popular style of monarchy, presenting the trophy at the Wembley Cup Final. In 1924, he made the first of a series of radio broadcasts, and in 1932 began the annual royal broadcast on Christmas Day.

The abdication of George's eldest son, Edward VIII, in 1936 was a major blow to any chance that monarchy would become more politically powerful. Edward had views of his own – over both domestic politics and foreign affairs. He did enough to convince critics that he was sympathetic to Hitler, while, at home, he appeared to favour doing more to develop social cohesion. After the General Strike, Edward made a donation to the relief fund for the miners, because, he claimed, 'it would be an unsatisfactory end to any dispute that one side should have to give in on account of the sufferings of their dependants'. Edward fell, however, because his determination to marry an American divorcee, Wallis Simpson, clashed with widely-held expectations about the public conduct of monarchs: Britain was still a Christian society. The Conservative Prime Minister, Stanley Baldwin, made it clear that Edward had to choose, and he abdicated. Baldwin's position was backed by the Cabinet, the Labour leadership and the Dominion Prime Ministers. In part, there was governmental concern about Edward's views on Hitler and on unemployment, but the central issue was the proposed marriage. Democratic royalism was not compatible with government hostility.

His brother and successor, George VI (reigned 1936–52), was less forceful in his personal opinions. He helped significantly with morale during World War Two, not least by remaining in London during the German bombing. The King was also Colonel-in-Chief of the Home Guard. He was concerned at the plans of the Labour

**Three generations of rulers**
George V (king 1910–36), Edward VII (king 1901–10) and Edward VIII (king 1936). The nature of monarchy changed during their reigns. George V was particularly adept at adapting to the rise of Labour. He played a major role in persuading Ramsay MacDonald to form a National Government in 1931. Edward VIII was less successful in responding to political trends. His wish to marry a divorcee caused the abdication crisis of 1936 and led to the succession of his brother, George VI (1936–52).

government elected in 1945 and greatly regretted the ending of the Indian Empire, but was not a political player. George's elder daughter, Elizabeth II (reigned 1952– ), was an experienced and skilful adviser of successive Prime Ministers. She had political opinions, not least a belief in the Commonwealth, but was careful not to take a public political stand, and to maintain constitutional conventions. Politicians helped to preserve the monarchy's neutrality. Under Elizabeth, the royal family maintained their important charitable role as patrons of good causes, especially voluntary organisations both at community and national level. This contributed to a strong sense that the royal family had an important purpose, and helped maintain social harmony. The monarchy was also important to the nation's sense of continuity.

In the 1980s and 1990s, the royal family, like other national institutions, was affected by increased public criticism and had to consider how best to respond both to the criticism and to the pressure of change. This problem was further posed and accentuated by the position of the Queen's four children, especially the role, and matrimonial difficulties, of the heir, Prince Charles, who finally divorced in 1996. He himself had sought to make the monarchy more 'relevant' and had indeed played a major role in addressing and highlighting issues of national concern and some that had been marginalised, not least alternative medicine, the environment, inner-city problems and the excesses of Modernist architecture (see Chapter 15).

Although republicanism has always been at the margins in Britain, the 1990s saw an upsurge in anti-monarchical sentiment and a more critical press. The tragic death in August 1997 of Princess Diana, the ex-wife of Charles, Prince of Wales, unleashed a wave of national grief which the royal family seemed totally unable to comprehend. After that, encouraged by the Labour government of Tony Blair, the monarchy tried to modernise. Royal visits became more informal and there was a conscious effort to link royalty with the younger generation. Whether or not Britain is in the process of developing a 'Scandinavian-style' monarchy (i.e., very low key, with few trappings of state), nevertheless remains to be seen.

### George VI (1895–1952)

Prince Albert, the second son of George V, was born at Sandringham in Norfolk. He went to Dartmouth Naval College and served in the Navy. He was present at the Battle of Jutland in 1916. After leaving the Navy in 1917 he spent a year in the Royal Air Force. He was made Duke of York in 1920. He married Lady Elizabeth Bowes-Lyon in 1923 and they had two daughters. Although he had never expected to be king he came to the throne in 1936 after his brother abdicated to marry Wallis Simpson, an American divorcee. During the Second World War he helped maintain morale by staying in London during the blitz, and he overcame a stammer to make many broadcasts to the public. His last public appearance was to open the Festival of Britain in 1951.

## The House of Lords

The House of Lords lost power and status. The Parliament Act of 1911 removed its right to veto Commons' legislation, and was pushed through by the Liberal government after strident social criticism of the aristocracy. Aside for Bills concerning money, which could be presented for royal assent after one month, even without the consent of the Lords, the Lords were still left with a two-year delaying power for other public Bills. They used this power to delay the passage of the Irish Home Rule Bill introduced in 1912. The Act also introduced payment for MPs and cut the duration of Parliament from seven to five years. This reversal of the Septennial Act of 1716 ensured that governments would have to go to the polls at more frequent intervals, although there was no return to the Triennial Act of 1694.

In 1947, the Lords delayed Labour plans for nationalising the steel industry. As a result, Attlee pushed through the Parliament Act of 1949, which reduced from three to two the number of occasions on which the Lords could block legislation passed by the Commons before it became law, and reduced the delaying power of the Lords from two years to one. Life peerages were introduced in 1958. The Labour governments of 1964–70 showed renewed interest in reforming the House of Lords, but did not persist with their plans. Opposition was led by Michael Foot, on the left of the Labour Party, and Enoch Powell, on the right of the Conservative Party. Foot believed that the reform did not go far enough: he wanted to abolish the House of Lords. Powell believed the reform went too far and might undermine the supremacy of the House of Commons.

The newly elected Labour government of Tony Blair proposed in 1997 to remove the right of hereditary peers to vote in the Lords, a measure that would ensure that only individuals who had been created peers could vote: this was likely to increase the power of the government through the extended use of patronage. The hostile reaction of the Conservative Party to this proposed change was such that the Blair government agreed in 1999 to retain 91 hereditary peers until the second stage of the government's reform relating to the composition of the House of Lords has been completed (the other hereditary peers were to lose their voting rights). It is generally agreed that a reformed upper house should include an elective element, but not on a scale which would lead to rivalry with the House of Commons.

The role of individual peers in politics also declined. This was a matter not only of the rise of Labour – a party that had few peers and even less deference to the aristocracy – but also of changes in the Conservative Party. In 1923, George, Marquess Curzon, an experienced Foreign Secretary, who expected to be appointed Prime Minister, was passed over in favour of Stanley Baldwin, in part because Arthur Balfour, a former Conservative Prime Minister whose advice George V sought, told him that the Prime Minister could no longer be a member of the House of Lords. When the Earl of Home became the Conservative Prime Minister in 1963, he renounced his peerage and stood successfully for election to the House of Commons.

## Working parts

The 'efficient' parts of the constitution, to adopt Bagehot's phrase, were the House of Commons and the Cabinet. He argued that real political power lay with the Commons. It was there that governments were made and broken. The Commons changed considerably during the twentieth century. It was affected by the professionalisation of national life. The number of professional, full-time politicians in the Commons rose and the nature of the job became more demanding. Most MPs became career politicians who sought governmental office from the outset of adulthood and in some cases before. As a consequence, they had less experience of the outside world, and less of an ability to understand it in anything other than political terms. Furthermore, career politicians were more prone to think in party terms, for the first point about parliamentary politics in twentieth-century Britain was that they were party politics. The emergence of the career politician affected the composition of the parliamentary Conservative and Labour Parties considerably, although they also altered in response to social shifts. In general, there was a decline in the number of MPs who had attended Oxbridge (Oxford or Cambridge Universities) and the major 'public' (i.e. private) schools. Conservative MPs became less likely to be large landowners and more likely to be employed in the professions. The number of Labour MPs with trade union backgrounds fell, whilst the number drawn from the public services increased.

The role of parties forced politicians to define themselves in terms of traditions (and tensions) within individual parties. MPs gained a political identity by virtue of whether they resided on the left wing or the right wing of their respective political parties. Traditionally, the Labour Left was characterised by its strong ideological commitment to Socialism; Labour's Right was prepared to work with capitalism to achieve Socialist aims. The left wing of the Conservative Party was long associated with the Disraelian-inspired tradition of one-nation Conservatism; the Conservative Right placed greater emphasis upon individual rights and the free market. At the close of the twentieth century, it could be said that the Labour Party has become less left-wing as Tony Blair has sought to position New Labour in the centre ground of politics. In actual fact, New Labour looks suspiciously like one-nation Conservatism of old with its emphasis upon the need to combat social exclusion and the excesses of unfettered free-market activity. The Conservatives, meanwhile, had moved to the right as the Thatcher revolution succeeded in transforming their party into a free-market entity. During the 1990s, changes within the parties themselves were making it more difficult to think in conventional left–right terms. Attitudes towards Europe were to complicate matters further, as neither pro-Europeanism nor Euro-scepticism could be confined either to one party or to one particular wing of that party. Europe was perhaps the one issue over which Margaret Thatcher and Tony Benn could agree.

Parties also helped link Parliament and the nation, for political parties provided a bridge between the two. In the 1990s, however, this bridge started to look less secure as the public became disillusioned with politicians (and politics in general). The atmosphere of sleaze that surrounded the Major government in its final years, with allegations of 'cash for questions', created the impression that politicians were on the make. That MPs put the national interest a poor second was a view that had been gaining greater credence among the public since the mid–1970s. It was strongly held in the late 1990s, as opinion polls and survey data revealed, and this might explain why indices of active political participation, turnout levels at elections and party membership figures, recorded falls. It would be wrong, however, to ignore signs of disillusionment earlier in the century, for example in the early 1900s, early 1920s and early 1930s.

Another major change during the century was the growth in the government's representation in Parliament. The number of ministers increased, and thus the percentage of MPs who held or had held government office rose. The number of MPs who were ministers rose to about 100 in the 1990s, close to one-third of a governing party's parliamentary following. This lessened the potential division between ministry and Parliament, and, as all ministers have to vote with the government in Parliament, made it less likely that a government would be overthrown by any means other than a general election. The only government to fall at the hands of the House of Commons was the minority Labour government of James Callaghan in March 1979. The Conservative-dominated National Government of Neville Chamberlain was fatally damaged at the hands of the Commons in a censure motion in 1940, although the government won the particular division with a majority of 80; 120 Conservative MPs voted for the motion or abstained.

The Cabinet, the regular meeting of ministers to discuss policy, became more effective and important. The crucial break occurred during World War One, after Lloyd George became Prime Minister in December 1916. Asquith's Cabinet had been unwieldy and was said not to be up to the complex task of managing the war. In both peace and war, collective responsibility was difficult in such a large body. As a result, only certain ministers were informed of key issues, most particularly the decisions of Anglo-French Staff Talks in 1909. Lloyd George, Britain's first modern presidential-style Prime Minister, instead created a War Cabinet of five members. Meeting every other day, this body was given a secretariat, and made responsible for creating and coordinating policy, corresponding directly with government departments. Lloyd George gave unity to government by controlling the executive authority of the War Cabinet.

Such a scenario sounds desirable, and it did, probably, lead to greater efficiency in the conduct of the war. It also, however, created problems. After the war, Lloyd George used the Cabinet Secretariat, as well as his Private Secretariat, to override the views of ministers. Thus, for example, the views of the Foreign Office and Foreign Secretary, Curzon, over British policy towards the Greek–Turkish conflict were ignored, and Britain followed an ultimately unsuccessful policy of backing Greece. After Lloyd George fell, a larger Cabinet was restored, but the expectation of a more effective body was sustained, in part by maintaining the Secretariat.

In 1940, Churchill revived Lloyd George's position with a similar War Cabinet. More generally, during the century, Cabinet government developed with a series of Cabinet sub-committees, the remit and membership of which was determined by the Prime Minister of the day. The development of the Cabinet Committee system represented a significant accretion of prime-ministerial power which successive Prime Ministers have not been afraid to use to bolster their own position in Cabinet.

The growing power of the Prime Minister, evident since the days of Lloyd George, and the limited constraints on his/her power, gave rise to fears that Cabinet government had given way to prime-ministerial government. This was true of Churchill, Eden and Macmillan, and the debate became very heated from the 1960s. It admits of no clear-cut conclusion, not least because the careers of prime ministers tended to end in failure. Through a series of key reshuffles, Thatcher created a Cabinet of like-minded individuals which she found very easy to control, but it was these same ministers who turned on her in October 1990. Under Tony Blair, since May 1997, the Cabinet appears to have lost much of its significance, with meetings known to last for only thirty minutes. Some commentators have referred to Blair as an 'elected monarch' who runs his government through a small court of key officials and ministers. Recent wars (over the Falklands in 1982 and Kosovo in 1999) were controlled by a small group surrounding the then Prime Minister.

As a political body, the Cabinet has many disadvantages. It is big and can be factionalised. However, it limits departmental autonomy and offers an institutional coherence at the centre of policymaking that is valuable. As such, it offers a focus different from the two other principal forms of governmental coherence: first, the authority of the Prime Minister, and secondly, the control of the Treasury over expenditure, and its consequent determination to influence, if not dictate, policy. The Treasury has tended to operate as an alliance of the Chancellor of the Exchequer with senior civil servants, but such bureaucratic regularity has been less consistent in the case of Prime Ministers. Many looked outside the ranks of the Civil Service and sought their own advisors who lacked any form of scrutiny or control other than from the Prime Minister. This was true of both the Wilson and the Thatcher governments, but less so of Callaghan and Major. Such advisors frequently contributed to poor relations between Prime Ministers and senior colleagues. In the same period, Prime Ministers became more assertive across the entire field of government policy.

The Cabinet directs the Civil Service. One of the major changes during the century was the marked expansion of the latter. In part, this was an aspect of the bureaucratisation that affected all organisations during the century, so that, for example, by the 1970s the Coal Board was employing large numbers of typists as well as miners. In the case of government, however, the expansion of scope led to a major increase in the total numbers employed, and the management of these resources became a central problem. This expansion took place without the processes of government becoming open to parliamentary and judicial scrutiny and control, although attempts were made to strengthen the review of government activities, particularly in the 1990s. Thus, when the position of 'Ombudsman', the Parliamentary Commissioner for Administration, was created in 1967, he could investigate individual complaints against the actions of government departments, but was not permitted to investigate cases of 'maladministration' in the Civil Service, local government, the nationalised industries, the NHS, the police, or the armed forces. Local government was brought into the Ombudsman's scope in 1969, but, in general, the Civil Service remained outside the control of anyone bar ministers (and the fiscal constraints of the Treasury).

# ◼ Continuity and change

In several respects, the political system changed very little during the twentieth century. The essential features remained the same as in 1914. There was still a hereditary monarchy with limited, essentially consultative powers, a bicameral Parliament, with the House of Commons being the most powerful and only elected chamber, national political parties with recognisably different policies and bases of support, a largely two-party system with a weaker third party, an absence of proportional representation, and a state in which power is concentrated in London. The Prime Minister remained head of both the executive and the leading party in the legislature, and national leader of that party. The power of the Prime Minister owed something to the absence of proportional representation and the concomitant need for compromise. For example, in the 1997 general election, Labour took 63.6% of the seats on 43.3% of the votes, while the Conservatives and Liberals between them took only 32.0% of the seats on 47.5% of the votes.

Civilian control over the military was also maintained during the century. In World War One, there had been much tension, as Lloyd George sought to impose control on the generals. In World War Two, there was far less tension, in large part because the generals were under control. This situation did not change thereafter. Unlike in France, de-colonisation did not lead to serious differences between civilians and military. Names such as Montgomery still resonate with much of the public, and poppies are still worn with pride every November, but this did not have political consequences. The Falklands conflict, in 1982, served to bring home the reality of war to a new generation of citizens, but Thatcher went on to win the 1983 general election, not suspend the constitution. Unlike in Germany and Italy, ex-servicemen's organisations did not become a political force. The British Legion, founded in 1921, did not become a Fascist front. The National Union of Ex-Servicemen, a Socialist body founded in 1919, collapsed the following year, in part because it was clear that there would not be a serious right-wing populist movement and in part because the trade unions offered only limited support.

It is considerably less clear how far British governments have consistently controlled the intelligence services, both foreign and domestic. There have been persistent rumours about the attitude of the intelligence services, or sections thereof, towards Labour governments. These rumours have been given solid substance where Harold Wilson's minority Labour government in 1974, is concerned. Peter Wright, a former MI5 officer, confirmed the existence of a plot against Wilson, in his controversial memoirs, *Spycatcher*, published in 1987. It is also unclear whether the

## Box 8.3

### The secret service

The 'secret state' was a creation of the turn of the century with the foundation, first, of the London Police Special Branch, and then of Divisions 5 and 6 of the British Directorate of Military Intelligence, which became MI5 and MI6. MI5 was responsible for counter-espionage, including the surveillance of those seen as subversive, MI6 for espionage outside Britain. Both grew appreciably in peacetime size during the Cold War, although MI6 was affected by Soviet penetration, particularly that by Kim Philby, who became liaison officer with the American intelligence agencies. In

November 1962, Macmillan told the House of Commons that 'hostile intrigue and espionage are being relentlessly maintained on a very large scale', and the following September, Sir Roger Hollis, the head of MI5, warned the Americans that his deputy might have been a Soviet agent. The same charge was to be brought against Hollis, again probably unfairly. The Security Services were accused of plotting against Labour governments in 1924 and 1976, and appear to have been sympathetic to Thatcher.

intelligence services have followed policies abroad without the knowledge of the government, for example during the Suez Crisis of 1956. In the mid–1990s, the Major government took the first steps towards making the security services accountable to Parliament. Stella Rimington, the first female head of a British secret service, and Sir Colin McColl became the first heads of MI5 (British Security Service) and MI6 (British Secret Intelligence Service) to have their names made public, even though Sir Colin refused to be photographed. The Intelligence Services Act (1994) led to the establishment of the Intelligence and Security Committee which provided a forum for parliamentary scrutiny of the work of the security services.

There was also much that is different from the situation in 1914. The nature of the party system changed. The Irish influence in British parliamentary politics, which was important until 1914, disappeared. Scottish politics, in contrast, became more complex. They were four-party from 1967, which led to pressure for an Alternative Member System, or Proportional Representation, in the Scottish Parliament (which opened in 1999). The rise of the Scottish National Party (SNP) also served to give the party system a regional dimension. Demands for self-government in Wales, though less vocal than in Scotland, established Plaid Cymru as the political face of Welsh nationalism. These parties co-existed alongside the established 'third' party in the political system, the Liberal Party, which was renamed the Liberal Democrats in 1987 after its merger with the Social Democratic Party (SDP). The use of proportional representation in the 1999 elections for the Scottish Parliament and Welsh Assembly left Labour as the largest party but without a majority. In Scotland, this led in 1999 to a Labour–Liberal coalition (see Chapter 12).

Both World Wars led to major extensions in state power. Some were long-term, others seen as temporary. The outbreak of war itself led to the passage of the Defence of the Realm Act of 1914 and the Emergency Powers (Defence) Act of 1939. These brought both controls and the habit of control, and the latter proved more insistent and lasting than had been intended. Furthermore, the size of government bureaucracy increased with each war, as did its legal powers. Restrictions on state power declined and were not pressed. Conscription, in 1916 and 1939, represented and symbolised the authority and needs of the state. In World War One, new ministries included Munitions, Labour, Shipping, and Information. A Food Production Department was created, and the food supply was regulated in order to cope with the impact of German submarine attacks on food imports. Instructions to the milling and baking industries led to a dilution of wheat flour, so that bread included more barley, beans and potatoes. The dirty-white colour of the resulting bread was a striking consequence of government regulation. The government took over the control of the railways (1914), the coal mines (1917) and the flour mills (1918). Essential food prices were fixed in 1917, and coal and food rationed from that year. Licensing hours were regulated. The government also increasingly intervened to fix wages (see Chapters 6, 7, 9).

Experience of state intervention in World War One ensured that it was more effective in World War Two. Economic regulation and conscription were introduced more rapidly and comprehensively than in World War One (although conscription was not introduced in Northern Ireland in World War Two). New ministries were created in 1939 for Economic Warfare, Food, Home Security, Information, Shipping and Supply, Power, and Production. National wage-negotiating machinery was established in the coal industry, although it did not prevent a serious miners' strike in early 1944. Agriculture was subject to a hierarchy of control. Each county was administered by a separate War Agricultural Executive Committee, the members of which were appointed by the Ministry of Agriculture, and was in turn divided into districts controlled by district sub-committees.

The war also transformed the State's relationship with society. Everything was brought under the scrutiny of government. Food rationing, for example, remoulded the nation's diet in accordance with nutritional science (see Chapters 6, 7, 10). A tremendous boost was given to the expansion of the Civil Service, which was one of the central administrative themes of much of the century. This was a matter not only of greater numbers but also of enhanced organisation and effectiveness, and wider public acceptance of its role. Thatcher spoke of 'rolling back the state' and 'hiving off' departmental services. She created self-financing agencies, but there was only limited rolling back.

The impact of the two world wars on the extension of government power was major, although much of it was intended as temporary and, indeed, contained. In contrast, membership of the European Union involved more fundamental long-term changes. They are discussed in greater detail later in the book (see Chapters 10, 13), but, at this stage, it is sufficient to note that the political and governmental systems had to make many more adaptations to membership of the European Union than they did to the running and/or loss of Empire. Control of the world's largest and most populous empire was the essentially hidden aspect of the constitution in the first half of the century, but it was hidden precisely because it did not determine, or greatly affect, the conduct of government and politics; however, the future government of India was a major issue in 1933–5 and Churchill's campaign against the 1935 India Act consumed a colossal amount of parliamentary time, and also helped isolate Churchill (see Chapter 13).

There was one major exception: Ireland. After the union of the Dublin and Westminster Parliaments in 1801 and Catholic Emancipation in 1829, Irish politics became more central to those of Westminster. Yet, it was only clear after Irish nationalism had succeeded in breaking the union for most of the island in 1920–1, that Ireland should be seen as a question in imperial rather than British history, and it is important not to adopt a determinism that ignores the Irishness of much British history. Thus, excluding Ireland, it is remarkable how far Empire did not dominate government or politics (see Chapter 12).

Aside from the changes in the constitution arising from membership of the European Union, the other major changes reflected the general shifts in society and public culture discussed in earlier Chapters (see Chapters 6, 7). Influence over information proved very important in an age of mass politics. The government determination to control the flow of information led to the first Official Secrets Act of 1889 and, subsequently, to a series of attempts in war and peace to ensure that this control was maintained. Attempts were made to increase the information available to government in order to assist in planning. This was particularly important in wartime. For example, in June 1940, a farm survey was begun in order to assess productive capacity. By early 1941, about 85 per cent of the agricultural land had been surveyed. A more comprehensive farm survey of England and Wales followed from the spring of 1941. The government also created and improved systems for using the information it possessed, for example with the Police National Computer Unit, which was established in 1969 and became operational in 1974. This initially owed much to World War One. Attempts then to rally public opinion included the foundation of the Department of Information, which, in 1918, became the Ministry of Information. In

World War Two, this became the officially recognised means of supervising and coordinating the publicity output of all the other ministries. The Ministry was responsible for most of the nearly 1,900 official films produced during the war. In the second half of the century, peacetime information flows became more important – in both politics and economics – and increasingly helped to define society.

New means for, and expectations of, information transmission greatly affected the character of politics, particularly from the 1960s, as calls for both greater controls and easier access were made. In essence, the impact of democratisation and of television enhanced the role of the Prime Minister as spokesman of government and as intermediary between the public and the political system. Television led to a focusing on the spokesman and the sound bite, rather than the lengthier space provided by newspapers (see Chapter 5). Parliament seemed less relevant in a public politics that increasingly seemed presidential, and this was not changed by the televising of debates. Even broadsheet newspapers ceased in the 1980s to devote a daily page to reporting speeches and business in both Houses of Parliament.

# Local government

This presidential focus is one aspect of another major shift in government during the twentieth century: the lessened independence of local government. A reconsideration of the character and expansion of the role of local government had been a major feature of the 1880s. The directly-elected London County Council (LCC), created in1888, had been the world's largest municipal authority. Furthermore, it took an activist role in trying to improve London life. This was based on a strong sense of mission, and a capacity to produce information on which policy could be based. The LCC, for example, had had inspectors of such diverse spheres as midwives, labouring children and music-halls. Most county councils had been less activist, but they also had taken a major role in shaping the life of their communities.

In the twentieth century, however, the greater role of local government was not matched by an ability to formulate policy. The expanded role for government led to a development in the power and pretensions of the central state, rather than of local government. In part, this was due to the traditionalism of local authorities, but the dynamic of central planning and financial control was more important. There was no major reform in local government during the late 1940s and 1950s but, instead, a reduction in local authority autonomy.

Disputes between central and local government stemmed not only from political differences and clashes over jurisdiction and responsibility, but also from serious tensions over spending policies and levels. In part, this reflected an inability to agree on how to fund rising commitments. This inability owed something to policy disputes, but much to the problems stemming from limited economic growth. Thus, the relationship between central and local government was a prime instance of the clash for scarce resources that affected and shaped government and politics throughout the century. Incomes policy in the public sector was another contentious example of the same clash.

Local councils were given many responsibilities during the century, but they were frequently as agents of central government and as often against the wishes of local electorates, although, across much of Britain, involvement and interest in local government was very limited, and increasingly so. The role of independents in local government diminished, although it had earlier been important, and in Northern Scotland remained so into the late 1990s.

The shift in the balance between central and local government was one of the major stories of the British constitution in the twentieth century. On one level, it reached a highpoint with the total redrawing of long-established local government boundaries. Under the London Government Act of 1963, the Greater London Council was formed in 1965, adding all of Middlesex, and much of Essex, Hertfordshire, Kent and Surrey, to the London County Council area; while, within the new area, the boroughs were totally reorganised. The following year, the Labour government established a Royal Commission into Local Government in England under Lord Redcliffe-Maud. Reporting in 1969, it led to the Local Government Act of 1972. Coming into force in 1974, the Act redrew the map in order, it was hoped, to create a more efficient system. New counties were created, including Avon, Cleveland and Humberside, and some others were merged, including Huntingdonshire and Cambridgeshire, and Herefordshire and Worcestershire. Furthermore, there were major changes in the boundaries between counties, a reorganisation of the Yorkshire ridings, and new administrative districts within counties.

All this was pushed through in the name of rationality. New units were supposed to be the best for the provision of services, such as education or the fire services. Little consideration was given to local views or to the value of traditional identities in providing a sense of place and belonging (see Chapters 12, 16). There were even greater changes in Scotland and Wales, but they were reversed in 1996 when county authorities were largely restored.

The balance between central and local government also altered quite dramatically in the post–1945 period because power became centralised in Westminster to a greater extent. The process began with the Labour governments of 1945–51, as they introduced the National Health Service and nationalised key industries. In social and economic terms, power was transferred from localities to the centre. New requirements were placed on local government. Under the Town and Country Planning Act of 1947, county councils had to prepare development plans that were to be revised every five years.

The most significant bout of centralisation in more recent years took place under the Thatcher governments in 1979–90. Since 1979, some fifty Acts of Parliament have been passed reducing the power of local government. Their purpose was to reduce the financial autonomy of local councils and transform them into agents of governance (not governments). After clashing with the government, the Greater London Council was abolished in 1986. Thatcher's policies represented a major break with past traditions and she was largely successful in her goal (see Chapter 10). The powers and autonomy of local government were also lessened by judicial decisions. For example, the freedom of local authorities to move on 'travellers', such as gypsies, was limited in the 1990s by parliamentary statutes and judicial decisions. Under Blair from 1997, central government power was accompanied by moves towards devolution.

# The role of the state

Another related area of constitutional change occurred in the economy. Although not formally understood as part of the government, the extension of government control, with widespread nationalisation in 1946–51, greatly expanded the power of the state. Nationalisation brought some two million workers under direct government control, and consolidated the trend towards national control, planning, products and conditions, pricing and wage settlements. Such peacetime control had been prefigured by the Post Office. This expanded greatly after the establishment of the Penny Post in 1840, so that by 1914 the Post Office was the largest business operation in Britain, responsible for the nationalisation of the telegraphs, and, in 1912, the telephone system. This second nationalisation, like those later in the century, was seen as a means to improve the economic infrastructure. It also reflected a belief that state control was efficient. Thanks to state control, the Post Office could be used to distribute pensions.

World War Two was particularly important in encouraging confidence in and reliance upon state control and action. Nationalisation accentuated the post-war tendency of the state to intervene in labour relations and limit free collective bargaining. Bitter industrial disputes encouraged such intervention, but led to a quasi-corporatism that diffused responsibility away from individual companies and unions, with, it has been argued, detrimental consequences for efficiency and responsiveness to change. After World War Two, there was also an increased governmental concern with industrial efficiency. This had been apparent from the 1930s, but became more marked from the 1940s. The Attlee governments were concerned to manage and boost industrial efficiency (see Chapter 11).

Political as well as economic idealism lay behind the widespread nationalisations of 1947–51. Clause IV of the Labour Party constitution of 1918 called for state ownership of coal, electricity and transport. The Bank of England was nationalised in 1946, followed by coal (1947), railways (1948), road transport (1948), the electricity supply (1948), gas (1949), and iron and steel (1951). This reflected the parliamentary strength of Labour and the nature of a heavily regulated economy in which state ownership could be extended easily by exchanging shares for government stock. The extent to which the planned wartime economy was demobilised after the war was lessened by state ownership, the continuation of high rates of taxation, and the crucial role of the state both in allocating raw materials until 1948 and in fixing the sterling exchange. The attitude of government towards planning and control was reflected in the Town and Country Planning Act of 1947, under which county councils were given powers of compulsory purchase. In addition, property owners had to obtain planning permission for changes of use or alterations to building (see Chapters 6, 7, 10).

However, the nationalised industries were not good examples of effective management structures. They suffered from over-centralisation and also variable quality among the management staff. State ownership did not lead to cooperation, as the British Transport Commission rapidly demonstrated. Furthermore, state ownership encouraged management to act as lobbyists for government funds, rather than to heed economic pressures. Labour was more interventionist than the Conservatives, and the Ministry of Technology founded by Harold Wilson became, in effect, by the late 1960s, a Ministry of Industry. The 1964–70 Labour governments also created a Department of Economic Affairs (1964), which produced a National Plan (1965), a National Board for Prices and Incomes (1965), a Ministry of Land and Natural Resources and a Regional Development Fund. Greater government control of the economy led to further nationalisations, for example of aircraft manufacturers in 1977 (see Chapters 10, 11).

The greater role of the state in the economy was an aspect of one of the major changes in political structure and expectations, namely the growth of state power. This was a matter not only of legal powers and a growth in government bureaucracy, but also of information at the disposal of the state. Such power was deployed in many spheres, including moral regulation. Furthermore, there was scant erosion in the scope of government. As liberties were given they were regulated. For example, in the 1960s, gambling, bingo and off-course cash-betting were all permitted, only to be heavily regulated by the state-appointed Gaming Board established by the Gaming Act of 1968. The rights of potential players were limited by a system of restrictions that mostly remained in place until the mid-1990s.

Thatcher tried to 'roll back the state' from 1979 and had some success in so doing, especially in economic management (see Chapter 7), although, in certain spheres, there was an extension of the power of central government. This particularly arose from the government's determination to control public expenditure. This led to a marked extension in state power over local government, especially with 'rate capping': fixing the limits of local taxation. In addition, the ideological thrust of Thatcherism led to an extension of control over aspects of local government. Thus, state education was brought much more under central supervision, especially with the creation of a national curriculum. Universities also experienced more central supervision and control. The government's determination to ensure that local government services, such as the collection of rubbish, were put out to competitive tender, rather than only being carried out by local government employees, also led to an extension in control.

Another sphere of such extension arose from the privatisation of most of the nationalised industries (see Chapter 10). Once privatised, these industries were mostly not treated like other companies but instead were subject to special regulatory regimes with Regulators empowered to fix charges and comment on operating procedures. This compromise between nationalisation and the free market was matched by other compromises. For example, the decline in council-house building under Thatcher and Major (1979–97) and the encouragement of purchase by tenants (see Chapter 10) was qualified by support for Housing Associations, which came to be an increasingly important alternative to local government control of housing. The role of regulators was also an aspect of the extent to which the practice of Thatcherism was frequently different from its ideology and rhetoric, although that owed much to the need for Thatcher to operate through a governmental and political system that she did not fully control. Another aspect of the same process was the continuation of planning mechanisms. The decisions of planners to refuse development permission could be overturned by the Secretary of State for the Environment, but, in most cases, there was no such intervention.

Government thus sought to control aspects of the market-led economy of the 1980s and 1990s. These regulatory inclinations were affected, however, by a desire to attract investment and, more generally, by the problems of economic management in a competitive and unpredictable world economy. In many respects, the fragility of the state was revealed by the latter, as with the impact of the oil price rise of 1973 and the failure to protect sterling's membership of the European Exchange Rate Mechanism in 1992 (see Chapters 10, 11). An emphasis on state power thus has to be qualified by an understanding of the difficulties of government, not least in terms of the expectations created by this very power. This was amply demonstrated by the National Health Service (see Chapter 2).

Discussing nationalised industries as an aspect of the constitution is designed to remind us that the identity and extent of the latter is not fixed, and that change in the constitution was not an innovation of the 1990s. Nevertheless, the late 1990s was a period of marked innovation. Although centralisation was a key feature of Britain's constitutional development in the fifty years from 1945, a major change was introduced in the late 1990s, with the devolution of an elected Parliament in Scotland and an elected Assembly in Wales. Both were elected in 1999. While the UK government retained important powers, for instance in external relations, and the Welsh Assembly was not granted tax-raising powers, the act of devolution provided formal recognition of the regional distinctiveness of the United Kingdom. Furthermore, the Scottish Parliament ratified the choice both of the executive (government) and of Scotland's senior law officer, a type of democracy different from that seen in Westminster. As throughout the century, the requirements of politicians continued to pose new problems for the processes of government (see Chapter 12).

## Summary

◆ Britain has an 'unwritten' constitution. There have been important constitutional changes during the century. The monarchy and the House of Lords have seen their power decline.

◆ Within the 'elective dictatorship', the power of Parliament has declined in favour of a more 'presidential' Prime Minister. In addition, power shifted from local to central government.

◆ Democratisation stemmed from democracy, the extension of the franchise, but was much wider in its impact. Democratisation was as much about trying to elicit a response from new state institutions and other consequences of the extension of state power, as concerned with the overthrow of the earlier Establishment.

## Questions for discussion

◆ What have been the strengths and weaknesses of the British constitution?

◆ Why did the House of Lords lose power? (See also Chapter 9.)

◆ Why did Prime Ministers acquire more power?

◆ What aspects of democratisation have you encountered in your work on the period?

◆ What is the relationship between democratisation and the agenda of individual political parties at particular moments during the century?

## Further reading

Barber, James, *The Prime Minister since 1945* (Oxford, 1991).

Baxendale, John, and Pawling, Christopher, *Narrating the Thirties: A Decade in the Making* (London, 1996).

Bradford, Sarah, *George VI* (London, 1989).

Clarke, P., *A Question of Leadership: Gladstone to Thatcher* (London, 1991).

Eccleshall, R., and Walker, G. (eds), *Biographical Dictionary of British Prime Ministers* (London, 1998).

Fielding, Steven (ed.), *The Labour Party: 'Socialism' and Society since 1951* (Manchester, 1997).

Foley, M., *The Rise of the British Presidency* (Manchester, 1998).

Holt, Richard, *Sport and the British* (Oxford, 1989).

Kuhn, William M., *Democratic Royalism: The Transformation of the British Monarchy, 1861–1914* (London, 1996).

Lawrence, Jon, *Speaking for the People: Party Language and Popular Politics in England, 1867–1914* (Cambridge, 1998).

McCrillis, Neal R., *The British Conservative Party in the Age of Universal Suffrage: Popular Conservatism, 1918–1929* (Columbus, Ohio, 1998).

Meadowcroft, James, *Conceptualizing the State: Innovation and Dispute in British Political Thought, 1880–1914* (Oxford, 1995).

Pennybacker, Susan D., *A Vision for London, 1889–1914: Labour, Everyday Life, and the LCC Experiment* (London, 1996).

Prochaska, Frank, *Royal Bounty: The Making of a Welfare Monarchy* (New Haven, 1996).

Rhodes, R. A. W., and Dunleavy, P. (eds), *Prime Minister, Cabinet and Core Executive* (London, 1995).

Strachen, Hew, *The Politics of the British Army* (Oxford, 1997).

Taylor, Rogan, *Football and its Fans: Supporters and their Relations with the Games, 1885–1995* (Leicester, 1992).

Tomlinson, Jim, *Government and Enterprise since 1900: The Changing Problem of Efficiency* (Oxford, 1994).

Vincent, David, *The Culture of Secrecy: Britain, 1832–1998* (Oxford, 1998).

Weinberger, Barbara, *The Best Police in the World: An Oral History of English Policing from the 1930s to the 1960s* (Aldershot, 1995).

Witherell, Larry L., *Rebel on the Right: Henry Page Croft and the Crisis of British Conservatism, 1903–13* (London, 1997).

Young, Ken, and Rao Nirmala, *Local Government since 1945* (Oxford, 1997).

# Politics, 1900–45

## Contents

A political narrative does not come first and foremost in this book. Instead, politics are treated as an aspect of the history of the century and not, necessarily, a determining aspect. Nevertheless, the political history of the century is still important. Restricted to two chapters, the narrative is necessarily selective, but it is important to note again a frequently unstated point. Throughout the century, Britain remained a democracy, and governments changed without violence or the threat of violence. This was different from the history of many other European states, including France, Germany, Italy and Spain. With the important exception of Ireland, British elections overwhelmingly returned MPs who did not believe in the use of violence. Extremist parties had little impact in British politics, and extremist tendencies within the major parties were contained. Within the parliamentary system, the major shift was from a Conservative–Liberal two-party system to a Conservative–Labour system. A **first-past-the-post electoral system** ensured that, although parties did not usually win majorities of votes cast in elections, they were still generally able to win the majority of seats.

## Key issues

▶ Why did the Liberals collapse?

▶ Why did Labour rise?

▶ Why were the Conservatives so successful in the 1930s?

▶ Why were extremists unsuccessful in the 1930s?

▶ What was at stake in national politics in this period?

## Pre-war politics

**first-past-the-post electoral system:** System in which the individual candidate with the most votes is elected, even if they have less than half the total votes cast.

There was no Edwardian calm to British politics. Instead, Edward VII's reign (1901–10) was a period of uncertainty and tension. The century opened with Britain at war (the Second Boer War, of 1899–1902, in South Africa), the National Debt rising, and politicians uncertain of how best to respond to growing industrial militancy, as well as concern about national efficiency and pressures for social reform. To pay for the war, the government raised taxes, including income tax from 8d to 1 shilling and 3d,

**The khaki election (1900)**
Benefiting from wartime patriotism, Robert, 3rd Marquess of Salisbury, won re-election for his Conservative government. The hunting image employed in Tenniel's cartoon for *Punch* (10 October 1900) reflected a popular upper-class sport.

and borrowed £135 million. War and domestic issues were linked in a concern about Britain's strength relative to other powers, particularly Germany. Far from there being any general complacency, there was a widespread feeling that something had to be done. This was exacerbated by serious defeats in the early stages of the war.

What was to be done was less clear. Salisbury and the Conservatives (then called Unionists because of their support for the existing constitutional arrangements in Ireland) won a 'khaki election' held in October 1900. It was held when the Boer War was arousing patriotic sentiment and going well and the Liberals were publicly divided over its merits. Most of the electorate had no such doubt about the expansion of Empire. Only 184 Liberals were elected and no fewer than 163 government supporters were elected unopposed. However, this victory could not, for long, conceal important weaknesses in the Conservative position, including the inability to respond positively to the growing demands of organised labour. The Liberals were also helped by the declining, but still considerable, strength of their Nonconformist constituency. Salisbury failed to take advantage of the 1900 general election in order to reorganise and strengthen the government. Very few middle-class politicians were brought into office.

More generally, in the 1900s, there was a freneticism that reflected a sense that real issues were at stake. There was no consensus over how best to analyse and respond to Britain's relative decline. The first lightning rod was cast by Joseph Chamberlain (1836–1914), Colonial Secretary from 1895 to 1903. Chamberlain, a major Birmingham manufacturer of screws, who employed 2,500 workers by the 1870s, and became Mayor of Birmingham, had sold his holdings in the family firm and become a professional politician. A former Radical, who had broken with the Liberals, Chamberlain was convinced that the British Empire had to be strengthened and British society and the economy protected from decline, although his imperial vision was very much a 'white' view and even so it is by no means clear that his vision was welcomed in Australia and Canada. Chamberlain sought a new relationship with the outside world, namely a replacement of free trade, the powerful economic creed of nineteenth-century liberalism, by tariffs (import duties) with a system of Imperial Preference to encourage trade within the Empire. The revenues tariffs produced were to be spent on social welfare, thus easing social tension, without increasing

**Joseph Chamberlain**
One of the leading politicians from the 1880s until the 1900s, Chamberlain (1836–1914) was a radical Liberal who abandoned Gladstone when he supported Home Rule. He then led the Liberal Unionists into alliance with the Conservatives, only to resign in 1903 in order to campaign against free trade and for imperial preferences.

taxes, the last a necessary strategy for the Conservatives, because their supporters were increasingly sensitive to rising rates of taxation.

To Chamberlain, this appeared to offer populist revival and an opportunity to strengthen the Conservative government, but, in fact, his policy divided and weakened the Party. Conservative free traders were put in a difficult position and several joined the Liberals, including Winston Churchill in 1904. The popularity of the tariff policy was compromised, because it was presented as a taxation on food imports that would hit the urban working class by increasing the price of food. Furthermore, the issue united the Liberals and increased their popularity, thus demonstrating the political limitations of tariff reform for the Conservatives. Never underestimating the credulity of their audience, Liberal speakers focused on the price of food and ignored the wider questions posed by the challenges to the British economy represented by free trade, especially the competition for British industry. On the other hand, given the developing New Liberalism, the Liberals were also far better placed than the Conservatives to give voice to popular pressure for social reform and, more generally, for change. In the 1906 general election, the majority of Liberal candidates included pledges for social reform in their election addresses.

Unable to unite the party over tariff reform, or to offer solutions on questions such as social reform, the Conservative Prime Minister, Arthur Balfour, resigned on 4 December 1905. He hoped that the Liberals would divide in office, but, instead, they were better placed to win the general election in January 1906 with a landslide, gaining 401 seats to the Conservatives' 157. The Liberals had recovered well from earlier divisions over Ireland and the Boer War. Since 1903, the Liberals in England and Wales had been allied with the Labour Party, agreeing not to fight each other in certain seats lest they help the Conservatives. This cooperation was helped by common hostility to tariffs and by Labour anger with the government's attitude towards trade union rights. Furthermore, Balfour was unable to unite his party. He was also no populist and a poor campaigner. The Conservatives in government were seen as overly linked to sectional interests – the employers, the agricultural interest, the Church of England, and the brewers – and had not acquired any reputation for competence. They were blamed for the mismanagement of the Boer War and suffered from the sour taste the conflict had left. Furthermore, the Conservatives did not seem a credible source for the changes necessary to ensure the 'national efficiency' that was widely called for. Conservative policies were also unwelcome. Tariff reform was rejected in favour of free trade. Workers preferred to think about the cost of food rather than the threat to their jobs. In the election, the Conservatives lost some of their urban working-class support, while the Liberals took the former Conservative strongholds of London and Lancashire, and also made important gains in rural and suburban parts of southern England, the Conservative heartland. Many of the latter gains were lost in the two elections of 1910, but the Liberals then retained Lancashire and London, ensuring that they were the major party in all the leading industrial areas.

Victory gave the Liberals a mandate for action. As President of the Board of Trade in 1905–8, David Lloyd George increased state regulation of the economy. The Trade Disputes Act of 1906 gave trade unions immunity from actions for damages as a result of strike action, and thus legalised strike action, rejecting the attempts of the courts, through the Taff Vale Judgment of 1901, to bring the trade unions within the law. That Judgment had made the trade unions liable to damages for strike action, and had specifically awarded the Taff Vale Railway Company damages against the

### Herbert Henry Asquith (1852–1928)

Herbert Henry Asquith was to have a very mixed reputation, but, at the time he became leader of the Liberal Party, he was an impressive and powerful figure, Prime Minister without a break from 1908 until 1916, and, with his allies, the victor in two elections in 1910. His ability took him from a modest background among small employers in the Yorkshire cloth industry, via Oxford and the law, into Parliament where he was a skilled debater. Home Secretary in 1892–5, Asquith became Chancellor of the Exchequer when the Liberals returned to office in 1905. Succeeding Campbell-Bannerman in 1908, Asquith led a talented ministry that introduced ambitious reforms, limited the powers of the House of Lords, and passed Irish Home Rule through Parliament. He was less successful as a wartime Prime Minister, and was replaced by Lloyd George in December 1916. This divided the Liberals and they were further weakened when Asquith refused to abandon the party to the new Prime Minister. Until he resigned the leadership in 1926, Asquith was a divisive force.

Amalgamated Society of Railway Servants arising from the rail strike of 1900. The Salisbury government had rejected trade union pressure to change the law, strengthening union concern about Conservative views and the commitment to intervene in electoral politics. The Workmen's Compensation Act of 1906 met Trades Union Congress (TUC) demands for the enforcement of national standards. The government intervened to prevent a rail strike in 1907. The Mines Regulations Act of 1908 limited the number of hours that miners could spend underground.

The Liberals, however, found themselves thwarted by the conservatism of the House of Lords, especially over attempts to modify the Education Act, and the Licensing Act that determined pub licences. The latter issue opposed the Nonconformist lobby to the brewers, most of whom were close to the Conservative Party. The Prime Minister, Sir Henry Campbell-Bannerman, ably held his talented Cabinet together, but, until he resigned in April 1908, there was only limited drive to Liberal government; Campbell-Bannerman was content with a policy of 'filling up the cup'. Rather than producing a coherent blueprint for change, he responded to the Liberal lobbies, and this encouraged a somewhat *ad hoc* feel to government policies.

Campbell-Bannerman was replaced by the abler and more decisive Herbert Henry Asquith. He managed the rare trick of combining intellectual ability and political skill, leading a Cabinet of much ability. Asquith faced a difficult financial situation. The government wanted both new battleships, to keep a lead over the Germans (see Chapter 13), and old age pensions in order to fulfil the expectations that New Liberalism could enhance social welfare (see Chapter 2). In 1894, Balfour had stated that 'the best antidote to Socialism was practical social reform'. It was the Liberals who seemed most determined to implement this policy.

Current taxes could not meet the bill; the deficit rose from £700,000 for 1908–9 to an estimated £15 million for 1909–10. The Old Age Pensions Act of 1908 cost £8.5 million in its first full year of operation and over £12 million by 1913. So, in 1909, Lloyd George, now Chancellor of the Exchequer, introduced what, with a characteristically popular flight of rhetoric, he called the 'People's Budget'. This raised direct taxation, on higher incomes, and prepared the way for taxes on land. He proposed a redistributive budget, designed to maintain free trade and to heal divisions within the Liberal Party at the cost of landlords. The Conservatives, in contrast, argued that revenues should be raised by tariff reform. They were also concerned about the principle and the practice of significant redistribution by taxation. The Liberals had lessened concern about the issue, by planning no tax increases on annual earned income below £2,000, a figure that then excluded the middle class; but the notion of redistributive taxation was indeed a threat to this group, as was to be shown clearly under Labour in the 1970s. The Conservatives were also anxious about the impact of the budget on the landed interest. The House of Lords, in which this interest was well represented, rejected the budget on 30 November 1909, claiming that they were doing so in order to refer the measure to the electorate.

The Liberals called an election in January 1910. Public excitement was great, and the turnout rose considerably, in part because there was a new electoral register. The Conservatives increased their percentage of the vote over the 1906 election, and gained 116 seats, especially in rural southern England. Much of the electorate rejected the 'Socialism' that New Liberalism appeared to offer. However, Conservative support for tariffs prevented them from regaining the working-class support in Lancashire and London they had lost in 1906, and, although the Conservatives gained more votes than the Liberals, the latter were able to remain in office, thanks to winning more seats, and to support from Labour and the Irish Nationalists. The Conservatives won 273 seats, the Liberals 275, Labour 40, and the Irish Nationalists 82. Conservative policies helped to keep both of these groups behind the Liberals. Liberal success led the Lords to accept the budget.

Another election, in December, confirmed the result. Balfour was to be a Prime Minister who never won an election, but instead lost three. The Labour Party had advanced rapidly since the formation of the Labour Representation Committee in 1900, and the creation of the Labour Party itself in 1906, winning more seats each election, but it was still less powerful than the Liberals as a party of the Left. Campbell-Bannerman did not see Labour as a threat, was happy to cooperate with it, and appointed John Burns, the first member of the working class to join the Cabinet. Labour had problems of identity in the face of Liberal welfare reforms and its electoral performance after 1910 was mixed at best. It enjoyed no by-election successes and even the municipal advance involved strengthening support in areas already won over to Labour.

Yet, it was unclear how far the Liberals could adjust to the rising number of working-class voters and the growing importance of class issues by backing social reform, and thus lessening Labour's appeal in class-based politics. In 1907, Philip Snowden urged the Durham miners' gala to reject the Liberals and support only Labour. Many prominent Liberals did not favour a focus on social reform, because, more generally, the Liberals were unhappy with class politics. The Liberals did not adopt working-class candidates to any great extent, were unhappy with using the language of class, unenthusiastic about powerful trade unions, and unwilling to accept working-class power. Furthermore, the Liberal leadership was opposed to votes for women, and this encouraged many female and male activists to switch their support to Labour.

Yet, there was a powerful radical strain to 'New Liberalism'; and the government was definitely out to appeal for working-class support. The National Insurance Act of 1911 sought to provide security against sickness and unemployment (see Chapter 2), although employee contributions were unpopular with many and led the Conservatives in 1913 to promise repeal. The pace of reform was maintained. In late 1913, Lloyd George proposed state-funded rural house-building and a minimum agricultural wage. When war began in 1914, it cut short government initiatives that were being planned for health, housing, education, and a minimum wage.

Although the Lords had passed the budget, their own powers were now a major political issue. The Irish Nationalists insisted that the Lords' veto be reduced in order to pave the way for Home Rule. The Lords themselves, however, were unlikely to pass such a measure unless the King threatened to create a large number of Liberal peers, the same threat that had been employed in 1832 in order to push through the First Reform Act. Edward VII refused to make such a threat unless a second election produced a clear mandate, and Asquith was able to persuade his successor George V (reigned 1910–36) to pledge to do so. This led to the election in December 1910: 272 Liberals, 272 Conservatives, 42 Labour and 84 Irish Nationalists, were returned. The threat of a mass creation of peers led the Conservative leaders to accept the legislation, although a 'Diehard' right-wing opposition rejected such concessions. On 10 August 1911, the Parliament Act was pushed through the Lords under the threat of such creations. The Lords lost their veto on legislation, although they retained the power to delay it for up to two years. This was a major blow to traditional constitutional, political and social assumptions, and one inflicted in the full glare of publicity (see Chapter 8).

Irish Nationalist support, and the new limitation in the power of the Lords, led the Liberals to return again to Home Rule, a policy that the Conservatives were pledged to resist. They had established themselves as the defenders of the Union when Gladstone introduced his first Home Rule Bill in 1886 and this helped both to provide the Conservatives with their identity and to divide the Liberals. Indeed, the Liberal Unionists were formally amalgamated with the Conservative Party in 1912. Home Rule moved to the forefront. The Protestant majority in much (but not all) of Ulster had no intention of yielding to rule from a Dublin Parliament, which would be Catholic dominated, and felt abandoned by the government. The Asquith administration, indeed, paid insufficient attention to the particular character of Ulster society.

Tensions rapidly escalated. Andrew Bonar Law, who became leader of the Conservatives in November 1911, dropped hints about supporting armed opposition in Ulster, in a famous speech at Blenheim Palace on 27 July 1912, an extremist step that suggested that Conservative support for the status quo was putting them in an exposed position. Bonar Law's Presbyterian Ulster–Scottish background made the fate of Ulster particularly urgent to him, but he also saw Ireland as an opportunity to reunite a party divided by tariff reform and to attack the government. Bonar Law also abandoned support for taxes on food imports.

Having lost three successive general elections, the Conservatives were both divided and unable to reach out to new electoral constituencies and other political parties. The Party was only rescued from this by the course of World War One, a reminder of the major role of events in political history. The Home Rule Bill passed the Commons in 1912 and 1913, under the terms of the Parliament Act, but opposition and the escalating crisis in Europe ensured that the Act was finally passed in 1914 with the proviso that it was not to be implemented until after the War and that the Ulster situation was to be reconsidered.

# World War One, 1914–18

The outbreak of World War One did not transform British politics. Although the Liberal Party and Cabinet were divided over declaring war on Germany, the German

**The Wartime Coalition**
Asquith and Bonar Law, the Liberal
and Conservative party leaders with
their 'winner' (*Punch*, 1916). In fact,
the Coalition was to unseat Asquith
as Prime Minister within a year,
although it then survived the coming
of peace and lasted until 1922.

decision to attack neutral Belgium, as well as France, with which Britain had a defence understanding, contained divisions, and only two Cabinet ministers resigned
(see Chapter 13). A coalition government was not formed, but the parties agreed an
electoral truce, so that in by-elections the sitting party would be re-elected. The outbreak of the war left the Conservatives with few opportunities, not least because their
patriotism and pragmatism led them to accept government policies, including
higher taxation and a massive expansion in state power. The Conservatives supported the government in all matters connected with the war under the terms of the
party truce agreed in August 1914. The government's decision to place the Home
Rule Bill on the statute book did create problems, but Conservative criticism took
the form of a symbolic withdrawal of MPs from the House of Commons when the
vote was taken.

Politics changed in 1915 when problems with the war effort, specifically the
unsuccessful Gallipoli expedition and a shortage of shells, led Asquith, in May, to
establish a coalition government in order to prevent Conservative and newspaper
attacks. The key posts were retained by the Liberals, and the eight Conservatives in
the Cabinet made less of an impact than Labour was to do during World War Two.
Labour was also brought in, and the Labour leader, Arthur Henderson, became the
first Labour Cabinet Minister. This was a testimony to the major role of the trade
unions in the wartime economy. Political instability followed, however, because the
most dynamic minister, Lloyd George, having now moved to the key Ministry of
Munitions, had lost confidence in Asquith's ability to lead the country. Lloyd George
wanted to mobilise all the country's resources for war, and this attitude and determination found more favour with the Conservatives than with many Liberals.

There was powerful opposition within the Liberal Party to conscription. It was
seen as opposed to the Liberal tradition of civil liberty, and prominent Liberals, such
as Reginald McKenna, Lloyd George's replacement as Chancellor of the Exchequer,
resisted the measure. Nevertheless, Lloyd George and the Conservatives were determined to see it through in order to provide sufficient men for the trenches on the
Western Front. A fudge, Lord Derby's semi-voluntary scheme, introduced in

October 1915, failed to produce sufficient recruits and, faced with Lloyd George's threat to resign that December, Asquith gave way. The Military Service Act of January 1916 introduced conscription for single men, and, in response to a sudden surge in weddings, the married followed in April.

Nevertheless, there was still widespread dissatisfaction with the conduct of the war and particular pressure from backbench Conservative opinion. Differences between Conservatives and Liberals who looked to Asquith prevented coalition unity and contributed to a sense of malaise. The management of the war seemed inadequate. This led to pressure in November 1916 for a small War Committee to direct the war effort. Asquith saw this as directed against his premiership, but his effort to preserve his position collapsed in the face of the growing alignment of Lloyd George and the Conservatives.

In December 1916, Lloyd George took control of the war effort. Less skilful than in the past, the over-confident Asquith was displaced, and the government was recast. Lloyd George became Prime Minister, and both Conservatives and Labour continued to offer support. Asquith, however, refused to hold office in the new government and was supported by most of the Liberal ministers. Lloyd George had thus divided the Liberals, even as he brought new vitality to the government, not least with the formation of a War Cabinet. Conservative support for the government was more important than when Asquith had been the coalition Prime Minister. Bonar Law became Chancellor of the Exchequer and Balfour Foreign Secretary. There were three Conservatives in the War Cabinet. This was a government for war.

Politics was not banished for the rest of the war. Important issues were raised, especially about the possibility of negotiations in 1917, an unsuccessful proposal that led to the resignation of its sponsor, Arthur Henderson, from the War Cabinet, although Labour remained in the Coalition. Henderson's attitude was a response to the possibility that Russia would leave the war, but also an echo of trade union and Labour Party disquiet about consequences of the conflict, including food shortages and rising prices, as well as a rise in workers' grievances. These were directed both against aspects of the war, such as wage controls, labour direction and profiteering, and also against facets of social difference that appeared less acceptable in a period of total war. The following year, Lloyd George's war leadership was challenged by Asquith in a debate over the availability of troops for the Western Front, an issue on which Lloyd George had given the House of Commons misleading information. Lloyd George survived, in large part thanks to Conservative support, but the Liberals were now very bitterly divided.

The Liberal division continued after the war. It led, in the post-war 'coupon election' of 14 December 1918, to the Asquithian MPs being denied the letter of endorsement (or 'coupon') by Lloyd George and Bonar Law. Held in the relief and euphoria of victory, the election, the first since 1910, brought the Coalition more than 500, and maybe up to 523, out of 707 MPs: the precise figure is unclear as not all the Coalition's supporters had received the 'coupon'. The Liberals were badly hit, being passed by Labour in percentage of votes cast. The latter was no longer subordinate to the Liberals, since the 1918 Representation of the People Act enfranchised more of its potential constituency. The Act was very important for Labour, although the extension of the franchise was not restricted simply to 'natural' Labour supporters. The reduction in the cost of elections after 1918 was also to be of great benefit to Labour as it could now afford to fight virtually all seats. In the 1918 election, Labour gained 60 seats.

The Liberals were hit both by long-term trends and by short-term pressures, not only divisions but, also, the essential illiberalism of the war years. State action became coercive during the war with the introduction of the Defence of the Realm Act in 1914 and conscription in 1916. Individual liberties which Liberals had long thought sacrosanct were trampled under foot due to the requirements of total war. Much of the traditional Liberal concern with temperance (restrictions on the drink trade), Church schools and Church disestablishment no longer seemed of interest or relevant to most of the electorate. Furthermore, the social welfare platform of pre-war Liberalism now seemed better, and certainly more popularly, represented by the Labour Party. The Liberals lacked new or attractive policies and leaders. Asquith lacked charisma, and lost his seat in 1918. Lloyd George, 'the man who won the war', was Prime Minister, but his prestige was personal. The radical and Edwardian social reformer was now dependent in Parliament on the Conservatives. They had recovered from their pre-war electoral failures under the banner of coalition government in the war years and now held 382 seats. Having lost three general elections before the war, and drifting to the Right (and further from electoral popularity), the Conservatives had been offered by the war an unexpected way back to the centre of politics from where they were able to benefit from their skills in flag-waving.

## ■ Peacetime divisions

The Lloyd George Coalition continued until 1922. However, its leader's attempt to give it coherence by creating a new centre party that would accommodate the Conservatives, who dominated the Coalition in Parliament, with the social reform of the Lloyd George Liberals, fell foul of incompatible views, especially the determined Liberalism of his supporters. The Conservatives limited Lloyd George's freedom of action over peace terms with Germany, as well as towards Ireland and labour relations. They were also unenthusiastic about social reform policies that would lead to high taxes. Taxes had already risen greatly during the war and the number of income-tax payers had been considerably increased. Nevertheless, Lloyd George used the Conservatives' fear that if they broke with him that might pave the way to a Labour government, in order to retain power and have some leeway over policy, which served to give his government an aura of progressiveness. Most of the Conservatives were initially keen to maintain the Coalition in order to strengthen opposition to Socialism. They were disturbed by Labour's success in the recent election, by trade union militancy, and by the spectre of Communism sweeping Europe. Yet, some Conservative opinion was very opposed to the Coalition. In 1918, the National Party ran about 26 candidates against the Coalition. They were opposed to Indian and Irish nationalists, trade unions and 'Bolshevism', and became part of the die-hard tendency which affected Conservative support for the Coalition.

The Coalition was put under stress both by the settlement of the Irish Question and by the problems of post-war social policy. The Anglo-Irish Treaty of 1921 gave effective independence to what became the Irish Free State. A government dominated by Unionists (Conservatives) thus ended the Union, not a move that won their enthusiasm for the Coalition, and one that particularly harmed Lloyd George's position among the backbench Conservative MPs who were to turn against him in 1922. Forty voted against the Act. Liberals, in turn, were angered by the tough tactics used earlier to fight the Irish Republican Army (see Chapter 12).

Post-war economic problems were serious. A world-wide depression in 1921–2 hit British exports. In 1921, unemployment rose markedly (to 1.8 million insured workers), as did industrial disputes, including an unsuccessful miners' strike. Lloyd George no longer seemed able to control social unrest or ensure industrial peace. His value to the Conservatives was now far less clear. Abroad, the government was over-extended, with its interventionism in the Russian Civil War against the Communists, and also new commitments in the Middle East, in both Iraq and, more seriously, Turkey (see Chapter 13).

At home, the level of government expenditure could not be sustained. In 1922, a committee under the chairmanship of the businessman Sir Eric Geddes, appointed to recommend government cuts in the face of an anti-waste campaign in the Conservative heartlands, urged deflation. The armed forces were cut, as was expenditure on social services, education and housing, the last the policy of building council houses and thus providing homes for the demobilised troops. This 'Geddes Axe' did not improve Lloyd George's popularity. The social politics of the government seemed clearly different from what Labour offered. The Labour Party made important gains in council and by-elections in 1921–2.

Yet Lloyd George was to fall because he lost Conservative support, not because he increasingly alienated radicals. Much of the Conservative leadership, including the leader since March 1921, Austen Chamberlain, a son of Joseph Chamberlain, did not want to divide the anti-Labour vote. Nevertheless, concern about Lloyd George and his policies led many Conservatives in 1921 to decide that they would not fight a second election in alliance with him. Indeed, Lloyd George failed to persuade the Conservatives to fight a second 'Coupon' election in December 1921. Support ebbed further in 1922 as Lloyd George's sale of honours – peerages and baronetcies – led to a public scandal, and in September Chamberlain was informed that 180 Conservatives would not fight the next election as Coalition candidates. Chamberlain wanted to continue the Coalition; but a meeting of Conservative MPs at the Carlton Club on 19 October 1922 decided otherwise by 185 to 88 votes. The energetic and talented but inconsistent and dishonest Lloyd George was no longer trusted, admired, or felt necessary by the majority of the MPs, and they also lacked confidence in party leaders who seemed too close to him, particularly the aloof Chamberlain. The National Union of Conservative and Constitutional Associations was also against the continuation of the Coalition, as were the executives of many constituency associations. They put pressure on MPs, and, in part, the fall of the Coalition reflected the pressure of activist politics. The Newport by-election victory for an independent (i.e. Anti-Coalition) Conservative confirmed the anxiety of many Conservative MPs about the Coalition. After the meeting decided that the Conservatives should fight the next election as an independent party, not part of the Coalition, Lloyd George resigned as Prime Minister and Chamberlain as party leader. The Conservatives, now again under Bonar Law, who had spoken against the Coalition at the Carlton Club meeting, took office.

The Coalition was over and the party system was back. It had to adjust to a new electorate. The Fourth Reform Act of 1918 brought universal male suffrage, and gave women the vote, albeit at a higher age; but, as in the nineteenth century, existing political groups accommodated themselves to the extension of the franchise. However, plans for significant changes to the political system, including proportional representation, which had been part of a 1918 Reform Bill, remained just plans.

Yet the political world had also changed. The Conservatives were stronger than before World War One, although plans to restore the powers of the House of Lords were not pursued. The Conservatives also had to find a new role now that Lloyd George had apparently settled the Irish issue.

A more broadly-based Labour had replaced the divided Liberals as the leading party of opposition. Labour was therefore the party that opposition to the Conservatives had to cohere round, were it to be successful. Although there were important exceptions, for example in Liberal-dominated Cornwall, Labour had become the natural first-choice party of the working class, and, as such, was strong in all major conurbations and industrial areas. Labour benefited from the rise in class politics and from the growing prominence of class issues, such as industrial relations. Labour also enjoyed a measure of support in rural areas among agricultural workers, although that was to ebb as the agricultural workforce declined, while the rural workforce anyway tended to be less unionised than their urban counterparts. Labour benefited much from the greater prominence that the trade union movement had won during World War One and from shifts within the movement so that it was more clearly aligned with Labour. Arthur Henderson, the effective leader in 1908–10, 1914–17 and 1931–2, had been a trade union leader. The reformist policies of Labour influenced many town and county councils and widened the appeal of the party. Furthermore, Labour, not the Asquithian Liberals, had benefited from opposition to the Coalition and become the home of anti-Coalition views from a variety of backgrounds. Labour won fourteen by-election gains in 1919–22. It was far from restricted to the working class or Socialists.

Labour also benefited from the weakness of its radical challengers, Communism and the Independent Labour Party (ILP). Yet, Labour also contained both Communism and Socialism. The relationship between the Labour Party and Socialism is a matter of controversy. Some scholars argue that Labour helped Socialism advance, while others claim that Socialism became stronger due to World War One, the example of the Communist Revolution in Russia in 1917, and the decline of the Liberals, not thanks to the Labour Party.

The Liberals suffered from this shift in working-class support. They no longer had a strong working-class identity, although, in parts of the country, working-class Liberalism remained important. Furthermore, many of the Labour voters were new voters enfranchised in 1918. Thus, rather than the Liberals losing support to Labour, Labour gained much from the new electorate, while the Liberals lost more heavily to the Conservatives. The Liberals also suffered from their divisions. This was not a case of tension within a political party, but of two competing organisations.

More seriously, the Liberals – together and separate – were hit by the nature of the electoral system, specifically the absence of proportional representation. Winning from 18 to 30 per cent of the vote in the elections of 1922, 1923 and 1924, the Liberals suffered because their electors were evenly spread across the country, far more so than Labour, and thus were perennially coming second to Labour victors in working-class seats and to their Conservative counterparts in middle-class areas. In former strongholds, such as West Yorkshire, the Liberals were in a weak parliamentary position by 1924. Thus, despite the continued liveliness of liberalism as an intellectual philosophy, seen, for example, in the writings of the economist John Maynard Keynes, the Liberals failed to recover their pre-war position. Across much of the country, the Liberals were more likely to attract support from Conservative supporters than from Labourites, just as they tended to defect to the Conservatives, not Labour, and this affected the way in which policy was presented. The Liberal alliances with Labour in 1924 and 1929 were in part tactical, although there was also a common hostility to protectionism. Furthermore, these alliances cost the Liberals part of their middle-class support. Angered by Lloyd George's radicalism, Alfred Mond, founder of ICI, the Liberal MP for Carmarthenshire, joined the Conservatives in 1926. Winston Churchill had already done so in 1924.

The collapse of the Coalition led to a return of party warfare. Easily winning the general election of 15 November 1922, Bonar Law formed a totally Conservative government, the first since 1905; only to serve for 209 days before resigning in May 1923 as a result of the throat cancer that killed him that October. The decision to abandon Lloyd George had helped the Conservatives to victory with 344 MPs elected. Bonar Law had fought on the platform of stability and 'tranquillity', and, in office, he sought both, promising, in order to lessen the divisiveness and unpopularity of tariff reform, not to introduce protectionism without seeking a mandate in a second general election. The shape of Bonar Law's long-term strategy was unclear.

Bonar Law was succeeded not by Austen Chamberlain, who was discredited by his support for the Coalition, nor by the Foreign Secretary, George, Marquess Curzon, a peer who felt that he had the strongest claim to the post, but by the less grand (and less experienced) Chancellor of the Exchequer, Stanley Baldwin, who was to remain leader of the Party until 1937. Baldwin was crafty, not sparkling, but his tactical skill helped prevent the Conservative divisions from having the same effect as their Liberal counterparts. He also played a major role in making the Conservatives appear to much of the electorate to be conservative, but not reactionary, consensual, not divisive, and the natural party of government. Baldwin was to prevail in the General Strike of 1926, the financial–political crisis of 1931, and the abdication confrontation of 1936.

Initially, however, Baldwin was less successful. He swiftly lost office, because his call for tariffs, in order to protect industry and reduce unemployment, united both branches of the Liberals and Labour in defence of free trade. The Asquith and Lloyd George Liberals formally reunited. Baldwin was convinced that tariffs were necessary in order to improve the economy, and had supported tariff reform when he entered Parliament in 1906, but the policy was distrusted, unpopular, and widely perceived in class terms as a measure that would help the few, not the many. Furthermore, Baldwin campaigned poorly and did not make sufficient effort to lessen public anxieties. In the general election of 6 December 1923, the Conservatives took 38% of the votes, but only 258 seats, while Labour took 191 and the Liberals 158. The shift in the share of the vote had been small, but this was sufficient to give the Conservatives a net loss of 88 seats. The Liberal reunion was crucial. The Baldwin government was voted out by the new House of Commons in January 1924, and Labour took office as a minority party. A Labour government depended on the Liberals, not, as before World War One, vice versa. Led by Ramsay MacDonald, who was determined to replace the Liberals, this brief government was important because it showed that Labour could rule. There were no serious upsets, and financial policy was particularly prudent, with the orthodoxy of Philip Snowden making him an ideal Treasury-minded Chancellor of the Exchequer. Far from introducing a capital levy or wealth tax, Snowden was a supporter of tax cuts. The Labour government kept the Trades Union Congress at a distance and used emergency powers to defeat a strike by London tramwaymen.

Although dependent on the Liberals in Parliament, and drawing, in part, on the ideas of radical Liberalism, this was no coalition government, and in October

1924 the Liberals turned on Labour in a vote of confidence over the treatment of a Communist agitator. The government had had a charge of inciting soldiers to disobedience, brought against a Communist journalist, John Campbell, dropped. Earlier that year, the formal recognition of the Soviet Union had led to controversy, while, in August, the proposal to make a trade treaty with the Soviet Union, and to include a British loan, was unacceptable to both Liberals and Conservatives. The supposed (in practice *very* limited) sympathy of Labour for the Soviet Union and Communism was an issue in the following general election, not least due to the publication on 25 October of an apparently compromising letter allegedly by Zinoviev, the President of the Communist International, giving instructions to British sympathisers to provoke a revolution.

This did not greatly hit the Labour vote, which was larger, in terms of both number and percentage of votes, in the general election of 29 October 1924 than in earlier elections. Labour lost 40 seats, leaving them with 151; but the Liberals, who had done badly in by-elections during 1924, were hit very hard. The number of their seats fell from 158 in the December 1923 election to 40 in October 1924. They were hit by serious financial problems in the 1924 election (the third in quick succession) and did not contest 207 seats, helping the Conservatives to dominate the anti-Labour vote. Liberal weakness cost Labour seats. The Liberals lacked a viable alternative strategy. Their role in putting Labour into power had alienated much of their middle-class support. It also helped reunify the Conservatives by making it clear how far the Liberals had moved from the Lloyd George Coalition.

Liberal problems helped the Conservatives, who appeared as the party best placed to protect property. During their months in opposition, the Conservatives ended the division that had stemmed from the Carlton Club meeting, abandoned tariff reform, and improved their organisation. In October 1924, they took 48.3% of the votes and 419 seats, winning the largest majority (223 seats) for a single party since 1832. In so far as one party could lay claim to the position, this was the national party. They were overwhelmingly the middle-class party, and benefited from the expansion of this sector of society; but the Conservatives also received a large share of the working-class vote.

Yet, the new, larger electorate was potentially volatile, and winning its support posed a considerable challenge to politicians, both Conservatives and others, similar to that which had earlier confronted Disraeli and Gladstone. Politics became more professional: the management of constituencies and political parties more a matter of full-time activity. The Conservatives printed 97 million leaflets for the 1929 election, and also used mobile cinema vans. Under Baldwin, the media were harnessed to create a political image for a mass electorate, with frequent radio broadcasts helping to cultivate the folksiness which the Conservative leader sought to project, while Conservative Party propaganda, often geared towards the female electorate, emphasised the dangers of Socialism to family life and property in general. Unlike in much of Europe, Britain had a strong and confident centre-right party that did not reject democracy. Equally, again unlike most of Europe, the Left was willing to work within the system. The duality left little role for the Liberals, who Baldwin saw as the obstacle to Conservative hegemony. His account of society and politics left scant room for them.

Baldwin offered in his speeches a vision of England in which Christian and ethical values, an appeal to the value of continuity, pastoral and paternalist themes, and a sense of national exceptionalism, were all fused. This was not intended to exclude the Scots, Welsh and people of Ulster, each of whom were presented as possessing a distinctive character and tradition, but also qualities that had enriched and been enriched by the English. Although the rural themes in Baldwin's speeches and their impact can be over-emphasised, in the 1920s he frequently employed rural imagery as an important way to address the issue of the national character, not least in his stress on the country as representing eternal values and traditions, which could sustain 'peace in our time'. The countryside symbolised the natural fecundity that was important to his romance of a stable prosperity without serious problems (see Chapter 3).

Baldwin was particularly keen to promote peace between the two sides of industry in the 1920s. He strove to bring masters and men together in one industrial nation. Baldwin believed that his own background in industry- he had run the family iron works before entering politics – gave him a unique insight into the world of industrial relations. He opposed the Trade Union (Political Fund) Bill in 1925, which proposed to replace 'contracting-out' with 'contracting-in', thereby modifying the political levy in a way disadvantageous to the Labour Party, on the grounds that it would provoke an unnecessary confrontation between capital and labour.

Yet the importance which Baldwin attached to continuity did not mean that he and his 1924–9 government were opposed to reform. Indeed, two of its prominent members sought important changes. Neville Chamberlain, son of Joseph and half-brother of Austen, was a former Lord Mayor of Birmingham, who was Minister of Health in 1923 and 1924–9. His Housing Act of 1923 provided a subsidy per house to housebuilders – both local authorities and private – for two years. This was designed to deal with the housing problem and to help the economy and the unemployment figures. Chamberlain also sought to improve the provision of pensions, with the Widows', Orphans' and Old Age Contributory Pensions Act of 1925, which introduced contributory pensions to cover those aged from 65 until they reached the non-contributory scheme at 70. With the Local Government Act of 1929, Chamberlain created a new structure for the provision of social welfare, including for the unemployed. Local authorities – counties and county boroughs – took over the bulk of the responsibilities of the Poor Law Guardians; although the long-term unemployed were transferred to new Public Assistance Committees (see Chapter 2).

Chamberlain's schemes were helped by the support of the Chancellor of the Exchequer, the ex-Liberal Winston Churchill. He reorganised the financial relationship between central and local government. However, by returning Britain to the Gold Standard in 1925, and fixing the exchange rate at the pre-war rate of \$4.86 to the £, Churchill overvalued sterling, and helped deflate the economy. The return to the Gold Standard has long been regarded as a central reason why the British economy experienced so many problems in the inter-war period. The basic problem was that, as the pound was overvalued, exports suffered (see Chapter 11).

This exacerbated difficulties in the coal industry by pushing up the price of coal exports, and thus played a role in causing the 1926 coal strike and the General Strike. Coal exports had also been hit by the development of competing power sources and of mining in other countries, and, as exports fell, the employers tried to cut wages. The miners rejected the report of a Royal Commission under a Liberal MP, Sir Herbert Samuel, that recommended the rationalisation of the numerous pits, many of which were uneconomic, and a cut in wages, and the TUC called out 1½ million workers in a selective 'General' Strike. They feared that otherwise the TUC would be

**The General Strike of 1926**
The strike brought many unaccustomed scenes to Britain's streets, including stockpiles. It briefly threatened to lead to a degree of organisation comparable to wartime, but its rapid collapse ended many fears and plans.

seen as weak, and that this might lead to the rise of more radical options, such as syndicalism.

Beginning on 3 May 1926, the strike had variable support, and most of the South of England, outside London, did not strike. While the dock, rail and tram workers gave good support to the strike, the Seamen's Union did not, and there was only limited support in the road haulage industry. There was a firm government response, that included moving police, deploying troops and warships, and encouraging about 100,000 volunteers. The last were most numerous in London and the South-East. There was also a vigorous government propaganda response, with Churchill editing the *British Gazette*.

The TUC called off the strike on 12 May. It did not want revolution and the unions could not afford a long strike, and the miners were left to continue the strike alone. They eventually had to accept the owners' terms.

The amazing thing about the General Strike was the extent to which both sides, government and trade unions, went out of their way to avoid antagonising each other. Baldwin resisted Conservative backbench pressure for retribution against the trade unions until tempers had cooled, and the Trades Disputes Act of 1927 was a relatively moderate measure, but it still left a sour taste in trade unionists' mouths, and helped Labour and the trade unions recover cohesion, unity and morale after the General Strike. Alleging support for subversion, in 1927 the government also ended the 1924 Anglo-Soviet trade agreement and broke off diplomatic relations with the Soviet Union. Furthermore, thereafter, Conservative measures continued modest and uninspiring, winning the government little popularity. Baldwin's lack of energy had a detrimental effect in so far as creating any impression of drive was concerned.

Nevertheless, the leadership was confident of winning the next election, which was, in fact, to be its major inter-war electoral failure. Prosperity had not been achieved. The return to the Gold Standard was damaging, industrial relations remained cool, and unemployment above a million led to repeated opposition attacks. It also pressed hard on government finances. Chamberlain's reforms of the Poor Law and local government brought scant popularity, and de-rating was allegedly unpopular. There was a widespread sense that it was time for a change: the government, and certainly many of its ministers, seemed tired and lacking in direction.

Some individual policies, such as the Low-Church Home Secretary's attack on 'vice' in nightclubs, failed to rouse widespread support. Labour benefited from a desire for new ideas and faces. It seemed moderate, and the defeat of the General Strike helped lessen anxiety about Socialism. MacDonald, still the leader, did not arouse fear or anger. Indeed, in his *Where is Britain Going* (1926), the prominent Communist Leon Trotsky attacked MacDonald for being ideologically confused and barren, as well as dull and untalented.

Labour and the TUC were vindicated on 30 May 1929, when the Conservatives lost power in the next general election, the first contested on a fully democratic franchise, for the age at which women could vote had been brought into line with that of men (21 in 1928). Fighting on the platform of 'Safety First' (which was suggested by an advertising agency), but with little else to offer by way of policy, the Conservatives won more votes, but Labour won more seats, although, again, not enough for an absolute majority. Their number of MPs had risen from 29 in 1906 to 288 in 1929, and, the same year, they contested their highest number of constituencies so far: 569, compared with 427 in 1923. Furthermore, for the first time, Labour was the largest party in the Commons. MacDonald formed his second minority Labour government.

The general election in 1929 was also the Liberals' last serious bid for power. They put up 513 candidates and overwhelmingly failed. Lloyd George, leader after Asquith died in 1926, had managed to unite the Liberals momentarily with a Keynesian-influenced programme designed to conquer unemployment. The election was a disaster for the Liberal Party, however, as it only increased the number of MPs from 40 to 59. The appeal of Liberalism, even on the pressing issue of the day, was insufficiently strong to challenge the hegemony of the two main parties. As in 1923, the Conservatives suffered from their loss of marginal seats in the industrial parts of Lancashire and the West Midlands. Their working-class support was far from solid, and may have been hit by the limited nature of economic expansion. The Conservatives were criticised for failing to secure prosperity. They lost over 150 seats. The increase in the Liberal vote was insufficient to win many seats, but it sufficiently hit the Conservatives to let Labour win many.

## The 1930s

Labour was to be brought down in 1931, as in 1924, through the complex manoeuvres of three-party politics, but that was not the principal issue for the second Labour government. Instead, it was badly hit by the serious world economic crisis that began in October 1929, the Slump and the Depression, although the economic situation was already serious when Labour came to power. Baldwin had left an inheritance of unemployment of 1.16 million, a government deficit, and high interest rates to protect the gold reserves. The impact of the dramatic fall in world trade after the collapse of New York share prices greatly exacerbated the situation. Devaluation was rejected by the Governor of the Bank of England as likely to lead to a collapse of the currency, and instead, in 1930, the government relied on modest public works schemes to combat unemployment, and an increase in taxation to fund unemployment benefits. MacDonald was willing to overturn the maxims of the past, and the Wall Street Crash led him to become an advocate for industrial protection.

Nevertheless, the Treasury warned that unemployment benefits threatened

### Ramsay MacDonald (1866–1937)

James Ramsay MacDonald took the Labour Party into office. From a poverty-stricken background in Scotland, where he was the illegitimate son of a servant and a farm labourer, MacDonald became a key figure in the Independent Labour Party and in the Labour Representation Committee, which, in 1906, became the Labour Party. Elected an MP in 1906, MacDonald suffered from his opposition to Britain's entry into World War One, but he became party leader in 1922, and in 1924 headed a minority Labour government that helped make Labour seem a safe party in government. Head of another ministry in the Labour government from 1929, MacDonald was hit by the Slump and parted company with many of his Cabinet colleagues over whether to cut unemployment benefit. In 1931, MacDonald became head of a National Government in which the Conservatives were the leading force. Expelled from the Labour Party, he remained Prime Minister until succeeded by Baldwin in 1935, and was then Lord President of the Council.

national bankruptcy, and the government was under growing pressure from the Conservatives over welfare expenditure and the budget deficit. In early 1931, MacDonald pressed his Cabinet colleagues to support a cut in benefit rates, only to find the majority unwilling to support him, certainly without equivalent sacrifices from other sections of society. While this impasse continued, a European banking crisis gathered pace. The Kreditanstalt bank in Vienna collapsed in May 1931 and this led to a major run, first on the German banks and then elsewhere, leading to pressure on British gold reserves. At the same time (31 July), the report of the government-appointed Committee on National Expenditure under Sir George May projected a more serious budget deficit and urged that the majority of the cuts it deemed necessary should come from unemployment benefit. Other sections of society were not called upon to make equivalent losses. The Cabinet, however, was opposed both to cutting benefits and to introducing means testing, and this left a rise in taxation as the remedy. MacDonald found the Conservative and Liberal leaders unwilling to accept this, and was pressed by the Bank of England on the threat of national bankruptcy. The government was divided over the cuts that were believed necessary to balance the budget in order to restore confidence in sterling. The cut in unemployment benefit, pressed by Philip Snowden, the Chancellor of the Exchequer, and supported by MacDonald, was rejected by the TUC and the bulk of the Labour Party. Trade union loyalty to the Labour government had been tested too much by 1931. Snowden was not willing to follow alternative strategies, such as introducing tariffs, increasing taxes or increasing borrowing. This can be seen as a cautious, but unimaginative, response, yet Labour's lack of a parliamentary majority limited its options.

The Cabinet seemed unable to cope with the crisis and to provide the decisive leadership MacDonald thought necessary. He was worried that financial collapse would hit the working class more than cuts in social expenditure. On 23 August, the Labour Cabinet split over the economy programme recommended by MacDonald as acceptable to the financial markets and the opposition leaders. This included a 10 per cent cut in unemployment benefit rates. The Cabinet accepted the proposal by eleven votes to nine, but the nine were not willing to remain part of the government, and on the evening of the 23rd the Cabinet resigned, only to find MacDonald still Prime Minister. George V convened a conference of the party leaders and this led to a cross-party National Government. Unable to rely on his party, the Prime Minister had turned to the opposition. MacDonald and a few supporters joined the Conservatives and the Liberals (though not Lloyd George who was convalescing after an operation) in forming a National Government on 24 August 1931. This was designed to tackle the crisis and push through the necessary changes without destabilising society. A widespread fear of economic collapse and social and political disruption, combined to encourage the formation of such a government.

As, however, with the wartime coalition of 1915–22, the National Government continued beyond the immediate crisis. It continued in power, indeed, until a new wartime coalition was formed in 1940. MacDonald, who was not a great success as leader of the National Government, was succeeded as Prime Minister by Baldwin in June 1935 and he, in turn, as Prime Minister and Conservative leader, by Neville Chamberlain in May 1937. Both Baldwin and Chamberlain saw off challenges from Churchill, who did not return to office (as First Lord of the Admiralty) until 1939.

As with the wartime coalition, the National Government was dominated by the Conservatives, while the opposition was dominated by Labour, although the Lloyd George Liberals also played a role, while the Samuelite or 'official' Liberals left the government when it introduced tariffs in 1932, although they didn't move into opposition until 1933. MacDonald's Foreign Secretary in 1929–31, and his predecessor as Labour leader, Arthur Henderson, returned to lead Labour in 1931–2. It became more left-wing in opposition while the Liberals were badly divided. The old Liberal Party was split three-ways into Samuelites, the Lloyd George family group, and the 'Simonites'.

The National Government convincingly won the general elections of 27 October 1931 and 14 November 1935, in large part because it was in tune with majority opinion. Labour lost working-class votes as a result of the economic problems of 1929–31, and, to the electorate at large, appeared a divided party, while the Conservatives benefited from the economic upturn of 1934 and from the consolidation of propertied and business interests into one anti-Socialist bloc. This was a major benefit flowing from the notion of a National Government. As in 1924, many former Liberals voted Conservative. The Liberals had attracted over five million votes in 1929, but they were hit by the Liberal–Liberal National split of 1931–2, and declined seriously at constituency level. Liberal weakness was to be a condition of Conservative strength. Labour proved far less effective at winning their backing. In 1931, the National Government won 554 seats, the Conservative share rising from 260 in 1929 to 473. Labour won only 52, down from 288. The bulk of the non-Conservative National MPs elected in 1931 were right-wing Liberals, a reflection not only of Conservative support but also of the Liberals' role as a largely middle-class party. In 1935, when the percentage of unemployed insured workers was 16.4, the Conservatives and their allies won 429 seats on 53.3% of the vote. Labour, which had just discarded its leader, George Lansbury, won 154, although the Labour share of the vote was 37.9%, a swing of 9.4%. The Liberals took 21 seats with 6.8% of the vote. The National Government was represented all over the country winning *all* the seats from such industrial towns as Blackburn, Bolton, Derby, Leicester, Newcastle, Oldham, Plymouth, Salford and Sunderland. The Conservatives won at least half the working-class vote.

The consolidation of the anti-Socialist vote was democratic, as was the opposition. There was no equivalent to the political polarisation across most of Europe in the 1930s. During the decade, the number of democratic states in Europe fell dramatically. In Britain, in contrast, the extremists did not gain control of the political parties and their own movements were unsuccessful. There was no crisis of conservatism to generate a powerful radical right. The right-wing extremism of Sir Oswald Mosley's British Union of Fascists (BUF) was unacceptable, not only to the bulk of public opinion, but also to the Conservative establishment who marginalised the BUF. Mosley saw himself as a second Mussolini, but it proved easier to borrow the latter's black-shirts as a party uniform, than to recreate the political circumstances that had permitted the Fascist seizure of power in Italy. The membership of the BUF, launched as the New Party in 1931 and renamed by Mosley after he visited Italy in 1932, peaked at maybe 50,000 in June 1934, but was below 25,000 thereafter. The BUF won no parliamentary seats, and it did not prove necessary to repress the BUF or to encourage the development of a rival loyalist movement. The BUF was launched late, after the worst was over and when the economy was beginning to recover. In addition, there were not the same number of 'politically homeless' in Britain as in Germany and, again unlike Germany, no collapse of middle-class centre parties to open a legitimate route to power for extremists. The demagoguery of Mosley and the violence of his supporters helped discredit the BUF. More generally, they revealed the limitations of a populist movement in a political culture that had little time for those seeking the overthrow of the system. In response to Mosley, the government in December 1936 passed the Public Order Act banning political uniforms and para-military organisations and controlling marches. The Act sought to limit street violence. Marginalised by its methods, the BUF was unable to benefit from the widespread uncertainties and fears that it tapped. Mosley's move into more aggressive anti-Semitism in 1936 brought him no benefit, and when, in 1937, the BUF contested East London seats in the London County Council elections, it did badly. Due to Mosley's peace campaign, membership rose to between 20,000 and 25,000 in 1939.

Nor was Communism so strong that the Establishment sought to create a counter movement, either by looking to the BUF or by creating a populist movement of its own. The antagonism of many Labour politicians and trade unionists meant that the Communist Party was effectively marginalised in the 1920s and 1930s. Even the disaster of 1931 did not provide an opening for the extreme Left. Indeed, the Labour vote held up surprisingly well in 1931. Communist membership rose in the 1930s, but was still no more than 18,000 in 1939. Suffering from the close links of Labour with the trade unions, the Communists were strongest in East London and parts of the industrial zones of South Wales and Central Scotland. They were able to win Council seats in their areas of strength. The United Mineworkers of Scotland operated as a Communist trade union in 1929–36. In 1935, the Communists won only one seat, the mining constituency of West Fife gained by William Gallacher, while the Independent Labour Party took four Glasgow seats. Communist attempts to create links through a Popular Front strategy, as in France and Spain, were rejected by Labour. The Communists suffered from often poor leadership and from the ambivalent reputation of Stalin's Soviet Union (see Chapter 7).

Thanks in part to the economic upturn and fall in unemployment from 1933, and to the general prosperity of the metropolitan region, opportunities for extremism were limited. The absence of any tradition of the violent overthrow of authority was also important. Had the General Strike of 1926 led to widespread violence or to a change of government, neither of which was the intention of the trade union leadership or membership, then the situation in the 1930s might have been less propitious. The Communist-led National Unemployed Workers Movement, the 'trade union' of the unemployed, launched marches and demonstrations demanding work, but support was limited – only 700 marching in 1934 – and it was concerned to remain within the bounds of the politically possible. Riots in 1936–7 by striking miners at Harworth in Nottinghamshire were ended by police action. Force was used to maintain order in Northern Ireland. In 1932, the police shot dead two men in Belfast. In 1935, troops were brought in to back up the police after sectarian riots in North Belfast claimed eleven lives.

The National Government, therefore, maintained stability and avoided radical change. It was a governing presence, unlike the Popular Front of Labour and Liberals advocated by left-wing intellectuals, or the unsuccessful Communist attempt to affiliate with Labour after the National Government's electoral victory in 1935. In January 1937, the Communists, the Independent Labour Party, and the Socialist League, a left-wing ex-ILP pressure group within Labour, published a Unity Manifesto, only for Labour to disaffiliate the Socialist League. A left-wing Popular Front government was indeed attempted in France, but it was short-lived. Disunity affected Labour's reputation. Although the Party did not move as far to the left as some urged, it came to support more radical policies than MacDonald had sponsored in office. The nationalisation of the banking sector became a Party goal, and, in general, Labour came to support more state intervention in the economy.

As well as maintaining stability at a particularly difficult time, nationally and internationally, the National Government was prepared to countenance a greater degree of intervention in the economy than previous governments had believed desirable. Through the adoption of such policies as protectionism, the National Government served as a link between the old world of *laissez-faire* and the new world of peacetime interventionism which came into existence after 1945. Protectionism was enacted in 1932, although it was linked with Imperial Preference.

Nevertheless, the National Government's conservatism ensured that the more activist and interventionist policies pressed by some younger Conservative MPs, such as Robert Boothby and Harold Macmillan, were ignored in favour of the fiscal caution supported by Neville Chamberlain, who was Chancellor of the Exchequer from November 1931 until he became Prime Minister in May 1937. Reflationists inside and outside the Conservative Party were thwarted by the government and the Treasury. There was a determination to balance the budget and keep both expenditure and taxation low. This was what 'sound finance' was assumed to mean and there were few opponents of 'sound finance'. This was to be criticised subsequently by those who cited John Maynard Keynes' *General Theory of Employment, Interest and Money* (1936), a complex work that called for public spending to be raised in order to cut unemployment. It is far from clear, however, that such a policy would have worked. It is too easy to be wise with hindsight, especially that of some naive 1960s Keynesians. It is more appropriate to note the degree to which, for many academics and politicians, the performance of the economy between the wars was almost incomprehensible. Furthermore, it took the greatest economist of the age until 1936 to work out and publish his ideas. Foreign New Deals, such as those in the USA and Sweden, still left unemployment high.

There was, however, some interventionism. Government support for industrial location in 'special' areas was important in some, but not all, depressed communities. The cuts in unemployment benefits and public-sector salaries made during the fiscal crisis of 1931 were reversed. A corporatist approach was adopted in some areas, for example agriculture, with Marketing Boards. These were established for bacon, hops, milk and potatoes. Far from government policy being tied to free trade, the

### Harold Macmillan (1894–1986)

Harold Macmillan went to school at Eton and then studied Classics at Oxford. After recovering from injuries received during the First World War he joined the family publishing firm, and married Dorothy, the daughter of the Duke of Devonshire. He was Conservative MP for Stockton-on-Tees (1924–9 and 1931–45) and for Bromley (1945–64), but did not hold office until World War Two. As Minister of Housing and Local Government (1951–4) he achieved a target of 300,000 new houses in a year. He became Prime Minister in 1957, and fostered relations with the USA and Russia (exchanging visits with Khrushchev), and supported independence for British colonies, being famous for his 'wind of change' speech in South Africa. In 1963 he failed to take Britain into Europe because of French opposition, and his government was undermined by the Profumo scandal. Suffering from ill-health, he resigned but remained Chancellor of Oxford University, and was given an Earldom at the age of 90.

adoption of tariffs in 1932 helped sections of the economy and this was important to the success of the National Government in the 1935 general election.

In agriculture, for example, protectionism led in 1932 to the Wheat Act, which guaranteed minimum prices and encouraged a rise in the arable acreage. This became part of a more general protectionist environment in which, aside from subsidies on a number of farm products, there were also import duties on food and restrictions on the quantity of imports. For example, the Pig Marketing Board established in 1933 restricted the imports of Danish bacon, although it remained popular with consumers. Furthermore, the level of subsidy was not such as to protect British farmers from the problems of agriculture in a competitive environment. In general, unemployment remained high. 2.96 million people received unemployment benefit in January 1932 and 2.25 million in March 1935. The real unemployment figure was higher.

The National Government has been vilified since, in large part because of the response to appeasement and, also, due to the nature of the government's collapse at a time of military defeat in 1940. Furthermore, the replacement of Chamberlain as party leader by Churchill in 1940 ensured a major change in the Conservative Party, and the Conservative leadership in subsequent decades was happy to share in the general rejection of the National Government. It is now time to ask whether its achievements have been underrated. Appeasement is reconsidered in Chapter 13.

It is unclear what would have happened had there been no World War Two – no election was due until 1940 – but, despite some Labour by-election successes in 1938–9, most observers were confident that Chamberlain would win. In public opinion polls, Chamberlain won approval rates of 55% and above until March 1940. However, the political situation was transformed by Hitler's growing aggression, the crisis over appeasement in 1938, Hitler's rejection of the Munich settlement in 1939, and the outbreak of World War Two in 1939: Britain declared war on Germany on 3 September. Chamberlain was no Lloyd George. During the winter of 1939–40, in what was later called the 'phoney war', the government attempted to wage war with as little disruption to society as possible.

## The 1940s

This policy was swept aside by Hitler's successful *blitzkrieg* in Western Europe in the spring of 1940, which began with the attack on Denmark and Norway. The failure of the attempt to prevent the German conquest of Norway led to a Labour censure motion in the Commons that attracted enough Conservative support to lead to the search for a coalition that could encompass Labour: 41 Conservative MPs voted against the government and many more abstained. Chamberlain still had the backing of most Conservative MPs, many of whom regarded Churchill, a vocal and bitter critic of appeasement, as a dangerous maverick. However, Conservative divisions were growing, Chamberlain was losing heart, and the Labour and Liberal leaders were unwilling to serve under Chamberlain.

Churchill was asked to form a new government on 10 May 1940. This was to be a coalition government. A War Cabinet of five, including two Labour members, was made responsible for policy, and Churchill became more powerful when Chamberlain resigned as party leader that autumn and was replaced by him. The Labour leader since 1935, Clement Attlee, was an effective Deputy Prime Minister. His appointment was intended to highlight the notion of national unity. Other prominent Labour politicians obtained major posts, Herbert Morrison as Home Secretary and Ernest Bevin as Minister of Labour.

The combination of an effective coalition and a popular wartime leader helped the country and its politicians bear wartime problems and initial serious setbacks, such as defeat in Greece in 1941 and the loss of Singapore in 1942, without debilitating division. Churchill's rousing oratory, bull-dog spirit, and sheer capacity for work, all the more remarkable in a man who was already 65, made him the motive force as well as the public face of the government. Through the War Cabinet, he was able to exercise a degree of central control which had even eluded Lloyd George in 1916–18. Unlike Lloyd George, Churchill had the backing of the largest parliamentary party.

Furthermore, as in World War One, there was no general election during the war. The parties declared an electoral truce, although it was rejected by unofficial left-wing challengers, who won four seats from the Conservatives in 1942, and by the Common Wealth Party, an idealistic left-wing party established in 1942 by Sir Richard Acland, Liberal MP for Barnstaple. Common Wealth set out to contest by-elections against 'reactionary' candidates, and won three by-elections in 1943–5. There were demands for a commitment by Churchill over the Beveridge Report (see p. 39). His unwillingness to give any immediate commitment to legislation based on the Report had significant political results. On 16 February 1943, 119 MPs went into the division lobby against Churchill on the issue of the report being implemented. In the 'little General Election', as the press called the six by-elections in January and February 1943, the Conservatives vote dropped in four of the six, and the Conservative candidate was lucky to hold North Midlothian against a Common Wealth challenge. However, the war was conducted with less public criticism and ministerial dissension than World War One, let alone the French Revolutionary and Napoleonic Wars (1793–1815) when there had been both elections and several changes of government. Two Labour left-wingers, Aneurin Bevan and Emanuel Shinwell, were the only serious parliamentary critics who the Churchill coalition had to contend with. Churchill remained very popular in the country and easily won the two votes of confidence he faced in Parliament, that in July 1942 by 476 to 25 votes. There was of course criticism of Churchill within both the government and the coalition. However, he benefited not only from being Prime Minister in wartime, but also from the weakness of his Conservative rivals and critics. Partly as a consequence of his focus on the war and his own self-confidence, Churchill was insufficiently sensitive to shifts in the public mood towards attitudes and policies associated with Labour. The consequences were to be made brutally clear in 1945 when he and the Conservatives were rejected by the electorate.

Churchill was active politically both at the start and at the close of this period. In many respects, there was much that was similar. Yet, in political terms, the differences were also striking. The rise of Labour had had a greater impact than changes in the franchise. It forced politicians to come to terms with a working-class electorate that had a political party specifically pledged to its interests. The presence of such a party and the possible implications of it gaining a parliamentary majority (implications that were not fulfilled until 1945), roused fears and encouraged the consolidation of an anti-Socialist party. Churchill's move from the Liberals back to the Conservatives was a part of this process. It was by no means inevitable that such a party should take the form that it did, and, indeed, the political history of the period was strewn with uncertainties, some of which claimed or compromised the careers of talented individuals. The interaction of issues with the changing political structure was particularly complex, and ensured that it was frequently inappropriate to think in terms of clear-cut alignments. However, politicians had to try to adapt these issues to the party structure and to an electoral system based on first-past-the-post constituencies. The last proved constant, although the loss of most of the Irish seats was important, and greatly helped the Conservatives. The party structure itself buckled under the strain. Both the Liberals and Labour split, although the Labour splits (MacDonald and his supporters in1931 and the ILP in 1932) were small-scale, and the Conservatives were riven by serious tensions, most obviously in 1922 over continuing the Coalition. These strains and divisions remind us that real and difficult issues were at stake, and that politics involved far more than the quest for power.


Summary, Questions for discussion, and Further reading follow at the end of Chapter 10.

# Politics after 1945

## Key issues

▶ Why were the Conservatives so successful in the 1950s?

▶ What did Harold Wilson achieve?

▶ Was the United Kingdom ungovernable in the 1970s?

▶ Has Margaret Thatcher's impact been exaggerated?

## Contents

## Labour wins power, 1945

The war years were very important for what came after. At their close (the war with Germany was over, although that with Japan not yet), a general election held on 5 July 1945 removed the Conservatives and gave Labour an increase of 10% on its pre-war share of the vote and its first clear parliamentary majority. The wartime coalition was not maintained, as after World War One. The Labour Party conference in May had turned down Churchill's suggestion that the coalition continue until Japan was defeated. Instead, Labour left the coalition in May, and Churchill formed a caretaker government that lasted until the general election.

At the election, the change to Labour was far more abrupt and sweeping than anyone had dared predict. Labour strengthened its working-class support, which was not seriously challenged by the Communists, and gained a large portion of the middle-class vote. Labour took 393 seats on 47.8% of the votes cast, to the Conservatives' 213, the most miserable Conservative result since 1906, although their share of the poll was still 39.8%. Conservative organisation had been poor, but the lack of attractive policies was more important. The Liberals took 12 seats on 9.1% of the vote. The Labour net gain was 227 seats. Aside from doing very well in industrial constituencies, Labour also took such southern seats as Cambridgeshire, St Albans, Taunton, Wimbledon and Winchester. Having won none of the twelve Birmingham seats in 1935, Labour now took ten of the thirteen available. Labour also dominated the Left. The Independent Labour Party had only three MPs, the Communists only two, and the Common Wealth only one, and he subsequently joined Labour. So also did Common Wealth's leader, Acland, while, after the death of the ILP's leader James Maxton in 1946, the Party's MPs joined Labour.

**Labour victorious, 1945**
Ernest Bevin, Foreign Secretary (1945–51), celebrates Labour's first election with a parliamentary majority. The Prime Minister, Clement Attlee, is fourth from the left in the front row. The role of public meetings has since declined in a television age.

Labour's victory in what Michael Foot was later to call 'the blissful dawn of July 1945', reflected political, social and cultural shifts during the war. State control, planning and Socialism increasingly seemed normative [the norm]. Keynes's ideas influenced the 1941 budget. The cost of living was subsidised, taxation rose, and attitudes towards what was quintessentially British changed. A language of inclusiveness and sharing became important, and wartime aspirations were focused by the Beveridge Report of December 1942 which called for the use of social insurance to abolish poverty, and pressed the case for child allowances, a national health service and the end to mass unemployment (see Chapter 2). This formula for post-war reconstruction encouraged the sense that the war had to lead to change, and that Labour offered the best chance of change. Trade union membership rose by 50% during the war, while the role of the Labour Party in the coalition was important to its revived standing and provided an apprenticeship in power. This role confounded claims that Labour was inexperienced and therefore unfit for government.

Yet, the Labour landslide in 1945 owed just as much to the unpopularity of the Conservatives as it did to an upsurge in positive support for Labour. Memories of the past, of mass unemployment and appeasement, were just as potent as any hopes for the future which the electorate may have had. The Conservatives were not willing or able to offer the more optimistic scenario proposed by Labour. This was the first election since the universal male franchise was granted in 1918 in which working-class Conservative support (difficult as that is to measure) dipped to come close to 30%, while Labour took a majority of the working-class vote. The *Daily Mirror*, the most popular newspaper in the country, supported Labour, but presented it in a non-partisan, wartime spirit, not as a working-class, still less a Socialist party.

## Labour in power

The Labour government elected in 1945, and led by Clement Attlee, set out not only to confront the problems of post-war reconstruction and international competitiveness,

### Clement Attlee (1883–1967)

Clement Attlee, the first head of a majority Labour government (1945–51) and the head of the Party from 1935 until 1955, came from a comfortable middle-class background and went to public school and then Oxford. He turned to social work after seeing poverty in the East End of London, had a distinguished war record in World War One, and became an MP in 1922, holding minor posts in the first two Labour governments. Rejecting the National Government, Attlee succeeded the pacifist George Lansbury in 1935 and helped to keep Labour moderate in the late 1930s. Joining the War Cabinet in 1940, Attlee was to be Deputy Prime Minister before beating Churchill in 1945. As Prime Minister, Attlee was responsible for coordinating the establishment of the Welfare State and the National Health Service, and for widespread nationalisations. Under Attlee, Britain joined NATO.

but also to fulfil its supporters' hopes of a New Jerusalem. Labour emphasised its pragmatism, but also had a strong ideological thrust compounded of ethical Socialism, Fabianism, a belief in planning, and a measure of Marxism. Labour intended to make capitalism work for the benefit of the people. It was also frightened of the disorder that extremism on left and right had caused in Europe since 1917, and saw planning and social welfare as the necessary means to contain and overcome chaos and the threat of breakdown (see Chapter 7).

The election had seemed to indicate that the public sought better social welfare and housing, and the government created the National Health Service and a more comprehensive system of national insurance (see Chapter 2). Nationalisation extended state control over the 'commanding heights' of the economy, including the Bank of England, the railways, coal, and iron and steel. The combination of these tasks ensured that there was an extensive legislative agenda. The years 1945–7 were a hive of activity. Working very hard and ably coordinated by Attlee, the government achieved much in a relatively short space of time. The achievements were equally marked in overseas affairs. The first phase of de-colonisation took place in 1947–8.

There were, however, problems. The continuation of wartime austerity was unpopular, and the end of the Lend-Lease agreement with the USA put fresh pressure on the economy and the financial system. Crisis led in August 1947 to an austerity plan designed to limit domestic consumption and in October 1947 to a Control of Engagement Order providing powers to direct labour. Rationing was extended to include bread in 1946 and coal and potatoes in 1947, and support for state controls waned. Trade union unwillingness to abandon the free market in wages both limited and undermined economic planning. In 1946, the government had repealed the Trade Disputes Act passed by the Conservatives in 1927, but labour relations were not trouble-free. Troops and the Supply and Transport Organisation were used to suppress strikes, which were illegal until 1951. Strikers did not receive unemployment pay and the government claimed that Communist conspiracies were behind the strikes, for example the London dock strike of 1949. The docks were particularly prone to unofficial strikes, in part because the dockers resented the discipline of the Dock Labour Scheme introduced in 1947. This brought a measure of security, but lessened the freedoms enjoyed under the earlier casual system. There were dock strikes during each year of the Labour government. Despite the tensions indicated by these disputes, the Attlee governments contained Communism, although that owed more to the avoidance of defeat and German occupation in World War Two. Aside from the docks, there was relatively little confrontation between the government and the trade unions.

The Conservative Party had responded to its defeat in 1945 by undertaking a thorough review of its policies. The outcome was the Industrial Charter (1947), which showed that the Conservatives accepted the existence of the mixed economy with a role for nationalised industries. By the 1950s, the Attlee governments looked tired; many of the senior members had first been given office by Churchill during the war, and seemed to lack direction. The Conservative percentage of the vote rose in the general election held in February 1950, particularly in South-East England, while the Labour percentage fell (from 48.0 to 46.1), and the Labour majority fell greatly, to only five seats.

## The 1950s

Nevertheless, Attlee was re-elected in February 1950. His last period in office was made difficult by renewed international and financial problems, and by a rise in Labour dissension, which hitherto had been largely contained. Expectations about social welfare were far higher than they had been hitherto. The National Health Service had proved far more expensive than anticipated, in part because of pent up demand (see Chapter 2). This combined with the costs of rearmament during the Korean War, which began in 1950. Britain played a major role on the Allied side, second only to that of the USA, and heightened international tension led to an increase in military expenditure. In January 1951, a rearmament programme of £4,700 million was announced. As in 1906, it was unclear how best to pay both for an extension of social welfare and for new defence needs, but both problems now seemed more acute. In place of rivalry with Germany, there was now a Cold War with the Soviet Union in which Britain was in the front line (see Chapter 13).

The result was a financial and political crisis in 1951. The immediate crisis was short-term. Charges were imposed on the provision of false teeth and spectacles within the National Health Service, and in protest, in April, Aneurin Bevan (the creator of the Health Service, a prominent radical determined to keep Labour Socialist, then Minister of Labour), Harold Wilson (the President of the Board of Trade) and John Freeman resigned from office. In the long term, the problem of popular expectations within a nationalised service that placed a heavy burden on the national budget had become clear, as was the political sensitivity of the National Health Service (see Chapter 2). Bevan's resignation also set the scene for a conflict which was to tear the Labour Party apart during the 1950s – that is, whether the party could afford to remain wedded to public ownership at a time when nationalisation seemed to have been pushed as far as possible.

Labour divisions did not prevent Labour polling its highest ever total of votes hitherto (and 48.8% of the votes cast) in the general election held on 25 October 1951. However, the Conservatives, with slightly less backing (48%), won more seats (321 to 295). They had benefited from a marked fall of the Liberal vote: 9.1% in 1950, 2.6% in 1951 (6 seats), and also were allegedly helped by seat re-distribution. Furthermore, much of the gain in the Labour vote was achieved in seats they already held, as their core constituency underlined their support. Such an increase brought no benefit in terms of seats, an important aspect of the first-past-the-post system.

Churchill became Prime Minister again, but the Conservatives did not return to the policies of the 1930s. Instead, there was much with which Churchill would have been familiar as a reforming Liberal imperialist. Accepting the consequence of 1945, the adaptable Conservatives continued the welfare state and, indeed, much of Labour policy. Only iron and steel, and road haulage were denationalised (both in 1953); the railways, gas, coal and electricity remained in the public sector. Furthermore, the denationalisation of steel was not a top priority for the government. It had been in the election manifesto, but neither Churchill nor his Cabinet acted with zeal in the matter.

A continuity of economic policy between the Labour Chancellor of the Exchequer, Hugh Gaitskell, and his Conservative replacement, R. A. Butler, including a fixed exchange rate for sterling, Keynesian demand management, and a commitment to 'full' employment, led to the phrase 'Butskellism'. The Conservative government decided that it was not sensible to legislate against trade union rights (or privileges, depending on one's viewpoint), such as closed shop agreements and the legal immunities the unions had gained in 1906. It was felt that such legislation would be difficult to implement and would exacerbate labour relations. Harold Macmillan was particularly against such legislation. The Minister of Labour, Walter Monckton, avoided clashes with the unions and, instead, offered concessions. Neither side of industry was in favour of major reform and the government did nothing to secure it. There was also continuity in foreign and imperial policy after 1951: this should be emphasised too. The Churchill government was equally, if not more, supportive of the Atlantic Alliance, NATO, and the Commonwealth. There was little time for Europe and nothing more than a passing interest in European integration. The consensus of the 1950s was not a new departure, but, in many senses, a reworking of the consensus policies and attitudes of the 1920s and of the war years.

This consensus hit the Liberal Party and made it difficult for it to project a viable identity as a centre party. The 1950s were a time when the two-party system swept all before it with both major parties receiving more than 40% of the vote. Not until the end of the decade, could the beginnings of a Liberal revival be observed. Nevertheless, in May 1950 and October 1951 the Liberals rejected Conservative advances. On the latter occasion, the Liberal leader, Clement Davies, turned down the offer of a place in Churchill's Cabinet.

In practice, consensus was not universal, and should not be exaggerated. Although continuing the welfare state, the Conservatives did not make it more generous, as Labour, in opposition, advocated. There was a determination to resist higher taxes. Very different policy goals between the major parties ensured that elections mattered. Support for Keynesian methods was not the same as similar views on the future of British society. Aside from these differences, there were also contrasting responses to circumstances. In opposition, Labour sought to replenish its ideological identity and to distinguish itself from the government. Furthermore, many Conservative activists rejected aspects of the consensus that did exist, including the failure to restrict trade union powers. Subsequently, both Labour and many Conservatives were to see 1951–64 as years of missed opportunity.

The Conservatives held office until 1964, with Churchill as Prime Minister until 1955, and then the former Foreign Secretary Sir Anthony Eden, until 1957, Macmillan until 1963, and Sir Alec Douglas-Home, until Labour won the October 1964 election. Most readers will associate Conservative governments with those of Margaret Thatcher and John Major in 1979–97, but that is not the background from which to look at their predecessors in 1951–64. There were comparisons, not least a determination to support the American alliance and a reluctance towards furthering European integration, but there were also differences. In 1951–64, there was no attempt to change dramatically, or even significantly, the welfare state or labour relations. Instead there was a 'one-nation', Tory paternalism (to both working and middle classes) that was later to be anathema to Thatcher. This was true even of the Macmillan years (1957–63). Macmillan and Home both became Prime Minister at the expense of the more liberal Butler, but Macmillan was ready to go with change, and he kept the Conservative right wing at a distance. The successive Conservative governments benefited from the economic growth of the period, and in the general election held on 26 May 1955 they raised their already high support, winning 49.7% of the vote and 345 seats. Labour won 46.4% and 277 seats. The Conservatives had an overall majority of 60. The election had been brought forward from the autumn, for which it had originally been planned, because of concern about the balance of payments, wage-claims and the problems of sterling.

The elderly Churchill was ill for some of his period of office, and should have resigned in 1953 when he was very ill. When fit, he concentrated on foreign policy. He showed only limited interest in domestic policy, and resigned, on grounds of ill-health, on 5 April 1955. Illness and a focus on foreign policy also characterised Eden's premiership. He was also less than adept at managing his ministers, parliamentary party, rank and file, and government image. An impression of complacency and weakness sapped support in late 1955 and 1956 (see Chapter 13). Eden's time at the helm was brief, because confidence in his leadership was shaken by his failure to overcome Colonel Nasser, the ruler of Egypt, in the Suez Crisis of 1956 (see Chapter 13). Eden resigned on 9 January 1957 and the majority of ministers supported Macmillan, rather than Butler, as his successor.

## The Macmillan years, 1957–63

Like his two predecessors, Macmillan devoted much of his effort to foreign policy, in particular to rebuilding the American alliance after the Suez crisis. He also ensured that Conservative divisions were less intense and damaging than their bitter Labour counterparts. Labour was bitterly divided over nationalisation and, by the end of the decade, nuclear disarmament. Macmillan tried to keep unemployment low, and his refusal to accept cuts of £153 million in public spending for the financial year 1958–9 that Peter Thorneycroft, the Chancellor of the Exchequer, thought necessary to hit inflation, led the entire Treasury team to resign on 6 January 1958. This was the first time three ministers had resigned together since 1903. In 1958, interest rates and taxation (both income and purchase taxes) were cut and in 1959 the economy grew by 4%. This fuelled a consumerism that the populist Macmillan was happy to benefit from.

It also helped Macmillan to a resounding victory in the general election held on 8 October 1959. The Conservative percentage of the vote was slightly down (49.3%, compared with 49.7% in 1955), but it was still high, the Labour fall was greater (46.4% to 43.9%), and the Conservatives won 365 seats, their best post-war figure until Thatcher's second victory in 1983. This was the first time during the age of mass democracy in Britain that a party had won three successive general elections, and the last time that there had been three successive victories was in the 1830s. The achievement was to be repeated by the Conservatives under Thatcher in 1979, 1983 and 1987, and surpassed when her successor, Major, narrowly won in 1992, so it is difficult to appreciate the extent to which the 1959 result was seen as an achievement. It had also been far from obvious. The Conservatives did badly in by-elections in 1956–8, and in late 1957 Thorneycroft had been worried about losing the next general election. Conservative Area Offices had warned that concern about inflation was leading to a rise in Liberal support. This crisis was surmounted thanks to economic growth, but is an indicator of political and economic tensions during the years of Conservative dominance. These tensions were masked by Macmillan's studied public air of complacency and, more generally, by growth, low inflation and full employment, but they were to become important when growth faltered and divisions emerged over economic management.

The Conservative hoardings proclaimed 'Life's better with the Conservatives. Don't let Labour ruin it', and there was little doubt that a sense of affluence had helped greatly. 'Most of our people have never had it so good', a phrase Macmillan had employed in a speech in 1957 was much used during the election campaign. The Conservative Party organisation also proved effective. Labour itself had had little to offer, although, at least in the election campaign of 1959, they avoided the serious public dissension of the previous years and of the early 1960s. The Labour percentage of the poll had successively fallen since 1951, in 1959 the modest revival of Liberal support (5.9% compared with 2.7% in 1955) was won at the expense of the Labour share, and in 1960 *Must Labour Lose?*, by Mark Abrams and Richard Rose, appeared. Thanks to affluence, the austerity of the late 1940s was a fading memory. Rationing had ended and real incomes risen.

Macmillan soon appeared less happily in control and less able to provide adequate leadership. Having boomed in 1959 and 1960, the economy put great pressure on the trade gap (balance of payments), as imports rose faster than exports. British companies proved unable to keep up with rising demand, in part because they were less productive than foreign competitors and in part because of rising wage costs. This led, in 1960, to a rise in interest rates and to credit restrictions for consumers, and in 1961, to a fiscal squeeze and a 'pay pause', an unpopular attempt to control wage rises. This worked only in parts of the public sector and was ignored by the unions and by private-sector employers. The Conservatives proved unable to maintain their record for effective economic management. Concerned about economic problems, Macmillan, who had called in the 1930s for state intervention, showed now an interest in government economic planning, a policy that was to be developed when Labour took power in 1964. In 1961, there was support for French-style 'indicative' planning. This led, in 1962, to the creation of 'Neddy', the National Economic Development Council, with its task of creating a national economic plan and its membership drawn from employers, unions and government. It had no real effect on policy. The National Incomes Commission, which Macmillan saw as the arbitrator of incomes policy, was boycotted by the unions. Macmillan, however, called for a 'New Approach' including more planning and better labour relations.

Entry into the European Common Market (EEC) was seen as an aspect of this change of direction, but Macmillan increasingly seemed weak. The decision to seek entry in the first place was also a sign of weakness, in this case the underlying weaknesses of the British economy, which the levels of growth existing within the EEC made more dramatic. The government lost popularity in 1961–2, and the French veto of January 1963 on Britain's application to join the EEC made Macmillan seem

## Harold Wilson (1916–95)

Harold Wilson won four out of the five general elections he contested as Party leader and was Prime Minister in 1964–70 and 1974–6. Very talented and a shrewd opportunist, Wilson entered the Cabinet at the age of 31 in 1947, resigned from the Labour government in 1951 over rearmament, and was a major figure on the centre-left of the party in the 1950s, eventually succeeding Hugh Gaitskell as Party leader in 1963. Narrowly elected Prime Minister in 1964, Wilson supported important social reforms, but was unable to get to grips with economic problems, failed to secure trade union reforms and entry into the EEC, and was soon regarded as devious and unsuccessful. Returned to power in 1974 as a result of Heath's failures, Wilson shelved disputes over the EEC by holding a referendum on continued membership in 1975, but economic and other problems steadily mounted. In 1976 Wilson resigned unexpectedly.

irrelevant as well as unsuccessful. The government's policy of European-style modernisation had failed (see Chapter 13).

In the summer of 1963, Macmillan was hit by consumerism in a different guise, the Profumo affair. John Profumo, the Minister of War, was shown to have shared a lover with others, including a Soviet naval attaché, and then to have lied to the House of Commons about the affair. The scandal helped to create an impression of a decadent and troubled government, but Macmillan fell in October 1963 for a more mundane reason: a prostate illness. He was succeeded not by the qualified and popular Butler, but by Lord Home, the Foreign Secretary, Macmillan's choice, and the cause of much critical ridicule. Both the method of selection and the choice of Home were bitterly criticised. Two leading Conservatives, Iain Macleod and Enoch Powell, refused to serve under Home.

Home renounced his peerage, and, as Sir Alec Douglas-Home, was elected to the Commons. He was less maladroit than his critics suggested, but he was no match in populist politics for the younger and more dynamic leader of the Labour Party, Harold Wilson. Wilson, a Bevanite who had opposed the moderate leadership of Attlee's successor, Gaitskell (1955–63), succeeded him when Gaitskell unexpectedly died in January 1963. Wilson was to be revealed in office as a fixer, largely concerned to keep his Cabinet together, but in 1963–4 he was able to portray himself as the leader able to take Britain forward, in particular by linking science and Socialism so as to provide effective planning and solutions (see Chapter 4). Condemning in 1964 what he termed 'thirteen wasted years' of Conservative government, Wilson sought the mantle of John Kennedy, the Democrat President of the USA, who had used similar language in 1960 about the need to end Republican rule, in his successful campaign against Richard Nixon.

## Labour in power, 1964–70

The general election of 15 October 1964 was closer run than had seemed likely the previous year, and indeed Conservative support in opinion polls by Gallup rose from 29.5% in July 1963 to 40% in September, at the expense of Liberals and, even more, 'Don't Knows'. The electorate had become wealthier in the 1950s, but the percentage willing to vote Labour in 1964 was only slightly below that of 1951. The

Conservatives were again to discover in 1997 that rising real wealth under their government did not prevent a Labour victory.

Labour's percentage of the vote rose from only 43.9 in 1959 to 44.1 in 1964, but that of the Conservatives fell from 49.3 to 43.4, in large part because of a strong increase in the Liberal vote. Liberal support stemmed from a variety of sources. There was a distinctive Liberal political tradition, especially in parts of the 'Celtic fringe' in Cornwall, Wales and Scotland. However, many Liberal votes were protest votes against the government, rather than support for specific Liberal policies. The Conservatives were hit by the scandals of the previous two years. These helped demoralise the party and contributed to a sense that it had little to offer. The abolition of Resale Price Maintenance, the system by which industry fixed retail prices, had been the major political issue in early 1964, but it had divided the Conservative Party, for small manufacturers and shopkeepers opposed the abolition, which was pushed through by Edward Heath, the President of the Board of Trade, in the name of encouraging competition, and thus providing a route for modernisation (see Chapter 4). Meanwhile, the expansionist 1963 budget led to pressure on the balance of payments, which was highlighted by Labour.

More generally, the Conservatives seemed dated, as in the prosecution of the publishers of *Lady Chatterley's Lover* for obscenity in 1962 (see Chapter 15). The impact of repeated attacks by satirists is difficult to assess, but could not have been helpful. Yet, the Conservative vote did not collapse. That is the crucial fact to note: we are discussing a fall in support, not its disappearance. This fall is explicable not only in short-term political terms, but also by the inability of the Conservatives to respond effectively to socio-cultural shifts. In all, the Conservatives lost 1.75 million votes. Labour took 317 seats to the Conservatives' 304 (and the Liberals' 9). This was only the second time that Labour had won a majority.

Labour came to power with high hopes, including plans to use economic planning to improve economic performance, harness new technology, and end the 'Stop–Go' cycle. A Department of Economic Affairs was created in 1964, and in 1965 it produced the National Plan, an optimistic blueprint for growth. A National Board for Prices and Incomes was also created in 1965. A Ministry of Technology was designed, to encourage new industrial processes. Prices and incomes policies were joined by active policies for regional regeneration, with the establishment of a Regional Development Fund. It was hoped that growth would fuel improved social welfare. Prescription charges were abolished and pensions increased. An Industrial Reorganisation Corporation followed in 1966.

Labour policies lacked a sound economic basis, not least because Wilson refused to tackle acute balance-of-payments problems by devaluing, but the show was all, and the Conservatives had no surge of support under their new leader, Edward Heath. In the general election held on 31 March 1966 to strengthen its parliamentary position, Labour's share of the vote went up from 44.1% (1964) to 48% and the Conservatives down from 43.4 to 41.9, but the shift in seats from 317 to 364, compared with 304 to 253, was more dramatic. With a majority of nearly 100, Wilson had a parliamentary position that left him with fewer excuses for subsequent mistakes.

The general election had been held then to take advantage of apparently propitious circumstances, but the economy rapidly reasserted itself, first with a seamen's strike, which Wilson blamed on agitators, and then with the sterling crisis of July 1966. The Treasury used the opportunity to press the case for deflation, and the Department of Economic Affairs' attempt to eclipse the Treasury failed. Its head,

George Brown, once Wilson's rival, lost power and was moved to the Foreign Office. The National Plan was ditched.

The deflation of 1966 and the accompanying wage-freeze only bought time. British industrial productivity was lower than that of other leading industrial powers, and an overvalued currency helped to price exports out of markets. The trade gap widened in 1967, and that November the pound was devalued by 14.3% after strenuous attempts to prevent the inevitable that called Wilson's judgement into question. Britain's lessened status was further shown by the rejection of a second application to join the EEC, Wilson's failure to mediate in the Vietnam War, and the drawing up of plans for Britain's withdrawal from east of Suez (see Chapter 13).

The balance of payments remained weak, and there were serious doubts about the quality of economic management. More generally, Wilson came to be regarded as stronger on image than on substance. The failure of his attempt to improve industrial relations and reform the trade unions in 1969, by giving government powers to demand strike ballots or impose cooling-off periods, encouraged a sense of broken hopes (see Chapter 11). It also presaged the crises that were to face Heath in 1974 and Callaghan in 1979. Wilson's pragmatic efforts to keep the party united led to claims of duplicity and opportunism, while his populist gestures did not commend him to all. Wilson was criticised from the Left for betrayal. In *The Politics of Harold Wilson* (1968), the radical journalist Paul Foot claimed 'What is required is not a new leadership, but a new Socialist politics, with roots deep down in the Labour rank and file.' Foot criticised Wilson for an absence of coherent Socialist theory and a rootless pragmatism. Aside from this critique, it can be argued that Wilson was more successful as an opposition leader than as Prime Minister. This owed much to divisions within the Labour Party, but also to the intractability of the task. Wilson's failure to inspire and lead was also important.

The years 1964–70 may not have led to fundamental economic change or Socialism, but they were certainly a time of social advance. The Wilson government captured the prevailing mood of the time for progressive change, and, without its support, a number of key legislative moves would not have taken place. Liberalisation of the laws concerning abortion, homosexuality, capital punishment, censorship and divorce, and the passage of the Race Relations Act in 1965, were intended to transform Britain into a more tolerant and civilised society (see Chapters 6 and 7). This, when taken together with important reforms in the education system, including the changeover to comprehensive education and the establishment of the Open University (see Chapter 2), and the deep-seated concern for such disadvantaged groups as the elderly and the handicapped, revealed a government guided by a genuine humanitarian imperative. Increased pensions and reform of the Rent Act made a major difference to much of the population.

In 1969, Wilson benefited from a measure of economic recovery, including a balance-of-payments surplus. Deflation had solved that problem. More generally, the problems of the period, and the shock of the new represented by the government's social policies, were both lessened by a peacefulness that was only compromised in Northern Ireland (see Chapter 12). Wilson refused Lyndon Johnson's pressure to send troops to Vietnam, as both Australia and New Zealand had done. As a consequence, there was no equivalent to the American anti-war movement and draft dodging, no issue that really brought government and youth culture into violent opposition. The abolition of National Service in 1959–63 and the fact that only volunteers were sent to serve in Northern Ireland contributed to the same end; and

"She'll never make it with all that lot."

**Common Market entry unsuccessful**
Harold Wilson's attempt to join the European Economic Community (now European Union) was rejected by the French. The caption refers to the problems created by Britain's commitments and the government's wish to protect farflung interests.

is a reminder that we need to look at what did not happen in order to have a better understanding of what did.

In addition, there was no issue or symbol around which Conservative forces could rally. Thanks to the winner-takes-all system of British elections, it is easy to neglect the Conservatives in the 1960s, but, in the general elections of 1964 and 1966, they polled more than 40% of the votes, in the first case less than 1% behind Labour, and in 1970 Heath defeated Wilson. Yet the Conservative Party lacked a cause. Having established the National Economic Development Council in 1962, it could hardly criticise the Wilson governments for continuing with its planning experiment. Having given independence to most of the Empire in 1957–64, it was not in a position to criticise the abandonment of most of the rest. Having applied, unsuccessfully, to join the EEC in 1961, and put entry into the Common Market in their 1966 election manifesto, the Conservatives were in no position to complain about Labour's application in 1967. The populist nationalism offered by Powell, when he began to attack the consequences of immigration in April 1968, was rejected by Heath, distrustful of Powell and unwilling to associate the Party with racialism.

Powell, who had resigned with Thorneycroft in 1958, was also an early monetarist, who believed that the fight against inflation was crucial and that this should be accomplished by limiting the money supply, even at the cost of higher unemployment. Powell supported what he regarded as true capitalism. He was opposed to state intervention and wanted, instead, to see a free market in operation. This was to be the political economy of Thatcherism, and serves as a reminder that the ideas and policies associated with her period as Conservative Party leader (1975–90) did not originate in the crises and pressures of 1972–5. However, in the 1960s, although such views enjoyed much support among Conservative activists, many of whom were far more concerned about inflation than unemployment, they were not the policies of the leadership. The Conservative Party began to emphasise the effects of rising prices in 1969–70, but it failed to develop a coherent anti-inflationary policy of its own. This was a failure which would come back to haunt the Party after victory in the 1970 election.

# The 1970s

In 1970, the public opinion polls suggested that Wilson had been correct to call the election a year earlier than he needed, but the Conservatives unexpectedly won. This appears to have reflected doubts about Labour's economic management, that were focused by a poor set of trade figures, although the failure of Labour to inspire its own supporters was important. The turnout (percentage of the electorate who voted) was the lowest since 1935, and, before that, 1923, in part because the electoral register was old. The voters turned against Wilson, rather than towards the unpopular Heath, and there were few signs of a widespread rejection of Labour ideas and policies. Instead, Labour management seemed flawed. This was, at best, a weak basis for Conservative government during what was to be a difficult period. It is also important to look at the wider context; in this case a more general move to the Right at the end of the 1960s. In the USA, the Republican Richard Nixon had won the 1968 presidential election. Whatever the reasons, the Labour percentage of the vote fell to 43, the lowest since 1935 (1966: 48), while the Conservative percentage rose to 46.4 (41.9), the highest since 1959. In terms of seats, the figures were Labour 287 (364) and Conservatives 330 (253).

Heath pushed through change in what he saw as an attempt to modernise Britain. The decimalisation of the currency in 1971 discarded centuries of usage and contributed to inflation. The Local Government Act of 1972 drastically altered the historic territorial boundaries of local government, although regional governments were not created. Measures were taken to improve Whitehall efficiency. Joining the European Economic Community was central to Heath's plan to modernise Britain and make it more effective internationally and domestically. Membership was his focus, part of a long tradition of British leaders devoting attention to foreign issues at the expense of serious problems at home. Heath fused the two. He saw membership of the EEC as crucial to the revival of Britain's economic fortunes. It would provide the competition which the British economy needed in order to prosper. The intransigent French President, Charles De Gaulle, had gone, Labour had opened negotiations in its last weeks in office, and Heath was able to join on the basis of accepting the EEC's terms, which included the higher food costs of the Common Agricultural Policy, with its agricultural subsidies, and the progressive prohibition of cheap food imports, especially from suppliers in the British Commonwealth. After negotiations were successfully concluded in July 1971, and the Commons voted in favour of entry by 356 to 244 on 28 October 1971, the Common Market Membership Treaty was signed on 22 January 1972. On 1 January 1973, the United Kingdom became a full member. Large majorities against entry in public opinion polls were ignored.

However damaging it might turn out to be, Heath at least had achieved his major objective. He was less successful elsewhere. When he came to office, Heath had outlined an economic policy different from that of Wilson, one that was more prudent and far less ready to intervene in the economy, not least in a refusal to subsidise inefficient industries. Income tax and public spending were to be cut. This was the policy described as that of Selsdon Man, named after Conservative planning sessions at Selsdon Park, Surrey, in January and February 1970. Wilson referred to them as 'Stone Age economics'. This policy was seen as essential in order to help Britain compete effectively within the EEC. John Davies, the outgoing Director-General of the Confederation of British Industry (CBI), was appointed head of a large Department of Trade and Industry, and Davies announced that taxes were not well spent propping up 'lame ducks'. Industrial corporatism was reversed, and the legislative and administrative structures dismantled. Seven of the regional development agencies were abolished, and the Mersey Docks and Harbour Board was allowed to go into liquidation.

This policy was not sustained. In February 1971, the government intervened to nationalise Rolls-Royce, Britain's leading manufacturer of aero-engines, when it was threatened by bankruptcy. Later in the year, Upper Clyde Shipbuilders was rescued under pressure from a union work-in and following an initial refusal to provide support. This contributed to a sense of weak government responding to pressure. The Industry Act of 1972 was designed to provide for manufacturing companies that were in difficulties.

The problems of economic management, however, were far more widespread. Wage inflation accelerated and price inflation also rose significantly. British goods became uncompetitive, putting great pressure on the balance of payments, which deteriorated to a record deficit of over £1 billion in 1973. Unemployment rose to over a million, a shock after three decades when it had been generally low, and sterling declined in value. Government revenues also fell, as taxes were cut. The money supply (provision of money and credit) was greatly expanded. It rose 20% between 1971 and 1973. Public spending also shot up by nearly 50% in real terms during the government's period of office, in large part in an attempt to reflate the economy that was launched in the summer of 1971 and persisted until 1973. As credit became much easier to obtain, price inflation surged ahead, spectacularly so in house prices.

Price inflation put pressure on wages. Heath had come to power pledging to end interventionism in setting wage rates. The Prices and Incomes Board created by Wilson had been abolished. Instead, Heath sought to leave wages to the market, while levelling the playing field by reforming the position of trade unions. The Industrial Relations Act of 1971, passed despite protest strikes and bitter TUC opposition, established an Industrial Relations Court with extensive powers to try to limit strikes, for example, by enforcing strike ballots. However, as most unions unexpectedly refused to register, the legislation was fruitless. The unions that did register were expelled from the TUC, and the Labour Party undermined the legislation by making clear that it would repeal it if elected. A de facto incomes policy was operated in the public sector.

The situation was blown apart by the National Union of Miners (NUM). In 1972, it staged the first national coal strike since 1926 in pursuit of a large pay claim. Mass picketing closed access to coal stocks, and the government declared a state of emergency, only to give in and accept the award of a 32% increase by a court of inquiry. This wrecked the government's wage policy and also made Heath seem weak. It set the scene for nearly a decade of the so-called crisis of governability, as successive governments found themselves forced into a corner by the excesses of trade union power (see Chapter 11).

Economic problems, not least the existence of record post-war levels of unemployment, which Heath was reluctant to exacerbate, led him to change policy and to adopt interventionism, with a statutory income policy involving first, in November 1972, a wage and price freeze, and then, it was hoped, more modest increases.

This 'U turn' was to be bitterly attacked by Thatcher, who prided herself on being consistent, and was an ideologue. Heath was also stubborn, but he saw himself as a pragmatist, although he was singularly unsuccessful as such, in part because of his difficult personality and limited political skills. Having been bought off in 1972, the NUM, however, was unwilling to accept the constraints of the statutory policy in late 1973. The union's policy was motivated as much by political considerations as by labour relations. They began an overtime ban in November 1973 and, the following month, the government put industry on a three-day week to conserve power supplies. The miners pushed their £138 million pay claim hard. The Communist Vice-President of the NUM, Mick McGahey, told the Union's policy-making conference that if they did so 'we shall speed the day when not only will we establish decent wages and a decent standard of living, we will end this Tory Government and create conditions for a rapid advance to Socialism in this country'. This was a marked example of union leaders seeking to wield political power.

Unwilling to compromise, and unused to responding to the views of others, Heath was hit hard by the impact of the oil price shock that followed the outbreak of another war in the Middle East: the Yom Kippur War of October 1973 between Israel, and Egypt and Syria. In order to put pressure on the West, OPEC (the Organisation of Petroleum Exporting Companies) quadrupled prices. This hit the balance of payments, fuelling inflation. The prospects for growth in the world economy were thus undermined, and it was clear that the British economy faced a difficult situation. The massive rise in oil prices was part of an increasingly damaging international economic context. Other commodity prices had already risen, while the Bretton Woods system of fixed exchange rates, that had brought a measure of stability since World War One, collapsed when the USA abandoned it.

Heath called a general election to bolster his position and try to overawe the miners. Held on 28 February 1974, it left the Conservatives with the biggest percentage of the popular vote (37.9 to 37.1 for Labour), but with fewer MPs (297 to 301),

**Britain bankrupt**
The London satirical magazine *Private Eye* reflected a sense of national collapse in the mid-1970s. Oil-rich King Faisal of Saudi Arabia appears able to buy indebted Britain. Ironically, the discovery of oil in the North Sea shortly beforehand helped ease Britain's balance-of-payments.

and with the Liberals (19.3% and 14 MPs) under Jeremy Thorpe holding the balance of power. They had grown in electoral strength since their nadir in 1945–59, and had won by-elections during the Heath government, but were unable to 'break the mould' of two-party politics. Heath initially held on to office, in the hope of persuading the Liberals to enter into a coalition, but the Liberals rejected this idea and Wilson returned to power. Heath's had been the first government since MacDonald's second Labour government (1929–31) that lasted for only one term. In addition, much of the legislation of the Heath years was swiftly reversed and the policies abandoned. It was looked back on as a period of failure.

Labour was to hold office until 1979, thanks to another general election, in October 1974, in which Wilson won a small overall majority, and a bigger majority over the Conservatives. He was, however, unable to govern effectively, and in 1974–6 Wilson completed the process begun by Heath. An economy, state and society that had been muddling through for decades, operating far below the level of effectiveness of other countries, but nevertheless at least avoiding crisis and breakdown, slid into chaos.

The overall situation was far from propitious. The inflationary pressures and economic problems arising from the oil shock affected the entire world, and Britain, as yet, was not a major producer of North Sea oil. The collapse of the long post-war boom triggered a combination of rapid inflation and rising unemployment. This posed problems for Keynesian economists as an adverse relationship of the two had been assumed. Yet, Wilson compounded Heath's inability to control wages by positive measures that let them rip. As, at the same time, controls were placed on prices and dividends, company profits collapsed, there was a massive fall on the stock market, and there was no incentive to invest. As a result of this economic illiteracy, 1974–6 was the closest that Britain has come to the fall of capitalism.

This crisis is well illustrated by the two covers of the satirical magazine *Private Eye* shown here.

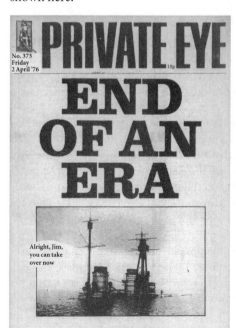

**All at sea**
The resignation of Labour Prime Minister Harold Wilson and his succession by James (Jim) Callaghan as perceived by the satirical magazine *Private Eye* (1976). Wilson was mistrusted as a fixer who could no longer fix anything. A copy of *Private Eye* now cost 25 per cent more than a year earlier. Inflation was biting.

Wilson had become a fixer who could no longer fix anything. In 1974, he had repealed the Conservatives' Industrial Relations Act and legal sanctions on pay bargaining and announced, in its place, a 'social contract' with the TUC, but that could not contain a massive wage explosion that began with buying off the miners. Other unions sought to follow the lead, and industrial earnings, which had increased by an average of nearly 14% yearly in 1971–3, itself a very high figure, went up by 19% in 1974 and 23% in 1975. As prices also rose fast, there was pressure for further wage increases. Wilson was unwilling to take on union leaders who refused to accept wage restraint, and unable to move the economy from recession. At last, in June 1975, the TUC responded to the initiative of Jack Jones, the Transport Workers' leader, and offered a voluntary agreement on wage restraint that the government accepted. This agreement, which held firm until 1978, was to effect a significant reduction in the rate of inflation, which eventually fell to below 10% in 1978.

Union leaders themselves were under pressure from their members. The power of union leaderships had declined since the 1950s as the Shop Stewards movement became stronger. This led to greater power for plant bargainers, and ensured that agreements reached between employers and union leaderships frequently did not stick. This situation exacerbated, and was exacerbated by, the heavily fragmented nature of the trade union movement and its tendency to compete at plant level. As a consequence, the issue was not only 'Who governs Britain?', the question asked by Heath in 1974, when he sought to defeat the miners, but 'Could Britain be governed?' The lead sectors of the British political economy were institutionally weak, for the Confederation of British Industry also had serious weaknesses. The problems of the union sector worried thoughtful union leaders, such as Clive Jenkins, who sought reorganisation. These institutional weaknesses made it difficult to make corporatism work, as opposed, for example, to Germany and Sweden where strong unions could deliver deals. In Britain in 1975, union leaders signed up for an income policy without any real support from their members. This was to be a major problem for the Labour government.

It also provided a parlous background for a further extension of public ownership in the economy. In 1975, the Industry Act established the National Enterprise Board, while the government took the majority of the shares in the newly consolidated car manufacturer British Leyland (see Chapter 11). The British National Oil Corporation was created in 1975, and British Aerospace and British Shipbuilders in 1977. These were major nationalisations.

Now aged 60, Wilson surprised commentators by resigning in April 1976, and his choice, the 64-year-old Foreign Secretary, James Callaghan, won the ballot of MPs for the Labour leadership, beating, on the second ballot, the candidate of the 'soft left', Michael Foot. Callaghan was only to face the electorate once as Prime Minister and was defeated then, in 1979, by Margaret Thatcher, but he had considerable talents, both as Party leader and as Prime Minister. He was more popular than his colleagues, was not an ideologue, and was more honest than Wilson.

Callaghan and his Chancellor of the Exchequer, Denis Healey, did not believe, like Tony Benn and the 'hard left', that it would be possible to resist economic pressures by a policy of state Socialism – nationalisations, high taxation and tariffs. Instead, they advocated pragmatism, and were willing to rethink the Keynesian prescriptions of the previous thirty-five years. The government confronted lower economic growth than hitherto, high inflation, and deficits both in the balance of payments and in spending (the government spent more than it received). Lower growth reduced anticipated revenue, while higher unemployment pushed up social-welfare costs and cut tax yields. In April 1976, Healey introduced heavy spending cuts, but, that September, a sterling crisis forced the government to turn for a loan to the International Monetary Fund (IMF), as if Britain was a bankrupt banana economy.

The IMF demanded cuts in government spending, and, after a political battle within the Cabinet, they were accepted. Cuts were imposed in December 1976. The government lost popularity, and also by-elections. Its parliamentary majority disappeared and Callaghan was obliged to rely on a pact with the Liberals. This lasted from spring 1977 until autumn 1978, during which time the Callaghan government presided over a relative improvement in the country's economic fortunes. So much so that if the Prime Minister had called an autumn 1978 election, as many expected him to do, then Labour could very well have won. The Liberals, now under David Steel, gained neither a share in government nor proportional representation, but were happy to support the government's plans for elected assemblies in Scotland and Wales. The Liberals regarded the Lib–Lab pact as a way of preventing a minority Labour government from pursuing radical policies.

In the meanwhile, the economy remained under strain. Big cuts in government expenditure had led to a small reduction in the government deficit, and inflation fell in 1978; but the level of industrial disputes remained high. In 1977, violent mass picketing in support of a union-recognition strike at the Grunwick film processing factory in North London again raised serious issues about public order. Industrial disputes discouraged investment and, given the downward pressure on public expenditure, caused a particular crisis in the public sector. The crisis culminated in the 'Winter of Discontent' of 1978–9. Callaghan lacked a message and policy to keep Labour united. The TUC and Labour Party Conference both rejected the norm of 5% in wage increases, proposed by the government. The selfishness of union leaders was summed up by Moss Evans, the General Secretary of the Transport and General Workers Union, who declared in January 1979, 'I'm not bothered by percentages. It is not my responsibility to manage the economy. We are concerned about getting a rate for the job.' Strikes by petrol-tanker drivers and lorry drivers were followed by attempts by public-sector unions to 'catch up'. Hospital ancillary staff, ambulancemen, and dustmen went on strike. Hospitals were picketed, the dead unburied, troops called in to shoot rats swarming round accumulated rubbish. The large number of simultaneous strikes, the violence and mean-mindedness of the picketing (which included the turning away of ambulances), and the lack of interest by the strikers in the public, discredited the rhetoric and practice of trade unionism for much of the public. Labour clearly could not handle the unions (see Chapter 11).

A sense that Britain was out of control made both Labour and the unions seem harmful, and led to a surge in support for the Conservatives under the largely unknown Margaret Thatcher, who had become Party leader in 1975 in a determined rejection of Heath and his policies. The political crises of 1972–4 had discredited the Heathites and created a sense of breakdown that provided Thatcher with her opportunity. She had been far weaker in 1972. By February 1975, however, in the battle not to be Edward Heath, Thatcher won in large part because she most clearly was not Heath and because she was willing to stand against him in a first ballot of the Party's MPs. Yet, Thatcher's elevation to the leadership owed more to the fact that Heath had lost three out of four elections than it did to support for policies which would later become known as 'Thatcherism'. Indeed, the Conservative Party's support for trade union reform after the 'Winter of Discontent' simply reflected the popular desire for change: it had less to do with ideological fixation.

Callaghan made a serious error in not risking a general election in the autumn of 1978. In early 1979, the weakened Labour government did not yet need to risk a general election, but it lost control of the parliamentary arithmetic. The Lib–Lab pact having ended in 1978, Labour rule depended on the compliance of the Scottish Nationalists (SNP). The referendum on Scottish devolution held on 1 March 1979 did not deliver the necessary percentage of the electorate in support, and the SNP then joined the Conservatives and Liberals in throwing out Labour in a vote of no confidence at the end of the month (see Chapter 12).

Labour support fell in the general election held on 3 May 1979 (36.9% compared with 39.2%), although less than that of the Liberals (13.8%–18.3%). The two combined to boost the Tories to 43.9% (35.8%), providing a working majority of 43 seats. Thatcher had benefited from a marked fall of Liberal votes which helped in many key constituencies, as well as from a widespread sense of despair with both Labour and the unions. She indeed won the support of about one-third of union voters and the percentage lead over Labour of 7% was the largest since 1945. This reflected a national swing of 5.2%, born of frustration with Labour. The country had embarked on 18 years of Conservative rule. It had voted for change, although it was not clear what that change would be.

## ■ The Thatcher years, 1979–90

Margaret Thatcher was a figure of great controversy, and, for those who remember her period as Prime Minister (1979–90), this controversy has not ebbed. She was indeed a phenomenon, holding continuous office for longer than any other Prime Minister in the age of mass democracy, indeed than any since the Earl of Liverpool in 1812–27. Thatcher attracted peculiar hatred on the Left, far more so than any other Conservative Prime Minister this century, and was intensely disliked by most of the intelligentsia of the country. 'Thatcherite' became a term of abuse to a degree that 'Heathite' or 'Majorite' could never match; indeed the comparison is absurd. Furthermore, within her own party Thatcher aroused strong negative passions. Her predecessor as Conservative leader, Heath, hated her, and the 'one-nation' paternalists who had dominated the party since Churchill replaced Chamberlain in 1940, were appalled at what they saw as her divisive language and policies.

Thatcher, in her turn, had contempt for those she called the 'wets' (Thatcher's critical term for one-nation paternalists – she thought them 'spineless') and a dislike of a tradition, ethos and practice of compromise and consensus, that she felt had led to Britain's decline. Arguably, Thatcher had more contempt for 'wets' in her own party (such as Jim Prior and Ian Gilmour) than for her opponents in other parties. She blamed previous Conservative governments, from Macmillan's to Heath's, as well as the Labour governments of Wilson and Callaghan, for causing Britain's problems, although Callaghan had abandoned Keynesian policies, and there was an element of continuity in fiscal policy between him and Thatcher.

Thatcher openly attacked what she termed 'the progressive consensus'. Conversely, she called for a return of what she saw as older values, for example telling the *The Times* on 10 October 1987 that children 'needed to be taught to respect traditional moral values'. Pleased to be known as the Iron Lady and promising strong leadership, Thatcher relished her determination to weather the storm. It endowed her politics with a sense of virtuous struggle. Thatcherism was just as much a moral as an economic creed. She had no time for doubt, or even debate. The Cabinet became less important and, instead, Thatcher relied on personal advisors. She sought to transform the political culture and, self-consciously, to implement an ideology.

Thatcher and her supporters, such as Sir Keith Joseph and Nicholas Ridley, sought to rewrite British history. In particular, they applauded aspects of the 1930s, and rejected the Keynesian analysis of the period. Thatcher referred positively to her youth in 1930s Grantham. The Thatcherites also criticised post-1945 economic management and 1960s social policies. Keynesian economics was condemned for a willingness to accept dangerous levels of inflation, and inflation itself was seen as socially disruptive, as well as a threat to core Conservative constituencies. Thatcher offered an apparently straightforward solution to Britain's economic problems (control the money supply) at a time when other politicians seemed lacking in both insight and determination. Thatcher benefited from the extent to which the views towards poverty and the poor that had contributed to the welfare state created in the late 1940s were insecurely rooted, and, in particular, were compromised by concern about tax implications. Furthermore, Thatcher argued that, in 1945–79, both Conservative and Labour governments had failed to restrain trade union power.

In practice, as with all politicians, there was much compromise: Thatcher was not the most Thatcherite. Indeed, there was to be criticism that her rhetoric of 'rolling back the state' was misleading, and that government expenditure did not fall as anticipated. In part, this was due to factors she had not anticipated, especially a major rise in unemployment during the first Thatcher government and the consequent rise in unemployment payments.

Yet, rhetoric and policies were fused, because, although there was less unalloyed Thatcherism or indeed a consistent body of policy that could be called Thatcherism than Thatcher suggested, there was, nevertheless, a stated determination to persist that was different in degree and style from that of her predecessors. This aroused both widespread hostility and genuine doubt. Both owed much to the particular policies and problems of the first years of the government.

After coming into office, the government rapidly signalled its intentions with a budget on 12 June 1979 that was seen by its supporters as an attempt to provide incentives in society and the economy, and by its critics as grossly unfair. Public expenditure was cut by £4,000 million. The basic rate of income tax fell from 33% to 30%, and the top rate on earned income from 83% to 60%, while the top rate on 'unearned' income – interest from savings and other investments – was cut from 98% to 75%. In contrast, Value Added Tax (VAT) rose from 8% to 15%, although there were important exemptions.

This was a major shift from direct to indirect tax. It was criticised as regressive, in that taxes on the wealthy fell, while the poor were hard hit. However, cuts in direct taxation were popular, and helped provide Thatcherite Conservatism with both a value system and popularity. Rising prosperity and more widespread taxation had ensured that 80% of households were paying direct taxation by 1975. As a result, taxation levels became more central in public awareness and public debate, and were the principal factor in the response of many throughout society to government policy. Public expenditure was cut by another £1,275 million in the second budget – on 26 March 1980 – and the Public Sector Borrowing Requirement (PSBR) was restricted to £8,500 million.

Lower tax rates released purchasing power. The net effect was to push up inflation. It rose to 18% in 1980. Interest rates rose markedly in order to cope with inflation. Combined with the impact of North Sea oil, now being produced and exported in large quantity, high interest rates led to a rise in sterling. The combination of a high exchange rate for sterling and high interest rates hit the economy, especially export industries, while the high exchange rate also led to a fall in the price of imports. Much of the economy became uncompetitive. Company bankruptcies pushed up unemployment. Social security payments thus rose, driving up public expenditure at a time when the economic recession was hitting national income and government revenues.

The government responded, on 10 March 1981, with another budget in which spending was cut by £3,290 million and some taxes (not income tax) increased. This was an attempt to cut the budget deficit as a percentage of GDP, specifically the PSBR, which had increased by 130% in 1977–9. Far from following Keynesian precepts, and trying to invest and spend its way out of crisis, the government was following a deflationary policy, a course that aroused great controversy.

Unemployment rose further. By the winter of 1982–3, it reached the unprecedented post-war figure of 3.3 million. The shrinking of the economy hit manufacturing industry particularly hard (and services far less so). In terms of public perception, these were 'real' jobs. They were predominantly male and in traditional industrial tasks, such as 'metal-bashing'. Furthermore, many factories that were closed, such as the Consett steelworks in County Durham and the Corby steelworks in Northamptonshire, were crucial to entire communities. The rapid rise in unemployment was completely out of line with recent experience and thus had a heavier impact than the comparable recession in the early 1990s. The toll was repeatedly driven home because unemployment figures were published monthly, and not, as with many other indices, quarterly.

To critics, both inside and outside government and the Conservative Party, these figures suggested policies that had failed, and a government that must change direction, as Heath had done in 1971. Far lower unemployment figures then had seemed disastrous. Thatcher's response defined her government: 'The lady's not for turning', she told the 1980 Party conference, and the delegates applauded. Throughout her period as Prime Minister, Thatcher was popular with the Conservative Party conference, more so than in the Cabinet and the parliamentary party.

She remained adamant the following year, despite an outbreak of rioting not seen (except in Northern Ireland) since 1832. These were not industrial disputes involving violent secondary picketing, and thus answerable to some sort of control. Instead, from April 1981, in Brixton and Southall in London, Toxteth in Liverpool, Moss Side in Manchester, and, to a lesser extent, other centres, such as Derby, crowds rioted, looted, and fought with the police. From the perspective of today, these were small-scale disturbances, many of which reflected specific local problems, especially relations between black youth and the police, which became the focus of the report from the Scarman Inquiry that was set up after the Brixton riots. At the time, however, it was unclear how far these riots would spread and how they would stop.

Evidence of the strains on social cohesion of government policy did not lead Thatcher to change direction. Instead, she sought to lessen disunity within the government in September 1981 by bringing forward supporters, especially Nigel Lawson, Cecil Parkinson and Norman Tebbit, and removing prominent 'one-nation' critics, Sir Ian Gilmour, Christopher Soames and Mark Carlisle. The reshuffle did not cut unemployment, but it made it easier to see out the crisis until the next election, which was not due until 1984, a suitably apocalyptic year for those who remembered George Orwell's novel. Nevertheless, the reshuffle seemed to make it even more probable that Thatcherism would be a one-term phenomenon. This encouraged her opponents in their attempts to determine policy after the likely removal of the Conservative government.

Thatcher was far from alone in the quest to transform British politics. To her left (a very large area), there was a process of adjustment in which efforts were made to remake first the Labour Party and then British politics as a whole. Callaghan's defeat demoralised the Labour realists and, in opposition, the Party drifted leftwards, an important aspect of the political polarisation of the decade as ideas and practices of consensus were put under pressure. Michael Foot, a veteran left-winger, defeated Healey for the leadership in November 1980, and Benn and his left-wing union allies pushed through a conference programme that was designed to entrench a radical agenda. A future Labour government would seek to extend public ownership in the key sectors of the economy. A policy of protectionism was advocated. The House of Lords would be abolished. Britain was to leave the Common Market, and abandon the nuclear bomb whatever other nuclear powers did (unilateral nuclear disarmament). The Labour Party was to become more responsive and tighter-knit, by making it easier for constituency parties to deselect sitting MPs as official candidates. In future, the Party leader would be elected by an electoral college, consisting of three sections, MPs, trade unions and constituency associations.

There were two problems. First, Labour was not in office, and secondly, the programme helped to split the Labour Party, thus ensuring, under the British first-past-the-post, constituency-dominated electoral system, that the Conservatives were better able to win re-election. The 'Gang of Three' former Cabinet Ministers – David Owen, William Rodgers and Shirley Williams – sought to resist the Left within the Labour Party, and, when they became dissatisfied with their lack of success, joined another former Labour Cabinet Minister, Roy Jenkins, in forming the Social Democratic Party (SDP) on 26 March 1981. The decision to deprive Labour MPs of the sole power to elect the Party leader proved to be the final straw for Owen, Rodgers, and Williams. In the 1979 Dimbleby lecture, Jenkins had spoken of the need for a revived centre in British politics. In pursuit of this aim, the newly founded SDP quickly made overtures to the Liberal Party, which, still led by David Steel, was eager to reciprocate.

Designed to 'break the mould' of British politics, the SDP was intended to be a third force, and to make the impact that the post-war Liberals had failed to do. In terms of electoral calculation, the SDP, in alliance with the Liberals, sought to benefit from Tory unpopularity and from the leftward drift of Labour. In 1981, indeed, the Alliance (SDP and Liberals) benefited from defections by Labour MPs, by-election and local election success, and ratings in the public opinion polls that put it above the other parties. As 1981 gave way to 1982 the popularity of the Alliance, the unpopularity of the Conservatives, and Labour's lack of credibility seemed to indicate that the mould was indeed about to break.

Politics, however, is the art of taking advantage of the unexpected. Thatcher was able to regain the initiative, thanks to an Argentinian invasion of the Falkland Islands on 2 April 1982. This was to be a make-or-break moment for the government. A stronger ministry might have negotiated, but a weak one could not afford to lose, and Thatcher was not by temperament a negotiator anyway. An expeditionary force was sent to the South Atlantic on 5 April, and the Argentinians were totally defeated, surrendering on 14 June. The victory raised Britain's international prestige, and won the government, and Thatcher, widespread support in Britain. It also increased Thatcher's already strong sense of purpose and self-confidence, her disinclination to adapt to the views of others. The Falklands War also helped Thatcher within the Conservative Party. It cemented her already strong relations with party activists, relations never enjoyed by Macmillan, still less Heath. This enabled Thatcher to push an agenda that had not hitherto enjoyed widespread support within the Party, especially privatisations of nationalised industries.

The gut patriotism released and displayed in 1982 made many commentators uncomfortable, but Thatcher knew how to respond. It helped give her leadership a dynamic reputation enjoyed by no Conservative leader since Churchill. Thatcher's defence of Britain's interests struck a chord across party boundaries. Most of the Labour Party supported the recovery of the Falklands.

Victory abroad was joined to a measure of success at home. The recession had been so strong that it was easier subsequently to demonstrate growth, whether in output or, to a lesser extent, employment. Growth in 1982–3 was accompanied by a fall in inflation; although unemployment remained very high and was still at, or close to, 3 million in 1983. However, again, as so often with politics, a sense of relative achievement was crucial. Unemployment was no longer rising, and was even modestly falling. This greatly lessened the insecurity that is a major part of the wider impact of unemployment. Furthermore, to some, higher unemployment (for others) was the acceptable cost necessary to ensure weaker unions and lower inflation. In addition, the fall in interest rates, and thus in mortgage payments, greatly contributed to a rise in the living standards of many of those who were in work and owned houses. This was taken further with a pre–election budget on 15 March 1983, in which personal allowances were raised by more than the rate of inflation. Furthermore, in order to encourage home ownership and a sense of well-being, the maximum loan eligible for mortgage interest relief was raised from £25,000 to £30,000.

Increasingly confident, Thatcher decided to call the election early, and it was held on 9 June 1983. This was to be a curious landslide. The Conservatives won 397 seats (339 in 1979), Labour 209 (269), and the Alliance 23, giving Thatcher the biggest working majority since 1945, and one that easily surpassed Macmillan's in 1959 and Wilson's in 1966. This success was particularly strongly marked in London and southern England.

Yet, the Conservative percentage of the vote (42.4%) was the lowest of any Conservative government since Bonar Law's short-lived ministry of 1922–3. It was lower than that of Thatcher in 1979 (43.9), let alone Heath in 1970 (46.4), and Macmillan in 1959 (49.3). In short, despite the rhetoric, there was no Thatcherite tide among the electors. They remained wedded to the National Health Service: Thatcher was forced to declare that it was safe in her government's hands. Instead, Conservative victory owed much to the state of the opposition, which was divided, and more equally so than at any stage since Bonar Law's victory in the 1922 election. Labour gained 27.6% in 1983, the Alliance 25.4%, a major success for third-party politics. The SDP and the Liberals jointly endorsed candidates.

Labour's programme had not appealed to the traditional Labour voter, let alone swing-voters. Foot did not seem a potential Prime Minister, and the manifesto, described by Gerald Kaufman, a shadow minister, as 'the longest suicide note in history', was regarded as extreme. The defence policy, particularly unilateral nuclear disarmament, failed to convince many Labour supporters. This extremism – not the existence of the Alliance – made Labour unelectable, and helped the Alliance win votes, even though its leader, Roy Jenkins, proved a poor campaigner. The Alliance, however, came second in all too many seats. In southern England, it supplanted Labour as the major opposition party, but the Conservatives won the seats. In northern England, SDP MPs who had defected from Labour lost their seats, and attempts to dislodge sitting Labour MPs failed, even in constituencies, such as the City of Durham, where the MPs were unpopular and there was a significant number of non-traditional Labour voters.

The Alliance had not broken the mould of British politics. It suffered not only from the electoral system, but also from its parliamentary counterpart, specifically the traditional bi-polarity of government and opposition, the latter understood as the leading party. This affected procedures in the House of Commons, media coverage and popular attitudes. After the 1983 election, David Owen replaced Roy Jenkins as SDP leader.

The Conservatives had done better in the 1983 election than subsequent arguments that they won because of opposition divisions might suggest. The appeal of the Alliance ensured that there were apparently two viable alternatives to voting Conservative in England. This had not been the case in 1959, 1970 or 1974. In this context, it was impressive to retain so much of the Conservative vote. As in 1935, Conservative victory was not prevented by a high rate of unemployment. Indeed, to some commentators, the period was reminiscent of the 1930s. There were indeed similarities, but the differences were more striking. The Labour Party was more radical than in the 1930s, as was the Conservative government. Thatcher both sought to reverse decades of government policy and social attitudes (as the National Government had not sought to do), and also had to face serious trade union opposition.

In 1983, Thatcher rushed ahead, revelling in victory, and remoulding the Cabinet to reduce the number of 'wets'. On 11 June, Francis Pym, the Foreign Secretary, who in the election campaign had been so imprudent as to suggest that big majorities were bad as they encouraged extremism in government, was left out of the government while Nigel Lawson, an ardent Thatcherite, became Chancellor of the Exchequer.

Thatcher was soon to find another fight on her hands, one with the miners. Union rights had already been reduced, especially with the banning of secondary picketing (see Chapter 11), and the government had done its best to defeat strikes in the public sector. A major steel strike in 1980 was unsuccessful, and the industry was restructured.

Traditions of militancy were stronger in the coal industry, and the leadership was determined to resist a programme of pit closures that reflected the very different levels of profitability between pits. A first wave of closures was reversed in 1981, when unofficial stoppages forced the Cabinet to restore the subsidies it had been seeking to remove. McGahey declared 'I want the Tories to be the anvil, and I will be a good blacksmith.' The government was better prepared for the second round. Arthur Scargill, the President of the NUM, was as little interested in compromise as Ian MacGregor, appointed Chairman of the National Coal Board (NCB) in 1983, and his backers in the government. Thatcher was determined to be more successful than Heath in defeating what she saw, with much reason, as a 'political strike'. She was greatly helped by poor and divisive leadership in the NUM, the willingness of

**The miners' strike, 1984–5**
The attempt by the National Union of Miners to prevent pit closures developed into a bitterly divisive dispute. Many miners continued working and the government under the determined Margaret Thatcher deployed massive police resources to keep coal supplies moving. Extensive stockpiling of coal before the strike also helped.

50,000 miners to remain at work, and the availability of energy, including stockpiled and imported coal.

The long dispute exacerbated divisions within the NUM, the union movement, and the Labour Party, rather than among the Conservatives. Uncertain of his members' backing, Scargill had refused in April 1984 to call a national strike, as that would have required a national ballot. Instead, he hoped that the individual areas of the NUM would strike. Many did, but Nottinghamshire crucially would not, and the strike-breaking Union of Democratic Mineworkers was formed. Thus, Scargill found that mass picketing was directed as much against working miners as against attempts to move coal to the power stations. This intimidatory and violent picketing helped to alienate much of the public from the miners' cause. It was brought home to them by television reporting. In the meanwhile, Thatcher was able to focus the government's resources on defeating the strike. The NCB was kept firm and police resources were concentrated on keeping the Nottinghamshire pits open. The police benefited from the establishment of a national system to allocate police resources. The fact that the minister who would have been most predisposed to negotiate with the miners, Peter Walker, was Secretary of State for Energy, ensured that Thatcher had complete Cabinet backing for her 'no surrender' policy.

The strike collapsed in 1985, as poverty and helplessness sapped support. Scargill had to call it off in March. Pit closures were pushed through, and the defeated NUM remained divided. Thatcher's recasting of labour away from the traditional heroisms, and towards new industries in which the workforce had different social and political values, had been taken a long way forward.

Instead of trade unions, nationalised industries, and council houses, Thatcher wanted a property-owning democracy in which corporatism was weak, and capital supreme. Institutions and opinions that resisted were marginalised, and one centre of opposition, the Labour-controlled Greater London Council, then led by a vocal left-winger, Ken Livingstone, was abolished in 1986. This was part of a wider process of centralisation which took place during the Thatcher years. Some fifty Acts of Parliament were passed restricting the powers of local government. These powers were transferred to the centre, to Westminster and Whitehall (see Chapter 8).

Under Thatcher, in a deliberate rejection of the Attlee legacy, the past was sold: nationalised companies and council houses alike. In 1979, part of British Petroleum was sold; and, in 1980, British Aerospace followed, while the Housing Act allowing tenants to buy their homes, a major boost to home ownership, was passed. This process was directly encouraged by giving the purchasers favourable deals, and by a tax system designed to provide money for purchases. State holdings in British Petroleum, Cable and Wireless, Britoil (1982, 1985), British Telecom, British Gas (1986, 1990), British Airways (1986–8), Rolls Royce (1987), the British Airports Authority, the National Bus Company (1984–5), British Steel (1988), and the water companies (1989) were all sold, with an under-valuation of assets to encourage sales and ensure that the share issues were fully subscribed, especially with the tranche of British Telecom shares sold in 1984. British Telecom brought in the greatest pro-ceeds. The electricity generating companies, coal (1994), and rail followed in the 1990s. The sales of the nationalised companies subsidised government as the income was added to Treasury revenues rather than being treated as capital for investment.

Under Thatcher, mortgages continued to attract tax relief, and taxes were cut. In the 1987 budget (17 March), the threshold for inheritance tax was raised from £71,000 to £90,000, while the basic rate of income tax was cut from 29% to 27%. Personal pension plans were launched, allowing large numbers without company pensions to gain tax relief on retirement savings. This was designed to increase share ownership. Share and home ownership became the coping stones of the new property-owning democracy. In 1987, as more generally, Thatcher was concerned to reward not only her core constituency but also her vision of British society, those she termed 'our people'.

The budget contributed to a strong 'feel-good' factor, and, on 11 June 1987, Thatcher held another general election, again a year early. Unemployment had fallen from a peak of 3.4 million in January 1986, the economy was growing, and interest rates had fallen. Even so, popular support for Thatcherism was less than total. The Conservative percentage of the vote declined very marginally to 42.3 (from 42.4), although the number of Conservative MPs fell from 397 to 376. This still offered a comfortable majority. Labour under Neil Kinnock, its leader since after the 1983 election, looked more attractive than it had under Foot, but its policies were still to the left of the bulk of the electorate. Labour's share of the vote went up from 27.6% to 30.8% (209 to 229 MPs), and Labour became more clearly the leading opposition party, because the divided Alliance had fallen from 25.4% to 22.5% (23 to 22). The Conservatives continued to do very well in London and southern England, but Labour was far more successful in Scotland and Wales. Labour won 50 of the 72 Scottish seats, while the Conservatives got only 10. The failure of the Alliance to break through was followed by the merger of the major part of the SDP with the Liberals in 1988. David Owen led a rump SDP, but, after poor results in by-elections, that collapsed in 1990. Owen was subsequently to urge his supporters to vote Conservative in the 1992 election.

Having won, Thatcher characteristically avoided all temptation to consolidate. She was determined to end Socialism and to entrench her changes. Income tax was cut further – by the 11 March 1988 budget – to a basic rate of 25% and a top rate of 40%. Combined with lax credit, seen, for example, in the ease with which credit cards could be obtained, this fed through into a consumer boom. Thatcher argued that public, not total, borrowing was crucial, and sought to contain inflation through this means. As a result, despite the much vaunted monetarist determination to control the money supply, private borrowing was largely unchecked. Thatcher abandoned Heath's limited control of bank lending as part of a general 'bonfire' of financial regulations. This left only short-term means of control, principally raising interest rates, which hit manufacturing. They were briefly raised to 15% in October 1989.

Thatcherite economics led to an uneasy co-existence of private wealth, and the public poverty of a state sector that was not able to invest sufficiently in 'infrastructure', such as school buildings. The consumer boom pressed on an economy that had lost much of its 'excess capacity' in the recession of the early 1980s. As a result, domestic production could not rise to match demand. Instead, inflation shot up, as did imports, pushing the balance of payments into a record deficit of £20 billion in 1989. Government revenues were also under pressure. Privatisations led to one-off gains that helped produce a budget surplus in 1988–9, but by late 1989, the situation seemed out of control. The Conservatives lost their reputation for economic competence.

Simultaneously, the political position of the government was under acute pressure. Much of this was self-inflicted. The Poll Tax became one of the most unpopular pieces of legislation passed since the post-war austerity years, although the essentially law-abiding nature of the population ensured that most people paid it (as they had paid the unpopular Ship Money imposed by Charles I in the 1630s). In place of funding local government by rates charged on property owners, the government proposed a 'community charge' from every adult, with all those in a given council area paying the same amount. This was designed to forge a link between expenditure and revenue, for now all inhabitants would bear the consequences of rises in the former, as they would lead to higher rates. It was hoped that this would lead voters to turn away from Labour councils, which tended to spend more and levy higher rates.

The Poll Tax ignored the dictates of progressive taxation, that the rich should pay more than the poor, and, in addition, the introduction of the tax was poorly handled. In part, the level was simply set too high – the electorate paid, and continues to pay, an equivalent poll tax called the Television Licence Fee. Only a small minority took part in violent demonstrations, such as the riot in Trafalgar Square on 31 March 1990, but the furore over the tax both hit the government's popularity, especially in Scotland, where it was introduced a year early, and encouraged restless Conservative MPs to feel that Thatcher had lost the ability to respond to popular moods. Many of the MPs were vulnerable to any fall in government support in a future election, and they were worried by by-election results. Thatcher was now less popular than the government. In the autumn of 1989, a backbench Conservative MP, Sir Anthony Meyer, decided to challenge Thatcher for the Conservative Party leadership. It was a challenge which was bound to fail, but Sir Anthony succeeded in securing 33 votes.

There was to be no further general election under Thatcher. Instead, the Conservative leadership fell apart over the issue of Europe. Speaking on 20 September 1988, at the opening ceremony of the 39th academic year of the College of Europe at Bruges, Thatcher declared 'We have not successfully rolled back the frontiers of the state in Britain, only to see them reimposed at a European level, with a European super-state exercising a new dominance from Brussels.' Instinctively suspicious of the European Economic Community (EEC), Thatcher fell out with the Deputy Prime Minister, the distinctly uncharismatic Geoffrey Howe, over further European integration. The crux of their disagreement related to British membership of the

Exchange Rate Mechanism, which constituted stage one of economic and monetary union (see Chapter 13).

Howe resigned on 1 November 1990, and then announced his support for a leadership bid by the ambitious Michael Heseltine, a man who believed in the EEC as well as himself. The first ballot, on 20 November, gave Thatcher, whose campaign had been poorly managed, 204 votes to Heseltine's 152. This was not enough to prevent a second ballot, and raised the prospect of Heseltine gaining sufficient momentum to win then, as Thatcher herself had done in 1975. Determined to block Heseltine, a persistent critic and the candidate of the left of the party, Thatcher stood down as Prime Minister and leader of the Conservative Party on 22 November. For her successor, she backed the relatively inexperienced Chancellor of the Exchequer, John Major. On 27 November, on the second ballot, he beat both Heseltine and the Foreign Secretary, Douglas Hurd. The 1980s were over.

The long-term impact of Thatcher and Thatcherism is unclear. In part, it depends on how far changes within Labour in the 1990s and the policies of the Labour government elected in 1997 are, at least in part, attributed to the influence of the Thatcher years, not least the changes in society that were encouraged. It is also misleading to exaggerate the impact of government, and, indeed, of a particular period of government by one party, and to attribute all or most change in a period to state initiative or policies. Nevertheless, it would be idle to deny that there were important shifts in the social fabric. One of the most important was in housing. The rise in home ownership took many people outside the direct control of the state, at least in the shape of accommodation rented from local councils. This reflected Thatcher's marked preference for freedom and market mechanisms as opposed to planning and state pricing. The shift was apparent even in Scotland, where public housing had been more prominent than in England. The percentage of the Scottish population living in public-sector rented accommodation fell from 52.1 in 1981 to 38.4 in 1991, while that in owner-occupied property rose from 36.4 to 52.8. Furthermore, the number of new homes built in the public sector dramatically fell. An absence of newly-available affordable accommodation was a result, and this helped push the number of homeless up. In Scotland, it rose from 16,034 in 1978–9 to 30,859 in 1986–7 (see Chapters 3, 7).

# The 1990s

Initially a stop-gap, John Major proved both more and less successful than might have been expected. More, because he was Prime Minister for six and a half years – from 28 November 1990 until defeated by Tony Blair in the general election held on 1 May 1997. To do so, he both saw off challenges from within the Conservative Party and, in 1992, won a general election that he had been widely expected to lose. Less successful, because Major's years in office witnessed serious blows to government policy, a disunited ministry that lost public confidence, and a party that was increasingly tarnished. Furthermore, the election in 1997 saw not only a widespread rejection of the Major government, but also widespread opposition to much for which it stood.

The root problem was that the pleasant, but uncharismatic, Major was less able to control developments than most prime ministers and, crucially, unable to create a sense that he was in control. From this, flowed many of his problems with colleagues, party and public. Initially, Major was helped by the less than first-rate leadership of Labour by Kinnock, but, after Kinnock resigned, following the general election of 9 April 1992, and was replaced by John Smith (1992–4), and then Blair, the quality of Labour leadership cast a harsh light on Major. He lacked any distinctive ideas or policies with which to win favour with the electorate. Major continued the direction of Thatcherite policies, but without her charisma or, from 1992, parliamentary strength. When Major did attempt to strike a new note, as with his campaign for family values, the private lives of some of his ministers led to accusations of hypocrisy.

The inheritance was difficult, although Thatcher's departure led public opinion to swing back to the Conservatives in late 1990. The European issue seriously and publicly divided the Conservative Party, inside and outside Parliament; while the economy faced serious problems. Although unemployment was below 2 million (a figure still far higher than that for most of the post-war period), inflation was in double figures. The situation became more, not less, difficult in the early 1990s, as recession bit. Unemployment was heavily concentrated in the old industrial areas, such as North-East England, but the recession was more widely spread, and in 1992 unemployment also rose appreciably in London and the Home Counties, as the financial-services industry and other service-sector employers shed staff. By January 1993, when there were over 3 million unemployed, the unemployment rate was 10.6%. In contrast, the previous month's average EEC unemployment was 9%.

The resulting hardship was not restricted to a small 'underclass'. The substantial increase in individual debt in the 1980s, as a consequence of the liberalisation of the financial system and government encouragement of the widespread desire to own property, ensured that many now were in a vulnerable situation. By June 1992, repossessions of houses by creditors were at an annual rate of about 75,000, while 300,000 mortgage-holders were six months or more in arrears with their payments (see Chapter 7).

A Labour victory was widely anticipated in the 1992 general election, but the electorate was wary of Kinnock, and the triumphalist note he struck towards the close of the campaign in the Sheffield rally, although a one-off slip after he was plunged into a situation not of his making, was unwelcome. There was a suspicion that taxes would rise sharply if Labour gained power, and this affected an electorate keen to retain the cuts in income tax introduced by Thatcher. In the pre-election budget, the Conservatives introduced a 20% income tax band for the first £2,000 earned in excess of personal allowances, halved the rate of car tax, and doubled the value of personal equity plan tax shelters. In contrast, Labour offered higher rates of income tax and National Insurance contributions for much of the middle class. Furthermore, the Conservatives misled the electorate about the possibility of avoiding tax increases in the future. In some respects, both major parties competed to debauch the electorate with false assumptions, but then, as on many other occasions, much of the electorate wished to be misled. Major was a popular Prime Minister, seen as honest and, crucially, not as abrasive or divisive as Thatcher. Ditching Thatcher enabled the Conservatives to shed some of the unpopular legacy of the 1980s. Despite the recession, the Conservatives were also seen as more competent managers of the economy, a reputation they were swiftly to lose after the election.

The swing away from the Conservatives in the South of England and the Midlands in 1992 was less than anticipated, in Wales it was only 1%, and in Scotland there was a small swing towards them. Nevertheless, the Conservative majority of

21 was small (disproportionately small in comparison to their share of the vote), in part because of tactical voting by their opponents: Labour and Liberal supporters voted for whichever of the two candidates was most likely to defeat Conservatives. They did so far more than they had in 1983 or 1987, because then each party was competing with the other, as much as with the Conservatives. The Liberal Democrats had the same level of electoral support in 1992 as the Liberals had enjoyed in the 1970s: the SDP had made scant difference; 326 Conservatives were elected, compared with 376 in 1987, while Labour won 271 seats compared with 229 in 1987. Labour had also benefited from an above-average swing in London and the East Midlands, in both of which there were many Conservative marginal seat.

The small majority that followed the 1992 election hamstrung Major, especially because it made it very difficult to follow a policy on Europe that was not at risk from wrecking opposition from within the Conservative Parliamentary Party, particularly from the 'Eurosceptics', who focused on the outcome of the Maastricht summit of EEC leaders in December 1991. On 21 May 1992, 22 Conservatives voted against the government over the Maastricht agreement; on 4 November 1992 and 8 March 1993, 26; on 20 May 1993, 41. Votes on 8 March and 22 July 1993 led to government defeats and forced Major to seek (and win) a vote of confidence on 23 July. Confidence in the government's financial competence and European policy collapsed on 'Black Wednesday' – 16 September 1992, when speculators forced sterling out of the Exchange Rate Mechanism in a humiliating defeat for government economic and fiscal policy. The government's position in the public opinion polls collapsed. As Major, himself, later admitted, thereafter the public was never prepared to give his government the benefit of the doubt. As accusations of 'cash for questions' (MPs receiving money from interested parties in order to raise questions in Parliament) engulfed the Major government in an atmosphere of sleaze in the mid-1990s, the public had little reason to. In June 1993, Gallup polls suggested that Major was the least popular Prime Minister since opinion polling began.

Divisions sapped Conservative unity, purpose, and popularity, even when the economy recovered from the mid-1990s. The recovery, however, brought less of a 'feel good' factor than in the recoveries of the 1980s, in part because property prices did not rise. Unemployment fell and purchasing power rose, but many of the new jobs were part-time and, anyway, the electorate was not minded to reward the increasingly exhausted Conservative government. It performed terribly in public opinion polls, had major swings against it in by-elections, and lost very heavily in European and council elections. The local elections of 6 May 1993, 5 May 1994, and 4 May 1995 brought awful results for the Conservatives. In 1993, on an unprecedentedly low percentage of the vote, they lost control of every county council apart from Buckinghamshire, including former strongholds in rural England such as Dorset. In 1994, the percentage fell another 4%, to 27%, and in 1995 to 25%. The party's local power base was devastated. A strongly hostile media did not help: the press took great delight in chronicling the misfortunes of the Major government. In June 1995, Major felt it necessary to resign as leader of the Conservative Party and stand for re-election in order to reassert his authority. He beat John Redwood, a critic on the right of the party, in July, but this did not end the divisions.

Major limped on until the 1997 election, held on 1 May, but its result surprised few. Major delayed the election until the last possible moment, a sure sign that he expected his government to be defeated. The only real success which he could claim, the beginnings of a peace process in Northern Ireland, was not enough to secure the Conservatives a fifth consecutive term of office. The biggest surprise in the 1997 election was the scale of the defeat. Thanks, again, in part, to tactical voting, the Conservatives lost heavily in England, while a collapse of their support cost them all their seats in Scotland and Wales. Labour, with 418 seats, won a big majority, and the Liberals won more seats than in 1992, although, in terms of the percentage of electoral support, they failed to benefit greatly from Conservative unpopularity.

The victorious Blair fought on the platform of 'New Labour'. It is too soon to come to any firm views about its success or lasting impact. Suffice it to note here that the changes within the Labour Party were as important to the political history of the period up to the 1997 election as those within the Conservative government. Once Major lost direction, and it looked as though he would not be re-elected, attention shifted to Labour, increasingly seen as a government in waiting. Under Smith, Labour leader 1992–4, and then, with more determination and clarity, under his successor, Blair, Labour moved away from collectivist solutions based on interventionism and state planning, and prepared to embrace aspects of Thatcherism, not least the market place and modest rates of taxation.

The organisation of the Labour Party was also transformed. This change in policy and organisation had begun under Neil Kinnock, after the electoral defeat in 1987, although he was a less than wholehearted moderniser. Nevertheless, *Meet the Challenge, Make the Change*, the Labour Party policy review of 1989, dropped many recent policies including price and import controls, high income tax, unilateral nuclear disarmament, wealth tax, and the restoration of union legal immunities. The review borrowed from Thatcherism in its favourable references to the free market, and it discarded much of the rhetoric and substance of Socialism. It was a key document in the conversion of Labour to the market place.

Changes in organisation were taken further under Smith and Blair, and were more important because Labour seemed closer to power. Smith moved away from the block vote of trade unions at Party conferences and in constituency parties, and, instead, favoured a one member, one vote approach. It was designed to democratise the party, and also both symbolised and made effective the growing breach between Labour and the unions. Under Blair's leadership, the Labour Party became a more disciplined entity whose organisational structures were geared towards electoral victory. From the Party's new base, Millbank Tower, its instant rebuttal system gave Labour the campaigning edge in 1997. Image became all-important under Blair, as the very name New Labour suggested, and 'spin doctors' and focus groups assumed centre stage. Yet even here, New Labour owed something to the Kinnock years: Peter Mandelson, spin doctor supreme, had been Director of Campaigns and Communications under Kinnock.

In 1995 'Clause IV' of the Labour Party's 1918 constitution – its commitment to public ownership of the means of production, distribution, and exchange – was abandoned at Blair's instigation after a ballot of Party members. This was seen as the end of an era. Hugh Gaitskell had singularly failed to achieve the same goal when he tried to push it through in 1959. Blair was also careful to limit spending pledges and to avoid talk of higher taxes. There were still important differences, however, between Conservatism and what Blair termed 'New Labour', and the charge of being a Thatcherite brought against Blair tells us more about tensions within the Labour Party than about Blair's ethos and policies. Nevertheless, as with 'Butskellism' in the 1950s and, although less clearly, the absence of Socialism from the minority Labour governments of the 1920s, similarities are as striking as differences. The reconfiguration of the Left extended to the Communist Party of Great Britain. Discredited by the collapse of Communism in Eastern Europe, the Party was wound up at its Congress in 1991, and became the Democratic Left, although a minority that refused to accept this seceded and kept the original name.

The scale of the Conservative defeat in 1997 left the Party in a very difficult state. Conservatives found themselves facing a Labour government that had appropriated the rhetoric of 'one-nation' Conservatism in all but name. New Labour appeared to offer a more appealing vision of life in post-Thatcher Britain, by championing a society in which the dominance of the market place was not to be allowed to undermine social cohesion. The Conservatives, in effect, were hoist by their own petard. Labour support for devolution was different, and was part of a wide range of constitutional initiatives; but the debate about the desirability of government intervention in the economy came to an, at least temporary, end. As a result of the steps that successive Conservative governments took to 'roll back the frontiers of the state' between 1979 and 1997, and the shift in Labour policy, especially the abandonment of Clause IV, there was widespread support for the free market.

Similarities between governments should not surprise. One of the recurrent features of the political history of the century was that problems were persistent or recurred. Furthermore, the pressures of office diluted ideology and blurred apparently sharply-etched differences. Politicians who were effective as polemicists in opposition had to adjust to the exigencies and compromise of government, or go. Some adjusted well – Lloyd George being a prime example, Thatcher less successfully so – but others failed and fell. For some, such as Wilson and Heath, the process of compromise helped discredit them.

Yet, in conclusion, it is necessary to look for a wider significance than the quest for power. Here, as so frequently during the century, it is possible, Janus-faced, to point in two directions. On the one hand, the political system avoided the extremism and collapse that affected so many other European countries. However, it is unclear if this owed much to the politicians – the ability of the English Channel to act as a

**Labour Leader Tony Blair launching the party's election poster campaign, 1997.**
The stress on all sections of the community in this carefully staged event was deliberate. The posters captured the problems created by commitments to improve social services without increasing taxation.

defensive shield was as, if not more, important. Furthermore, Britain declined relatively, and, in some respects, absolutely, during the century (see Chapter 16). It is difficult to see how individual political leaders, and possibly the entire system, can escape a portion of the blame. Decline can be, and has been, variously explained. Economic factors, such as poor management and labour relations, have received much of the blame, and are discussed in the next chapter. Yet these cannot be divorced from the political context, while, more generally, many politicians have sought, with limited success, to address these, and other, problems. Thus, a narrative of political fortune has to end on a sombre note. Different parties have held office, but the century saw a major fall in Britain's fortunes, and this was not a fall hidden from contemporaries.

## ◼ Summary

◆ A short political narrative of the twentieth century reveals important continuities, as well as major shifts. Elections have repeatedly revealed that there is no majority party in the popular vote, even though there has generally been one in Parliament. Parliamentary politics saw off extremism.

◆ Major figures have been brought down by ministerial divisions (Asquith, 1916; Thatcher, 1970) as much as elections (Churchill, 1945), although the former have sometimes reflected concern about elections (Thatcher).

◆ The replacement of Liberals by Labour in the 1920s was the most important shift in party politics. It indicated the dominant role of two parties in a first-past-the-post system. Thereafter, there has been no comparable shift despite a major attempt by the Social Democratic Party in the 1980s. Third parties could be important in electoral and parliamentary politics. Coalition politics in some form were very important in the first half of the century, but far less so in the second half.

## ◼ Questions for discussion

◆ Why did Liberalism collapse?

◆ Why were the Conservatives so successful in 1931–64?

◆ What was the political impact of the rise of Labour?

◆ Why did Labour fail in the 1970s?

◆ What did Thatcherism amount to?

◆ How would the political history of the century have been different if elections had been decided by proportional representation?

◆ Was British politics responsible for the decline of the British economy?

## ◼ Further reading

Brookshire, Jerry H., *Clement Attlee* (Manchester, 1996).

Charmley, John, *A History of Conservative Politics, 1900–1996* (London, 1996).

Crewe, Ivor, and King, Anthony, *SDP: The Birth, Life and Death of the Social Democratic Party* (Oxford, 1996).

Davis, John, *A History of Britain, 1885–1939* (London, 1999).

Evans, Brendan, and Taylor, Andrew, *From Salisbury to Major: Continuity and Change in Conservative Politics* (Manchester, 1996).

Francis, Martin, *Ideas and Policies under Labour, 1945–51* (Manchester, 1997).

Jefferys, Kevin, *Retreat from New Jerusalem: British Politics, 1951–64* (Basingstoke, 1997).

Jones, T., *Remaking the Labour Party: From Gaitskell to Blair* (London, 1996).

Kavanagh, Dennis, and Morris, Peter, *Consensus Politics from Attlee to Thatcher* (Oxford, 1989).

Morgan, Kenneth, *Labour People, Leaders and Lieutenants: Hardie to Kinnock* (Oxford, 1987).

Packer, Ian, *Lloyd George* (London, 1998).

Pearce, Robert, *Attlee* (London, 1997).

Pimlott, Ben, *Labour and the Left in the 1930s* (London, 1977).

Pimlott, Ben, *Harold Wilson* (London, 1992).

Searle, Geoffrey, *The Liberal Party: Triumph and Disintegration, 1886–1929* (London, 1992).

Seldon, Anthony (ed.), *How Tory Governments Fall: The Tory Party in Power since 1783* (London, 1996).

Smart, Nick, *The National Government, 1931–40* (London, 1999).

Smith, Jeremy, *The Tories and Ireland, 1910–1914: Conservative Party Politics and the Home Rule Crisis* (Dublin, 2000).

Stewart, Graham, *Burying Caesar: Churchill, Chamberlain and the Battle for the Tory Party* (London, 1999).

Thorpe, A., *A History of the Labour Party* (London, 1996).

Williamson, P., *National Crisis and National Government: British Politics, the Economy and Empire, 1926–1932* (Cambridge, 1992).

Williamson, P., *Stanley Baldwin: Conservative Leadership and National Values* (Cambridge, 1999).

Wood, Ian, *Churchill* (London, 1999).

# Economic Worlds

## Contents

**supply side:** Economy led by
the requirements of industry, in
contrast to a demand-led
economy catering to the needs
of consumers.

The economic fortunes of the country are an important aspect of its history. As with many other themes, for example democratisation and secularisation, it is necessary to note that many central features of economic change were not unique to Britain, but were shared by other countries. This was true, for example, of the decline of heavy industry and the rise of the service sector. Much discussion of British economic history concentrates on the macro-economic picture, aggregate (total) indices of activity, and overall trends. It focuses on quantitative indices and economic theories. These are important, but it is necessary to be cautious in applying theories without due consideration of social and political contexts. In addition, there are marked differences between the various theories on offer. In particular, discussing, for example, management and labour problems, '**supply side**' explanations that focus on the domestic economy clash with others that emphasise the dynamics of the international economy. Furthermore, the statistical records that are used in such studies are not without serious problems. It is difficult to define and measure growth rates or to decide how best to reconcile national trends with the experience of particular sectors and areas.

We will come to discuss aspects of the economy as a whole, but it is also important to notice that there were many economic worlds, many different economic experiences, both by sector of the economy and by region. We shall illustrate this by considering two examples – the economic history of Wales and, briefly, Scotland, and the British motor car industry. We will then turn to consider major themes during the century. This is not a conventional approach, but is deliberately adopted in order to make it clear that the general economic history of the century both meant different things in different areas, and is, in large part, an amalgamation of a variety of histories.

## Key issues

▶ What happened to heavy industry?

▶ How has the economic geography of the country varied?

▶ How far and why did the British economy decline?

▶ What was the role of service industries?

▶ What was the impact of changes in labour relations?

# Introduction

The history of the economy varied by sector, company and, indeed, employee. Nevertheless, there are overall trends. First, Britain has remained a leading economy in the world, and this has underpinned much else discussed in the other Chapters in the book. This may be a surprising point of departure and the stress is generally on *relative* decline. That indeed was important, not least in the perception of economic, political, social and cultural problems (see Chapters 7, 16). Britain was no longer one of the leading economies in terms of absolute gross domestic product (GDP), or GDP per capita (living standards), or GDP/worker-hour (labour productivity). Yet, it is also worth understanding the impact of continued success, particularly in terms of providing far more revenue for government and more work for a larger labour force, which grew particularly rapidly in the 1920s. The nature of employment has also become more often part-time work. This has suited a labour force in which women with children have played a greater role, but has also posed major problems, not least with the uncertainties, and limited protection and returns, of part-time work. In addition, the value added by employment has been larger than ever before. This value added is a matter of productivity. That has risen greatly during the century, but, nevertheless, below the rate in other leading Western countries, especially since World War Two. Prior to then, productivity rose less than in the USA, but was still above most other leading economies, including Germany. The cause of this failure is a matter of controversy. It is frequently ascribed to poor investment, management, and labour-relations policies. It has also been most acute in the industrial sector.

Manufacturing has faced the most serious problems, having to adapt to **de-industrialisation** and (less marked) **re-industrialisation** arising from new demands. Services faced fewer problems. This has owed something to commercial policy, specifically the management of the exchange rate, which has often been too high for manufacturing exporters. At the beginning of the century, aside from her major, sometimes leading, role in the production of traditional goods, such as coal, textiles, iron, steel and ships, Britain was also playing a major role in the development of new sectors, in the growth of production in chemicals, and in, for example, new consumer goods, such as motor cars and telephones. However, there were growing worries as the rate of economic growth slowed before 1900. Also, there was concern about low productivity and about a slowness in moving into new industries such as new chemicals and dyes. Nevertheless, the sheer scale of activity was impressive. The cotton industry was well established, but in 1900–9 15 million spindles (35%) was added to the capacity of the industry. Despite pressure in particular sectors, Britain was doing well in the liberal international economic order, but that order was greatly challenged in World War One.

In the 1920s, the British sought to recreate the liberal order, but with only limited success. Britain's economy grew less than that of the USA, and, although it compared well with other major Western economies, there was a serious recession in 1920–1, GDP only rose above 1913 levels in 1927, and the trade balance with most of the world had deteriorated since 1913, a major argument against free trade and in favour of tariffs. Exports remained well below 1913 figures.

To many contemporaries, the economy appeared to be in the doldrums, and this view was confirmed by subsequent economic analysis. However, there were

**de-industrialisation:** A run-down in the extent and role of industry, such that there is a reduction in the proportion of industry in a country's economy.

**re-industrialisation:** The creation of new industries in order to boost a country's economy.

## Box 11.1

### The Gold Standard

Until the outbreak of World War One, the pound sterling had been fixed against other currencies on the basis of its value in gold. Gold and sterling were thus convertible. The financial strains of war led Britain in effect to come off the Gold Standard (as she had done in the French Revolutionary and Napoleonic Wars), and, in 1919, she formally came off the Standard in order to avoid deflation. Nevertheless, the financial community pressed firmly to return to the Gold Standard in order to provide stable finances, and it succeeded in persuading Winston Churchill, the Chancellor of the Exchequer, to do so in the April 1925 budget. This was proclaimed by Churchill as a return to, and sign of, economic normality, but led to an overvalued currency, which hit exports, and one that was protected by higher interest rates that affected the rest of the economy. The Gold Standard was abandoned in September 1931 as a result of pressure upon sterling during the Slump. The pound was therefore allowed to 'float', to find its own value against other currencies.

developments, not least the growth of demand-led consumer industries, rather than the more supply-led heavy industrial sector.

The return to the Gold Standard in 1925 was seen as a return to pre-war normality, but it did not help export industries as sterling was overvalued. The Treasury, however, shared the general lack of interest of the City of London in Britain's industry (and agriculture). Churchill felt that Montagu Norman, the powerful Governor of the Bank of England, was prepared to see Britain have 'the finest credit in the world simultaneously with a million and a quarter unemployed'. The neglect of industry was to be a serious problem for the British economy throughout the century, and one that encouraged a number of suggested remedies. These included bringing businessmen into government, an approach attempted by both Lloyd George and Thatcher, and also the notion of creating a powerful ministry with specific responsibility for the economy.

No such remedy was on offer in the 1920s, for confidence in peacetime planning was limited until after World War Two. In part, it was discredited by its association with the Five-Year Plans of the Soviet Union, but, more generally, such planning was unacceptable to the powerful financial community whose views were central to economic strategy until the 1940s. From 1945, the combination of a more powerful government, a belief in planning, a different intellectual consensus, a greater concern with unemployment, and a rejection of past attitudes and policies associated with the Depression and mass unemployment, led to a more interventionist strategy.

The world-wide Slump of 1929 and the subsequent Depression, destroyed the liberal economic order. World trade collapsed, dragging down British export industries, such as shipbuilding, and hitting confidence. Protectionism was introduced in 1932. There was then, from 1933, a measure of recovery, thanks, in part, to Britain coming off the Gold Standard early, although it brought scant benefit to the heavy industrial sector, which did not grow appreciably until rearmament in the face of the Nazi threat.

Unemployment fell substantially in World War Two, but the conflict also created major problems. Trade objectives and routes were totally changed, and the economy was completely subordinated to military ends. Due to air attack, much industrial plant was destroyed or damaged, far more than in World War One.

After 1945, there was a protracted period of economic recovery and growth until 1973, with low levels of unemployment and no major recessions, although Britain's relative economic position deteriorated. Most British trade was still with the Empire

## Box 11.2

### Registered unemployed

In thousands to nearest 10,000. Methods of recording figures changed from 1992.

| | |
|------|-------|
| 1937 | 1,480 |
| 1940 | 960 |
| 1945 | 140 |
| 1950 | 310 |
| 1955 | 230 |
| 1960 | 360 |
| 1965 | 330 |
| 1970 | 580 |
| 1975 | 870 |
| 1980 | 1,670 |
| 1985 | 3,150 |
| 1990 | 1,600 |
| 1994 | 2,790 |

and the USA, but the fastest post-war growth was in Europe. The size of the economy fell from being the second largest in the Western world after World War Two to fifth largest by the mid-1990s: France, Germany and Japan had passed Britain. They have benefited from a process of post-war economic catch-up and, arguably, from more general political and social modernisation after World War Two. This decline was particularly marked in some areas. Thanks, in part, to wartime destruction of Dutch, French, German, Italian, Japanese, Norwegian and Soviet shipping, British companies in 1950 still owned 30% of the ships afloat, although that was way down on the 50% figure for 1900. By 1960, however, the percentage was down to 15; by 1970, 11; and by 1980, below 5. This was due not only to the growth in the shipping industry of other countries, but also to problems in the British industry. Coal, another major industry, benefited from considerable investment in the 1950s, but production costs remained above those of international competitors, and this caused major problems in the 1970s. Similarly, there was post-war growth in engineering, again, in response to an expanding economy, but it proved impossible to sustain this across the entire sector. In part, this was due to international competition, but there were also important changes in demand, due to reduced needs in markets that declined, for example locomotives, marine engines and textile machinery.

Nevertheless, despite serious economic problems, there was, by the standards of what followed, relatively full employment, an annual average growth rate of real GDP of 2.8% for 1951–73, and rising government revenues. The energy (oil and coal) crisis of 1973–4 ushered in a more traumatic period, although analysis of these years is highly controversial, and it is not clear that explanations devised for this period are also appropriate for earlier in the century. This is particularly true of the assessment of the policies associated with the Thatcher governments (1979–90). There were sharp recessions in 1974–5, 1979–81, and 1990–2, and the latter two defined the public perception of the Conservative revanche of 1979-97. The extent to which de-industrialisation and high unemployment were necessary to economic restructuring, and the relationship between manufacturing problems and the strength of the service sector, are controversial. More generally, there was a lack of confidence in economic policy and government management in the last third of the century, which contributed to a public rejection of interventionism, first by the Conservatives in the late 1960s and, more decisively, from the mid-1970s, and then by Labour in the 1990s.

# Wales

The economic history of Wales indicates many of the general themes of the century, including the crisis of heavy industry, the development of new industries, and the rise of the service sector. The first, for long, predominated, ensuring that Wales seemed a case of economic despair, but the situation improved from the 1960s, in part due to the combination of regional economic aid and the transformation of attitudes and economic experience.

In 1938, the Earl of Plymouth, President of the National Industrial Council of Wales and Monmouthshire, a body established in 1932, declared:

the problem of the Welsh industrial areas will never be overcome until we have succeeded in finding a solution of the difficulties which confront our great basic, the coal trade . . . to achieve a balanced state in industry . . . essential we should have light industries.

## Box 11.3

### Coal production in the UK

In million tonnes

|  | |
| --- | --- |
| 1940 | 225 |
| 1945 | 182 |
| 1950 | 216 |
| 1955 | 222 |
| 1960 | 194 |
| 1965 | 188 |
| 1970 | 133 |
| 1978 | 122 |
| 1988 | 104 |
| 1993 | 81 |

The Welsh economy was indeed in difficulties. The key industry in South Wales was coal, but the industry was hit by international competition, an overvalued pound until September 1931, inadequate investment, and industrial problems. Production fell from 56 million tons in 1913, to 48 in 1929, and 20 in 1945. Related activities also suffered. The iron and steel, and tinplate industries were badly hit. All the Cardiganshire lead mines were closed by 1931.

Heavy industry remained in serious problems. The expansion of the late 1940s, in particular with the massive and modern Port Talbot steelworks opened in 1951, was succeeded, in the 1970s and 1980s, by closures and massive layoffs. The Ebbw Vale iron and steel plant, located in South Wales, rather than Lincolnshire, as a result of government pressure in the 1930s, closed in 1975–6, with many redundancies; the Shotton steelworks on Deeside following in the 1980s. The best coal seams had been dug out, and cheaper coal from elsewhere spelt the end of the South Wales pits and their especially militant labour force: there were only 17 pits left in Wales by 1986. Economic decline hit employment, health, morale, and the environment. By 1957 it had already left large areas of derelict land, including 8,227 hectares of disused spoil-heaps, 3,090 of disused mineral workings, and 7,567 of disused buildings and installations.

The situation in the coal industry deteriorated further in the 1990s. The impact on local communities was traumatic. For example, Taff Merthyr colliery closed in 1992. It had been crucial to employment in Bedlinog and Trelewis. The loss of the 485 jobs at the pit came on top of a fall in employment in the coal industry in Mid-Glamorgan, from 52,000 in 1947 to less than 1,000 in 1992.

Yet there was also development and a new workforce, much of it white-collar, for whom traditional loyalties had scant interest. This was a workforce living not in the valleys, but on the north and south coasts and in the urban region around Cardiff, which had been declared capital of Wales in 1955. Expansion in service industries and, in particular, in administrative agencies based in Cardiff, created much new employment, as did investment, especially from Japan, in new industrial plants. These were concentrated in South Wales, the economic importance of which was boosted by a new proximity to markets, thanks to the opening of the Severn Bridge in 1966 and the extension of the M4 motorway into South Wales.

A new geography of wealth and employment greatly favoured Cardiff and, to a lesser extent, Bridgend, Newport, Swansea and Wrexham. BP Chemicals developed petro-chemical production at Baglan Bay. Ford invested £180 million in its Bridgend engine plant. The combination of new technology and foreign investment was well illustrated with the new purpose-built colour television plant at Plencoed, Mid-Glamorgan, opened in 1993. The plant exemplified two features of modern industrial location: road links and 'greenfield' sites. It was located on a 150-acre site off the M4. Tourism was another industry that expanded greatly, becoming the biggest employer in the 1990s. Restoration of the valleys and countryside was an important consequence of the virtual disappearance of the coal mines. The industrial heritage was used increasingly in the leisure industry.

Thus Wales exemplified the key trends in twentieth-century British economic history. There was much hardship in Wales, but also, in the last quarter-century, alongside continued structural weaknesses, an impressive transformation that included a greater stress on higher-productivity sections of the economy.

# Scotland

Scotland had many regions with widely differing economic fortunes and living standards. The West Central Belt was hard hit by the fate of the traditional heavy industry sector. This had been very important into the early twentieth century, and was the basis of the prosperity of much of the population. Formed in 1903, the Glasgow-based North British Locomotive Company was the largest private loco-motive-builder in Europe and able to build over 500 locomotives annually. In 1929, Clyde shipyards still provided 25% of world tonnage, as well as being the leading source of demand for the Scottish steel industry. However, thereafter, the size and economic importance of the coal, heavy engineering, shipbuilding and steel industries all declined. Their closely inter-linked nature ensured that the decline of shipbuilding had disastrous effects. The industries of the West Coastal Belt had all been seriously affected by World War One, but they suffered even more seriously from the Slump. So also did Dundee's jute industry. Heavy unemployment was the result, both there and elsewhere. The failure of locomotive building was largely due to the failure to adjust to standardisation and mass markets. Scottish engineering specialisation had got caught into one-off, custom-built items.

The decline in manufacturing in turn hit much of the rest of the economy, for example the service sector. The decline also reduced the potential demand for foodstuffs and consumer goods. The Scottish economy was less diversified than its far larger English counterpart. In particular, the marked emphasis on heavy industry, that had characterised the nineteenth century, was not complemented to the same extent by a development in light industry. This was to be a serious problem as domestic and international markets declined for the products of heavy industry, while those from light industry, such as consumer durables, became more important at home and abroad.

In the second half of the twentieth century, Scottish heavy industry suffered similar problems to those in other areas of British heavy industry. These included foreign competition, labour problems, and a lack of consistency in government and managerial policy. The high profile Ravenscraig steelworks (the strip mill was commissioned in 1963) rapidly turned from evidence of hoped for regeneration to a symbol of failure, and was closed in 1992. In general, the late 1940s and 1950s were years of post-war recovery in which it proved possible to benefit from sustained international economic growth. However, industry in Scotland, as elsewhere in the UK, suffered increasingly from a loss of competitive advantage, particularly as a consequence of expansion in the productive capacity and efficiency of Britain's rivals. In addition, the Scottish economy in the nineteenth century had developed on the basis of cheap labour. Standardisation of labour costs across the UK made it less attractive.

Given the importance of shipbuilding to Scotland's economy, the decline in competitiveness in this sphere was both symptomatic of a wider problem and significant in its consequences. In the late 1940s and early and mid-1950s, Scottish shipyards benefited from rising world demand, but by 1960, they were losing orders to the lower charges of foreign yards. In addition, the latter were able to promise earlier and more reliable delivery dates, a consequence of the absence of modern yards in Scotland able to offer flow-line production and the consequent higher productivity. This absence reflected a lack of investment, born of short-term attitudes and limited planning for the longer term. As the market became more competitive from the 1960s, Scottish yards lost business and were closed. This led to nationalisation in 1977, but that did not prevent further savage closures.

The textile industry was also badly hit by international competition and by rapid changes in fashion. For example, what was once the biggest linen damask factory in the world, that of Erskine, Beveridge and Co. in Dumfermline, closed, and was converted to flats in 1983–4. The knitwear industry in Border towns such as Hawick, was badly hit in the 1980s and 1990s.

Light industry was actively encouraged after World War Two. It helped to diversify the industrial base, although by the 1980s the new enterprises of the late 1940s and 1950s were frequently in serious difficulties, and post-war optimism seemed very transient. New technology led to new industry and employment. North Sea oil was first landed in 1975, and Britain became an exporter of oil. The oil industry brought much prosperity and many jobs to North-East Scotland, although many of the jobs were clerical or cleaning. Aberdeen lost jobs because of the high cost generated by the oil industry. Nevertheless, for the first time ever, average earnings in North-East Scotland rose to above the national average. The computer industry developed in Fife. The long-established financial-services industry expanded in Edinburgh, while service-industry employment in Glasgow, the 'city of culture', brought a measure of prosperity in the 1980s and 1990s. Scotland developed as a customer-service base for many companies, with call-centres based in Glasgow and elsewhere. Edinburgh and North-East Scotland, in the late 1990s, had average per capita income over 130% of the UK average, and Aberdeen had the highest average car values in the United Kingdom.

As elsewhere, however, jobs and prosperity did not flow to all the people and areas that had lost them. The pattern of the workforce was very different. Much of the new work in the 1980s and 1990s placed little stress on manual strength and traditional skills. Male workers dominated the oil industry, but the situation was very different with computers. As a result, in areas like Glenrothes, there were higher rates of female than male employment in the mid-1990s. New jobs did not flow to traditional manufacturing centres, and economic decline hit Clydeside particularly hard.

## Box 11.4

### An instance of failure: car production

The history of the British motor industry has been less than happy. Problems were multiple. They included industrial structure, weak management, poor labour relations, investment and marketing policies, and the role of political interference and government. It was easy in the 1960s and 1970s, when strikes were frequent, for commentators to blame the unions, but in practice, the problems were long term. The fragmented structure of the industry in the early decades of the century, with many companies and factories, was a serious drawback. It led to too many models, and this reduced the scope for the high-volume flow of mass production, because there was a lack of standardisation of components. The resulting small-scale production led to high unit costs, and thus reduced opportunities for investment. This was more generally a characteristic of British industry in the early decades of the century, much of which found it difficult to abandon the older traditions of engineering and, instead, embrace mass production and what was known, after the successful American car manufacturer Henry Ford, as Fordism.

There was significant rationalisation in the 1930s, leading to six major firms by 1939. Morris Motors, Wolsley and MG merged in the Nuffield Organisation in 1936. Nevertheless, in 1945 the National Advisory Council, commenting on limited pre-war exports, argued that the industry was divided into too many small-scale units and pressed for standardisation. The difference in scale and modernity between the Ford Dagenham plant built in the 1920s, and British motor plants that had been developed from small factories, was readily apparent. Low productivity and lack of investment were also highlighted in successive reports, for example that of the Central Policy Review Staff in 1975. Attempts in the 1950s to persuade manufacturers to standardise parts were left to individual companies to implement and fell foul of their competitiveness.

**Box 11.4 continued**

In the 1960s, the car industry fell victim to government intervention. Intent on reducing long-term unemployment in regions of declining heavy industry, especially Clydeside, South Wales and Merseyside, the government encouraged companies in growing industries, particularly the motor industry, to locate there. Encouragement took the form of subsidies, but also the refusal of the industrial development certificates necessary for building new plants elsewhere. Thus, in part, the motor industry was moved away from the established centres of production in South-East England and the West Midlands (British Leyland). Vauxhall, instead, expanded at Ellesmere Port, Ford at Halewood, and companies that were to become part of British Leyland at Speke and Linwood. This was an ultimately unsuccessful policy. Although the extensive use of rail to move components and car bodies helped alleviate the factor of distance, there were, nevertheless, problems that contributed to the continued fragmentation of the industry. Furthermore, there were difficulties in building up new concentrations of skilled labour.

Poor management was also an issue. It proved difficult to create an effective attitude towards planning for national production within company structures. After the formation of the British Motor Company (BMC) in 1952, when Austin merged with the Nuffield Organisation, car assembly continued to be dispersed within the company's factories. In an attempt to maintain goodwill, and reflecting a widespread unwillingness to rethink operations completely, the BMC continued to produce the models associated with the constituent enterprises in their original location. Austin and Nuffield retained their separate identities until the early 1960s, each with a separate board of directors. This was not the best basis for rationalisation and coherent company strategy. As more generally in the industry, there was a lack of adequate investment, and of an effective system of financial control and product planning, and a preference for engineering quality over financial control. Thus, although the company launched a very successful design in 1959 with the Mini, it was poorly marketed and the production was poorly priced.

The Labour governments of 1964–70 sought to reform the industry as part of Labour policy of economic planning, and also because the motor car industry appeared a part of the industrial base that could be used both to compensate for decline in old-established industries and to win crucial exports. Naturally favourable to big units, which seemed the best means for effective planning and achieving vital economies of scale, the government encouraged a process of consolidation through mergers. The BMC merged with the recently merged Jaguar Group in 1966, while, the following year, the Leyland Motor Corporation was formed from Leyland, Rover and Standard Triumph. In 1968, the two companies merged to form the British Leyland Motor Company (BLMC), which was to be renamed British Leyland (BL) in 1975. This was seen as a new start, and the new company was given an immediate loan of £25 million for retooling.

However, the new company hit many problems. Its inheritance was unwieldy. Across its 48 factories, it produced the full range of cars and goods vehicles, yet again offering many models, to the detriment of volume production. Out-dated and poorly-maintained plant and machinery was a major problem that reflected insufficient investment, certainly in contrast to global competitors.

Labour relations were also a major problem. This was true both of the areas into which the industry had expanded in the early 1960s, where the ex-shipyard workers and ex-miners had a strong culture of trade union militancy, and of factories in traditional areas of motor manufacture, both Cowley near Oxford and Longbridge in the West Midlands. The report on labour relations drawn up in 1966 by the industry's Joint Labour Council criticised the nature of union organisation, specifically the failure to enforce collective agreements, which led to numerous unofficial strikes. The frequent laying-off of production workers and changes in overtime, in response to shifts in demand, helped exacerbate labour relations. They remained poor. Although strike activity nationally fell in 1980, in part due to the consequences of the deflationary policy of the Thatcher government, labour disputes in the car industry remained a problem in the early 1980s.

By then, a determined effort had been made to improve productivity by cutting excess capacity. This had become necessary as a consequence of the readily apparent failure of the industry in the 1970s. By 1975, imported cars accounted for 33% of new registrations, while BLMC's share was only 31%; the American-owned manufacturers in Britain, Ford and Vauxhall, were more successful. BLMC lost £76 million in 1975, working out as a considerable sum on each car sold. The Labour government could not let such a major employer go bankrupt, and in the mid-1970s governmental interventionism was at its height. Large sums of public money were invested, especially in 1975 and 1977, and the company was reorganised with the car-making division, known as British Leyland, separated from bus and truck manufacture. The workforce was heavily cut from 1977.

These changes were unsuccessful. BL could not respond sufficiently fast to match developments in domestic and international markets. It was poor both as a manufacturing company and as a competitive enterprise. By 1978, BL had a smaller market share in Britain than Ford; by 1988 than Vauxhall. By 1987, the car division held only 15% of the home market. In 1984, Jaguar/Daimler had been floated off from BL. It was bought by Ford in 1989. In 1987, Leyland Trucks was sold to DAF, a Dutch company, and the buses division went to Volvo. In 1988, the car division, now called the Rover Group, went to British Aerospace, but sales continued to decline, and in 1994 it was sold to BMW, a leading German car manufacturer. In contrast, Nissan, the Japanese car maker that located near Sunderland, was far more successful. Benefiting from the newness of its plant and continued investment, Nissan's factory at Sunderland built 98 cars per assembly line worker in 1997, compared with 62 at Honda's plant in Swindon, 62 at Ford's plant at Dagenham, and 33 at Rover's plant at Longbridge, which was badly in need of fresh investment and made heavy losses in 1998. The following year, BMW threatened to close the plant, although this threat was withdrawn and fresh investment was promised.

Even where there were jobs, there was also much uncertainty. The oil industry was hit in the 1980s and 1990s by falls in the price of oil that reflected developments in the Middle East. The microchip industry came to suffer from over-capacity in the late 1990s. The bitter dispute over attempts to introduce new working practices at the US-owned Timex plant at Dundee in 1993 indicated that economic change was not welcomed by all. It also revealed the consequences of growing foreign ownership of Scottish concerns: the management decided to shut the plant.

Scotland's economic history had many points in common with that of Wales, but also some important differences. Wales was more attractive to foreign investors. Nevertheless, both managed the transition from heavy industry without social breakdown, and created new worlds of work that contributed greatly to economic growth in the 1990s.

# Government intervention and labour relations

The example of the car industry, as described in Box 11.4, can be contrasted with other more successful sectors, such as pharmaceuticals, but is nevertheless important because it exemplified many of the themes of British industry during the twentieth century, including three that were present, but far less pronounced, over the two previous centuries: government intervention, poor labour relations, and foreign competition. It cannot be said that any of these three have produced a benign context for economic growth. Government intervention was defended as crucial for planning, but it was frequently unsuccessful and inconsistent. The latter was especially true of regional aid and state ownership. The steel industry, for example, was nationalised in 1949 and 1967, and privatised in 1953 and 1988. Aside from this lack of consistency, there was also poor management of nationalised industries by governments, and the enforcement of unrealistic pricing policies, which, together, made investment by the industries themselves difficult. Government attitudes towards, and legislation for, incomes policies also varied greatly. So also did interest-rate policy.

Given this context, it was scarcely surprising that industries experienced great difficulty in planning ahead. This became more acute from the 1970s, as EEC policies and attitudes came to play a role alongside, and, in some cases, in conflict with those of national government. EEC policies were particularly important in agriculture. Prices were subsidised above market rates and food mountains built up. It is possible that a third level of intervention will be added with the creation of sub-Westminster parliaments. From 1997, Scottish business interests expressed concern that an Edinburgh parliament with tax-varying powers would affect economic activity in Scotland.

Government intervention was especially pronounced in labour relations. Some aspects of this have already been considered in Chapter 10, but it is important to discuss them again here, because labour relations were a major issue in the economic as well as the political history of the country. Much of the discussion tends to focus on disputes. However, it is important to note that these were far from constant in rate or scope. Some sectors, such as the coal mines and the docks, and later, car manufacturing, were particularly prone to labour disputes, but most workplaces did not suffer from strike action. Furthermore, strikes were scarcely unique to Britain. Having accepted this, there were, nevertheless, problems with labour relations that are not simply measured by the frequency of strikes. First, the possibility of disputes discouraged both investment and attempts to raise productivity. Secondly, disruption, or the prospect of disruption in key industries, particularly energy and transport activities, affected production and confidence elsewhere. Thirdly, so many strikes were unofficial, 'wildcat', and therefore especially disruptive. More generally, the greater integration of the economy increased interdependence, and thus vulnerability to disruption.

Trade union membership rose from 1.5 million in 1895 to 13.5 million in 1979. Labour relations deteriorated from the 1880s, causing growing militancy among unskilled and semi-skilled workers. The deterioration in labour relations arose as employers sought to push through the changes in work methods necessary in order to meet the growing challenges of competition. There were major strikes in the London gasworks and docks in 1888–9, in the South Wales coalfield in 1893 and 1898, and in the engineering industry in 1897–8. These helped to radicalise sections of the workforce, as did the major strike over union recognition at the Penrhyn slate quarry in 1900–3. These disputes led to a questioning of the ability of the system to solve disputes, and this had political consequences. In 1899, the Trades Union Congress advocated an independent political organisation to return sympathetic MPs to Parliament, and by 1906 there were 29 Labour MPs.

Labour relations deteriorated anew from 1909, when there were major strikes in the shipyards. Difficult economic circumstances led in 1910 to downward pressures on pay, industrial disputes, sabotage and riots. Disputes in the coal industry arose from pressure on the profitability of pits and on miners' living standards due, in part, to geological factors which reduced pit productivity. Employers sought to restrict customary rights and payments. Sabotage by striking miners in South Wales in 1910 against colliers, strike-breakers and the trains attempting to bring them in, as well as some looting, was resisted and led to much violence. At Tonypandy, a miner was killed by police. Troops were sent in by the Liberal Home Secretary, Winston Churchill, although he held them back, and was criticised for allowing the rioters to destroy property. The following year, the first general rail strike led to sabotage at Llanelli, and also to the deployment of troops who killed two strikers in Liverpool. As with other such disputes, there was a potent mixture of dissatisfaction with specific conditions, and demands for political transformation.

The availability and attitude of labour attracted more government attention during World War One, and this led to a measure of state regulation. For example, the effort to increase agricultural production led to the establishment of wages boards. They fixed minimum wages and regulated working hours. The need for labour both at the front and in the workplace led to substantial bargaining gains for those in work. After the war, there was an upsurge in labour disputes, as economic problems hit home alongside deflationary problems. The coal industry, which employed about one-tenth of the male workforce, was especially disturbed and this was crucial to the General Strike of 1926: it arose from a crisis in the coal industry. Firm government action and a lack of certainty on the part of the TUC led to a rapid end of the strike, and the miners were left alone. They eventually had to accept the employers' terms. This left a legacy of bitterness and also ensured continued distance between trade unionism and the Conservatives (see Chapter 9). There was no system of Conservative trade unions to compete with Labour counterparts. Equally, there was no attempt to bring the unions within the fabric of government. They remained under the control of their members. Furthermore, successive governments and the Ministry of Labour opposed state intervention in labour relations. They were left to free collective bargaining between employers and trade unions, a free market. However, the market was controlled by the employers, many of which were firmly anti-union and unwilling to consider the wider social needs of their workers.

The sense of distance between the trade unions and the Conservatives was exacerbated during the Depression of the 1930s. The major rise in unemployment affected long-established industries, such as shipbuilding, particularly hard, and these tended to be heavily unionised and influential within the union movement. The unwillingness of the government and Treasury to support reflation and major rises in public spending led to criticism, but the unions were able to do little. Nevertheless, the corporatism of the 1930s led to union leaders being included on government committees.

The critical need for labour during World War Two altered the situation, although perhaps just speeding up processes that were already underway. In 1940, the National Government was replaced by a coalition government in which Labour played a prominent role. Union leaders such as Ernest Bevin, General Secretary of the Transport and General Workers Union 1921–40, Walter Citrine, General Secretary of the TUC 1926–46, Vic Feather, General Secretary of the TUC 1969–73, Jack Jones, General Secretary of the Transport and General Workers Union 1968–78, and Hugh Scanlon, the engineers' leader, wielded great influence from the creation of the wartime coalition until Thatcher came to power in 1979. They played key roles in what was a corporatist state. During World War Two, trade union membership rose from about 6,250,000 in 1939 to nearly 8 million in 1945, in part because union membership was officially encouraged. Despite strikes, labour relations were far better than in World War One, and the institutional freedom of the unions was preserved alongside central planning and wage restraint. The post-war Labour governments (1945–51) realised many of the unions' political aims, including nationalisation of much of industry, universal statutory social services, and the goal of full employment. Free collective bargaining continued, and there was no government regulation of labour relations comparable to that of many other sections of the economy or, for example, to the Irish Industrial Relations Act of 1946. Nevertheless, strikes remained illegal until 1951 and the Attlee government called out troops eleven times to deal with them (see Chapter 10).

The Conservative ministries of 1951–64 sought to avoid labour disputes. They preferred to leave employers and unions to settle disputes and to persuade the unions to control their own members. The Churchill government (1951–5) only called out the troops once, and there were few strikes. Government conciliation helped, but so also did the avoidance of the attempt to tackle poor productivity. This was a period of economic growth and, therefore, with profits good, employers made concessions. However, labour relations came to be seen as a major issue during the 1964–70 Labour governments. In part, this was a consequence of the extension of government control over much of industry and a conviction of the value of planning. The nationalised industries were a major strain on government resources, while, more generally, wage demands set the pace for inflation. In addition, labour relations were deteriorating. Wilson hoped to transform the situation. A wages policy had been maintained by the Attlee government until 1950, and less effectively by the Wilson governments in the 1960s, and Wilson produced a Bill based on the 'In place of strife' White Paper in early 1969. This proposed state intervention in industrial relations and legal penalties for wildcat strikes. It was withdrawn, however, in face of trade-union and Labour Party opposition, including a protest strike on 1 May 1969.

Heath inherited the problem. At first he sought to return to the free market, but, under the pressure of concerns about rising unemployment and inflation, shifted towards a policy of wage controls. Relations between his government (1970–4) and the unions were more acrimonious than under Wilson, not least because political differences were matched by an absence of common assumptions, experiences and history. The Industrial Relations Act (1971) inaugurated a new era of confrontation in the field of industrial relations. Some prominent unionists saw labour relations as an aspect of class war. In the 1970s, thanks to television and power cuts, people became accustomed respectively to the immediacy of picket-line violence and to taking baths in the dark. Far more working days were lost in strikes than in the 1960s. The labour-relations crisis of the 1970s discouraged investment and thus made it harder to maintain productivity increases and economic growth.

Trade-union power and economic problems helped to discredit the post-war social democratic consensus, especially the notion of the planned, corporatist state. With unemployment rising, unions engaged in wasteful demarcation disputes, many shop stewards adopted the language and attitudes of class conflict, and the net effect was to add an ugly side to the general impression of an economy in which it was foolish to invest and a country in decline. The role of the unions was vilified in Anthony Burgess's novel *1985* (1978), in which 'TUCland' is revealed as callous and destructive, and also in Lindsay Anderson's film *Britannia Hospital* (1982). As the Labour government's social contract crumbled in the winter of 1978–9, TUCland seemed all too real.

Anger with the trade unions helped the Conservatives greatly in 1979, not least by sustaining their determination during the last months of the Callaghan government and in the subsequent election campaign. Furthermore, public opinion polls had revealed a steadily growing percentage convinced that unions were overly powerful (even among Labour supporters). The Conservatives fought the election pledged to change aspects of labour relations, including the 'closed shop' and secondary picketing, and to enforce the use of secret ballots before strikes. Many workers, including trade unionists, disliked the pre-entry closed shop and voted Conservative.

Thatcher had little time for discussions with trade union leaders, believing that they played too large a role in the economy, and that this role was harmful. She saw them as 'the enemy within', hostile to her politics and to entrepreneurship, and, more specifically, as slowing the pace of productivity growth. In 1980, Thatcher pushed through an Employment Act that banned secondary picketing, by restricting picketing to workers involved in disputes, and to their place of work. Exemptions from 'closed shops' were expanded and the Act offered funds for secret ballots before strikes, and for the election of union officials. A second Employment Act of 1982 banned pre-entry 'closed shops' and allowed 'closed shops' to exist only where a ballot revealed 85 per cent support, a very high threshold.

These changes were not accepted without protest. A one-day 'Day of Action', i.e. strike, in 1980, however, achieved little, and in 1983, the National Graphical Association was fined and had its assets sequestered following its attempt to enforce a closed shop at the Warrington printing plant of the *Stockport Messenger*. The Association had to give way. In 1984, another 'Day of Action' failed to shake the government's decision to ban unions at the Government Communications Headquarters (GCHQ) at Cheltenham, a branch of the spy system.

After the failure of the Miners' strike in 1984–5 and the unsuccessful violent picketing of News International's new printing plant at Wapping in 1986–7, fresh Employment Acts were passed in 1988, 1989 and 1990. These successive acts proved far more effective than Heath's attempt at one-stage total change. The Acts of 1988–90 gave trade union members the right to ignore a union ballot on industrial action, banned strikes to establish or retain 'closed shops', introduced restrictions on industrial action, election ballots, and cases going to full industrial tribunals, and forced unions to repudiate unofficial action. This incremental approach towards trade union reform proved to be very successful, as it created a series of new status quos which were given time to establish themselves before being bolstered by further measures. In turn, such an approach made it more difficult to undertake concerted opposition to the reforms that were introduced. Ultimately, both the Labour Party and the trade unions had little choice but to accept the changes that had been made. The demonising of trade unions also proved a very successful strategy for Thatcher. The Major governments also kept the momentum of trade union reform going in the 1990s: the Trade Union Reform and Employment Rights Act was passed in 1993. It established the principle that pre-strike ballots should be by post and decreed that strike action could not begin until seven days after the result of a ballot was known. Having ended the Burnham Committee, the negotiating machinery for teachers' pay, in 1986, the government abolished twenty-six wage councils in 1993. The market was to set wages.

These changes were part of the 'bonfire of controls' which took place under Thatcher and which continued under Major, at least controls in the economy. In 1986, the City of London was deregulated in what was called the 'Big Bang'. Thatcher's support for market-oriented measures helped to characterise the 1980s with its pronounced individualism (see also Chapter 7). It is unclear how far these measures were responsible for the rise in the rate of economic growth, which, in the mid and late 1980s, accelerated beyond its previous trend, although, in part, this was a matter of recovery from the severe recession of the early 1980s. The crude monetarism of policy in her early years was relaxed. Furthermore, for the first time since 1945, in 1979–89 the British rate of growth surpassed that of France and Germany. This trend, however, was not to continue into the 1990s.

The legislative changes of the 1980s and 1990s had an impact, not only on high-profile disputes but also on the general climate of labour relations. In the late 1980s, trade union militancy became less common, and the level of industrial action continued to fall in the early 1990s, especially in the private sector. The number of stoppages beginning in a year fell from over 2,000 throughout the period 1967–1979 to below 1,100 throughout 1985–92. By 1990, only 48 per cent of employees were union members, and the number covered by closed-shop agreements had fallen to 0.5 million, compared with 4.5 million a decade earlier. This was good for some trade unions as they had to explore new services to members, such as insurance and legal services. Trade union membership fell from 13.5 million in 1979 to 10.5 million in 1986, 7.3 million by 1994 and 6.7 million by 1998. Thanks to privatisation in the 1980s and early 1990s, fewer trade unionists were the employees of state-owned companies. Furthermore, economic changes and shifts among the labour force ensured that trade unionists were increasingly in white-collar jobs.

More generally, far more wage negotiations were at a local level, there were fewer demarcation disputes, and the spread of 'single-union agreements' eased industrial tension. The introduction of these agreements had caused disruption in the mid-

1980s. In 1985, the new *Today* newspaper had secured such an agreement with the electricians, and, in 1986, Rupert Murdoch and News International also turned to the electricians, breaking the restrictive practices of the print unions. After the Wapping dispute of 1986, in which the print unions were hit by fines and sequestrations, such agreements became common. They became a prerequisite of any decision by a multinational corporation to establish a British-based operation. More flexible labour practices were also linked to the decline of 'jobs for life', although the extent of these had been exaggerated.

Although the lessening of trade union influence was the work of the Conservative government, similar attitudes were adopted by the Labour Party, both because they saw that such measures were popular and because they appeared appropriate to the cause of 'modernisation' that was heavily pushed by Labour in the 1990s, particularly under Blair after 1994. As a result, the Labour Party constitution changed, with the ending of the trade union bloc vote, and even talk of a formal severing of the institutional link between Labour and the unions. After Labour was elected in 1997, the influence of trade union leaders on the government was far less than it had been during the Labour governments in 1964–70 and 1974–9. The unions were less influential in economic policymaking in the late 1990s than many of their European counterparts, crucially so in not securing shorter working weeks. This was significant, and very different from the case in France and Germany, because the relatively low productivity of British workers was in part alleviated by their willingness to work the longest average hours in Western Europe. This has been linked to problems in relative levels of public health, but it certainly permitted a higher standard of living than would otherwise have been the case.

# Management

A focus on trade unions should not lead to a neglect of other aspects of the economic context and climate. Management, its quality and ambitions, is one of the most important. It has been argued that this bears a large part of the responsibility for Britain's relative decline. Managers, of course, varied, but it has been claimed that, on the whole, they lacked the necessary calibre and vision, not least compared with their American and German counterparts. Instead, they have been seen as drawn from a narrow section of the community, poorly educated for their task, and complacent. For decades, many managers were gentlemen and amateurs, rather than being equipped with the necessary technical understanding to encourage, and respond to, innovation. This failing became more important as the pace of innovation increased and as British industry dropped behind. The maintenance of the economic status quo was not enough, and the failure of managers, bankers and trade unionists to appreciate this was serious. These attitudes became strongly entrenched throughout much (but by no means all) of industry in the second half of the nineteenth century, and they became normative (the norm that conditioned the response to new circumstances). As a consequence, the domestic economy performed poorly, encouraging British investment abroad.

The poor performance of the domestic economy was exacerbated by World War One, but the war did not cause it. Difficulties both before and after the war encouraged many economic interests to support protectionism and the development of the Empire as a secure zone for British exports. This was not, as it turned out, an economic strategy that addressed the problems of productivity that handicapped the domestic economy. Politicians, union leaders and managers all failed to address the latter, especially over-manning and restrictive practices. Too little effort was devoted to raising the educational attainment of managers and workers, specifically the lack of sufficient vocational training, particularly apprenticeships. In industries such as coal mining, there was a failure to match the rate of technological and organisational change shown by foreign competitors. Thus, in the inter-war coal industry productivity gains were too low. This can be attributed as much to a managerial failure to adopt, and invest in, technological innovation as to an unwillingness on the part of miners to respond to change. There was also a failure to restructure the industry by amalgamating the large number of mines, many of which were uneconomic.

Management failure has been linked to mistaken investment strategies, both within companies and more generally in the economy. It has been argued that the institutional providers of investment in the City of London, especially the banks, shared in a culture of complacency and gentlemanly amateurism. This has been traced to a series of interrelated cultural norms and practices, such as a suspicion of expertise and technical skills, that inhibited efficiency and encouraged false patterns of investment. Difficult to prove or quantify, such analyses suffer from an inability to demonstrate that the whole interpretative structure they give rise to can account for particular facets of the British economy.

More specifically, it has been suggested that there was a preference for investing in well-established companies, rather than in developing sectors. Risk or venture capital was thus insufficient and too expensive: interest rates were too high. Furthermore, aside from this pattern of industrial investment, there was also a preference for non-industrial investment, both on the 'money markets', for example in British and foreign government bonds, and in housing. Even when there was investment in industry – old or new – it has been argued that much of it was poorly-directed, because of an absence of sufficient professionalism in information flows within the capital market. Furthermore, much British investment was short-term, responding to myopic institutional shareholders unwilling to commit sufficiently to long-term investments. In contrast, it has been suggested that American and German capital markets were more effective in providing large flows of investment income for technologically advanced industries, such as cars, chemicals and electrical engineering, before and after World War One, and computers after 1945, although the former claim has also been queried.

Investment choices are also linked to politics and to socio-cultural assumptions. The latter is especially true of state encouragement, through the tax system, for home ownership. The former has been seen in the influence of commercial considerations and the City of London in fiscal and economic policymaking and the lesser weight of manufacturing, let alone agricultural, influences. This emphasis on the City has been blamed for deflationary policies, for repeatedly keeping sterling too high, and thus hitting exports, and also for failing to give due weight to protectionist interests. Policy in the 1920s, specifically the return to the Gold Standard in 1925 at too high a rate, has been seen in this light, but the charge has also been made, more generally, throughout the century. However, protectionist interests were apt to underrate the general economic value of expanding trade. Furthermore, protectionism reduces competition and thus the pressure for productivity gains. This argument has been made both about economic policy in the 1930s and about the consequences of Britain's failure to enter the European Economic Community until 1973. There was greater exposure to global competition both prior to 1932 and after 1973, especially after Thatcher came to power in 1979. Aside from the debate over free trade or protectionism, it has been argued that government has failed to create a suitable business climate. Specifically, there have been claims that corporation taxes (taxes on business profits) have been too high, discouraging investment, and that there has been insufficient governmental support for Research and Development other than to the benefit of the defence (i.e. war) industry. Both these factors are held to have limited the potential for productivity gains.

**consolidation:** The merging of companies in order to create national brands and reduce overhead costs.

# Consolidation

Trade unions and the car industry both exemplified a more general feature of the economy during the century: **consolidation**. Just as the number of unions fell with mergers, so the same process affected companies. Company mergers led to a consolidation in the private sector, albeit one that was generally less sweeping than nationalisations. Public limited companies developed, and they used their borrowing capacity to fund expansion and consolidation. Products, such as beer, that had provided a degree of local identification were replaced by national brands. Local breweries were taken over. Consolidation had begun in the Victorian period. The number of breweries in Scotland fell from 220 in 1860, to 125 in 1900, and 45 in 1930. The following year, the two largest, William Younger and William McEwan, merged to form Scottish Brewers. Consolidation continued after World War Two, and brewing ceased in traditional centres such as Aberdeen and Dundee. Major companies, such as Scottish and Newcastle, dominated the industry, and microbreweries played only a minor role.

The same process occurred in England. In the early twentieth century, for example, ownership and production became more concentrated in the Northumberland and Durham brewing industry. In Portsmouth, during the century, all the other breweries became incorporated into Whitbreads; which, in turn, ceased brewing in the city in 1983. In Berkshire, there were 42 brewing companies in 1902, but only two by 1970. There had been extensive consolidation there in the inter-war period. Simonds of Reading became a major regional brewer, not least by purchasing brewers in Newbury. Morland of Abingdon bought brewers in Wantage and Reading, while out-of-county brewers also made purchases. Takeovers led to the closure of local breweries, such that in 1939 there were only eight brewing companies in Berkshire. Consolidation continued after the war, leaving Morland as an independent brewer, and Simonds – merged with Courage in 1960 – as part of a national firm. In the UK as a whole, 22 breweries were taken over in 1959 and 28 in 1960. The related malting industry also had similar consolidation.

Consolidation, and attendant exposure to national and international policies and pressures, can also be seen in other industries. In publishing, for example, once-independent companies, such as Bartholomew, Collins, Longman, Macmillan, and Nelson, became part of international conglomerates. In the chocolate industry, Rowntree took over Mackintosh in 1969 and was, in turn, taken over by the Swiss company Nestlé in 1988.

The leisure industry was also affected by consolidation and rationalisation. Local and regional newspapers and cinemas were taken over by national chains, and had to respond to their requirements. Companies like the Westminster Press became a national force. Local independents were absorbed: the *Shields Daily News*, for example, by the Westminster Press in 1934. The Portsmouth and Sunderland Newspaper Group indicated the geographical spread of that company. There was a similar process in retail and services. Big retail chains became important from the Victorian period. By 1900, J. Sainsbury had 47 provision stores, by 1906 there were over 500 shops in Julius Drewe's grocery chain, and by 1914 another grocer, Thomas Lipton, had 500 shops.

Banks amalgamated, leading, by 1918, to the formation of the 'big five' banks: Barclays, Lloyds, Midland, National Provincial, and Westminster. Local banks were taken over. In 1896, twenty private banks merged to form Barclays. Strongest in East and South-East England, the bank spread by amalgamating with the Consolidated Bank of Cornwall in 1905, the United Counties Bank, an important Midlands bank, in 1916, the London, Provincial and South Western Bank in 1918, and the Union Bank of Manchester in 1919. When Nevile Reid and Co. merged with Barclays in 1914, it ended nearly 140 years of private county banking in Berkshire. National mergers also affected local facilities, as in 1909, when the London and County merged with the London and Westminster. The process of merger continued. The National Provincial and the Westminster merged. In 1969, Barclays and Martins, both themselves the product of numerous amalgamations and takeovers, merged. Martins was the last national English bank to have its headquarters outside London; but, with the merger, Liverpool lost this status.

In banking, mergers between British companies were not related to any loss of domestic banking business. Foreign banks developed a profile in London and played a major role in financial services there, but they made little impact elsewhere, although the Hongkong and Shanghai (HSBC) bought the Midland. In manufacturing consolidation was, in part, driven by the attempt to gain economies of scale in the face of serious foreign competition. It was designed to lead to a rationalisation of production, with larger units and more efficient processes.

In many cases, this proved unsuccessful, as the example of the car industry has shown. In part, amalgamation was not accompanied by the necessary rationalisation. In part, there was insufficient investment, whether or not industries benefited from amalgamation. In part, foreign competition remained relentless. This was the case, for example, with the cotton industry. Based in Lancashire, this was a major industry, which, at the beginning of the century, had been a major exporter. By 1937, however, exports to the Far East, and especially India, had fallen dramatically. This reflected problems in particular markets, but also major competition from Indian and Japanese manufacturers. As a consequence, the industry contracted in Britain. In the 1930s, the workforce fell from 564,000 to 398,000 workers, and 22 million spindles were scrapped.

After a brief period of post-war expansion, there was renewed decline in the 1950s, in large part due to foreign competition. Britain became a net importer of cotton goods in 1958. The Cotton Industry Reorganisation Act of 1959 offered compensation for the removal of now-excess capacity. In 1959–60, about 300 mills closed, and half the industry's spindles and 40% of looms were laid aside. This was a major change for the economy of North-West England and for many individual towns. Contraction was the drastic counterpart to the development of large, integrated companies, especially Courtaulds and Viyella. The industry could not, however, match foreign competitors, and it continued to lose ground in both British and foreign markets.

The Yorkshire wool-textile industry was also hit, although less savagely; in part, because exports, which fell in the inter-war period, had played a smaller role than they did in the cotton industry. Whereas the cotton labour force fell by 42% in 1912–37, that in wool declined by 11%.

The inter-war period was far more favourable for another important branch of industry, the chemical industry. The British had dominated this on the global scale in the mid-nineteenth century, but had then been surpassed by the USA and Germany, both of which had made more effective use of new techniques, such as electro-chemical processes. World War One, however, led to important government support, with, for example, the demand for explosives causing the development of a British petro-chemical industry and the beginnings of a chemical industry on the Tees. The importance of the industry having been demonstrated by the war, it was then protected by post-war legislation directed against free trade: the Dyestuffs (Import Regulations) Act of 1920 and the Safeguarding of Industries Act of 1921. The opportunities and costs of the chemical industry also led to consolidation, and eventually, in 1926, to the creation of Imperial Chemical Industries (ICI). With its major base at Billingham, ICI brought important development to the Tees estuary. Other major companies included Courtaulds, Fisons and Unilever. These companies and others developed the manufacture of synthetic textiles such as rayon and nylon, synthetic pharmaceuticals, and soap powders.

After World War Two, the petro-chemical industry expanded, petrol became the major raw material for organic chemical manufacture, and the range of products grew. The use of synthetic textiles rose. The oil link led to the growth of manufacturing complexes where oil was imported, for example with BP at Grangemouth and Esso at Fawley.

This growth in production in the chemical industry was achieved without an expansion in the number of companies involved. More generally, capital-intensive production throughout industry was concentrated into fewer concerns. Yet, there was also important growth in smaller-scale activity, both in specialist manufacture and, more particularly, in services. A good example was Corby in Northamptonshire. This steel town was devastated in 1980, when British Steel closed the works, ending more than 5,000 jobs. By 1981, unemployment was up to 22%. By 1999, however, it had fallen to less than 3%. In part, this was due to diversification. Corby gained Enterprise Zone status and this helped to lure in a wide range of companies, many also attracted by good road links via the A1 and M1. Many of these companies – such as Rank Hovis and Allied Foods – were big, but by 1999 Corby had more than 700 employers and a range of production – from electronic components to foods and pharmaceuticals. More generally, such diversity helped many areas to weather the economic shocks of the twentieth century.

Corporatism and collectivism affected society and politics from the 1940s. The nationalisation policies of the Attlee governments (1945–51) made the legislative realm of the government the economic space for Britain. Regional autonomies and variations, and corporate identities, were eroded as the Bank of England (1946), coal (1947), railways (1948), road transport (1948), the electricity supply (1948), gas (1949), and iron and steel (1951) were nationalised. All these moves brought more of the economy under direct government control, including about two million workers. Nationalisations also consolidated the trend towards national control, planning, products, conditions, pricing, and wage settlements. The new British Railways, for example, began to standardise carriages with the introduction of the all-steel British Railways Mark 1 carriage in 1951. The printing of tickets was concentrated on one site. British Railways, alone, employed 681,000 workers in 1948. Nationalisation led to the rationalisation of the coal industry, with the closure of many small pits, although it soon came to use state subsidies in order to delay further rationalisation to cope with the competition from alternative energy sources and from foreign coal production. The Attlee government's nationalisation policy reflected a commitment to economic planning, a belief in the importance of public ownership, and the specific problems both of particular industries and of the 1940s, not least the lack of investment during World War Two.

## ■ The way ahead?

To draw attention to the rise of new industries and to less divisive labour relations may appear to suggest that problems have been successfully overcome. Indeed there has been a great increase in national wealth since 1945 and Britain remains a major industrial power. Yet, it would be foolish to ignore continued problems. First, de-industrialisation has affected not only traditional heavy industries, such as shipbuilding, iron and steel, and heavy engineering, but also newer light industries. Thus, in Northern Ireland, synthetic-fibre plants established in the 1960s closed in the early 1980s, and in 1998 computer-chip factories in Tyneside and in Scotland's 'Silicon Glen' were hit. By the mid-1980s, Britain was importing more manufactured goods than it exported. This was unprecedented during the century and led to considerable alarm, but, in part, reflected a different balance of priorities within the British economy that was responsive both to the sectors in which Britain enjoyed competitive advantages, and to investment opportunities. In 1998 the numbers employed in manufacturing fell, both below 4.05 million and below those employed in wholesale and retail.

Secondly, Britain has fallen behind in international competitiveness. There has been growth, but Britain's relative economic performance declined appreciably by comparison with traditional and new competitors, although the indices used are not free from uncertainty and the employment of different indices can produce very varied rankings and trends. Between 1960 and 1981, Britain's annual growth in gross domestic product was lower than that of the other OECD countries, although, in part, this reflected the earlier development of manufacturing in Britain and the scope elsewhere for catching up. After 1960, the average standard of living fell behind that of Germany, Japan, France and Italy. Individual industries, both old – steel, iron – and new – electronics – were hit by competition, as was mining, agriculture, fishing and forestry. The service sector was also hit. Indeed, Britain lost part of its world market share in internationally traded services, in large part because of competition from the USA and Western Europe. This fall was faster than that in manufactured goods in the 1970s and 1980s.

There was protracted debate about the causes of this decline throughout the century. As government intervention in the economy became more important, so the debate was increasingly politicised. Before 1979, modernising economic strategies sought to use an expanded state and to encourage such expansion, but this diminished after 1979. Thus, debate over economic policy was bound up with disagreement over the desirable extent of state power and intervention (see Chapters 7, 10).

The study of recent British economic history and, indeed, the collection, publication, and analysis of economic statistics were also matters for contention. It was unclear whether the re-allocation of resources from industry towards services was desireable or harmful, and whether excessive resources were devoted to long-established manufacturing at the expense of more modern sectors. There were different views on the optimum form of labour relations and on wage rates. The relationship between different factors, particularly between market and non-market developments, was unclear. Economists disagreed and it is scarcely appropriate therefore to offer firm statements. Nevertheless the following captures the main points.

# Summary

◆ The British economy grew during the twentieth century, despite serious and painful recessions especially in the 1930s, early 1980s and early 1990s.

◆ The rate of growth was below that of many other countries, and this led to much talk of national decline.

◆ There have been important qualitative changes in British industry. Heavy industry declined. Despite difficulties, the 'new' industries of the inter-war period remained important and were joined by other new industries from the 1960s.

◆ Employment patterns have changed in response to industrial shifts. Different skills have been emphasised, and physical strength is far less important than in the past. Women have become far more important in the labour market.

◆ Labour relations and government intervention caused great contention during the century. Both affected economic activity.

# Questions for discussion

◆ How far has Britain declined, and why?

◆ What was the economic history of your area in the twentieth century?

◆ How did employment patterns alter during the twentieth century?

# Further reading

Alford, B. W. E., *Britain in the World Economy since 1880* (London, 1996).

Booth, Alan, *British Economic Policy: The Crucial Years, 1939–51* (Oxford, 1987).

Booth, Alan, *British Economic Development since 1945* (Manchester, 1995).

Campbell, Alan, Fishman, Nina, and Howell, David (eds), *Miners, Unions and Politics, 1910–47* (Aldershot, 1996).

Church, R., *The Rise and Decline of the British Motor Industry* (London, 1994).

Clarke, Peter, and Trebilcock, Clive (eds), *Understanding Decline: Perceptions and Realities of British Economic Performance* (Cambridge, 1997).

Cooper, Richard, and Woodward, Nicholas, *Britain in the 1970s: The Troubled Economy* (London, 1996).

Floud, Roderick, and McCloskey, Donald (eds), *The Economic History of Britain since 1700* (2nd edn, Cambridge, 1994).

Johnson, Christopher, *The Economy under Mrs Thatcher* (London, 1991).

Lloyd-Jones, Roger, and Lewis, Merv, *British Industrial Capitalism since the Industrial Revolution* (London, 1997).

McIvor, Arthur, *Organized Capital: Employers' Associations and Industrial Relations in Northern England, 1880–1939* (Cambridge, 1996).

Middleton, Roger, *The British Economy since 1945: Engaging with the Debate* (London, 1999).

Pope, Rex (ed.), *Atlas of British Social and Economic History since c.1700* (London, 1989).

Tomlinson, Jim, *Problems in British Economic Policy, 1870–1945* (London, 1981).

Weir, R. B., *The History of the Distillers Company, 1887–1939: Diversification and Growth in Whiskey and Chemicals* (Oxford, 1995).

# The Parts of the
British Isles

CHAPTER 12

In 1900, the British Isles was a unified state, although not under this name, with one Parliament – in Westminster. Earlier parliaments in Dublin and Edinburgh had long ceased to exist. By 2000, there were two states – the United Kingdom of Great Britain and Northern Ireland, and Eire (the Republic of Ireland) – and, within the United Kingdom, there were powerful separatist tendencies in Scotland, Northern Ireland (Ulster), and, albeit to a considerably lesser extent, Wales. It is easy to treat this change as part of a process of inevitable dissolution in which only the timetable was (and is) uncertain. Such an approach is unhelpful. It was unclear from the outset how relations between the parts of the British Isles would develop, and it is necessary to write an account of the history of England, Ireland, Scotland and Wales, without employing the tactics of teleology: assuming that what did happen was bound to do so.

## Key issues

▶ Why did Eire leave the Empire?

▶ What was the political situation in Scotland and Wales prior to the 1980s?

▶ How did nationalist support develop in the 1960s and 1970s?

▶ Why was Northern Ireland affected by the 'troubles' from 1968?

▶ Why did nationalism become stronger in Scotland and Wales from the 1980s?

## Contents

# The nineteenth-century background

## Nineteenth-century Ireland

The Union of 1801 ensured that the politics of Ireland were far more closely linked with those of Britain than heretofore. The Union was to dissolve in violence, and it is possible to write a brief survey of Ireland in this period centred on hardship and discord: the potato famine of 1845–9 and the struggle for Irish political autonomy. Both were of great importance. Emigration represented a widely-held desire to leave. The population fell from 6,552,385 in 1851 to 4,458,775 in 1901 and 4,390,219 in 1911. Yet, it is also important to recall that other themes can be advanced. Ireland remained within the Empire, largely speaking English, although Catholic and Celtic in culture, rather than Protestant and Anglo-Saxon. There was no collapse into anarchy or civil war, and the Irish economy developed as part of the growing imperial economy, although the railway system grew more slowly than elsewhere in Britain. Belfast became a centre of manufacturing industry, based on linen, shipyards and tobacco. Its expansion, however, saw the development of patterns of urban segregation based on religion. More generally, housing, employment, education and leisure were all sectarian. Furthermore, the far more agricultural South and West of Ireland were very different from the more industrial North-East.

Throughout Ireland, the closing decades of the century brought economic and social change, commercialisation, anglicisation, and the dismantling of landlord power. By 1914, Ireland had gained a large share of its economic independence. Thanks to legislation in 1860, 1870, 1881, 1885, 1891 and, especially, Wyndham's Act of 1903, landlords were obliged to settle the land question largely on their tenants' terms: farmers increasingly owned their holdings, a change achieved with little violence. This was described as 'killing Home Rule by kindness'. Wyndham's Act provided long-term low-interest government loans to buy out landlords. The position of the Catholic Church also markedly improved, not least thanks to the disestablishment of the (Protestant) Church of Ireland in 1869. In Kildare, for example, a convent was established, soon followed by a church and schools, and in 1889 a magnificent Catholic Gothic church, whose spire dominated the town, was opened. Ireland was more closely linked to Britain by economic interdependence and the rapid communications offered by railways and steamships, and yet its Catholic areas were at the same time becoming more socially and culturally distinct. Catholics were in the majority everywhere apart from parts of Ulster.

The reform process that characterised Britain was matched in Ireland. The Irish Local Government Act of 1898 brought to Ireland the system of elected local councils introduced in England by Acts of 1888 and 1894. Thus, alongside the far greater peasant proprietorship stemming from land legislation, local government was also transferred to the control of the largely Catholic bulk of the population. Landlords were a declining power economically and politically. In Ulster they also declined, but, because of the power of local Unionists (unlike in the South, where Unionists were few), they managed to retain a shaky foothold in politics. The Belfast and East Ulster business classes took over the leadership of the Ulster Unionists from 1906, a year after the formation of the Ulster Unionist Council, and, although the landlords were a presence and had some influence, they were not a major force.

Nineteenth-century Ireland also had had an important and growing nationalist movement. Part was violent, mounting terrorist attacks in England, Ireland and elsewhere. The Fenians, a secret organisation founded in 1858, tried to launch a rebellion in Ireland in 1867, and were responsible for terrorist acts in England and for an attempted invasion of Canada from the United States. The Fenians, reconstituted as the Irish Republican Brotherhood in 1873, decided on a policy of waiting until a propitious time for another uprising. But in 1882 another society, the Invincibles, murdered Lord Frederick Cavendish, the Chief Secretary for Ireland, in Phoenix Park, Dublin, leading to new measures designed to maintain order. Some Irishmen served with the Boers against the British army.

Most Irish nationalism, however, was non-violent. Daniel O'Connell organised a party that, in the 1830s and 1840s, campaigned for the repeal of the Act of Union. The government responded by attempts to improve the lot of the population

THE ILLUSTRATED LONDON NEWS

REGISTERED AT THE GENERAL POST-OFFICE FOR TRANSMISSION ABROAD.

No. 2295.—VOL. LXXXII.          SATURDAY, APRIL 14, 1883.          WITH TWO SUPPLEMENTS | SIXPENCE. By Post, 6½D.

1. House and Shop occupied by Whitehead.    4. Kitchen behind the Shop.
2. DetectiveSergeant Richard Price.    5. Carboy containing 170 lb of Nitro-Glycerine.
3. The Scullery, used as a Laboratory.    6. Vat containing explosive liquid discovered in the cellar.

THE FENIAN DYNAMITE PLOT IN ENGLAND: THE SECRET FACTORY OF NITRO-GLYCERINE IN
LEDSAM-STREET, BIRMINGHAM

**Irish terrorism in England**
In April 1883 police discovered a nitroglycerine factory in the Ladywood district of Birmingham. The nitroglycerine was followed to London where the conspirators were arrested.

through reform and by firm action aimed at limiting extra-parliamentary agitation. The extension of the franchise in 1868 and 1884 greatly increased the number of Catholic voters and most of them supported **Home Rule**, which would have left an Irish Parliament and government in control of all except customs and excise, defence and foreign policy. The Home Government Association of 1870 was followed by the Home Rule League (1873). Charles Parnell became leader of the MPs pressing for Home Rule in 1879, and this became the powerful Irish Parliamentary Party, with 85 MPs in 1886. Their role in Parliament, where Ireland was over-represented, ensured that Home Rule came to play a major part in the political agenda, and they also helped push through land reform. Resisted, however, by Conservatives

**Home Rule:** The movement demanding self-government for Ireland in the period before 1914.

**nationalism:** The search for independence on the part of peoples who regard themselves as distinct.

and Liberal Unionists, who saw Home Rule as likely to undermine the Union, proposals for Home Rule were defeated at Westminster in 1886 and 1893.

At the beginning of the twentieth century, the future of Ireland depended apparently on the arithmetic of Westminster politics. Nevertheless, a broader current of **nationalism** was having an impact in Ireland. An interest in Irish culture led to the formation of the Gaelic Athletic Association in 1884, which was designed to safeguard traditional sports, and to the Gaelic League in 1893, which sought to protect the Irish language. Sinn Féin, a new nationalist organisation, was founded by Arthur Griffith in 1905; Eamon de Valera became leader in 1917. The nationalism backed by these groups was Catholic and Gaelic. Like the United Irishmen movement of the 1790s, it had originally sought to incorporate Protestants, but was quickly transformed into a separatist nationalism that excluded Unionists, Protestants, and non-Gaels.

## Nineteenth-century Scotland

Home Rule was not a major issue in Scotland. Much of Europe was inspired by nationalism, or, depending on one's perspective, suffered from it, in the nineteenth century. Multinational Empires, especially Austro-Hungary, Russia and Turkey, were challenged by the rise of nationalist politics, and the same was true for Britain in Ireland and India. Yet, in Scotland, this was less the case, largely because of Scottish identification with the idea of Britain and the Empire and with the economic and other benefits of the Empire. The semi-autonomous position that Scotland enjoyed in the United Kingdom was also important. Scotland had its own currency, legal system, education system and Established (Presbyterian) Church.

Scotland was affected by the same trends as England and Wales, not least industrialisation and urbanisation. There was a development of a sense of national identity centring on a re-emergent cultural identity that did not involve any widespread demand for independence: kilts, the Wallace cult (which caused English unease), literary consciousness, and support for Home Rule, but no Home Rule party. The religious dimension to nationalism so obvious (and so divisive) in Ireland was lacking.

The principal point of violent tension was in the Highlands. There, the clan system had declined during the eighteenth century, to be replaced by a more aggressively commercial attitude towards land tenure, social relations and economic activity, helping to lead to extensive emigration. After the Napoleonic Wars, the labour-intensive economy, in which fishing, military employment and illicit whisky-making had played a major role, was replaced by a more capital-intensive economy based on sheep-ranging. This required less labour. Most of the Highland population possessed no secure and long-term legal rights to land, and were, therefore, easily displaced in the 'clearances'. The initial clearances were for sheep, but from c.1850 they were largely for game: by 1884, 1.98 million acres, over 10% of Scottish land, was reserved for deer, and thus the hunting interests of a small minority.

Many Scots emigrated from the Highlands and Islands, but those who remained reacted with increasing bitterness to the effects of change. In the 1880s, crofting MPs, opposed to clearances, won five seats in northern Scotland, while the 'Battle of Braes' in Skye grew more intense. There was an Irish-type resistance to clearing: the Land League, modelled on the Irish Land League, had 15,000 members by 1884. The crisis led to the Napier Commission and the Crofter's Holding Act of 1886, which established crofting rights and ended the major phase of the clearances. The Napier Commission was influenced by Skene's *Celtic Scotland* (1880), with its vision of the social rights of Celtic society. This also influenced Irish nationalists.

The issue was less explosive than land rights in Ireland: the Highland peasantry were being evicted by their clan chiefs, although it was widely held that the English-ness of the Duke of Sutherland was the catalyst for the Sutherland clearances. Furthermore, later clearances were often by new businessmen, both Scots and English, who were absentee. Nationalism was slow to develop in Scotland. The National Association for the Vindication of Scottish Rights was launched in 1853. 2,000 people came to its first meeting at Edinburgh; 5,000 in Glasgow. It strongly urged Scottish rights, but was not *explicitly* nationalist. Later, some Scottish national-ists, such as Theodore Napier, identified with the Boers. The Scottish Patriotic Association, the Scottish Home Rule Association (SHRA), and other small-scale bodies all played a part. The cross-party SHRA, founded in 1886, regarded the exert-ing of pressure on the most sympathetic political party as the best political strategy.

Scottish consciousness did not therefore subvert the identity of Britain. In place of the notion of North Britain, which was rejected by the late nineteenth century, that of Scotland returned, but it was a Scotland in part increasingly anglicised and yet also prone to countervailing and complicating currents. The Secretaryship for Scotland was restored in 1885, but it was not a post designed to hold Scotland down. National parties won the Scottish seats and electoral shifts reflected those elsewhere in Britain: the Conservatives and Liberal Unionists took 38 of the 72 seats in 1900, the Liberals 58 in 1906. Labour made gains from 1906. Five of the ten Prime Ministers in 1880–1935 were Scottish, and another two had important Scottish links. In the 1890s, English-based trade unions made important inroads and these UK-wide unions gained ground at the expense of Scottish unions, in part by amalgamation. For example, the Scottish Railway Servants became part of the Amalgamated Society of Railway Servants in 1893.

Nevertheless, from the 1880s many Liberals backed Home Rule, and it was widely expected that the Irish Home Rule Bill of 1912 would, once passed, by followed by Home Rule for Scotland. The emerging ILP also favoured Home Rule. Scottish cultural identity was strong and there was a belief that Scotland could reconcile this with 'Britishness', and enjoy and enhance both.

## Nineteenth-century Wales

In Wales, unlike Scotland, language was a key aspect of identity and there was agitation for education in Welsh, but Welshness was not dependent on the use of the language. The continued existence of Anglican privileges in a predominantly Non-conformist country became the burning issue in nineteenth-century Wales. There was a reaction against the political control of the landed gentry, and radical Liberal-ism was the most important political strain in Wales at the beginning of the twentieth century. No Conservative was elected for Wales in the 1906 election, a landslide not repeated (and then to the benefit of Labour) until 1997. With David Lloyd George, Welsh Liberalism reached the apex of political power, but, as later with the Scot Ramsay MacDonald and Labour, this was as part of a British political consciousness. At the same time, there was a potentially uneasy relationship with the rise of Welsh cultural and political nationalism, although the key Welsh issues of the late nineteenth century – land, disestablishment and education – could be presented in radical Liberal terms and thus incorporated in British politics. Cultural national-ism proved to be a more potent force than political nationalism. Agitation over rents and tithes led to riots, especially in 1887, but landlords were not shot: the

Welsh wished to differentiate themselves from the more bitter contemporary agitation in Ireland.

# Independence in Ireland

The situation in Ireland shifted with the narrow Liberal victories in the two 1910 elections and the Liberal triumph over the House of Lords in 1911. A Home Rule Bill was introduced in April 1912. It provided for an Irish Parliament, but also continued representation in Westminster where extensive powers over defence and taxation were retained. However, the response among the Ulster Protestants was very strong. It led to the signing of the Solemn League and Covenant in 1912, pledging resistance; the formation of the 90,000-strong Ulster Volunteer Force in 1913; and gun-running from Germany in 1914. Asquith, the Liberal Prime Minister, had failed to allow for Protestant views and their fears about Dublin rule. In reaction to the prospect of an unwelcome constitution, Ulster had retreated from constitutional politics. As the situation escalated, bellicose speeches were made, not least by Conservative leaders, and the Catholics organised the National Volunteers, to 'defend' Home Rule. The links between Liberals and Nationalists on the one hand and Conservatives and Ulster Unionists on the other helped radicalise the situation and made it impossible to devise a bi-partisan policy. Such a policy was not without a possible basis in legislation to settle the land question and to introduce a measure of devolution, but it was not pursued. Instead, Ireland became a divisive issue in British politics, and a touchstone of differences between Liberals and Conservatives.

Civil war and effective partition were avoided thanks to a compromise produced in September 1914 under the shadow of European conflict. Parliament passed the Home Rule Bill, suspended it for the duration of the war, and made provision for the possibility of special treatment thereafter for Ulster. By then, however, the situation had changed greatly.

Initially there was little suggestion that this would be the case. Over 270,000 men, both Protestant and Catholic, served in the armed forces, all as volunteers, for conscription was not introduced in Ireland. Most of the Volunteers who had been organised prior to the war served. In contrast, fewer than 2,000 rose in Dublin in the Easter Rising of 1916, an unsuccessful attempt to create an independent Irish Republic, which was proclaimed on 24 April. The numerous soldiers' wives of Dublin, when informed by the Volunteers that the establishment of a republic meant that the payment of separation allowances had now ended, responded not with nationalist

## Box 12.1

### Easter Rising

The 1916 rising in Ireland was planned by the military council of the Irish Republican Brotherhood. A general rising throughout Ireland was intended, but, instead, it was largely restricted to Dublin. There was supporting action in parts of Ireland, but nothing of note. This ensured that the rising would fail militarily, and instead it became a bold gesture. About 1,200 rose in Dublin on Easter Monday, 24 April, and seized a number of sites, but, under heavy British pressure, including the shelling of the city centre, the insurgents were forced to surrender on 29 April. The rising won considerable sympathy for the nationalist cause. The Irish Volunteers were swiftly re-established and, by the end of 1917, began public drilling exercises.

**The Easter Rising, 1916**
British soldiers using barrels as an improvised barricade. Although militarily unsuccessful, the Rising showed that militancy could not be contained within established political divisions and practices. The majority of the Irish population, however, loyally supported the war effort against Germany.

enthusiasm but with anger. Outside Dublin, due to divisions in the leadership, the planned nationalist uprising failed to materialise. In Dublin, the rebel Irish Volunteers suffered from bad planning, poor tactics, and the strength of the British response, which included an uncompromising use of artillery. After six days' fighting, the Volunteers unconditionally surrendered.

The firm British response, however, served to radicalise Irish public opinion. Martial law was declared and a series of trials, fifteen executions, and numerous internments provided martyrs for the nationalist cause. More generally, supporters of Home Rule were alienated by the role of the Conservatives in the Coalition. This included blocking Lloyd George's offer of immediate Home Rule with an exclusion of six Ulster counties. Constitutional nationalists were increasingly losing their ability to lead the Catholic community. In a by-election in South Longford in May 1917, the Sinn Féin candidate, Joe McGuinness, beat the Home Rulers of the Irish Parliamentary Party. He was helped by better organisation and the support of the Archbishop of Dublin. The Irish Volunteers were also rejuvenated in 1917.

A proposal to introduce conscription in March 1918 was very unpopular. In the 1918 general election, 47% of the vote and 73 out of the 105 Irish parliamentary seats, including most of those outside Ulster, were won by the Sinn Féin party, nationalists under Eamon de Valera who refused to attend Westminster and demanded independence. They rejected the policy of 'Home Rule within the Empire' which John Redmond (1856–1918), the leader of the Irish Parliamentary Party, had supported and which had been the basis of the Home Rule Act in 1914. Redmond's brother, an MP, had died fighting for George V in World War One. Catholicism was very important to Sinn Féin. Religious and political identities and commitments were interwoven.

Contingency was the key factor in Irish independence. The role of World War One was crucial in that it destroyed the basis for the Home Rulers who, under Redmond, had been imperialists as well as nationalists. Redmond hoped to be the Irish equivalent of a Canadian or Australian Prime Minister: 'local but loyal'.

In January 1919, a unilateral declaration of independence was issued by a new national assembly (Dáil Eireann), and the nationalist Irish Volunteers, soon to rename themselves the Irish Republican Army (IRA), staged their first fatal ambush. The Volunteers' leaders rejected the idea of a constitutional settlement in favour of a more militant solution. They were opposed to conventional politics, which they saw as likely to lead to compromise. British refusal to accept independence led to a brutal civil war in 1919–21, with IRA terrorism, guerrilla warfare and ruthless British reprisals, especially by reinforcements for the Royal Irish Constabulary, called the 'Black and Tans', many of whom were ex-soldiers. The British were unable to maintain control. They partitioned Ireland between what were designed to be two Home Rule states, under the Government of Ireland Act of December 1920, establishing Northern Ireland, and in June 1921 opened the first parliament of the new Northern Ireland. The following month, a truce was agreed between the British and the IRA.

This was followed by the Anglo-Irish Treaty of December 1921, which accepted both partition and effective independence (rather than Home Rule) for the new Irish Free State (Eire) which became the governing body over most of the island, excluding a large part of the province of Ulster in the North. This treaty superseded the Government of Ireland Act of 1920 in the South. The Irish Free State became a self-governing dominion within the British Empire, with a Governor-General appointed by the Crown, the same status in the 'Community of Nations known as the British Empire' as Australia, Canada, New Zealand and South Africa, although the new dominion was far more alienated from Britain and the Empire than the others. In its own constitution, the new state was described as 'a co-equal member of the community called the British Commonwealth of Nations'.

Six out of the nine counties of Ulster had become Northern Ireland; six rather than nine because the balance of population in the six counties, overwhelmingly Protestant, made the Unionists feel secure in their new state. Initial proposals for an Ulster made up of the historic nine counties, which would have entailed a Catholic majority, were rejected, and a new Ulster of the six counties came into existence. This remained part of the United Kingdom and was represented at Westminster by twelve MPs; increased after 1979 to seventeen. This division of Ireland was in part a consolidation of a longstanding difference in social, economic, religious and cultural factors, but their territorialisation, in a new political unit, created serious problems, not least because of the size of the Catholic minority in Northern Ireland: one-third of the population. Nevertheless, the creation of a separate Ulster recognised a different identity compounded of demographics and history, from that of the rest of Ireland.

The settlement also helped end the divisiveness of Ireland in British politics. It played only a minor role in parliamentary and electoral politics thereafter, a process assisted by the massive shrinkage in Ireland's parliamentary representation. There was to be no movement to regain Ireland, and nothing comparable to the bitterness that territorial loss had brought to France from 1871 or to Germany and Hungary after World War One. 'Self-determination' had been a key idea in the settlement of Europe after the war and the Irish Free State could be seen in this light. Furthermore, the British government had acted to rid itself of the problem of Ireland, although not at the cost of Britain's own best interests.

Northern Ireland was self-governed, with a Parliament at Stormont: a measure of political power had been transferred from London. It was very much a Protestant state and publicly affirmed its British and Unionist identity. The Unionist fear of abandonment had been overcome, although southern Unionists in fact had been abandoned. In its place, in Northern Ireland came the fear of betrayal by the Catholic enemy within. Under the Civil Authorities (Special Powers) Act, the Northern Ireland government interned over 900 men and women between 1922 and

1925. Martial-law tactics were judged necessary to respond to what was seen as a threatening situation.

The large Catholic minority claimed to suffer discrimination in voting arrangements, school support, employment and policing; although the extent of this is controversial. The assertion that Catholics were worse treated in the allocation of public housing has been challenged. Nevertheless, inter-communal relations were very poor. There were riots in Belfast in 1922 and 1935, and the government of Northern Ireland had scant sympathy for the Catholic minority. Despite original statements of good intentions, it made little effort to accommodate them, and ignored the economic problems of the border counties where Catholics were numerous. Catholics were, in effect, reduced to the status of second-class citizens. Protestants were in a similar position in the Irish Free State.

The partition was opposed by much of the IRA, the anti-Treaty forces known as the Irregulars. They were unable to accept a settlement that entailed anything short of the national goal of a united Ireland. Compromise was unacceptable. The Irregulars mounted a terrorist campaign in Northern Ireland in 1921. Unwilling to accept the Anglo-Irish Treaty because it had not secured full independence, the Irregulars also fought the newly independent government in the South in 1922–3 in what was a more bloody conflict than the so-called War of Independence of 1919–21. The IRA was beaten in both Northern Ireland and the Irish Free State. The Northern Ireland Police were given 'special powers', the National Army in the Free State emergency powers. IRA terrorism led to a vigorous response from the Irish government under William Thomas Cosgrave, which executed 77 rebels and imprisoned 12,000. Thereafter, IRA terrorism remained a minor irritant, in both North and South, until the late 1960s.

Cosgrave's government sought to improve relations with Britain. It defeated Sinn Féin in the 1923 general election, and in 1925 ratified the border with Northern Ireland. This confirmed partition, and was important to the process by which the new governments in the Irish Free State and Northern Ireland were consolidated. The administrative structures remained those of British Ireland, the policy of buying out the landlords was completed, and the Free State essentially maintained its earlier economic relationship with Britain, selling agricultural goods and importing manufactured products.

The Irish Free State developed as a democratic constitutional state. De Valera, who had been leader of Sinn Féin in 1917–26 and had rejected the Anglo-Irish Treaty in 1921, gained power after the 1932 election, with the Fianna Fáil party he had founded with moderate Sinn Féin support in 1926. He was, thereafter, President of the Executive Council (1932–7), Prime Minister (1937–48, 1951–4, 1957–9), and President (1959–73). When he gained power in 1932, de Valera successfully pressed the British to recall the Governor-General. He was replaced by a nonentity nominated by de Valera who undertook no public duties. The Executive Authority (External Relations) Act of 1936, limited the role of the Crown in the Free State to diplomatic formalities, and then only as advised by the Executive Council. After coming to power, de Valera had set off an 'Economic War' with Britain by suspending the payment of land annuities from Irish farmers to the British government. A cycle of retaliation led to protectionism by both sides, hitting Irish agricultural exports to Britain. The 'Economic War' was ended by agreement in 1938. Its costs had helped to lead to the formation of the Fine Gael Party to oppose de Valera's Fianna Fáil.

Much of the IRA was willing to accept de Valera's leadership and, indeed, he took some of its members into the government and the police. Others, however, wished to fight on for a united Ireland and this led them into conflict with de Valera, not least when they raided army bases, in order to gain arms, and accepted money and arms from Hitler. De Valera responded with imprisonment and executions, and, like the British government in Northern Ireland in the early 1980s, faced down IRA hunger-strikers. He was unwilling to fight to push Ireland's territorial claim to Northern Ireland, although it was expressed in the 1937 constitution.

Under that constitution, passed after a referendum, the oath of allegiance to the Crown that MPs had been obliged to take under the Anglo-Irish Treaty of 1921 was abolished. Appeals to the Privy Council had already been abolished. The constitution was republican. It described the Irish State, now rechristened Eire (Ireland), as a 'sovereign, independent, democratic state'. The head of state was to be a directly-elected President, while Irish was to be the first language, an important declaration of cultural independence from Britain.

Irish neutrality in World War Two was a more powerful affirmation of independence; and was not shared by Northern Ireland, which made an important contribution to the war effort. The war dramatised the difference between the two parts of Ireland, and also led to much bitterness in Northern Ireland, which suffered, not least when Belfast was heavily bombed by the Germans. Eire's neutrality posed serious problems for Britain, particularly because of the exposed nature of Atlantic shipping routes and the denial of ports in Eire to British warships: these ports had only been transferred to Irish control in 1938. De Valera's government promised that it would not open Eire to German forces, but an inability to rely on the country led Churchill seriously to consider invasion. The IRA had launched a bombing campaign in England in 1939. This was not related to Eire policy, but did not encourage British warmth towards Irish nationalism. Nevertheless, Irish policy did not prove divisive in British party politics.

After World War Two ended, de Valera tried to reopen the issue of partition. However, the 1945 Northern Ireland general election to Stormont showed majority support for continued union with Britain. The possibility of a settlement was further lessened in 1948. De Valera was replaced by a new government under John Costello, and vestigial British authority was extinguished by the Republic of Ireland Act of 1948. Proposing the Bill in the *Dáil*, Costello claimed it would 'end forever, in a simple, clear and unequivocal way this country's long and tragic association with the institutions of the British Crown'. The new Act repealed the External Relations Act and took Eire out of the Commonwealth. On Easter Monday 1949, Eire became a republic. This move clashed with the views of the British government, and led to a clarification of the position of Northern Ireland that entrenched Unionism. In October 1948, the House of Commons was told that the government would not accept any change 'in the constitutional status of Northern Ireland without Northern Ireland's free agreement', a promise that was condemned by the Irish government and by Labour opponents of partition.

## Scotland and Wales, 1920–65

The loss of most of Ireland in 1921 was not, however, followed by any change in the situation in Scotland or Wales. Far from reducing the cohesion of the British state, this loss had removed its major cause of instability. There was some pressure for

## Box 12.2

### Inter-war Scottish politics

Although the foundation of the National Party of Scotland (1928) and the Scottish National Party (1934) may appear important in hindsight, inter-war Scotland was dominated by the same three-party politics as England. As in England, the Liberals, who had been very strong in Scotland in the 1906 and 1910 elections, collapsed. Labour became more important, and the 1924 Housing Act, which encouraged local authority house construction, helped to win the party support. However, Labour was hit by rifts, especially between the radicals of the Independent Labour Party and the Labour leadership, and these were exacerbated by the débâcle of the Labour government in 1931. Labour did very badly in Scotland in the 1931 election. The National Government sought to combat unemployment with the 1934 Special Areas Act. Although nationalism became more vociferous in the 1930s, there was scant sign of a major political change in Scotland.

Home Rule in Scotland and Wales, but it was of limited importance. The Labour government failed to deliver on hopes of Scottish Home Rule in 1924, and the other parties were also unforthcoming. The Scottish Home Rule Bill of 1913 had proved a disappointment and the Bill introduced in 1926 had also failed. In the 1920s and 1930s, there was a loss of faith in Home Rule by Labour. It was no longer confident that Scotland's social and economic problems could be solved without English aid. Instead, there was an increased Labour belief in centralisation.

Elements in the Scottish Home Rule Association began to think that a national party would be more effective. The National Party of Scotland, founded in 1928, pledged 'to secure self-government for Scotland with independent national status within the British group of nations'. The Scottish Party followed in 1932. It was more Conservative in background and sought a sovereign Scottish Parliament with co-operation for defence and foreign policy on a UK basis. The two united in 1934 to form the Scottish National Party (SNP), but it did not win a parliamentary seat – Motherwell – until 1945. Scotland was hit hard by the Depression of the 1930s. Its heavy industry lost markets and unemployment rose sharply. Public discontent, however, was contained. Compared with the large-scale government intervention after 1945, government initiatives in the inter-war period were limited, but they included a major programme of house construction. Scotland benefited in the 1940s from the interventionist economic policies introduced by the Labour MP Tom Johnston who became Secretary of State for Scotland in 1941. A firm believer in economic planning, Johnston supported hydro-electric power, reafforestation and industrial location initiatives. He also helped improve the social infrastructure, in health, housing and education.

Politically, Scotland was dominated by the Conservatives and Labour. Labour's breakthrough in Scotland came in 1922 when it won 32.2% of the votes cast there and took 29 of the Scottish seats at Westminster. The Liberals were more important than the SNP. Labour in Scotland was hit by the consequences of the crisis of 1931 and did very badly in the general election of that year, but began to recover in 1935. The BBC in Scotland, both radio and, from 1952, television, produced relatively little and broadcasts were dominated by material from the national network.

In Wales, the Liberal Party declined, but in favour of Labour, not nationalists. The Labour Party took ten Welsh seats in the general election of 1918, eighteen in 1922, and twenty-five in 1929. Much Welsh nationalism was directed to electing a Labour government for Britain. Separatist belief and activity grew, but were still limited. Plaid Cymru, the 'Party of Wales', was formed in 1925 to campaign for self-government, but it had little impact. Its 'back to the land' policy extolled agriculture and sought to obtain cultural and economic integrity and political autonomy. The party was concerned primarily with the Welsh language and was opposed to urban and industrial society, but these goals were not shared by the bulk of the Welsh population, whose background was anglophone. In 1932, Plaid Cymru became committed to Welsh Home Rule.

Not only was self-government for Wales a minor issue in the inter-war period, but institutions for distinct administration also made far slower progress than that for Scotland. Whereas the Secretaryship of State for Scotland had been revived in 1885 and the Scottish Office created in Edinburgh in 1934, the Welsh equivalents were not created until 1964, when Labour, which had opposed the idea until 1959, came to power. In 1941, Councillor George Williams of Cardiff, Chairman of the National Industrial Council, complained that that body was 'the only organisation which can speak for the whole of the local authorities of the Welsh region on economic affairs'. Nevertheless, there were some moves towards devolved government. A separate Welsh Department of Education was created in 1907, and other devolved executive departments, such as the Welsh Board of Health (1920), thereafter. A Council for Wales and Monmouthshire was created in 1948, but it had no power. The same was true of the Ministry for Welsh Affairs created in 1951.

The severely depressed economy of inter-war Wales, affected by large-scale emigration and requiring financial support from the national exchequer, was not the best basis for widespread demands for Home Rule. Furthermore, radicals in the 1930s did not tend to look to constitutional reform, and this helped to marginalise them. In 1936, Plaid Cymru's leaders were imprisoned for burning the RAF bombing school at Pen-y-Berth. Communists won council, but not parliamentary, seats. Welsh nationalism led Plaid Cymru to oppose Britain's role in World War Two, which was seen as a clash of rival imperialisms. Some of its members were pacifists, products of a strong strain in Welsh Nonconformity, others refused to be conscripted, and several – Arthur Owens and his group – may have been German spies and saboteurs.

The hardship of the 1930s helped cement an identity between Wales and Labour that persisted in the post-war decades of economic growth. The militant South Wales Miners' Federation came close to Labour, sponsoring 13 MPs in 1945. Wales remained a Labour stronghold until the 1960s, Labour taking 32 of the 36 seats in the 1966 election; although a Liberal recovery there played a key role in the national revival of the Liberal Party from 1945 onwards. Whereas Lloyd George was the dominant Welsh figure in British politics in the opening decades of the century, in the 1940s and 1950s this role was assumed by Aneurin Bevan, MP for Ebbw Vale, a radical Socialist who, as Labour Minister of Health, played a key role in the foundation of the National Health Service in 1948. Labour enjoyed a degree of electoral support in Wales greater than that of the Liberals during their heyday.

In the 1940s, 1950s and early 1960s, nationalism had little impact in the UK. The IRA terrorist campaign of 1954–62 in Northern Ireland, which concentrated on border attacks, had no success, although a small-scale bombing campaign in Scotland in 1952–3 led to the removal of 'ER II' from pillarboxes: the Queen was Elizabeth I in Scotland. The ballot box brought Welsh and Scottish nationalists scant joy. The SNP-backed Scottish Covenant movement obtained two million signatures for a covenant signed at its 1949 convention calling for Home Rule within a federalist system.

Home Rule for Scotland was demanded in the 1950 general election, but Liberal support was more than counter-balanced by Conservative and Labour opposition. The Attlee governments (1945–51) were centralist, not federalist, and despite supporting Home Rule legislation for Scotland in the 1945 general election campaign, showed scant support for it once in office. Labour itself rejected Home Rule at its 1958 conference. Furthermore, the Conservatives, who were firm supporters of the Union (with both England and Northern Ireland), enjoyed considerable support in Scotland. In 1955, they even won 50.1% of the popular vote there. This reflected the benefits of post-war economic recovery, the affluence of the 1950s, the government's housing record, the weakness of the Liberals in the same period, and Labour's fall in popularity.

The nature of Plaid Cymru's appeal was illustrated by the adoption speech made by Gwynfor Evans in launching his parliamentary campaign in Merioneth in 1959: 'There is a great awakening in Merioneth and throughout Wales – the sound of chains and fetters breaking. Wales is experiencing an awareness of its nationhood, becoming proud of its ancestry, and gaining mental and spiritual freedom which will inevitably lead to national freedom. . . . If we make a breach in this wall, we shall soon see the people following.' The electors did not agree. Evans came bottom with 22.9 per cent, no real improvement on his performance in 1955. Labour, not the nationalists, were the beneficiary of Conservative unpopularity in 1964 and 1966. In Scotland, Labour gained 45 seats in 1964, in part because of the appeal of planning and industrial modernisation. The Conservatives seemed complacent and the Conservative Party in Scotland (the Scottish Unionist Party) seemed to offer little. Furthermore, the anti-Catholic/Irish dynamic of much of Scottish Conservatism seemed less relevant and appealing.

# Nationalism in 1966–79

The situation in Wales, Scotland and Northern Ireland changed in the late 1960s. The most dramatic transformation occurred in Northern Ireland. It was scarcely surprising in a period in which there were numerous demands for change that the situation there should be scrutinised critically. However, the background was not totally bleak. An IRA campaign launched in 1954 had had little success, had declined in intensity from 1958, and was formally suspended in February 1962. Captain Terence O'Neill, who became Prime Minister of Northern Ireland in 1963, sought greater harmony between Catholics and Protestants, and hoped that economic growth would help to ease sectarian tensions. O'Neill sought reconciliation in order to make the Union secure. In 1964, he held talks on reconciliation with Seán Lemass, the Prime Minister of Eire, and in 1968 launched a programme for the removal of discrimination against Catholics in housing, local government, and voting arrangements.

However, despite encouragement and some pressure from the Labour government in London, the pace of change proved insufficient to diffuse a sense of discrimination, and the continued Unionist ascendancy, backed up by the police, led to tension. A civil rights movement, essentially complaining about the position of Catholics, developed. It was modelled on the civil rights movement which had emerged in the USA. The Campaign for Social Justice in Northern Ireland was launched in 1963, and the Northern Ireland Civil Rights Association was founded in 1967. A harsh and insensitive response led to fighting in October 1968, beginning in

Derry/Londonderry on 5 October, when the attempt to prevent a banned protest demonstration led to violence. O'Neill was supported by the British government under Wilson, but support within the Unionist community fell badly, and the current of violence rose. Fighting in January 1969 led to counter-violence, and in the summer of 1969 there came a breakdown in law and order, with open communal violence.

The Labour government was determined not to use troops to maintain order, and on 30 July 1969 the Cabinet agreed to the use of CS gas by the police in an attempt to avoid such a deployment. However, in the face of rioting in Derry and Belfast, on 14 August 1969, the Cabinet had reluctantly to accept the use of troops to restore peace. They were intended as a short-term measure, to be withdrawn as soon as peace was restored, and to protect Catholics as much as Protestants, but instead, their very presence became an issue and a cause of violence. The Labour government did not wish to impose direct rule from London, and succeeded, in the short term, in restoring order, but no long-term solutions were provided, and order remained fragile. The attempt to impose a curfew on the Falls Road in Belfast in July 1970 was rejected by its Catholic community, while the authorisation in August 1970 of the internment (imprisonment without trial) of suspected terrorists increased tension in 1971, including, on 5 February, the first killing of a British soldier 'in the Troubles' by the Provisional IRA; 1971 saw the first major offensive by the Provisional IRA. The following year, there was widespread shooting and bombings, including 'Bloody Sunday' in Londonderry and 'Bloody Friday' in Belfast. In the first, fourteen civilians were shot dead. The Catholic population and the army increasingly saw each other as enemies. The events of 'Bloody Sunday', 20 January 1972, marked the moment when the Nationalist community in Northern Ireland came to regard British troops as an occupying force. The Provisional IRA, founded in 1970, and the (Protestant) Ulster Volunteer Force and Ulster Freedom Fighters pushed terrorism up the political agenda, as both communities in the province became engulfed in paramilitary-led violence. The British government reacted with a determined attempt to re-impose control. In Operation Motorman, the IRA's 'no-go' areas in Londonderry and Belfast were reopened for military and police patrols. This obliged the IRA to abandon attempts to stage a revolutionary war and, instead, to turn to terrorism. The number of troops rose from 6,000 in 1969 to 20,000 by 1972. The Provisional IRA also undertook bombing missions to mainland Britain.

The continued intractability of the situation led to the imposition of 'direct rule' from London: the Unionist regional government and the Stormont Assembly were suspended in March 1972. The Heath government re-imposed direct rule on the assumption that it would be a temporary measure. There was no attempt to integrate Northern Ireland into the United Kingdom. The Heath government wanted to establish the conditions under which Northern Ireland could become self-governing again, but on a different basis than before: this time there would be a genuine cross-community government in Northern Ireland. The government sought, with the Sunningdale Agreement of 1973, and the creation of a non-sectarian power-sharing Executive, which took office in 1974, to negotiate a settlement, but they did not command sufficient cross-community support, and the Ulster Workers strike of May 1974 led to the resumption of direct rule that spring. The collapse of the power-sharing Executive convinced the British government that direct rule would have to continue indefinitely. Under these circumstances, Britain now sought to give its Ulster problem an Irish dimension. The government of the Republic of Ireland was brought into the equation. The British government's efforts to bring the Republic in led to the Anglo-Irish Agreement of November 1985. This gave the Eire government a formal role in the affairs of Northern Ireland, through an Anglo-Irish Secretariat and Inter-Governmental Conference, but the Unionists responded with fury, regarding such steps as the prelude to a British sell-out in the province.

Despite greater Conservative sympathy for the Unionists, Conservative and Labour governments essentially followed a bi-partisan policy. There were traditional Labour sympathies for the nationalist cause, but this bi-partisanship represented a more serious abandonment of tradition for the Conservatives. In one respect, it was an aspect of the 'modernisation' that Heath sought (see Chapter 10), combined with a desire on the part of central government to make the decisions, that clashed with Unionist support for devolved government in Northern Ireland.

The situation elsewhere was less violent. Scottish nationalism was a peaceful cause, as was the mainstream of Welsh agitation. However, more violent nationalist groups in Wales used bombs to attack what they saw as alien presences, such as reservoir dams, and pipelines taking water from drowned Welsh valleys to English cities. This cause first led to violent action in 1952, and there was a rise in sporadic terrorist activity in 1966–9. The second homes of English-speaking holidaymakers became a target. Very few second homes were burnt, but the tensions between in-comers and Welsh residents were significant, especially in regard to Welsh-language education. The Welsh Language Society, *Cymdeithas yr iaith Gymraeg*, launched in 1962, painted out English names on road signs from 1963. The Labour government helped lessen tension with regional development policies and the creation of the Welsh Office. In 1967, the Welsh Language Act gave Welsh equal legal validity with English.

Language was far less important as an issue in Scotland. Nevertheless, efforts were made to encourage Gaelic and Scots. The Western Isles Council began a bilingual English/Gaelic policy in 1975, but its impact was to be hampered by the dominant role of English, especially on television. Although Gaelic-medium schools became more important in the Highlands and the Western Isles in the 1980s, the 1991 census revealed a pronounced fall in the use of Gaelic by children.

Plaid Cymru also had an impact at the ballot box, with an upsurge of support from 1966. That year, its President, Gwynfor Evans, won its first parliamentary seat – Carmarthen. In by-elections in 1967–72, Plaid Cymru also made an impact in English-speaking South Wales. This upsurge owed much to the unpopularity of Labour's economic policies, and was a consequence of disillusionment with Wilson, as well as a reaction against the self-interested and occasionally corrupt dominance of most of Welsh local government by Labour. Plaid Cymru won 175,000 votes in the 1970 general election, and in 1974 took three seats from Labour.

Similarly, in Scotland, the SNP benefited from Labour's unpopularity, although hopes based upon local elections in 1968 and by-election victories in Hamilton (1967) and Govan (1973), proved deceptive. Nevertheless, in 1970, the SNP gained 11% of the Scottish votes, the first time a fourth party had achieved a significant share of the vote in mainland UK. In October 1974, the SNP took eleven seats with 30% of the Scottish vote. The discovery of North Sea oil appeared to make Scottish independence credible. The Conservative Party began a period of long-term decline in Scotland from the late 1960s, a decline that both hit the Unionism it represented and was reflected by its decline. Working-class Scottish Conservatism/Unionism was particularly badly hit. A sense of a distinctive Scottish viewpoint frequently

**devolution:** The granting of governmental power to smaller areas of a country, for example, Wales or Scotland within the United Kingdom.

opposed to that of London was encouraged by the activities of the two Scottish independent television companies (Scottish Television, 1958– ) and Grampian Television (1962– ). Unlike the BBC, they operated only in Scotland. They also took at least half the viewing audience.

The activism of the 1960s and 1970s culminated with pressure for **devolution** of power from London. In the case of Scotland, the discovery and exploitation of North Sea oil allowed the SNP to argue that a self-governing (even independent) Scotland was a viable proposition. In Wales, calls for self-government, more muted than in Scotland, centred upon the need to protect the ailing Welsh language. Concerned about Nationalist gains in the 1974 elections, the minority Labour government under Callaghan also sought to win the support of Plaid Cymru and the SNP. A Scotland and Wales Bill introduced in 1976, proposed an assembly for each with control over health, social services, education, development and local government, but with no taxation power and with the Westminster Parliament retaining the veto. The Bill met opposition from nationalists, who felt that it did not go far enough, but, more substantially, from Conservatives and some Labour politicians who were opposed to nationalist aspirations. This was especially strong in English-speaking South Wales. The Bill was defeated in February 1977. That November, separate Bills were introduced for Scotland and Wales, and they passed the following spring. To secure the legislation, the government conceded referenda in Scotland and Wales. The referenda, held on 1 March 1979, required the support of 40% of the electorate, not simply the majority of votes cast. This was not obtained in Scotland, although the majority of votes cast there was favourable to devolution (52%). Devolution was heavily defeated in Wales: 11.8% of the electorate voted for, and 46.5% voted against. The SNP responded to the Callaghan government's refusal to enact devolution in Scotland by tabling a fatal vote of 'no-confidence' at the end of March 1979.

## Nationalism from 1980

Thereafter, the nationalist issue interacted with the generally hostile response to Conservative government in 1979–97. Election results in Scotland were very different from the Conservative triumphs in England, and this provided the nationalists with ammunition, although Scottish electors were as capable of contributing to British politics, as, for example, when Roy Jenkins helped establish the Social Democrats by winning Glasgow Hillhead in a by-election in March 1982.

The Conservative Party's historic claim to be the Unionist Party, for long its official title, was fatally undermined during the Thatcher years, as the parliamentary Party became predominantly representative of the more affluent parts of southern England. Thatcher was very unpopular in Scotland. In 1979, there was a pro-Labour swing of 0.1% in Scotland, and in 1983 another anti-Tory swing. The Conservatives won only 10 of Scotland's 72 parliamentary seats in 1987 and only 11 in 1992. The Community Charge, or Poll Tax, a new form of domestic rating, was particularly unpopular in Scotland, because Scotland was used as a guinea-pig and the tax was introduced in 1989, a year earlier than in England and Wales. This provided the SNP with a significant boon. The SNP ran a non-payment campaign, and took Govan from Labour.

Labour, however, decided not to promote civil disobedience and refused to campaign for non-payment. Labour was put in a difficult position, especially in

Scotland, as it sought to act as an effective national opposition party without being outflanked by the nationalists. In March 1989, the first meeting was held of a Constitutional Convention designed to produce plans for a Scottish Parliament. Supported by Labour and Liberal Democrats, it was rejected by the Conservatives, who supported the Union in its current form (and vigorously defended it in the 1992 election); while the SNP proposed independence. Labour had only embraced the idea of a Constitutional Convention after the SNP won Govan. This was a good example of the role of the SNP in driving Labour policy, specifically into a stronger and stronger commitment to Home Rule.

Scotland avoided the lawlessness seen in Wales. There had been a marked decline in terrorist activity in Wales in the 1970s as devolution seemed a serious prospect, but its failure and the unpopularity of the Thatcher government led to a fresh upsurge. Arson attacks on houses bought by outsiders and on estate agencies were met with a firm response from the security services. They were fearful of parallels to the situation in Northern Ireland, and benefited from support from the national government. In 1980–2, there were widespread arrests, as activists were subject to Special Branch surveillance. The arrests led to controversial court cases, and to disquiet about police tactics. Yet the militants were resorting to a terrorism that threatened a measure of destabilisation.

A campaign of public protest that included Gwynfor Evans's threat to starve himself to death forced the government to establish a Welsh-language television channel, S4C, that began transmitting in 1982. Language carried with it an emotional force denied most political issues other than religion, and in the case of some people, a transfer of energy from religion can be discerned. An emphasis on language also served as the basis for a partial account of the Welsh past, one in which the emphasis was on Welsh versus English, rather than divisions within the Welsh. This was taken further with the tourist industry's development of heritage sites.

It was Labour, not the nationalists, that was to be instrumental in changing the situation. The Labour victory in 1997 was even more a Conservative disaster. They lost all their Scottish and Welsh seats. The collapse of the Conservative vote in Scotland and Wales was structural, not tactical, although it is still worth noting that the Conservatives gained 19.6% of the votes cast in Wales. The government elected in 1997 had such a powerful position in Parliament that it had no need to consider nationalist moves there, but Labour had decided to support devolution, as a means, it hoped, to assuage nationalist sentiment. Devolution also sat easily with New Labour's drive to create a new Britain with modernised institutions and to replace what was seen as the over-centralised character of the British constitution and government. In September 1997, referenda held by the government provided support for an Assembly in Cardiff and a Parliament in Edinburgh, with the latter wielding powers of taxation. The outcome of the referenda revealed the different degrees of support which devolution continued to enjoy in Wales and Scotland. Whereas only 50.3% supported devolution in Wales, 74.9% did so in Scotland.

It is unclear whether this will be a lasting solution or a half-way house to independence. The latter is sought by the nationalists, but not by their major leading opponent, Labour, which benefits greatly from the existing situation. Scottish independence would weaken the Labour position in Westminster, especially because Scotland is heavily over-represented there. Scottish MPs looked after an average of 54,000 voters each in 1999, compared with 59,000 for the average Welsh MP and 65,000 for his or her English counterpart. Equal representation would reduce the number of Scottish MPs from 72 to around 58. Labour strategy is, in some respects, a cynical attempt to use the idea of a Scottish Parliament to undercut the SNP, while using Scotland for its own ends south of the border.

If the SNP succeeds, Scottish independence will be constrained by the European Union, for all the SNP and Plaid Cymru's support for a 'Europe of the regions', but there will still be a marked discontinuity in Scotland's history. This will lead to a need to re-focus public identity, that will be potentially divisive. It may also fail to address the regional theme that is so strong, both there and in Wales, with its own marked north–south divide. Alongside the vitality of Scotland and the Scots, there are, also, tremendous differences between Glasgow and Shetland, Ayr and Aberdeen.

The fact that just under 50% of the electorate abstained in the Welsh referendum in 1997 led to questions being asked about the legitimacy of the new Assembly. Eighteen months later, Tony Blair's use of the trade union bloc vote to ensure that his preferred candidate for the position of leader of the Welsh Assembly, Alun Michael, was elected, revealed a degree of central control inimical to the whole logic of devolution, and cost Labour support in the election for the new Assembly. Using a PR system, the 1999 elections for a Scottish Parliament and Welsh Assembly left Labour as the largest party in both, but without a majority in either. The failure of Labour to win a majority meant a Labour–Lib. Dem coalition executive in Scotland and a minority Labour executive in Wales. Labour won 56 of the 129 Scottish seats, the SNP 35, the Conservatives 18 and the Liberal Democrats 17. In Wales, Labour won 28 of the 60 seats, Plaid Cymru 17, the Conservatives 9 and the Liberal Democrats 6. Thus, the nationalists in each became the official opposition party. This was particularly apparent in Scotland where the SNP came first in 7 and second in 54 of the 73 constituencies; the other 56 seats were regional top-up seats calculated with reference to the proportion of votes cast after allowing for representation among the constituency MPs.

# ◼ Northern Ireland in the 1990s

A sense of new beginnings also affected Northern Ireland in the late 1990s, although the path towards it was more troubled and the prospects less optimistic. By September 1992, 3,000 people had died in the 'Troubles', many as a result of terrorism by the IRA, although with an increasing number killed by Protestant paramilitary groups, such as the Ulster Volunteer Force and the Ulster Freedom Fighters, who determined that Ulster should remain part of the United Kingdom. IRA terrorism on the British mainland began in 1973, included attacks on the Conservative Party conference at Brighton (1984) and the Cabinet (1991), and led to the deaths of three Conservative MPs. It also affected aspects of the political culture. The Birmingham pub bombings of 1974 led to the limitation of the civil rights of suspected terrorists in the Prevention of Terrorism Act. In October 1988, the Home Secretary, Douglas Hurd, announced a ban on the use of the direct speech of terrorists on radio and television. Defended as an opportunity to prevent the dissemination of attempts to justify 'criminal activities', the ban captured the dilemmas arising from a strange situation of what was at once war and peace, a deadly struggle but also one conducted in a peacetime democracy, most of whose inhabitants were not directly affected. In 1971, there had been a clash within the BBC when Lord Hill, the Chairman of the Board of Governors, made it clear that the BBC could not be impartial between the Army 'and the gunmen'. The controversy over the programme *Real Lives: At the Edge of the Union* led in 1986 to the first one-day strike by journalists in the history of the BBC.

It became apparent that the Anglo-Irish agreement of 1985 for continued partition and more cross-border cooperation was not going to serve as the framework for a settlement. Alongside specific acts of directed terrorism, there were also 'tit for tat' killings: the random murder of members of the other denomination in order to instil terror. Indeed in 1992, more Catholics were killed than Protestants, although not all Catholics were killed by Protestants. This emphasised the failure of nationalist politics and of terrorism to protect the Catholic community. At the same time, the bloody disintegration of Yugoslavia, and the development of 'ethnic cleansing' there, led to new fears about the future of Northern Ireland. Since the Troubles began, there had been a process of concentration, with Protestants moving to the east and Catholics to the west.

The situation was bleak, but, as before, the impact of terrorism in Northern Ireland was both all-pervasive in its effect on the general political environment, and yet also very specific. The violence of the sectarian housing estates of working-class north Belfast was not matched in leafy middle-class south Belfast. Indeed, a significant number of the Catholic middle class, who had benefited greatly from moves against discrimination over the previous quarter-century, moved from largely Catholic areas to the hitherto mostly Protestant south Belfast. Sinn Féin, the political wing of the IRA, only enjoyed the electoral support of about 10 per cent of Northern Ireland's population; but, in 1993, IRA terrorism in small towns that had hitherto been largely exempt from the 'Troubles', and in particular, the devastation of their commercial centres by bombs, underlined yet again the danger of assuming that violence could be restricted. These attacks, a counterpart to the use of car bombs to attack financial targets in the City of London in 1992–3, revealed the IRA's awareness of the economic weapon that terrorism offered; in London there was great concern about the insurance implications.

Mainland terrorism increased the cost of the 'Troubles', although, influenced by pan-Celticist ideas and possibly hopeful of winning nationalist support, the policy of the IRA Army Council was not to attack targets in Scotland or Wales. The cost to the United Kingdom of supporting social welfare in Ulster was also heavy. In 1938, the UK had agreed to subsidise Northern Ireland social welfare payments to UK standards. In the summer of 1994, unemployment was 40 per cent higher than the British average and male earnings 11 per cent lower. As a result, the net transfer of resources to Ulster was far higher than that to Scotland and Wales, although they all benefited greatly. In 1993, there was a net transfer to Ulster of £3.4 billion, excluding the cost of the security forces.

Attacks on the small towns in Ulster led Unionist politicians to declare in 1993 that the terrorists were winning. Angry at what they saw as inadequate policing, and suspicious of a dialogue between the government and the IRA, they pressed unsuccessfully for the reintroduction of internment and increased their criticism of the Anglo-Irish agreement. Gerry Adams, President of Sinn Féin, was also engaged in secret talks with John Hume, leader of the Social Democratic and Labour Party. The British and Irish governments feared that these talks would gain a momentum of their own and so tried to regain the initiative. New talks between the British and Irish governments produced, on 15 December 1993, the Downing Street Declaration, in which John Major and Albert Reynolds, the Prime Ministers of the two countries, agreed to a shared sovereignty that would guarantee the rights of nationalists, while Unionists were assured that they would not be forced into a united Ireland. Sinn Féin was to be allowed to enter the talks if the IRA ended their violence.

A paramilitary ceasefire followed in 1994: the IRA announced a ceasefire on 31 August, the Loyalist paramilitaries on 13 October. The first meeting between government officials and Sinn Féin took place on 9 December. Preliminary talks based upon a joint framework document published in February 1995 followed. The broadcasting ban was lifted. On 10 May 1995, leaders of Sinn Féin met a British government minister, the first such public meeting for seventy-five years. The cease-fire was followed by inward investment and a rise in house prices, both indicators of a widespread desire for peace and its opportunities. The ceasefire broke down on 9 February 1996, in large part over the decommissioning (handing over for destruc-tion) of terrorist arms, when there was a devastating IRA bomb attack on Canary Wharf in London, the symbol of Thatcherite enterprise. The IRA was unwilling to accept decommissioning, which was then regarded as a condition for Sinn Féin entry to all-party talks. Major devoted much effort to the negotiations, but his efforts floundered as his government became increasingly dependent upon Ulster Unionist support in the House of Commons.

The peace process was carried forward from 1997 by his successor, Blair. On 19 July 1997, the IRA declared a resumption of the 1994 ceasefire. Blair was assisted by American pressure on Sinn Féin, and, in 1998, the Good Friday (10 April) Agree-ment laid the basis for the resumption of provincial self-government. An Assembly and an Executive were both created, and the Assembly met for the first time on 1 July 1998. A North–South ministerial council was established to discuss matters of mutual concern and develop common policies. There would also be a new British–Irish Council with members drawn from the British and Irish governments, the Northern Ireland Assembly, Scottish Parliament and Welsh Assembly. The Irish government agreed to amend Articles 2 and 3 of its Constitution in line with the principle of consent. Despite its subsequent endorsement by 71% of the people in Northern Ireland in a referendum on 23 May 1998, the character and longevity of the settlement remained unclear. The refusal of the IRA to decommission its vast armoury proved to be a significant stumbling block to peace in the province. More fundamentally, both sides of the sectarian divide view the Good Friday Agreement in a different light. For Unionists, the Agreement offered a final word on their constitu-tional status, that is, they could remain British for as long as a majority of them wished to do so. For nationalists, Sinn Féin made it clear that the Good Friday Agreement was a beginning rather than an end, the first stage in a process leading to a united Ireland.

## A diversity of perspectives

This chapter has hitherto been a political narrative, and it is important that that dimension is understood. Yet it is also necessary to stand aside and ask about non-political developments. In large part these have been covered in other chapters, because England, Ireland, Scotland and Wales are not removed from themes such as the impact of the motor car. However, it is still useful to touch on particular aspects of their development and to draw attention to the view of British history from their perspective.

# Ireland

This book is not a history of the British Isles. Nevertheless, it is still important to note briefly the major features of post-independence Irish history. In its early decades, Eire was very different from Britain. It was predominantly rural and had little industry, despite the opening of the Shannon hydroelectric scheme in 1929 and the development of small domestic industries by de Valera in the 1930s. Eire was poor and the difficulty of finding opportunities for its growing population ensured that there was much emigration, especially to Britain. The country was also very conservative, in its politics, society and culture, and in the dominance of the Catholic Church and Catholic morality. The import and sale of contraceptives were banned in 1935. Opposition from the Catholic Church helped to block an attempt in 1951 to reform the health care for expectant mothers and young children. Catholicism and Gaelic culture were seen as crucial to the identity of the new state. The failure of the system to provide for its population was shown by a revival in emigration to levels not seen since the 1880s. Whereas 166,751 people had emigrated from Eire in 1926–36, 408,766 left in 1951–61. This reflected a fall in the agricultural labour force, due to industrialisation, and a lack of opportunities across much of Eire. The population fell throughout the South and, in particular, the West. The fall in the marriage rate was another consequence of poverty and lack of confidence.

This remained the overwhelming picture until the 1970s, and, even more, 1960s, although there were important earlier changes, such as the mid-century campaign against tuberculosis. The Programme for Economic Expansion, published in 1958, recommended the ending of protectionism and a policy of self-sufficiency, and instead, one of free trade, and a determination to make Eire more attractive to foreign investment and a base for exports. That year, Seán Lemass replaced de Valera as Taoiseach (Prime Minister) and leader of Fianna Fáil, encouraging the move towards new policies, especially greater intervention in the economy, health and education. In 1961, however, Eire's attempt to join the EEC failed. In the 1960s, there was a measure of industrialisation, although much in the form of multinational branch plants with restricted local linkages. Employment and output rose, emigration fell, and many of those who had left in the 1950s returned. As an indication of optimism, the average age at marriage fell. A new social politics was born, with free secondary education and the establishment, in 1961, of a national television station, Radio Telefís Éireann. Eire's entry into the EEC in 1973, after massive support in a referendum, transformed the economy, although it was then hit by the oil crisis. Membership of the EEC led to a substantial infusion of development aid; part of the transfer of wealth from richer to poorer states within the EEC/EU. In addition, the stress on agricultural production and protectionism in the EEC/EU benefited Eire, protecting her large farming sector from world competition. Thus, more people lived, and live, close to the land than in Britain. More generally, the economy grew. Ireland's economic strength owed much to heavy involvement in high-tech industries and computer-based technologies. Thanks to strong export expansion, the annual average growth rate in GDP in Ireland in 1990–4 was over 5 per cent, the highest in the EU: Britain's, in contrast, was only 0.7 per cent, the lowest bar Sweden.

Eire also experienced significant social change. Secondary and university education expanded considerably and the television became important. There was a substantial measure of secularisation. The authority of the Catholic Church was contested over abortion, contraception, divorce and homosexuality. The ban on contraceptives was relaxed in 1979. There were bitterly-contested referenda on social issues: on abortion in 1983 and divorce in 1986. These confirmed the existing bans, continuing the flow of Irish women to Britain for abortions; but another referendum, in 1996, narrowly permitted civil divorce and re-marriage. Irish society remained more sectarian than that of Britain; but a lesser role for the Church than hitherto in Irish society, culture and politics became more apparent from the 1960s. This was linked to a measure of emancipation for women that culminated with the election of the youthful and progressive Mary Robinson as President in 1990: hitherto, public life had been very male-dominated. New money helped to change the character of Irish politics, which were far more unstable after the defeat of Fianna Fáil under Jack Lynch in 1973 than they had been since 1958. Charles Haughey, Taoiseach in 1979–81, 1982 and 1987–92, was associated with new social forces and accused of corruption. A charismatic figure, Haughey's opportunistic policies and favouritism helped to divide Fianna Fáil, leading eventually, after charges of illegal telephone-tapping, to his replacement by Albert Reynolds in 1992, but Reynolds's apparent misuse of government patronage led to his fall in 1994. He was replaced by Bertie Aherne who played a crucial role in the events leading up to the Good Friday Agreement in April 1998.

The instability of the republic's politics reflected the strength of sectional interests and the difficulty of moving beyond a politics of personality, but, thanks to EU money, the Irish were spared the worst consequences of their politicians. In the 1990s, it seemed that economic growth, secularisation and social change in Eire had greatly eroded the legacy of the catastrophic dimension of much Irish history: conquest, expropriation, colonisation, discrimination, poverty, myth-making and bitterness. The situation was very different in Northern Ireland. There 'extremists' played a more central role in politics, the danger of violence was ever present, and civil society rested on threatened foundations.

## Scotland and Wales

Scotland and Wales are, as they always have been, different countries from England, although differences were less distinctive than in the cases of Eire and Northern Ireland. Scotland and Wales lacked any equivalent to Stormont or the Troubles in Northern Ireland, while, in contrast to Eire, they shared essentially the same electoral system, government practice and economic parameters as the rest of Britain. Interest and tax rates were set in London for Cardiff and Edinburgh, but not for Dublin. Economic and social trends were also similar in England, Scotland and Wales, whether the decline of heavy industry or secularism, the broadening out of the middle class or the strains on the nuclear family.

Yet there were also major differences, especially in the case of Scotland. To give only a few examples of differences in the case of Scotland since the 1970s, there were separate professional bodies, infrastructures for tourism and business promotion, housing markets, and house-purchase systems. No national core curriculum was imposed in Scotland, the school exam system was much closer to that of Eire than to the rest of the UK, and due to strong opposition, there were no full secondary opt-out schools or City Technical Colleges in Scotland. Furthermore, there was only one denominational non-Catholic school in Scotland's state sector.

Homosexual acts between consenting adults were illegal in Scotland, while legal in England and Wales, from 1967 to 1981. For non-nationalist devolutionists, the level of administrative independence in policymaking, without democratic control, was a major reason for supporting change. Immigration had far less of an effect on Scotland and Wales than on England. Furthermore, the people of both were more dependent on the state than were people in England. Scotland enjoyed a disproportionately high share of government expenditure, especially in health and education, and had far more of its population in council housing. Politically, voting patterns markedly diverged: both Wales and, from the 1960s, Scotland were far more attached to Labour, and less to the Conservatives, than England. These points serve as a reminder of diversity, and more specifically, of the existence of several public cultures and societies in Britain and the United Kingdom. It is unclear whether these will lead to different states, but they certainly ensure that there were, and are, many contrasts behind the terms Britain and the United Kingdom. The role of the envisaged British–Irish Council, a council of the isles, has to be seen in that context.

# England

The village that symbolizes England sleeps in the subconsciousness of many a townsman. A little London factory hand whom I met during the war confessed to me, when pressed . . . that he visualized the England he was fighting for – the England of the 'England wants You' poster – as not London, not his own streets, but as Epping Forest, the green place where he had spent Bank Holidays. And I think most of us did. The village and the English country-side are the germs of all we are and all we have become: our manufacturing cities belong to the last century and a half; our villages stand with their roots in the Heptarchy [Anglo-Saxon period].

This passage comes from a book much of which now seems curious, if not embarrassing, H. V. Morton's *In Search of England* (1927). Henry Canova Vollam Morton (1892–1979) grew up in Birmingham and followed a career as a journalist and a travel writer. Although now largely forgotten, he was one of the most popular writers of his day and was close to many leading figures. Indeed, Morton accompanied Churchill to the Atlantic Charter negotiations with President Roosevelt in 1942. Morton's views were matched by many other ruralist writers and their impact powerfully contributed to inter-war ideology and culture.

This mindset, however, was displaced in the 1940s. World War Two, national mobilisation, and Labour government led to powerful calls for modernisation and provided many opportunities for modernisers. Citizenship and national identity were redefined, culminating with the 1951 Festival of Britain. Marking the hundredth anniversary of the Great Exhibition, this offered a Labour vision of progress.

That vision, however, was to be powerfully challenged, so that modernisation became an ambivalent and controverted cause. Modernity and social progress proved inadequate as the bedrock for identity, but traditional notions were also unworkable. Morton's call for a rural England, 'a happy country-side . . . guarding the traditions of the race' seemed anachronistic.

The anxiety about identity and change widely in the early decades of the twentieth century was also mirrored at its close. First, the drive for devolution in Scotland and Wales led to talk of the break-up of Britain, as well as the United Kingdom. This raised the question of what, if anything, England would amount to. Secondly, the drive for closer European integration led to uncertainty and dispute about identity and nationality. In the case of England, this was taken further as a consequence of the Blair government's stated support for regional assemblies and governments.

**Festival of Britain, 1951**
The festival reflected a mood of post-war optimism and confidence, or at least interest, in new solutions. The immediate background was bleak: the South Bank site of the Festival had been extensively bombed. In fact, most British people were less confident than at the time of the Great Exhibition a century earlier.

Thirdly, there were some interesting manifestations of re-found local identity in Cornwall and even in Yorkshire.

To discuss England alongside Scotland, Wales, and Northern Ireland in a chapter on the parts of the British Isles thus seems appropriate at the cusp of the millennium in a way that it would not have done several decades earlier. Then the history of Great Britain in the nineteenth and twentieth centuries was essentially a history of a state based in England – and Scotland, Wales and Ireland were given separate treatment.

Yet to say that this is inappropriate does not make clear how this subject should be discussed. The identity of England and the meaning of Englishness was something that only came to be addressed anew in the late 1990s. There is no tradition of nationalist politics or culture in England, other than on an extremist fringe, and certainly nothing to compare with Scotland, Wales and Ireland. It would definitely be a new consciousness if England is seen as in opposition to these, but there is little evidence of such attitudes. Furthermore, to abstract England from a wider British history is suspect. The forces that moulded English history were also those that moulded the rest of Great Britain (Northern Ireland is, in part, an exception), certainly until the creation of separate assemblies for Scotland and Wales in 1999. The major political parties in England were not English nationalist parties; nor were they restricted to England. The Church of England did not serve as a substitute.

In addition, it would be misleading to pretend that there is *an* English identity. The notions of place and race advanced by Morton and many other inter-war writers are now dismissed, and, although their critique of modernism still strikes many chords, it has to adopt a different ideology and vocabulary. In post-war England, inclusive notions of nationality sought to accept differences and to overcome divisions that might be based on race or religion, thus ensuring that neither could serve as the basis for an English identity. The impact of national economic and commercial policies, trends and products was matched by national education, leisure, broadcasting policies, practices and institutions.

Allowing for this, there are very wide variations within England. In population terms, there is no single dominant area comparable to South Wales or the Central Belt of Scotland. London might aspire to dominance, and was helped by the growing prominence of the central government and the financial interest, both of which were centred there; but 'the' Midlands and 'the' North are both important and different. They are also very varied in themselves. Such differences undermine any attempt to argue that, but for the 'Celtic fringe', in other words Scotland and Wales, England would have had a Conservative, comfortable, middle-class history in the twentieth century. Certainly, without Scotland and Wales, Labour would not have held power so often, but, nevertheless, there would still have been an important culture and consciousness that was not comprehended within a Conservative England. More specifically, rural romanticism and its construction of an essentially Southern (South Downs) England was misleading even as an account of southern England.

The tension between the attitudes and interests that were most strongly represented in London and the South-East and those that focused in 'the North' was important to the dynamics of twentieth-century England. It challenged, and at times undercut, attempts to suggest that there was a consensus. The tension also provided much of the emotional dynamo behind class politics: a different sense of 'place', as well as of class attitude, was at issue.

More than image and perception were involved. There are important differences between parts of England, and, also, a frequent use of geographical terms, such as East Anglia, the North-East, or the West Country. Yet, it is unclear that there are coherent, clearly defined units to match terms such as the 'West Country'. This area has a vague geographical existence, but, despite frequent references to it in the local media, plays no part in defining residents' sense of identity: counties remain the primary focus.

To take the two regions that are most frequently held to have a clear identity, the North and the South-West: it is apparent that attempts to suggest that the 'North' or the 'North-East' – for there is a crucial lack of clarity here – has a separate identity that can emulate that of Scotland are deeply ahistorical. It is not simply that Scotland was a separately governed nation until 1707. Scottish identity was also expressed and sustained in a distinctive established church, legal system, educational system, and local government. Scotland retained clear boundaries. Thus, a sense and practice of Scottish identity remained strong, at the same time as conceptions of Britishness were advanced in Scotland. Identity was and is neither exclusive nor a constant: a sense of collective self-awareness can include a number of levels or aspects of identification.

The situation in northern England is radically different. There is no continuity with past identifications to lend historical roots and rationales to present-day demands. The north of England was absorbed by the West Saxon state in the tenth century and, since then, distinctive political structures have been essentially administrative in character, representative of the local authority of the national state, as with the Palatine jurisdiction of Durham, and the Yorkist and Tudor Councils of the North. Similarly, there has been no autonomy in religious or cultural terms: the archdiocese of York was scarcely the basis of a separate identity.

Indeed, any reading of the history of the last millennium will offer cold comfort for those who wish to suggest a separate Northern or North-Eastern identity. This is also apparent if the cartography of identity is concerned. If there is a North, where does it begin, where does it reach to, and how far do overlapping senses of identity challenge any clear regional spatiality? This is also true of the North-East. Geographically this is more coherent, essentially because the established image of the region reflects several urban nodes from Tyneside to Cleveland, centred on Newcastle,

Sunderland and Middlesbrough, with sparsely populated largely rural areas to north, west and south that can seem to serve as buffer zones for the region – part of it, but unable to challenge the manner in which the urban nodes define its interests and culture.

Yet this 'construction' of the North-East is open to question. The extent to which the dominant image and images of the North-East can be seen as an accurate reflection of the region as a whole is open to debate. Alongside, or is it interacting with, this world is that of a largely rural region, of isolated farmsteads, small towns and open spaces, and again another, of suburban developments, out-of-town shopping centres and 'executive' housing estates. It is a rash individual who says that one is more 'true' to a regional identity than another. If out-of-town shopping centres, most famously the Metro Centre at Gateshead, were a novelty of the 1980s, the world of coal and heavy industry that was, and is, so important to the area's traditional identity was not an immutable feature of the region.

A sense of identity often develops, or is expressed most clearly, in hostility or opposition to other groups, and their real or imagined aims and attributes, and these groups are frequently ones with which relations are close. Indeed, the reality of overlapping senses of collective self-awareness can be very difficult. This can be seen in current discussion of Northern identity, much of which expresses a depressingly repetitive and small-minded hostility to London and national government. This sense of hostility looks back on a century of relative decline. Regions that collectively were the 'workshops of the world' became areas requiring special assistance from the 1930s. In February 1938, 35% of all benefit claimants in northern England had been unemployed for a year or more. The experience of mass unemployment in the 1930s was, for many, part of a continuing process, for unemployment levels in the 1920s remained above one million, while in the period of 'full employment' after World War Two unemployment figures in the northern industrial regions remained higher than those in the South. Thus long-term unemployment, associated poverty and the even more widespread threat of unemployment, helped to shape the experience of much of the working-class population in the North of England. This contributed to a strong sense of alienation, and to a political world in which collectivist solutions and the Labour Party took a dominant role. The welfare state, for example municipal housing, played a greater proportional role in the North than in the South, not that such housing was not very important throughout the country. As a consequence, dependence on the welfare state, and sensitivity to real or apparent challenges to it, became more marked in the North. This was an aspect of the lower average incomes of the North, and these were important not only because they took more people into a dependency culture, but also because the benefits and attractions of consumerism were, at least in part, outside the pockets of much of the poor.

It would, however, be misleading to present a stark counterpoint of North and South. Averages are no more than that, and an image of northern decline and poverty is, at least in part, as important as the reality of a more complex situation. If regional identity is dependent on a feeling of dispossession and alienation then it will be profoundly unattractive. Rather than thinking in terms of metropolitan (London) versus regions, national versus regional, it may be more pertinent to address the issue of how best to conceptualise interacting national attitudes and cultural languages and their local resonances and sources. This is especially pertinent as the mobility of the population remains high, adding to the sense of impermanence and fluidity.

The overriding theme of much discussion of the history of 'the North-East' is conflict, and, in that perspective, regionalism offers a new dimension to class conflict, a new way to re-state social identity, alienation and defiance. However, the repeated emphasis on conflict and coercion as the means by which social, and thus, by extension, intra-regional, relations are allegedly 'structured' is very questionable. It assumes a process that it frequently does not demonstrate, and mistakes assertion and emotion for analysis and exposition. Founding the North-East on a polemic of regional alienation, socio-cultural expropriation or oppression, and politico-historical myth, will be limiting.

In the case of the South-West, it is also very unclear where the boundaries and centres should be, and the notion of a distinct and separate identity is questionable. In Cornwall there is a strong sense of dissatisfaction with national government, but it is very unclear that control from Bristol, or even Plymouth or Exeter, would be more welcome. The distance from Penzance to Bristol, Swindon or Bournemouth is great, and accentuated by poor communications, and all three look more to London than to Devon, let alone Cornwall. Shared economic interests are limited, and there is little sense of a cultural or political consciousness that can define and unite a region.

The regional situation is even more obscure elsewhere. To take the Midlands, where two separate regions, West and East, are often discerned, it is unclear how far counties such as Cheshire, Derbyshire and Oxfordshire should be seen as integral, or as transition zones to neighbouring regions. The East Midlands to the north, and even immediately south, of the Trent can be seen as part of the North, Oxford is, in part, a commuter town for London, while Cheshire is as much part of the North-West as of the West Midlands. The role of counties such as Essex and Cambridgeshire in East Anglia is unclear, as is the extent to which the Welsh Marches can be separated from the West Midlands.

In April 1994, the government established ten regional administrations by combining existing regional offices of the Departments of the Environment, Transport, Trade and Industry, and Employment, and appointing a single director to take charge of these 'integrated regional offices'. They were designed to act as a single contact point between the central government and the localities. The ten were the South-West, South-East, London, Eastern, West Midlands, East Midlands, Yorkshire and Humberside, North-East, North-West, and Merseyside, the last where cross-departmental teams of civil servants were deployed to deal with problems after the 1981 Toxteth riots. The regions varied greatly – in population (from 1.5 to 7.7 million) as well as in size. Their coherence is a matter for debate. There were, also, many specific points that invited question. For example, London's suburbia was divided between South-East and Eastern, not united. In the South-East there is the 'bagel problem': London is central to it and without London it is unclear how far the constituent parts have any identity or unity. Yet London and the South-East would be a region far more populous and wealthy than any other, and this might lead to an inherent instability in the process of regionalisation.

In 1999, in a new initiative, eight Regional Development Agencies (RDAs) began operation. One of their first tasks was to prepare an economic strategy for each region. The RDAs were under a statutory duty to consult Regional Chambers (non-elected bodies, of whom 70% were representatives from all the local authorities in the region), if such bodies met government standards for their composition. This process was pressed further in April 1999, when, following the Scottish model, the

North-East Constitutional Convention, charged with drawing up a blueprint for a directly elected regional assembly, first met. A similar body for the North-West followed later in the year.

It is unclear what these moves will lead to. The uncertainty of identities and units at the close of the century is an important corrective to any attempt to provide a simple and uniform account of England, the largest, wealthiest, most powerful and most populous of the parts of the British Isles.

## ■ Summary

◆ It was far from inevitable that nationalism would lead to an independent Ireland, but the First World War swept away the prospect of Irish Home Rule.

◆ Nationalism was weak in Scotland and Wales until the 1960s. Instead, both were dominated by national political parties.

◆ The 1960s was also a decade of change in Northern Ireland. The attempt by the Unionist government to introduce reforms and also retain control collapsed and the situation spun out of control, leading to the introduction of British troops.

◆ The reaction to Thatcherism helped the cause of nationalism in Scotland and Wales. In 1999, both gained separate representative bodies.

◆ There have been important contrasts in development within both Britain and England.

## ■ Questions for discussion

◆ Why was Ireland partitioned?
◆ How distinctive are the parts of Britain?
◆ Why did devolution fail in the 1970s but succeed in the 1990s?
◆ How far have differences within Britain been related to the country's political history?

## ■ Further reading

Bennie, Lynn; Brand, Jack; and Mitchell, James, *How Scotland Votes* (Manchester, 1997).

Boyce, D. G., *The Irish Question and British Politics, 1868–1996* (2nd edn, London, 1996).

Dunphy, Richard, *The Making of Fianna Fáil Power in Ireland, 1923–1948* (Oxford, 1995).

Follis, Bryan A., *A State under Siege: The Establishment of Northern Ireland, 1920–1925* (Oxford, 1995).

Harkness, David, *Ireland in the Twentieth Century* (London, 1995).

Hennessey, Thomas, *A History of Northern Ireland, 1920–96* (London, 1997).

Kendle, John, *Federal Britain: A History* (London, 1997).

Laffan, Michael, *The Resurrection of Ireland: The Sinn Féin Party, 1916–1923* (Cambridge, 1999).

Loughlin, James, *The Ulster Question since 1945* (London, 1998).

Matless, David, *Landscape and Englishness* (London, 1998).

Morgan, Kenneth O., *Rebirth of a Nation: Wales, 1880–1980* (Oxford, 1981).

Peatling, G. K., *From Unionism to Liberal Commonwealth: The Transformation of British Public Opinion towards Irish Self-government, 1865–1925* (Dublin, 2000).

Robbins, Keith, *Great Britain: Identities, Institutions and the Idea of Britishness* (Harlow, 1998).

Walker, Graham, *Thomas Johnston* (Manchester, 1988).

# 13

# Britain and the Outside World: Political Aspects

## Contents

'Fog in Channel. Continent cut off.' The old joke about British insularity has never been an accurate reflection of the many and varied factors that link Britain to the outside world. This relationship made up much of the country's history in the twentieth century. At the outset, Britain ruled the greatest Empire in the world; at the close, it was surrendering its sovereignty as part of the membership of a supra-national union of European states. This was an important shift, not some minor appendage to the domestic history of the country. Furthermore, international developments greatly affected domestic developments, while comparisons with the situations in other countries provide a context for judging what happened in Britain. As a consequence, two chapters have been allocated to examine Britain and the outside world, and the decision to devote these chapters to the subject reflects a belief that it is important and should not be treated as a postscript to some account organised round the domestic perspective. Any division between categories is necessarily artificial, but, nevertheless, offers a valuable focus. In this chapter we concentrate on the political dimension, always remembering that it did not exist in some kind of vacuum.

## Key issues

▶ What was the course of Empire before its loss?

▶ Why was the Empire lost?

▶ What were the consequences?

▶ Why did Britain get involved in the two World Wars?

▶ Why was she on the winning side in both conflicts?

▶ Why did Britain join the European Union, and with what consequences?

## ◾ Empire at its height

The inclusion of this section may appear curious, a product of reprehensible nostalgia or an inappropriate anachronism. However, for many in the world, the experience and legacy of British control was the importance of British history. Furthermore, for many Britons, Empire was a tap-root of self-identity underpinned by families with relatives in Australia, New Zealand, Canada and South Africa, and one of its consequences was a reluctant Europeanism. In the second half of the nineteenth century, the British fought across the globe as never before. It is easy to underrate these conflicts, as none was a war for survival and none transformed British society, but for Britain their cumulative impact was important, while their individual impact on other societies was formative. Britain's role was part of the wider story of European **imperialism**, but greater than that of any other state, because of her limited involvement in power politics on the continent of Europe, her unprecedented naval and commercial strength, and the extensive character of the Empire already. As a consequence, Empire was more central to British history than to that of France or Germany.

**imperialism:** The attempt of a state to spread its power over a number of countries.

In the mid-nineteenth century, the Empire included Ireland (although represented in the Westminster Parliament), Australasia and Canada, much of India, and parts of the West Indies, of southern Africa, Burma and Malaya, as well as a host of islands across the oceans. Britain was the leading naval power. From the 1860s, the pace of British expansion increased, and by 1899, Britain had conquered much of Africa. She remained the leading naval power, as well as the strongest power in South Asia. Britain's most difficult transoceanic conflict was the Second Boer War with the Afrikaner republics of the Orange Free State and the Transvaal in southern Africa in 1899–1902. The British were initially outnumbered and poorly led. Their opponents' superior marksmanship with long-range Mauser magazine rifles, and their effective combination of the strategic offensive and a successful use of defensive positions, inflicted particularly heavy casualties on the British in the winter of 1899–1900.

More effective British generalship and more plentiful resources changed the situation in 1900. The ability of Britain to allocate about £200 million and to deploy 400,000 troops was a testimony to the strength of both her economic and her imperial systems, although the dispatch of so much of the regular army left it far below normal strength in the British Isles. Other colonies, especially Australia and New Zealand, also sent troops. Once the Boer colonies had been overrun in 1900, their mounted infantry challenged British control, leading to a blockhouse system with barbed-wire fences, scorched-earth policies and reprisals. This led to the Treaty of Vereeniging in 1902, a bitter but conditional Boer surrender.

The severe difficulties encountered in the Second Boer War, which took the lives of 22,000 British troops, might suggest that imperial expansion had run its course. The unexpectedly high cost of the war certainly placed a severe burden on British public finances. The battlefield defeats in the early stages of the war undermined Britain's imperial prestige (see Chapter 9). Yet the potency of Empire remained clear for all to see: the euphoria surrounding the relief of the siege of Mafeking, in May 1900, was indicative of this.

It is easy to present the British Empire as foredoomed to failure, and that is how it looks from the close of the twentieth century, and how it looked from the 1960s at the latest, if not from the 1950s. Already, at the start of the century, thanks, in part, to the diffusion within the Empire of British notions of community, identity and political action, and British practices of politicisation, specifically nationalism and democratisation, there was opposition to imperial control, although it was limited in scope. In 1885, the Indian National Congress was formed; in 1897, the Egyptian National Party.

Yet, the Empire continued to expand, while the granting of dominion status to 'settlement colonies' became a peaceful evolutionary route to independence, reducing what might otherwise have been difficulties in relations with Australasia and Canada. Australia became a dominion in 1901 and New Zealand in 1907. The search for reconciliation after the Boer War led to the formation of the Union of South Africa in 1910. The constitution gave power over the whole of South Africa to the Afrikaners, a form of responsible government that was very much a 'white' solution. There was to be no third Boer War. Alongside the support for close links with 'white' colonies, which were pushed by Chamberlain and the tariff reformers, there was also interest in the development of a powerful Asiatic Empire. This was advocated by Curzon, Viceroy of India (1898–1905). He pushed a forward policy in Tibet, on the North-West Fronier of India, and in the Persian Gulf, and sought to strengthen British government of India.

The USA, which had seized independence from Britain in 1775–83, was rising as a great economic power, and expanding her possessions across the Pacific, but Britain managed her disputes with her, for example over the Canadian frontier, and over the Venezuelan border in 1895, skilfully, and accepted American hegemony in the Western hemisphere. In turn, the Americans did not seek to overthrow the British Empire. In 1908, the Committee of Imperial Defence and the Foreign Office concluded that the possibility of war with the USA was remote.

British troops were sent where they had never gone before. On 31 March 1904, a force under Colonel Francis Younghusband, advancing through the Himalayas towards Lhasa, opened fire at Guru on Tibetans who were unwilling to disarm. Due to their two Maxim (machine) guns, four cannon and effective rifles, the British killed nearly 700 Tibetans without any losses of their own. Younghusband then proceeded to Lhasa. Thanks to the resources of the imperial state, his advance had been supported by 16,000 draught animals, and 10,000 human porters. A year earlier, the British had smashed the army of Sokoto at Burmi in Nigeria, with vastly disproportionate casualties, and had brought resistance in northern Nigeria to an end.

**Imperial identity**
Victoria's Jubilee in 1897 provided an opportunity to strike imperial themes, as seen with this *Punch* cartoon of her multi-ethnic people. The Queen was the first Empress of India, and the British empire was continuing to expand, especially in Africa. British forces were to be victorious at Omdurman in the Sudan a year later.

"FOR QUEEN AND EMPIRE!!"

A lost world of British power, far from the country's shores, indeed; but as much part of British history as the doings of modern ministries. Furthermore, the impact of those years of imperial might were to reach deep in affecting subsequent attitudes. Politicians like Churchill, who had been present at Kitchener's decisive victory over the Mahdists of Sudan at Omdurman in 1898, found it impossible to forget the legacy of power, and subsequently developed a romantic attachment to the idea of Empire. So also did the army and navy, and this was part of the reason why, after the loss of Empire, Britain continued to spend a higher proportion of her revenues on 'defence' (i.e. the military) than other European states. More generally, Empire was part of British identity and ceremonial. The Golden and Diamond jubilees of Queen Victoria, in 1887 and 1897 respectively, proved that. In 1896, the Earl of Meath launched Empire Day on 24 May, Queen Victoria's birthday.

However, as Younghusband crossed the Himalayas, British ministers and commentators were having to consider a threat nearer home – Germany. The German issue has remained a central problem for British policy throughout the twentieth century, and, today, is an important aspect of public uncertainty over the European Union. The philosopher and traveller David Hume travelling through Germany in 1748 had observed, 'Germany is undoubtedly a very fine country, full of industrious, honest people, and were it united it would be the greatest power that ever was in the world.' That was before American independence in 1776, but, anyway, it was then implausible, because Germany was divided, especially between Austria and Prussia.

German unification in 1866–71 transformed the situation, and, as Germany became more assertive, it became more important in British thinking. In December 1899, the rising journalist J. L. Garvin decided that Germany and not, as he had previously thought, France and Russia, was the greatest threat to Britain. Rejecting the view of Joseph Chamberlain, Secretary of State for the Colonies, that Britain and Germany were natural allies, their peoples of a similar racial 'character', Garvin saw 'the Anglo-Saxons' as the obstacle to Germany's naval and commercial policy. A German threat also became a theme in imaginative literature. A projected German invasion was central to *The Riddle of the Sands* (1903), a novel by Erskine Childers, which was first planned in 1897, a year in which the Germans indeed discussed such a project.

In addition, there were governmental tensions. British resources and political will were tested in a major and expensive naval race between the two powers, started by the German Minister of Marine, Alfred von Tirpitz, in 1897, in which the British launched HMS *Dreadnought*, the first of a new class of battleships, in 1906. The number of dreadnoughts being built, rapidly became an issue of public anxiety and government concern. It affected the fiscal planning of Lloyd George and the Liberal government's confrontation with the House of Lords in 1909–11 (see Chapter 9). The navy was concentrated in home waters in response to the German threat. An alliance with Japan became crucial to the security of Britain's position in the Far East.

Britain also came to play a greater role in European power politics, turning away from the non-interventionism, indeed isolationism, that had characterised her policy for over forty years, essentially since the Crimean War of 1854–6. Britain and France moved closer together with an *entente* in 1904. Thereafter, alliance with France came to play a bigger role in British thinking. The defeat of France's ally Russia in the Russo-Japanese war of 1904–5 weakened Russia as a balancing element within Europe. This exposed France to German diplomatic pressure and created British alarm about German intentions, as in the First Moroccan Crisis of 1905–6. This crisis, provoked by Germany, was followed by Anglo-French staff talks aimed at

dealing with a German threat. Their consequences were to play a major role in leading Britain towards World War One. In 1907, British military manoeuvres were conducted for the first time on the basis that Germany, not France, Britain's leading
colonial rival, was the enemy. That year, fears of Germany contributed to an Anglo-
Russian *entente*. Thus Britain moved closer to a power with whom it had competed
for hegemony in South Asia for decades.

Yet, political opinion is rarely uniform. It was, and is, difficult in any state to
determine what the notion of national interests entailed and how best to secure
them. Alongside hostility to Germany in political and official circles, there were
politicians, such as Balfour, Prime Minister 1902–5, the 5th Marquess of Lansdowne, Foreign Secretary 1900–5, and his fellow Liberal-Unionist, the Earl of
Selborne, First Lord of the Admiralty 1900–5, as well as Lord Sanderson, Under-
Secretary at the Foreign Office, who sought to maintain good relations. Lansdowne
also negotiated the *entente* with France, but the *ententes* were not alliances. Britain
failed to make her position clear. This encouraged Germany to hope that she would
not act in the event of war. Britain had not intervened when the two powers had last
fought, in 1870–1.

## World War One, 1914–18

Tension between Serbia and Austria (which then also ruled what are now Hungary,
the Czech Republic, Slovakia, Slovenia, Croatia and Bosnia) spun out of control in
1914 when Serbian nationalists killed the Archduke Franz Ferdinand, the heir to the
Austrian Empire, in Sarajevo. This produced an international crisis over the Balkans,
in which Britain was not initially involved. The crisis led to the outbreak of a conflict
that spread through the pressures of competing alliance systems. Austria and her ally
Germany found themselves opposed to Serbia and her ally Russia. Germany decided
to strike at Russia's ally France, in order to defeat her before the slower-moving
Russian army could act. As France's German border was well protected, she did so by
invading through vulnerable Belgium. Britain was a guarantor of the neutrality of
Belgium, but the Germans did not think that their invasion would provoke British
entry. The Liberal government was indeed divided about war with Germany, but the
attack on Belgium helped unite most of the government behind war. Only two
members of the Cabinet resigned. Thereafter, the war spread. Turkey and Bulgaria
joined Germany, while Italy entered the war on the Allied side in 1915, and the USA
entered in 1917, the year in which Russia collapsed through revolution.

This war was to be terrible for both Britain and the British. It was widely, but
erroneously, assumed that the conflict would be short, and Sir Edward Grey, the
Foreign Secretary, even told the Commons in August 1914 that the burdens of
taking part would be little more than those of remaining neutral. British participation also had many important consequences, both short and long term, some of
which have already been discussed in other chapters. Partly as a result of these, the
war should not be treated simply as an episode in military history. The military history of the conflict has to be understood, nevertheless, in order to appreciate much
of its impact. It was crucially different from Britain's recent experience of conflict,
even the initially unsuccessful Second Boer War of 1899–1902, because of its seemingly intractable character, the threat to the British home base, the possibility that
Britain might lose, with very serious consequences, and the massive quantity of
resources that the war required and destroyed.

**The trenches**
The nature of the fighting in World War One was as ghastly as the casualties. Justified revulsion at both has tended to make many commentators underrate the reasons for Britain's entry into the war – to prevent German domination of Europe and in particular her unprovoked attack on neutral Belgium – and also the success of the British on the Western Front in outfighting and defeating the Germans in 1918. The development of effective artillery–infantry coordination played a large part in this success.

The euphoria of the war's outbreak and the general confidence in its speedy conclusion were followed on the Western Front in France and Belgium, by October 1914, by the emergence of stalemate. The troops were not going to be 'home by Christmas'. The concentration of large forces in a relatively small area, the defensive strength of trench positions, especially thanks to machine-guns with their range and rapidity of fire, and to quick-firing artillery, but also helped by barbed wire and concrete fortifications, ensured that, until the collapse of the German position in the last weeks of the war, the situation there was essentially deadlocked. It proved very difficult to translate local superiority in numbers into decisive success. It was possible to break through opponents' trench lines, but difficult to exploit such successes; as yet, aeroplanes and motor vehicles had not been effectively harnessed to help the offensive. Furthermore, once troops had advanced, it was difficult to recognise, reinforce and exploit success: until wireless communications improved in late 1917, control and communications were limited. Frontal attacks, for example by the British at Neuve-Chapelle and Loos (1915), the Somme (1916), and Arras and Passchendaele (1917), led to heavy casualties, not least when a strategy of attrition was followed, as at Passchendaele – a hell of shells and mud.

The ratio of troops and firepower to space pushed up losses. The British used 2,879 guns – one for every nine yards of front – for their attack near Arras in April 1917; 58 per cent of British battlefield deaths were from artillery and mortar shells, and just below 39 per cent from machine-gun and rifle bullets. German 150mm field howitzers could fire five rounds per minute. Air-burst shrapnel shells increased the deadly nature of artillery fire. Machine-guns were especially devastating against the British troops advancing slowly and in close order on the Somme in 1916: 21,000 men were killed on 1 July, the first day of the offensive, most of them in an hour.

The impasse of trench warfare was broken in 1918. The British blocked the last German offensive in the spring, and in July–November, with French and American support, launched a series of attacks in which they outfought the Germans, overrunning their major defensive system in September. The massed use of tanks was a major shock, and, on 8 August, no fewer than 430 British tanks broke through the German lines near Amiens. Although they rapidly became unfit for service, tanks

**Tanks**

First used by the British at the Somme on 15 September 1916, tanks were to symbolise the mechanisation of war, although their actual impact in World War One was limited. In November 1917, the Germans regained most of the ground near Cambrai that the British had recently seized thanks to their first use of massed tanks. The Germans also deployed tanks in 1918, but they did so in far smaller numbers and to less effect than the British. The Germans were unable to manufacture as many as the British. Other new British weapons included the Stokes Mortar, and in August 1918, HMS *Argus*, the first clear-deck aircraft carrier, was commissioned. The British also sought to match German advances in air, submarine and gas warfare.

could be hit by rifle bullets and machine-guns without suffering damage and could smash through barbed wire and cross trenches. More generally, the Germans had lost their superiority in weapons systems. British gunnery inflicted considerable damage on German defences, and was well coordinated with infantry advances.

Successes elsewhere were also important. The British navy retained control of their home waters, checking the German high sea fleet at the battle of Jutland in the North Sea in 1916, and, after very heavy shipping losses, eventually thwarted the German submarine menace, in part through the belated introduction of convoys in 1917. Britain was, therefore, able to avoid blockade and invasion, to retain trade links that permitted the mobilisation of British and Allied resources, crucially links with the USA, and to blockade Germany. The German colonies were overrun, the Suez Canal and oil supplies in the Persian Gulf were both protected from Germany's ally Turkey, and the Turks eventually driven from Palestine and Mesopotamia (now, Israel, Palestine and Iraq).

Germany was defeated, not 'stabbed in the back' by domestic opposition (as German nationalists later claimed), but euphoria in Britain was limited. The war had seen virulent patriotism and a widespread conviction that it had to continue until Germany could be driven from Belgium; but the discontent of many soldiers led to thousands of court martials, while shell-shock affected large numbers. Several war poets, most famously Siegfried Sassoon and Wilfred Owen, presented war as an epitome of military futility and incompetence, and Richard Aldington, who had been affected by gas and shell-shock, denounced society in his anti-war novel *Death of a Hero* (1929). Such views, however, found scant echo in public opinion or in the inscriptions on the numerous war memorials erected after the conflict. The last were, and are, one of the more eloquent testimonials to the heavy cost and loss of this war. For example, 10 per cent of male Scots between 16 and 50 were killed, a figure which was to give rise to the idea of a 'lost generation'.

## Empire, 1919–39

The war carried Britain to the apex of Empire. She played a leading role in the peace conferences held in Paris, most importantly that with Germany which led to the Treaty of Versailles of 1919. Germany lost territory in Europe and had to agree to both reparations (payments for war damage) and demobilisation of most of its armed forces. The German fleet sailed to the British naval base at Scapa Flow in the Orkneys where it was scuttled. The German overseas Empire was distributed among the victors, Britain gaining League of Nations mandates for Tanganyika, part of Togo, and a sliver of the Cameroons, all in Africa, and Nauru Island in the Pacific, while the Dominions of Australia, New Zealand and South Africa also all made gains. The partition of Turkey led to the acquisition of British mandates over Palestine, Transjordan and Iraq, and Britain had already annexed Cyprus and Egypt, both formerly part of the Turkish Empire. Ardent imperialists, such as Lord Milner and Leo Amery, pressed for the strengthening of the Empire, partly in the hope that this would never again be dragged into the Continental mire. British influence increased in both Persia and Turkey, and British forces, operating against the Communists in the Russian civil war that followed their coup in 1917, moved into the Caucasus, Central Asia, and the White Sea region, and were deployed in the Baltic and the Black Sea. In 1919, Lord Curzon, the Foreign Secretary, suggested the annexation of parts of the Russian Empire.

Such ambitions could not be sustained. The high tide of Empire was to ebb very fast. The strain of the war was heavy enough, and it left a burdensome debt, but, in addition, the expansion of imperial rule and of Britain's international commitments involved intractable problems. Armed intervention in Russia, which had been supported by Churchill, was a failure and was abandoned in 1919. It had been opposed by British left-wingers, sympathetic to the Communists, and by conscripts eager for demobilisation, but failed, essentially, because of the intractability of the task. In the Middle East, revolts in Egypt (1919) and Iraq (1920–1) led to Britain granting their independence in 1922 and 1924 respectively, although she maintained considerable influence in both, in what was to be a successful exercise in informal Empire. The Third Afghan War in 1919 underlined the difficult situation of the 'North-West Frontier' of India. British influence collapsed in Persia in 1921, and the British backed down in their confrontation with Turkey in 1922–3, the last being a crucial factor in Lloyd George's fall. As is discussed in Chapter 12, most of Ireland was lost, and this was a major blow to imperial self-confidence: the Empire began at home. At the Washington Conference of 1921–2, the British accepted the principle of equality in naval strength with the USA.

There was a lack of resources and will to sustain schemes for imperial expansion. Such schemes were expensive. It had cost £40 million to suppress the Iraq rising, and the garrison cost £25 million a year. Retrenchment and judging between commitments were increasingly the order of the day. The Geddes Axe cut most heavily into military expenditure (see Chapter 9). Even retaining the Empire involved major efforts. This was increasingly so in the 1930s, as nationalism became a stronger force, and British military resources were put under mounting pressure from the need to consider German rearmament, Japanese aggrandisement, and the constraints created by domestic financial problems. There were Greek Cypriot nationalist riots in 1931, Arab violence in Palestine in 1936–9, and pressure from the non-violent Indian National Congress.

Yet, much effort was expended in defending the Empire. Over 60,000 men were deployed in 1936 to crush a rising under the Faqir of Ipi on the North-West Frontier; two years later, 50,000 troops were employed against the Arab rising in Palestine. Both problems were brought under control. Empire was important in British consciousness. On Empire Day every year, schools staged pageants and displays, souvenirs were issued, and large parades were held in Hyde Park. The British Empire Exhibition in 1924–5, for which Wembley Stadium was built in 1923, was a major public occasion. Another followed in Glasgow in 1938. The Empire Marketing

Board, created in1926, sought to encourage trade within the Empire. New air routes linked the Empire to Britain, and the British tried to develop imperial links, for example by encouraging the settlement of British demobilised soldiers elsewhere in the Empire after World War One. The awarding of British university degrees through extension courses was more successful. These disparate elements interacted to create a sense of imperial partnership, camaraderie, even nationalism, but one that was not free from tensions and other identities. These tensions varied. There was a crisis in Anglo-Australian relations in 1932–3 over the 'bodyline' cricket tour, as aggressive English bowling roused Australian anger. Acculturation worked best at the level of colonial elites.

Imperial federation was an influential idea in this period. Its origins can be traced back to the late nineteenth century. The development of the notion of a Commonwealth – unity in independence – proved useful in maintaining the support of the Dominions. An imperial conference in 1926 defined the Commonwealth as 'the group of self-governing communities composed of Great Britain and the Dominions'. This formed the basis of the Statute of Westminster (1931), which determined that Commonwealth countries could now amend or repeal 'any existing or future act of the United Kingdom Parliament . . . in so far as the same is part of the law of this dominion'. This notion of devolved Empire did not, however, settle the question of India, which was not a Dominion, while Irish nationalist sentiment was not satisfied with the Dominion status that followed the treaty of 1921.

The crucial political issue was India. As with Ireland in 1914, it is not clear what would have happened had there not been war, in this case World War Two, which broke out in 1939. The Amritsar massacre in April 1919, when General Dyer ordered troops to fire on a demonstrating crowd, causing nearly 400 fatalities, had dented British authority in India by exposing its inherently repressive nature. That same year, a Government of India Act established the principle of dyarchy, that is, responsible self-government in certain areas. This reflected Liberal aspirations that were not shared by all Conservatives. The Government of India Act of 1935 moved towards self-government, an aspect of a wider democratising process (see also Chapter 8), but was designed to ensure British retention of the substance of power. However, the provincial elections of 1937 were a success for the Indian National Congress.

A section of the Conservative Party, led by Churchill, bitterly opposed the 1935 Act. They saw the moves towards self-government as a crucial step to the abandonment of Empire. For Churchill, the new policy on India was more than a tactical step. From the embittered luxury of exclusion from office from 1929, he offered an apocalyptic vision that appeared out of place to many. The Viceroy of India described Churchill in 1929 as an 'Imperialist in the 1890–1900 sense of the word', and that world now appeared less relevant. The bitterness of the parliamentary rebellion against the 1935 Act was a testimony to the pull of Empire and the rebels' sense of danger, but also to their failure. In part, divisions within the Conservative Party and domestic political considerations were at issue: the anti-Baldwinites uniting around an issue, and being defeated by Baldwin. There was also a more general sense that Empire had to change, and that reform of the government of India was, alongside Imperial Trade Preference and more equal relations with the Dominions, the best means to give the Empire a future. Imperial Preference was introduced in 1932. It was to that end, that Leo Amery, an ardent imperialist, supported the legislation in 1935, while Lord Irwin (later Earl of Halifax), the Viceroy of India, backed eventual Dominion status for India.

# Britain and the Continent, 1919–39

The debate over the future nature of the Empire might seem to mark Britain's distance from the Continent. In fact, the debate seemed urgent in part because of Britain's relations within Europe. The Empire had helped Britain survive World War One. It was Britain's lifeline as a great power. Foreign protectionism in the 1920s and, especially, 1930s stimulated fresh consideration of Empire as an economic resource and lifeline. The failure to produce a lasting international settlement at Paris in 1919 also affected attitudes towards Empire, and this was accentuated by the hostility of particular expansionist powers, first the Soviet Union and, from 1933, Nazi Germany.

Aside from specific challenges, there was a more general shift to a situation in which foreign policy became more central to British government and to public debate. This was one of the legacies of World War One and of the manner in which it was wound up. The Napoleonic Wars had been followed by a system of collective security in which Britain played little role, but the situation was very different after 1918. Not only did Britain now play a major role, but in addition, the Paris peace settlement did not bring peace to Eastern Europe. One of the major features of the twentieth century was that of greater British concern with European power politics than in the Victorian period. The process led, via World War One and the subsequent attempts to consolidate and defend the peace settlements, and World War Two and subsequent confrontation with the Soviet Union, to the modern search for stability and order in a post-Communist Europe. British Foreign Secretaries in 1919–39 devoted more time to Continental affairs than had been the case when major changes had been taking place there in the 1860s and 1870s, or, indeed, since 1815.

At Paris in 1919, Lloyd George had supported President Wilson of the USA in a stress on national self-determination, and, thus, the creation of a state system based on **nation-states**. This, however, produced a situation in Eastern Europe in which a number of weak states were vulnerable to any revival in the strength of Germany or Russia. In the 1920s, British governments sought to bring stability to the Paris peace settlement and to manage German revival so that it did not overturn the European system. A similar policy had been successfully followed towards France from 1815.

In the 1920s, Labour and Conservative governments shared similar goals, but there were also differences. Labour sought to reconcile realism and idealism, and to compensate for what they saw as the unreality and unfairness of the 1919 peace settlement, specifically the exclusion of Germany and the Soviet Union from the League of Nations, which had been created to maintain peace. Reparations also seemed excessive to many commentators. A stronger League, representative of all peoples, seemed to Labour to be the means to peace. Labour was also keen on international arbitration and disarmament. The 1924 Labour government cut naval construction and stopped work on the naval base at Singapore.

The process of adapting to German revival broke down in the 1930s, in large part because there was no managing Adolf Hitler, the Nazi leader who took power in Germany in 1933. In addition, the economic problems of the 1930s made Britain less able to sustain its global military presence.

Initially, the British and French governments had hoped that Hitler would be tamed by the responsibilities and exigencies of power, or that he would restrict his

**nation-state:** A politically independent country consisting of a single nation.

energies to ruling Germany. Mussolini, the Fascist ruler of Italy, was strongest on bombast, although Italy was weaker than Germany. The British government had been concerned when Japan invaded the Chinese province of Manchuria in September 1931, but was unwilling to act on its own against Japan, and the USA was not prepared to help. In December 1933, the First Sea Lord urged the government to stay on good terms with Japan.

There was also a feeling in Britain that the Versailles terms had been overly harsh on Germany, and that it was, therefore, understandable that Hitler should press for revision. Provided this could be done peacefully, Hitler did not appear to threaten British interests or possessions. It was anticipated that German revisionism could be accommodated, and that Hitler would be just another episode in European power politics, rather as Napoleon III of France, the reviser of the Congress of Vienna in the mid-nineteenth century, had been, and, possibly, less threateningly so. Both Britain and France were unsure whether Soviet Russia was not a greater threat to the European system than Nazi Germany. They also wanted to avoid war, and that indeed was the objective of rearmament. In both Britain and France, pacifism was strong, as shown by the 'Peace Ballot' in Britain in 1935, and fiscal restraint even stronger, although, outside Europe, both powers used troops to sustain their imperial interests.

Baldwin tried to rely on the League of Nations, cooperation with France, and modest rearmament. The support of the French and the Foreign Secretary, Sir Samuel Hoare, for a settlement of the dispute between Abyssinia and her invader Italy at the expense of the former, in late 1935, was seen as **appeasement** and led to Hoare's enforced resignation. Hoare, in fact, had been authorised by the Cabinet to accept Italian conquests. The government then considered oil sanctions against Italy, but France was only willing to cooperate if Britain undertook to guarantee the demilitarisation of the Rhineland in accordance with the terms of the 1919 settlement. The British government, which had no intention of fighting over the Rhineland, refused, and when, in March 1936, the Germans sent troops into the region the British did not respond. Instead, they sought to discourage the French from acting. In hindsight, the failure to prevent this action marked a major step in Nazi expansionism, but, at the time, it was not seen in such a stark light.

Neville Chamberlain, Prime Minister from May 1937, was unsuccessful in his handling of foreign policy, in part because of inexperience, ignorance and obtuseness, but also because he suffered from the effects of growing Nazi confidence. Chamberlain thought it both necessary and possible to negotiate with Hitler. He seems to have believed that he could win Hitler over, but the fatal flaw of appeasement (however noble its intentions, and they were not always noble) was that Hitler (unlike Stresemann, German Foreign Minister in the 1920s) did not want to be appeased. This became increasingly obvious with the passing of time, but there were relatively few critics of British government policy even in 1938.

Chamberlain's first flight abroad was to see Hitler at Berchtesgaden in September 1938, when he went to see Hitler in an effort to prevent war over the latter's intimidation of Czechoslovakia, one of the new states created at Paris, and one in which Britain had no vital interests. If Chamberlain was personally unprepared, both for flying and for dealing with Hitler, he was more generally unready for the challenge posed by the deteriorating international situation. The policy of the appeasement of dictators, particularly Hitler (but also Mussolini and the military regime in Japan), with which Chamberlain was to be associated, was, in practice, not a coherent policy,

**appeasement:** The unsuccessful attempt to maintain peace by granting concessions, particularly to Germany but also to Italy and Japan, before the Second World War.

still less ideology, but the sum of a diverse set of responses to very varying problems. In general, appeasement rested on the belief that it was possible to reach settlements with dictators. Following the first meeting, peace was maintained at Munich (on 29 September 1938) by forcing Czechoslovakia to accept most of the German terms, especially the cession of the Sudetenland. Chamberlain then sought a broader agreement with Hitler in order to bring stability to Europe.

Chamberlain himself, and sympathetic papers, most clearly *Truth*, which was run by Sir Joseph Ball, the head of the Conservative Research Department, were strongly anti-Communist, and, for long, regarded Hitler and Mussolini as lesser threats. Their anti-Semitism owed much to hostility to Communism and was a darker side of the Conservative emphasis on a vision of England/Britain with its clear counter-pointing of 'unEnglish/unBritish' values. Yet, for much of the 1930s, it was by no means clear to many commentators in Western Europe whether Nazi Germany or Soviet Russia under the Communist dictator Stalin, was more of a threat, and it was also unclear how best to confront the threats. The eventual outcome – alliance with the Soviet Union from 1941 and then 'cold war' with her – was far from inevitable. Chamberlain feared that war would lead to the collapse of the British Empire and would also wreck the National Government's domestic policies, and he was indeed correct on both counts. It was assumed that if conflict broke out with Germany, then Japan might be encouraged to attack Britain's Asian Empire. An American alliance did not seem a welcome solution, as the Americans were regarded as a threat to British imperial interests and unlikely to provide consistent support. Thus, appeasement was designed to avoid both war and unwelcome alliances.

As late as 9 March 1939, Chamberlain gave a very positive account of the prospects for peace to a lobby briefing in Downing Street. Next day, Sir Samuel Hoare, the rehabilitated Home Secretary, predicted an imminent 'golden age' of European peace and plenty based on cooperation between Britain, France, Germany and Italy. On 15 March, however, Hitler occupied Prague, the capital of Czechoslovakia, and renounced all the guarantees he had earlier made in the Munich agreement. Appeasement had failed, obviously so.

# Judging appeasement

Appeasement, and the nature of Britain's role in the origins and early stages of World War Two, were highly controversial at the time, and became so again in the 1990s. Fundamental questions were raised, including the role of a moral perspective in international relations. In some respects, all foreign policy involves a process of compromise that can be negatively described as appeasement. The process of establishing goals and priorities, and compromising with both the views of other powers and the apparent limitations presented by British resources, was (and is) difficult, and liable to give rise to controversy. This was shown in relations with China over Hong Kong in the 1980s and 1990s, when Hong Kong's newly introduced, fragile democracy was left with no guarantees, and in British policy towards Serbia in the 1990s.

The controversial nature of foreign policy was seen with the response to the Spanish Civil War of 1936–9 in which a left-wing Republican government was overthrown by a right-wing uprising led by Franco. The British response was very mixed. Under the Foreign Enlistment Act of 1870, the government prohibited recruitment for service in Spain, but 2,000 British volunteers served in the International Brigades against Franco, and 526 died. Most were left-wing and many were recruited through the Communist Party. Conversely, most of the trade union movement, both leaders and workers, were only cautiously committed to the Republican cause, which they generally saw as a foreign issue, and many Catholic workers refused to back the Republicans, who were anti-clerical. Churchill and many Conservatives backed Franco, seeing him as a bulwark against Communism.

Those who went to fight Fascism in Spain had a worldview in which developments in Britain could be understood in terms of those on the Continent, and vice versa. This was particularly held by those who were hostile to the nature or content of contemporary British politics. A search for new solutions, especially in the face of the Depression of the 1930s, led critics to turn to radical alternatives that were associated with foreign regimes. Thus Mosley turned to Fascism, some elements in Plaid Cymru looked to Mussolini and were denounced as neo-fascists, and from 1933, Communists and left-wing Labour activists in Wales proposed the formation of workers' defence groups or militias on Continental lines.

The bulk of the population, however, preferred to see Britain in isolation. Furthermore, with, unlike much of the Continent, only a relatively small standing army and no peacetime conscription, Britain was not prepared for sustained and extensive Continental warfare. Her society was patriotic and, at times, jingoistic, but it was not militaristic. Unlike in much of the Continent, there were few men in military uniforms on the streets. Furthermore, even if mobilised, Britain could do little in Central or Eastern Europe. Commenting on Hitler's threat to Austria, Harold Nicolson noted in 1934, 'We cannot send the Atlantic fleet to Linz.' The Dominions did not want war with Germany, and their leaders applauded the Munich agreement. The British service chiefs also urged caution. They were well aware of Britain's numerous commitments throughout the world and warned about the dangers of military action on the Continent. Servicemen anxious about British readiness for war secretly informed Churchill of the low state of armaments, especially aircraft. The Treasury was against an arms buildup, and concern about the German air force, particularly an exaggerated fear about what German bombing could achieve, also induced caution. In 1938, the Royal Air Force had only 103 modern fighters.

Labour, as well as the Conservatives, was for long unsure about how best to respond to Hitler. Due to a strong pacifist component, Labour was divided over rearmament, and in the 1935 election Chamberlain was denounced as a warmonger by Labour politicians. Initially, the official Labour line was one of reliance on the League of Nations, but, as the League became clearly unable to stop Hitler, the Labour leadership pressed for a firmer British response and for rearmament.

Britain's limitations as a military power do not answer the question of whether British policy could have been more effective in achieving its goals. Rearmament was pressed hard, and defence expenditure rose to 30% of government spending in 1938. As Prime Minister, although not earlier as Chancellor of the Exchequer, Chamberlain was especially keen to boost production of fighter aircraft. That was not enough. Britain needed allies if she was to deter effectively, but there was no powerful alliance system comparable to that in 1914. France had been greatly weakened by World War One, and confidence in the ability of an Anglo-French alliance to prevent German expansionism in Eastern Europe was limited. This caution may have been excessive, given the weaknesses of the Nazi regime, not least a lack of enthusiasm among the generals, but it is possibly too easy in hindsight to criticise the leaders of the period, and, not least, to underrate their fear of causing a second 'Great War'.

**Neville Chamberlain (1869–1940)**
Although he had been an important Minister of Health and Chancellor of the Exchequer, Chamberlain's career was overshadowed by deteriorating relations with Germany while he was Prime Minister (1937–40). He is seen here with Hitler and his Foreign Minister in 1938. Having failed to limit German expansionism, Chamberlain gave the guarantee to Poland in 1939 that led to war later that year. He resigned in 1940 when the successful German invasion of Norway sapped confidence in his leadership.

Unlike in 1914, Russia was no longer an ally, and nor was Japan. Furthermore, isolationist America had passed Neutrality Acts from 1935, and was seen as self-interested. The British government was suspicious of America, seeing her as a threat to the British economy and, in particular, to the system of British Imperial Preference, to which, in truth, the Americans were hostile. Chamberlain was particularly suspicious of American intentions and policies, although a trade agreement was signed in 1938.

Unhappy with Britain's allies and potential allies, the government preferred to negotiate directly with the expansionist powers. This policy focused on Germany, because it was felt that Japan would be cautious if peace was maintained with Hitler. Italy was not treated as a serious threat, and instead, was regarded as a possible ally. Hitler was seen as impulsive but ready to do a deal on the basis of a revision of the 1919 terms. A trade agreement in 1934 had been followed by a naval convention in 1935, but, thereafter, the British government had little to offer, especially as Hitler did not want the return of the colonies lost as a result of World War One. Nevertheless, a sense that compromise was possible, combined with a lack of interest in the areas threatened by German expansionism, encouraged a conciliatory search for a settlement that led to the Munich agreement. This was unsuccessful and also discouraged potential allies against Germany.

In 1939, there was a breakdown of confidence in negotiating directly with Germany, but the attempt to create a powerful opposing alliance left Britain offering implausible guarantees to the exposed states of Poland and Romania as well as being unable to prevent the Soviet Union from joining Hitler; instead she was reliant on the French, who were to be revealed, when Germany attacked in 1940, as a flawed ally, both militarily and politically.

Had the 1939 negotiations for a triple alliance of Britain, France and the Soviet Union succeeded, then Hitler might have been deterred from acting. They collapsed, however, in August 1939, largely because Britain and France could not satisfy the Soviets on the issue of Polish and Romanian consent to the passage of Soviet forces in the event of war. This should be considered when assessing claims that Britain could have done more to win Soviet support. Earlier, the idea of a four-power declaration by Britain, France, Poland and the Soviet Union had fallen foul of Polish opposition.

This failure reflected the nature of the Anglo-French alliance system in Eastern Europe, especially the concern of Britain, France, Poland and Romania that the Soviet Union was a threat. Given Soviet cooperation with Germany in 1939–41, and Soviet control of much of Eastern Europe in 1945–89, this was a reasonable supposition, although there is a danger of reading back from the war and post-war experience, and British fears may have been exaggerated. Stalin was interested in some form of agreement with Britain, but the Foreign Office was highly suspicious. The Nazi–Soviet Pact of August 1939 was crucial in encouraging Hitler to invade Poland, given the failure of Italy to act in Hitler's support and the unexpected determination of Britain and France to fulfil their guarantee of Polish independence given after the Nazi seizure of Prague.

Hitler persisted despite the guarantee. He believed that Britain and France would not fight, especially as a result of his pact with Stalin. Indeed, the British Chiefs of Staff had advised that it would not be possible to offer Poland any direct assistance. Chamberlain sought to abandon the guarantee to Poland when Hitler attacked.

Nevertheless, the German attack led Britain and France to declare war on

3 September 1939. It seemed necessary to help Poland in order to prevent German domination of Eastern Europe and the collapse of the alliance with France. Further-more, domestic opinion had moved against appeasement, and this affected both the Conservative Party and the opposition. Both Parliament and public opinion now saw war with an untrustworthy Nazi Germany as inevitable. Churchill, who had been a harsh critic of appeasement, told the Commons that day:

This is not a question of fighting for Danzig or fighting for Poland. We are fighting to save the whole world from the pestilence of Nazi tyranny and in defence of all that is most sacred to man. This is no war for domination or imperial aggrandisement or material gain; no war to shut any country out of its sunlight and means of progress. It is a war, viewed in its inherent quality, to establish on impregnable rocks, the rights of the individual, and it is a war to estab-lish and revive the stature of man.

# ■ World War Two, 1939–45

Once war had broken out, Chamberlain hoped that a limited war, including the naval blockade of Germany, would lead Hitler to negotiate or would lead to his over-throw. Poland was quickly conquered by Germany, and the Soviets joined in to overrun part of it. Britain and France were determined to fight on to prevent German hegemony. This led Hitler to plan the attack on France eventually launched in May 1940. France collapsed nearly as fast as Denmark, Norway, the Netherlands and Belgium, all of which fell to Germany in early 1940. The British were driven from the Continent, although much of the British army was successfully evacuated from the beaches near Dunkirk. Britain appeared to have lost the war. Churchill replaced Chamberlain as Prime Minister in May 1940. Several leading politicians, including Chamberlain, felt it necessary to consider a negotiated peace. In May 1940 Viscount Halifax, the Foreign Secretary, was ready, if Hitler made one, 'to accept an offer which would save the country from avoidable disaster'.

Churchill, however, was unwilling to trust Hitler and determined to fight on. He successfully outmanoeuvred his rivals in the government, but the military situation was still parlous. Late 1940 and early 1941 was the nadir of Britain's twentieth century. Isolated, apart from the crucial support of the Empire, and effectively bankrupt, she suffered further defeats with the fall of Greece to Germany in 1941. Operation Sealion, the planned German invasion of southern England, had been called off, after the German air force failed to gain air superiority over the invasion beaches in the Battle of Britain in July–September 1940. Crucial as this was, it was a victory only in that it denied Germany triumph. There was no sign that Britain was strong enough to challenge German control of the Continent. Furthermore, German pressure on Britain increased in the winter of 1940–1. The 'Blitz' – the bombing of Britain, that began in August 1940 and lasted until May 1941, with later less intensive, but still serious, revivals – was very damaging, and made it clear how far Britain had been pushed back onto the defensive. Cities such as Coventry, London and Southampton were devastated. Submarine attacks on British trade routes, especially the crucial supply route from North America, raised the pressure on the British economy and on food supplies. The fall of France had increased British vulnerability, as German submarines could now be based on the west coast of France. In 1941, German surface warships also attacked British trade.

The Germans also challenged Britain's position in the Middle East. Italy under

**London Blitz, 1940**
London was frequently attacked between September 1940 and May 1941. About 19,000 tons of bombs were dropped and there were heavy civilian casualties. The bombing failed to drive Britain out of the war.

**Vickers-Armstrong Supermarine Spitfires flying in formation, 1939.**
The following year these and other fighters outfought the German Luftwaffe in the Battle of Britain. Between 10 July and 31 October 1940, 915 British and 1733 German fighters were destroyed. This was crucial as the British were building twice as many as their opponents per month.

Mussolini had entered the war in 1940, and he launched attacks on British positions in East Africa and Egypt. These were swiftly checked and the Italian armies in Ethiopia and Libya were heavily defeated in early 1941. However, the Germans sent a force under Rommel that in April 1941 drove the British back into Egypt. Churchill's future as Prime Minister was in doubt.

The total change in the situation in 1941 owed little to Britain. Hitler's attack on the Soviet Union, Operation Barbarossa, launched on 22 June, and his declaration of war on the USA following his ally Japan's attack on her (and on British and Dutch colonies) that December, were what led to the defeat of Germany and Japan in 1945. German and Japanese advances in 1942 were still very serious. The British lost Hong Kong, Malaya and Burma to the Japanese. The surrender of Singapore on 15 February 1942 was a major disaster. The British had been outfought by a smaller Japanese army in the Malaya campaign, and the surrender shattered British prestige in Asia. The Germans pushed into Egypt, while German submarine attacks continued to inflict heavy losses in the Atlantic.

However, the Germans and Japanese were held in 1942 – by the British in Egypt and on the India–Burma border respectively; and serious defeats were inflicted. The Americans beat the Japanese at Midway in the Pacific, the British beat the Germans at El Alamein in Egypt, the Soviets beat the Germans at Stalingrad. Germany and Japan were driven back the following year. Germany's ally Italy was successfully invaded in 1943, followed by France, with the D-Day landings on 6 June 1944. By the end of 1944, France had been cleared. Meanwhile the Soviets advanced across Eastern Europe, and the Americans 'island hopped' towards Japan.

In 1945, Germany was invaded from west and east, and Hitler committed suicide in the ruins of Berlin as the Soviets captured the city. His successors were forced to surrender unconditionally. Japan was driven to the same fate by the American use of atomic bombs. Although subsequently the cause of considerable criticism, this spared the Allies (and the Japanese) the very heavy casualties that had been anticipated had Japan itself been invaded. In the closing months of the war against Japan, the British had recaptured Burma. The Allied bombing of Germany was also controversial, and doubts about its morality had been raised at the time, for example by the Bishop of Chichester. Leaving aside the moral dimension of raids, such as that on Dresden in 1945, there is also the question of whether the heavy losses of manpower in bombing Germany was justified. At the time, however, the bombing campaign was widely seen as a return for German air attacks and also as likely to disrupt the German war effort and hit morale. There is only limited evidence for the latter, and, although the German war economy was seriously damaged by bombing, the night-time attacks on cities contributed little to this goal.

**Planning the post-war world**
Churchill, Roosevelt and Stalin (*seated from left to right*) with their respective Foreign Ministers behind them (Eden, Stettinius and Molotov) at the Yalta conference (February 1945). Such conferences helped sustain the impression of Britain as a great power, but in fact the strains of war had seriously weakened her, and the post-war world was to be dominated by the USA and the Soviet Union.

World War Two bore hard on Britain. She suffered greatly in casualties and resources. Britain lost 25 per cent of its national wealth in World War Two and was the world's greatest debtor nation by 1945. However, despite this, and Churchill's participation in a series of wartime conferences of Allied leaders, the USA and the Soviet Union, not Britain, provided the crucial fighting power and economic strength to win. The degree of British financial dependence upon the USA was marked; it would become more so after the war. It has been claimed that in order to win American support, Britain surrendered her existence as an independent power and was transformed into an American satellite; although it is not clear that there was any real alternative after the defeats of 1940. It was difficult to have any confidence in the idea of negotiating with Hitler. His treatment of France in 1940, and later his seizure of the satellite state of Vichy France, was scarcely an encouraging comparison.

# The Cold War

Wartime alliances frequently do not survive peace. This was particularly true of World War Two, because of the ideological division between Communism and the anti-Communist powers. Arguably the alliance did not survive the war itself: by early 1945 differences over the fate of Eastern Europe were readily apparent. The Soviet Union soon appeared to pose a threat comparable to that of Nazi Germany. Soviet actions in Eastern Europe appeared to vindicate Churchill's claim in March 1946 that an 'Iron Curtain' was descending from the Baltic to the Atlantic. Europe was thus presented as divided between free and unfree. The Labour government quickly came to accept his view, and the Foreign Secretary from 1945 until 1951, Ernest Bevin, was particularly concerned to contain Soviet expansion and to persuade the USA to this end. On 14 March 1946, the British embassy in Moscow asked if the world was not 'faced with the danger of the modern equivalent of the religious wars of the sixteenth century', with Soviet Communism battling against Western-European social democracy and American capitalism for 'domination of the world'. Early 1946 was a period of mounting crisis, with anxiety about Soviet schemes in Greece, Iran and Turkey, and concern about Communist strength in Western Europe. The Soviet government was increasingly anti-British in tone.

The débâcle of 1940 had revealed that an alliance of Britain and other European powers was unable to guarantee their territorial integrity, although, after the war, there was interest in alliance with France, leading to the Treaty of Dunkirk of March 1947 (Churchill had proposed a Franco-British union in 1940). However, in response to fears about Soviet plans, an American alliance appeared essential. In February 1947, the British acknowledged that they could no longer provide the military and economic aid deemed necessary to keep Greece and Turkey out of Communist hands. Instead, the British successfully sought American intervention. Concerned about Communism, the Americans did not intend to repeat their inter-war isolationism. This became more important to British policy than earlier ideas of Western European collaboration. Similarly, in 1949, the British encouraged the Americans to become involved in resisting Communist expansion in South-East Asia: the French were under pressure in Indo-China, the British in Malaya. Bevin's policies were criticised from the left of the Labour Party, especially in the 'keep left' campaign of May 1947, in which Richard Crossman, Michael Foot and others on the Left attacked what they saw as dependence on America.

### Ernest Bevin (1881–1951)

A longstanding trade unionist, General Secretary of the leading union, the Transport and General Workers' Union, in 1921–40, and Minister of Labour in 1940–5, Bevin was Foreign Secretary from July 1945 until March 1951. As such, he was instrumental in organising Britain's response to the post-war world. A firm anti-Communist, from his trade union days, Bevin was concerned about the expansion of Soviet power in Eastern Europe and helped to negotiate the creation of NATO.

Bevin was also a supporter of the decisions to make a British atom bomb and to take part in the Korean War. Bevin was committed to the continuation of the British Empire, but found it impossible to negotiate a peaceful end to the Palestine mandate.

Confrontation with the Soviet Union was to be the main theme of the late 1940s and early 1950s, but it did not drown out two other themes: first, a period of fundamental change in the Empire, and secondly, faltering steps with regard to European cooperation. World War Two was far more damaging than World War One for the Empire. The British occupied both Italian Somaliland and Libya, another part of the Italian empire, during the war, and Churchill considered the annexation of the latter; but such views were now anachronistic. They were also inimical to the new world order of independent, capitalist democracies which the USA wanted to see. Instead, the Labour government elected in 1945 withdrew from much of the Empire. The granting of independence to the Indian sub-continent, which became the separate states of India, Pakistan, Ceylon (Sri Lanka), and Burma, in 1947–8, was followed by the ending of the Palestine mandate in 1948, and of Crown Colony status for Newfoundland in 1949. The sterling crisis of April 1949 underlined British weakness.

These steps were not intended to mark the end of Empire, but rather, they were intended to provide the means for continued informal control. Indeed, the government sent troops to maintain the British position in the economically crucial colony of Malaya, in the face of a Communist insurrection. Bevin hoped to use imperial resources to make Britain a less unequal partner in the Anglo-American alliance. The government, for example, sought to develop the economy of British East Africa, with an ambitious, and ultimately unsuccessful, Groundnuts Scheme, designed to increase the supply of vegetable oils and fats within the sterling area, in order to cut imports from non-sterling areas. Bevin acted in a lordly fashion in the Middle East. Nevertheless, India had been the most populous and important part of the Empire and the area that most engaged the imaginative attention of the British. Once India had been granted independence, it was difficult to summon up much popular interest in the retention of the remainder of the Empire.

## ◼ The formation of a European Community

With the hindsight of the late 1990s, the big question over British foreign policy in the fifteen years after World War Two is why Britain did not join what was initially called the Common Market (European Economic Community: EEC), which became the European Union (EU). In large part, this is a poorly posed question, because most commentators in the late 1940s did not foresee such an outcome. Nevertheless, even had they done so, there was still a sense of British difference and distance. Western European cooperation, actively pressed by the French, was an option after World War Two, but British willingness was lessened by a suspicion of federalist intentions and a determination to preserve independence. Although there was interest, especially in 1945–6, in the idea of a Western European 'Third Force', independent of the Soviet Union and the USA, and of a related economic and commercial 'Western Union', the British saw the USA, the Commonwealth and the Empire as more vital economic and political links. This view was strengthened by the economic, political and military weakness of the Western European states, and by the willingness of the USA to avoid isolation, unlike after World War One. The North Atlantic Treaty Organisation (NATO), created in 1949, replaced the idea of a Western European 'Third Force'.

In 1950, the Labour government rejected an invitation to join negotiations for a European Coal and Steel Community. Attlee told the Commons, 'We on this side are not prepared to accept the principle that the most vital economic forces of the country should be handed over to an authority that is utterly undemocratic and is responsible to nobody.' Having nationalised these industries, Labour did not wish to transfer control to a predominantly non-Socialist organisation.

Churchill pressed the case for a 'United States of Europe' in 1946, but he saw Britain as a friendly outsider and stressed the need for a partnership between France and Germany as the basis for this new Europe. Churchill declared, at a 'United Europe' rally in May 1947, that the international order rested on four principal pillars: the USA, the Soviet Union, the British Empire and Commonwealth, and Europe. Bevin was similarly opposed to seeing Britain treated simply as part of Europe, and wanted Britain to be treated differently from the rest of Europe in her acceptance of American Marshall Aid for post-war reconstruction. In 1950, he replied to an American proposal by claiming that:

Great Britain was not part of Europe; she was not simply a Luxembourg. . . . The people in this country were pinning their faith on a policy of defence built on a Commonwealth–USA basis – an English-speaking basis. People here are frankly doubtful of Europe. How could he [Bevin] go down to his constituency – Woolwich – which had been bombed by Germans in the war, and tell his constituents that the Germans would help them in a war against Russia.

The government was distrustful of French plans for a European Army, although, following Eden's return as Conservative Foreign Secretary in 1951, the British gave active support to the European Defence Community, and they only abandoned the European Army concept in June 1954 when its failure seemed certain. A more traditional problem was captured in 1951 when the Conservative Selwyn Lloyd became Minister of State at the Foreign Office and admitted that he disliked foreigners, did not speak any foreign language, and, except for World War Two, had never visited a foreign country. This was an admission of what was a more widespread lack of sympathy.

There was a deeper reason, however, for distance from Europe. In Western Europe, many earlier political parties, especially those on the Right, had been discredited by the events of the 1930s and 1940s, and political structures had been found inadequate. This created a situation of political and governmental fluidity, and led to a sense that change was necessary. The creation of the EEC was part of a process in which the political structures and party politics of France, Germany and

Italy were transformed between 1945 and 1958. Britain was separate from this process. She also lacked the direct experience of territorial invasion and devastation that affected France and Germany. Controlling the sinews of war meant far more to them than to Britain.

In political and institutional terms, therefore, the creation of the EEC in 1958, as a result of the Messina conferences of 1955 and 1956 and the Treaty of Rome of 1957, was both effect and cause of a divergence between Britain and the leading Western European states. The difference was seen further in 1959 when the British inspired a European Free Trade Association (EFTA) of countries not in the EEC, including Eire, Denmark, Norway and Portugal. It was restricted to commercial matters, and lacked the idealistic and federalist flavour of the EEC.

# The 1950s: Cold War and the ebbing of Empire

The Cold War gathered pace from 1947, as Britain and the USA responded to the consolidation of Soviet power in Eastern Europe, a consolidation that climaxed with the Communist coup in Prague in 1948. Attlee had decided by January 1947 to develop a British nuclear bomb. This policy was regarded as necessary for Britain's security and influence, and, throughout, the British sought to play more than a secondary role. The Berlin Crisis of 1948 led to the stationing of American B-29 strategic bombers in Britain. In the event of war, they were designed to bomb the Soviet Union. The threat of the use of the nuclear deterrent helped bring a solution to the crisis, but the bombers remained. East Anglian bases, especially Lakenheath and Mildenhall, became little Americas. The following year, the foundation of the North Atlantic Treaty Organisation (NATO) created a security framework for Western Europe. Bevin took a prominent role in its formation.

The USA was thus anchored in the defence of Western Europe. Yet, there were heavy costs. Under American pressure, Britain embarked in 1950 on a costly rearmament programme that undid the economic gains made since 1948 and strengthened the military commitment that was to be such a heavy post-war economic burden. The British were to devote a higher percentage of national resources to defence than economic rivals such as Germany. Furthermore, high defence spending was to influence economic policy. British forces also played a role in resisting Communist aggression in the Korean War of 1950–3. They were the second largest foreign contingent after the Americans. It was difficult to defend the commitment in terms of

---

**Box 13.2**

### Atomic vulnerability

After Britain became a base for American aircraft armed with atomic bombs, Brendan Bracken, a Conservative MP and the manager of the *Financial Times*, wrote in 1950: 'What a wonderful thought it is that President Truman, can ring a bell and give an order that American aircraft can load their bombs and fly from London to Moscow. The interest of their visit will not be returned on Washington, it will be returned on poor old London. All this talk about . . . national sovereignty doesn't mean much when the President of the United States of America can use England as an aircraft carrier without the knowledge of the ship's company.'

traditional British interests, and the Americans tended to take decisions without much or any consultation, but, nevertheless, the Attlee government played a major part in encouraging a firm response, including the broadening of the Allied role to encompass driving the Communists from North Korea.

The policy of the Attlee government was supported by the vast majority of the Labour Party and trade union movement. Communist and Soviet sympathisers within both were isolated and the Communist Party was kept at a distance. This helped prevent the development of a radical Left and was linked to the alliance between labour and capital that was to be important in the post-war mixed economy. At the same time, from the winter of 1950–1, the Attlee government was keen to explore the possibility of better relations with the Soviet Union. Furthermore, in 1950, Britain recognised the Communist government of China, rather than following America in treating the exiled government in Taiwan as that of China. In response, the Americans refused British requests to join the ANZUS Pact of 1951 between the United States, Australia and New Zealand.

Britain still saw itself as a major imperial power, and, when Churchill regained power in 1951, he had no intention of dismantling the Empire. However, Britain lacked the resources to sustain the Colonial Office policies outlined in the successive Colonial Development and Welfare Acts of 1940, 1945, 1949, 1950 and 1959, and government action was able to provide only a portion of the investment necessary for colonial economic development. Other ministries opposed colonial industrialisation as a threat to British interests at a time when the war-ravaged economies of Western Europe were beginning to recover their strength. In 1956, Harold Macmillan, then Chancellor of the Exchequer, revealed anxiety about the cost of colonial aid.

Nevertheless, there was still a determination to act as an imperial power. Although global commitments were reduced in some areas, elsewhere they were maintained and even expanded. In south-west Arabia, Britain pursued a forward policy involving a vigorous assertion of British interests. Aside from an attempt to create a federation in the Aden Protectorates, there were also ambitious plans for economic development, a drive into the interior in search of oil, and a determined attempt to exclude Yemeni and Saudi influence. However, these measures led to an increased political and military commitment to the region which proved unsustainable against the local and external opposition which the new policies stimulated.

In 1956, the weakness of the imperial response and the limited domestic popularity of Empire were exposed in the Suez crisis. Britain and France attacked Egypt, an intervention publicly justified at the time as a way of safeguarding the Suez Canal, which had been nationalised by the aggressive Egyptian leader Gamal Abdel Nasser (the British had withdrawn their troops from the Canal Zone in 1953). Nasser's Arab nationalism was also seen as a threat to the French position in Algeria and to Britain's Arab allies.

Just as references to the appeasement of dictators in the 1930s were initially to be expressed when the Argentinians invaded the Falklands in 1982, and it was thought, misleadingly, that the Thatcher government would not respond, most prominently by the Labour leader Michael Foot; so, in 1956, the Prime Minister, Anthony Eden, was determined to act. He had resigned as Foreign Secretary in 1938 ostensibly in protest at appeasement, and saw Nasser as another Fascist dictator. The invasion was poorly planned, but it was abandoned, in large part, because of American opposition. Concerned about the impact of the invasion on attitudes in the Third World, the Americans, who were ambivalent about many aspects of British policy, refused to extend any credits to support sterling, blocked British access to the International Monetary Fund until she withdrew her troops from Suez, and refused to provide oil to compensate for interrupted supplies from the Middle East. American opposition was crucial in weakening British resolve, and led to a humiliating withdrawal. It underlined the vulnerability of the British economy. President Eisenhower was dubious about many aspects of the special relationship, especially in the Middle East, and had made this clear to Churchill in 1953. In January 1954, Sir Roger Makins, the British Ambassador in Washington, had expressed concern that 'the Americans are out to take our place in the Middle East'. The crisis strained British relations not only with America but also with other powers, both Commonwealth such as Canada, and non-aligned, and, not least, with France. It can be seen as the end of Britain's ability to act wholly independently; from then on, there was an implicit reliance on American acceptance.

Prime Minister in 1957–63, Macmillan set out to restore relations with the USA, rather than to preserve, let alone try to strengthen, the Empire. He put much effort into this task, but he was a suppliant, as American policy over the provision of missiles for Britain's nuclear bombs was to demonstrate. In October 1957, Macmillan claimed to have succeeded 'in regaining the special relationship with the US which we had previously enjoyed'. In 1960, he described 'the British as Greeks in the Roman Empire of the Americans', in other words, the providers of wisdom.

The overthrow of the pro-British Iraqi government in 1958 underlined the limitations of British power, and was followed by Britain encouraging the USA to take over its former responsibilities in the Middle East. There was a wave of de-colonisation, and much of the Empire was dismantled, especially in Africa, but also in the West Indies and Malaysia. Churchill and Eden would have been less willing to abandon the Empire at this rate. De-colonisation was hastened by a strong upsurge in colonial nationalist movements, particularly in West Africa, which policy-makers did not know how to confront. De-colonisation proceeded on the simple assumption that Britain would withdraw from those areas which it could no longer control (or, equally importantly, from those areas where the cost of maintaining a presence was prohibitive). Although criticised by some right-wing Conservatives, especially the Suez Group and the Marquess of Salisbury, who resigned over the issue, de-colonisation was not a central issue in British politics. Colonies appeared less necessary in defence terms, not least because Britain had in 1957 added the hydrogen bomb to the atom bomb.

Independence was granted to Ghana and Malaya in 1957, and to British Somaliland, Nigeria and Cyprus in 1960, the last being especially significant as it had been said that Cyprus would 'never' be independent, and because, with a small population, it set the precedent for the cession of independence to such territories. Sierra Leone, Southern Cameroons (as part of Cameroon), and Tanganyika followed in 1961, Jamaica, Trinidad, and Uganda in 1962, Sabah, Sarawak, Singapore, Zanzibar, and Kenya in 1963.

 The departure from Empire led added force to Macmillan's unsuccessful bid to join the EEC. It also provided one of the might-have-beens of post-war British history. There was fighting in the last stages of Empire, not only the Suez crisis of 1956, but also resistance to nationalists in Aden, Kenya and Malaya, and confrontation with Indonesia over Malaysia; but nothing on the scale that the French faced in their attempt to retain Indo-China (1946–54) and Algeria (1954–62), or that the Portuguese confronted in their African colonies. The defence of imperial pretensions depicted in the popular film *Zulu* (1964) was an incident from 1879. It is unclear how far a major nationalist rising in, or foreign invasion of, a British colony would have led to a substantial response that might have proved bitterly divisive within Britain. Certainly, de-colonisation did not prove as divisive for the Conservatives as Europe was to be in the late 1980s and 1990s. In part, this was because the Empire was seen as being transformed into the Commonwealth, rather than lost. The British view of Empire was important. The logic of Britain's imperial mission, bringing civilisation to backward areas of the globe, allowed Britain to present the granting of self-government as the inevitable terminus of Empire. The contraction of Empire was also relatively painless, because interest in much of it was limited. This was not the case with some traditional Conservative interests, such as the military, but was the case with much of the party's middle-class support.

If imperial diehards represented one critique of government policy and the foreign-policy consensus, another was provided by the Campaign for Nuclear Disarmament (CND) launched in 1958. That year, 9,000 people marched in protest from London to the Atomic Weapons Research Establishment at Aldermaston. In 1960, the philosopher Bertrand Russell organised a campaign of non-violent civil disobedience. Its impact, however, was limited.

# Joining Europe

Support for joining the EEC became more widespread in British political circles as it became clear that the organisation would be a success, particularly in terms of the level of economic growth enjoyed by the member states. The loss of British influence in Washington was also an issue, as America was keen for Britain to join. Macmillan, who saw himself as a moderniser, able to fill his sails with the 'winds of change', applied to join in 1961, in part because he thought the Americans wanted a stronger Europe, as, indeed, they did (see Chapter 10). In June 1962, however, the French President, Charles De Gaulle, made it clear to Macmillan that he preferred an EEC without Britain. He told him that British entry would totally alter the character of the EEC in political as well as economic terms, and that Britain was too close to America. Anglo-American relations also played a major role in the disagreement between the two men over possible cooperation in nuclear weaponry. In January 1963, notwithstanding the support for British entry from the other members of the EEC, France vetoed the British application, De Gaulle declaring at a press conference at the Elysée Palace, 'England is insular . . . the nature and structure and economic context of England differ profoundly from those of the other states of the Continent.'

Even though there was a degree of what could be described as proto-Euroscepticism in the Conservative Party, the Labour Party was more ambivalent about the EEC than the Conservatives, in part because of fear that Continental workers would accept lower levels of social protection and welfare, and thus price their British counterparts out of work. Hugh Gaitskell, Labour's leader in 1955–63, declared, in a television interview on 21 September 1962, that entry into the EEC 'means the end of Britain as an independent nation; we become no more than Texas or California in the United States of Europe. It means the end of a thousand years of history'.

There was a rethink when Labour came to power in 1964 under a new leader, Harold Wilson. Wilson had initially hoped to maintain Britain's role as a major independent power. This, however, had to be abandoned in the face of the country's severe financial problems. As a result, the government decided to abandon Britain's military position 'east of Suez'. British forces were withdrawn from Aden in 1967, and from the Persian Gulf and Singapore in 1971. Unlike Australia and New Zealand, Britain did not come to the assistance of the USA in Vietnam: for Britain, Vietnam was to be no second Korea. Britain became increasingly irrelevant to Pacific states. De-colonisation continued. Gambia and the Maldives gained independence in 1965, Bechuanaland, Basutoland and Barbados in 1966, Aden in 1967, Mauritius, Nauru and Swaziland in 1969, and Tonga and Fiji in 1970. There was little left, apart from such far flung outposts as the Falkland Islands, Gibraltar, and Hong Kong.

Britain's international commitments were increasingly centred on Western Europe. Defence priorities were focused on deterring a Soviet invasion of Western Europe. The government launched a new bid to join the EEC, securing a massive Commons pro-entry vote of 488 to 62. Wilson was motivated largely by commercial reasons, although some of his colleagues, such as Roy Jenkins, were more enthusiastic about the political possibilities. Britain seemed more enthusiastic about entry in 1966–7 than it had been in 1961–3. Wilson and his pro-European Foreign Secretary, George Brown, undertook a tour of those countries which were already members of the EEC. De Gaulle, however, blocked this second attempt. This time he emphasised the underlying weaknesses of the British economy. The Wilson government responded by saying that it would not take 'non' for an answer: Britain would leave the application 'on the table'. The appointment of Christopher Soames, a prominent pro-European Conservative, as British Ambassador to Paris showed that there was now a domestic political consensus in favour of Britain's membership of the EEC. Negotiations were set to begin again at the end of June 1970.

This still left Britain in a difficult position. It was increasingly cut off from an EEC that was benefiting from higher growth rates and pressing ahead without consulting Britain. The 'special relationship' with the USA, that Macmillan had worked hard to restore after the Suez débâcle, was in difficulties. President Johnson was angered by the failure to send troops to Vietnam, by the rundown of the British role east of Suez at a time when the USA was poorly placed to replace it, by British defence cuts, and by British attempts to mediate in the Vietnam War.

These attempts reflected Wilson's desire to act as a major figure on the international stage. He sought to be a peacemaker: to end the unilateral declaration of independence by the white settlers in Southern Rhodesia, to end conflict between Pakistan and India, and to try to ease Cold War tensions, the last following a course set by Churchill, Eden and Macmillan. However, the effect of the devaluation of sterling in 1967 weakened British prestige, and the attempt to act as an independent power brought scant benefit. Britain also lacked the necessary diplomatic strength. The Commonwealth was not able or willing to provide necessary support, EFTA was not intended as a political force, and, anyway, was weak, and Britain faced intractable problems, including a Rhodesian government unwilling to abandon white supremacy. Britain's options seemed no longer to be those of independence and alliance from a position of strength, but, instead, to be those of joining the American or European systems. This indeed was to be the theme of British power politics over the following quarter-century.

In the early 1970s, a decision for Europe was made again. This reflected both positive feelings about the advantage of joining the EEC, and concern about the alternatives. The USA, under Richard Nixon, President from 1969, seemed an unattractive ally. Although he was keen to withdraw from Vietnam, Nixon's policies led to fresh American commitments in Cambodia and Laos. These seemed far distant from Britain's interests.

Edward Heath, Prime Minister in 1970–4, was not keen on close cooperation with the USA, and was determined not to be branded as the American spokesman in Europe. Instead, he pushed hard for British membership in the EEC, seeing this as crucial to his vision for the modernisation of Britain (see Chapter 10), and as a way for it to play a convincing role on the world stage. De Gaulle's resignation in 1969 was a necessary prelude to the invitation by the EEC the following year to four applicants – Britain, Ireland, Denmark and Norway – to resume negotiations for membership. By the time they resumed at the end of June 1970, Heath had replaced Wilson as Prime Minister. De Gaulle's successor, Pompidou, was concerned about German strength, rather than Anglo-American links. The four signed the treaty of accession in Brussels on 22 January 1972. The negotiations were relatively easy for two reasons. First, Heath was prepared to surrender much in order to obtain membership. He accepted the EEC's Common Agricultural Policy, although it had little to offer Britain. Cheap food from the Commonwealth, especially New Zealand lamb, was to be excluded, in order to maintain the market for more expensive, subsidised Continental products. Secondly, there was only limited opposition within the Conservative Party, still less the government. Membership was criticised most strongly by the left wing of the Labour Party, whose dominance forced Wilson to declare that he opposed entry on the terms which Heath had negotiated, although Labour supporters of EEC membership, led by Jenkins, were willing to vote with the government, thus providing crucial parliamentary support. Heath pushed membership hard on its economic merits, arguing that it opened up markets. In contrast, he said little about possible political consequences. Heath claimed that there would be no lessening of national identity, and ignored warnings to the contrary. He followed up EEC membership by further coolness towards the USA. In April 1973, Heath did not respond positively to the call for a new Atlantic Charter from the American Secretary of State, Henry Kissinger. Instead, he followed the French lead.

Policy changed when Labour returned to power under Wilson in February 1974. The new Foreign Secretary, James Callaghan, at once called for very close cooperation with the USA. This signalled a reassertion of Atlanticism in British overseas policy. In contrast to Heath's exploration of Anglo-French nuclear collaboration, the Labour government was to renew the nuclear alliance with the USA through the Chevaline programme. The end of the Vietnam War and Nixon's departure helped to make the USA seem a more acceptable ally.

EEC membership was re-examined, in large part in an effort to quieten critics on the Labour Left, not the first occasion on which foreign policy was subordinated to domestic considerations. The Wilson government entered into a protracted and largely cosmetic re-negotiation of Britain's terms of entry. The divided government scarcely displayed a principled commitment to a European cause. Wilson launched a constitutional novelty: a referendum campaign in which the principle of collective Cabinet responsibility would not apply. This was seen as the best way to surmount party divisions and keep the government together.

In the referendum on Britain's continued membership of the EEC, held on 5 June 1975, 67.2% of those who voted favoured membership, the only areas showing a majority against being the Shetlands and the Western Isles, while Protestant suspicion of Continental Catholicism was probably responsible for the limited support in Ulster. The available evidence suggests that public opinion was very volatile on the EEC, implying a lack of interest and/or understanding, and that the voters tended to follow the advice of the Party leaderships, all of which supported continued membership. The opposition was stigmatised as extreme, although opposition was from across the political spectrum, from Enoch Powell on the nationalist Right to Tony Benn on the Socialist Left. As he was a Cabinet minister, Benn was best placed to articulate concern about the EEC. He saw it as an undemocratic 'capitalist club', and told the Cabinet that 'on the EEC Commission, unlike the Council of Ministers, there is no British veto at all. You don't elect these people, they are Commissioners, and they are not accountable.' Benn also presented the EEC as incompatible with a truly Socialist Britain, not least by ending the possibility of national economic management. He argued that economic problems required the retention by the British government of powers to introduce import surcharges, devalue the pound and control capital movements, all of which would be threatened or lost if sovereignty was pooled within the EEC.

Benn saw the size of the opposition vote as 'some achievement considering we had absolutely no real organisation, no newspapers, nothing'. This was scant consolation. The referendum result was decisive. Britain stayed in. As a consequence, relations between Britain and the other members of the EEC were not to become as divisive a domestic political issue again, until they emerged in the late 1980s as the focus for divisions within the Thatcher government. There was no real controversy in 1979 when, fearful of the deflationary consequences of tying sterling to a strong Deutsche Mark, the government decided not to join the Exchange Rate Mechanism (ERM), the only one of the then nine EEC states not to do so. This decision was symptomatic of the reluctant Europeanism of the Callaghan government (Callaghan had succeeded Wilson as Prime Minister in April 1976). This, in turn, reflected Callaghan's ingrained Atlanticism, which was emphasised, on a personal level, when he appointed his son-in-law, Peter Jay, as Ambassador in Washington.

In the late 1970s, other issues took centre-stage in Britain. The economy and union relations were more pressing as domestic issues. The international body that seemed most powerful and effective was not the EEC, but the International Monetary Fund (IMF), from which the government sought a loan in 1976 and had to accept policy dictation. The constitutional issue that was most prominent was relations within Britain, specifically Scottish and Welsh devolution, not relations within the EEC (see Chapter 10). Outside Europe, the Labour governments of 1974–9 took a much less assertive stance than their predecessors of 1964–70 had done. Callaghan, nevertheless, ordered a continued naval presence in the South Atlantic in order to deter Argentinian action against the Falklands. Imperial fragments continued to gain independence – the Solomon Islands, Ellice Island and Dominica in 1978, the Gilbert Islands and St Vincent in 1979 – but the Empire's replacement, the Commonwealth, amounted to little in the international system, or even in British foreign policy; although it was vocal on Britain's relations with southern Africa. Policy towards Rhodesia and South Africa proved contentious, with Britain under pressure to take action against white minority regimes.

## The Thatcher years, 1979–90

Margaret Thatcher sought to centre Britain's international position on alliance with the USA, not membership of the EEC. She told a dinner, held in Washington in 1985

**Box 13.3**

## The Falklands War, 1982

The Falkland Islands in the South Atlantic were under British control from 1833, but were claimed as the Malvinas by the Argentinians, who were convinced by 1982 that the British government was not certain of the desirability of holding on to the colony. On 2 April, the virtually undefended islands were successfully invaded. The Thatcher government decided to respond with a task force and rejected American mediation attempts that would have left the Argentinians in control. On 25 April, the British recaptured the subsidiary territory of South Georgia, and on 2 May large-scale hostilities began when a British submarine sank the Argentine battleship *General Belgrano*. Landing on 21 May, British troops forced the Argentinians to surrender on 14 June. The conflict strengthened Thatcher's reputation for resolve, and led to the fall of the military junta in Argentina.

to celebrate 200 years of diplomatic relations between Britain and the United States: 'There is a union of mind and purpose between our peoples which is remarkable and which makes our relationship truly a remarkable one. It is special. It just is, and that's that.' This was not simply a matter of sentiment. Thatcher was fortunate that in the 1980 American presidential election the sitting President, the Democrat Jimmy Carter, was defeated by the Republican, Ronald Reagan. Reagan went on to win the 1984 election easily.

The two leaders were very close, not only in their attitudes to society and domestic politics, but also in their foreign policy views. Both were firmly opposed to Communism, and Cold War tensions revived with the Soviet occupation of Afghanistan. Thatcher backed Reagan with public support over Afghanistan, the deployment of American Cruise and Pershing missiles in Britain and Western Europe, and over the American Strategic Defence Initiative or 'star wars' project designed to protect the USA from Soviet missiles and to give the Americans a commanding lead in the arms race. Like Reagan, Thatcher maintained the anti-Communist propaganda and intelligence dynamic of the Cold War. During the Falklands War of 1982 the two did not discuss the crisis nightly by phone, because, according to Reagan, 'She knew where we stood with each other.' American logistical and intelligence support greatly aided the British recapture of the Falklands.

Furthermore, Reagan was willing to let Thatcher take a role that was disproportionate to the respective strength of the two countries. Although she did not always take the lead, the relationship was indeed special to Thatcher, for it gave her great influence on the world stage. The relationship also proved divisive within Britain, because the Labour Party's move to the left in the early 1980s led to a rejection of key aspects of British foreign and defence policy. These included the country's status as an atomic power. In 1981 the annual conferences of both the Labour Party and the Trades Union Congress passed motions in favour of unilateral nuclear disarmament (see Chapter 10).

The nature of the Anglo-American relationship affected Britain's position within the EEC. Thatcher instinctively preferred to side with the USA and to adopt American attitudes when there was a choice. This helped to lead to a domestic political crisis in 1986. The fate of the Westland Helicopter company – acquisition by either American or European companies – divided the Cabinet and led to the departure of Michael Heseltine, who had supported the European option against the wishes of Thatcher.

Differing attitudes towards the USA were part of a wider contrast between Britain

## Box 13.4

### Thatcher and Europe

Mrs Thatcher encapsulated her views at her speech at the opening ceremony, at the start of the academic year, of the College of Europe in Bruges, given on 20 September 1988: 'We have not successfully rolled back the frontiers of the state in Britain, only to see them reimposed at a European level, with a European super-state exercising a new dominance from Brussels.'

and her European partners. Thatcher was especially critical of what she saw as a preference for economic controls and centralist planning in the EEC. She felt closer to Reagan than to Continental conservative leaders, such as President Giscard d'Estaing of France and Chancellor Kohl of Germany, let alone their Socialist counterparts. In describing the 'Social Chapter' as Marxist, Thatcher testified to her sense that the EEC posed the danger of alien values. Her government was more influenced than its Continental counterparts by the emergence of neo-liberal free-market economics in the 1980s. This reflected the hostility of the right wing of the Conservative Party, the source of Thatcher's support, to the corporatist and regulatory state, while such a state accorded with the attitudes of Continental Christian Democrats. This contrast was accentuated by the exigencies of coalition politics on the Continent, for their systems of proportional representation tempered any abandonment of centrist policies. As a consequence, the economists of, and those linked to, the 'Chicago School', most obviously Freedman and Hayek, were more influential in Britain than elsewhere in Europe, and the liberalisation of the financial system was pushed furthest in Britain.

Thatcher favoured the extension of free trade within the EEC, but was critical of the process of convergence within the EEC and of the pretensions and policies of EEC institutions. She can be criticised from this perspective for failing to appreciate the consequences of her own actions. By signing the Single European Act in 1986, Thatcher gave new powers to the European Parliament and abolished the veto rights of a single state in some key areas of decision-making, but she no more realised what would flow from this, as the momentum for the creation of a single market gathered pace, than she understood the consequences of her failure to retain support among Conservative backbenchers. As a politician, Thatcher was gravely weakened by her inability to appreciate the potential strength of those she despised. Her own attitude towards the EEC was more bluntly put by Nicholas Ridley, a minister close to her who was forced to resign from the Cabinet in 1990 after calling the European Community 'a German racket designed to take over the whole of Europe'.

Thatcher's alienation from the EEC, by then the European Community (EC), became more serious as the EC developed in a more ambitious direction. The Delors Report of 1989 on economic and monetary union proposed a move towards a single currency. Thatcher found herself pushed towards closer links by her leading ministers, especially Nigel Lawson, the Chancellor of the Exchequer, and Geoffrey Howe, the Deputy Prime Minister. She eventually took Britain into the Exchange Rate Mechanism (ERM) of the European Monetary System (EMS) in October 1990, but made it clear that she would never accept a single currency. However, her reluctance over European integration had fractured Cabinet loyalty and this provided the lightning rod for dissatisfaction with her leadership within the Cabinet and parliamentary party. Challenged for the leadership by the Euro-enthusiast Heseltine, Thatcher stood down as leader after a less than impressive showing on the first ballot (see Chapter 10).

## The 1990s

Thatcher was succeeded in 1990, however, not by Heseltine nor by Douglas Hurd, but by the least pro-European of the three candidates for the leadership, John Major. Sceptical about European integration, although less so, and less determined than Thatcher, he initially spoke about his desire to place Britain 'at the heart of Europe'.

Major, nevertheless, resisted the concentration of decision-making within the EC at the level of supranational institutions. In the Maastricht agreement of December 1991, Major obtained an opt-out clause from Stage Three of economic and monetary union, the single currency, and from the 'Social Chapter' which was held likely to increase social welfare and employee costs and to threaten the competitiveness and autonomy of British industry. Major also ensured that the word 'federal' was excluded from Maastricht.

Major's reputation was, nevertheless, wrecked by Europe. He had supported entry into the ERM in October 1990 at the rate of 2.95 Deutsche Mark to the pound, an overvalued exchange rate, because he believed that this would squeeze inflation out of the economy, and thus create an environment for growth. The government, however, found itself forced to respond to the financial policies of the strongest economy in the ERM, Germany, and unable to persuade the German Bundesbank to reduce its interest rates. The Bundesbank put the control of German inflation, threatened as a consequence of the budget deficit arising from the unification of East with West Germany, above the prospects for British growth. The British government was therefore obliged to raise interest rates to defend the pound when its value reached the bottom of the permitted exchange-rate band at 2.82 Deutsche Mark to the pound. This hit British industry hard. The policy was nevertheless maintained until, as a result of heavy speculation against sterling, Britain was forced, in a humiliating and damaging fashion, to leave the ERM on 'Black Wednesday', 16 September 1992, a day on which interest rates were raised substantially and large sums of money were spent in a fruitless attempt to defend the exchange rate. The reputation of the Major government for economic competence was destroyed.

Thereafter, Europe continued to be a divisive issue within the Conservative Party and government. It became more so, because the general election of 9 April 1992 had left the government with a parliamentary majority that was so small that it was very vulnerable to dissent. This became even more the case with successive by-election defeats. Britain's enforced withdrawal from the ERM and the Danish rejection of the Maastricht Treaty in a referendum fanned the flames of Conservative Euroscepticism. The parliamentary rebellion over Maastricht in 1992–3 eventually encompassed one-fifth of backbench Conservative MPs. The Major government found itself sidelined in Europe with its 'wait and see' line over British participation in the single currency. Not even a pre-emptive leadership contest in July 1995 could help Major to heal the Conservative Party's wounds over Europe (see Chapter 10).

Conservative disunity and failure over Europe – an inability to shape the EEC, or to limit its consequences and its impact on British politics – contrasted with a more assertive stance elsewhere abroad. The expulsion of Argentinian invaders from the Falkland Islands in the South Atlantic in 1982 brought crucial prestige to Thatcher. Britain's prominent role in the American-led coalition that drove Iraq from Kuwait in 1991 was both successful and did not have divisive consequences at home. The end of the Cold War in 1989 brought one era of competition between the great powers to a close, and Britain was on the winning side.

Yet, such actions and developments could not compensate for failure over Europe, a dramatic contrast with the situation a century earlier, when European developments had had far less consequence for British politics and the economy. Blair took office in May 1997 intent on changing the situation. He was more sympathetic to the European ideal than his Conservative (and indeed Labour) predecessors. Like Heath, Blair came to power convinced that closer European integration was central to his strategy for modernisation. In a House of Commons statement on 27 October 1997, Gordon Brown, Chancellor of the Exchequer, stated that there were no constitutional reasons why Britain could not join the single currency. This significant admission was followed, on 23 February 1999, with the announcement of a government-sponsored national changeover plan. This step, declared Blair, showed that his government had 'changed gear' in its approach towards the single currency. Yet he felt obliged to be cautious both because of the more sceptical nature of public opinion, displayed again in European elections in June 1999, and because the British economy was on a different cycle from the rest of the EU. Blair has also been reluctant to antagonise the Murdoch-owned press, and its influence on public opinion is such that he is unlikely to risk a referendum on the single currency before the next election. As a result, Britain did not join the European currency, the Euro, when it was launched on 1 January 1999 (Brown had made this clear on 27 October 1997); and by the end of 1999 the Blair government had still to set a target date for British entry into the Euro.

It remained unclear in 1999 whether Blair would find the EU much more sympathetic to his policies – domestic and foreign – than Thatcher had done. In particular, the left-wing governments elected in France and Germany in 1997–8 had scant sympathy for Blair's determination to move Labour away from Socialism. Just as Thatcher had been concerned that changes within Britain would be reversed at the European level, so Blair rapidly acquired the same concern, although, unlike Thatcher, he hoped to be able to change European minds. In particular, it seemed apparent that the modernisation project that Blair championed, and his desire to revive the economy by following pro-business policies, were threatened by the policies and attitudes of European institutions and the dominant Franco-German axis. In more general terms, the outcome of the 1997 election should not be seen as a turning-point in Britain's relationship with Europe. This is because New Labour has never expressed support for federalism. The Foreign Office Mission Statement launched by the new Foreign Secretary, Robin Cook, embodied the traditional British view of Europe. Britain hoped to play a leading role in a Europe of independent nation-states. Under Blair, Britain was set to remain the awkward partner in the European enterprise.

Difficulties and dilemmas at the close of the century are a reminder that the international dimension cannot be treated as a minor issue, important only in wartime. Instead, the dimension has to be seen as important for two reasons. First, it has had a major impact on the course of British history. Secondly, it provides a context within which it is possible to consider, even judge, British developments in a comparative dimension. The two are linked. It is clear that all states, societies, economies and cultures have been increasingly affected by others and by participation in a system in which the ability of individual states to take different decisions and follow their own course was limited. That was the argument of governments concerned about German aggression in 1914 and 1939, and was the argument subsequently taken by those supporting greater commitments to the Continent, whether membership in European organisations, or political and military commitments. Yet an argument about interdependability did not, and does not, dictate the contours and consequences of such relationships. Throughout the century, it was apparent that choices existed, but that this was denied by politicians and polemicists keen to advocate a particular point of view.

It was also apparent that Britain's role in the world was diminishing, but that many politicians and commentators and much of the public were reluctant to accept this and to think through the possible implications. For long, the situation was partially disguised by the generally pliable attitude of Dominion governments and colonial populations and because Britain was fortunate that her major ally was America. When, however, the latter alliance was absent or weak, as in the 1930s, the situation was far more difficult. Furthermore, within the EEC and then the EU, Britain lacked any such ally to shield her or protect her interests. This became increasingly apparent from the 1980s.

## Summary

◆ The loss of Empire was the major theme in the first half of the century. Strong and relevant in the 1900s, it appeared to be neither by the late 1940s, and was rapidly dismantled between 1947 and the late 1960s.

◆ Britain suffered greatly from playing a leading role in the resistance to German aggression in both World Wars, but was fortunately on the winning side.

◆ Britain played a much greater role in European affairs than was the case during the nineteenth century. The transition was a difficult one, especially after she joined the Common Market in 1973.

## Questions for discussion

◆ What are Britain's national interests?
◆ Should Britain have fought Germany in 1914?
◆ How large a role did Empire play in British policymaking?
◆ What was wrong about appeasement?
◆ What were the consequences of World War Two for Britain?
◆ Why did Britain play a major role in NATO?
◆ Was it a mistake not to be a founder member of the EEC?
◆ What role did Britain play in the Cold War?
◆ Why did relations within the EEC cause political divisions in Britain in the 1980s and 1990s?

## Further reading

Bartlett, C. J., *British Foreign Policy in the Twentieth Century* (Basingstoke, 1989).

Bell, Philip, *France and Britain, 1940–1994: The Long Separation* (London, 1997).

Bourne, John, *Britain and the Great War, 1914–1918* (London, 1989).

Boyce, D. G., *Decolonization and the British Empire, 1775–1997* (Basingstoke, 1999).

Bullock, Alan, *Ernest Bevin, Foreign Secretary, 1945–51* (Oxford, 1983).

Butler, L. J., *Britain and Empire: Adjusting to a Post-Imperial World* (London, 1999).

Cockett, Richard, *Twilight of Truth: Chamberlain, Appeasement and the Manipulation of the Press* (London, 1989).

Doerr, Paul W., *British Foreign Policy, 1919–1939* (Manchester, 1998).

Greenwood, Sean, *Britain and the Cold War, 1945–91* (London, 1999).

Lucas, Scott, *Divided We Stand: Britain, the US and the Suez Crisis* (London, 1991).

Marshall, Peter (ed.), *The Cambridge Illustrated History of the British Isles* (Cambridge, 1996).

McIntyre, W. D., *British Decolonization, 1946–1997* (London, 1998).

Naylor, John, *Labour's International Policy: The Labour Party in the 1930s* (London, 1969).

Orde, Anne, *The Eclipse of Great Britain: The United States and British Imperial Decline, 1895–1956* (London, 1996).

Ovendale, R., *Anglo-American Relations in the Twentieth Century* (Basingstoke, 1998).

Parker, R. A. C., *Chamberlain and Appeasement: British Policy and the Coming of the Second World War* (Basingstoke, 1993).

Purdue, W., *World War Two* (Basingstoke, 1999).

Young, J. W., *Britain and European Unity, 1945–92* (Basingstoke, 1992).

# Britain and the Outside World: Economic, Social and Cultural Aspects

# CHAPTER 14

This chapter is no mere sequel to the previous one, but reflects the view that social, economic and cultural developments cannot simply be fitted into the gaps in a predominantly political narrative. They are sufficiently important to merit their own coverage. This chapter addresses not simply links, but also comparisons and contrasts. All are important in forming and sustaining national identity.

## Key issues

▶ How have the economic relations between Britain and the rest of the world altered?

▶ How far has British society developed in line with the rest of the West?

▶ What has been the cultural impact of the USA?

## Contents

## Economic aspects

Britain's shift from being one of the leading economies of the world, one of the workshops of the world, to being a far less significant industrial power was one of the narrative themes of the century. It was also a theme that was worked out through economic relations with the remainder of the world. The British economy declined in relation to the outer world, and this decline was measured out through links with the world (see Chapter 11).

At the close of the nineteenth and beginning of the twentieth century, German and American competition became more apparent. In the last quarter of the nineteenth, British industries no longer benefited from cheaper labour and, in some cases, raw materials; and foreign competition was responsible for factory closures. British exports increasingly found markets difficult or closed. Tariffs rose significantly on the Continent from the late 1870s, leading to complaints before the Royal Commission on the Depression in Trade and Industry appointed in 1885. In the last quarter of the century, the rate of export growth fell and imports of manufactured and semi-manufactured goods rose. Germany, for example, was the main source of pharmaceutical products (see Chapter 1).

The growth of German economic power posed a stark contrast with the situation earlier in the century. The annual average output of coal and lignite in million metric tons, in 1870–4, was 123 for Britain and 41 for Germany; by 1910–14, the figures were 274 and 247. For pig-iron, the annual figures changed from 7.9 and 2.7 in 1880, to 10.2 and 14.8 in 1910; for steel, 3.6 and 2.2 (1890), 5.0 and 6.6 (1900), 6.5 and 13.7 (1910). Germany not only forged ahead in iron and steel production, but was also particularly successful in chemicals, electrical engineering, and optical goods. The number of kilometres of railway in Germany, a larger country, rose from 11,089 in 1860 to 33,838 (1880) and 63,378 (1913); in Britain, where the railway boom had started earlier, the comparable figures were 16,798, 28,846, and 38,114. Germany was helped by a large home population: in 1900, her population was 56.4 million, that of Britain, 41.5 million, excluding Ireland, 37 million. Although British gross domestic product per man-hour was 42% higher than that of Germany in 1913 and her gross national product per head 30% greater, the gaps were dropping and the impact was, anyway, lessened by Germany's larger population.

The American economy, with its greater natural resources and markets, and more innovatory ethos, easily surpassed that of Britain. Indeed, by 1914, American output was equivalent to that of the whole of Europe. In large part, America's innovatory ethos derived from skilled labour shortages throughout the nineteenth century. Britain, by contrast, invented and invested in heavy machinery in the early phases of the Industrial Revolution, making wholesale replacement expensive, while her plentiful supplies of cheap, skilled labour in any case militated against maximising technological inputs. During World War One, the British war effort was to be heavily dependent on American financial and industrial resources.

Attitudes towards America were ambivalent. Thanks to the steamship, the Atlantic shrank in the nineteenth century: crossings became faster, more comfortable, safer, and more predictable. In 1914, it took only a week to cross between Britain and the USA, as compared with six weeks in the 1850s. The USA thus became closer, and the real cost of travel fell. The USA also came to play a greater role in British consciousness, although far less than it was to do. Many Victorians wrote about the USA. Dickens, Trollope and the historian James Bryce were all among the leading figures taken by America's energy and drive, yet often shocked by its populist politics. They were seen as vulgar and dangerous, an attitude that looked towards twentieth-century criticism of American culture. A standard means of castigating a politician was to accuse him of the 'Americanisation' of British politics, and Gladstone and Joseph Chamberlain both suffered accordingly.

Competitive pressures ensured that, at the close of the nineteenth century, there was less confidence that British institutions and practices were best, and far less confidence than earlier in the century, and also a sense that reform was necessary. The 3rd Marquess of Salisbury, Prime Minister in 1885–6, 1886–92 and 1895–1902, was not alone in being pessimistic about the future of the Empire. There was much interest in the German educational system in the 1890s and early 1900s, and the National Efficiency movement publicly looked to German models.

Concern about Britain's position in the global economy fuelled attempts to re-work the Empire into a strong economic unit, attempts that linked the tariff reformers of the 1900s to the inter-war attempt to develop the Commonwealth. Lobby groups, such as the Empire Industries Association launched in 1925, pushed the case for protectionism. Economic relations between Britain and the Dominions, however, were a source of disagreement, not least because economic problems were encouraging a general move towards protectionism. The Dominions wished to protect their industries from British competition, and were concerned that free trade within the Empire

**Box 14.1**

## The Commonwealth

The product of the British Empire, the Commonwealth originated as the partnership between Britain and the Dominions, the self-governing parts of the Empire – Australia, Canada, New Zealand, South Africa, Newfoundland and the Irish Free State. The 1931 Statute of Westminster clarified the Dominions' legislative autonomy and this provided the basis for the expansion of the Commonwealth with de-colonisation. British hope that this would enable her to continue as a great power rapidly faded in the 1950s, as the newly independent states developed their own views, and as the non-aligned movement sapped the willingness of some to follow the British lead. From the 1960s, there were serious divisions over British government policy towards South Africa and Southern Rhodesia (now Zimbabwe). Britain's membership of the EEC from 1973 weakened economic ties. Nevertheless, the Commonwealth continues to have some institutional flesh and provides links between Britain and some of her former colonies.

would harm them. The response was Imperial Preference, eventually established in agreements reached at the Imperial Economic Conference held at Ottawa in 1932. These involved bilateral understandings on a large number of products, although British exporters benefited less than Dominion producers. The Dominions raised tariffs on non-British imports, but were unwilling to cut tariffs on British imports as they feared the impact on Dominion producers. The Ottawa agreement was a cautious arrangement, that contrasted with the bold views of the Conservative politician Leo Amery, who pressed for a common economic policy and currency. Nevertheless, it was promising, especially in light of rising protectionism elsewhere during the Depression of the 1930s. Furthermore, the tension and lack of warmth shown at Ottawa suggested that it would be difficult to achieve more. This imperial conference was far less harmonious than those of the 1920s.

The protectionism introduced with the general 10% tariff under the Import Duties Act of 1932 reflected an awareness of economic decline and a loss of confidence in free trade. Imperial Preference made protectionism more politically acceptable, but its essential thrust was concern about the economic position in Britain. There was pressure not only from industrial interests, but also from rural counterparts affected by falling prices in agriculture. The rural interest was particularly important in the Conservative Party, and it was a Conservative-dominated National Government that pushed through protectionism in 1932. In the process, the National Government lost its support from the Samuelite or 'official' Liberals (see Chapters 3, 9).

The Imperial Preference aspect of protectionism made the Empire more important in the 1930s. The Empire took 49% of British exports in 1935–9, compared with 42% a decade earlier. British exports to the Empire actually fell in value, but, as those to the remainder of the world fell even more, the economic importance of the Empire became more important. Instead of thinking primarily in terms of the global economy theoretically made possible by free trade, British policymakers were increasingly thinking in terms of an economic bloc led by Britain, in which the Dominions played a major role, and that operated as a sterling area. Both Baldwin and Neville Chamberlain thought in these terms. Until the 1967 devaluation of sterling, the currencies of most Commonwealth countries, bar Canada, were fixed in value relative to sterling, and they conducted their international trade in sterling. Many of these states held large sterling balances, which helped support the currency.

Box 14.2

## Trade figures, 1930–90

Annual averages of balance of trade in millions of pounds. The figures are net balances including both visible trade (in deficit throughout this period) and invisible (services) trade (in surplus throughout period).

| | | | |
|---|---|---|---|
| 1930–4 | −27 | 1966–70 | +144 |
| 1935–40 | −24 | 1971–5 | −1,044 |
| 1946–50 | −56 | 1976–80 | +424 |
| 1951–5 | −19 | 1981–5 | +3,608 |
| 1956–60 | +132 | 1986–90 | −11,870 |
| 1961–5 | −42 | | |

Inflation and the growth in trade and services both encouraged a rise in the figures.

In 1951, colonial sterling balances held in London amounted to about £920 million. The importance of Malaya's sterling balance helped account for the determination to defeat the Communist insurgency there. World War Two had shown the vulnerability of British overseas investments, income from which was vital to the British economy.

The role of sterling declined, however, alongside Britain's economic and military position. Devaluation was particularly damaging to sterling's international role, but so, also, was the declining role of British investment and trade. The USA replaced Britain as the biggest source of foreign investment in Canada in the 1920s, and as Canada's biggest export market after World War Two. The British share of this foreign investment in Canada fell from 85% in 1900 to 15% in 1960, while the American share rose from 14% to 75%. The Canadian assets of American insurance companies already exceeded those of British companies by 1911. In 1992, Canada signed the North American Free-Trade Agreement with the USA and Mexico. New Zealand and, even more, Australia came increasingly to look to East Asia for economic partners. In 1970, 49% of Australian exports went to Asia; in 1991, 67%.

Links with the 'informal' Empire, the parts of the world where British influence was very strong, but which were not part of the Empire, also declined. By the late 1980s, Latin America, once a major field of British trade and investment, supplied only 1.5% of British imports and took only 1.4% of its exports. Investments in the region were only 6% of British foreign investment. Britain's economic role in Asia was also substantially reduced in the second half of the century. This was the case both in former colonies, such as Malaya, where British companies lost control of the palm oil, rubber and tin production they had developed, and in other countries where Britain's role had been important: China, Iran and Japan.

Despite the loss of Empire, the British economy still differed from that of Continental Europe. The special financial status and influence of the City of London was distinctive. Even in relative decline, the City became more closely linked into a world network of financial centres, the other key-points in which were New York, Tokyo and Hong Kong. Furthermore, foreign investments remained important throughout the century. Foreign investments had yielded 3.9% of gross national product in the 1870s, and rose from about £500 million in 1870 to an estimated £3,132 million in 1914. Their increased importance contributed greatly to the enhanced role of the

City of London in the British economy. There were massive sales of foreign investments during World Wars One and Two, but fresh investment in the inter-war period. Much of it was in the Empire, for example copper-mining in Northern Rhodesia (Zambia), and cotton and coffee production in Uganda. Foreign investment picked up again in the later decades of the century, especially with financial liberalisation under the Thatcher governments. This investment was characteristically private enterprise, not governmental. Investment outside Europe focused on the USA. In the 1990s, it was more important there than German or Japanese investment. Nevertheless, British investment in Continental Europe also grew appreciably in the 1980s and 1990s.

This reflected a major growth in British trade with the Continent. Trade had been inhibited by war and protectionism during the first half of the century, but became more marked after World War Two, especially after Britain's entry into the EEC in 1973. The EEC steadily became more pronounced as a trading zone. Between 1985 and 1991, exports between its member states grew by 40%, while those to other countries fell by 3%, as European economies with their high wage costs, lost their competitive edge. As a consequence of the creation of the Single European Market (SEM), the EC legally became the domestic market for Britain in 1993: it was necessary to comply with the SEM in order to operate within the EC, and, therefore, in Britain.

As a member of the EC, with, from the 1980s, less restrictive labour and financial conditions than elsewhere in Western Europe, Britain attracted considerable 'inward investment', from Japan, Korea, the USA, and other states. In 1991, 53% of all Japanese direct investment in the EC came to Britain. By April 1993, Japanese car-makers had invested £2.4 billion in Britain, transforming local economies with factories such as the Nissan works near Sunderland, and the chairman of the French car-maker Peugeot called Britain a 'Japanese aircraft carrier' ready to attack Continental markets. Britain was second only to Canada in 1991 for the number of new American foreign manufacturing projects. This created many jobs, helping to ease the impact of the decline of heavy industry in Britain. Similarly, American and Japanese securities houses and investment banks used London as the base for their European operations. Aside from the creation of new concerns by foreign companies, they also found it easier to purchase existing businesses in Britain than on much of the Continent. The flow of investment capital remained free even after free trade had gone. British businesses were, and are, public companies with shares quoted on the stock market, and therefore, open to purchase to an unusual extent. Successive governments were willing to accept, and sometimes welcome, such takeovers. Inward investment was not new. Ford had been a major investor in the 1920s, developing a major car factory at Dagenham.

Growing trade with the rest of Europe affected Britain's economy and geography. Aside from the creation, alteration or loss of particular markets, there were also structural changes in the economy. The British and French national electricity grids were linked in the 1980s, leading the British power distribution system to become less dependent on electricity generated in Britain, and thus on British coal. The growing importance of trade with the Continent helped ports on the east coast, such as Dover, Felixstowe and Hull, to boom, while oceanic Liverpool declined.

There were, therefore, significant changes in Britain's economic relationship with the remainder of the world. These were of particular note, because foreign trade has been crucial to Britain's economy for centuries, and played a larger role in the economy than in those of France, Germany and the USA. Much British manufacturing was for export, and the service sector included a high-skill, high-value part focused on foreign trade for example, by providing insurance and banking. These characteristics became more pronounced during the nineteenth century. In the twentieth, there was a relative decline in British manufacturing, while services became far more important in Britain's economic relationship with the outside world.

Trade was also crucial to the world of goods and this affected senses of identity. This was as true of the British breakfast, with its Danish bacon, American cereals, and Swiss-style muesli, as of the cars that were so important as aspects of personality. As imports of manufactured goods became greater, especially after World War Two, so British products became less distinctive and characteristic. In addition, within Britain, they became less effective as signifiers of style and quality (see Chapter 4).

## ■ Social and cultural developments

This economic displacement was an aspect of a wider socio-cultural shift in Britain's relations with the wider world. Nevertheless, it is necessary to be cautious in analysing this shift. Cultural and economic trends are different. The former cannot be readily quantified, and what can be quantified was, and is, not necessarily crucial. Furthermore, it is dangerous to reify [turn into things] cultural influences, still less treat them as necessarily in competition. 'America' and 'Europe' were not polar opposites. To think of cultural and intellectual fashions and choices in hegemonic and adversarial terms can be very unhelpful.

The intellectual and cultural world of Britain in the eighteenth and early-nineteenth centuries had not been closed to Continental influences, especially in Scotland. Nevertheless, in the second half of the nineteenth century, Continental influences increased, in philosophy, political and economic theory, and science. For example, the work of the German philosopher Hegel had an impact on Oxford, while, in the 1880s, Karl Marx's views were disseminated in Britain. In 1883, H. M. Hyndman's *The Historical Basis of Socialism in England* appeared, offering a view of class development that drew heavily on Marx. In 1885, the group variously termed the 'Hampstead Marx Circle' or 'Hampstead Historic Society', which included George Bernard Shaw and Sidney Webb, began meeting to discuss Marx's work, which they approached through the French translation. Two years later, an English translation of *Das Kapital* appeared in London.

Britain also shared in the artistic movements of the period. Just as the French Impressionists reacted against the particular conventions of academic painting, so their British counterparts, such as the 'Glasgow Boys' – James Guthrie, E. A. Walton and W. Y. MacGregor – adopted a new and vigorous style, which, in their case, drew on the French Barbizon School and the naturalist artist Bastien-Lepage. Thanks to the dealer Alexander Reid, who was painted by his friend Van Gogh, the Glasgow artists acquired international sales and reputation, while Degas and the Impressionists were introduced to Scotland.

**avant-garde:** The writers, musicians, artists, etc., who are in the forefront in the development of new ideas and methods. The term particularly refers to Modernist writers and artists in the first half of the twentieth century.

At the same time, British writers played a role in the *fin de siècle* movement. The Irish writer Oscar Wilde wrote his play *Salomé* in French in 1891. An English translation, with illustrations by Aubrey Beardsley, first appeared in 1894, but, as the play was banned by the Lord Chamberlain, it was first performed in Paris in 1896. *Salomé* inspired Richard Strauss's opera. At a distance from the **avant garde**, other arts also

## Virginia Woolf (1882–1941)

Virginia Stephen, daughter of the writer and critic Leslie Stephen and his second wife Julia Duckworth, was born in London and educated at home. After her father died in 1904 she moved with her brother Thoby and sister Vanessa to Bloomsbury, where they formed the Bloomsbury Group of writers, artists and philosophers. In 1912 she married Leonard Woolf, and set up the Hogarth Press with him in 1917. Her first novel, *The Voyage Out*, was published in 1915. Subsequent novels, including *Mrs Dalloway* (1925) and *To the Lighthouse* (1927), showed an increasingly experimental and fluid structure and lyrical use of language, developing the 'stream of consciousness', a kind of interior monologue. Her interest in feminism is shown in *A Room of One's Own* (1929). She continued to write novels, essays, stories and letters, but suffered from recurring bouts of depression, which had started at the time of her mother's death in 1895 and became more and more serious until in 1941 she drowned herself. Her final novel, *Between the Acts*, was published after her death.

were influenced by Continental developments and practitioners. For example, in the fashionable field of portraiture, Franz Winterhalter and Jacques Tissot were key figures; the British painter John Everett Millais was also important.

Continental developments continued to have an impact in the early decades of the twentieth century. The stress on the subconscious and, in particular, on repressed sexuality, in the psychoanalytical methods developed by the Austrian Sigmund Freud and the psychological theories of the Swiss psychiatrist Carl Jung, challenged conventional ideas of human behaviour, and affected both literature and drama as many writers sought to explore psychological states. Continental composers were also influential after World War One: Rimsky-Korsakov, Schönberg, Hindemith and Prokofiev. Ballet was greatly affected by the Ballets Russe, a company created by the Russian impresario Sergei Diaghilev.

Yet, there was also much resistance (and even more indifference) to Continental trends. Literary modernism, for example, had a smaller impact than on the Continent. There were important British Modernists, including the novelist D. H. Lawrence (1885–1930), who left England in 1919, Virginia Woolf, and the Irish writers James Joyce and W. B. Yeats. All were outsiders in a British cultural world largely focused on more conventional styles and authorities. Realism in literature and art remained more influential, as did empiricism in philosophy. In music, Vaughan Williams was more popular than Hindemith, and not all critics or audiences enjoyed Schönberg's atonal and serial music (see Chapter 15).

This response was cultural in the widest sense, part of a suspicion of the foreign that was strongly marked in the period. The sense of challenge to Britain's economic and political position, combined with widespread immigration and an awareness of cultural shifts, led to a fear of alien forces and an overt racism, as in the forcible re-patriation of gypsies in the 1900s. Attitudes towards refugees in the mid-nineteenth century had been open, although, in part, this was due to a chauvinistic sense of British superiority. Attitudes closed up, however, in the late nineteenth century, in reaction to tensions arising from Jewish immigration, fears about anarchists, and anxieties about the national 'stock' (see Chapter 2). One aspect was concern from the 1890s about sinister Chinese using opium dens to corrupt British men and, in particular, women. Limehouse in East London, with its Chinese population and docks, became synonymous with the seductions of opium. Thomas Burke's *Lime-*

*house Nights* (1917) and the *Fu-Manchu* stories of Sax Rohmer (the pseudonym of Arthur Sarsfield), the first of which, *The Mystery of Dr Fu-Manchu*, appeared in 1913, sustained this concern into the 1920s, and, indeed, Brilliant Chang, a Chinese drug-dealer, became the most notorious criminal of the period. Sarsfield had been a crime reporter in Limehouse. Imaginative fiction more generally registered a theme of foreign threats to Britishness operating in Britain, as in the popular *Bulldog Drummond: The Adventures of a Demobilized Officer Who Found Peace Dull* (1920) by Sapper (Lieutenant-Colonel H. C. McNeile), a novel that spawned a number of sequels.

More generally, Communism could be grafted onto the sense of alien challenge. It was generally presented as foreign, and the prominent role of Jews in the movement was emphasised. Jingoistic tendencies had been encouraged during World War One, leading to propaganda such as Horatio Bottomley's newspaper *John Bull*. After the war, a sense of threat to what was seen as traditional patriotism led in 1923 to the foundation of the British Fascists.

World War One, Britain's problems, and the threat of Communism, combined to challenge cosmopolitanism in British life and to encourage a search for national character. This had a number of cultural manifestations, not least the cultural style termed 'realism' and also a stress on supposedly rural values (see Chapters 3, 10, 12). From this perspective, many sought to look abroad, within the Empire, to new Britains. The Society for the Overseas Settlement of British Women hoped that the women would 'marry and produce the children essential to the preservation of a white Australia or a British Canada', instil in the young a love of Britain, and ensure the purchase of British goods. National culture was celebrated in a number of works. One of the most weighty was completed in 1928. The first edition of the *Oxford English Dictionary* contained 240,165 main words and 400,000 entries. Started in 1859, it was a triumphant statement of the importance, longevity and character of the language, and a presentation of English as just that, not American.

America did not offer the security of the Empire. It could seem a source of competition, commercially and internationally, and of values challenging British social, cultural and political norms, although political and economic tensions between the two powers were handled peaceably. Disagreements in the New World in the 1900s – over both South America and the Canadian frontier – were settled. The USA supported Britain in World War One, coming into the conflict in 1917. More generally, the transition from one great power to another was managed without conflict between the two.

America had a strong appeal, itself, to many British commentators, and this was part of its competitive threat. Those who looked to the USA for new developments in jazz or the cinema were looking in some respects to a very different America from that seen by those attracted by a notion of Anglo-Saxon cultural or racial affinity, but their common element was a potentially challenging frame of reference. Any stress on America represented a very different cultural emphasis from that of Europe, with its much stronger sense of the living past and its greater hesitation about novelty. Jazz for example was very much a novelty. American soldiers introduced it during World War One. In 1919, the Original Dixieland Jazz Band visited London, and, in the 1920s, British emulators took up dances such as the Charleston and the Black Bottom. Part of the appeal of jazz was that it was American, itself a cultural development of importance. In the 1930s, jazz was increasingly successful as dance music. British bandleaders, such as Ted Heath and Ray Noble, used the opportunities of radio to trumpet their big brass sound.

In the cinema, British culture, history, and society were interpreted and presented for American, and thus, also British, audiences by American actors, directors and writers, or by their British counterparts responding to the American market. Thus, Lord Peter Wimsey, a fictional epitome of the best of the British aristocracy, was played by an American, Robert Montgomery, in *Busman's Honeymoon* (1940). British audiences were encouraged to 'buy British', but generally preferred American films.

American links, a positive image of the USA, and a habit of looking at Britain through the American prism, were all greatly accentuated by World War Two (1939–45). Britain's eventual role was as a junior Alliance partner, more obviously saved and supported by the Americans than in World War One. This cooperation was sustained after the war when the situation was very different from the aftermath of World War One. The Anglo-American geopolitical and strategic alignment in the early stages of the Cold War was supported by a stress on common Anglo-American values. President Truman's Democratic administration (1945–53) was far from identical with the Attlee Labour governments (1945–51), with their nationalisations and creation of a welfare state, but it was possible to stress common language and values, certainly in comparison with the Communist Soviet Union. This was supported by the memory of wartime cooperation and fraternisation. The large number of British women who went to America as GI brides was an obvious indicator of the latter: the length of the American forces' stay in wartime Britain ensured that the number was far greater than comparable figures from elsewhere in Europe.

Cooperation with the USA did not separate Britain from the Continent. Other European states were founder-members of NATO, American economic assistance under the Marshall Plan was important in the recovery of Western Europe, and the Americans played a role in thwarting Communist activity in France and Italy. Cultural Anglo-Americanism was matched by closer links between America and Western Europe as a whole: France, Italy, and in particular, Germany were exposed to strong American cultural forces. The sway of Hollywood reached to the Elbe, which, in part, marked the frontier between what was to become West and East Germany. In 1947, G. M. Trevelyan, a leading historian, spoke of living in 'an age that has no culture except American films and football pools'. Its cultures weakened or discredited by defeat, collaboration or exhaustion, much of Western-European society was reshaped in response to American influences and consumerism, which were associated with prosperity, fashion and glamour. Changes in consumer taste were to have important economic consequences. Britain's economy and society were wide open, like others in Western Europe, to the stimuli coming from the most developed and powerful global economy.

At the same time, the impact of Empire declined. Britain's cultural, social and political influence in former imperial possessions ebbed rapidly. The percentage of the Australian and Canadian populations that could claim British descent fell appreciably from 1945, as they welcomed immigration from other countries. Constitutional links with Britain, for example the right of appeal to the Privy Council in Great Britain from the superior courts of Commonwealth countries, were severed or diminished in importance. Republican sentiment grew markedly in Australia in the 1980s and 1990s. America came to play a more important cultural role in both Australia and Canada, with, for example, American soap operas being shown frequently on the television. In 1951, Australia and New Zealand independently entered into a defence pact with the United States (ANZUS). Britain had little role to play as the Pacific became an American lake.

In some respects, the USA served as a surrogate, for both Britain and the Dominions, providing crucial military, political, economic and cultural links for both, and offering an important model. The strength of these links compromised Britain's European identity, but, from the 1970s, they slackened, not least because anglophilia became less important in the USA, and Britain had less to offer in terms of any special relationship.

On the other hand, encouraged by the role of American programmes on British television, and American or American-derived products in British consumer society, the American presence in the British economy, and the more diffuse, but still very important, mystique of America as a land of wealth and excitement, grew. America thus became very important to British culture in the widest sense of the term, and helped to alter the latter. The suburban culture and society that was prominent in Britain in the 1950s was particularly accessible to American influences. This was seen in popular music, for example Perry Como, the cult of the car, the use of 'white goods', especially washing machines, and electricity, rather than coal, the rise of television, and well-kept lawns.

Although there are obvious problems with 'measurement', it is apparent, not least for linguistic and, to a certain extent, commercial reasons, that post-war American cultural 'hegemony' was stronger in Britain than in the other major Western-European countries. Through popular music and the increasingly ubiquitous television, American influence grew rapidly in the 1950s. It became the currency of the affluence that replaced the austerity of the 1940s. American soap operas and comedy programmes (such as *I Love Lucy*) set standards for consumer society. America also became a topic for study. The Atlanticism of the 1960s led to the creation of Schools of English and American Studies in new universities, such as East Anglia and Sussex, separate from those of European Studies.

There were also important Continental influences, although far less so at the level of popular culture. These influences, in part, reflected strong personal links. Many British artists trained or travelled abroad, and they were affected by what they found there. In the two decades after World War Two, British culture was greatly influenced by existentialism, a nihilistic Continental philosophical movement closely associated with Heidegger, Kierkegaard and Sartre, that stressed the vulnerability of the individual in a hostile world, and the emptiness of choice. Novels affected by these notions, such as those of Camus, had an impact in Britain, as did plays, most obviously the work of Sartre. From the war until the mid-1950s, French plays, especially the works of Sartre and Anouilh, were frequently performed, in translation, both in London and elsewhere. Sartre's work, for example, greatly affected the novelist Iris Murdoch.

The popularity of French plays was eventually affected by the indigenous 'kitchen sink drama' of, in particular, John Osborne. This was not, however, a simple case of 'British' versus foreign; for other Continental playwrights became influential from the mid-1950s, moulding authors, directors and audiences. Bertolt Brecht died in 1956, but it was only from the mid-1950s that his works had a major impact in Britain; major productions were staged by leading national companies, such as the National Theatre and the Royal Shakespeare Company, especially in the 1960s. Brecht's works also became very popular as school plays.

Another powerful Continental influence on British drama was the 'theatre of the absurd'. This term was applied in 1961 to a type of non-realistic modern drama that was centred in Paris, but followed in London. There the works of Samuel Beckett, an Irishman resident in Paris, and the Romanian Eugene Ionesco were produced frequently. The author of *Waiting for Godot*, Beckett influenced Harold Pinter, one of the leading British playwrights from the 1960s.

British classical music was also influenced by Continental composers. The works of the Russian Dmitri Shostakovich were frequently performed in the 1950s and 1960s. In the 1970s and 1980s, living Continental composers whose works were often heard included the Italian Luciano Berio, Pierre Boulez, the French conductor of the BBC Symphony Orchestra (1971–5), and the Pole Witold Lutoslawski. Such foreign influence was scarcely new, and there were also noted British composers whose work was distinctive, most obviously Benjamin Britten (1913–76) and Michael Tippett (1905–98), both of whom produced important operas.

British popular music was far less affected by the Continent. Instead, it was greatly influenced by American popular music in the 1950s. Rock 'n' Roll arrived with the playing of Bill Haley and the Comets on the soundtrack of the film *Blackboard Jungle*, which was released in Britain in 1956. Later films, such as Haley's *Rock Around the Clock* and Elvis Presley's *Jailhouse Rock* and *King Creole*, had a big impact on British youth audiences.

British singers, both male and female, modelled their performance on Americans and sang their songs, as they had done from the 1920s, although they also drew on British light entertainment. Thus, Marion Ryan, one of the most successful singers in 1956–62, recorded versions of Perry Como's *Hot Diggity* and Peggy Lee's *Mr Wonderful*, while Cliff Richard initially sought to emulate Elvis Presley. American culture also affected British youth through film stars, especially James Dean and Marlon Brando, and films such as *Rebel without a Cause* and *The Wild One*. Bebop – improvised jazz with complex rhythms that was developed in the USA – was played in London by Ronnie Scott and John Dankworth, and in 1959 Scott opened the jazz club named after himself.

Jazz, however, became far less popular as dance music in the 1960s; part of a wider rejection of American musical styles. From the early 1960s, British groups developed their own sound and became the most popular of all on the Continent.

**Coffee bar culture, Soho (1958)**
Popular music, especially from the USA, helped to develop and reflect a distinct youth culture in the 1950s. Many of the features characteristically associated with the 1960s, including higher rates of illegitimacy and divorce, were already present.

The Beatles were to lead a musical invasion whose sounds were to be heard across the Atlantic. In many cases, Continental groups had to produce their material in English – not primarily in the hopes of reaching a world market, which none did (save ABBA, who essentially became British by adoption), but because, if they did not do this, they appeared parochial and out of date, even in their own countries. With the pop explosion of the 1960s and British leadership in such areas as fashion, design and photography, London displaced Paris as the cultural capital of Europe.

One of the most important sources of Continental influence on Britain was the large number of refugees who fled the traumas of Continental politics. Large-scale immigration from Eastern Europe, especially Poland, in the late-nineteenth century, was followed in the 1930s by refugees from the Nazis, not only from Germany, but also from Austria and other countries threatened or occupied by the Germans: Freud came from Vienna to Hampstead in 1938. In addition, Communist takeovers led to immigration, both after 1917 and in the late 1940s. Although London was not as cosmopolitan as Beirut or Constantinople at the beginning of the century, it was more so than it had been in the past.

Immigrants brought different interests and new methods. In some spheres, they were particularly important. Many found university posts and greatly influenced the intellectual life of the country. Foreign economists, such as Thomas Balogh and Nicholas Kaldor, had an impact on the economic policies of the Labour governments of 1964–70. F. A. von Hayek wrote his highly influential text *The Road to Serfdom* in 1944 while he was Professor of Economic Science and Statistics at London University. His views on the evils of collectivism influenced the Conservative Party during the 1945 election and, more powerfully, in the 1980s, and he was made a Companion of Honour in 1984 for his achievements in economic thought.

The arts were also enriched. This was especially true of the performance of music. Soloists, such as Alfred Brendel, strengthened the musical life of the country. Architecture was also greatly affected. The leading British architect of mid-century, Berthold Lubetkin (1901–90), was born in Tbilisi, the son of a Georgian mother and a Russian Jewish father. Trained in Moscow, Berlin, Warsaw and Paris, he was influenced by Marxist method, and by the German art philosopher Wilhelm Worringer, and proclaimed his affiliations with his responsibility for the short-lived Lenin Memorial in Finsbury.

By the early 1990s, most of the immigrants had died or retired. There was no new wave from the Continent to replace them. Nevertheless, their influence had been considerable. If it entailed a greater openness to Continental influences, it did not, however, imply a sympathy for political developments there. As with many immigrants to America, those who took refuge in Britain had no reason to feel much warmth towards Continental political cultures.

Immigrant professors and architects can be more widely influential than might appear apparent at first glance, but, nevertheless, their influence is generally indirect. There have also been more direct links between Britain and the Continent. One of the most important has been tourism. This is crucial to the relationship between Britain and the outer world, for it obliges people to be aware that there is an 'other': other places, other peoples, and other ways of organising life. The impact of such experience can be lessened by many of the aspects of 'package holidays', specifically going abroad to 'cocoons', environments in which the foreign is tamed or lessened, and in which there are aspects of Britishness, not least other British tourists. Nevertheless, tourism is still important. In the first half of the century it was limited. War was a factor, but the relative cost of foreign travel was more so; and for those in the middle class who could afford it, fashion and habit helped to limit the lure of abroad. Thus, the working class was apt to go to the seaside resorts developed in the Victorian period, such as Blackpool, Skegness, and Southend, while much of the middle class went to more 'select' coastal resorts, such as Torquay. The more affluent were familiar with the Alps or the French Riviera.

Far greater numbers travelled for pleasure from the late 1950s. This was a consequence of greater disposable wealth among the working class, especially skilled artisans, the development of the package holiday, the use of jet aircraft, and the spread of car ownership (see Chapter 4). As a consequence, although a large number never went abroad, in part because of poverty, far more inhabitants of Britain than ever before visited the Continent. Furthermore, far more than ever before made a regular habit of doing so, and some went several times a year. If many visited 'little Britains' in resorts such as Benidorm, which was purpose-built from the 1960s to cater to the mass-tourism market, others did not. A growing percentage of the population chose to live abroad, especially in retirement, or had second homes there. This became particularly the case in France and Spain in the 1980s and 1990s, and was a consequence of the liberalisation of financial controls under Thatcher. It became easier to transfer funds abroad and to own foreign bank accounts. There was, however, a darker side to the British presence in such countries as Spain. The number of ex-patriates whose residence on the Spanish riviera was dictated by past misdemeanours led to the area becoming known as the 'costa del crime'.

Such links were an important aspect of a reconceptualisation of relations with the Continent in which the latter became more familiar. This was related to a shift in the notion of patriotism. Patriotic sentiment was less frequently expressed from the 1960s, and attitudes towards abroad became less adversarial. The expression of hostile views was frowned on. Sensitivity to criticism of the Continent was shown, for example, during the 1996 European football championships. England was drawn against Germany in the semi-final, and much of the popular press employed martial images or language. The *Sun* declared 'Let's Blitz Fritz', while the *Daily Mirror* of 24 June carried headlines such as 'Mirror Declares Football War on Germany' and 'Achtung! Surrender . . . For you Fritz, ze Europe 96 Championship is over'. In the face of complaints to the paper, the editor was severely reprimanded and had to apologise. In the 1990s there are signs of a growing Australian influence in British television, with Australian soaps such as *Neighbours* and *Home and Away* becoming ever more popular, and spawning a whole new sub-culture.

Thus notions of identity and habits of expressing identity were both in flux in the closing decades of the century. It would be mistaken to pretend that they had ever been constant, but the last half-century was one of particular fluidity. The loss of Empire, alliance with the USA, and membership of the European Union were far more than simply political issues.

In the 1990s, issues of identity focused on Europe. Britain was, and is, a European country affected by similar social, and other, trends. That does not mean that British participation in the movement that successively spawned the EEC, EC and EU should be seen as inevitable. Europe could, and can, have different forms and meanings, and it is difficult to argue that they were, and are, inevitably reduced to the European Union. Although some opponents of the movement for European unification might have been, and may be, self-confessed 'Little Englanders', others could quite legitimately claim that they were in no way 'anti-European', but simply wanted to see 'Europe' developing along different lines. This was Thatcher's position in her famous Bruges speech of 1988. In addition, she prided herself on the role that Western firmness had played in the freeing of Eastern Europe from Soviet hegemony and Communism. Her vision of Europe was far from restricted to the EC, and at Bruges she spoke in terms of a wider 'Atlantic community'. Nevertheless, the identification of Europe with the EC had much impact: British politicians talked in the 1960s and 1970s of 'entering Europe', and, in the 1980s, Thatcher's views on the EC led to her being presented as 'anti-European'.

This Chapter has tried to show that such debates were, and are, not narrowly political. Instead, they had a wider meaning in terms of cultural, social and economic identities and interests. These were, and are, fluid, and have never been hermetically sealed from the outside world. Furthermore, they were not simply a matter of government and elite attitudes and consciousness. Instead, as part of the process of democratisation, discussed in chapter 8, debates, for example over relations within Europe or with the USA, that might have been thus confined were increasingly played out in a public sphere. Yet to use the term 'debate' is to intellectualise excessively the nature of cultural impact, and, also, to imply a misleadingly formalised process both of contention between pressures and of the creation of identity. If the situation in practice was less open to precise description and analysis, that did not make it any less important.

In the twentieth century, openness to the outside world became more intense, and did so as part of the process of accelerating change that characterised the age. That, however, should not lead us to assume that shifts in national identity have largely been a response to this changing relationship. It is also important to note changes within Britain, both between and within areas and between and within social groups. Indeed, the impact of the outside world rested in part on its interrelationship with developments within Britain. Thus, for example, in the 1950s, the availability of American role models, such as James Dean and Elvis Presley, was important in the definition of youth identity (see Chapter 6). In the 1980s, the autonomy gained by some regions elsewhere in the Continent, for example Catalonia in Spain, served as an important example for supporters of Scottish and Welsh devolution (see Chapter 12).

More generally, thanks to film, television and travel, the immediacy of foreign exemplars became more urgent. Yet, this was more than a matter simply of opportunity. In addition, there was an important loss of confidence within Britain that encouraged the search for foreign models. This was not new – Germany had been a source of models in the late nineteenth century (not least with regards to state welfare provision) – but it became more insistent. The process was facilitated by the presentation of the USA as an ideal, in both film and television. This was the most important source of change in terms of Britain's relations with the outside world, in large part because it drove expectations and habits within Britain. In particular, the USA was a model of individualism and consumerism and, albeit to a lesser extent, for democratisation. Britain was an ally of the USA, not simply in political and military, but also in wider social and cultural terms, unlike, say, American allies such as Iran in the 1970s or Saudi Arabia. Sensitivity to this was lessened greatly by the sense that the resultant changes stemmed in large part from Britain, not the American example. As a result, there was not a reaction against American culture as there was, for instance, in inter-war Germany or post-war France. Thus, in culture, as in politics, the shift from the period of British great-power status to that of American hegemony was managed without conflict. The process of decline was largely hidden from British eyes, and Britain successfully adapted to the consequences, in some cases eagerly so. We are all consumers now.

# ■ Summary

◆ The two major sources of external influence have been Continental Europe and the USA. The first has had more of an impact at the intellectual level, and the latter at the popular level.

◆ No other part of the world has had comparable influence, although immigration from 'New Commonwealth' countries was of increasing importance from the 1950s.

◆ External influences have not necessarily competed with each other, or with domestic trends. There has been a more complex process of interaction.

◆ External influence became more important in the second half of the century. Britain was especially open to American influence. The history of Britain and the British in the twentieth century cannot be told without consideration of this subject.

# ■ Questions for discussion

◆ How far have your families and neighbourhoods been affected by shifts discussed in this chapter?

◆ What impact did Hollywood have on British culture and society?

◆ Is Britain a European country, and what does Europe mean?

# ■ Further reading

Cain, P. J., and Hopkins, A. G., *British Imperialism: Crisis and Deconstruction, 1914–1990* (Harlow, 1993).

Ellwood, D. W., *Rebuilding Europe: Western Europe, America and Post-war Reconstruction* (Harlow, 1992).

Heater, D., *The Idea of European Unity* (Leicester, 1992).

Jarvie, I., *Hollywood's Overseas Campaign: The North Atlantic Movie Trade, 1920–1950* (Cambridge, 1992).

Louis, W. R., *In the Name of God, Go! Leo Amery and the British Empire in the Age of Churchill* (New York, 1992).

# Cultural Trends

## Contents

For most readers culture means **high culture**, the world of poets and painters. Yet culture can also be understood in a much broader fashion. This is true not only of its products – from pop music to opera – but also of the way in which they are produced, and the contexts of cultural activity. Culture, in other words, can mean both the products of 'high' and 'low', 'elite' and 'popular' culture, and the way in which these are received or 'negotiated' as part of a whole way of life. There is a push–pull tension. Styles are important, but so also is the consumption of culture and its impact on the consumers. This wider approach will be the subject of this chapter. As far as examples are concerned, emphasis will be on the culture of print – published material – because it is more accessible, throughout the country and further afield, than, for example, architecture or paintings. A network of school and public libraries holds many of the works and they are also generally available in inexpensive paperback editions. This chapter is organised in order to reflect some of the major divisions in twentieth-century cultural history, for example World War Two as a watershed and the 'sixties' as a particular cultural 'unit'.

## Key issues

▶ What have been the principal changes in popular culture in the sense of the whole way of life of the community?

▶ How far is culture an expression of identity?

▶ What has been the relationship between culture and consumerism?

## ■ Triumphant marketplace

The triumph of the market is the major theme in twentieth-century British cultural history. By the market, we mean the role of consumers in determining the success of particular art forms and artists. Such a situation was scarcely new. The cultural marketplace indeed had come to the fore in Britain in the eighteenth century, as patronage by individual wealthy patrons was largely replaced by the anonymous patronage of the market. This entailed producing works for sale to individuals the artist had not met. It led to a new series of cultural meeting points and places of cultural consumption: art galleries and auctions, concert halls and choral festivals.

**high culture:** The more prestigious and intellectual areas of the arts, such as poetry, classical music, etc.

The crucial links were provided by entrepreneurs: concert organisers, art auctioneers, and most significantly, publishers. Publishers financed book production and arranged the sale of the finished product. These entrepreneurs treated culture as a commodity, a commodity whose value was set by the market. Furthermore, this was a particularly fluid market, one in which style and novelty were crucial.

This situation remained the case during the nineteenth century, but the market greatly changed. This was largely due to the movement of the bulk of the population into a market that had been hitherto defined essentially in terms of the middling orders. In the Victorian period, the bulk of the working class, especially the skilled artisans, gained time and money for leisure. Much of this was spent on sport, and, in the Victorian period, football emerged as a very popular spectator sport, while other sports, such as horse racing, also attracted a large working-class following: greyhound racing was not introduced to the United Kingdom until 1926. Aside from sport, there was also a marked growth in leisure facilities catering for the urban working class. Much focused on the large music-halls that were built in this period. They offered both spectator entertainment and an opportunity to participate, by singing along or engaging in repartee with the performers.

During the same period, *organised* middle-class cultural activity greatly expanded. This owed much to the expansion of the middle class in cities, and their pursuit of culture not only for pleasure, but also as a way of defining their purpose and leadership. The middle class patronised a great upsurge in art, poetry, and the performance or production of music, leading to popular art movements such as the Pre-Raphaelites – William Holman Hunt, John Millais and Dante Gabriel Rossetti – who enjoyed considerable popularity from the mid-1850s. Cities such as Birmingham, Glasgow, Leeds, Liverpool, Manchester and Newcastle, founded major art collections and musical institutions, such as the Hallé Orchestra in Manchester in 1857. There was also a boom in middle-class sports such as golf and lawn tennis, whose rules were systematised in 1874. Sporting institutions and facilities were created across Britain, creating foci for local sociability. Northumberland Cricket Club, for example, had a ground in Newcastle by the 1850s, while Newcastle Golf Club expanded its activities in the 1890s. Civic organisations played a major role in such expansion, but the essential dynamo was commercial. This was even more obviously the case with individual activity, whether the growth of private music-making (by individuals and by families) or the great increase in reading. The purchase of books, magazines and newspapers expanded greatly.

This was the situation as the twentieth century began. By Western standards, Britain had a buoyant cultural world. It rested on mass literacy, a highly urbanised society, and the wealth of one of the leading economies in the world. The metropolitan settings of culture were lavish and expanding in number. The London Coliseum, which opened in 1904, included tea rooms, a cigar bar, and an American bar. The London Palladium, which followed in 1910, included facilities for gentlemen changing into evening dress. From the 1890s, theatre syndicates from existing music-hall managements built new venues such as the 'palaces' for more respectable customers. The prime inequality was class-based, but those in jobs still had access to inexpensive forms, such as newspapers and music-halls. While not synonymous with mass entertainment, popular culture was well served by it. Furthermore, although the situation was very far from being one of equality, especially as far as the entrepreneurs were concerned, women were not denied the opportunity to be performers. Indeed, some of the leading music-hall artistes were women, most famously Marie Lloyd. Women also played a prominent role in the more conventional theatre. Nevertheless, men enjoyed far more opportunities.

Mass culture was viewed with dismay by Socialists, who sought to transform the working class into a moral, united and educated force able to transform society. They hoped for self-improvement and 'rational recreation', not the rowdyness and vulgarity of football or music-hall, and founded bodies such as the Cooperative Holidays Association and the Clarion Vocal Unions and Cycling Clubs. These, however, made scant impact on the bulk of the working class.

# State intervention

In organisational terms, the principal tension in the culture industry in the twentieth century arose from the issue of state intervention. It would have been surprising in a century in which government increasingly intervened in large areas of British society, and taxation played a greater role than earlier, for the world of culture and leisure to have escaped intervention. There were also particular reasons for intervention in this sphere. An inherited concern with morality, or at least propriety, had left the government with powers of censorship and, more significantly, a widespread expectation that censorship would be exercised in order to 'protect society'. This ensured that established cultural forms, such as books and theatre, were subject to censorship. The Lord Chamberlain, through the Examiner of Plays, had to give a licence before any public performances on the stage. This, in particular, restricted new and different works. George Bernard Shaw's play *Mrs Warren's Profession*, with its sympathetic discussion of prostitution, was written in 1893, but denied a licence on the grounds of immorality, and not publicly performed until 1925. D. H. Lawrence's novel *The Rainbow* (1915) was banned on grounds of obscenity, and when his novel *Women in Love* was published in Britain in 1921 (it had first appeared in America in 1920), it had been altered to avoid both a similar ban and a threatened libel action. Lawrence's novel *Lady Chatterley's Lover*, written and privately printed in Florence in 1928, was published in England in an expurgated version in 1932, and in a complete version only in 1960. The publishers were prosecuted, unsuccessfully, for obscenity in 1962. In 1929, thirteen of Lawrence's paintings were seized in a London exhibition. James Joyce's novel *Ulysses* (1922) was banned until 1936 and copies were seized by the Customs. In addition, censorship was extended to new media: film, radio, television and videotapes. Cinema censorship began in 1912.

Censorship was exercised in a number of ways. The most obvious was the suppression of works that were disapproved of. The three editors of the satirical magazine *OZ* were imprisoned in 1971 for publishing obscene literature. Aside from government action, there was also self-censorship by authors or publishers in order to avoid the prospect of action. Thus, D. H. Lawrence was initially unable to find a publisher for *Women in Love*. Films were designed to avoid certificates by the censor that would limit viewing: in the late 1950s, the Rank Organisation refused to show any X-rated films in its cinemas. Yet, more significant, was the censorship created by the institutional structure of particular industries, as well as the expectations about their goals and roles.

These expectations and institutional structures combined with the state control of radio and television for much of the century. Although not a government body, the BBC was a public one and, more significantly, it enjoyed a monopoly on television

### George Bernard Shaw (1856–1950)

George Bernard Shaw was born and grew up in Dublin. He began to work for an estate agent but in 1876 he left Ireland to join his mother, a music teacher, and his sister, an actress, in London, where he wrote several unsuccessful novels. He became a book reviewer, art and music critic, and a drama critic in 1895, greatly admiring Ibsen and Wagner. He was a socialist free thinker, who believed in individual responsibility and integrity. He gave many lectures and wrote many essays supporting such causes as women's rights and voting reform. In 1898 he married Charlotte Payne-Townshend, who had nursed him when he was ill. Shaw wrote over 50 plays, including *Man and Superman* (1902) and *Pygmalion* (1913), which was later made into the musical *My Fair Lady*. He also wrote many letters – his correspondence with the actresses Ellen Terry and Mrs Patrick Campbell has been published. He was a lifelong vegetarian and drank neither spirits nor tea and coffee. He continued to write until he died aged 94. He accepted the Nobel Prize for Literature in 1925 but refused all other honours.

transmissions until 1955 and on radio broadcasts until 1973. Furthermore, even when permission was granted for an independent television channel – ITV – the times within which television could be broadcast were still set by the government. Partly in response to the Pilkington Committee on Broadcasting, which in 1962 condemned the 'trivial' nature of many television programmes, particularly on ITV, only the BBC was allowed a second television channel in 1964. Independent television had to wait until 1982 (see Chapter 5).

Both the BBC and ITV were expected to conform to an agenda that reflected the established culture of polite society. Thus, they were expected not to broadcast material that was deemed obscene, cruel or blasphemous, or to encourage people to break the law. In the widest sense, the prime agency for cultural transmission became an adjunct of a certain view of society. This was a matter not only of proscriptive (what could not be broadcast), but also of prescriptive (what was encouraged or prescribed) content. Thus, for much of the century, radio and television encouraged a sense that 'family values', as traditionally understood, were normal. Television was the predominant cultural technology from the 1960s. There was a period when challenging television drama did have a popular audience, for example the television plays of Dennis Potter (1933–95), such as *Pennies from Heaven* (1978), but, on the whole, television contributed to a situation in which not only was popular culture the dominant culture, but also the former set out to offer few challenges. 'Difficult' work was marginalised. Potter's *Brimstone and Treacle* (1977) was banned by the BBC.

State intervention was fairly apparent as an issue in radio and television; although the government has not been so much a fixed agent on the proscriptive/prescriptive boundary as a reasonably flexible body that also reflects change in cultural trends. Elsewhere, state intervention was frequently important, but not always so apparent. One obvious sphere in which the role of the state was important was patronage. In the twentieth century, the state was not only the single most important patron of the arts, but also far more active than any other body. This reflected, in part, the extension of the state's role in the economy with nationalisations, but also, more generally, the growth of government.

Patronage was most apparent in architecture. Public bodies were the biggest commissioners of buildings. This was true both of large individual works, such as universities and hospitals, and of multiple units, especially council houses. Once constructed, buildings also had to be decorated. The *avant-garde* sculptors Jacob Epstein and Eric Gill produced important work for the London Transport headquarters. The importance of public commissions encouraged the production of designs that were believed likely to appeal, and this moulded the profession more widely than the actual commissioning process itself. Furthermore, the impact of approved techniques and styles was extended through the planning process. New buildings required planning permission and this provided opportunities for the propagation and enforcement of specific agendas.

In architecture, the roles of proscriptive and prescriptive public pressures were (and are) readily apparent. They were (and are) less so in other fields where state patronage has been less important and where planning permission was not required. Nevertheless, the state still played a role in these fields, and increasingly so during the century. This owed much to the institutionalisation of state patronage. Such patronage was not new. In the 1910s, James Joyce received grants from the Royal Literary Fund and the Civil List while working on his novel *Ulysses*. Nevertheless, as with much else, total war was important as a trend-setter. The notion of total war in World War Two led to government support for measures to raise morale, as well as an important War Artists programme that was responsible for much important work. John Piper produced atmospheric paintings of bombed buildings, while another painter, Stanley Spencer, celebrated shipyard work on the Clyde.

The situation changed greatly with the formation of the Arts Council in 1946 (Keynes was the first chairman; autonomy for Scotland followed with a separate Scottish Arts Council in 1967), and the beginning of a programme of continual public subsidy of the arts. This was both an opportunity and a problem. It was an opportunity because it freed the arts from dependence on the marketplace, but it was a problem because it created another marketplace. This was politicised, not so much in terms of public politics, but rather, less public, but still bitter, artistic politics. Stylistic fashions and notions of relevance played a major role in this marketplace, but so also did pressure on behalf of particular cultural institutions, for example the Royal Opera House at Covent Garden in the 1990s. The National Lottery grant in 1997 of £78.5 million to update the building was very controversial.

Public patronage attracted much attention and considerable controversy. Each year, grants led to debate, especially with particularly difficult works of art, such as those of Damien Hirst in the 1990s. Whatever the views on their individual merits, the common note in these controversies was whether public funds should be used for such ends. In one sense, this was an aspect of a culture war between the criteria and ranking set by the artistic Establishment that influenced and directed government funding, and those that made sense in the vernacular culture of popular taste. This led, and leads, to issues of taste and influence that divided commentators. Were, for example, the most influential and 'best' novels of the 1950s, the James Bond novels of Ian Fleming (1908–64) or the early novels of Iris Murdoch (1919–99), for example *Under the Net* (1954) and *The Bell* (1958)? Whatever judgements are made, it is the case that the latter type of work tended, and tends, to attract far more critical attention. That, indeed, was central to the cultural politics of the twentieth century. Critics such as Q. D. Leavis in *Fiction and the Reading Public* (1932) were sceptical, if not hostile, to bestsellers. The most commercially successful British films of 1959, 1962, and 1974 respectively – the smutty comedy *Carry On Nurse*, the Cliff Richard musical *The Young Ones*, and the soft-core *Confessions of a Window Cleaner* –

have not attracted much critical or scholarly attention. In 1963, however, Sir John Davis, Managing Director of the Rank Organisation, the owner of the Odeon cinema chain, commented on the critically-acclaimed realist films of recent years: 'I do feel that independent producers should take note of public demand and make films of entertainment value. The public has clearly shown that it does not want the dreary kitchen sink dramas', the last made clear to Rank by the commercial failure of Lindsay Anderson's film *This Sporting Life* (1963). In *Comedians* (1975), by the left-wing playwright Trevor Griffiths, those comedians who remain true to their trainer's ideals and believe that jokes should not exploit prejudices and sustain stereotypes are rejected by the agent, who is 'not looking for philosophers but for someone who sees what the people want and gives it to them'. In the 1990s, there was criticism of the 'dumbing down' of culture, and critics such as William Best, in his *The Strange Rise of Semi-Literate England* (1991), blamed institutions, such as public libraries and the BBC, for failing to maintain cultural standards.

The Establishment emphasis in cultural politics was challenged not only by the marketplace, but also by increasing critical interest in popular culture, especially from the 1960s on; although much of that attention was from a self-consciously intellectual position. This was the case with the treatment of the two most successful categories of novel produced in the century: the adventure novels, which reached their height in the works of John Buchan and Fleming, and the detective novel, most famously the works of Agatha Christie (1890–1976), the best-selling novelist of the century.

Both the latter two categories indicated an aspect of popular art: namely that it tended to be **Realist** in style, rather than **Modernist**. To use the term 'realist' to describe the generally improbable plots and limited characterisation of Fleming and Christie may appear confusing, but they were realist in that they purported to represent the world as it is, using traditional means to do so.

**Realist:** A practical point of view, dealing with things as they really are, in contrast to the romantic or idealised vision.

**Modernist:** A movement, particularly in the first half of the twentieth century, which aimed to make a break with the past and find new forms and means of expression.

# Modernism

Modernism, in contrast, was a characteristic of a range of international artistic movements that challenged traditional forms and assumptions and, instead, preferred an experimental moulding of form in order to shake the reader and viewer from established patterns of response. Modernism was a reaction against the positivism and representational culture that had dominated the Victorian period. In part, it drew for inspiration on the new social sciences and their challenge to established assumptions, for example on works such as Sigmund Freud's *The Interpretation of Dreams* (1900) and Sir James Frazer's classic of anthropology, *The Golden Bough* (1890–1915).

**Box 15.1**

## Imagist poetry

A poetic movement of the 1910s that offered a poetic Modernism of clarity and precision. Richard Aldington, James Joyce and Ezra Pound were prominent in the movement. A verse from *At the Window* (1916) by D. H. Lawrence, better known as a novelist:

'Further down the valley the cluttered tombstones recede
Winding about their dimness the mists' grey cerements, after
The street-lamps in the twilight have suddenly started to bleed.

## T. S. Eliot (1888–1965)

Thomas Stearns Eliot was born in St Louis, Missouri. He went to Harvard and spent a year at the Sorbonne in Paris before returning to Harvard to study philosophy. He came to England to study at Oxford, but had already started writing poetry. In 1914 he met Ezra Pound, who encouraged him to stay in England. In 1915 he married Vivien Haigh-Wood. He worked in a bank for some years then joined the publishers Faber and Faber. He met Bertrand Russell and was introduced to the Bloomsbury Circle, becoming known as a poet, critic and dramatist. In 1927 he took British nationality and became an Anglo-Catholic. Among his best known works are *The Waste Land* (1922), *Four Quartets* (1944) and *Old Possum's Book of Practical Cats* (1939), which was made into the musical *Cats* in 1981. He was awarded the Nobel Prize for Literature in 1948.

On canvas, the first chance for many to see the works of Manet, Cézanne, Gauguin and Van Gogh was offered by Roger Fry, when, in 1910, he organised the Manet and Post-Impressionists Exhibition. The impact this had on British artists was indicated two years later with the contents of Fry's 'Second Post-Impressionist Exhibition'. Modernism had an impact in a number of movements, including Vorticism, Expressionism and Surrealism. The very terms used by the Vorticists symbolised their determination to shock. In 1914, the Vorticists led by Wyndham Lewis (1882–1957) founded the Rebel Art Centre, and Lewis adopted the term Vorticism to describe the transforming energy of Modernism. The Vorticist magazine was called *Blast: The Review of the Great English Vortex* (1914–15). Its first issue, that of June 1914, stated 'We only want the world to live, and to feel its crude energy flowing through us.' Vorticism helped open British art to Modernism. Such activity centred on London, but there were also important provincial centres. In 1903, Alfred Orage and Holbrook Jackson founded the Leeds Arts Club in order to propagate the most recent departures in the cultural world. Orage lectured on Nietzsche, while the club sponsored exhibitions of *avant-garde* paintings. Although Orage left for London in 1906 the club continued until 1923.

Modernism's impact in literature was multifaceted, although more in poetry and the novel than in drama. Its distinctive characteristics included the use of the stream of consciousness and a fascination with myth, both characteristics of the novel *Ulysses* (1922) by James Joyce (1882–1941), in which Dublin life ironically counterpoints Homer's *Odyssey*. Free verse was used to throw together very different voices and fractured ideas in the influential poem *The Waste Land* (1922) by T. S. Eliot (1888–

### Box 15.2

## The style of Woolf

So boasting of her capacity to surround and protect, there was scarcely a shell of herself left for her to know herself by; all was so lavished and spent; and James, as he stood stiff between her knees, felt her rise in a rosy-flowered fruit tree laid with leaves and dancing boughs into which the beak of brass, the arid scimitar of his father, the egotistical man, plunged and smote, demanding sympathy . . . the blue went out of the sea and it rolled in waves of pure lemon.

Virginia Woolf, *To the Lighthouse*, 1927

1965). Major Modernist works are held to include the novels of Dorothy Richardson (1873–1957) and Virginia Woolf (1882–1941), as well as the novel *Nostromo* (1904) by Joseph Conrad (1857–1924). Richardson's fictional sequence *Pilgrimage* (1915–67) created an impact with its early use of stream of consciousness writing. Conrad had been born in Poland, Eliot in the USA, but both settled in England. Their careers are a reminder of the difficulties of placing national categories on writers. They also underline one of the central features of British culture, its use of the most influential language in the world. English benefited from the spread of the British Empire and trade, but, increasingly, from the impact of American power and culture. Due to this linguistic link, the British were best placed among Europeans to benefit from the American century (see also Chapter 14). Alongside Americanism, there was also anti-Americanism, an important factor in cultural matters since World War One.

# Ireland, Scotland and Wales

Language was important to British culture, for it not only linked Britain to the American world, but also ensured that, whatever its political problems, the British Isles could operate, at least in part, as a cultural unit. The leading Irish, Scottish and Welsh writers published in English. This was true of Joyce as well as W. B. Yeats (1865–1939), although Yeats was also committed to Irish literature and culture. Dylan Thomas (1914–53), in his lifetime an extremely successful Welsh poet, wrote in English and spent much of his adult life in London. Language was shared by all social groups, but artistic styles and themes tended to lack such range, and displayed an approach, indeed vocabulary, that could exclude many.

However, there were also important differences between the countries of the British Isles. Scotland had a steadily, and often significantly, diverging high culture from England during the twentieth century. Scottish literature was an effectively separate tradition from the 1880s. The Scottish Renaissance of the inter-war period was originally concerned with the revival of Scots as a literary language, but then focused on the poetry of Hugh MacDiarmid (1892–1978). MacDiarmid sought to revive the use of Scots and Gaelic, in his poetry but also by developing institutions and literary practices directed against England and anglicised Scots. MacDiarmid became a founder-member of the National Party of Scotland in 1928. He was also a Communist. The use of English was rejected by Sorley Maclean (1911–96), who gave Gaelic poetry a new vigour for the twentieth century. This transformation of a traditional form greatly influenced younger poets.

Aside from Scottish high culture, in which there have been important differences from England in agenda and expression since the 1920s at the latest, there were many other cultural and socio-cultural shifts during the century. They increased the divergence between England and Scotland, and made the strength of Scottish nationalism in the 1990s less surprising. For example, in the 1880s there were over 100 cricket clubs in north-east Scotland; by 1910 close to none. In a different format of popular activity, Scottish folk music was revived during the twentieth century.

# A survey of the century

This book does not have space to list, still more describe, discuss and assess, the leading artistic figures of the century, even supposing that an agreed basis for definition existed. It is as well to recall the background of growing production. Far more words, images and sounds claiming to be art appeared than in any previous age. A greater quantity was, and is, not the same as more diversity, but that was also a feature of the society. The following section is intended to give some slight guidance, but there is no substitute for detailed works on the subject or, indeed, for reading, looking and listening yourselves.

At the risk of considerable simplification, two broad categories are offered at the outset. First, works that engage with human society at a large scale, and secondly, those that focus on more intimate relations, especially issues of gender, family and self. These classifications can be contested, but they are a start.

## 1900–40

Human society can be seen as an issue in the works of two of the most influential writers at the start of the century, George Bernard Shaw (1856–1950) and H. G. Wells (1866–1946). Science fiction played a major role in Wells's work. It was not simply a matter of scientific futurism. Instead, he used fantasy to discuss what he saw as social realities in *A Modern Utopia* (1905), and also offered portraits of the travails of those born without silver spoons, as in *Love and Mr Lewisham* (1900), *Kipps: The Story of a Simple Soul* (1905), and *Tono-Bungay* (1909). In the last, landed wealth, religion and commerce all appear as weak panaceas, and scientific experimentation, instead, is revealed as fulfilling, although not always profitable. Education as a means for personal development and social advancement was also an important theme in Wells's work, as it was to be in many novels of the century, such as those of C. P. Snow (1905–80).

In *The New Machiavelli* (1911), Wells attacked the obsession for bureaucratic reform, and this links his work to the far more sombre vision of Aldous Huxley (1894–1963), in his *Brave New World* (1932). Set in the twenty-sixth century, this used a vision of the future to criticise powerful intellectual trends in the present. People in *Brave New World* are engineered biologically to make them fit for their tasks, and drugs are used to keep them happy. Technology offers not heaven but a bureaucratic hell of ordered control. George Orwell's *Nineteen Eighty-Four* (1949) did not range so far into the future, and its target was political rather than technological. Nevertheless, the theme of control and its dangers was again at the forefront. Winston Smith is punished for thought crimes in a Britain that is dominated by a Party, under Big Brother, that rewrites history and manipulates the language in order to control thought.

If the future could be a discussion of the implications of the present, there was also much social comment that was more directly pointed. Bernard Shaw was a determined opponent of social hypocrisies, which he saw as morally destructive, as well as poisonous for society. He directed his vigour against both bourgeois greed and do-gooding liberalism, the latter satirised in his play *Major Barbara* (1905). In the preface to the play, published the following year, Shaw claimed that by giving the workers a sense of the immorality of the system, 'we produce violent and sanguinary revolutions, such as . . . the one which capitalism in England and America is daily and diligently provoking'. This was a world away from the playful probing of hypocrisies in the plays of Oscar Wilde, who had died, in exile, in 1900.

A less cerebral account of social problems was offered by the successful novelist Arnold Bennett (1867–1931). In *Anna of the Five Towns* (1902), there is not only paternal pressure and the harshness of religious conviction, but also the divisiveness of wealth and poverty in the Potteries. The debtor Prices both commit suicide. *The Old Wives' Tale* (1908) was about the travails of two sisters and their frustration by life's problems. The difficulty of escaping one's background was also a theme of Bennett's novel *Clayhanger* (1910).

John Galsworthy (1867–1933) was another popular writer of the period, although his role as a dramatist tends to be forgotten. His plays frequently commented on social problems: *Strife* (1909) on the impact of a strike, *Justice* (1910) on solitary confinement in prison, and *The Skin Game* (1920) on social inequality. Galsworthy's plays frequently contrasted wealthy and poor families. His sequence of novels *The Forsyte Saga* (1906–21) focused on social mores and matrimonial break-up, not political or social issues. Galsworthy was rewarded with honours – the Order of Merit in 1929 and the Nobel Prize for Literature in 1932 – but was criticised in fashionable literacy circles. A far harsher account of social problems can be found in such works as the poems and novels of the Irish-born Patrick MacGill (1891–1963), who left school at twelve, emigrated to Scotland, and worked as a potato picker and a navvy. His *Songs of a Navvy* (1911) and novel about navvy life, *Children of the Dead End* (1914), were bleak accounts based on his own experience, while in his novel *The Rat Pit* (1915) he dealt with the social origins of prostitution.

Fashionable circles had little time for popular writers of the period, such as Bennett, Galsworthy, Rudyard Kipling (1865–1936), who received the Nobel Prize for Literature in 1907, G. K. Chesterton (1874–1936), and Hilaire Belloc (1870–1953), let alone for adventure writers such as John Buchan. Chesterton and Belloc offered a Catholic critique of modern society, as well as detective fiction (Chesterton), literary biography (Chesterton), travelogue (Belloc), and poetry for children (Belloc). J. M. Barrie (1860–1937), the author of many successful plays, most famously *Peter Pan* (1904), received the Order of Merit in 1922, as well as a baronetcy and honours from the Universities of Cambridge, Edinburgh, Oxford and St Andrews.

Instead, the Bloomsbury Group sought to further the *avant garde* in a deliberate reaction against Victorian styles and assumptions. Bloomsbury was essentially a group of friends with similar views who saw themselves as playing a crucial role in reviving a stale literary tradition, although they also contributed to painting and the promotion of psychoanalysis. The best known novelist in the group was Virginia Woolf (1882–1941). She had no time for what she presented as the 'materialist' writing of Bennett and Galsworthy, and, instead, sought a Modernist focus on aesthetic sensibility. In 'Mr Bennett and Mrs Brown', an essay of 1924, Woolf distinguished between what she considered Bennett's false 'realism' of surface description and a 'modernism' that searched for true realism. In place of narrative, Woolf advocated a view of life as a 'luminous halo'. Her novels explored such ideas. In *Mrs Dalloway* (1925), she employed interior monologue and stream of consciousness to reveal character; in *To the Lighthouse* (1927), Woolf offered a pointillistic meditation on time and fulfilment; and in *The Waves* (1931), provided another experimental form, including a series of interior monologues, to reveal personality and consider the role of memory. Another such form was offered in 1923 when *Façade*, an innovative set of poems by Edith Sitwell, was performed with music composed by William Walton.

Woolf was scarcely alone among inter-war writers in focusing on people as individuals, building up or frustrating the personalities of others (and themselves), rather than as vehicles for narrative and/or commentators on social issues. An emphasis on imagination and the emotional focus was clear in D. H. Lawrence's

*Women in Love* (1920). These subjects were not incompatible with comments on wider issues, however, as E. M. Forster (1879–1970) showed in *A Passage to India* (1924), at once a novel about sensibility and a searching investigation of the psychological tensions of Empire.

Modernism had only a limited appeal, compared with many of the 'middle' and 'low' brow writers of the period, and had little airing on the radio. Although 'middle' and 'low' brow writers might not find favour with Bloomsbury and the reviewers of the *Times Literary Supplement*, such writers tended to dominate sales. They benefited from the rising disposable income of the inter-war period, especially the 1920s, from the ready availability of inexpensive books, and from increased leisure. Women readers were of growing importance, as indeed were children. There are suggestions that British society was more literate in the 1920s than it was to be in the 1990s.

These markets did not necessarily see themselves as 'middle' brow. Their favoured authors were not always too different in style from Kipling or Galsworthy, who had both won the Nobel Prize for Literature. In *The Herries Chronicle*, a family saga set in Cumberland, Hugh Walpole (1884–1941) produced a work that was closer to *The Forsyte Saga* than to *The Waves*. Well-known works in this saga included *Rogue Herries* (1930). Walpole also wrote popular school stories.

Walpole's one-time collaborator, J. B. Priestley (1894–1984), also won popularity with an accessible novel, *The Good Companions* (1929), an engaging account of a touring theatrical company. A Yorkshireman, Priestley had an interest in English character, but his distance from cosmopolitanism did not make him a provincial drudge. In his plays of the 1930s, such as *Dangerous Corner* (1932), he used time cleverly for intellectual as well as dramatic effect, a theme to which he was to return in *An Inspector Calls* (1945). Another Yorkshire writer, the feminist Winifred Holtby (1898–1935), also offered a strong sense of place in *South Riding* (1936). This tradition of writing continued in much of the popular novel writing of the later twentieth century, for example the works of Catherine Cookson (1906–99), which were mostly set in her native Tyneside.

A musical equivalent can be sought in the pastoral work of Ralph Vaughan Williams, for example his *Pastoral Symphony* (1921), and Percy Grainger. This was criticised by the composer and critic Constant Lambert as the 'cow pat school' of British music. Elgar emphasised an elegiac tone, and remained popular in concert programmes, gramophone record sales and BBC broadcasts. The cult of the countryside was also seen in A. A. Milne's dramatisation in 1929 of *The Wind in the Willows* by Kenneth Grahame (1859–1932), as well as in Milne's books *Winnie-the-Pooh* (1926) and *The House at Pooh Corner* (1928). The Scottish Renaissance writers overwhelmingly concentrated on rural themes. Similarly, many of the painters of the period produced portraits or landscapes that paid scant tribute to fashionable themes. In the inter-war years, the Royal Academy Schools were characterised by a conservatism greatly at odds with Modernism. Works by painters such as Picasso could be bought in the galleries in Cork Street, but their impact on the wider world was limited. Scottish art patronage was even more conservative and most Scottish painting was conventional in subject and approach. There was only limited interest among Scottish painters in theoretic Modernism.

It was only in 1945 that the Trustees of the Tate Gallery in London agreed to the opening of a small room devoted to abstract art. The Gallery, founded in 1897, was way behind the Museum of Modern Art in New York, not least because it lacked funds. In the inter-war period, the Treasury was loath to increase support for the

**Ralph Vaughan Williams (1872–1958)**
A leading composer, Vaughan Williams was prominent in the revival of English music. His interest in folk songs contributed to his song cycle *On Wenlock Edge* (1909), and his concern with the works of early English composers led to his *Fantasia on a Theme by Thomas Tallis* (1909). His influence was eventually overshadowed by younger composers more influenced by continental developments.

arts, and this lack of vision contributed to a weak, in many respects absent, cultural policy. Yet taste was also an issue. James Bolivar Manson, the Tate's Director in the 1930s, was a painter of flowers and was opposed to Post-Impressionism, Cubism, Expressionism, Surrealism and to living British artists such as Sickert and Moore. This affected the Tate's acquisition policies.

'Low' brow works of the inter-war period included popular romantic stories, for example those published by Mills and Boon, as well as adventure stories and detective novels. These works were not especially profound, but they were important, and are valuable today as accounts of the mores of the period. Thus, for example, Dorothy L. Sayers's detective novels – *Whose Body?* (1923), *Clouds of Witness* (1926), *Unnatural Death* (1927), *The Unpleasantness at the Bellona Club* (1928), *Strong Poison* (1930), *The Five Red Herrings* (1931), *Have His Carcass* (1932), *Murder Must Advertise* (1932), *The Nine Tailors* (1934), *Gaudy Night* (1935), and *Busman's Honeymoon* (1937) – are still in print. They are fantasies, in that Lord Peter Wimsey, the detective, although shell-shocked at the outset, is wealthy and improbably perfect, but they also offer guidance on contemporary attitudes to women, in the person, in particular, of the independent-minded and free-living Harriet Vane. Furthermore, they show such milieux as the new world of advertising. On the stage, the equivalent were readily accessible domestic comedies, such as the plays of Noel Coward, for example *Hay Fever* (1925), or Priestley's *When We Are Married* (1938). P. G. Wodehouse's comic novels about Bertie Wooster and Jeeves, characters first introduced in 1917, were adapted for the stage by Ian Hay.

Despite works by architects such as Berthold Lubetkin, Modernism also had little impact in architecture. Liberty's in Regent Street, built in 1924, using Elizabethan timber, better expressed the widespread desire for a style suggesting continuity, not the new. It was matched on the screen by the success of Alexander Korda's *The Private Life of Henry VIII* (1933). The architectural Modernism that looked to Continental figures, especially Le Corbusier and Walter Gropius, also had only a limited impact in Scotland. As in England, pre-war styles – both revived classicism and Arts and Crafts – remained very strong.

Much of the culture of the period was not designed to challenge established practices and the social order. Sayers's Harriet Vane was more independent than the women in Agatha Christie's detective novels. Other female novelists aside from Christie, for example Ivy Compton-Burnett (1892–1969) and Daphne Du Maurier, focused on stable sexual and class identities. This was part of a conservative disposition that was very pronounced in the 1930s. Du Maurier's novels, such as *Jamaica Inn* (1936) and *Rebecca* (1938), had a particularly strong sense of place, in this case Cornwall. The upper middle-class satire produced by 'the Bright Young Things', such as Evelyn Waugh did not challenge established ideas.

Alongside works that were about and/or for the affluent, there was also much that might be termed 'Condition of Britain' culture – attempts to present the life of the less fortunate. These included George Orwell's social criticism in his *Down and Out in Paris and London* (1933) and his bleak and bitter description of working-class life in northern mining communities in *The Road to Wigan Pier* (1937), as well as Walter Greenwood's depiction of the harshness of unemployment in *Love on the Dole* (1933) and Walter Brierley's *Means Test Man* (1935) on a similar theme. A Scottish equivalent was the account of Depression Clydeside offered by George Blake in *The Shipbuilders* (1935). A sense of the nobility of ordinary people was presented in *The Dustman* (1934), a painting by Stanley Spencer (1891–1959), that showed a dustman

**Edward Elgar (1857–1934)**
A varied and much honoured composer, popularly seen as the bandwriter for late Empire, but in fact a very sensitive and often lonely figure, with the ability to probe emotion through sound. Elgar, Vaughan Williams and Walton were very different twentieth-century composers, yet each was seen as quintessentially 'English'. They took certain elements of tradition, bonded them with foreign or modern influences, and produced something entirely fresh yet seemingly eternal, the invention of tradition in action.

and other labourers being reunited with their wives after the Last Judgement. A more accurate portrayal of working-class life was offered by *10am* (1937) by Harry Wilson (1899–1972). This view of North Seaton depicted daily routines such as cleaning boots, and the scene included the ubiquitous coal heap. *The Road to Wigan Pier* was published by Victor Gollancz for The Left Book Club, a scheme to encourage the reading of committed works, launched in 1936, that had over 56,000 subscribers by 1939. The British film documentary tradition of the period also helped provide an idea of the condition of the country.

## 1940–60

Sayers abandoned detective stories in the 1940s. As for many authors, World War Two (1939–45) provided the occasion, if not the cause, for a shift to a new seriousness, in Sayers's case a series of radio plays about the life of Christ, *The Man Born to be King* (1941–2). Artists found less demand for landscapes and portraits. Many, instead, recorded the impact of war. Under the War Artists' Scheme established by the Ministry of Information, several thousand paintings and drawings were commissioned. Some showed bomb damage, including works by John Piper, and Graham Sutherland's *Devastation in the City* (1941). Henry Moore and Feliks Topolski depicted people sheltering from German air raids in tube stations. The Ministry gained the services of the GPO Film Unit, renamed the Crown Film Unit, and they produced propagandist documentaries. This seriousness did not drown out other themes or styles, and the war years saw, for example, the introduction of vigorous jive and jitterbug dances by American soldiers (GIs). Such exuberance was rarer in the world of high culture. Graham Greene (1904–95), author of *Ministry of Fear* (1943), was employed in the Ministry of Information. Michael Tippett's oratorio *A Child of our Time* (1944) incorporated Negro spirituals.

After World War Two, George Orwell's bleak political satires *Animal Farm* (1945) and *Nineteen Eighty-Four* (1949) made a considerable impact. Carol Reed's film *The Third Man* (1949) was set not in the future but in a corrupt and devastated present where occupied Vienna could serve to suggest similarities with austere Britain. The screenplay was by Greene. The previous year, in *The Heart of the Matter* (1948), Greene tackled the failure to maintain moral standards in the face of a pitiless world. *Brideshead Revisited* (1945), by another Catholic convert, Evelyn Waugh (1902–66), also dealt with faith assailed and the search for some sign of divine purpose.

The music of Vaughan Williams and Elgar was criticised as too nice or overly florid by young composers, especially Benjamin Britten and Tippett. Britten's operas, the most important British ones of the century, notably *Peter Grimes* (1945), *Billy Budd* (1951) and *The Turn of the Screw* (1954), were disturbing works. The Ealing (film) comedies of the late 1940s and early 1950s, such as *Passport to Pimlico* (1949), *Kind Hearts and Coronets* (1949) and *The Lavender Hill Mob* (1951), were far less bleak, but their satire could not conceal a sense that the world was rarely benign. On radio, Britain was challenged by sinister schemes that had to be thwarted by *Dick Barton, Special Agent* (1946–51), and he also starred in three British films (1948–50). The Boulting Brothers made *High Treason* (1951), the nearest British equivalent of the Hollywood 'red scare' films, about Communists trying to sabotage power stations.

In the visual arts of the period, *avant-garde* ideas competed with a more conventional mainstream. The latter prevailed at the 1951 Festival of Britain. Alongside a show of the future, the dominant artistic mood was neo-Romantic. Only one abstract work was selected for display in connection with the Festival, and that work caused a public controversy. The Director of the Tate Gallery in the 1950s, John Rothenstein, was criticised for his lack of enthusiasm about Cubism, although he was an enthusiast for Wyndham Lewis. In Scotland, the Edinburgh painters, particularly W. G. Gillies (1898–1973), William McTaggart (1903–81), Anne Redpath (1895–1965) and John Maxwell (1905–62), did not engage with theory. Far from trying to be *avant garde*, they emphasised expressiveness and the use of colour in a conventional manner to produce decorative works. In contrast, other artists such as the sculptor Barbara Hepworth (1903–75) were experimenting with abstract forms. 'New American Painting', a big exhibition of large abstract works held in 1958, had a major impact. Looking at art and design from a different perspective, there was a shift in fine and decorative arts, graphics and industrial design from the austerity and functionalism that had characterised the late 1940s to a more affluent tone, as shown, for example, in the Coventry Cathedral exhibition of 1962.

Architecture was now dominated by Modernism. The progressive style of the 1930s became an orthodoxy that was used for the widespread post-war rebuilding, for urban development, and for the new construction made possible by the investment in hospitals, schools and New Towns. A centrepiece was the first major post-war public building, the Royal Festival Hall (1951), designed for the Festival of Britain's South Bank Exhibition, by Robert Matthew, the Chief Architect to the London County Council. The Modern movement in architecture was visibly important in the transformation of British cities from the 1960s, although less so in domestic architecture.

The novelists of the 1940s were concerned, at times despairing, but not angry. The late 1950s, in contrast, were to be the stage for the 'Angry Young Men', a group of writers who felt very much at odds with their Britain. Their problems were not those of faith in a hostile world (Greene, Waugh) or the pressure of totalitarianism (Orwell), but, rather, a sense that the post-war reforms of the Labour government and 1950s affluence had produced a vulgar materialist society that was disagreeable in itself and frustrating to them as individuals. They were impatient alike with the values of ITV and with traditionalism. In contrast to the liberal worthiness of C. P. Snow's Lewis Eliot, the protagonist of his sequence *Strangers and Brothers* (1940–70), came Charles Lumley in John Wain's novel *Hurry On Down* (1953), a graduate who flees self-advancement and becomes a window-cleaner, and Jim Dixon, the hapless protagonist in Kingsley Amis's *Lucky Jim* (1954). The latter novel also struck at the 'phoniness' of social mores in the period. Social values were lacerated in John Osborne's play *Look Back in Anger* (1956), John Braine's novel *Room at the Top* (1957), Alan Sillitoe's novel *Saturday Night and Sunday Morning* (1958), and David Storey's novel *This Sporting Life* (1960). Sillitoe's account of working-class life in his native Nottingham was an example of the 'grim up north' school that became fashionable in the 1950s.

More generally, this extended to a stronger interest in the 'North'. This had a number of manifestations in the early 1960s. Northern accents became fashionable; northerners, such as the dramatist Alan Bennett, 'made it' on the national stage; and northern males were said to benefit from the alleged southern preference for a bit of 'rough'. The films of Marlon Brando had revealed the limitations of the southern matinée idol. Northern men (and Welsh men, such as Richard Burton) addressed this lack; however, some of the most famous 'northern' figures in the films of the period were not northern at all.

The works of the 'Angry Young Men' were a long way from the successful staples of the West End stage, the lending libraries, and the standard bookshops. In the West End, audiences flocked to see plays by Noel Coward, both old (such as *Private Lives*, 1930) and new (for example *Look After Lulu*, 1959) alike, as well as plays by Terence Rattigan (*The Winslow Boy*, 1946) and William Douglas-Home (*The Chiltern Hundreds*, 1947; *The Manor of Northstead*, 1954). The audiences were also very large for the short stories Agatha Christie adapted for the stage: *The Mousetrap* (1952) and *Witness for the Prosecution* (1953).

The 'Angry Young Men' were not the only voices in print. There was fresh energy in Scottish and Irish writing, while in England, studies of middle age by Angus Wilson (1913–91) – *Hemlock and After* (1952), *Anglo-Saxon Attitudes* (1956), and *The Middle Age of Mrs Eliot* (1958) – enjoyed solid sales. The lending libraries continued to buy and lend large quantities of Christie and other secure genre writers. American popular novelists also made a greater impact than hitherto. At the cinema, Hammer's *The Curse of Frankenstein* (1957) began a series of successful horror films that made the reputation of their leading actors, Peter Cushing and Christopher Lee.

## 1960–70

The 1960s destroyed a cultural continuity that had lasted from the Victorian period. This reflected the impact of social and ideological trends, including the rise of new forms and a new agenda moulded by shifts in the understanding of gender, youth, class, place and race.

To approach the 1960s from the perspective of fiction will not work. Other cultural forms were so much more powerful as expressions of the age and as ways in which we can approach it. Nevertheless, one feature of the literature of the period that should be noted is the major role of women novelists. This was scarcely new, but was more pronounced than in the 1950s. Aside from the already well-established Iris Murdoch (1919–99) and Doris Lessing (1919– ), women writers who made an impact included Margaret Drabble (1939– ) and Angela Carter (1940–92). Lessing's *The Golden Notebook* (1962), a key text of the decade, engaged with feminism and psychoanalysis. Like many earlier novelists, Drabble took the familiar theme of a sensitive individual's attempt to break free from the limitations of a conventional background, and her novels, such as *A Summer Birdcage* (1963), *The Garrick Year* (1964), and, in particular, *Jerusalem the Golden* (1967), permit us to see the working out of that theme for 1960s women.

It would have been difficult for the latter to escape the Beatles. Youth culture was not an invention of the 1960s (see Chapter 6), but it became much stronger then and also had a far more powerful influence on the overall cultural life of the country. Furthermore, the Beatles were home-grown. In the late 1950s, British singers had essentially imitated American models. Cliff Richard, for example, had initially looked towards Elvis Presley. 'Rock 'n' roll' was popular. In the winter of 1960–1, however, the Beatles established themselves as the band for Liverpool teenagers and developed the distinctive Mersey sound.

To become national, the Beatles had to be repackaged. In 1961, the band abandoned their leather jackets for smart suits, and their manager, Brian Epstein, got them a recording contract with the music giant EMI. It was newly responsive to the commercial possibilities of pop and understood that it was no longer appropriate to expect performers to behave as they had been told to do in the 1950s. The Beatles' debut single, 'Love Me Do', was released in October 1962, followed in January 1963 by 'Please Please Me'. They set the sound for change. Other Merseysiders – Cilla Black, Gerry and the Pacemakers, and the Swinging Blue Jeans – sustained the Liverpool impact on London.

Yet the Beatles also left the North. Just as, in film, working-class dramas set in the North of England, especially *Room at the Top* (1959), *Saturday Night and Sunday Morning* (1960), *The Loneliness of the Long Distance Runner* (1962), *Billy Liar* (1963), *This Sporting Life* (1963) and *Get Carter* (1971), had a vogue, but were absorbed by a more metropolitan focus (see Chapter 6), so the same was true of popular music. British youth culture was reconfigured towards fashionable middle-class interests. Thus, the hippies and drugs of the 1960s reflected the affluence, ethos and American-ism of middle-class South-Eastern youth, rather than their Northern working-class counterparts. The Beatles came from the latter, but took to the new culture, especially to drugs and Asian mysticism, providing it with a 'sound'. The role of students in the 'pop culture' of the 1960s was particularly important, and the majority of them came from a middle-class background. Many of these students had the money to spend on drugs and attending pop concerts, in large part because of the affluence of their parents.

Pop art was an aspect of a determined assault on conventional understandings of artistic content, meaning, and production. 'Just what makes today's homes so dif-ferent, so appealing?', a satirical collage by the influential pop art exponent Richard Hamilton, appeared in 1959. Pop art was deliberately unconventional and irreverent. Pop art was followed by Op art, the iconic, pulsating black-and-white spirals painted by Bridget Riley. Pop art of the 1960s included Peter Blake's collage for the album cover of the Beatles' *Sgt. Pepper's Lonely Hearts Club Band* (1967), as well as the Beatles' animated film *Yellow Submarine* (1968). 'Different' art had entered the mainstream and public consciousness. This was not only the case with the visual arts. In 1966, Tom Stoppard's play *Rosencrantz and Guildenstern are Dead* wittily and successfully reinterpreted *Hamlet*, one of the greatest Shakespearean classics. Stop-pard followed up with *The Real Inspector Hound* (1968), a play that subverted theatrical conventions, not least by playing on the audience's sense of certainty. Like many other innovative and influential figures of the period, Stoppard, born in 1937, was young.

In the 1960s, massive open-air concerts focused the potent combination of youth culture and pop music, but this music, and its commercialism, was, in turn, to be challenged by punk, a style that set out to shock and to transform popular culture. Yet, to reach a wider audience, punk, in turn, had to be taken up by record com-panies and television. It also entered the cultural mainstream, affecting style in fashion and design. The role of punk in style and design was but part of a more general bridging between popular culture and design themes, a bridging that was driven by the pressures of commercialism in a society that affected novelty. Thus, design values came to be seen as more important in manufacturing and retail, and they changed more rapidly. Attitudes towards shape and colour that owed much to cultural currents, rather than functionalism, affected the context of everyday life, from the lines of motor cars to 'kitchen design'. Experimentation with new forms that were still functional became widespread and affected much of the world of goods. For example, the potter Walter Keeler (1942– ) made pots with practical uses, taking particular interest in attractive domestic tableware. To that end, he, like other potters, sought inspiration from foreign forms, in his case *raku*, the moulded earthen-ware used in Japanese tea ceremonies, and also probed the possibilities of the medium. Keeler developed salt glazing, using changes in texture to highlight design. Bernard Leach was also an important cultural mediator of Japanese forms.

At the same time, aspects of 'high' culture, especially architecture, were in-fluenced by design values and a striving for relevance in a 'post-industrial society'. This was clearly seen in museums and art galleries. New attitudes to building design and layout and to the presentation of exhibits rapidly took hold. For example, in the Tate Gallery muslin ceilings and plywood walls brought brightness where there had earlier been heavier surfaces.

This was a *national* shift, as were most of the cultural developments in the period. The extent to which there were separate cultural experiences in parts of the UK was limited. There were of course variations, not least thanks to the role of Welsh and Gaelic cultures, but there was also much uniformity. Youth culture was universal. Scotland, for example, produced singers and bands that had a national impact: Lulu and Donovan in the 1960s, the Bay City Rollers in the 1970s, and Wet Wet Wet in the 1980s and 1990s. Northern Irish and Irish bands, such as Van Morrison, Thin Lizzie and UB40, also had a major impact, not least on the relationship between Irish and British culture. The role of radio, television and the record industry helped ensure the national, indeed international, character of popular music. Yet, alongside commercially-induced homogeneity, there was also a diversity of cultural roots. This was seen in interest in ethnic music, for example, in the 1990s, Bangra and the revival of Irish traditional music via Riverdance. Furthermore, those roots could influence the mainstream. This was true of Afro-Caribbean influence: Bob Marley had a major impact on popular music from the 1970s.

Working-class voices and themes were increasingly present. This was true not only of popular music, but also of fiction and theatre. The growing willingness of television to focus on working-class life was important. 'Situation comedies' ceased to be preponderantly middle class: both *Steptoe and Son* (1962) and the *Likely Lads* (1964) made a major impact.

## 1970–99

The 1970s opened on a cultural world of bewildering complexity. *The Mousetrap* was still running on the London stage (as indeed it still is in 1999), and James Bond was saving the world on screen: *Diamonds are Forever* appeared in 1971. Yet, alongside this apparent, but somewhat misleading, continuity in 'low' brow interests, it was harder to see the main outlines of *avant-garde* culture. In part, there was a tension in media in that, although 'arty' films and television programmes were produced, both those media were essentially populist in content. Furthermore, *avant-garde* film did not attract a major following.

If film remained dominated by Hollywood values, this was part of a general shift in which America became more influential among both the cultural elite and mass culture, certainly more so than the earlier influence of European models for part of the elite. However, cultural forms other than film were less influenced, still more set, abroad. British architecture enjoyed a boom in its international reputation with architects such as James Stirling producing major works at home and abroad. Never-theless, Modernism in architecture was increasingly criticised by conservation movements and on aesthetic grounds. It was attacked as the 'New Brutalism', lacking a human scale and feel, and this attack was popularised by Prince Charles in the 1980s and 1990s, not least with his description of the initial plans for the extension to the National Gallery as a 'monstrous carbuncle' [facial growth]. He also condemned the plans for the new British Library as 'a dim collection of brick sheds and worse'. By the 1980s, Modernism was being challenged by a neoclassical revival pioneered by Quinlan Terry. This again was true of all parts of the British Isles. Distinctive styles of architecture had been eroded by Modernism.

The prestige of British painting and sculpture was also high. It was recognised and celebrated with prominent exhibitions, such as the Hayward Gallery's account of British conceptual art, 'The New Art', in 1972. Established figures, such as Francis Bacon, Barbara Hepworth and Henry Moore, were joined by younger figures such as Patrick Heron and Peter Howson. Furthermore, with increased interest in performance art, there was a growing determination to break down the gap between performer and audience. This was especially true of sculpture and culminated in 1998 with Antony Gormley's *Angel of the North*. Situated on a panoramic hill south of Gateshead, overlooking both the A1(M) and the East Coast railway line, this work was seen by over 90,000 people daily, making it the most viewed piece of sculpture in Britain.

The *Angel of the North* was a product of public patronage. Gateshead Urban District Council was keen on sculpture as a way to raise artistic consciousness and improve the quality of life. There was also money available in the 1990s from a number of sources, especially the National Lottery. The Arts Council of England Lottery Fund provided £791,000 for the *Angel*. This was a very different cultural context from the working men's clubs, which were especially prominent in northern England, and in the 1990s still numbered more than 3,000, with a total membership of 3 million. Entertainers there had to be immediately responsive to their audiences, and they tended to focus on traditional themes. It was too easy to overlook such institutions and forget, for example, that Sheffield's Crucible Theatre was best known from 1977 as the venue for the world snooker championships.

The use of public money ensured that, in the 1990s, culture became increasingly a political issue, although it had scarcely been free from controversy in the 1970s and 1980s. In that period, although there was no consistent widespread popular interest in the place of the arts in society, individual artists had taken political positions. For example, influenced by Brecht, Howard Brenton probed the nature of power in plays such as *Magnificence* (1973), *The Churchill Play* (1974), and *The Weapons of Happiness* (1976), and caused controversy with his criticism of government policy in Northern Ireland in *The Romans in Britain* (1980). Edward Bond attacked capitalism and the Establishment in modern Britain from a Revolutionary Socialist perspective in plays such as *Saved* (1966), and *The Worlds* (1979). David Hare's powerful play *Plenty* (1978), which was subsequently made into a film, was a striking account of disillusionment with life in Britain. Culture was a highly political matter for Thatcherites and they attacked publicly subsidised 'left-wing' theatre. Community theatre, which had flourished in the 1970s, was hit as subsidies were withdrawn, on essentially political grounds, from companies like 7:84, Joint Stock, and Belt and Braces. Many arts figures, such as the playwright Harold Pinter, attacked the Thatcher government, and its appointment of businessmen as trustees to national museums and galleries led to controversy; although there was no issue comparable to that of the use of Lottery funds in the 1990s.

The 1990s also brought the Department of Culture in 1997, and a fierce controversy over whether it was appropriate to charge for entry to museums. This was related to concern about the social position of culture. The Labour government elected in 1997 attacked what it termed cultural elitism, and sought to redirect public patronage in line with its 'Cool Britannia' image. It quickly found itself embroiled in controversy, not least because it was unable to free itself from major commitments of public funds to the Royal Opera House. The geographical location of culture was also an issue. There was strong criticism of London's dominant position, not least over the decision to locate the Millennium Dome at Greenwich and because national institutions were important cultural investments. Nevertheless, a part of the Tate Gallery opened in Liverpool in the 1980s, another part opened in St Ives in Cornwall, there were major developments in Birmingham and Glasgow, and a National Armouries Museum opened in Leeds.

Debate in the 1990s did not only focus on institutions. There was also concern about the content and morality of modern culture. The presentation of pickled parts of animals by Damian Hirst and of the cast of a house by Rachel Whiteread did not strike everyone as art. This reached a height with the 'Sensation' show at the Royal Academy in 1997, which led to unprecedented media attention on British art. Much of this related to Marcus Harvey's large portrait of the sadistic murderess of children, Myra Hindley, a portrait painted in 1995 with the template of a child's hand. The painting led to controversy within the Academy with the resignation of four Academicians, while two artists threw ink and eggs respectively at the painting.

The range of printed opinion over the exhibition indicated the ability of the arts to focus attention. On the one hand, there was the clash between social convention and individualism, a clash that resonated throughout the century. One critical writer, Julie Burchill, felt herself in an age of 'the politics of Why Not . . . perfect for the ageing dirty-minded children . . . at the Nursery for Wayward Youth. These are the days in which the most obscenely oppressive images are not challenged but actually celebrated as some sort of liberation.' More informed critics saw the show as part of the rhythm of cultural change. Richard Cork of *The Times* claimed 'The rebels have stormed the bastions of conservatism'. This was a timeless process that could be seen at work throughout the twentieth century. Once-banned works became lauded classics. Whole areas of experience that had been expressed covertly, such as homosexuality, were given prominence. E. M. Forster's novel about homosexuality, *Maurice*, written in 1913–14, was not published until 1971, a year after Forster's death (it was filmed in 1987).

Much art, however, was far less controversial. Marcus Harvey's painting tells us less about the possibilities of painting in the 1990s than Howard Hodgkin's explorations of colour and its use to depict emotion. Winner of the Turner Prize in 1984 and knighted in 1992, Hodgkin was a member of a group of British painters who began exhibiting in the 1960s, including Patrick Caulfield and David Hockney, who were of international significance. A different aspect of culture was offered by the popular 'heritage' films of the 1980s and early 1990s, for example *Heat and Dust* (1983), *A Room with a View* (1986), *Maurice* (1987), *Howards End* (1992) and *The Remains of the Day* (1993). They were intelligently done literary adaptations that offered attractive period-costume accounts of upper-class life. There was an interesting tension here, as in BBC adaptations of the 1990s, such as *Pride and Prejudice*, *Martin Chuzzlewit*, *Our Mutual Friend* and *Vanity Fair*, which commanded prominent slots in the schedule, but remained critically respectable. This is a further reflection of the complexity of the relationship between 'high' and 'low' culture.

# Conclusions

Alongside the rhythm of cultural change can be seen a continuing fissure between elite and popular cultural forms, a wide disjuncture between 'high' and 'low' brow works. There were of course parallels. For example, both detective fiction and children's literature from the 1960s tackled issues that would have been generally regarded as inappropriate prior to that decade, and, by doing so, lessened the gap in content between them and more 'high' brow works. Roald Dahl produced surrealistic children's stories, such as *James and the Giant Peach* (1961) and *Charlie and the Chocolate Factory* (1964), as well as verses, such as *Revolting Rhymes* (1982). By the 1990s, Dahl's books were the most popular children's works in Britain.

Dahl was an experimenter, but the overwhelming characteristic of popular 'low' brow works was a reluctance to experiment with form and style. This division in approach was more widespread. It also affected other arts, such as architecture, music, painting, and sculpture. As a consequence, a pattern of contrast that was essentially set earlier in the century with the impact of Modernism remained important to the cultural life of the country. It ensured that there were very differing understandings and experiences of culture and the arts. This difference was more than a matter of stylistic pluralism. It also reflected the wider cultural politics of a society containing very different levels of income, education and expectation. There was no automatic link between these differences and the contents of cultural 'consumption' and 'production', or artistic awareness, but they were very important to the configuration of the cultural life of the people.

# Summary

◆ The relationship between 'high' and 'low' culture is complex.
◆ Cultural 'products' are interesting in themselves, and also a way to approach the society of the period.
◆ Public patronage played a major role, especially from the 1960s.

# Questions for discussion

◆ What is the importance of cultural history?
◆ How influential were leading writers?
◆ What was the importance of American models?
◆ What has been the role of public patronage?
◆ What examples from 'low' culture would you use?

# Further reading

Aldgate, Anthony, *Censorship and the Permissive Society: British Cinema and Theatre, 1955–1965* (Oxford, 1995).

Aldgate, Anthony; Chapman, James; and Marwick, Arthur (eds), *Windows on the Sixties: Exploring Key Texts of Media and Culture* (London, 1999).

Aldgate, Anthony, and Richards, Jeffrey, *Best of British: Cinema and Society from 1930 to the Present* (2nd edn, London, 1999).

Alexander, Michael, *A History of English Literature* (Basingstoke, 2000).

Armes, Roy, *A Critical History of British Cinema* (London, 1978).

Bamford, Kenton, *Distorted Images: British National Identity and Film in the 1920s* (London, 1999).

Barr, Charles, *Ealing Studios* (London, 1993).

Booker, Christopher, *The Neophiliacs: A Study of the Revolution in English Life in the Fifties and Sixties* (London, 1969).

Booker, Christopher, *The Seventies: Portrait of a Decade* (London, 1980).

Carey, John, *The Intellectuals and the Masses: Pride and Prejudice among the Literary Intelligentsia, 1880–1939* (London, 1989).

Chapman, James, *Licence to Thrill: A Cultural History of the James Bond Films* (London, 1999).

Dentith, Simon, *Society and Cultural Forms in Nineteenth-Century England* (London, 1998).

Dickinson, Margaret, and Street, Sarah, *Cinema and State: The Film Industry and the British Government, 1927–84* (London, 1985).

Durgnat, Raymond, *A Mirror for England: British Movies from Austerity to Affluence* (London, 1970).

Ford, Boris (ed.), *The Cambridge Cultural History of Britain* (Cambridge, 1992).

Hewison, Robert, *Culture and Consensus: England, Art and Politics since 1940* (London, 1995).

Johnston, John, *The Lord Chancellor's Blue Pencil* (London, 1990).

Marwick, Arthur, *The Sixties: Cultural Revolution in Britain, France, Italy, and the United States c.1958–1974* (Oxford, 1998).

Massey, Anne, *The Independent Group: Modernism and Mass Culture in Britain, 1945–59* (Manchester, 1996).

Richards, Jeffrey, *Films and British National Identity: From Dickens to Dad's Army* (Manchester, 1997).

Ryall, Tom, *Alfred Hitchcock and the British Cinema* (London, 1986).

Shellard, Dominic, *British Theatre since the War* (New Haven, 1999).

Spalding, Frances, *The Tate: A History* (London, 1998).

Walker, Alexander, *National Heroes: British Cinema in the Seventies and Eighties* (London, 1985).

Waters, Chris, *British Socialists and the Politics of Culture, 1884–1914* (Manchester, 1990).

Williams, Raymond, *The Country and the City* (London, 1975).

# Into the Twenty-First Century

# CHAPTER 16

This closing chapter is not a comparison with the opening one. Much of this comparison has been provided by the chapters that have followed, specifically their closing sections, and there is no need to repeat them. Instead, it is important to try to look for some wider significance for the years at the close of the millennium rather than presenting them as the tail end of the study. These, however, are difficult years to write about. There is nothing that dates so rapidly as recent history. If we look back from the start of the new century, it is possible to see abrupt and sweeping changes in political history, and there is no reason to imagine that this will cease to be the case. It is, therefore, very difficult to judge the long-term significance say of the Labour victory in 1997, the Good Friday Agreement in Northern Ireland in 1998, or the launch of the Euro (European currency) in 1999. Partly because of this, this chapter will concentrate on social and long-term developments. However, it has to begin with possibly the most important change in the political system, namely Britain's position in the European Union.

## Key issues

▶ What was/is the impact of European integration?

▶ How far was Britain changing as an environment at the close of the millennium?

▶ How vibrant was/is British culture?

In the spring of 1993, Cambridge University Press published a *Concise History of Britain, 1707–1975* by a leading English historian, W. A. Speck. In his Introduction, Speck claimed that his period of coverage 'spans the whole history of Britain in the precise sense' and explained that 'membership of the EEC was a partial surrender of British sovereignty'. In his Epilogue, Speck argued that the benefits or otherwise of membership of the European Community could not be appraised dispassionately because it was 'too early' and the issues too emotive and pressing, but he offered a comparison of membership with that of Scotland within Britain.

Applying the past to the present is, indeed, very difficult, and can lead to serious error, but historians are better placed to do so than anyone else, and it is part of their public duty to make an effort. It is clear, from British history, that close and important relations with Continental Europe have been a major theme of English, Scottish,

Welsh, Irish and British history. Yet that did not (and does not) imply a strong sense of European identity.

Identity of course was/is neither exclusive nor constant. A sense of collective self-awareness could/can include a number of levels or aspects of identification. These often developed/develop or were/are expressed most clearly in hostility or opposition to other groups, and their real or imagined aims and attributes, and these groups were/are frequently ones with which relations were/are close. Indeed, the reality of overlapping senses of collective self-awareness can be very difficult, as, also, can be the processes of often continual adaptation in these senses.

At present, there is a scholarly emphasis on the degree to which nations, like all communities, are mental constructs: bodies created and defined by thought and belief. As with much historical writing, this is, to a considerable extent, a matter of stating the obvious. It is readily apparent that Britain, as a political identity, was in large part created; and that this creation owed much to the formulation and dissemination of new images. It is also clear that notions of nationhood were politically charged. As constructs, nations are as powerful as the family, embracing all the same responses of pride, defence, aggression, etc.

The debate over relations with Europe led both to claims that Britain had for long had close contacts with the Continent, and to others of British exceptionalism: that Britain was unique and different from the other Continental countries. These arguments were compatible, for the history of European peoples and countries is one of considerable variety, a variety whose consequences can readily be grasped, not only in Britain, but also, throughout Europe. This relates directly to the question of what type of 'Europe' the European Union will propose. Arguably, it will be most successful if it can accommodate the particular interests and views of nation-states. A policy based on making them redundant appears unrealistic, certainly in the case of Britain.

In the late 1990s, the British state attracted decreasing support and respect, especially in Scotland and Wales. In both, there was a tendency to define unwelcome aspects of Britishness as English. Furthermore, respect in these areas for central concepts of Britishness, such as the monarchy, was contested. There was, however, throughout Britain, particularly in England, only a limited sense of European identity, certainly far less so than in many Western European countries. This opened up the possibility of a significant gap between popular attitudes and the views of powerful governmental and political circles. The central political problem in any community is the eliciting of consent. This is not simply a question of defining acceptable policies and selecting leaders who will be judged competent, but also reflects the nature of identification between people and government, which is a question of history, symbolism, and a sense of place and purpose. These, in turn, combine to produce an ideology that is more potent than the more intellectual and abstract creeds usually designated by that term. Thus, alongside talk in the 1990s of the failure and redundancy of the nation-state, and its need for replacement by power-sharing, supranational bodies and 'Euro-regions', it can be argued that it was the nation-state that was most effective at eliciting and securing consent. Indeed, much of the nationalist pressure within Britain from the 1960s testified to the strength of the idea of the nation-state, for this pressure sought to create new nation-states in Scotland and Wales, and to expand that of Eire to include Northern Ireland (see Chapter 12). All three efforts reflected the strength of nationalism, not its redundancy. For tactical reasons, they could align with the European ideal, but their essential logic was older and different.

**The Scottish Parliament**
The opening of the Scottish Parliament in 1999 represented a major success for supporters of devolution. Backers of Scottish independence, however, saw this step as only a staging post. It is unclear whether the Parliament will contain or encourage demands for independence.

Anti-Englishness was an aspect of this nationalism, certainly among nationalists in Scotland and Northern Ireland, to whom Britain all too often was England writ large. This is a reminder that the political history of twentieth-century Britain had an important geographical component. In particular, the Conservative presence in Scotland and Wales was generally weaker than that of their opponents, especially after 1960. Although Conservative support in Wales peaked in the mid-1970s and early 1980s, it remained considerably below that of Labour. Within England, the Labour Party was strongest in the North, the Conservatives in the South-East, and the West Midlands was a major battleground. As a result, Labour electoral triumphs registered shifts in political geography. In 1966, Labour victories included seats where it had never won before, such as Brighton, Cambridge, Hampstead and Oxford in the prosperous South of England, and non-industrial seats such as Cardiganshire, Lancaster and York. This was also true of the 1997 election. Conversely, the Conservatives took seats in northern England in 1983, only to lose them as their electoral fortune successively ebbed in 1987, 1992 and 1997. The degree of emphasis that should be placed on the regional dimension of identity and politics is unclear, certainly within England.

It is possible to exaggerate the effectiveness of the nation-state of Britain as a representative political unit during the twentieth century. There is a kind of circularity: the nation-state represented national interests effectively because its very existence *defined* those interests. What is less clear is that the interests thus defined and pursued by the nation-state were the primary interests of the people of that state. Nevertheless, given that these interests did not exist clearly, except in the most basic terms, outside the political process, the nation-state played a crucial role in the discussion, definition and validation of such interests. It is far from clear that a European political community can successfully fulfil the same function, certainly in terms of obtaining active popular support, and this is the case both for Britain and for its constituent parts.

Britishness, indeed, is historically specific, not timeless, and is generally seen as having been formed after the Anglo-Scottish Union of 1707. It can even be argued that Britishness then, and possibly until 1945, was quintessentially Imperial. If that view is taken, then the 'Little Britishness' characteristic of the post-war period, and Thatcherism, in particular, was of very recent origin, not as deeply rooted as is generally implied. The situation was naturally more complex and nuanced than any either/or approach, and it is crucially important to neglect neither the contingency, in the shape of the pressures of domestic and international developments, nor continuities, most obviously in terms of institutional, constitutional and political longevities.

A sense of fluidity was readily apparent in the period after 1945. The end of Empire, large-scale Commonwealth immigration, European integration, the 'Troubles' in Northern Ireland, and the re-emergence of Scottish and Welsh nationalisms all posed serious problems for conventional earlier assumptions, and were all seen in that light. Adjustments had to be made, legally, culturally and socially. This was especially true of policy towards Northern Ireland, Scotland and Wales, and towards immigration. Successive shifts in government policy towards Northern Ireland from 1969 indicated the major potential role of government policy in affecting (but not determining) developments, and also the contingencies that shaped this role.

Notions of nationhood increasingly accommodated immigrants. The Race Relations Act of 1965 sought to include immigrants in the nation. The diversity represented by immigrant communities was extolled by many commentators in the last quarter of the century. There were real problems, not least widespread discrimination, poor relations with the police, and the 1980s riots; but also positive aspects, such as the impact of Afro-Caribbean music and of Asian cuisine.

One 'adjustment', in the eyes of some critics, was a widespread refusal to accept change. This was seen by many commentators, particularly, but not only, on the Left, as producing a culture of nostalgia that was continued throughout the century, but reached a peak at particular moments. In the early decades, this culture focused on rural values, and idealised the contemporary countryside as a retreat from urban coarseness and frenetic change. From the 1960s, the 'anti-modern' culture increasingly focused on the past. It was no longer so credible to romanticise the rural present of agri-business. This focus on the past took many forms, including visiting country houses and enjoying films and television programmes set in the past. The membership of the National Trust rose considerably. In 1997–8, its membership rose above 2.5 million, more members than any political party, and in 1997 there were 11.7 million visitors to the 251 National Trust properties open at a charge.

The fashion for the past led to the 'heritage industry', to period styles, as seen, for example, in clothes, furniture, decorations, and architecture, and to works such as the film adaptation of classic English novels by the Merchant Ivory film company, including E. M. Forster's *A Room with a View* in 1985 and his *Howard's End* in 1992. Ironically, James Ivory was born in California and Ismail Merchant in India. Nostalgia was powerfully presented on television with programmes such as the hugely popular *Dad's Army*, *It Ain't 'alf Hot, Mum* and *Hi-De-Hi*.

The interaction of chance and long-term trends emerges repeatedly in any account of twentieth-century British history, as it also does in that of earlier centuries. It is possible to stress continuity, to emphasise a constant expression of a deep sense of history, an organic, close-knit society, capable of self-renewal, as well as the rooted strength of institutions and culture. The British certainly have a genius for the appearance of continuity, but the manufacture or repetition of traditions frequently masked, and masks, shifts in the centres of power. This process is breaking down. It is difficult to assimilate membership of the European Union or shifting political relationships within the British Isles with any emphasis on continuity.

Furthermore, it is possible to stress the role of chance, and thus to suggest that present options and future developments cannot be discussed with reference to a comforting view of the past. The relative stability of Britain over the course of the century, it can be argued, was due not only (or even at all) to deep-lying characteristics, forces and trends, but, instead, to victory in both world wars. Most Continental countries, in contrast, were defeated and occupied, with the accompanying strains. On the Continent, many right-wing political groupings were contaminated, or at least affected, by the rise of Fascism. In Britain, as in Ireland, in contrast, there was no foreign invasion, no seizure of power by undemocratic forces from Left or Right. Across much of Europe, but not in Britain, liberal democracy collapsed – from within, in the 1930s, or from German invasion in 1940. There was much, therefore, in the notion of British exceptionalism, as far as what could be fancifully termed the mid-twentieth-century crisis was concerned.

Yet, although not invaded, Britain scarcely survived the crisis unscathed. For her, this was a crisis in domestic government, economic management, social welfare, and international position. It indicates the problem of judgement. Britain emerged from the crisis with her parliamentary system intact and as part of the victorious wartime coalition. In 1945, British forces took part in the defeat of Germany and Japan, and in Britain there was a peaceful transfer of power from Conservative to Labour through the ballot box. Yet, there have also been claims that the 1940s were a decade of failure. These claims relate specifically both to a misguided sense of international mission that led to an excessive role against the Axis powers (Germany, Italy, Japan) and/or, later, against the Soviet Union; and also to a choice of post-war domestic priorities that unwisely focused on social welfare, rather than on investment for economic renewal.

These claims are controversial, but they also exemplify the problems of judging achievement and failure. It is unclear how far politicians (and whole societies if we can think in such abstract terms) can have been expected to understand trends and options. Such an understanding required an appreciation not only of developments in Britain, but also of those elsewhere.

Thus, in 1945, with Germany and Japan in ruins, and France only recently liberated, it is unclear how far contemporaries should have anticipated the rapid relative decline of British power over the following three decades. A world power in the early 1940s, albeit not at the level of the USA, Britain was a relatively unimportant off-shore island in Europe by 1975. The two central planks of British greatness – possession of a world-wide empire and global economic influence (partly as a trading nation but, increasingly, as a financial centre) – had been eroded and obviously so. Adjusting to the loss of Empire and to long-term (relative) economic decline, however, was difficult. This was true not only for economic and political elites, but for many others in society used to considering Britain powerful. Thus, workers in the 1960s and 1970s found it difficult to adjust working practices to respond to highly competitive imports from new and expanding industrial centres, such as Japan. More generally, there was a widespread sense that 'someone owes us a living', a sense that Thatcher set out to smash, but with only limited success.

Yet, at the same time, twentieth-century Britain witnessed very positive advances, although they were not such as to make Britain distinctive or a leading power. Relative economic (especially industrial) decline, symbolised by the fate of British companies in car manufacture, has to be set against improving living standards for all, including the poor. Most notably in the last quarter of the century, these brought levels of consumption to the majority of the population that would have been inconceivable to the generations born in the early part of the century. By March 1999, there were 10 million home owners and the average-priced house was £85,257. Mass-ownership of the car was a symbol of that social progress and of the ability of consumerism to mould society and put pressure on the environment. A world of out-of-town shopping centres and multiplex cinemas (the first at the new city of Milton Keynes) was what many wanted in the 1990s, although not all could afford it. Furthermore, although the standard of living of British producers and consumers rose considerably it fell relative to that of other Europeans, let alone Americans. This had an impact in terms of relative levels of consumption and, also, relative standing in social indicators, such as per capita welfare expenditure, life expectancy, infant mortality rates, and investment in education. There was a parallel to the situation in the late Victorian period. Average real earnings consistently rose in 1861–1901, but the growth rate in the economy slowed in the 1890s, and was slower than that of all other major European states. This raises the question of how far the problems of particular decades are best explained in terms of a long-term situation. This situation, in turn, requires analysis, not least discussion in terms of whether, as has been suggested, rising benefits for individuals, either in income or social benefit or both, have been won at the cost of necessary investment in, and improvement to, the structures and context of the national economy. That might be a false question: the two elements may not be related. Whichever is the case, it is necessary to set rising average real wages alongside economic problems.

Similarly, the loss of world-power status took place at a time when dramatic changes in communications, as well as patterns of consumption, resulted in a greater knowledge of, and access to, parts of the world than was ever the case in the heyday of Empire. Global travel and a global (pan-American) culture were opened to the many in the second half of the century.

A stress on chance, the contingent, and the difficulty of arriving at judgements, focuses attention on the uncertainties of history. It renders deterministic approaches to the past suspect. This also leads to the consideration both of other options and of those which were unsuccessful. For all their talk about being the natural party of government in Britain, only thrice in the century (the Conservatives and their allies in 1900, 1931 and 1935) did either the Labour or the Conservative Party gain more than 50 per cent of the popular vote. Furthermore the electoral system rewarded power to parties who polled fewer votes than their rivals (Conservatives, not Labour, in 1951; Labour, not Conservatives, in February 1974). Party cooperation had the same effect in 1910, 1923 and 1929, in each case keeping the Conservatives from office, in 1910 to the benefit of the Liberals, while, on the other two occasions, Labour was the beneficiary.

A reminder of the unpredictability of three-party politics draws attention to the consequences of the number of political players. It was by no means obvious that Labour would be the last major party to emerge in Britain during the twentieth century. The failure of the Social Democrats in the 1980s was far from certain, and there was much talk of the party 'breaking the mould' of British politics. Furthermore, the likely success of lesser parties was unclear. The early 1930s, for example, witnessed the creation of four independent parties – National Labour, National Liberal, Mosley's BUF, and the Independent Labour Party that disaffiliated from Labour in 1932. All failed, but it was far from obvious that the Slump and the formation of the National Government would not lead to a major permanent political reconfiguration. The same was true earlier of the Lloyd George coalition. Indeed the Conservative leadership was willing to fight a second 'Coupon' election in cooperation with

Lloyd George. Due in 1923, such an election would probably have led to a second victory, and there would have been no need for another election until 1928. Thus coalition politics might have become the inter-war norm from the outset.

War is also a sphere in which the contingent is crucial and counterfactualism (the 'what if?' approach) valid, especially if the counterfactualism focuses on options and possibilities that were considered at the time. This ensures that they were then part of the future possibilities that affected planning. To ignore them would therefore be to make the past seem misleadingly predictable. This was driven home, as far as war was/is concerned, with the possibility that Thatcher might not have triumphed in the Falklands crisis of 1982 and thus might have failed to win the 1983 general election. She could have been killed, as was intended, when the IRA bomb planted in the Grand Hotel at Brighton exploded during the Conservative Party conference in 1984.

It is foolish to view earlier crises as in some way more predictable. At the most basic level, Britain could have lost World War One or World War Two. The over-running of France in 1914 or the defeat of Russia in 1917 without the compensation of American entry might have forced Britain to negotiate peace. This would have been unlikely to involve any direct consequences for British domestic history, although defeat in war might have discredited the governmental system, thus encouraging radical political tendencies comparable, at least in part, to those that affected Germany in 1918. Furthermore, defeat might have led to greater pressure from within the governmental system/'Establishment' for changes in the organisation of the state.

Defeat in World War Two came far closer. In 1940, Britain's European alliance system collapsed and Britain was threatened with invasion. The consequences would have been more serious than defeat in World War One, as the Nazi regime would have demanded major changes in British government and political culture, and effective parliamentary government would have come to an end.

Even without defeat, both world wars underlined the role of contingency. Each had a major impact on British politics and society. Britain entered World War One with the Liberals ascendant and World War Two with the Conservatives in an even stronger position. Both conflicts saw their political position fade but, more significantly, saw substantial shifts in public culture. Thus, the Representation of the People Act of 1918 brought universal male suffrage and votes for women, while the election of the first majority Labour government in 1945 was followed by the nationalisation of much of the economy and the introduction of the welfare state and the managed economy. It can be suggested that the seeds of these changes were sown pre-war; that, for example, the Liberal ascendancy was fragile, with its middle-class support increasingly being lost to the Conservatives and its electoral agreement with Labour under mounting pressure. The ability of the National Government to repeat its 1931 and 1935 electoral successes in the election due by 1940 has been queried.

Yet, allowing for pre-war tensions in each case, there was still a wartime sea-change in both. Much clearly stemmed from the inability, during these conflicts, to continue with peacetime arrangements as it became clear that the wars would be difficult and long. The pressures of total war led to a re-examination of political, government, economic and social assumptions, while the need to assuage the possibilities of social discontent and to show the soldiers that there was much worth fighting for, encouraged a wartime egalitarianism that had, at least in part, a post-war impact, particularly after World War Two. Thus major changes can be traced to the contingencies of war.

The reminder of the contingent in war, international relations and domestic politics is also valid for other spheres. Labour failure in the Euro-elections in 1999, the first national election in Britain under a system of proportional representation, led the Labour government to abandon its commitment to holding a referendum on proportional representation before the next general election. Had such a system been introduced then, or earlier, it is likely that all governments would have been coalitions, and probable, therefore, that centrist tendencies would have been dominant.

Labour relations could have taken very different courses during the century. There might have been no legalisation of strike action in 1906, and this could have led to widespread violence during the major strikes of the early 1910s. It might have made Labour–Liberal cooperation impossible and encouraged the development of a more radical Labour Party and trade union movement. Furthermore, the Conservative government might have tried to ban or suppress the General Strike of 1926, or the situation might in some other way have turned violent. Again, the striking coal miners might have failed against Heath in 1974, but succeeded against Thatcher a decade later.

To turn to the economy, there might have been no means of exploiting natural gas or oil in the North Sea. Its absence would have put great pressure on Thatcherite public finances, making it harder to cut taxes and thus expand the private sector. Alternatively, earlier exploitation of the oil might have weakened the position of the coal industry and possibly saved the reputation of the Wilson government by enabling it to avoid devaluation in 1967, or enabled Heath to see off the miners' strikes.

Such counterfactuals are not idle speculation. It is important to remember that, at any one moment, various developments seemed possible to people in the past, and that the sole guarantee was that what was going to happen was not known. This last, however, is the very opposite of our position when we view the past, and we need a powerful leap of the imagination to recover the uncertainty of the past and to make judgements accordingly.

Contingency can even be extended to aspects of history that are not usually tackled through the 'what if?' approach. Thus, in the case of culture, we can ask how far public culture and consumerism would have been different had there been no commercial television, as was indeed the case until 1955. In the case of the environment and transport, we can speculate about the consequences had there been more stringent restrictions on house-building on greenfield sites, either in the inter-war or post-war periods, or both. The former might have led to restrictions on suburbia, and to higher-density housing, with important social and cultural consequences.

Both these questions direct attention to the state of culture and the environment at the close of the century. In both cases, there are possibilities of major change contained within existing circumstances, and it is unclear how they will work themselves out. This is true, for example, of the potential impact of computers and the internet on literature, or, more particularly, reading; and of the effect of environmental degradation on attitudes to social regimentation. It is possible that serious pollution may force the government to try to control driving, and it is also possible that this eventuality will not arise. Each option indicates the difficulty of prediction. So also, for example, do issues such as race relations.

'Culture' and 'environment' do not exist in isolation. They are shaped as issues by society. From the 1960s, there have been important changes in social aspirations.

Notions and practices of personal responsibility have altered in a more atomised and individualistic society. Ideas of social order have changed. These changes, common throughout the Western world, help to mark off Britain at the close of the twentieth century from the position at the start. It is not, for example, just that Britain no longer has an Empire, but also that the attitudes that gave rise to one have gone. The Falklands War of 1982 was followed by a national commemoration service in St Paul's Cathedral in which the clergy prayed for the defeated Argentinians. Thatcher's earlier call during the war to 'Rejoice' when South Georgia was recaptured did not strike a universal chord, and was heavily criticised in some quarters, as was the *Sun* headline 'Gotcha' when the Argentinian flagship the *Belgrano* was torpedoed with heavy loss of life. The emphasis had been different when Mafeking was relieved from Boer siege in 1900. More generally, pressure for expenditure on social welfare, health and education – aspects of the democratisation of modern Britain – lessened the availability of resources for the military, while concepts of manliness changed, as did the role of men in society.

Attitudes change. In the widest sense, that is our culture. At the close of both century and millennium, the British were more prosperous than ever before, but polls indicated that they were not content. Whether they would have been under other circumstances is unclear and unlikely. An essentially secular and individualistic society in an economic system without certainty, and with traditional family, gender and other practices and assumptions under great strain, was not one in which it was easy to feel secure. But then such security had generally been fragile. This is not a triumphalist note for the Conclusion; but triumphalism is out of place, itself a comment on attitudes at the close of the century.

## Summary

◆ There was nothing predictable in modern British history. International developments were especially unpredictable.

◆ Britain's loss of world-power status was a major theme that it is all too easy to forget.

◆ Britain also witnessed major advances, especially in health and social welfare, although they were not distinctive to the country but, instead, aspects of wide-ranging developments in the Western world.

## Questions for discussion

◆ What does British identity mean at the beginning of the new millennium?
◆ How does Britain differ from the USA and Western Europe?

## Further reading

Robbins, Keith, *Great Britain: Identities, Institutions and the Idea of Britishness* (London, 1998).

# Glossary

**appeasement**  The unsuccessful attempt to maintain peace by granting concessions, particularly to Germany, but also to Italy and Japan, before the Second World War.

**avant-garde**  The writers, musicians, artists, etc., who are in the forefront in the development of new ideas and methods. The term particularly refers to Modernist writers and artists in the first half of the twentieth century.

**benefit policies**  Policies for the government provision of pensions and allowances.

**capitalism**  The system whereby property and the means of production are privately owned, and regulated by market forces rather than by government intervention.

**collectivism**  Belief that agricultural or industrial units should be collectively owned, with the owners sharing the work and the profits.

**Communism**  A political system based on the teachings of Marx, in which the workers control the means of production.

**consolidation**  The merging of companies in order to create national brands and reduce overhead costs.

**consumerism**  The focus on the role in society particularly of manufactured goods, and the processes of buying and selling.

**Corn Laws**  Laws regulating and restricting corn imports, repealed in 1846.

**de-industrialisation**  A rundown in the extent and role of industry such that there is a reduction in the proportion of industry in a country's economy.

**democracy**  Government by freely elected representatives of the people.

**democratisation**  The process by which institutions and practices become more accountable to the public.

**deregulation**  The lifting of government restrictions, in order to encourage competition.

**devolution**  The granting of governmental power to smaller areas of a country, for example, Wales or Scotland within the United Kingdom.

**disposable income**  The money people have left to spend as they like after tax deductions.

**egalitarianism**  The belief that all people should have equal shares in society's rights, benefits and duties.

**the Establishment**  The people and organisations in authority who control public life.

**Eugenics movement**  The belief that the nation's stock could be improved by encouraging the healthier, more intelligent people to have children and restricting the reproduction of weaker or 'less desirable' groups.

**first-past-the-post electoral system**  System in which the individual candidate with the most votes is elected, even if they have less than half the total votes cast.

**franchise**  The right to vote in public elections.

**full employment**  The belief that everyone who is able to work should be able to find a job – it will never be 100 per cent because there will always be some people moving between jobs.

**Great Depression**  A period of decline in economic activity that began in the last quarter of the nineteenth century. There was a further serious Depression in the 1930s.

**high culture**  The more prestigious and intellectual areas of the arts, such as poetry, classical music, etc.

**Home Rule**  The movement demanding self-government for Ireland in the period before 1914.

**imperialism**  The attempt of a state to spread its power over a number of countries.

**individualism**  The belief that all people have individual rights and freedoms within society.

**internal market**  Trade within and between sections of an organisation such as the National Health Service.

**libertarianism**  The belief that people should be free to express their religious or political ideas.

**Modernist**  A movement, particularly in the first half of the twentieth century, which aimed to make a break with the past and find new forms and means of expression.

**monetarism**  The belief that the economy can be regulated by the control of the money supply.

**multi-culturalism**  The ability of people from different religions and ethnic groups to take a full part in society side by side without cultural conflict.

**nationalism**  The search for independence on the part of peoples whoc regard themselves as distinct.

**nation-state**  A politically independent country consisting of a single nation.

**neo-liberalism**  A renewed interest in liberal principles regarding social and political affairs.

**privatisation**  The transfer of government-owned industries to private ownership through the selling of shares on the stock market.

**Realist**  A practical point of view, dealing with things as they really are, in contrast to the romantic or idealised vision.

**redistributive taxation**  The system whereby wealthier people pay higher taxes, which are used to provide benefits for the poor or disadvantaged.

**re-industrialisation**  The creation of new industries in order to boost a country's economy.

**revolutionary Marxism**  The belief based on Karl Marx's teaching that the working class would rise up and take power from the property owners.

**secular ideologies**  Belief systems and philosophies that are not based on religion.

**suburbia**  The areas on the outskirts of towns and cities where most people live and from where they travel to work or to shop.

**supply side**  Economy led by the requirements of industry, in contrast to a demand-led economy catering to the needs of the consumers.

**trickle-down**  The benefits that come to poorer sections of society as a result of more successful people having, and spending, money.

**universal adult male suffrage**  Voting rights granted to all men over the legal age of majority.

**universalism**  The belief that no one should be excluded from the provisions of the welfare state.

**Welfare State**  The system by which the government provides benefits and services such as health services and pensions for all members of society.

# Bibliography

It is all too easy to offer a list of books stretching off towards the horizon, but that serves particularly little point for this subject, for fresh information and insights arrive with great rapidity. It is more useful to encourage readers to turn to sources from the period. Most libraries will hold newspapers either in hard copy or on microfilm. It is very instructive of course to read national newspapers, such as *The Times*, which survive in widely-available microfilm editions, but local newspapers can also offer much insight. They show how national developments – the General Strike or rationing, the creation of the NHS or the end of the grammar school – affected communities and were perceived.

Aside from newspapers, it is very useful to turn to visual images, not least newsreels. Museums can also be very helpful. The Castle Museum at York is especially valuable for its collections of household items and their display in, for example, kitchens and living rooms of particular periods. The Victoria and Albert Museum includes material up to the present. National and local art galleries are valuable. Another aspect of visual culture and comment is provided by cartoons and caricatures, for example those in magazines, especially *Punch* and *Private Eye*, and newspapers.

Maps are also important. Changing editions of the Ordnance Survey show some aspects of how particular areas have altered. *Mapping the Past: Wolverhampton 1577–1986* (Wolverhampton Libraries and Information Services, 1993) is a particularly fine collection of successive maps. Historical atlases of particular localities are also very useful. Recent ones of value include D. Dymond and E. Martin, *An Historical Atlas of Suffolk* (Ipswich, 1988); Hugh Clout (ed.), *The Times London History Atlas* (London, 1991); *Newcastle's Changing Map* (Newcastle, 1992); *An Historical Atlas of County Durham* (Durham, 1992); Joan Dils (ed.), *An Historical Atlas of Berkshire* (Reading, 1998); and Roger Kain and William Ravenhill (eds), *The Historical Atlas of the South West* (Exeter, 1999). Lincolnshire, Norfolk and Sussex have also been covered. At present, however, there are no good historical atlases for much of the country, including the West Midlands. A good thematic historical atlas is provided by Andrew Charlesworth and others, *An Atlas of Industrial Protest in Britain, 1750–1990* (London, 1996).

Literary sources tell us much about society. Servants, for example, frequently featured in detective stories of the 1930s, but not those of the 1950s. There are many guides to the literature of the period. Aside from the British dimension, it is also worth considering David Daiches (ed.), *The New Companion to Scottish Culture* (Edinburgh, 1993). There are numerous memoirs. Important political ones include Roy Hattersley, *Fifty Years On: A Prejudiced History of Britain Since the War* (London, 1997); Denis Healey, *Time of My Life* (London, 1989); Roy Jenkins, *A Life at the Centre* (London, 1991); Margaret Thatcher, *The Downing Street Years* (London, 1993). Diaries include Richard Crossman, *The Diaries of a Cabinet Minister* (3 vols, London, 1975–7). Travel accounts of Britain, by British and foreign writers, offer much. J. B. Priestley's *English Journey* (1933) was less pungent than George Orwell's *The Road to Wigan Pier* (1937).

To turn to scholarly books, the best introduction is Peter Clarke's *Hope and Glory: Britain, 1900–1990* (London: Penguin, 1996). It is overly political, but, throughout, it provides a clear narrative that is illuminated with perceptive insights about many aspects of society. Before mentioning any other national surveys, it is important to note the vital local and regional perspective. The Longman series 'A Regional History of England' includes such valuable works as Norman McCord and Richard Thompson's *The Northern Counties from AD 1000*, C. B. Phillips and J. H. Smith's *Lancashire and Cheshire from AD 1540*, David Hey's *Yorkshire from AD 1000*, Marie Rowlands's *The West Midlands from AD 1000*, J. V. Beckett's *The East Midlands from AD 1000*, J. H. Betty's *Wessex from AD 1000*, and Peter Brandon and Brian Short's *The South East from AD 1000*. Histories of smaller localities in the twentieth century have generally not been of this standard, and local and regional history journals tend to give too little space to the twentieth century. Nevertheless, they are still worth reading.

Other national surveys of note include Keith Robbins, *The Eclipse of a Great Power: Modern Britain, 1870–1975* (London, 1983); Bernard Porter, *Britannia's Burden: The Political Evolution of Modern Britain, 1851–1990* (London, 1994); Ross McKibbin, *Classes and Cultures: England, 1918–1951* (Oxford, 1998); David Childs, *Britain since 1939* (London, 1995); John Davis, *A History of Britain, 1885–1939* (London, 1999); and Martin Pugh, *Britain: A Concise History, 1789–1998* (Basingstoke, 1999).

Valuable work on economic history includes Peter Dewey, *War and Progress: Britain 1914–1945* (London, 1996), and Rex Pope, *The British Economy since 1914: A Study in Decline?* (London, 1998). The essays in Paul Johnson (ed.), *Twentieth-Century Britain: Economic, Social and Cultural Change* (London, 1994) offer much.

For social history, it is best to turn to recent works. The following are important: Andrew Adonis and Stephen Pollard, *A Class Act: The Myth of Britain's Classless Society* (London, 1997); Sue Bruley, *Women in Britain since 1900* (London, 1999); M. Durham, *Sex and Politics: The Family and Morality in the Thatcher Years* (London, 1991); David Gladstone, *The Twentieth-Century Welfare State* (London, 1999); Harry Goulbourne, *Race Relations in Britain since 1945* (London, 1998); David Hirst, *Welfare and Society, 1832–1991* (London,

1999); Hugh McLeod, *Religion and Society in England, 1850–1914* (London, 1996); Arthur Marwick, *British Society since 1945* (3rd edn, London, 1996); and N. L. Tranter, *British Population in the Twentieth Century* (Basingstoke, 1995). Major constituencies are covered in David Vincent, *Poor Citizens: The State and the Poor in Twentieth-Century Britain* (London, 1991); and John Benson, *Prime Time: A History of the Middle Aged in Twentieth-Century Britain* (London, 1997). General surveys of value include Edward Royle, *Modern Britain: A Social History, 1750–1997* (2nd edn, London, 1997); and Martin Pugh, *State and Society: A Social and Political History of Britain, 1870–1997* (2nd edn, London, 1999).

For Scotland see I. G. C. Hutchison, *Scottish Politics in the Twentieth Century* (London, 1999).

For Ireland: D. G. Boyce, *The Irish Question and British Politics, 1868–1996* (2nd edn, London, 1996); David Harkness, *Ireland in the Twentieth Century: Divided Island* (Basingstoke, 1995); and Charles Townshend, *Ireland: The Twentieth Century* (London, 1999).

For British political history: John Charmley, *A History of Conservative Politics, 1900–1996* (London, 1996); Kevin Jefferys, *Retreat from New Jerusalem: British Politics, 1951–64* (Basingstoke, 1997); Ian Packer, *Lloyd George* (London, 1998); David Powell, *The Edwardian Crisis: Britain, 1901–1914*

(London, 1996); Geoffrey Searle, *The Liberal Party: Triumph and Disintegration, 1886–1929* (London, 1992); Nick Smart, *The National Government, 1931–40* (London, 1999); Andrew Thorpe, *A History of the British Labour Party* (London, 1997); and Ian Wood, *Churchill* (London, 1999).

For empire and foreign relations: C. J. Bartlett, *British Foreign Policy in the Twentieth Century* (London, 1989); Sean Greenwood, *Britain and the Cold War, 1945–91* (London, 1999); W. D. MacIntyre, *British Decolonization, 1946–1997* (London, 1998); Anne Orde, *The Eclipse of Great Britain: The United States and British Imperial Decline, 1895–1956* (London, 1996); Ritchie Ovendale, *Anglo-American Relations in the Twentieth Century* (London, 1998); and John Young, *Britain and European Unity, 1945–1992* (London, 1993), and *Britain and the World in the Twentieth Century* (London, 1997).

For culture: Steve Hare (ed.), *Allen Lane and the Penguin Editors, 1935–1970* (London, 1995); Joseph McAleer, *Popular Reading and Publishing in Britain, 1914–1950* (Oxford, 1992); and Ralph Negrine, *Television and the Press since 1945* (Manchester, 1998).

A wider context is offered by Mark Mazower, *Dark Continent: Europe's Twentieth Century* (London, 1998). Most histories of Britain, however, fail to direct sufficient attention to the wider context.

# Index

and general election results
206, 207

and the Heath government
214, 217

and local government 173, 175

and the Major government
228

and neo-liberalism 140–1

as Prime Minister (1979–90)
218–27

and the state 171, 175

and television 99, 100

and trade union reform
217–18, 245–6

and the 'wets' 218

Thatcherism 127–8, 140–1,
143–4, 219

and Britishness 355

economic policies 211–12,
218–20, 225–6

and New Labour 230, 231

and trade union reform
217–18

theatre of the absurd 326–7

Thomas, Dylan 339

Thorneycroft, Peter 206, 207, 211

Thorpe, Jeremy 215

Tippett, Michael 327, 344

Tirpitz, Alfred von 287

Tissot, Jacques 323

toiletries and cosmetics 80–1

Topolski, Feliks 344

tourism 328–9

and Wales 238

Town and Country Planning Acts
(1944/47/50) 61, 64, 173,
174

town planning 25, 61–2, 63

Town Planning Act (1909) 25

towns see urban Britain

trade

with Continental Europe
320–2

figures (1930–90) 320

imperial 318–20

see also free trade; tariff reform

Trade Boards Act (1909) 37

Trade Disputes Act (1906) 180

trade unions

bloc votes 154

and the Conservatives 243–4,
247

and egalitarianism 141

fall in membership 126

and the Heath government
213, 214

and Labour governments
**1964–70** 210
**1974–9** 216, 217

and the Labour Party 188

labour relations and state
intervention 242–7

and the Macmillan
government 205

and political funds 191

post-war 202, 203, 243

and socialism 110

and the Spanish Civil War 296

and the Taff Vale Judgment
(1901) 180–1

and Thatcherite Conservatism
223–4

in Victorian Britain 14

and women 113

and World War Two 244

see also strikes

Trades Disputes Act (1927) 133,
192, 203

trams, electric 87, 92, 93

transplant surgery 28, 70

transport 86–96

development of new forms of
69, 86

public transport and health 31

and urban growth 58

Trevelyan, G. M. 325

trickle-down thesis of prosperity
145

Truman, Harry S. 325

tuberculosis 27, 30, 38, 127, 275

TUC (Trades Union Congress)
191–2, 216, 243

Tudor Walters Report (1918) 60

Turing, Alan 70

'Two Cultures' debate 70

## U

Ullmann, Walter xii

underclass 95, 127–8

unemployment

in the 1970s 213, 217

in the 1990s 228, 229

in the inter-war years 25, 58,
114, 115–16, 192, 193–4,
198; and economic policies
194, 197, 236

middle class 128

National Unemployed
Workers Movement 196–7

in northern England 280

in Northern Ireland 273

in Scotland 239, 265

and social welfare 37–8

and Thatcherite Conservatism
220, 221, 223

and women workers 122

Unemployment Assistance Board
37

Unemployment Insurance Act
(1924) 38

United States of America

Britain's 'special relationship'
with 308, 310–12

and the British Empire 286,
297, 305–6, 326–7

and British foreign policy
308–9

Civil War (1861–5) 7

and the Cold War 301, 302,
304–5

economic growth 318

influence on British culture
324–6, 327, 330–1, 339

investment in Canada 320

and post-war Europe 303

and Victorian writers 318

and World War One 318, 324

and World War Two 300, 301

universal adult male suffrage 2,
40, 113, 150, 187, 359

universalism 119

universities 175

and science 72

and women 110, 122

urban Britain

changing townscapes 58–65

Garden City movement 25,
37, 58–9

and health 24–5

and high-street shopping 80

house-building 46, 59–63

images of 64–5

New Towns 22, 24, 58–9, 61,
62

suburbia 53, 59, 61

town planning 25, 61–2, 63

## V

Vagrancy Act (1898) 10

vagrancy laws 10

VAT (value added tax) 219

Vaughan Williams, Ralph 53,
323, 342, 344

VCR (video cassette recorder)
98, 102

Vickery, Alice 18

Victoria, Queen 1, 7

Diamond Jubilee (1897) 286,
287

Victorian Britain 1–15, 131–2,
333

Ireland 255–8

Scotland 258–9

and the United States 318

Wales 259–60

Vietnam War 210, 308, 309

violence

absence of revolutionary
155–6, 178

subcultures of youth 125

voluntary organisations

and social welfare 38, 39

women's 115

and World War Two 118–19

Vorticism 338

## W

Wain, John 345

Wales

administration 266

Anglican Church in 6, 14, 132,
133

Conservatism in 355

devolution 270, 271, 272, 277,
330

economy 237–8, 266; and
environmental change
48–9, 238

and English national identity
278, 279

local government 173

nationalism 254, 265–6, 269

nineteenth century 9, 259–60

Plaid Cymru 170, 266, 267,
269, 270, 272, 296

population 17

'pub and chapel' culture 10

second homes in 54

unemployment 116

Walker, Peter 224

Walpole, Hugh, *The Herries
Chronicle* 342

Walton, E. A. 322

waste disposal and recycling 50

water supplies 50

and cholera 6

and rural areas 27

Waterworks Acts (1869/76/90)
11

Watson, James 70

Watt, James 3

Waugh, Evelyn, *Brideshead
Revisited* 344

wealth

distribution of 108, 128

private, and Thatcherite
Conservatism 226

Webb, Sidney 322

welfare state 39, 119, 158, 202

costs 40

in northern England 280

and post-war Conservatism
205, 206

and Thatcherism 219

see also social welfare

Wells, H. G. 68, 340

*When the Sleeper Awakes* 26

Welsh Assembly 170, 176

Welsh language 259, 269, 271

Welsh Language Act (1967) 269

West Country 279

Westland helicopter company
311

Westminster, Gerald Grosvenor,
Duke of 56

Whitehouse, Mary 99, 121

Whiteread, Rachel 350

Widows', Orphans' and Old Age
Contributory Pensions Act
(1925) 191

Wiener, Martin 71

Wilde, Oscar 144, 152, 340

*Salomé* 322

wildlife 45–7, 57, 64

Wildlife and Countryside Act
(1981) 64

Wilkins, Maurice 70

Wilkinson, Ellen 41

*The Town that was Murdered*
58